SECOND EDITION

Social Work:
Issues and Opportunities
in a Challenging Profession

Diana M. DiNitto

The University of Texas at Austin

C. Aaron McNeece

Florida State University

and Contributors

Allyn and Bacon

Boston • London • Toronto • Sydney • Tokyo • Singapore

Dan, the years go by, but you are missed every day.
Diana

For Carl McNeece, 1912–1995

Series Editor, Social Work: Judy Fifer
Editor-in-Chief, Social Sciences: Karen Hanson
Editorial Assistant: Jennifer Jacobson
Marketing Manager: Quinn Perkson
Production Coordinator: Thomas E. Dorsaneo
Editorial-Production Service: Melanie Field, Strawberry Field Publishing
Composition and Prepress Buyer: Linda Cox
Manufacturing Buyer: Megan Cochran

Copyright © 1997, 1990 by Allyn & Bacon
A Viacom Company
160 Gould Street
Needham Heights, Mass. 02194

Internet: www.abacon.com
America Online: Keyword: College Online

Library of Congress Cataloging-in-Publication Data

DiNitto, Diana M.
    Social work : issues and opportunities in a challenging profession
/ Diana M. DiNitto, C. Aaron McNeece, and contributors. — 2nd ed.
        p.   cm.
    Includes bibliographical references and index.
    ISBN 0-13-063827-7
    1. Social service—United States.   I. McNeece, Carl Aaron.
    II. Title.
    HV10.5.D56   1996
    361.3'2—dc20   96-23669
                                                             CIP

Printed in the United States of America
10 9 8 7 6 5 4 3 2 1 00 99 98 97 96

Contents

Preface

This book is our attempt to portray the profession of social work in a realistic light. Many introductory texts describe social work in ways that make the profession seem devoid of controversies and struggles. For example, social workers are portrayed as people helping clients who want their services, and the clients all do better in the end. In fact, anyone who has practiced social work knows that many clients have little interest in seeing social workers and that social workers often feel they do not have the power or abilities to solve many of their clients' problems. Social workers do have a positive impact on the lives of many people whom they serve, but painting too rosy or placid a picture of the profession fails to represent the field accurately to students. In this text we present a balanced picture of the many rewarding aspects of social work practice as well as the difficulties, struggles, and problems that social workers face as they do their jobs and attempt to uphold the values and ethics of the profession.

This book also addresses controversial issues within the profession. For example, we consider what the roles of social workers should be today and debates over the movement of social workers toward psychotherapy and private practice. In addition, many social work students receive their education without much understanding of the roles of organizations such as the Council on Social Work Education and the National Association of Social Workers in these issues. Through this book, we hope to help students become more knowledgeable consumers of their social work education by making them aware of the roles of these organizations in shaping social work education and practice.

Another distinguishing feature of this book is that it addresses controversies faced across the board by human service professionals and the interrelationships among these professional groups. For example, where do social workers stand in relation to others practicing in the fields of mental health and substance abuse? These issues are particularly relevant in an era of managed health and mental health care and conservative attacks on the kinds of services that social workers provide.

We also do the things that most other introductory social work texts do. We cover the social work practice methods, a number of fields of practice, women's issues, and ethnic minority concerns, as well as the knowledge, value, and skill bases necessary to practice social work.

Social work is no easy profession. Students generally recognize this from their early days in field placement. We hope that this text serves as one resource that those interested in a social service career can turn to in making their decisions about whether or not social work is right for them.

In doing this second edition, we have called on a number of colleagues in the profession to assist us. We are grateful for their contributions and acknowledge them on the first page of the appropriate chapter. Diana also wishes to thank Kelly Larson, Mary Margaret Just, and Phyllis Bassole for their assistance in completing this manuscript. And thanks to the following reviewers: Sally Spill, Concordia College; Patricia Johnson-Dalzine, Central State College; Harv Leavitt, Heritage College; Richard Blake, Rutgers University; Martin Hope, Winthrop College; Ronald W. VanderWiel, Temple University; Elaine Leeder, Ithaca College; William C. Berleman, University of Washington; and Thomas D. Oellerich, Ohio University.

Diana M. DiNitto
C. Aaron McNeece

1

Origins of a Diverse Profession

Photo courtesy of the Cincinnati Historical Society

Social Workers on the Job

Mainstream Social Work

James works for the Children's Protective Services Division of a large state human services agency. He is assigned primarily to investigating reports of suspected child abuse and neglect, although he occasionally recruits and trains foster parents for his office when his schedule permits. A typical day includes an early morning review of reports from the local hospital, the county sheriff's office, and the local schools, which are all required by state law to report suspected child abuse to the county child abuse registry. James spends part of his day talking to the alleged victims and the doctors, nurses, neighbors of the family, and anyone else who may be able to shed light on the child's circumstances. He spends a considerable amount of time in court, pursuing legal efforts to have children removed from their homes and providing the court with periodic reports on the progress of children in foster care. He has seen several badly injured children die from their injuries, but he has also placed many other children into safe, nurturing environments, and he takes a great deal of pride in knowing that he may have saved them from further abuse.

Emerging Roles in Social Work

Kim is in a management position at a large manufacturing firm. Unlike most of her executive counterparts, however, she is not directly concerned with production, marketing, or accounting. She is director of the firm's employee assistance program. Several years ago her company discovered that it was losing money because of high turnover and personal problems among production workers. She supervises a staff that works with these employees concerning marital difficulties, substance abuse, and emotional problems. In addition to supervising staff and making sure that all appropriate paperwork is completed, she spends much of her time training supervisors and working with other management personnel.

Social Work Serves a Wide Range of Clients

Fred works with chronic alcoholics—the kind of clients some people used to call "winos." They are mostly men, but the number of women in these circumstances seems to be growing rapidly. Many of them are only passing through town on their way to or from South Florida, and quite a few are homeless. Every morning Fred makes his rounds of local hangouts—alleys in the center of town where a few down-and-out men gather around a fire in an old barrel and share a bottle of MD20/20 or Wild Irish Rose. He also visits the city jail's "drunk tank" daily and attempts to convince a judge to release one or two of its residents to him. Sometimes he takes them to the shelter where his office is located, provides them with a hot meal and a bed, and sees them off at the bus station the next day. Sometimes he manages to get them a minimum-wage job busing tables or washing dishes. Occasionally Fred will accompany them to a local mental health or social services office to request counseling, financial assistance, or placement in a halfway house. A few of the clients he helps have quit drinking, found steady employment, and become solid citizens. These are the cases that keep him going.

Social Work and Social Planning

Gina, a planner in a state social services department, is responsible for collecting and analyzing data regarding foster care for dependent, neglected, and abused children. Her reports are used by departmental administrators (and sometimes legislators) to make decisions on such matters as the appropriate level of payments for foster care, the number and location of foster homes, and the types of families that should be recruited as foster parents.

A Common Bond

Fred and James spend much of their time working directly with clients, while Kim and Gina are involved primarily with supervisory and administrative matters. They all have something in common, however: They are all professional social workers who earn a living helping others. Although in different helping efforts, they are all pursuing similar goals—goals that are bound together by a common value base.

Values and the Profession

Most people are concerned enough about their friends, family, and neighbors to be willing to help them occasionally in difficult times. Some people feel so strongly about helping others that they volunteer a considerable amount of their time to that end, while other people, such as doctors, nurses, teachers, and *social workers,* help others as a vocation. Before we define exactly what social workers do, let's look at the values underlying this profession.

In 1960 the National Association of Social Workers (NASW), the largest professional membership group of social workers in the United States (see Chapter 2), adopted its first official code of ethics; in 1967 a preamble, or philosophical introduction, was added that states:

> *Social Work is based on humanitarian, democratic ideals. Professional social workers are dedicated to service for the welfare of mankind, to the disciplined use of a recognized body of knowledge about human beings and their interactions, and to the marshaling of community resources to promote the well-being of all without discrimination.*

The preamble to the new proposed revision of the code of ethics states that "the primary mission of the profession is to enhance human well-being and help meet basic human needs, with particular attention to the needs of vulnerable, oppressed and poor people" (National Association of Social Workers [NASW] 1996, p. 19). It continues to stress the role of social workers in promoting *social justice* and *social change* on behalf of clients. The six core values of social work are identified as service, social justice, dignity and worth of the individual, importance of human relationships, integrity, and competence.

Of course many other groups are concerned about the welfare of society. They are as diverse as the Junior League, "candystripers," and members of the Socialist Labor Party. But social work is different from these groups because it is a *profession* based on the importance, dignity, and well-being of the individual, commitment to the service of others, and professional preparation for practice. The last characteristic is perhaps what most distinguishes social workers from others who serve as volunteers.

The Summary of Principles from the current code of ethics (NASW, 1980) follows. You should review these principles to see whether your own personal values are generally consistent with professional social work standards of ethics.

I. The Social Worker's Conduct and Comportment as a Social Worker

A. *Propriety.* The social worker should maintain high standards of personal conduct in the capacity or identity as social worker.

B. *Competence and Professional Development*. The social worker should strive to become and remain proficient in professional practice and the performance of professional functions.

C. *Service*. The social worker should regard as primary the service obligation of the social work profession.

D. *Integrity*. The social worker should act in accordance with the highest standards of professional integrity.

E. *Scholarship and Research.* The social worker engaged in study and research should be guided by the conventions of scholarly inquiry.

II. The Social Worker's Ethical Responsibility to Clients

F. *Primacy of Clients' Interests.* The social worker's primary responsibility is to clients.

G. *Rights and Prerogatives of Clients*. The social worker should make every effort to foster maximum self-determination on the part of clients.

H. *Confidentiality and Privacy.* The social worker should respect the privacy of clients and hold in confidence all information obtained in the course of professional service.

I. *Fees*. When setting fees, the social worker should ensure that they are fair, reasonable, considerate, and commensurate with the service performed and with due regard for the client's ability to pay.

III. The Social Worker's Ethical Responsibility to Colleagues

J. *Respect, Fairness, and Courtesy.* The social worker should treat colleagues with respect, courtesy, fairness, and good faith.

K. *Dealing with Colleagues' Clients.* The social worker has a responsibility to relate to the clients of colleagues with full professional consideration.

IV. The Social Worker's Ethical Responsibility to Employers and Employing Organizations

L. *Commitments to Employing Organizations.* The social worker should adhere to commitments made to the employing organization.

V. The Social Worker's Ethical Responsibility to the Social Work Profession

M. *Maintaining the Integrity of the Profession.* The social worker should uphold and advance the values, ethics, knowledge, and mission of the profession.

N. *Community Service.* The social worker should assist the profession in making social services available to the general public.

O. *Development of Knowledge.* The social worker should take responsibility for identifying, developing, and fully utilizing knowledge for professional practice.

VI. The Social Worker's Ethical Responsibility to Society

P. *Promoting the General Welfare.* The social worker should promote the general welfare of society.

Much important information is contained in this code of ethics that delineates the official mission of the social worker as perceived by the major professional organization. Throughout this book we discuss many issues that directly concern the six sections of this code. Not every social worker agrees with each and every aspect of the code, and not all social workers are members of NASW. Nevertheless, this code serves as a guide to action and a check on professional conduct for many of us.[1]

Knowledge for Social Work Practice

Knowledge for social work practice has traditionally been derived from other fields, especially the social and behavioral sciences. In fact, until the latter part of the nineteenth century, social work in the United States was undifferentiated from the so-called social science movement (Miller, 1995). As the profession matures and grows, however, social workers are beginning to rely more and more on knowledge derived from within social work practice itself (Bartlett, 1970). A problem often noticed in a young profession such as this is that practitioners may frequently substitute conventional practice wisdom for empirically derived knowledge. Sometimes that unverified practice wisdom may be misleading and unproductive. The profession is becoming increasingly concerned with the evaluation and validation of practice knowledge through standard research methodologies (NASW, 1984). This is one of the reasons that schools of social work universally require coursework in research methods. We will return to this important issue in Chapter 2.

[1]After much study and deliberation, the Delegate Assembly of NASW formally reported its recommendations for revisions to the code of ethics in the January 1996 *NASW News.* A final decision on the proposed changes is scheduled for August 1996.

Defining Social Work

According to NASW (1973), social work is the professional activity of helping individuals, groups, or communities enhance or restore their capacity for social functioning and creating societal conditions favorable to this goal. Social work practice consists of the professional application of social work values, principles, and techniques to one or more of the following ends:

helping people obtain tangible services
counseling and psychotherapy with individuals, families, and groups
helping communities or groups provide social and health services
participating in relevant legislative processes

Social work practitioners are a diverse group of people. If a visitor from another planet reviewed the daily schedules and tasks performed by a dozen social workers, the alien being might think that this particular group of earthlings have very little in common. At best, our visitor might think that there are at least *two* different groups of persons representing two different professions. Historically there has been tension in the profession between social work practice relying on *direct intervention efforts to help individuals* and efforts to accomplish *institutional and policy changes*. To add to our visitor's confusion, there are many other professions that help people *directly,* such as nursing, medicine, and psychology, and many other groups of people, including political reformers, religious institutions, and advocacy organizations, helping *indirectly.*

The integration of these many activities into one profession depends in part on the value base mentioned earlier. It also depends on the *purpose* of the helping efforts. The purpose of social work practice can be seen as effecting deliberate changes in the interaction of people and their environment, with the goal of improving the capacity of individuals to cope with their life tasks in a way that is satisfying to themselves and to others, and in so doing, enhancing their capacity for a fuller realization of their aspirations (Compton & Galaway, 1975).

Throughout this text we provide examples of how social workers using different perspectives attempt to solve particular problems. These different perspectives are commonly referred to as *micro-, mezzo-,* and *macrolevel* strategies. Micro approaches focus on the individual either alone or as part of a family or small group, while macro approaches are directed at the larger social system. Mezzo approaches fall between these two. Micro approaches are often direct service interventions with individuals or small groups. Macro approaches are frequently considered indirect interventions, even though they may result in the establishment of programs that provide direct services to clients.

Some social scientists use the term mezzo, or meso, to describe community-level strategies and reserve the term macro for strategies targeted at larger social systems, such as state and national governments. For example, a drug abuse prevention program at a high school utilizing small-group techniques would be considered a microlevel approach to addressing the problem. A mezzolevel approach to this same problem might involve the county commission appropriating funds to build a youth recreation center to provide alternative activities for children. A macrolevel strategy could involve increasing legal penalties for drug dealers who sell to minors.

Functions of Social Work Practice

According to a major curriculum study in social work education (Boehm, 1959), social work practice can be viewed as having three primary functions: restoration of impaired capacity, provision of individual and social resources, and prevention of social dysfunction. A later textbook on social work practice broadened these functions to seven:

Help people enhance and more effectively utilize their own problem-solving and coping capacities

Establish initial linkages between people and resource systems

Facilitate interaction and modify and build new relationships between people and society's resource systems

Facilitate interaction and modify and build relationships between people within resource systems

Contribute to the development and modification of social policy

Dispense material resources

Serve as agents of social control (Pincus & Minahan, 1973, p. 9)

Underlying both descriptions of social work practice are the assumptions that (1) the individual is important, (2) persons having problems arising from their interactions with others deserve help, and (3) something can be done to alleviate these problems. The focus on social relationships is perhaps the most distinguishing characteristic of the profession. Individuals are always considered in relation to others and to the social environments in which they function.

It is important to note that both the *clinical* social worker (Chapter 4) and the *policy advocate* social worker (Chapter 5) are actually pursuing very similar objectives. James, Kim, Fred, and Gina may be pursuing different paths in their helping efforts, but each is attempting to apply social scientific knowledge as a way of improving or restoring *individuals'* capacity for social functioning. Sometimes this requires social workers to intercede directly between a client and the environment; sometimes it requires a change in the policy that puts the client at a disadvantage in relation to others in the environment.

Roots of the Profession

Practically every organized society in recorded history has placed a high value on helping. This altruistic value may have contributed to the survival of the group (Macarov, 1978). Many cultural anthropologists (Kropotkin, 1925) convincingly argue that social organizations that provided mutual aid for individuals belonging to the system were the most likely to survive and evolve into advanced social systems. This is quite different from the Darwinian theory of the survival of the fittest, which says that the strongest breeds develop from the destruction of inferior individuals. Species that have survived and flourished have not been those most able to dominate or destroy others, but those most able to cooperate with each other. Individual survival has always been subjugated to the survival of the *tribe* or the *community*. Mutual support seems to be just as ingrained as territoriality, aggression, and other primitive urges.

Religious beliefs in all civilized societies have promoted efforts to help individuals in need (Macarov, 1978). Almost all religions have required their followers to engage in acts of charity toward other members of their group. In ancient Egypt, grain was routinely stored for famines through a centralized system, and religious injunctions obligated the Egyptians to provide food even to strangers during a famine.

In other ancient desert societies, traditions often developed out of a harsh existence in which each person was required to show certain responsibilities to the group and to the community. In Jewish societies, gleanings (corners of the fields and forgotten produce) were reserved for the poor. Poor persons, even aliens, were free to take food when they needed it.

In China, government granaries were established during the first century B.C. to provide free grain to the poor. So concerned were the Chinese with the welfare of their citizens that a common greeting was not "Good morning" or "How are you?" but "Have you eaten?"

The early Christians carried their concern with charity to an extreme, emphasizing two major themes: the near sanctification of the poor, and the denigration of conspicuous consumption. An example of this philosophy is found in the Gospel of Luke, where Jesus said, "Blessed are you poor, for yours is the kingdom of God" and "But woe to you that are rich, for you have received your consolation." Early Christians in Jerusalem sold their possessions and distributed them to "all as they had need." Christian charity had become well organized and institutionalized by the second century A.D.

In many of these societies, special roles or offices were often reserved for those persons who had major responsibility for helping others. In some systems it was a priest; in others it was a shaman. St. Francis of Assisi founded the Franciscan order, which was particularly active in helping the poor. This order, as well as several others, renounced material possessions and led lives of poverty as a way of emphasizing their commitment to the poor.

Needless to say, our conceptions of charity and the values attached to helping have gone through significant transformations during the past two thousand years. Our philosophy of social welfare was radically altered by the English Poor Laws and subsequent reforms. A number of social work textbooks describe in greater detail the *history* of social welfare (Axinn & Levin, 1982; Romanyshyn, 1971; Pumphrey & Pumphrey, 1961), while others focus on social welfare *policy* (DiNitto, 1995; Gilbert & Specht, 1974; Dolgoff & Feldstein, 1984).

In this book our focus is on social work as a professional discipline. As a student preparing for a career in social work, you may be studying the history of social welfare along with social work as a profession, or these subjects may be presented in two separate courses. Most social work education programs offer a separate course on social welfare *policy* (as well as other courses on human behavior, social work practice methods, research, and a field practicum).

Roots of American Social Work

According to Popple (1995) the history of social work in the United States is "embedded in the general history of social welfare, which, in turn, is related to broad patterns of economic, social, intellectual, and political history" (p. 2282). It is impossible to separate the study of the history of social work from the evolution of U.S. social institutions.

Throughout the American experience many notable individuals have devoted much of their time and efforts to doing social work, long before it was recognized as a profession. (Some still argue that it is not yet a profession, but more about that later!) One of the most important but least recognized of these was John Augustus, a Boston shoemaker. In 1841 Augustus convinced a judge to release to his custody a number of young people who had been convicted of minor offenses. He believed that these persons would have a better chance of going straight if they were not kept with other hardened offenders in jail, and he was willing to take a personal risk in guaranteeing their good behavior. In the eighteen years until his death in 1859, Augustus "bailed on probation" 1,152 men and 794 women. This system of releasing offenders rather than jailing them eventually evolved into the system that we now know as probation, and it is the most common method of handling both juvenile and adult offenders (Allen, Eskridge, Latessa, & Vito, 1985).

Women and Black Prototypes

Another notable helper was Dorothea L. Dix, who pioneered reforms in the field of mental illness. Before the Civil War she lobbied for more humane treatment of people with mental illness. In 1848 she asked Congress to dedicate five million acres of public land for the support of institutions for the "insane." Congress eventually passed a bill allocating twice that amount, only to have it vetoed by President Pierce, but the debate generated by Dix engendered many institutional reforms at the state and local levels (Axinn & Levin, 1982). In 1889 Jane Addams established Hull House in Chicago, an organization that emphasized neighborhood services and community development. The settlement house movement that she began was geared toward social change. When problems arose for the family unit, correction was sought through societal change and social reform as well as casework. "To adjust an individual to civilization as he finds it round him, to get him to the pitch which shall induce him to push up that civilization a little higher... is perhaps the chief function of a settlement" (Addams, 1897, p. 339).

Forerunners of professional social workers also included African-Americans, such as Christian Fleetwood and Maggie Walker. Fleetwood served with distinction in the Union army during the Civil War and moved to Washington afterward to work for the Freedmen's Bureau, which was created in 1865 to provide relief to the recently freed slaves (Lindsey, 1956). In the late nineteenth century Maggie Walker became the first secretary of the Independent Order of St. Luke, one of the first black private social welfare organizations in the country. In 1902 she established a bank in Richmond, Virginia, which helped to finance many projects in the African-American community (Hammond, 1922).

Using his Abyssinian Baptist Church as an organizational base, the Reverend A. Clayton Powell (not to be confused with Congressman Adam Clayton Powell) sponsored many social service projects in "applied Christianity" just after the turn of the century. These included building a community center, providing education for adult African-Americans who were not eligible to enroll in New York City's public schools, and dispensing emergency relief to the poor (Powell, 1923).

Emergence of a Profession

It has been suggested that it was through social investigation and attempts to understand family situations that social work began to develop as a profession (Dolgoff & Feldstein, 1984). Professions, according to Greenwood (1957), are characterized by

1. Possession of systematic theory
2. Authority recognized by the clientele
3. Sanction of the community to operate
4. A code of ethics for client and colleague relationships
5. A professional culture (p. 263)

Greenwood feels that social work meets each of these criteria and, therefore, has attained the status of a profession. Not everyone agrees, however.

Social work as an occupation developed out of the early volunteer and reform efforts mentioned earlier. During the Civil War, paid employees of the Special Relief Department of the U.S. Sanitary Commission assisted Union soldiers and their families who were experiencing social and health problems because of the war (Kidneigh, 1965). Social work again appeared as a paid occupation in the Massachusetts Board of Charities in 1863, and in the Charity Organization Society of Buffalo in 1877 (Morales & Sheafor, 1986).

There is still quite a leap from being a *paid occupation* to being a *profession*, however. When charitable organizations received contracts to administer programs, they hired a few individuals to recruit, organize, and train volunteers. These paid employees, often called executive secretaries, eventually began holding conferences and talking about establishing standards and developing training courses. In 1898 a summer training course was offered to charity workers by the New York Charity Organization Society. Six years later a one-year program was developed by the newly organized New York School of Philanthropy. By 1919 a number of schools had organized the Association of Training Schools for Professional Social Work, and the American Association of Social Workers was formed two years later (Boehm, 1971).

At the 1915 meeting of the National Conference on Charities and Corrections, Dr. Abraham Flexner addressed the group on "Is Social Work a Profession?" He insisted that in order to qualify, social work must meet six criteria:

1. Professions are essentially intellectual operations with large individual responsibility;
2. they derive their raw material from science and learning;
3. this material is worked up to a practical and clear-cut end;
4. professions possess an educationally communicable technique;
5. they tend to self-organization;
6. they become increasingly altruistic in motivation.

Flexner's conclusion was that social work was not yet a profession, and he admonished social workers to "go forth and build thyself a profession" (Morales & Sheafor, 1986, p. 47–48). Mary Richmond, one of the eminent founders and early practitioners of social work, had said in 1890 that "only two things are necessary to do good work among the poor; one is much good will, and the other is a little tact" (Lubove, 1971, p. 46). More than eight decades after Flexner's admonition, social work has developed into a discipline that requires several years of specialized college or university training in order to qualify, yet the rest of the world is still not convinced that social workers have achieved the status of a profession. (We will return to this debate in later chapters.) Meanwhile, having a little goodwill and a little tact is probably still a valuable asset.

Social Work's Conservative Origins

In the current conservative political climate, public opinion would probably view social work as a liberal profession and, compared to accounting, finance, or marketing, it is. This liberal reputation, however, is probably due to the highly publicized actions of a relatively small number of social workers. Social work has its roots in the ideology of voluntarism, which as Roy Lubove notes, became a regressive influence during the twentieth century (Lubove, 1968). Voluntarism became the great American substitute for social action and social policy. It was closely allied with principles of limited government, individual freedom, and capitalist economics. Social workers were generally not in favor of liberalizing and broadening governmental social welfare programs until after the passage of the Social Security Act of 1935. When compared to the efforts of other reform movements in the late nineteenth and early twentieth centuries, social workers have "lacked the necessary zeal or strength to influence social policy changes" (Sanders, 1973, p. 176).

A predecessor of NASW, the National Social Workers Exchange, was organized in 1916 and changed its name to the American Association of Social Workers in 1920. Although it maintained an active lobby in Washington, it never undertook any major responsibility or active leadership in attacking poverty, and it never claimed the problems of destitution as a primary obligation of the profession (Klein, 1971). Social work lost much of its potential as a promoter of social change during its early years while it was devoting an increasing amount of its organized energy to its own development and security, as well as attaching itself to Freudian psychoanalytic theory. Although some argue that a new "activist spirit" that developed during the civil rights era of the 1960s and early 1970s brought the profession closer to a real commitment to social justice (Specht, 1972), others claim that the increasing concern with licensing, third-party reimbursements, and private practice are leading the profession in exactly the opposite direction (Frumkin & O'Connor, 1985). By the early 1990s, however, even the once optimistic activists conceded the apparent trend toward private practice, calling those social workers "unfaithful angels" (Specht & Courtney, 1994).

Social Work and Related Professions

Psychology

Social workers and psychologists, especially clinical psychologists, often work together as part of a team, and there is a great deal of overlap in what they do. Both are interested in the behavior of people and in their patterns of interaction. Both deal with the thinking and feeling processes of people. The psychologist, however, is interested primarily in understanding individual behavior. Silverman (1972) says of psychology that it "is the science that seeks to measure, explain, and sometimes change the behavior of man and other animals" (p. 1). While the psychologist focuses on individual behavior, the social worker is interested in the social functioning of the individual. While the psychologist, especially the *clinical* psychologist, may work with individuals on an intensive basis in an attempt to change their behavior, the social worker is just as often interested in changing the individual's *environment* as in changing the individual. Social workers focus more on the social role of the client and on the utilization of community resources in order to meet a client's needs.

In recent years the field of psychology has become increasingly specialized, with divisions such as social, industrial, counseling, and community psychology. Some of these newer areas may resemble social work more than experimental or clinical psychology inasmuch as they deal with environmental conditions that affect clients.

Let's look at an example of how a social worker and a psychologist might handle a particular case differently.

Juan has been in and out of juvenile institutions most of his life. Abandoned by his mother at an early age, and never having known his father, he went first to a church-operated orphanage and then to a foster home. After running away he stole a car and was apprehended by the police. By the time he was thirteen he was committed to a public "training school" for delinquent boys. Immediately after he got there, he saw a psychologist who gave him a battery of psychological tests. The purpose of these tests was to determine (1) his level of intellectual functioning, (2) his emotional state, and (3) the prospects for "adjustment" to his new environment. On the basis of these test results, a treatment plan was recommended. He now sees a clinical psychologist once a week. This psychologist thinks that it is important for Juan to change the way that his thought processes operate in order for him to adapt to the pattern of life in the institution.

Juan is also assigned to a social worker who will be his case manager while he is in the training school, and who will also be responsible for planning Juan's eventual return to the community. His social worker is interested in how and what Juan thinks, but he is more concerned with problems in his social relationships that have gotten him into the institution. He realizes that if Juan is ever to readjust successfully to a normal life in the community, he must try to build relationships for Juan that will be supportive and provide incentives for normal, healthy behavior. The social worker's job actually requires him to spend more time building a network of support systems for Juan in the community than in counseling Juan about his psychological problems.

Students who are interested in a job that allows them to engage exclusively in counseling clients might want to consider counseling or clinical psychology. On the other hand, for students who are "turned on" by a job that challenges them to manipulate and change the environment as well as to provide direct counseling as a way of helping clients, social work might be a better choice.

Sociology

The sociologist is interested in the *study* of social organizations and institutions, or as one text puts it, "the analysis of the structure of social relationships as constituted by social interactions" (Abercrombie, Hill, & Turner, 1984). The key words are *study* and *analysis*. Although there have been some radical or reform-minded sociologists whose political beliefs led them into social *action,* they are generally a much more theoretically oriented group of persons than are social workers. While sociological literature has contributed heavily to modern social work practice, it has been the social worker who has attempted to apply theories of social organization and interaction to improve social functioning. The sociologist is more interested in *understanding;* the social worker in *doing.*

Counseling

There are probably as many different types of counselors as there are shades of green—rehabilitation counselors, vocational counselors, guidance counselors, marriage counselors, and so forth—but they all differ from social work in one important aspect: They emphasize the establishment of a relationship with the client as a way of helping (Timms & Timms, 1982). In other words, counseling does not necessarily consider the manipulation of factors in the client's environment as a primary intervention technique. If a student is having problems at school, a counselor is likely to use some form of talk therapy as the primary method of intervention. The school social worker, on the other hand, is likely to consider such factors as relationships with parents, whether the family has the financial resources to provide the student with breakfast, and whether being a member of a racial or ethnic minority group affects the student's behavior. Instead of (or in addition to) counseling, the social worker may intercede with the parents, try to help the family obtain food stamps, or develop a program to improve race relations among students in the school.

Psychiatry

Social workers are also quite likely to work with psychiatrists as part of an interdisciplinary team, but there are vast differences between social work and psychiatry. Psychiatrists are medical doctors who use a medical model in their treatment of illness. The psychiatrist prescribes a treatment (which could include medication, rest, counseling, and so forth) for the client in the hope of effecting a cure (Noyes & Kolb, 1961). While psychiatrists deal with disordered and undesirable functionings of the personality, social workers often work with normal people (at least as normal as you and I) who simply have problems coping with certain situations or factors in their environment. While a psychiatrist might view Juan's delinquency as the consequence of a personality disorder, the social worker might see it as normal coping behavior for a youth in his situation. The problem then becomes one not of changing Juan but of changing Juan's *situation*.

Nursing

In one sense the profession of nursing, as defined by Urdang (1983), probably has more in common with social work than any of the other professions previously discussed. Nursing is "the practice in which a nurse assists the individual, sick or well, in the performance of those activities contributing to health or its recovery . . . that he would perform unaided if he had the necessary strength, will, or knowledge" (p. 3). The nurse would seem to have a mandate to pay attention to client-environment interaction, not just to the physiological or intrapsychic functioning of the client.

The major difference, of course, is that the specific skills employed by the nurse are based on medical training, and the nurse is more likely to be concerned with the client's physiological functioning. Some nurses focus their professional activities specifically on psychiatric nursing, while others work in nursing homes or other settings. There is still a great similarity between nursing and social work. In fact, the public health nurse and the social worker may sometimes be indistinguishable. (Both professions may frequently perform many of the same functions in nursing homes and hospices.)

Public Administration

How can there be any similarities between social work and public administration? Why do we even bother to make this comparison? We do it because the managers or directors of large public welfare organizations are just as likely to have been trained in public administration as in social work (McNeece, DiNitto, & Johnson, 1984). We also do it because a growing number of social workers—some with specific training in *social welfare administration*—are managers or directors of such agencies. Administrative training for professional social workers became available on a significant scale only within the past three decades. Today there is continuing debate over the appropriateness of dividing the profession between clinicians and administrators.

Some members of the profession question whether social work administrators have more in common with public administrators than with *real* social workers. On the other hand, some wonder whether clinical social workers are becoming more like psychologists than *real* social workers (Frumkin & O'Connor, 1985). The similarity between social workers with administrative training and those with clinical training rests partly on a common knowledge base in such areas as human behavior and the social environment, social welfare policy, and social work practice. It rests more heavily, however, on the common value base of the profession, discussed earlier. The *difference* between the social work administrator and the public administrator with no professional social work training depends also on values and skills. The public administrator is trained in management methods that can be applied to any public organizations—state highway department, a bureau of fisheries, or the Internal Revenue Service. The social work administrator, however, would not be comfortable working in an agency that did not seek to help clients with problems of social functioning or advocate for clients who were oppressed or disadvantaged. The public administrator may be guided more by values such as economy and efficiency, and the social work administrator by the well-being of the client.

Summary

Social work is a diverse profession. It is also relatively new and still trying to gain legitimacy among the more established professions. One of the hallmarks of this profession is its value base that is summarized in NASW's comprehensive code of ethics. The essence of social work practice is its focus on helping individuals, groups, or communities enhance or restore their capacity for social functioning and creating societal conditions favorable to those ends.

The evolution of American social work is a logical extension of the historical development of a helping profession that is as old as recorded history. Throughout the ages, those societies that have flourished have been those that organized systems for helping individuals with inadequate resources to care for themselves. What separates social workers from other persons performing similar functions as *volunteers* are those qualities that identify a *profession*.

Overview

Five themes that emerge from Chapter 1 appear throughout this book:

1. Social workers have struggled to develop a comprehensive definition of the profession, but no consensus has been reached.
2. Social workers must compete with a variety of traditional and new human service professionals in today's job market. Many of these newer professions have borrowed heavily from social work practice models, yet social work is still struggling to prove its effectiveness.
3. The value base of the profession is an important distinguishing feature of social work, and social workers frequently face value dilemmas that threaten their ability to deliver services to clients.
4. Social workers bring a broader perspective to assisting clients than most other human service professionals. Social workers consider the environment as well as the client in developing appropriate intervention strategies.
5. Social work's multilevel perspective makes the profession particularly well equipped to develop social welfare policies and to administer social welfare programs.

Throughout the book we discuss some sensitive issues and pose some difficult questions. The history of social work has not always been without strife. Major professional organizations have not always been on good terms. Social workers have frequently failed to reach a consensus on important social issues. Some fear that social workers have become too highly specialized and that diverse interests have carried the profession in too many directions, risking loss of identity as a profession. Others see this great diversity as a strength and welcome a debate of honest differences between factions with different points of view. We will not settle most of these issues; in fact, we will raise more questions than we will answer. However, we do promise you an interesting intellectual journey. In the end, you may agree with us that it would be difficult to find a more exciting or challenging profession.

Suggested Readings

Axinn, J., & Levin, H. (1982). *Social welfare: A history of the American response to need* (2nd ed.). New York: Harper & Row.

DiNitto, D. (1995). *Social welfare policy: Politics and public policy* (4th ed.). Boston: Allyn & Bacon.

Pumphrey, R. E., & Pumphrey, M. W. (1961). *The heritage of American social work*. New York: Columbia University Press.

Specht, H., & Courtney, M. (1994). *Unfaithful Angels: How social work has abondoned its mission*. New York: Free Press.

2

Educating and Credentialing Social Workers

The original chapter from the first edition of this book has been revised by DANIEL HARKNESS, Department of Social Work, Boise State University.

Social workers practice in many different areas—child welfare, drug abuse, mental health, corrections, gerontology—and use many skills to help their clients—case management, grant writing, legislative advocacy, program planning, psychotherapy, and supervision. Later in the book we explore a number of social work practice areas and skills. But before considering these subjects, we examine other aspects of the profession.

We begin by exploring social work education. How do social workers prepare for careers in social work, and what credentials must be acquired before an individual is considered ready to practice social work? As we will see, there is conflict about the degrees offered and whether certification and licensure are always in the best interests of social workers and their clients. We will also describe organizations in the United States and abroad that represent social workers' interests. They are a diverse group of organizations, and although their members share many viewpoints about the profession, there are also areas of substantial disagreement. Like other professions, social work has many internal concerns. Some concerns discussed in this chapter are pay scales, the job market, the declassification of social work positions, and privatization—topics that are likely to concern those deciding whether social work is the field for them.

Controversies in the History of Social Work Education

Training or education programs for social workers first developed during the 1890s as the need for workers in voluntary organizations such as the Charity Organization Society (COS) increased.[1] Since the inception of formal education, a series of issues about social work education have been addressed by the profession. Some of them were resolved early. For example, one controversy was whether schools of social work should be independent or affiliated with a university. Some social workers warned of relinquishing control of social work education to university faculty who might not appreciate the need for practical as well as theoretical education, but others emphasized the benefits for the legal and medical professions that had resulted from university affiliation. By 1923 most social work education programs were university affiliated. However, concern remained about maintaining the integrity and separate identity of schools of social work *within* academic institutions. For example, Edith Abbott, the first dean of the School of Social Administration at the University of Chicago, fought to maintain the school separate from the sociology department. Today, no one questions university affiliation, but some social work programs that are administratively located within other academic departments may still be dealing with issues that Abbott raised.

Another issue that has influenced social work since the early 1900s is professionalization. Since 1915, when Abraham Flexner gave his long-remembered speech de-

---

[1]Much of this section draws on Austin, D. (1986). *A history of social work education*. Austin, TX: The University of Texas at Austin, School of Social Work.

claring that social work was *not* a profession, social workers have been preoccupied with achieving professional status. One way social workers have done this is by refining their educational programs, but today considerable conflict remains over what the content of social work curricula should be and whether social work degrees should be offered at the baccalaureate as well as the master's level.

Graduate and Undergraduate Education

In the early days of professional social work education there were basically two types of students. One type had already earned baccalaureate degrees in other fields. Often these were women who had attended private northeastern universities and whose fathers or husbands were professionals. The other type of student was more likely to be a middle-class public high school graduate from the Midwest attending a public university. These students were seeking undergraduate degrees as a secure route to employment. With two types of students, social work education began to take two tracks—baccalaureate and graduate. Those with graduate education were more likely to take jobs in voluntary (private, nonprofit) agencies, whereas those with baccalaureate education tended to be employed by public welfare agencies.

In 1919 representatives of seventeen social work education programs joined together to address their common concerns by establishing the Association of Training Schools for Professional Social Work. Later the organization became the Association of Professional Schools of Social Work. In 1927 it changed its name to the American Association of Schools of Social Work (AASSW) and developed educational standards for all member schools. Although social work in many northern European countries continues to be a semiprofession or a trade taught in vocational schools, the AASSW in 1932 decided that the proper preparation for professional practice was graduate education. By 1939 full AASSW membership was granted only to programs that required two academic years of study. This model influenced social work education for many years. The strongest advocates for graduate-only education were graduate faculty and professionals with graduate educations; advocates of undergraduate education were agency administrators and college and university presidents. As more social service professionals were needed after passage of the Social Security Act in 1935, the debate over educational qualifications intensified.

In spite of the AASSW's decision, the number of undergraduate programs continued to grow. In 1942 a number of undergraduate programs and one-year master's programs formed the National Association of Schools of Social Administration (NASSA). NASSA was particularly concerned with preparation for public welfare practice. With two bodies representing social work education, confusion and disagreements were bound to occur, and in 1946 the AASSW and the NASSA formed the National Council on Social Work Education to resolve their differences. This group commissioned a study, referred to as the Hollis-Taylor Report (after its authors), that included the recommendations that one organization represent social work education and that two years of graduate education be required of social workers. Other groups that were accrediting specializations in social work education programs, such as psychiatric and medical social work, also agreed to these recommendations. As a result, the

Council on Social Work Education (CSWE) was established in 1952 and became the accrediting body for social work education. It was decided that CSWE would accredit graduate programs only. But the debate about undergraduate education was far from over.

As the War on Poverty and the expansion of many social welfare programs in the 1960s and 1970s increased the demand for social service personnel, the profession once again gave serious consideration to accrediting undergraduate programs. In 1962 CSWE adopted some guidelines for undergraduate programs. Programs could declare self-compliance with the guidelines and become constituent members of CSWE. In 1974 CSWE finally extended official accreditation to baccalaureate programs. Still, some social workers are not convinced that this was the right move, and debate continues over such issues as what distinctions should be made between undergraduate and graduate education and whether it makes sense to restrict undergraduate education to preparation for generalist practice while graduate students may be educated for specialist practice.

Curriculum Content

One of the first issues addressed by early social work educators was curriculum—what to teach? There was an emphasis on applying social science theory to develop social reforms. The "social gospel movement," based on the teachings of Jesus that were directed at social reform, influenced many faculty. Students were taught to analyze social conditions and develop models for reform, such as social insurance programs. Additional curriculum content was derived from the practice experience of COS workers, especially diagnosis and identification of resources appropriate to meet clients' needs. Mary Richmond's *Social Diagnosis,* published in 1917, is a classic in the field.

One of the first curriculum debates concerned the weight to be given social science and reform content as opposed to information on the practical applications of social work. By the 1920s curriculum was leaning heavily in the direction of practice methods, especially casework. The Milford Conferences of the 1920s brought social workers together to discuss definitions and elements of social casework. It was also at this time that the fieldwork component of social work education programs developed. Many students divided their time between the classroom and supervised agency practice. The tradition of schools' maintaining responsibility for directing the fieldwork component of social work education also developed.

In order to meet Flexner's criteria of a profession, social work still needed a scientific base, and Freud's psychoanalytic theory provided this for many. Social workers adapted Freud's work to the teaching and practice of casework. But debates over the proper definition of casework and the purpose of social work ensued. The emphasis in Freudian casework was on the *intrapsychic,* while Mary Richmond's work emphasized *social factors.* In the practice community social workers argued over whether the profession should concentrate on casework or on social reform. These arguments intensified during the Great Depression.

In the 1930s and 1940s another debate surfaced over how casework should be taught. Those who espoused the *diagnostic school* remained concerned with Freudian concepts and psychological problems *underlying* the client's presenting problem (the problem for which the client is seeking assistance), while *functionalists* espoused the theories of Otto Rank and concentrated on helping clients resolve their *immediate* presenting problems. Most social work educators seemed to favor the diagnostic school, but shrinking resources during the Great Depression made the functional school attractive to practitioners (see Eisenberg, 1956).

Group work and community organization also emerged as social work methods. Both methods aimed to prepare people for citizen participation in a democratic society. Another perspective on community organization was learning about interagency coordination, fund raising, and social welfare planning. Initial interest in group work came from those working with young people in nonclinical settings, such as youth clubs, but expanded to include the treatment of behavioral problems.

Social policy courses tended to be descriptive of current programs rather than part of the methods or practice curriculum, but they often included proposals for federal, state, and local action. Research was also part of the curriculum. This subject area was strongly influenced by the university community and was often taught by a social scientist other than a social worker. Community surveys of social conditions were a popular research methodology and most master's programs adopted a thesis requirement. The *Social Service Review* also began publication and remains a well-known journal publishing articles primarily about social work research. Box 2-1 comments on the importance of social work research.

In 1959 the report of a group headed by Werner Boehm outlined content considered essential for social work programs. It included (1) social science theory

---

BOX 2-1   Social Work Knowledge

Social action and social policy were at the cutting edge of social work education in the 1960s, but in the 1970s and 1980s social work research took center stage. The profession refocused attention on knowledge for practice when Joel Fischer (1973) asked "Is casework effective?" Fischer's question sought to introduce science as the arbiter of truth in the relationship among social work values, the art of helping, and client outcomes. The response from the profession was mixed. Many actively questioned whether helping could "be patterned on the methods of science" (Germain, 1970, p. 29), and some suspected that the hue and cry about research and science was actually a battle for control of the profession itself (Karger, 1983). On the pages of *Social Work, Social Service Review,* and other journals, a stirring debate on the nature of knowledge and the role of research in social work education and practice ensued (Heineman, 1981; Goldstein, 1990; Imre, 1984; Saleeby, 1979). However, it became clear that social workers had to demonstrate that social work helped people if they wanted to be paid for their services (Parloff, 1982). Although the debate continues, the profession has responded by increasing its investment in social work research and science.

about individuals, groups, and the social environment, (2) applied content on human growth and development and social policy, and (3) methods content including casework, group work, community organization, administration, and research. Although all of Boehm's recommendations were not formally adopted, they influenced CSWE's 1962 Curriculum Policy Statement.

Current Curriculum Guidelines

Social work education continues to evolve. Contemporary debates in the profession mirror old conflicts between different schools of social casework, and new solutions to the tension between different practice traditions continue to emerge. Social work is a pluralistic profession, and social work education must synthesize the common base of social work practice from an alliance of many points of view. The Council on Social Work Education has the responsibility of unifying social work education. Unifying social work education requires the administration of curriculum policy standards that limit what is taught in order to guarantee a common core of values, knowledge, and skills for practice. However, in 1992 the CSWE adopted new curriculum standards that attempt to promote greater innovation in social work education.

CSWE mandates that baccalaureate and master's programs be grounded in a liberal arts perspective. Upon that foundation, social work education includes content in nine areas: social work values and ethics; diversity; promotion of social and economic justice; populations at risk; human behavior and the social environment (HBSE); social welfare policies and services (SWPS); social work practice; research; and fieldwork. These content areas are described in CSWE's current Curriculum Policy Statement (see Commission on Accreditation, 1994).

Internalizing social work values and committing oneself to ethical behavior are necessary for socialization into the profession. This process begins by developing awareness of your personal values and how they influence your actions. Social work espouses democratic values. That means that social workers respect the right of all people to determine their future and to participate actively in every sphere of human activity.

"All people" connotes a constituency that is diverse and inclusive. Clients, like colleagues, are individuals with different experiences, needs, and beliefs. Moreover, they are members of groups that can be distinguished by race, ethnicity, culture, national origin, social class, gender, sexual orientation, religion, ability, and age. Social work education prepares you to appreciate and work with people who may be quite different from yourself.

Appreciating human diversity means more than celebrating differences. It also means coming to terms with the consequences of social differentiation. Social work education examines the history, dynamics, and consequences of social and economic injustice, human oppression, and discrimination. Students also learn how to become agents for change and social justice. The concepts of social and economic justice signal the existence of historical inequalities that still limit people's rights to participate fully in the life of the nation. Barriers to full participation in social and economic opportunities put people at risk of poverty, malnutrition, undereducation, and disease. Thus, social work education addresses the effects of discrimination, deprivation, and oppression on people of color, women, gay men and lesbians, people with disabilities, and others.

HBSE courses generally devote considerable attention to human development and the life cycle. Developmental theories of childhood and adolescence, such as those of Jean Piaget and Eric Erickson, may be given specific attention in addition to developmental models that emphasize biological and social development. Social work practice also requires knowledge about human development across the entire life cycle. In addition to individual behavior, behavior of families, groups, communities, and organizations are considered essential HBSE content. At the graduate level, courses on topics such as psychopathology may also be offered.

SWPS content and courses generally cover the major federal and state social welfare policies and programs, including social insurance, public assistance, and social services to a variety of client groups. In addition to describing who is served and how these programs work, SWPS content usually includes methods and models of policy analysis in order to answer questions such as whether a policy and its related programs are meeting their intended objectives, and to compare the results that would be obtained using alternative approaches. These courses may also address practice in the social policy arena, for example, the ways in which social workers influence the passage of legislation. The history and philosophy of the profession are examined, too.

The foundation of social work practice is the integration of values, knowledge, and skills for helping people in systems of all sizes. The skills of direct practice with clients include interviewing, building professional relationships, defining issues, assessing client strengths, setting goals, choosing and applying interventions, and evaluating practice outcomes. Social workers must integrate practice skills with their knowledge of human diversity to respond with sensitivity to the particular experiences of clients from differing ethnic and cultural backgrounds. Graduate education builds on the professional foundation to prepare students for advanced social work practice in an area of concentration. Thus, courses may also cover practice with particular groups of clients, for example, those with developmental disabilities or those with mental illnesses, and certain types of therapeutic techniques such as crisis intervention, ego psychology, or behavioral methods. CSWE requires that these practice courses be taught by a social worker with a master's degree in social work and two years post-master's experience. At the master's level social workers may also concentrate on learning what is called indirect or macropractice skills, such as social welfare administration and planning.

Research courses are intended to teach students to be critical consumers of social science research and to evaluate their own practice. Content includes the design and conduct of research ranging from evaluation of work with individual clients using single-subject designs to studies of larger systems using experimental designs, survey research, and other techniques.

Fieldwork or the field practicum requires that students have the opportunity to practice their skills under supervision in agency and other settings where social workers are employed. CSWE accreditation standards specify the minimum number of hours students must earn in fieldwork and the qualifications required of those who supervise field placements. While students from other academic departments may be allowed to take some social work courses, only social work students are permitted to take fieldwork courses.

CSWE does not specify a particular list of courses or syllabi to be followed. Since each program identifies its own specific mission, its faculty designs a curriculum to meet the program's objectives, ensuring that all curriculum areas are addressed. The specific courses and structures of social work programs—both baccalaureate and graduate—vary, depending on the program; and faculty and students often debate whether the curriculum is meeting its objectives or whether changes should be made. These discussions seem particularly frequent in master's programs in which students may select concentrations and specializations in addition to the basic curriculum.

Structure of Social Work Education

Although CSWE accredits only four-year undergraduate programs and master's programs, community colleges may also offer some social work courses, and universities may offer a doctorate in social work. There are approximately 382 accredited undergraduate programs, 112 accredited masters programs, and 55 doctoral programs in social work in the United States (Lennon, 1995).

Undergraduate Programs

Accredited undergraduate programs prepare students for beginning or entry-level generalist social work practice. Many undergraduate programs call the degree they offer the bachelor of social work (BSW); others offer a bachelor of arts or bachelor of science degree in social work. Since accredited programs meet the same standards, these are considered equivalent degrees. Of course, colleges and universities differ in their basic education requirements, such as the number of credits in English, science, and other subjects needed to earn a degree. And although CSWE mandates that certain subjects be taught, the faculty of each program determine the number of social work courses and their specific content. Directors of all accredited undergraduate programs are members of the House of Delegates of CSWE. The directors also have an independent organization, the Association of Baccalaureate Program Directors (BPD). BPD holds an annual conference that brings together undergraduate program directors to discuss issues of mutual interest. BPD interfaces with CSWE and other organizations to represent the interests of undergraduate social work programs. In 1995, the BPD established the *Journal of Baccalaureate Social Work.*

Master's Programs

Master's programs generally call their degree the master of social work (MSW), but some offer a master of science or master of arts degree in social work. All accredited master's programs offer a two-year course of study, and many also offer a shorter course of study called "advanced standing" for those who have a baccalaureate degree in social work from an accredited program. Advanced standing programs recognize that students with baccalaureate degrees in social work have knowledge that students from other disciplines must acquire in graduate school. Rather than repeat course work that they have taken as undergraduates, students admitted to advanced standing move on to more advanced social work courses. Possessing an undergraduate social work degree does not guarantee admittance to advanced standing, but it is a requisite for applying. Applicants are also required to meet other admissions requirements of the individual programs, and some programs receive more applications from qualified students than they can accept.

Master's programs generally offer students an opportunity to select a concentration or track of study. Some programs offer students a choice of two tracks, one called something like Direct Practice or Clinical Social Work, and the other often called Indirect Practice or Administration and Planning. Master's programs may also educate social workers for advanced generalist practice, or they may provide education for practice in specialty areas such as gerontology, child welfare, chemical dependency, or occupational social work. The National Association of Deans and Directors (NADD) is composed of the heads of master's programs. It is an independent organization that operates similarly to the BPD.

Doctoral Programs

Most doctoral programs offer a doctor of philosophy (Ph.D.) degree in social work, although a few still offer the doctor of social work (DSW). Unlike the bachelor's and master's degrees in social work, the doctorate is usually not considered a professional practice degree. Doctoral programs generally prepare professionals for careers in teaching and research or high-level administrative or policy analysis positions, although a few emphasize clinical work. Doctoral programs usually require two years of classroom work followed by completion of a dissertation. The Group for the Advancement of Doctoral Education in Social Work (GADE) is composed of doctoral program directors, and members meet annually to discuss issues in doctoral education. Since CSWE does not accredit doctoral programs, their content and design can be quite flexible, and much of the course work may be structured around the student's individual interests. Doctoral programs must, of course, meet the parent university's regulations for conferring graduate degrees.

Program Structure

A college or university may offer social work degrees at all three levels—undergraduate, master's, and doctoral—or it may offer programs at one or two levels. The size of social work programs varies considerably, from two faculty (the minimum number needed for an accredited undergraduate program) and a handful of majors, to several dozen faculty and more than a thousand majors. Colleges and universities that offer a master's degree often have a separate school, college, or department of social work, and many of these programs are headed by a dean or director. Virtually all programs that offer a doctorate also offer the master's degree.

Undergraduate programs that are not associated with graduate programs are often administered with related academic disciplines in the university. For example, one department may comprise social work, sociology, and anthropology with the same faculty chairperson. However, every accredited social work program must have its own director and faculty who possess appropriate academic credentials in social work. Programs must also have an adequate budget to carry out their functions.

Students

The exact number and characteristics of students enrolled in social work education programs is difficult to determine. Although CSWE periodically collects statistics on enrollments, not all programs respond to requests for information. In 1994,[2] the 349 undergraduate programs that responded to CSWE's inquiry reported approximately 24,536 juniors and seniors enrolled as majors. Another 13,933 majors were enrolled as freshmen and sophomores; however, at some colleges and universities students do not declare a major until the junior year. Of the full-time junior and senior social work majors, 85 percent were women. Twenty-seven percent were ethnic minority students, including 17 percent African American, nearly 4 percent Mexican American, and 2 percent Puerto Rican. Representation of other minority groups is relatively small, although this varies by program. For example, the University of Hawaii attracts a considerable number of Asian American students because of the state's ethnic heritage, and American Indian students were 35 percent of the juniors and seniors enrolled at Northeastern State University in Oklahoma.

In addition, more than 7,000 students were pursuing undergraduate degrees on a part-time basis. Another 19,000 undergraduate students were enrolled in social work courses but were not pursuing a social work degree. There appears to be considerable interest in social work courses among students who are not social work majors. They are often psychology and sociology majors who are interested in broadening their understanding of the social sciences and learning more about the application of this knowledge to solve social problems.

Approximately 33,212 students pursued social work master's degrees in 1994. Enrollment in social work graduate programs declined in the early 1980s, but during the decade that ended in 1994, full-time student enrollment increased by more than 50 percent. Part-time student enrollment increased during the same period by nearly 46 percent, and now nearly 35 percent of the students enrolled in master's programs attend school on a part-time basis. With dwindling financial aid, many students are enrolled part time because they are working to support themselves and their families as they pursue a master's degree.

Among full-time master's students, about 82 percent are women and about 21 percent are ethnic minorities. Fifty-four percent of students are enrolled in direct

[2]Information on social work education programs and students in this section relies on Lennon, T. (1995). *Statistics on social work education in the United States.* Alexandria, VA: Council on Social Work Education.

practice concentrations, and less than 7 percent are enrolled in indirect practice concentrations (administration, management, community organization, and planning). The remaining students are enrolled in generic concentrations, a combination of direct and indirect practice, another type of specialization (such as mental health or child welfare), or they have not yet declared a concentration.

Many faculty have expressed concern about declining enrollment in indirect practice tracks. Some observers associate indirect practice with social change and interpret these thinning student ranks as a sign that social work has abandoned the core values of the profession to help the poor and oppressed. For others, it means that fewer social work students will be prepared to manage social welfare programs. However, figures suggest that the *proportion* of students in indirect practice has not changed much, and that enrollment reflects the practice market. For most of the past twenty-five years, the percentage of full-time students enrolled in indirect practice tracks has hovered between 7 and 11 percent.

Moreover, direct services are the primary function of professional practice for 70 percent of the social workers with master's degrees.[3] Although 30 percent describe their primary functions as macropractice, that category includes a broad array of functions. Direct-service experience and time-in-grade are the steadiest rungs on the ladder to social work administration, so the direct-practice curriculum may be the surest route to indirect practice. However, as social workers find themselves directing programs, they may require continuing education to learn administrative skills. Less than 3 percent of social workers devote their time primarily to policy, consultation, research, and planning, and there appears to be a downward trend in the proportion of the profession performing macrolevel functions. Many factors influence the concentrations that graduate students choose, and it remains to be seen what choices students will make in the turbulent political environment as we move into the twenty-first century.

Approximately 2,100 students were enrolled in doctoral programs in 1994, an increase of only 15 percent in the last ten years. There are nearly equal numbers of full- and part-time doctoral students. Of full-time doctoral students, about 70 percent are women, and about 22 percent are ethnic minorities. About 68 percent of doctoral degrees are awarded to women and 15 percent to individuals of ethnic minority backgrounds.

By now you are probably thinking about the social work program in which you are enrolled—the degree or degrees it offers, whether it is housed in a separate school or college or combined with other degree programs, the number of students enrolled, and their gender composition and ethnic composition. In addition to student composition, faculty composition is important, as are interactions among students, faculty, and program administrators such as the director or dean. For example, the program should have procedures for academic and professional advising of students and should allow for sufficient opportunities for contact between administrators, faculty, and students.

---

[3]This paragraph relies on Gibelman, M., & Schervish, P. H. (1993). *Who we are: The social work labor force as reflected in the NASW membership.* Washington, DC: NASW Press. Copyright 1993, National Association of Social Workers, Inc.

Membership Organizations

A number of organizations represent professional social workers in the United States. Each has a different purpose.

The Council on Social Work Education

CSWE continues to pursue its goals of providing leadership in social work education and ensuring a competent cadre of social work professionals.[4] The council is concerned that there be a sufficient number of high-quality social work education programs to meet the country's need for social work professionals. The organization is best known for its role in accrediting social work education programs, but conferences, publications, consultation, and curriculum development projects to improve social work education and social work practice are also important functions. Much of CSWE's work is conducted by its commissions and committees. These commissions are Accreditation, Educational Policy, Field Education, Gay Men and Lesbian Women, National Legislation and Administrative Policy, Women, Social Work Practice, Conferences and Faculty Development, International, Publications and Media, and Racial, Ethnic and Cultural Diversity. The current president of CSWE is Moses Newsome Jr., and the executive director is Donald Beless.

CSWE Governance

CSWE revised its governance structure by amending its bylaws in a 1993 membership referendum. Under the new bylaws, a board of directors, composed of twenty-seven or twenty-eight voting members, governs CSWE. The voting membership includes the officers of the council (the president, vice president/secretary, and treasurer, joined once every three years by the president-elect) and twenty-four additional voting directors elected from the membership (including three graduate and three undergraduate faculty from accredited social work education programs, five minority representatives, two practice representatives, and one member at large). At least ten of the elected board members shall be from the following groups: African American, Asian American, Mexican American, Native American, and Puerto Rican, preferably with one representative from the Commonwealth of Puerto Rico. In addition to voting members, the board has two ex officio nonvoting members, the chairpersons of the commissions on educational policy and accreditation. CSWE has approximately 3,754 organizational members (schools and social service agencies) and individual members (faculty and social work practitioners) (R. Lucas, personal communication, September 14, 1995).

CSWE Accreditation

The Commission on Recognition of Postsecondary Accreditation and the U.S. Department of Education recognize CSWE as the official accrediting body of social

---

[4]Much of this section relies on Beless, D. (1995). Council on Social Work Education. In R. L. Edwards (Ed.), *Encyclopedia of social work* (19th ed., Vol. 1, pp. 632–636). Washington, DC: NASW Press. Copyright 1995, National Association of Social Workers, Inc.

work education programs in the United States. The twenty-five members of CSWE's Commission on Accreditation are drawn from social work faculty, students, practitioners, and the public and are appointed by CSWE's president. Criteria for accreditation are outlined in the manual *Handbook of Accreditation Standards and Procedures* (Commission on Accreditation, 1994) and are discussed throughout this book. After a program receives initial accreditation, it is reviewed again in four years and every eight years thereafter. Failure to meet the standards can result in sanctions against the program, the most severe of which is loss of accreditation. Reports of site visits conducted by teams of peers (social work faculty and practitioners) and study of documentation provided by the programs are the major vehicles for reviewing programs.

Although more than 525 graduate and undergraduate programs voluntarily comply with accreditation, there is never a lack of discussion or concern about the process. Like most evaluative procedures, fairness of the process and the content of the standards are frequent topics of discussion. Some believe that the standards are too broad and vague. For example, undergraduate students must have direct knowledge of social, psychological, and biological determinants of human behavior, but the standards do not specify the nature and amount of content on these topics. Faculty must exercise their best judgment in determining that they are upholding the standards, but at the time of review, the Commission on Accreditation may decide that content is inadequate. Others argue that some aspects of accreditation are so specific that they stifle educational innovations because adherence to standards results in uniformity rather than creativity among programs. These issues were reflected in the adoption of revised curriculum standards that took effect in 1995. Many believe that the new standards are more streamlined and flexible.

CSWE Publications and Conferences

CSWE keeps its membership informed of curriculum innovations and other educational issues through its publications. The *Journal of Social Work Education* (formerly called the *Journal of Education for Social Work*) is a refereed, quarterly publication. CSWE also publishes statistical reports and directories of social work education programs and books on social work education and practice. The organization's newsletter is the "Social Work Education Reporter." CSWE's major conference, the annual program meeting (APM), is held in a different location in the United States each year. It provides an opportunity for social work professionals, particularly social work faculty, to present papers and discuss issues of interest. It is one of the profession's major vehicles for disseminating information to improve social work education. Presentations address new models for social work practice, curriculum innovations, and a host of other topics ranging from student advising to sexual harassment.

The National Association of Social Workers

In addition to CSWE and the other organizations primarily concerned with social work education, another group of associations addresses a broad range of professional concerns and attracts many practicing social workers as members.

The organization with the largest membership of social workers in the world is the National Association of Social Workers (NASW).[5] Before the mid-1950s, there were several groups of social workers in the United States, organized primarily by special fields of practice. In 1955 six of these organizations, composed of social workers in the areas of medical social work, psychiatric social work, school social work, group work, community organization, and research, joined forces with the American Association of Social Workers (AASW), a general membership organization founded in 1921, to become the NASW. In its early years, NASW retained a structure focused on specialty practice areas, but considerable attention was given to improving the status of the profession in order to attract members. Today, NASW's literature expresses its "overriding concern for the eradication of racism, sexism, and poverty." In recent years its agenda has been to "advance the profession, to influence public policy, to advocate on behalf of clients and of professional social workers, to promote the image of the profession, and to improve compensation for social workers" (Goldstein & Beebe, 1995, p. 1757). But concerns about specialization have re-emerged. In 1995 NASW again began to offer members the opportunity to join specialty groups within its organizational structure.

NASW's day-to-day operations are conducted by national and chapter staff. The national office is located on Capitol Hill in Washington, D.C. There are fifty-five chapters, one in each of the fifty United States, the District of Columbia, New York City, Puerto Rico, and the Virgin Islands, and an international chapter open to social workers around the world. State chapter offices are generally located in capital cities to facilitate access to state social service agencies and state legislatures. Cities and other localities may establish units to bring members together on a regular basis.

NASW Membership

Of the 153,500 members of NASW, 77 percent are female. The median age of employed NASW members is forty-one to forty-five, and about 40 percent are age forty or younger. Eighty-eight percent of members are white, 6 percent are black, 3 percent are Hispanic, and 1 percent are Asian American. Box 2-2 takes a closer look at ethnic representation in the profession.

NASW is supported by members' dues that are divided among the national and chapter offices. Regular members must hold a baccalaureate or graduate degree from a program accredited by the CSWE. Dues for regular members are $157.50 a year and $20.00 more for those who are also members of the Academy of Certified Social Workers. A special student membership category has dues of $39.50 for baccalaureate and master's students enrolled in accredited social work education programs. Students' dues are lower because their incomes are often limited, and NASW wishes to encourage them to join and to continue their membership after graduation.

---

[5]Much of this section relies on Battle, M. G. (1987). Professional associations: National Association of Social Workers. In A. Minahan (Ed.), *Encyclopedia of social work* (18th ed., Vol. 2, pp. 333–341). Silver Spring, MD: NASW. Copyright 1990, National Association of Social Workers, Inc.; Goldstein, S., & Beebe, L. (1995). National Association of Social Workers. In R. L. Edwards (Ed.), *Encyclopedia of social work* (19th ed., Vol. 2, pp. 1747–1764). Washington, DC: NASW Press. Copyright 1995, National Association of Social Workers, Inc.; Gibelman, M., & Schervish, P. H. (1993). *Who we are: The social work labor force as reflected in the NASW membership*. Washington, DC: NASW Press. Copyright 1993, National Association of Social Workers, Inc.

BOX 2-2   Is NASW Diverse?

The typical member of NASW is a white woman in her early forties who earned her MSW ten years ago and provides direct services in a mental health setting. However, the profession also includes substantial numbers of ethnic minorities and men. Enrollment in social work education programs gives a good picture of the current ethnic diversity in the profession. In academic year 1993–1994, African American students earned more than 13 percent of the baccalaureate degrees and 12 percent of the MSW degrees awarded in social work; Mexican American and Puerto Rican students earned 6.8 percent of the baccalaureate and 4 percent of the MSW degrees; Asian Americans earned 1.7 percent of the baccalaureate and 1.9 percent of

the MSW degrees; and American Indians earned 1.1 percent of the baccalaureate and 0.7 percent of the MSW degrees. However, the ethnic minority composition of NASW is only 5.9 percent African American, 2.6 percent Hispanic, 1.5 percent Asian American, and 0.5 percent American Indian. Since 21.5 percent of the full-time students enrolled in graduate social work education are ethnic minorities, they appear to be underrepresented in the flagship organization of the profession, which is 88.1 percent white. On the other hand, 62 percent of the 137 employees running the daily operations at NASW's national headquarters are ethnic minorities (J. Reed, personal communication, September 25, 1995).

Sources: Figures on social workers are from Gibelman, M., & Schervish, P. H. (1993). *Who we are: The social work labor force as reflected in the NASW membership.* Washington, DC: NASW Press. Copyright 1993, National Association of Social Workers, Inc. Figures on social work students are from Lennon, T. (1995). *Statistics on social work education in the United States: 1994.* Alexandria, VA: CSWE.

NASW has attempted to increase baccalaureate membership, but those whose highest degree is a bachelor's are only about 4 percent of the total membership. Although many individuals with undergraduate degrees who remain in the profession eventually earn a master's degree and are no longer counted as baccalaureate members, the number of members whose highest degree is a baccalaureate is disproportionately small. In 1994, baccalaureate social workers received approximately 44 percent of all degrees earned in accredited social work education programs (Lennon, 1995). Some believe that NASW's programming is more responsive to graduate than baccalaureate degree social workers (Sheafor & Shank, 1986) and that the dues are too high to encourage baccalaureate membership.

NASW Governance

Since 1956 NASW has convened a delegate assembly to help ensure broad participation among the membership. The assembly now meets once every three years, and representatives are elected by their respective chapters. Policy statements on a multitude of topics are discussed and voted on. Issues addressed at the assembly range from deciding whether there should be a dues increase to determining the positions NASW will take on social issues such as abortion, lesbian and gay rights, and tax reform (National Association of Social Workers [NASW], 1994). The current set of position statements is available in chapter offices.

The NASW board of directors consists of twenty-five members elected by the general membership who make policy decisions for the operation of the organization following the guidelines established by the delegate assembly. The board includes an undergraduate and a graduate student representative. Currently Jay Cayner is the president, and Robert Cohen is the executive director of NASW.

NASW Standards of Practice

The NASW Code of Ethics provides general standards of practice to guide professional social workers (see Chapter 1). NASW has also developed a series of publications defining standards for particular fields of practice, including health, schools, child welfare, long-term care, clinical, and settings serving people with developmental and functional disabilities. Recently, standards have been developed for mediation and case management.

Academy of Certified Social Workers (ACSW)

The ACSW was founded in 1962 and had 61,000 members in 1995. Initially, NASW members were "grandparented" into the ACSW. Current requirements include a master's degree in social work from a CSWE-accredited program; two years, full-time (or 3,000 hours), supervised, post-master's or post-doctorate experience; a passing score on a written examination; references indicating acceptability for ACSW membership; and membership in NASW. The Academy of Certified Baccalaureate Social Workers (ACBSW) was established in 1991 but discontinued in 1995. Few baccalaureate social workers belong to NASW, and NASW membership was required for this certification.

NASW Committees

The seven committees established under NASW bylaws are the Committee on Inquiry; the National Committee on Racial and Ethnic Diversity; the National Committee on Nominations and Leadership Identification that develops ballots and suggests members for committee appointments; the National Program Committee that is responsible for the NASW Symposium and other conferences; the National Committee on Women's Issues; the National Finance Committee; and the National Committee on Lesbian and Gay Issues. Each chapter also has a committee on inquiry that hears grievances filed against individual social workers who are NASW members and agencies that employ members. Cases of misconduct in which a member is accused of violating the Code of Ethics may be brought before the committee. Violations include such charges as engaging in sexual activity with a client, an act expressly forbidden by the Code of Ethics. The number of social workers charged with such violations is quite small. When a member is found to have violated the Code of Ethics, the committee can impose sanctions, such as revoking NASW membership or suspending membership and requiring the member to practice only under supervision for a stipulated period. Grievances against agencies and other employers usually arise when social workers believe they have been unjustly fired or that the agency uses discriminatory hiring and promotion practices. When a member or organization fails to take steps to correct a violation, the NASW board of directors may publish this in the *NASW News*.

NASW Publications

All NASW members receive the organization's newspaper, the *NASW News,* published ten times per year, which keeps them abreast of current events such as the latest policy developments in Washington, actions of the NASW board of directors, and news of conferences in the United States and abroad. Organizations conducting national job searches to fill high-level administrative, clinical, or faculty positions may advertise in the *News.* All members also receive *Social Work,* a refereed journal published six times per year. Articles address virtually any topic of interest to social workers including new practice techniques and the results of original research. Other NASW journals are *Social Work Research, Social Work Abstracts, Health & Social Work,* and *Social Work in Education* (concerned with school social work). NASW published the nineteenth edition of the *Encyclopedia of Social Work* in 1995. The organization has also published an extensive list of books, reports, and manuals on social work practice.

Other NASW Membership Benefits

Additional membership benefits include the opportunity to purchase several types of insurance—medical, term life, hospital indemnity, disability, accidental death and dismemberment, and professional liability. Members who do not have these coverages may find NASW's coverage less expensive than individually purchased policies, and the economical rates may encourage other members to purchase additional coverage.

Social workers who face lawsuits resulting from their professional practice may be eligible for assistance through the Legal Defense Fund. For example, criminal charges may be brought against a social worker who did not remove a child from a home before the child was seriously injured or killed. If it appears that the social worker acted with all regard for professional practice and obeyed the laws of the state, he or she may receive help with legal fees.

NASW's Legislative Arms

Political Action for Candidate Election (PACE) is NASW's political action committee established under the Federal Elections Campaign Act. The purpose of PACE is to back candidates in federal, state, and local elections who support the goals of NASW. The Education and Legislation Action Network (ELAN) provides information on social welfare issues to members and the public and promotes the passage of social welfare policy supported by NASW.

The National Federation of Societies of Clinical Social Work

In 1971, societies for clinical social work in California, Illinois, Kentucky, Louisiana, New York, and Texas formed a national association to promote clinical social work education, lobby for the legal regulation of social work, and support third-party reimbursement for social work services. Some social workers were alarmed by the development of the NFSCSW, fearing that it signaled a splintering of NASW and a return to the fractious politics of old. In response, NASW increased attention to clinical issues, convening a historic invitational forum on clinical social work in 1979 (Ewalt, 1980). Today, the NFSCSW has 10,000 members in thirty-four states, and affiliation agreements with the American Association of State Social Work Boards, the American Board of Examiners in Clinical Social Work, and the Council on Social Work Education. Although NFSCSW and NASW share many of the same goals and concerns, the two organizations remain unaffiliated.

International Organizations

In addition to the organizations representing the interests of social workers primarily in the United States and Canada, several organizations are primarily interested in international social work. Among these are the International Council on Social Welfare (ICSW), the International Association of Schools of Social Work (IASSW), and the International Federation of Social Workers (IFSW).[6] The ICSW is headquartered in Vienna, Austria and the IFSW in Geneva, Switzerland. The IASSW is moving its offices from Canada to The Netherlands. These three organizations hold joint conferences in a different country each year. They also collaborate in the publication of a journal called *International Social Work,* which publishes articles on social welfare policy, programs, and services, and social work education, practice, and research. The journal facilitates communication and exchange of information among the three organizations and among social workers in different countries.

In the United States, the Foreign Equivalency Determination Service (FEDS) of the Council on Social Work Education evaluates academic credits and credentials granted by universities and social work programs overseas in order to determine their equivalence to courses, degrees, titles, and licenses in the United States. NASW has a Committee on International Social Welfare that promotes interest in international social work through various means such as presentations at major conferences, and it maintains information on social workers interested in international social work and their areas of expertise.

Are We One Big, Happy Family?

The history of the organizations representing social workers, like many other professional groups, is marked by conflicts. Although a number of organizations reached a consensus and merged to form both NASW and CSWE, old conflicts resurface, and new issues emerge. For example, although NASW and CSWE have cooperated on many fronts, such as their mutual support of the Institute for the Advancement of Social Work Research, tension sometimes develops between the groups. CSWE has a relatively small membership compared with NASW, and most CSWE members are

---

[6]Much of this section relies on Healey, L. (1995). International social welfare: Organizations and activities. In R. L. Edwards (Ed.), *Encyclopedia of social work* (19th ed., Vol. 2, pp. 1499–1510). Washington, DC: NASW Press. Copyright 1995, National Association of Social Workers, Inc., and personal communication with Dr. Katherine Kendall and Dr. Ralph Garber, September 1995.

NASW members. From time to time the question arises as to whether the organizations should remain independent or merge.

In a pluralistic society no single organization can easily represent all the interests of a group as diverse as professional social workers. Multiple groups help ensure that the special concerns and different traditions of social workers are promoted. For example, the National Association of Black Social Workers believes that all of its interests cannot be adequately represented by NASW, whose membership is predominately white, even if a major goal of NASW is the elimination of racism (also see Chapter 15). Likewise, members of the North American Association of Christians in Social Work believe that their particular concerns cannot be addressed by social workers who do not share the same religious beliefs. Feminists also believe they need an independent voice through organizations such as the Association for Women in Social Work (see Chapter 17).

Licensure and Certification: Protection for Whom?

In any profession an important purpose of licensure or certification is to ensure that those engaged in professional practice meet certain qualifications or standards.[7] By specifying the knowledge and skills required for social work practice, licensure and certification are supposed to protect the people who utilize professional services. Of course, the rigor of qualifications and standards differs according to the particular methods used to grant licensure or certification, and established practitioners, through grandfathering clauses, are often exempt from meeting new standards. Although regulation does not guarantee professional competence, it usually allows for filing complaints against individuals accused of failing to provide services in a professionally competent way. It also provides sanctions for those who have violated professional standards.

There are also elements of self-interest in professional regulation. Depending on the system used, licensure or certification determines and limits who may use a certain professional title such as social worker, and who is permitted to provide certain types of services. From this perspective, the intent of licensure and certification is to make the profession more highly valued in the labor market by increasing the status of professionals. Although there is no evidence to indicate that regulation has increased the salaries of most social workers, regulation and vendorship laws may have contributed to increased earnings in the private sector (Gibelman & Schervish, 1993a).

[7]Much of the information in this section relies on Abernathy, L. (April 28, 1988). *State licensure of social workers in New Mexico—Who needs it?* Unpublished manuscript; Compton, B. R. (1980). *Introduction to social welfare & social work: Structure, function, and process.* Homewood, IL: Dorsey Press; Gilbert, N., & Specht, H. (1981). *Handbook of the social services.* Englewood Cliffs, NJ: Prentice Hall; Hardcastle, D. (1990). Legal regulation of social work. In A. Minahan (Ed.), *Encyclopedia of social work,* 18th ed., 1990 supplement, (pp. 203–217). Silver Spring, MD: NASW Press. Copyright 1990, National Association of Social Workers, Inc.; Whiting, L. (1995). Vendorship. In R. L. Edwards (Ed.), *Encyclopedia of social work* (19th ed., Vol. 3, pp. 2427–2431). Washington, DC: NASW Press. Copyright 1995, National Association of Social Workers, Inc.

Certification generally grants recognition that an individual has attained a certain level of knowledge and skill. Others may practice social work but cannot use certain job titles that are restricted to those who are certified. *Licensure* is usually considered a stronger form of regulation than certification since it is intended to prohibit those who are not licensed from practicing social work. One problem with establishing true licensing laws is that the work of social workers is not defined or distinguished in a way that clearly differentiates it from related professions. Some states license or certify social workers with bachelor's and master's degrees, while others recognize only those with a master's degree, or accord social workers with a graduate degree higher levels of certification or licensure. The weakest form of regulation is *registration,* which simply allows individuals to place their names voluntarily on a list maintained by the state. Registration is a part of certification and licensure.

The legal regulation of social work practice across the United States has taken sixty years to achieve (see Middleman, 1984; Biggerstaf, 1995). Puerto Rico, in 1934, was the first to have a licensing law. Eleven years later, California adopted "official registration and certification." Not until 1960 did seven more states adopt regulations, followed by fourteen more in the 1970s. By April 1989, forty-five states plus the District of Columbia, Puerto Rico, and the Virgin Islands had social work regulation, although Michigan, Oregon, and Rhode Island had voluntary registration only. NASW targeted the remaining states in order to achieve social work regulation nationwide. By 1993, every state had legal regulation of social work practice.

States with social work certification or licensure have boards responsible for overseeing these activities. In many states testing is a component of regulation. Applicants usually pay an initial fee for testing and processing their applications. Those who have successfully met requirements pay an annual fee to renew their certification or license. Generally, continuing education is required to keep social workers' knowledge and skills current.

Although most states now have licensure or certification laws, employees of state welfare and social service departments may be *exempt* from obtaining these credentials. On the other hand, voluntary and proprietary agencies may *require* that social workers have state credentials and perhaps additional credentials.

Depending on the provisions contained in each state's certification or licensing law, social workers with graduate degrees may be able to obtain third-party payments (payments from insurance companies) for their clinical or direct practice services. These provisions are known as *vendorship laws.* Many social workers have fought long and hard to obtain third-party payments, believing in their right to practice autonomously and to collect fees. Others contend that the focus on self-benefit has taken energy from the poor and truly needy to serve the "worried well." According to Specht and Courtney (1994, p. 105), "Social work has grown a rather large psychotherapeutic tail and now stands in danger of being wagged by it."

Some forms of recognition are also granted by national credentialing bodies such as NASW's Academy of Certified Social Workers. The ACSW is voluntary, and now that all states have some form of social work regulation, fewer social workers will likely seek this credential. Social workers with graduate degrees engaged in clin-

QCSW

ACSW

ical practice may also become a Qualified Clinical Social Worker or a Board-Certified Diplomate in Clinical Social Work. Diplomate status requires a graduate social work degree, clinical course work, clinical fieldwork or internships, substantial professional practice experience, supervised practice, certification or licensure in states that have such regulation, and an examination. With increased competition in the private practice arena, these credentials may be more appealing. There are no national credentials in addition to the ACSW's for social workers with master's degrees who are engaged in nonclinical practice.

Although some people believe that licensure, certification, and vendorship laws are elitist and are meant to limit rather than diversify the cadre of practitioners, the widespread acceptance of regulation by social workers and other human service professionals renders this argument nearly moot. Others, however, see the regulation of social work practice as an expensive and time-limited experiment. Many states have some form of sunset review legislation, providing for the extinction of "nonessential" government functions should legislators feel that the regulatory boards are not serving their functions in protecting consumers (Hardcastle, 1990). And given current conservative attacks on social welfare services, state governments may be less inclined to support these regulatory efforts in the future.

Another issue in professional regulation is unionization. Tambour (1995) estimates that one quarter of the profession is unionized in the United States, particularly in California and the industrialized states of the East Coast and Midwest. The largest unions representing social workers are the American Federation of State, County, and Municipal Employees (AFSCME) and the Service Employees International Union (SEIU) associated with the AFL-CIO. Social work faculty at colleges and universities are often unionized. Although there are no unions made up entirely of social workers, union membership is another form of professional protection.

Debates about the merits of unionization reflect a wide range of attitudes. Some believe that unions are detrimental to merit systems. Union members generally receive benefits negotiated by their unions whether or not they are particularly meritorious workers. Others believe that union protection is important because when many workers band together they have more clout with employers regarding wages, benefits, and working conditions. Some feel that unions are not professional and should be left to the trades, such as plumbing and house painting, rather than disciplines such as social work. After all, doctors and lawyers are not represented by unions, although they do have powerful national organizations to help protect their interests. Social workers' quest for professionalization did not stop with Flexner's enunciation of his criteria. Issues such as unionization, certification, licensure, and vendorship have simply replaced older items on the professional agenda.

Status and the Profession

In selecting a career, you must consider many factors. Among them are salary, demand, image, and others, that affect the status of the profession.

Salaries in Social Work

In a study of NASW members, Gibelman and Schervish (1993b) reported that 92 percent of those with baccalaureate degrees earned between $10,000 and $30,000 a year, that 82 percent of those with master's degrees earned between $20,000 and $40,000, and that 92 percent of those with doctoral degrees earned $30,000 or more. They also reported that salaries vary with ethnicity and gender. Although the number of social workers of color included in these data are small, the mean annual income was $35,274 for Asians, $35,115 for Mexican Americans, $35,000 for Puerto Ricans, $34,977 for African Americans, $33,580 for whites, and $31,941 for Native Americans. This 1993 survey is based on a much smaller sample than one done by Gibelman and Schervish (1993a) in 1991 in which Asians were also found to earn the most and Native Americans the least; however, in the 1991 survey, whites earned slightly more than African Americans. In 1993 about half of the women earned $30,000 or more a year compared with more than two thirds of the men. Social work salaries have just kept pace with inflation (Gibelman & Schervish, 1993b).

Salaries are also influenced by pay scales that differ by state and region. Incomes in New England, the Mid-Atlantic, and the Pacific states are generally higher than those in other areas (Gibelman & Schervish, 1993a). Other variables affect salaries, too. For example, a number of small, private nonprofit agencies such as battered women's shelters and rape crisis centers operate on small budgets and are heavily dependent on volunteer services. The few paid staff may earn relatively modest salaries, and they often work in these agencies out of dedication to this particular field of service. It is not uncommon for students who come to social work education programs to discuss their interest in a social work major to say that they have been dissuaded by family and friends from selecting a social service career in favor of something more lucrative. Given the generally modest salaries earned by social workers, students likely choose the profession because their primary motivation is service rather than salary.

Classifying and Declassifying Social Workers

The War on Poverty, begun in the 1960s under John F. Kennedy's administration and continued under President Lyndon B. Johnson, heralded a period of substantial growth for the profession of social work. The Office of Economic Opportunity was established to administer programs such as Head Start and the Job Corps. There was a considerable feeling of optimism that more could and should be done to help the poor and other disadvantaged groups. The Food Stamp Program, Medicaid, and Medicare were also begun during this period, dubbed the Great Society. The Community Mental Health Act was passed, and amendments to the Social Security Act mandated increased social services to the disadvantaged. It was an exciting period for social workers—unparalleled since the New Deal. Demand for social workers exceeded the available supply.

As a result of the increasing demands for social workers in the 1960s and 1970s, NASW developed a six-level classification plan for social service providers (National

Association of Social Workers, 1973; also see Hopps & Collins, 1995). The six levels, adopted in 1973, include two preprofessional and four professional levels. The preprofessional levels are *social work aide,* which requires a high school diploma, and *social service technician,* which requires a two-year degree in human services or a four-year degree in a nonsocial work program. These preprofessional levels indicate that not all social service activities require a bachelor's or master's degree in social work. For example, activities such as organizing youth groups and assisting clients to apply for food stamps could be done by individuals other than professional social workers.

The four professional levels include *social worker,* which requires a baccalaureate degree from an accredited social work program, and *graduate social worker,* which requires a master's degree from an accredited social work program. The other two professional levels are *certified social worker,* requiring the ACSW credential or similar recognition by a state certification or licensure board, and *social work fellow,* requiring a doctorate or substantial experience beyond the minimum ACSW requirements. If social service organizations use this schema, tasks can be assigned to individuals with the appropriate level of expertise, and services might be delivered more effectively and efficiently.

Of course, models such as this one adopted by NASW are never perfectly mirrored in the real world. The work of social workers at different levels of practice overlaps considerably. For example, both bachelor's and master's level social workers provide counseling, and their ability to counsel effectively may depend on their personal characteristics, such as the amount of empathy they convey to clients, in addition to their professional training and experience. The question arises as to whether the profession can truly make distinctions among these position classifications.

Other questions must also be addressed: Do administrators even try to use these distinctions? Do social workers know enough about professional competencies at different levels of practice to make adequate distinctions, or would broader categories better serve their purposes—or at least better reflect what goes on in the real world? Such a classification system also denies a career ladder to those who have considerable practice experience and continuing education but not an advanced degree. Some people believe this system of classification has not been particularly useful (Hardcastle, 1987).

The inability to differentiate many social work tasks at the levels just described has bothered social workers. The profession is not truly competency based, although it has taken steps in that direction (Shank, 1993). But a related issue—*declassification*—has bothered social workers even more. Rather than an increasing trend toward using NASW's job classification system, what has occurred instead is relegating more job responsibilities to workers at the *lower* end of the job spectrum. This trend to employ individuals with fewer educational credentials has occurred in large part because social service funding has not kept pace with the growing demand for social services.

Demand has increased for many reasons. The growing number of elderly persons requires more social services. Improved services for people with mental disabilities means that more staff are needed to serve clients intensively in many smaller community programs rather than large institutions. Increased awareness of problems such as child abuse has caused more cases to be reported. The stigma of receiving mental health and chemical dependency services has been reduced, also causing more people to request treatment.

The growing demand but shrinking dollars for services have combined to form a climate in which public officials and social service administrators may hire less-qualified social service personnel to do much of the work. The idea persists that some contact with social service providers is better than no contact at all, regardless of the preparation and ability of the worker to serve the client. Many times the individual with minimum rather than maximum qualifications for the job is hired. NASW estimates that more than one half of the current social service labor force practices without a social work education (NASW, 1994).

Another factor contributing to declassification is the growing number of human service and counseling degrees offered by colleges and universities at the associate, undergraduate, and graduate level. Many have no external mechanisms for accreditation. Universities may prefer to offer programs that are not accredited because they do not have to meet specific requirements or pay accreditation and reaccreditation fees. As a result, more graduates claiming to be qualified human service providers are competing in the job market.

It is incumbent upon social workers to make the public aware of the need to ensure that clients receive services from qualified personnel, and the profession has resolved to fight declassification (NASW, 1994). Building on public education and its successful state-by-state initiative to regulate social work practice, NASW is committed to ensuring that social work practice requires a social work education. A social work education may be the best predictor of how well workers perform in social work positions (Booz-Allen & Hamilton, 1987), and NASW has issued a statement calling for research on the mutual relevance of social work education and practice. However, some in the profession worry that educational requirements will go too far. The *New York Times* restricts the term "social worker" to those who have earned the MSW degree, inaugurating an editorial policy which ensures that those identified as social workers have a social work graduate education. On the other hand, most students enrolled in social work education programs are pursuing a baccalaureate degree (Lennon, 1995). Although the profession appears to be united in the fight against declassification, it has had difficulty distinguishing the appropriate roles of social workers with baccalaureate and master's educations. As a result, social workers remain divided on the question of the role of baccalaureate education in the profession.

The Image of Social Work

If you were asked to describe the public's general impression of social workers, what would you say? Would you reply that social workers are highly respected professionals, that there is a consensus that social work services are of critical importance in society, and that the public has a clear idea of what social workers do? Or would you say that the public would be at a loss to describe the functions of most social workers, that it views social work services as a drain on the public coffers, and that social workers are die-hard liberals who promote dependency on government services? Although the views of many people likely lie between these two extremes, social workers often encounter individuals with misconceptions about their profession. On large university campuses with social work degree programs, many students may not know that social work can be selected as a major. Members of the public may be unaware that social work positions require specific degree preparation.

Social work, like other professions, often gets its reputations from negative rather than positive publicity. Take the field of child welfare. These are the kinds of stories most likely to make the news: A child protective services worker does not remove a child from a home due to lack of evidence of neglect or abuse and the child is later severely injured; a child is removed from a home because there is sufficient evidence of neglect or abuse, but later the case is labeled unsubstantiated and the parents sue; a citizen calls to report a suspected case of neglect or abuse, but it does not meet the criteria for investigation and she calls her state representative complaining that the social workers are not doing their job. The many cases in which children have been protected from harm generally go unheralded. Social work is a rewarding career, but social work students should be mindful of stressors like these that professionals face in their everyday work.

During the 1960s and early 1970s, books such as *The Other America* (Harrington, 1962) and *Regulating the Poor: The Functions of Public Welfare* (Piven & Cloward, 1971), called for increased attention to the problems of the poor and challenged government to respond. In the 1980s these attitudes were displaced by the Reagan administration's philosophy that public assistance programs should provide as little as possible for the shortest amount of time, and that the War on Poverty and the Great Society contributed to the number of poor and the number "on welfare." Books such as *Wealth and Poverty* (Gilder, 1981) and *Losing Ground: American Social Policy, 1950–1980* (Murray, 1984), espoused this philosophy, arguing that social welfare, especially government social welfare, is destructive to society.

The idea that social welfare is destructive appeals to people who believe that "government handouts" destroy individual initiative and encourage a culture of dependency. Moreover, these beliefs lead to the view that social workers are the "vandals at the gates of civilization." When those attitudes become public policy, social workers do more with less. Even the *Wall Street Journal* has discussed the problems of the profession in an article entitled "Desperate Straits, Burgeoning Caseloads, Cuts in Funding Beset Public Social Workers, Other Problems Include Loss of Status, Low Salaries; More Leave the Profession, 'Society Just Doesn't Care'" (Ansberry, 1987).

However, after dwindling enrollments in the early and mid 1980s, *full-time enrollment in social work education programs increased by 60 percent in the last ten years* (Lennon, 1995), and the *Occupational Outlook Quarterly* predicts that the nation will add nearly 191,000 social work jobs by the year 2005 (Gradler & Schrammel, 1994). We are waiting to see if these trends will continue in the age of downsizing government and the Republican's "Contract with America."

Some believe that the backlash against the poor and an increase in social problems has caused more socially minded students to enroll in human service education programs in an effort to promote a more humane and just society. But another trend that may be influencing enrollment is that social work and social services are moving from the public to the private sector. The privatization of social work practice has been going on for some time, and 60 percent of the profession is now employed under private auspices (Gibelman & Schervish, 1993a). Paradoxically, the privatization of social work may contribute to the growing enrollment in social work education programs, because an MSW degree is often the quickest route to the higher earnings and status associated with private human service practice (Barker, 1992; Gibelman & Schervish, 1993a). There are many social problems to be addressed, and social work education has provided social workers in public agencies and private settings with many tools to meet the challenge. Unfortunately, the privatization of social work may forecast less to come for poor and disadvantaged people (Specht & Courtney, 1994), because helping the poor and disadvantaged is sometimes least among the motivations for private practice (Butler, 1992). However, the evidence on this issue is mixed (Abell & McDonnell, 1990; Butler, 1990), and it remains to be seen how the altruism of the social work profession will emerge in the private sector. In 1994, *Working Woman* magazine published an article on the twenty-five hottest career opportunities for women. Jobs for those with social work degrees ranked high among them as illustrated in Box 2-3.

BOX 2-3   Selecting a Career Path

If you are thinking about a social work career, *Working Woman* magazine suggests the following options.

Managing for Maximum Security

When Margaret Moore was hired in 1974 as a counselor in a Pittsburgh halfway house for women offenders, she remembers, "I figured I'd be there long enough to get my master's in social work while providing for my son, and then I'd get out."

But soon she no longer thought about leaving. "I felt I was making a difference in people's lives," she says. "In my first year, I became convinced I had the capacity to run the system." Twenty years later, Moore, 45, had risen to deputy commissioner, becoming the highest ranking woman in Pennsylvania's Department of Corrections. She has just taken a new job as director of the District of Columbia's Department of Corrections (salary: over $80,000).

After becoming director of the halfway house where she started her career, Moore was hired as director of treatment at the maximum-security men's state prison in Pittsburgh. Next, she was tapped to convert a juvenile facility into Pennsylvania's second women's prison. But it was her appointment in 1987 as superintendent of a new medium-security men's facility in rural Huntingdon County that really raised eyebrows. "Women could be superintendents of women's prisons, but not of men's prisons," Moore says. "People were thinking, 'Women are too soft, too indecisive for this work.'"

But Moore proved to be more than up to the task, and in 1991 she was selected to head the largest prison-expansion program in state history. Her mandate: to have five new prisons up and running by the end of 1993. It required overseeing everything from staff recruitment and operating policies to materials and equipment procurement. Bringing the project to completion early, she was rewarded last year with the promotion to deputy commissioner.

"Many women wouldn't even think of working in a maximum-security prison," says Moore, who is married to another veteran corrections professional. "When I walk through a prison yard with hundreds of inmates around me, I may feel some uneasiness, but it keeps me sharp. You don't try to shut that off." Moore says she has been "terrified" only a few times. On two occasions, inmates took members of her staff hostage—in one case for two hours, in the other for five days. "Most of the time we go about day-to-day matters without incident," she says, "but the possibility of an emergency is something we have to be prepared for."

"Many of the people we incarcerate are not nice; they hurt people and create havoc," Moore says, "But I care deeply about *all* people, so I get beyond what they've done and see what can be done with them."

Elizabeth Weiss

Working in Health Care

The [Bureau of Labor Statistics] says [jobs in] health care—with or without reform—will grow 47 percent by 2005. That's almost one out of every six new jobs.

Geriatric-Care Manager

By 2005, almost 36 million people in the United States will be sixty-five or older. The geriatric-care manager, a social worker specializing in long-term-care planning, works with families and doctors to assess an elderly person's physical and mental abilities and medical and nutritional needs. She [or he] then finds and recommends the most suitable care facility or home health assistance and appropriate community programs to keep an aging client autonomous for as long as possible.

"You're primarily working with older people who don't want to talk to you and with complex family systems," says Barbara Kane of Aging Network Services in Bethesda, Maryland. "When you're not at odds with the patient, you could be at odds with angry children." A background in psychotherapy can be helpful, but nurses, social workers, and gerontologists are all qualified.

Education: BS in nursing, social work, or gerontology and MSW; forty-five states require certification as a licensed clinical social worker.

Salary: $50–$100 an hour, depending on the market.

Related career paths: Some geriatric-care managers consult with nursing homes and home care agencies, but successful private practice offers the highest income and prestige.

Practicing in the Human Services

Jobs related to the traditional helping professions will grow 70 percent by 2005, with an increase in programs emphasizing child care, elder care, and mental health, according to [Bureau of Labor Statistics] statistics. Our listing highlights the better paying opportunities among them and those with the greatest career mobility. We include human resources, which has grown into a full-fledged managerial function.

Employee Assistance Program Counselor

The hottest track in social work serves clients in the workplace. Employee-assistance programs began in the late 1960s, when it became clear that timely intervention for substance abuse and other mental health problems could hasten treatment, help recovery, and limit productivity losses. The EAP counselor, working in-house (as part of human resources) or from an external agency or private practice (which doubly ensures confidentiality), performs conversational triage with an employee who has been referred. Assessment skills and expertise in treatment resources are essential. "You must know about everything from alcoholism to Alzheimer's," says Gail Fisher of Resources of Change, a Bethesda, Maryland-based EAP consultancy. John Lacey of Human Affairs International, a Salt Lake City-based EAP agency, says that 75 percent of his class deal with stress and workplace-related conflicts, relationships, and family issues.

Education: BA, MSW, and experience in counseling services or as a licensed therapist are essential. The Employee Assistance Professionals Association also gives a certification exam.

Salary: Company or organization employment, $42,000–$60,000; counselor in private practice or director of EAP for Fortune 500 company, $100,000+.

Summary

This chapter has addressed a number of issues related to the organization of the profession, including social work education and the professionalization of social work. We have mentioned some of the rewarding aspects of social work practice as well as some problems the profession is working to resolve. There is no doubt that social work is an exciting field of practice for those interested in tackling the social problems faced by individuals, groups, communities, and the larger society. The following chapters look more specifically at the knowledge, values, and skills social workers use to address social problems and the many client populations that social workers serve.

Suggested Readings

Edwards, R. L. (Ed.). (1995). *Encyclopedia of social work*, (19th ed.). Washington, DC: NASW Press.

Gibelman, M., & Schervish, P. H. (1993). *Who we are: The social work labor force as reflected in the NASW membership*. Washington, DC: NASW Press.

Ginsberg, L. (1995). *Social work almanac*. Washington, DC: NASW Press.

Morales, A., & Sheafor, B. W. (1995). *Social work: A profession of many faces* (7th ed.). Boston: Allyn & Bacon.

Social Work, Journal of the National Association of Social Workers.

3

In Search of Social Work Theory

Photo courtesy of Robert Harbison

The original chapter from the first edition of this book has been revised by CYNTHIA FRANKLIN, School of Social Work, University of Texas at Austin.

Social workers have long looked for viable theories to describe and explain their views of human behavior and the interventions they employ in their work. Most simply, a theory is an explanation or set of attributions we make to account for events. All humans seek to explain their world and justify their experiences through various ideas and explanations. The cognitive psychologist George Kelly (1955) used the metaphor of the "person as scientist" to communicate this idea and to emphasize the fact that we constantly hypothesize and seek to confirm our hypotheses through our experiences. For example, if your friend Patti's boyfriend Jack unexpectedly breaks up with her, she will likely have an explanation or "theory" as to why this happened. Different explanations may include that he was interested in another woman, that he did not like her friends, that he was not ready to settle down with one person, that he never really loved her but was just using her, or that they were not compatible with one another.

Each of these explanations carries emotional and behavioral consequences of its own. For example, the "other woman" is likely to predict hurt, jealousy, crying, confrontation, and a number of other similar responses. Theorizing and explaining events is tricky, however, because there is never any way to know if our explanations are completely correct. For example, we may never know if the "other woman" is the real reason that Jack broke up with Patti. Different people may argue for various theories that account for the situation. Jack's friend Todd, for example, may explain that it was the stress of school combined with Patti's demands on Jack. Jack's brother Joe may account for this behavior as being his fear of commitment at such a young age. Robin, who dated Jack in the past, may say that he is a flirty guy and just wants to play the field more before he makes up his mind. All the people involved in explaining Jack's behavior may cite examples and provide information that supports their explanations. Thus, their explanations may not be mere speculations. But some individuals may offer better or more complete information to support their explanations than others.

What Is a Theory?

Scientists and other professionals seek to formalize this human process of theory generation. According to Abraham Kaplan (1963), a theory is "a way of making sense of a disturbing situation so as to allow us most effectively to bring to bear our repertoire of habits, and even more important to modify habits or discard them altogether, replacing them by new ones as the situation demands" (p. 295). Theories are necessary for the survival of our social system. They help us to explain, understand, and predict events and behaviors that make sense of our existence. Scientists develop ways to generate theories at different levels. Three levels of theory building are (1) *deductive theory*, (2) *functional theory,* and (3) *inductive theory* (Miller, 1993).

A deductive theory is a logically organized system in which all the constructs and connections between ideas are spelled out in a formal way so they can be tested in statistical models. Basic assumptions and propositions can be broken down into other components, and the theory can be tested. There is a continual two-way relationship between the data that is collected for testing the theory and the development of the theory. The theory is postulated, and as research is conducted on the constructs of the theory, the theory consequently is modified based on the research. A functional theory is a pragmatic theory, and most current social work theories fall into this category. It relies on a similar process as the deductive theory but is not as elegant and far reaching in its explanations or implications. Functional theory building usually relies on data from one experiment or experimental situation. Grand theories such as the one generated by Sigmund Freud, for example, usually do not emerge from this type of theory building. Instead, smaller theories that relate to more discrete phenomena emerge. Inductive theory generation relies on descriptive statements that emerge directly from data. The researcher, as much as is possible, starts with the data, such as a single case study, and builds theory from those observations. Through further testing of observations against data, the researcher can confirm or disconfirm the emerging theory.

A formal scientific theory is defined as a set of "interconnected statements—definitions, axioms, postulates, hypothetical constructs, intervening variables, laws, hypotheses, and so on" (Miller, 1993, p. 5). This definition is most like the deductive approach just described, although it should be noted that all types of theory building may be scientific and are important to social work practice. Put more simply, the definition of formal theory implies that theories offer a framework with which to test certain facts, being understood as discrete observations and measurements—quantifiable or verifiable observations. This means that it is not enough to speculate that something is a certain way; instead, a scientist must offer empirical evidence of certain facts before a theory can be verified. Facts by themselves, however, do not offer the full explanations needed to understand events in our world. We must frame those facts into more complex meanings, and it is through this framing that theories come into play. According to Thomas (1992) a theory is "an explanation of how certain facts fit together" (p. 4). Theories propose which facts are most important for understanding a phenomenon and tell us which relationships between facts are most relevant. In a nutshell, theories provide the meanings that we attribute to facts. We in turn collect more facts to support, refute, or modify our frames of understanding.

Types of Theories

Both *descriptive* and *explanatory* theories are important in social work. Descriptive theories string together observations in a way that helps us describe a process that leads to an event. We can usually answer questions such as how did this occur and what was the first event that set other events in motion. Thus, in an individual case study, we can describe the process that leads a youth to drop out of school. We can document poor performance in school, the child's family problems, and the spiral of other events that happened in succession before he or she dropped out. Explanatory theories help us understand the relationships between causal sequences and antecedents (why) and further help us use facts to form new explanations.

Using a statistical model, for example, Franklin and Streeter (1992) demonstrated the multidimensional causes of dropping out of school and how dropouts differed along socioeconomic lines. In the study, middle-class dropouts were found to have high achievement test scores but more psychological and family problems than lower income youths. The authors thus refuted previous unitary theories that attributed dropping out of school to a group of characteristics associated with low-income, disadvantaged youths. Subsequently, these former theories proposed that intervention strategies should be based on remedial education efforts. However, based on their data—facts derived from psychological and social measurements—Franklin and Streeter offered an alternative explanation—that there are multiple reasons that youths drop out of school. Therefore, Franklin and Streeter propose that intervention must follow a multidimensional course, including psychosocial interventions (not previously emphasized), if efforts to stop youths from dropping out are to be effective.

Models

Theories are, in a certain sense, quite similar to *models*. Sometimes the words are used interchangeably. Models, however, differ from theories in that they provide a whole set of theoretical proposals and assumptions (based on theory) for how the world works. They further provide a set of heuristics and links between theories that we can use to explain human behavior and attempt to change that behavior. In another sense, models are representations that serve as metaphors or analogies for understanding ourselves and the world around us. In the social work profession, for example, the metaphor "person in environment" underlies the practice models. Metaphors used as a part of models can change, and the implications for those changes often signal new developments in theory. For example, at different points in history, psychologists have used different analogies or metaphors to explain human cognitive functioning and how the mind works. A mechanistic, machinelike *model* has been used continuously to explain cognitive functioning, but it has been updated to match our changing technology. In the 1800s people talked about the mind working like a clock, but in the 1970s and 1980s we referred to the information processing model—a model that explained cognitive functioning in accordance with the way computers work (Ashcraft, 1989). More recently, a new and different metaphor for cognitive functioning has been introduced. Borrowing from literary fields and linguistics, cognitive psychologists discuss the structure and process of human narratives and their role in explaining cognitive and behavioral functioning. The narrative metaphor, or model, is having quite an impact on contemporary social work theory and practice (Bruner, 1986; Saleeby, 1994).

A model, of course, is only a representation and is therefore never complete. It only provides partial truths. The differences between models and theories should become clear in our presentation in later chapters of several different models of social work practice. Those models serve to *interpret* theories as they apply to practice. Some other terms that are often used are *paradigm* and *metatheory* or *metaframework*. Paradigm is used by some to mean only a general model or overall world view (Kuhn, 1962). Others use it as a more specific set of beliefs that explains relationships between models. A metatheory is a theory about a theory or a set of beliefs that explain a theory. Certain theories, such as the systems theory that will be described in this chapter, serve as a metatheory or a metaframework that provides a broader perspective with which to view theory. Metatheories help us understand and gain knowledge about theories.

According to Greenwood (1957), professional expertise must be grounded in a body of theory that is relatively abstract, systematic, and communicable. It must also be constantly tested, clarified, and restructured. A theory is by definition an abstraction that is created to explain and predict the reality it represents. Theories and models are both abstractions, but models tend to be less abstract than theories. According to Kaplan (1963), we may say that "system A is a model of system B if the study of A is useful for the understanding of B" (p. 263). Mastering the body of literature that constitutes the theoretical underpinnings of any modern profession, whether social work, law, or medicine, requires a carefully planned college or university education and a well-designed curriculum.

Professionals are not simply technicians; they do not just apply rules in the exercise of their craft. They must learn to think in certain ways and to exercise judgment, in addition to mastering a base of professional knowledge. According to Macht and Quam (1986), social work practice is built upon three different levels: general theory drawn from related disciplines (psychology, anthropology, sociology, and so forth); practice theory that explains the ways social workers use knowledge in their practice; and specific social *methods*, that is, theories of practice.

We do not have to look far to see how concerned social work has been with the relationship between theory and practice. Some schools have a curriculum that neatly partitions courses into "theory" and "practice" categories. Social Work Practice with Individuals and Families is a familiar course title, as is Theories of Community Organization. Then there are other curricula that carry this bifurcation down to the level of each course, with such titles as Theory and Practice of Social Welfare Administration. One almost expects the instructor to announce, "Now this lecture is on theory; tomorrow we will do practice."

Students also seem to have compartmentalized the notions of theory and practice. It is important for us all to realize that practice and theory are inseparable—that effective practice is possible only when predicated on a sound theoretical foundation. If knowledge is useful in directing practice, it is made useful through theories that link problems, processes, and goals in a way that allows us to make sense of them.

Evaluating Theories

Although multiple theories exist for social work practice, not all of these theories are equal in their abilities to link problems, processes, and goals and provide effective interventions for practice. It is therefore necessary to have a set of guidelines for evaluating a theory. Ryckman (1994) provides six criteria for evaluating a scientific theory: comprehensiveness, precision and testability, parsimony, empirical validity, heuristic value, and applied value.

Comprehensiveness

If a theory is to be useful for an applied profession such as social work, it must be comprehensive. It should account for a diversity of data and must provide explanations that can guide practitioners. For example, focused experimental theories, such as those that explain why children smile, are not as helpful as more complex theories that can explain why children bond to parents who abuse them. Of course a single theory cannot explain everything, but the more comprehensive it is, the better it may account for the real-life experiences practicing social workers face.

Precision and Testability

In order to have precision and to be testable, a theory must have defined its concepts and set forth clear relational statements that are refutable. This way the theory can be tested empirically. The theory must also be internally consistent and logical in its explanations. For example, it is difficult to study the concept of ego from Freudian psychology because this concept may not be empirically verifiable. Many aspects of ego theory also remain to be worked out in order to make this explanation of human behavior logical and consistent with human experience. If the developing sense of self (ego) is likely to be damaged during the course of child abuse, and this damage is believed to account for the deviant behavior of adults, what accounts for the resilience of some children who have abusive experiences and grow into normal adults? Why do others, such as those who experience major depression, stop being depressed when they take antidepressant drugs? Can one's ego development logically account for these experiences?

Parsimony

A good theory should be as concise and efficient as it is logical and testable. The word parsimony is often used to describe an economical and efficient theory—that is, a theory that uses as few assumptions as are necessary to study its domains and phenomena. Therefore, meaningless abstractions and relationships are not studied. For example, concepts from learning psychology such as avoidant conditioning may more economically explain how people develop phobias than the oedipal complex from the Freudian theory. The former theory requires fewer relationships between complex variables and fewer abstractions to arrive at a meaningful explanation; it is more parsimonious.

Empirical Validity

If a theory is precise and testable, then it can produce predictions that have empirical validity. Determining the validity of a social work theory is never easy. Theories must be rigorously tested, including many replications of various findings to make sure that researchers are not drawing the wrong conclusions from statistical tests. It takes a long time to support a good theory through tests of its validity. Every theory is therefore a work in process, but those theories that are continually tested and found to have the most empirical validity are better than those that remain anecdotal and speculative. For example, in recent years practitioners have developed new methods for treating trauma and post-traumatic stress disorder (PTSD). People who experience PTSD suffer from persistent reexperiencing of traumatic events through dreams, intrusive recollections, or they may behave as if the traumatic event is recurring. One of the new methods to treat PTSD is known as Eye Movement Desensitization and Reprocessing (EMDR) (Shapiro, 1989). Initial research supported the effectiveness of this method for helping people overcome the symptoms of PTSD. However, these findings are not conclusive and much more research on the theory behind EMDR and its methods is necessary before social workers will have confidence that EMDR makes sense as an intervention and is safe and effective with most clients. Fortunately, researchers are continuing to do this research, which makes EMDR an example of a practice theory in process.

Heuristic Value

A good theory has heuristic value in that it promotes and stimulates thinking that leads to further questions and research. For example, in an effort to prove a theory correct, some researchers spend much time investigating its validity. Others are so moved by what they perceive to be the inaccuracy of a theory that they devote their lives to investigating alternative explanations. Heuristic value makes some theories, such as Freudian theory, extremely famous and influential even though they do not have much empirical support. The theory's contribution is that it promotes research and understanding and serves as an impetus for the development of other theories.

Applied Value

In social work the applied value of a theory is most germane. A good theory must lead to new solutions to social problems. As mentioned earlier, social workers must rely on theory to direct their practice activities. A good theory, therefore, must be practical and advise the work of those in the field. This usually requires some degree of field testing or study of the theory in a field setting.

Toward a Social Work Theory

In practice, social workers have always been engaged in the complexities of people's lives and the social systems (environments) in which they live. They have looked for theories to explain the metaphor of the "person in environment." Over the past thirty years the systems theory has been applied as a metaframework to guide theorizing and practice. Systems theory serves as a metaframework and not a practice model because it does not provide specific explanations concerning human behavior nor the technologies necessary to conduct practice. In other words, systems theory helps social workers think in complex ways about human behavior as being embedded in the context of social environment, but it does not prescribe what they should do to change a person's behavior. From the systems metaframework, however, numerous practice models and perspectives have emerged. In discussing systems theory we first consider some of the basic ideas associated with general systems theory, cybernetics, and ecosystems theory (as applied in social work) and proceed to describe briefly two social work practice models that have emerged from the systems theory.

In 1970 Ann Hartman commented that, "systems theory is highly abstract, and the task of translating it through middle-range theory into practice is immense" (p. 467). In the early years, a great deal of confusion grew from the many different variations of systems theories. Also, the vocabulary of systems theory, such as *input, throughput,* and *entropy,* was completely foreign to social workers. This mode of thought, however, has contributed a tremendous amount to family practice, spawning numerous models within family therapy. In particular, systems theory has influenced social work practice because it moved practitioners away from the once popular reliance on reductionistic theories, such as Freudian psychological theories of human behavior, to more comprehensive, holistic, and contextual views that are more compatible with the foundations of the profession.

Concepts of Systems Theory

Until quite recently, Western science was guided by a mode of thinking that valued rigorous, *specialized* knowledge above all else. The unfortunate consequence of such an approach is a fragmented view of the world. Early in the twentieth century, mechanistic and deterministic theories, even in disciplines such as physics, were questioned. Relativity and quantum theory became the favored theories in field physics and microphysics. The systems view grew popular in all scientific disciplines, from biology to pure mathematics, as a way of examining the *interrelationships* between smaller units of analysis (Laszlo, 1972). The systems perspective has now become so popular that it has inspired such lofty works as Kenneth E. Boulding's *The World as a Total System* (1985). (Boulding also used a unique definition of system—anything that is not chaos.) Systems theory is an intellectual tool for analyzing the relationship between the structure of a system and its functioning. Structure, function, and response are the basic concepts of systems theory (Cortes, Przeworski, & Sprague, 1974).

Elements of Systems Theory

Systems are composed of parts that interact to serve a particular function (some might say to accomplish a particular purpose or goal—but that ascribes to systems human qualities that may not be appropriate). These parts or *elements* of systems may, in turn, be systems in their own right; that is, they may be subsystems of other systems. Thus, a lake or river might be considered both as an individual element or as a subsystem of a larger ecosystem. In another example, an individual who is made up of many subsystems (central nervous system, respiratory system, etc.) is part of a family system, which, in turn, is part of a neighborhood, which is part of a community, which is part of a city, and so forth. We could keep going until we reached the entire world system, but you get the idea. Each level of the system adds a new level of analysis, and these complexities interact to produce specific effects. The word *recursion* is often used to explain how each element in a system mutually influences the other in a way that defies linear causality. *Reciprocal* causality and *mutual influence* are terms used to describe the functioning of systems. In other words, A does not cause B, which in turn causes C. Instead, A and B interact to cause C, which in turn causes A (or B, or A *and* B). For example, when the child of a family has a behavior problem such as disobeying the rules or running away, the mother and father may get into fights over the child's behavior. However, this does not mean that the child's behavior started or caused the fights. In fact, the opposite could also be true: the behavior of the parents could precipitate the child's disobedience. In this way, the parents and child mutually influence one another's behavior. The family gets locked into a vicious cycle that spirals into an endless recursion of difficulties.

Environment

Systems always operate within an enveloping environment, and they both affect and are affected by their environment. Defining this environment is no easy matter. It is a function of the individual who is observing the system. While one systems analyst studying a management information system might not include the *user* as part of the system, another might perceive the user to be an integral component. Could the system function without a user? Does a stereo system include the *listener?* Think about it!

In recent years systems theorists within cybernetics (Maturana & Varela, 1980) have explained the relationships between systems, their environment, and observers in even more complex ways. *Autopoiesis,* or the process of self-generation, is the way that parts of systems relate to one another. While it holds true that a boundary between a system and another system is defined by an observer, it is also true that a system becomes distinct from its environment due to a dynamic process of its own and that this process cannot be understood separate from the environment. In this way, the boundary between a system (e.g., a family) and the environment does not cause the system, and neither does the system cause the boundary between itself and the environment. They are both responsible for each and exist together in an autopoietic (self-generating) system. More concrete examples of the processes of autopoiesis are the ongoing reforms often initiated in human services and educational organizations. These reform efforts often bring forth reorganization after reorganization, but in the final analysis, the structure and processes inherent in these organizations and their relationships with the environment manage to find a way to stay the same. Autopoiesis means that systems are always trying to maintain themselves through the processes of negative feedback, described a little later in the chapter (Becvar & Becvar, 1995).

Two other concepts from cybernetic systems theory build on this idea that systems self-generate and seek to maintain themselves over time. First is *structural determinism,* a term that defines the autonomy of systems and their abilities to decide how much deviation they can tolerate without losing their identity and integrity. The basic thesis behind this idea is that systems are limited by their own inherent structure, and that whatever effects the environment has on a system will be determined by the system's own properties and not that of the environment. The environment acts to perturb or constrain the system, but the result of this constraining is contingent on the system itself. Becvar and Becvar (1995) use this analogy to explain the concept of structural determinism. Your foot (environment) may kick a ball and it will roll, but the fact that the ball rolls has to do with its shape (structure), which is round. In this analogy, it could also be said that a ball will always roll unless the environment constrains it in some way, such as if it runs up against a curb, for example. In this way it is also true that the system will do exactly what its structure dictates unless it is constrained by the environment. Systems just do what they do, and their behavior is only perceived as right or wrong by an observer.

The second idea is *structural coupling,* a concept from cybernetics that explains how systems coexist with other systems. Systems must constantly transform their structures to meet the demands of the environment if they are to survive. Thus, systems are always interacting and mutually influencing (changing) one another in order to maintain themselves in a given context. In a family, for example, if the parents lose their jobs, they may take other jobs for less pay, sell their house and car, and move to an apartment to keep their family together and maintain the children in the same neighborhood and school. Thus certain concessions are being made with the environment in a seeming turn of bad luck or economic hardships. At the same time, however, the environment is responding as well, in that the job loss may be associated with the closing of a company, and this in turn affects many other people and the community. In addition, the company's closing drives down the price of housing, which has both positive (good for when they rent the apartment) and negative (bad for when they sell their house) impacts on the family and community in our example.

Boundaries

The particular characteristics of a system's boundary may vary, but boundaries serve one universal function: to separate or distinguish the system from its environment. *Anything* outside the boundary belongs to the environment. A system's boundary is dependent on the observer's level of inquiry, the intent in drawing the boundary line, and the observer's perception of the functioning of the system. Boundary decisions are essential when studying *open* systems—systems that interact with other systems. (We can also conceptualize *closed* systems—systems that become depleted because of a lack of interaction with other systems.) An example from family systems may help clarify the importance of boundaries. A family is a system composed of subsystems of couples, parents, children, parent/child dyads, and siblings. It is important for each of these subsystems to maintain intact boundaries. So, it is not healthy if parents interfere too much in the sibling subsystem, and it may be even worse if a child is allowed to become a surrogate spouse to a parent or a parental figure to a child. Families with boundaries that are too tightly or too loosely drawn across subsystems and generations may become dysfunctional. The family systems therapist Salvador Minuchin (1974) referred to the former type of family as being an *enmeshed* family and the latter as being *disengaged.*

Inputs/Outputs

Anything entering the system from the environment is an *input,* and anything leaving it is an *output.* In this process, inputs and outputs necessarily cross system boundaries. This exchange of resources is regulated and monitored by input/output filters. Input that originally contacts the system as raw material may be transformed or converted into energizing or maintenance inputs. Energizing inputs are those that are acted on by the system to produce outputs. Maintenance inputs allow the system to avoid *entropy,* a state of disorder or disintegration. In order to maintain a state of maximum order, a system must receive a balance of inputs and outputs—a process known as *negentropy.*

In the field of health care, an input could be tax revenues to purchase services, an outbreak of a contagious disease, or a scientific discovery leading to a vaccination. Outputs could be cured patients, improved health within a community, or improvements in neonatal mortality and morbidity statistics.

Conversion Processes

Systems are endowed with processes by which elements or components in the system may be changed or *converted.* These processes change input elements into outputs. In an *organized* system, the conversion process generally adds utility or value to the inputs as they are converted. In the juvenile justice system, delinquent youths may be viewed as inputs that are converted into nondelinquents through a process such as probation. One might also view delinquent youths as the outputs of a larger social system characterized by racism and poverty. On a macrolevel, financial resources (in the form of tax revenues) are inputs that are converted into programs and services through the process of social welfare administration.

Structure

The structure of a system is described by the form of the relationships that bind the individual elements or components together. Structures may be quite simple or incredibly complex. Complex systems may include hierarchies that are ordered levels of other subsystems. The notion of *hierarchy* is important in systems theory in that for a structure or a system to function appropriately across subsystems, the hierarchical arrangements of the system must also be maintained, with each component part maintaining its integrity. For example, an automobile may be part of a larger transportation system; while the engine system of the automobile consists of a combustion system, an ignition system, and so forth, each of these lower systems may consist of hundreds (or thousands) of individual elements. The way in which these elements and subsystems are related to each other is called *structure.*

On a human level, the family is one type of structure found within the larger social system. We might view the nuclear family as a subsystem of a larger structure, the extended family. To maintain *integrity* within family systems, a hierarchy must be maintained across generations (from parents to children) and intergenerationally (from one generation to the next). Each of these structures might be integrated into the type of system that we call a community. On a bureaucratic level, we are all familiar with the way in which organizational structures are divided into smaller structures such as departments, divisions, bureaus, units, and so forth.

Feedback

Two essential types of feedback are important for system activities, *positive* (amplifying) and *negative* (attenuating) feedback. However, it is important to know that the terms do not mean good or bad but rather describe corrective processes that take place within the system. Negative feedback is corrective and helps maintain the system within a critical operating range or eliminates performance fluctuations around a norm. More of A means less of B. Negative feedback helps maintain the status quo. An automobile drifting across the median of the highway while the driver dozes eventually contacts a series of small metallic warning devices that make a loud thumping noise and call the driver's attention to the problem. Parents who remain calm and enforce the rules when a teenager blows up will likely attenuate the teenager's emotions, leaving them with a calmer child. A woman who calls her boyfriend while in a battered woman's shelter and listens to his pleas to return home and give him another chance is introducing negative feedback into their couple system. If she returns home without further intervention, the system will maintain the status quo and a *negative feedback loop* will be enacted.

Positive feedback corrects the system by reinforcing the operation of the system. There may be a multiplier effect between input and output so that output increases with an increase in input. In other words, more of A leads to more of B. Some might say that the cost-of-living adjustments in Social Security benefit levels that are tied to the Consumer Price Index are a positive type of feedback that tends to lead toward instability (increased payments) in the Social Security system. If a teenager blows up and parents also get upset, crying and screaming, they are likely to be met with an amplification of more emotional outbursts and defiance by the child. The family has created a *positive feedback loop.* Positive feedback may cause system instability, while negative feedback leads to system control. To make further use of our example concerning the battered woman, being assaulted by her live-in boyfriend led her to seek assistance from the shelter. Had the woman continued her counseling—sharing her relationship problems (output) and receiving input from the shelter—the system would have continued to become unstable and been forced to make some type of dynamic change or cease to exist (entropy). If the boyfriend then came to counseling at the shelter, the system might find a new balance between output and input that will lead to a new order in the system (negentropy).

Equilibrium

A system remains in relative balance with itself and with other systems in its environment. Feedback allows change in one part of the system to produce changes (achieve equilibrium) in other parts. This does not imply a *static* system however. If systems were merely to maintain the status quo throughout the range of circumstances they encounter, there would be no development or progress. According to Laszlo (1972), equilibrium means that "natural systems create themselves in response to the challenge of the environment" (p. 46). *Morphostasis* refers to a system's tendency toward stability or a steady dynamic equilibrium. *Morphogenesis* on the other hand refers to behavior that allows systems to grow, to be creative, to be innovative, and to change (Becvar & Becvar, 1995). In all healthy systems, both processes work at the same time. Systems are always changing under the umbrella of stability, so that they can maintain their equilibrium.

Earlier we discussed *structural coupling* as an example of how systems change and accomplish a "fit" within a dynamic environment with other systems. An example is cited here to help clarify the process of equilibrium. In the world of horseback riding some riders take up the art of jumping the horse over fences (obstacles). If the horse and rider are to meet the challenge of the fence (environment) and successfully jump the fence, then the rider must do two things. First, the rider must stay very still on the horse's back so as not to throw the horse off balance. Second, the rider must constantly adjust to the horse's movements and rhythms in a type of dance so that the balance between the horse and rider will not be lost. Like the process of equilibrium, the rider is in continual motion but constantly works to remain in the same position on the horse's back.

Equifinality and Multifinality

Equifinality (equal ending) is a concept of systems theory that implies that no matter where one begins with a system, the end will be the same. Different initial conditions, therefore, do not necessarily lead to different ends. Becvar and Becvar (1995) explain equifinality in this way:

> *People in relationships tend to develop habitual ways of behaving and communicating with one another. We refer to these habits and characteristic processes as redundant patterns of interaction; systems are comprised of patterns and these patterns tend to repeat. Thus, no matter what the topic, the way the members of a given relationship argue, solve problems, discuss issues, and so forth, will generally be the same. These redundant patterns of interaction are the characteristic end state referred to by the term "equifinality" (p. 69).*

Multifinality (multiple endings), or *equipotentiality*, means that the opposite also takes place in systems. Different end states may be accomplished through the same beginnings. For example, the same intervention may produce very different outcomes at different times and across different communities. Both equifinality and multifinality speak to the fact that no deterministic predictions or simple cause and effect relationships can be accomplished with systems.

First Order and Second Order Changes

First order change refers to changes or small adjustments that happen in systems within the parameters of the system's own rules and structure. *Second order change* is change that requires a major transformation within the system's rules and structure. Both types of change are important to systems, but in order for systems to grow dynamically and developmentally, second order changes are usually required. For example, as a child grows, parents have to make adjustments in the way they set the rules that govern the child's behavior. When a child is age five, for example, a bedtime of 8:00 p.m. is not unreasonable, but when the child is ten, the parents may raise the bedtime to 9:00 p.m. or even 10:00 p.m. This type of adjustment is like a first order change because the structure and rules of the family system keep operating the same way. The parents keep setting the rules and expecting the child to obey. When the child is age fourteen or fifteen, however, this type of structure may cause problems because adolescents who are seeking autonomy within the system may want to set their own bedtime. If the parents continue to autocratically set and enforce a bedtime without input from the child, adolescent rebellion may ensue. What is needed is a second order change—a change in the way bedtime rules are set. In this situation the adolescent and parents may negotiate the bedtime. This requires a change in the structure of the family in that the child is given more power and is now brought into the decision making, thus affecting the family rules and overall functioning of the system.

Systems Theory in Social Work

One of the early major applications of systems theory to social work practice came from Pincus and Minahan (1973). They defined social work in the following way:

> *Social work is concerned with the interactions between people and their social environment which affect the ability of people to accomplish their life tasks, alleviate distress, and realize their aspirations and values. The purpose of social work therefore is to (1) enhance the problem-solving and coping capacities of people, (2) link people with systems that provide them with resources, services, and opportunities, (3) promote the effective and humane operation of these systems, and (4) contribute to the development and improvement of social policy (p. 9).*

An important element of their framework is a focus on the inadequacies of the formal, informal, and societal resource systems for meeting human needs. Another equally important characteristic is its focus on the *interaction* of people with their network of resource systems. This led Pincus and Minahan to view problems as attributes of an individual's social situation, not as attributes of the individual.

Debates concerning whether the focus of social work practice should be social change or change in the individual have been going on for many years and are not likely to be settled here. There seems to be an evolving consensus, however, that *generalist* social work practice (a model discussed throughout this book) must take into consideration the client's situation in the environment, that is, a *systems* perspective. In discussing *open* systems theory, Martin and O'Connor (1988) describe three ways in which this approach is useful in social work practice: (1) it helps social workers perceive and better understand the social environment; (2) it helps identify practice principles that apply across different contexts; and (3) it can help integrate social work theories and unify the profession.

Ecological Systems Theory

A number of writers have used the ecological metaphor in a systems framework when discussing social work. Ecological and systems ideas have appealed to theorists because they encourage social workers to adopt a broad focus, examining not only the individual client, but the client's interactions with family members, coworkers, and even the physical environment of buildings, parks, and other structures. There are several related "ecological" models within the social work literature. Some authors distinguish them from one another and others do not. The best known of the ecological models are the "life" model, developed by Germain and Gitterman (1980), the "competence-oriented" model developed by Maluccio (1981), and the "family centered" model developed by Hartman and Laird (1983). The life model is undoubtedly the most famous of the ecological models (Franklin & Warren, in press).

According to Carel Bailey Germain (1979), ecological systems theory is a form of general systems theory in which there is concern with the relations among "living entities" and "between entities and other aspects of their environment" (pp. 7–8). If this sounds much the same as systems theory in slightly different language, you may be on to something! Many believe that there really is no difference, apart from the semantics. Germain's life model, however, is complex, drawing from ecological psychology, ego psychology, and general systems theory. Proponents claim that the ecosystems perspective focuses on the *total* picture, "with equal emphasis being placed on learning about the strengths and deficits of the environment and of the client" (Greif, 1986, p. 225). In particular, the ecological model focuses not only on the various systems but the interactions between the systems. This type of holistic and interactive assessment reveals more areas for intervention; it also places greater demands on the social worker. Writers are careful to state, however, that the ecosystems models are more of a metaframework than bona fide practice models. A practice model requires that a set of interventions follow from the model, and this is not the case with ecosystems. The model produces no practice interventions that it can claim as its own. In fact, writers such as Germain have reviewed a number of practice interventions, from behavioral to psychodynamic traditions in psychology, to show how all these methods may be used in relationship to the ecosystems model. More recently Mattaini (1990) has integrated the ecosystems perspective with contextual behaviorism from the behavioral traditions in psychology to formulate a more systematic assessment framework.

Some proponents of the general systems theory approach, especially those who espouse a radical ideology, believe that the ecosystems perspective unduly emphasizes adaptation and accommodation and does not allow for *conflict* as well as the general systems model. However, Boulding's (1985) understanding of an ecological system focuses on three specific cases of ecological interaction: (1) mutual competition, (2) mutual cooperation, and (3) predation. This third category of interaction seems to allow as much conflict as the general systems model. You may decide after further reading that there are some differences between the generalist and ecological approaches, but for our present purposes, we will treat them as being much the same.

Critical Evaluation of Systems Theory for Social Work

We should not leave our discussion of systems theory in social work without returning to our previous ideas about how to critically evaluate a theory. How does systems theory measure up to our criteria for a good theory? Remember that we said a good theory (1) is comprehensive, (2) has precision and testability, (3) is parsimonious, (4) has empirical validity, (5) has heuristic value, and (6) has applied value. Think about these criteria for a moment and come up with your own ideas. In our opinion, systems theory partially meets three of the criteria, but does not meet the other three.

Systems theory's strongest suit is its comprehensiveness. It accounts for a broad range of activities across living systems. Second, it has tremendous heuristic value in that it stimulates thinking and promotes research and development of other theories. It also has some empirical support in that many of its concepts emerged from bodies of research in fields such as ecological psychology, biology, and mathematics. Systems theory falls short, however, on its precision and testability for applied fields much as social work because it is so abstract that its ideas and concepts are difficult to define and study. It is also not very parsimonious because its explanations are very dense and abstract. You may have had difficulties understanding ideas such as *second order change* and *morphogenesis,* for example. (So do we!) Or you might have been thinking to yourself, couldn't this family process be explained in a simpler way? Finally, as mentioned previously, systems theory has limited applied value in that it does not offer any specific practice interventions. Its main utility is as an assessment framework, and for this purpose it is useful, but also very cumbersome (Jordan & Franklin, 1995).

New Directions in Social Work Theory

As discussed earlier, systems theory has been very popular in social work practice for the past twenty-five years. But you may be thinking, with all the weaknesses mentioned in our critique of the theory, why is it so popular? The answer to this question is complex. One idea is that systems theory offers a way to think about the complexities of human behavior as we transact with social environments. Recall that social workers are most interested in the person as he or she is embedded in social contexts; they frequently rely on the metaphor of "person in environment" to explain these views. General systems theory and its intellectual descendants provide comprehensive theoretical guidelines as to how complex systems, such as human social environments, behave. Developments in the fields of chaos and complexity studies have also begun to indicate the ways in which complex systems emerge and change. These recent developments offer a new era of theorizing for social workers who are interested in how complex systems work. According to Franklin and Warren (in press), chaos and complexity is a large and rapidly growing field. Social scientists have begun to use complexity theory as a lens through which to examine the growth of, and changes in, human social systems. Complex or chaotic systems differ from those we have described earlier in the context of general systems and cybernetic systems theories. The chemist Ilya Prigogine has dubbed such self-organizing systems, which are capable of increasing their complexity over time, "dissipative systems" (Franklin & Warren, in press).

According to the definition of Harvey and Reed (1994), both biological entities such as individual human beings and human social entities such as families, communities, and entire societies are dissipative systems. They have the capacity to import energy, matter, and information from their environment and export the entropy that inevitably results in their use of the imports. Thus, it should be possible to gain insight into human social systems from an examination of the characteristics of dissipative systems. Franklin and Warren (in press) point out that dissipative systems show the characteristics of deterministic chaos—complex and unpredictable behavior.

In a chaotic regime, systems with a small number of variables can exhibit complex and unpredictable behavior. Although this behavior is unpredictable, it is not truly random. Rather, its unpredictability comes from what is called sensitive dependence on initial conditions; an extremely small change at one point can lead to an enormous difference in a little while. There is no way to predict how small such a difference might be, and thus, no way of anticipating the future—at least not very far in advance—based on our knowledge of the present. This is also known as the "butterfly effect," a name which comes from the idea that the fluttering of a butterfly in Africa can set off a chain of events that will culminate in a hurricane in the Caribbean a few months later. Sensitive dependence on initial conditions arises because chaotic systems typically consist of a number of interrelated elements, each of which influences the other again and again over time. Under such conditions, small changes can grow as they bounce back and forth through the system (Franklin & Warren, in press).

If human social systems are indeed dissipative systems, an examination of the characteristics of dissipative systems could be expected to shed light on the way in which human social systems work and the way in which they influence their members. Some applications of these notions have already begun to influence family therapy. For example, adherents to brief therapy models and solution-focused practice models use the metaphor of the "butterfly effect" to explain and demonstrate that only small initial conditions are needed to bring forth rapid changes in family systems. Applications of chaos theory and complexity theory remain to be seen in social work practice.

Ideological Perspectives on Social Work Practice

No one, according to Babbie (1985), ever starts out with a completely clean slate to develop a theory. We already have a general point of view or frame of reference that organizes our thinking about any particular issue.

Paradigms

Recall from our discussion at the beginning of the chapter that a world view or frame of reference is called a paradigm. Three major paradigms dominate sociological inquiry at present. The *interactionist* paradigm views social life as a process of interactions among individuals. The *functionalist* paradigm focuses on the organizational structure of social life. The *conflict* paradigm views social life as a struggle among competing individuals and groups, much like Marxist theory that describes the struggle between "haves" and "have-nots" as the basis for all meaningful social interaction.

The third paradigm has had a definite impact on the development of social work practice, but probably not as strong an impact as the political paradigms of *liberalism* and *conservatism*. Morales and Sheafor (1980) suggest that an initial investigation of social work practice should begin with the "mainstream" perspective (liberalism) before seeking to understand the "tributaries."

Liberalism

The liberal perspective in the United States views capitalism as a basically benevolent system that has given most Americans a very high standard of living. Liberals perceive social problems as a natural dysfunction of the combination of capitalism and industrialization. They wish to modify capitalism only to minimize the number of persons not benefiting from the system, but not to make fundamental changes in the system itself. Social welfare institutions are legitimate functions of government in a capitalist, industrialized system and are intended to minimize fluctuations in the system and minimize the damage to individuals. Liberals agree with the basic values of individualism, acquisitiveness, and competitiveness.

Conservatism

Like liberals, conservatives assume that self-interest, free enterprise, capitalism, and the market system are good. Unlike liberals, they seek no modifications of the system by government. They would limit helping efforts to private, voluntary charities. Conservatism suggests that social problems are more likely to stem from the moral character of the individual. At most, conservative ideology is supportive of social welfare as a *residual* responsibility of government. Individual needs should be met primarily by the family and the market system. Only when these institutions fail to function properly is there a role for government. Even then, governmental intervention should be limited to the absolute minimum.

Ronald Reagan's election as president in 1980 signaled the beginning of a number of conservative reforms that have dramatically influenced the U.S. social welfare system. In general the Reagan administration was committed to reduce federal responsibility for basic social provisions, and to encourage greater state and community responsibility for social programs, volunteerism, and private sector initiatives. The free-market philosophy of this administration encouraged a growing number of for-profit firms to enter human service domains traditionally reserved for public and nonprofit organizations.

As an example of how strongly Reaganomics has influenced social welfare policy, the director of the Office of Management and Budget (David A. Stockman) distributed to his top assistants copies of George Gilder's *Wealth and Poverty* (1981), a book that presents as *facts* assumptions about the relationship between human motivation and the economic system. The maximization of human potential is predicated not on cooperation but on competition. (Or as Michael Douglas unashamedly said in the movie *Wall Street,* "Greed is good!")

Gilder's book, as well as the Reagan economic philosophy, accepts a utilitarian concept of the public interest in which individuals acting in their own self-interest and competing within a political system will arrive at a better definition of the public interest than could be achieved by central planning. Common ends, if there are any, have no special value simply because they are common. Citizens compete for different ends, and a public policy is eventually fashioned within the political system. Whatever the output may be is defined as "the public interest" (Myerson & Banfield, 1955). The fact that the decision-making system is heavily weighted in favor of middle- and upper-class interests is conveniently overlooked.

These conservative trends have been intensified in the Republican-dominated Congress of the mid-1990s. In 1995 the Speaker of the U.S. House of Representatives suggested that the child welfare system would be more efficient if we returned to a system of orphanages. It appears inevitable that welfare reform will include severe limitations on the length of eligibility for programs such as Aid to Families with Dependent Children. There is even serious talk of ending school lunch subsidy programs and nutrition programs for low-income expectant mothers. Republicans and Democrats alike are taking the conservative trend seriously.

Radicalism

Radical social work theory begins with the premise that the circumstances of poor and disadvantaged clients can be linked to political and economic relationships that exist in the larger social order. Radicals believe that capitalism benefits the "ruling class" and that government in such a system is designed to maintain the privileges of this ruling class. (It has been said that the only difference between radicals and conservatives is that while radicals believe this, conservatives *know* it.) Marlene Webber (1980) describes the state as "an organ of class rule, an organ for the oppression of one class by another..." (p. 41). Piven and Cloward (1971) also suggest that the social welfare system is an important instrument for maintaining class privilege.

> *Historical evidence suggests that relief arrangements are initiated or expanded during the occasional outbreaks of civil disorder produced by mass unemployment and are then abolished or contracted when political stability is restored. We shall argue that expansive relief policies are designed to mute civil disorder and restrictive ones to reinforce work norms (p. xiii).*

Radical ideology insists that the ruling class gains the most from welfare programs. In addition to ensuring stability and providing a pool of permanently cheap labor, welfare money goes almost directly from the hands of recipients to landlords and merchants. Radicals also suggest that human beings achieve their full potential when they produce without the compulsion of the capitalist system. Everyone should be allowed and required to contribute to society. Profit, competition, and inequality distort the value and meaning of human life.

Radical ideology, when transformed into practice, results in revolutionary activity (Galper, 1975). This process, according to Galper, should not be confused with *reformist* activity. He defines revolutionary activity as a process that discredits, delegitimizes, and eventually captures and replaces the present social welfare system. This activity should be "essentially nonviolent," but not necessarily nonmilitant. (see Box 3-1).

BOX 3-1   Code of Ethics for Radical Social Service Workers

Galper (1975, pp. 225–227) has suggested a Code of Ethics for Radical Social Service Workers, which provides an interesting contrast to the NASW Code of Ethics outlined in Chapter 1.

1. I regard as my primary obligation the welfare of all humankind [as opposed to the welfare of the client, Section II.F. of the NASW code].

2. I will work toward the development of a society that is committed to the dictum, "From each according to his or her ability, to each according to his or her need." [Section II.F.2. of the NASW code is concerned with nondiscrimination, and section VI.P.6. indicates a commitment to social justice, but there is no position on economic equality.]

3. I will struggle for the realization of a society in which my personal interests and my personal actions are consistent with my interests and actions as a worker. [The NASW code, Section I.A.3., strongly suggests that personal and private interests should be clearly differentiated. Radicals feel that this type of fragmentation has politically conservative implications for social work and social welfare.]

4. I will consider myself accountable to all who join in the struggle for social change and will consider them accountable to me for the quality and extent of the work we perform and the society we create. [This need for *collective* responsibility is *not* part of the NASW code.]

5. I will work to achieve the kind of world in which all people can be free and open with one another in all matters. [This is in conflict with the privacy and confidentiality provisions of the NASW code, Section II.H.]

6. I will use information gained from my work to facilitate humanistic, revolutionary change in the society. [The NASW code suggests only a commitment to social justice.]

7. I will treat the findings, views, and actions of colleagues with the respect due them.

This respect is conditioned by their demonstrated concern for revolutionary values and radical social change. [Respect for colleagues in the NASW code, Section III.J., is unconditional; here it is predicated on their acceptance of a radical ideology.]

8. I will use all the knowledge and skill available to me in bringing about a radically transformed society. [The NASW code calls for practice to be conducted within the recognized knowledge and competence of the profession, and there is no commitment to radical change.]

9. I recognize my responsibility to add my ideas and findings to our society's knowledge and practice, [There seems to be little conflict here with the NASW code, Section I.E.]

10. I accept my responsibility to help protect the community against unethical practice by any individuals or organizations in the society. [This is much more comprehensive than the NASW code's provision, which is addressed primarily to the profession, Section V.M.2.]

11. I commit myself to use myself fully in the struggle for revolutionary change. [There is no corresponding injunction in the NASW code, only a commitment to social justice and nondiscrimination, Section VI.P.]

12. I support the principle that all persons can and must contribute to the realization of a humanized society. [The collective obligation of *all persons* is not found in the NASW code.]

13. I accept responsibility for working toward the creation and maintenance of conditions in society that enable all people to live by this code. [The NASW code addresses itself only to *social workers;* the radical code purports to be a standard of conduct for *everyone*.]

14. I contribute my knowledge, skills, and support to the accomplishment of a humanistic, democratic, communal, socialist society. [There is obviously no such call in the NASW code!]

Radicals believe that the professional relationship between social worker and clients reinforces class and social distinctions. Similarly, professional social welfare organizations (or bureaucracies) fragment social problems into components that are amenable to treatment by social workers with highly specialized and, most often, *clinical* training. The effect of these relationships, structures, and practices is to deflect our attention from the clients' "real" problems, which are essentially *economic* and *political* in nature (Burghardt, 1980).

Forms of radical social work practice began to develop during the Great Depression of the 1930s out of concern that the New Deal programs were inadequate to deal with such massive unemployment. In its early years, radical practice was also closely allied to trade union movements, both inside and outside the profession. The leadership was philosophically committed to the dissolution of capitalism and its replacement by a socialist system. Conflict and confrontation were openly advocated as tactics of social change (Burghardt & Fabricant, 1987).

Saul Alinsky, a community organizer who epitomized the eclectic approach regarding the political empowerment of disadvantaged groups, had a major influence on radical social work. To Alinsky, the power that was concentrated in the hands of community elites and their organizations could be challenged, captured, and redistributed without radically restructuring the economic nature of society. Alinsky's tactics may have been just as militant and confrontational as earlier forms of radical practice, but his organizations were rarely class based, and their ideology was much less sharply focused (Alinsky, 1946).

During the 1960s, radical social workers were extensively involved in the civil rights movement. Their ties to trade unionism were strengthened, and many alliances were created with client groups. At the local level, many urban social workers were involved in tenants' unions and tenants' rights movements. By the late 1960s many radical social workers were working in client membership organizations such as the National Tenants Organization and the National Welfare Rights Organization. Although still following a socialist orientation, they focused their efforts mostly on increasing services or benefit levels, increasing access to entitlements, and equalizing power between the clients and the welfare bureaucracies.

During the 1970s and 1980s, radical theory retained its socialist ideological commitment and perspectives on professionalism, but it became more flexible in developing strategies for change. It appears that the original hope for a radical restructuring of the economic system has given way to a more pragmatic approach to providing clients with the available services of the welfare system, while working to equalize power and achieve social justice. The conservative backlash of the Reagan administration and the continuing conservatism in both major political parties, as well as the U.S. Congress, has been a major setback. With the Left (both social workers and other citizens) becoming as isolated and as small a group as it has ever been in the twentieth century (Burghardt & Fabricant, 1987), prospects for the future of radical social work seem rather limited.

Longres (1996) has documented some recent changes in radical social work. The leading radical journal, *Catalyst: A Socialist Journal of the Social Services,* became *The Journal of Progressive Human Services.* The nineteenth edition of the *Encyclopedia of Social Work* has an entry on progressive rather than radical social work. Longres remains optimistic; he believes that progressive may indeed be a better word than radical. Also, British, Canadian, and Australian social workers still write a good deal about radical issues (Fook, 1993). In the United States "the progressive forces in social work keep the spirit alive through their involvement with ethnic sensitive, feminist, empowerment, strengths, and other more current alternatives to mainstream social work practice" (p. 464). Nevertheless, it is clear that radical social work voices are relatively muted, and it is not clear whether we will hear their return any time soon.

The novice social work student may be surprised that in an essentially capitalistic system such as ours, radical social work has managed to survive at all. We should keep in mind, however, that in many nations radical practice has a much stronger following than in the United States. This is particularly true of third-world countries, where social workers are far more likely to be concerned with the problems of poverty, hunger, and housing than with the mental health problems that require so much attention in this country (Midgley, 1985). However, a large proportion of social workers in other Western, industrialized nations such as England and the Nordic countries also accept a radical ideology on social change (Gibson, 1988).

Summary

The theories and ideologies that shape social work practice are varied and complex and in a constant state of change. If we had to identify a dominant strain of social work only ten years ago, we would have said unflinchingly that it had a liberal perspective and that it relied heavily on general systems theory as a way of understanding social phenomena and devising solutions to social problems. Despite its weaknesses, systems theory continues to be a fertile area of intellectual inquiry. The growth of complexity theory and chaos theory in social sciences is likely to assure interest in systems for some time.

Nearly two decades after the advent of Reaganomics we also find that we are relying more often on private solutions to public problems, and increasing numbers of social workers aspire to private practice. Practitioners in both public and private sectors also face more competitive environments in which to work. More than ever we need viable theories for social work practice and effective interventions.

Divisions in the profession over what is the true nature of social work also have heated up. Social workers find themselves in the unenviable position of being criticized from all sides. Radicals are critical of the alliance with the state and increasing professionalism, both of which they say have facilitated the oppression of disadvantaged groups within our society. Conservatives, on the other hand, criticize social workers for having created dependencies on entitlement programs such as Aid to Families with Dependent Children (see Chapter 12). Students should be prepared to accept the fact that the profession is constantly changing due to its interaction with a dynamic environment. Systems theory may be a useful tool to apply in following the continuing development of the profession.

Suggested Readings

Boulding, K. E. (1985). *The world as a total system.* Beverly Hills, CA: Sage.

Germain, C. (1979). *Social work practice: People and environments: An ecological perspective.* New York: Columbia University.

Martin, P. Y., & O'Connor, G. (1988). *The social environment: Open systems applications.* New York: Longman.

Pincus, A., & Minahan, A. (1973). *Social work practice.* Itasca, IL: F. E. Peacock.

4

A New Look at Traditional Social Work Methods

Positioning the Profession for the Future

The original chapter from the first edition of this book has been revised by MAGGIE JACKSON and LONNIE R. HELTON, Department of Social Work, Cleveland State University.

The social work profession has developed specializations, generally based on the size of the client system being served. Each specialization is assumed to use particular methods that are characterized by distinctive knowledge and skills. In the early years of the profession, all social workers were classified into three practice areas: casework, group work, and community organization. Caseworkers ordinarily interact with *individuals and families,* group workers with *collectivities of related and unrelated individuals,* and community organizers with representatives of community *organizations* and with *citizens at large.*

More than three decades ago William Schwartz (1961a) noted the inappropriateness of defining a specialization based on the size of the client system involved. He suggested that these three divisions should refer not to a practice specialization, but to different relational systems in which *all* social workers may seek to implement change. However, Compton and Galaway (1989) noted that a major difficulty with this approach has been the encouragement of dichotomous thinking. That is, a dilemma confronting the social worker is whether to concentrate on changing the individual or changing the environment. As the profession grew and as social problems became increasingly more complex, social work professionals perceived the need to unify these traditional approaches into a *generalist* framework that views casework, group work, and community organization not necessarily as specializations, but rather as practice methods that should be woven into the foundation of knowledge and skills of all social workers.

The current Curriculum Policy Statement of the Council on Social Work Education (CSWE) requires a generalist approach rather than a specialist focus at the undergraduate level; however, at the graduate level it suggests specializations that may be developed around practice roles, fields of practice, specific problem areas, or population groups such as the elderly, homosexuals, urban residents, or children and families. (Also see Chapter 2.) Some schools allow specialization in as many as three of these divisions. Thus a student in some MSW programs might focus on casework in juvenile corrections, community organization practice with minority groups, or administration of programs for the elderly. In one sense specialization seems to be the antithesis of professionalism, which would seem to require a minimal amount of common knowledge, skills, and interests among members. Yet, it is against this backdrop that the search for the common principles of social work practice began.

The Generalist Model

The generalist model of social work practice took on a new meaning within the profession when the bachelor of social work degree, rather than the master's, was approved as the entry level credential. CSWE's Curriculum Policy Statement recognized the generalist approach as a basic framework for social work practice. According to Standard B 5.2, "the baccalaureate level of social work education must include a liberal arts perspective and the professional foundation content, which prepares students for direct services with client systems of various sizes and types." In addition, "the master's level prepares students for advanced social work practice in an area of concentration. These levels of education differ from each other in the depth, breadth, and specificity of knowledge and skill that students are expected to synthesize and apply in practice" (Commission on Accreditation, 1994, p. 98).

In recent years, many schools have developed curriculum for an "advanced generalist" course of study. It requires social work educators to define the specific nature of generalist practice. This definition is the driving force for the entire curriculum in that program.

Over the last twenty-five years, social workers have addressed generalist practice in an effort to define both its scope and purpose. This focus was further defined by Baer and Federico (1978/1979) who developed specific competencies for generalist social work practice. More recently, the generalist practice model has been described by Kirst-Ashman and Hull (1993); Hoffman and Sallee (1993); Compton and Galaway (1989); O'Neil-McMahon (1990); Johnson (1986); and Sheafor, Horejsi, and Horejsi (1991). Kirst-Ashman and Hull present a popular paradigm known as the Generalist Intervention Model (GIM), which provides a basis for understanding generalist practice by delineating four major characteristics: (1) foundational knowledge, skills, and values; (2) problem solving with individuals, groups, and community organizations; (3) problem analysis and action from multiple perspectives; and (4) the utilization of a specific, flexible problem-solving method.

Knowledge Base for Generalist Practice

Generalist practice requires that the social worker's background include certain knowledge, skills, and elements that can be transferred to all aspects of social work practice. Although there may be no generally agreed upon theory of generalist practice, social workers concur that the knowledge base should be eclectic and should include a systems or ecological framework.

Systems theory provides a basis for assessing client needs from a holistic perspective and enables the social worker to focus on links between clients and social support systems. (Also see Chapter 3.) It does not rely on the traditional micro/macro dichotomies, but rather assists the social worker in identifying the appropriate client system for intervention and underscores other relevant systems needing change. In applying the systems framework to generalist practice, social workers must continually strive for an ecological approach to intervention with all client populations that allows clients opportunities to influence environmental factors affecting them. The social worker assists in this process through the roles of enabling, mediating, advocating, brokering, and educating the client. To illustrate, an older adult male living in a high-rise complex persistently complains about periodic increases in Medicare costs, yet has not voted in the last few elections because he feels that one vote is not important. He uses the excuse that very few friends in the building are registered to vote. They have similar feelings regarding their ability to influence decision making at the federal level. In the enabling role, the social worker is fundamental in enhancing the client's motivation by encouraging him to register to vote and recruiting others in the building to do likewise. In the role of educator, the worker's presentation of a brief seminar for the residents concerning welfare reform and the impact on older adults may also be instrumental in this effort. Moreover, in the role of broker, the social worker might arrange transportation to the election polls through the local neighborhood center.

To illustrate the base of practice for the generalist social worker, we must first describe the steps involved in implementing planned change. The helping process is a mutually negotiated effort. The client has the problem and the social worker has the repertoire of skills necessary for improvement of social functioning. Included in these steps are activities reflecting preparation for the encounter, communication (verbal, nonverbal, and written), analysis, goal setting, and roles.

Engagement

The social worker begins the helping process by assisting the client in identifying problems and issues that need to be addressed. The social worker must also determine whether to continue with the intervention process or refer the client to another agency. The casework process begins with the client further describing the presenting problem (the issue initially voiced by the client). Some clients may expect the agency or the caseworker then to take over the situation and solve the problem. Caseworkers sometimes do this, but this is a common misconception of the casework process that may result from the client's contact with other human service professionals or agencies whose models of assistance rely primarily on telling the client how to proceed in addressing the problem. Examples of this can be observed as a doctor writes prescriptions; an attorney files a brief or asks for an injunction on behalf of a client; and a teacher determines what school activities are to be carried out by the student.

In this beginning phase, the client and social worker engage in problem solving, which may lead to elaboration of problems related to the presenting problem. The problem to be addressed may be either the initial problem or related problems shared during this interchange. For example, a client may come to a family service agency with a marital problem and request marriage counseling. In discussing this problem with the client, the social worker may determine that the marital problem results from the client's (or spouse's) alcohol abuse. Resistant clients present special problems for social workers. This is especially true of *involuntary* clients, such as those referred for mandatory substance abuse services or those in the correctional system. It is also true of many *voluntary* clients, however, who often have a different view of their problem than the social worker.

Assessment

This step involves the collection and analysis of data concerning the client and his or her family or support system. Assessment is a dynamic process that should result in an understanding of the problem. Initial impressions may be confirmed, modified, or rejected in light of information that comes to the caseworker's attention as the case progresses. Assessment includes a judgment by the caseworker concerning the strength of the client's capabilities in coping with the situation. The course of action to be followed, whether called treatment, provision of services, or intervention, is determined during the assessment phase.

Assessment is a circular process because it continues throughout intervention. The caseworker's and client's perceptions regarding the problem may change over time depending on the individual needs or concerns of the client system. Moreover, the caseworker may need to assess and prioritize identified problems based on professional interventionist skills. This reflective thinking must include environmental influences that may affect the agency, thus impinging on service delivery. Mutual feedback is necessary for the caseworker and the client to make any necessary modifications in the intervention plan. Feedback is crucial for positioning both client and caseworker for adequate problem solving.

Planning and Contracting

Essential to bringing about planned change, the caseworker and the client must consider the range of possible solutions and their implications. Both must then agree on the responsibilities that each will carry out in order to select the most viable approaches to change. A written contract must be developed, specifying the roles and responsibilities of all parties and including a time line for each identified goal. Each goal must be broken into specific, measurable objectives by which outcomes of the helping process may be evaluated.

Action/Doing

During this step of the helping process, action to achieve the intended change occurs. The caseworker and client system fulfills their assigned roles and responsibilities. One could say that intervention or treatment always begins with the first contact with the social worker. The process is intensified after the client and caseworker have identified and assessed the problems, agreed on the objectives, and have mutually determined the most appropriate methods to be applied.

The client's particular needs, rather than the caseworker's preferences or the agency's resources, should determine the type of intervention to be employed. However, this is not always possible. For example, a child needing an adoptive home may be placed in foster care until adoption plans can be finalized. Foster care may continue for years, and the child may be moved frequently from one foster home to another rather than placed permanently, simply because the social worker cannot locate the proper resources. Another example is a mental health program emphasizing short-term treatment to maximize the number of clients seen, even though clients could benefit from long-term assistance. If an agency is unable to provide the necessary services, it is the caseworker's responsibility to refer the client to other resources within the community. The social worker's quandary is to decide what alternatives might be provided to the client when necessary services are not immediately available.

The social worker's interventionist skills might include interviewing, assessing, contracting, and referring the client to other agencies. Assisting the client in obtaining housing or necessary medical services, interceding with the school system on behalf of a client (or the client's children), or building the client's self-esteem are other appropriate interventions. Ideally, efforts should support the client in using personal and other resources to deal with the problem.

Monitoring and Evaluation

Mutual feedback from actions is analyzed to determine the degree of success achieved by intervention, and based on this assessment, subsequent actions may need to be revised. This process then positions the practitioner to begin the monitoring and evaluation step. Monitoring and evaluation occur on three levels. The social worker evaluates the progress of the client in utilizing available sources of assistance. The social worker may also monitor and evaluate the services provided to the client by other professionals, both within the agency and outside the agency, in order to determine their effectiveness. Finally, the social worker may teach the client how to self-monitor his or her own progress. This is especially important in working with clients with chemical dependency problems, since relapse is a constant threat.

Termination

The social worker must help determine whether it is appropriate to discontinue services or suggest other strategies of helping that can satisfy unmet needs. Termination has been defined as, "the conclusion of the social worker-client intervention process; a systematic procedure for disengaging the working relationship" (Barker, 1995, p. 380). This definition connotes unilateral activity or perhaps a finite closing of the helping relationship. However, termination must be perceived as a process that begins at the start of intervention. That is, the practitioner must inevitably discuss termination (indirectly or directly) so that the client will have some understanding in advance of how closure will be facilitated.

Planning a conclusion during the earlier stages of the helping process helps avoid fostering dependency or a misconception on the part of the client that the responsibility for a problem can be totally shifted to the caseworker or the agency. The conclusion of services may signal that the caseworker has confidence in the client's ability to learn to cope with recurring problematic situations. Be aware, however, that many clients terminate services abruptly, with no warning and no time for the social worker to help prepare them for future crises. Sadly, some clients just disappear, and the social worker frequently will have no further contact and no way to find out what happened.

Social Casework

The origins of social casework can be traced to the method of helping developed by Mary Richmond and described in her book *Social Diagnosis* (Richmond, 1917). Two persistent themes grew out of her work: the need to individualize people and the need to understand (diagnose) situations. The term social "diagnosis" fit well into a medical framework for practice, since it was suggestive of the idea that cases (people) could be viewed as either sick or well.

There are several different models of casework. One of them involves a *behavioral approach*. The essence of this approach is that behavior is shaped by all learning. To clarify, an individual is a product of environmental influences throughout his or her life. Thus, if behavior can be learned, it can also be unlearned. This framework provides a foundation for activity with the client during intervention. The growth of this approach occurred in the social work profession four decades ago. The body of knowledge forming this framework stems from research on learning and behavior modification, largely focusing on classic and operant conditioning (Thomas, 1973).

The roots of the *psychosocial model* of social work practice are found in psychoanalytic theories and concepts of the 1920s. Twenty years later it was further refined and moved away somewhat from the medical model in the works of Gordon Hamilton (1940). She called her method an "organismic" approach and stressed cause and effect relationships between the individual and the environment. This model evolved from Freudian theory, but was adapted and modified for social work practice.

Functional casework, based partly on the psychological theories of Otto Rank, was developed at the Pennsylvania School of Social Work during the 1930s. Emphasis is on the *processes* of help, especially the client-social worker relationship, and the dynamic use of time. Rank's "will" psychology referred to the individual's ability to mobilize actions toward a desired goal. It was "the deliberate use of time to arouse an awareness of motivation, the focus on the immediate present as the arena for mindful change, and the purposeful focus on the active processes occurring within the helping relationship" (Goldstein, 1982, p. 546).

Robinson and Taft viewed social casework as a process that mediated between the client's need for help and the agency's *function* (Smalley, 1967). This model tends to avoid diagnostic categories as having limited usefulness in dealing with clients who are "unique." However, this school also emphasizes the agency's function rather than the client's need. Social workers using this approach are expected to know the helping process only as it relates to the employing agency's setting and function.

The *problem-solving* model was developed by Helen Harris Perlman (1957) at the University of Chicago. This method focuses on how the difficulties that clients bring to caseworkers are related to their own approach to problem solving. The assumption is that a person's inability to cope with a particular problem is due to a deficit or absence of problem solving. That is, the client may lack the *motivation* to attack the problem in appropriate ways, the *capacity* to work on the problem in appropriate ways, or an *opportunity* to mitigate the problem. The caseworker focuses on the client's abilities in identifying a problem, seeking a solution, making decisions, and taking appropriate action. The social worker using this model may also consider an intervention from outside to resolve many problems.

Behavior modification is a newer model of practice that draws heavily on Skinnerian psychology. Behavioral casework owes much to Edwin Thomas (1967) at the University of Michigan School of Social Work. Behavioral frameworks, which stress the identification of clear *objectives* and the observation of *behavior,* are much more amenable to investigation and research through social scientific methods. Part of the popularity of behavioral casework is undoubtedly due to the growing feeling among many social workers that evaluation of intervention should be a routine part of social work practice. Evaluating whether or not specific behavioral objectives have been met is thought to provide more concrete evidence of social work's effectiveness than assessing clients' feelings with the use of more introspective measures. Behavioral methods have also gained advocates because of the focus on clients' assets rather than pathology and the recognition of the importance of environmental factors.

Task-centered casework is an approach also developed at the University of Chicago in the early 1970s by Laura Epstein who stated that this approach was "addressed to problems in living that the client can, with help, resolve through his own actions" (Reid, 1977, p. 2). This method is a short-term model in which both the client and caseworker must reach an explicit agreement on the problem to be addressed and the duration of treatment, and in which *behavior* is emphasized as the focus of intervention. In addition, Epstein (1980) noted that the logical sequencing of task-centered steps provides a basic structure for problem solving.

Competency-based social work practice emphasizes "the importance of identifying and using specific competencies involved in offering effective services" (Gambrill, 1983). It also emphasizes the importance of increasing clients' own competencies so that they may enhance the quality of their lives. This method is similar to other methods, especially task-centered and behavioral approaches. For example, the competency-based model stresses the necessity for agreement on outcomes to be pursued, contracting, intervention based on the empirical research literature, and behavioral change.

Most social workers are *eclectic* in their practice, using whatever method seems most appropriate with a particular client and a particular problem. The *Social Work Dictionary* defines eclectic as "a collection of certain aspects of various theories or practice methods that appear to be most useful for practice interventions" (Barker, 1995, p. 114). The caseworker examples in Box 4-1 illustrate a variety of methods. (Names of all persons in the case examples throughout this book are fictitious.)

BOX 4-1 Casework Examples

Lisa Jones

Lisa Jones, age sixteen, is two months pregnant by her nineteen-year-old boyfriend, John Thompson, a college sophomore at a local university. Lisa informed John just last week of her pregnancy and he was very upset. He wants to continue his engineering studies at school and does not feel ready to take on the responsibilities of marriage and a family. Lisa's mother, Mary, age thirty-eight, is divorced and has two other children (Kyle, age seven and Billy, age fourteen). Lisa, an above average student, is hesitant to tell Mary for fear of her mother's rejection. Mary's sister, Julia, became pregnant at sixteen and Lisa

has always heard about how this event "ruined her (aunt's) life." Lisa's father, a psychologist, lives out of state and is remarried to a twenty-five-year old woman; they have a ten-month-old son. Lisa regrets her father and mother's divorce and still feels partially to blame. She had been running around with a rough crowd at the time and was using drugs heavily in junior high school. She now sees her father only twice a year.

Mary Jones, an accountant, is engaged to marry a widower, Jerry Chase, a salesman rearing his two daughters Vickie, age three, and Pamela, age ten; his wife died of cancer a year ago. Lisa was always close to her mother until

continued

Jerry started dating her. John Thompson's father is a Methodist minister and his mother is a teacher at Lisa's high school.

Besides John, Lisa has told only her closest friend, Amy, also age sixteen, about the pregnancy. Amy suggested that Lisa go directly to Planned Parenthood. This advice made Lisa even more fearful of facing the reality of her pregnancy. She has been crying and has skipped school the past three days, hanging out at a local mall. John has not called her since she told him of her pregnancy and she is fearful of calling him. She feels dejected and hurt. Her mother is seldom home due to working long hours, and when not working, she is with Jerry. Lisa is angry at her mother and misses their once close relationship. She thought that John really loved her, and now she feels "used" and vulnerable. Amy convinced Lisa that she should talk to someone at the local community mental health center.

The social worker on call at the mental health center talked with Lisa about her crisis and has helped her sort out her feelings of fear, hopelessness, and loneliness. They have also discussed what options might be available to her. Lisa has been concerned about making the "right" decisions for everyone involved. The social worker arranged a family meeting and assisted Lisa in talking with her mother and father about her pregnancy and what might be the best plan of action. After several individual and family counseling sessions, Lisa has decided not to have an abortion and has insisted that alternate plans include her being able to continue her education. The social worker has made arrangements for Lisa to attend evening classes at an adult evening program in her school district, which includes other pregnant teenagers. She also advised Lisa as to what extent to involve the father in decisions regarding the future of their child. Lisa has agreed to her father and stepmother's attending the next family session.

Lonnie R. Helton, Cleveland State University

Gwen Halbert

Gwen Halbert and her two children, Eric, age nine, and Carrie, age four, have been brought to the family violence shelter by the police. Mrs. Halbert discovered that her husband, George, an alcoholic and cocaine addict, had been sexually molesting Carrie. Upon confronting her husband, Mrs. Halbert was brutally beaten. She then called the police. She has bruises on her face, and her son Eric was beaten across the back, when he tried to defend his mother. Mr. Halbert fled the home and has not yet been located by the authorities. Both mother and children are extremely agitated and fear that Mr. Halbert will suddenly appear and further harm them.

In helping Mrs. Halbert address the presenting problems, the social worker at the family shelter first took all family members to the local hospital for a complete medical evaluation. Then she requested that the mother seriously consider taking out a restraining order to prevent her husband from having contact with the children and her. After obtaining the restraining order, the mother decided the family would stay at the shelter for thirty days to give her time to develop longer term plans. Meanwhile, the social worker contacted the local school district, which agreed to provide transportation for Eric to attend school and to enroll Carrie in preschool. Both mother and children received daily counseling. The social worker helped Mrs. Halbert to realize that the shelter could provide multiple services to meet the complex needs of the family. The police have informed the mother that Mr. Halbert has been located and incarcerated at the city jail.

Social Work Practice with Groups

The distinguishing characteristic of the group work approach to social work practice "lies in its emphasis on group relations—its inevitable identification with the interacting process between group members, consciously stimulated and directed by a worker" (Phillips, 1957, pp. 42–43). Schwartz (1961b) noted that the group involves mutual aid—that is, a cluster of individuals coming together to address common issues or problems of varying degrees of intensity. Social work educators and practitioners of group methods disagree on whether the primary unit of attention is the group or the individual within the group. According to Middleman and Goldberg, models identified as "social group work" or "social work with groups" use the *group* as the primary unit of attention; secondary focus is on individuals within the group (Middleman & Goldberg, 1987, p. 718). Others insist that group work, whatever it is called, always focuses primarily on the individuals within the group. According to Gisela Konopka (1963), group work recognized early that there is not necessarily a dichotomy between individual and group, and that individuals can fulfill their optimal potential and feelings of self-worth by group participation.

History of Group Work

Social group work developed as a model of practice within various religious and charitable organizations during the nineteenth century. By the end of the Civil War, the YMCA and YWCA were using group work approaches in their programs. Toynbee Hall in London was using group work methods by the beginning of the twentieth century, as were the Neighborhood Guild and Jane Addams's Hull House. The Boy Scouts, Girl Scouts, and 4-H Clubs also adopted group methods (Schopler & Galinsky, 1995).

By 1935 the National Conference on Social Work had established a group work division, and in 1936 the National Association for the Study of Group Work was formed. In 1939 a committee concerned with professional social work education launched a study of the courses in group work offered by schools of social work. This led to the adoption of an official policy statement on group work practice by the American Association of Group Workers in 1946. It was not until 1955 that this organization merged with several others to create the National Association of Social Workers (Schopler & Galinsky, 1995).

The first class emphasizing group work training was taught at the School of Applied Social Sciences of Western Reserve University in the 1920s. This course was taught by Grace Coyle (Quam, 1995, p. 2580). Today all graduate programs in social work offer content on systems of all sizes, including groups, and several offer a sequence of courses that emphasize group work methods (Commission on Accreditation, 1994). Many field placements offer students exposure to group work methods, perhaps planning a group or co-facilitating with an experienced practitioner. However, the level or intensity of involvement may vary from one agency to another depending on the student's learning needs and the way services are delivered.

Group Work Models

As mentioned earlier, group workers are primarily concerned with the relationships among the group members and between the group members and the worker. The group worker participates in the group's interactions but is not a regular member who identifies with the others, nor is he or she assimilated into the group's activities. The group worker's roles and functions are guided by an understanding of group dynamics and by the individual members' need for help. The group worker must be careful to control personal values, preferences, and advice while concentrating on enabling the members of the group to achieve their objectives. Group work methods can assist a group in achieving mutually determined goals, achieving desirable changes for individuals within the group, and developing self-enhancement and personal fulfillment for group members. Three different models of group work have been described by Papell and Rothman (1966): the *social goals model,* the *reciprocal goals model,* and the *remedial goals model.* The social goals model, as well as the reciprocal model, grew out of the settlement house movement. The social goals model emerged from the concept that group work yields a broader knowledge base and a competent citizenry (Macht & Ashford, 1991). Persons belong to a group because they hope to attain certain social gains for the group. This model is used to attack problems within a community, such as crime, inadequate housing, or poor sanitation. The social goals model is frequently used in neighborhood centers, community action agencies, and neighborhood health or welfare councils. It is heavily influenced by the principles of democratic group processes and encourages group work practitioners to strive to develop and maintain democratic procedures in small groups (Papell & Rothman, 1966).

The reciprocal model views the individual as an entity that can be analyzed, understood, and treated only in relation to the many systems and subsystems to which he or she is connected. This approach assumes an organic, systematic relationship between the individual and society, focusing on the interdependence between the individual and larger systems. The reciprocal model "does not begin with a priori prescriptions of desired outcomes... It is only from the encounters of individuals that compose a reciprocal group system that direction or problem is determined" (Papell & Rothman, 1966, pp. 74–75). The social worker's role in such a group is that of an enabler or mediator to the "needs system" that develops in the group. This group work model emphasizes individual mental health and assumes a strong bond between community participation and psychological functioning (Macht & Ashford, 1991). For example, a social worker in a children's hospital might organize a support group of parents whose children are on the neurosurgery service, both to relieve parental anxiety about being away from their children's bedsides and concurrently to offer play therapy groups for their children to relieve the young patients' stress related to hospitalization or impending surgery. Moreover, the social worker could attempt to connect the families with appropriate resources, such as transportation, temporary lodging close by, or a visiting nurse service, which are likely to make the hospitalization and discharge planning easier.

The remedial model is a clinically oriented treatment model in which the group is used as an agent of change. In this model a group worker facilitates interaction among members of the group in order to achieve change for the individual. The group worker applies professional skills in helping the individuals in the group gain self-awareness or improve social functioning. The group supports its members by encouraging more appropriate modes of functioning. Intervention focuses on the

---

BOX 4-2   Group Work Example

Alice, a social work intern at an after-school prevention program for males and females ranging in age from thirteen to seventeen, wanted to start a self-esteem and social skills group for the students with poor grades. Many of these young people had been referred to the program by school personnel or by child welfare workers. Many of them came from single-parent homes in which the mothers received public assistance. Most of them had told Alice that they did not want to be in the program and saw it as a punishment or a "total waste of time." A few of the teens said that they had already been made to feel rejected at school and did not want their lack of accomplishment to be further accentuated.

Although somewhat chagrined by this unenthusiastic response, Alice met with a group of eight teens, three females and five males. All had experienced significant learning problems in school and some had failed at least one grade. Although embarrassed and frustrated by this failure, the young people seemed to crave opportunities to compete and prove themselves. Just as some of the teens were beginning to share deeper feelings about school and peer relationships in the group, Alice developed a strategy to further enhance the participation of all group mem-

bers. Alice, herself an avid weight lifter and runner, shared her athletic talents and interests with the group and offered to integrate a weight lifting program as part of the weekly talk group. The group members were excited about this new activity and were eager to begin the next week. Alice was able to obtain limited funds from her fieldwork supervisor at the agency to buy weights and also was able to enlist the support of the YMCA athletic coordinator who donated several sets of used weights.

In each session, the youths would begin by talking about problems that had occurred since the last group meeting, and then they would begin warm-up exercises and weight lifting. Alice, and the group members themselves, were surprised at how group interaction and relationships were enhanced as they exercised together and discussed mutual problems. Alice devised several effective group exercises whereby the teens were challenged to make the connection between strong bodies and mental readiness and strong self-esteem, both vital components for learning. The program became increasingly successful and became an ingrained component of service delivery at the after-school prevention program.

---

dysfunctional patterns in the group and within each member's relationships. This model is used most often in correctional facilities, mental hospitals, family service agencies, and other treatment-oriented programs. Box 4-2 describes an example of group work.

Community Organization Practice

Social workers engaged in community organization today address the current trends and policies affecting the environment. Community organization is defined as

an intervention process used by social workers and other professionals to help individuals, groups, and collectives of people with common interests or from the same geographic areas to deal with social problems and to enhance social well-being through planned collective action (Barker, 1995, p. 69).

Community organization practice involves the identification and recruitment of members of the action system, as well as the development of organizational and interpersonal relationships among them. Practitioners are involved in tasks such as identifying social problems, analyzing factors that create or cause these problems, formulating plans, developing strategies, and mobilizing resources to take action.

History of Community Organization

Community organization has its roots in the Charity Organization Society (COS) movement. After the economic depression of 1873, industrialization, immigration, and the movement of rural populations into urban areas created new social problems. The COS movement was concerned with solving the problems of fraud, duplication of services, and indiscriminate giving that were sometimes associated with charitable giving.

Continuing in the patterns developed by the COS movement, Councils of Social Agencies were organized shortly after the turn of the century. Their goals emphasized efficiency, centralization, and specialization in the planning and delivery of services by private agencies within the community. By the beginning of World War I, the term *community organization* had come into general use. During the war, community agencies designed services to meet the needs and problems of servicemen and their families. Fund-raising agencies, called "Community War Chests," were developed to centralize planning and administration and achieve greater efficiency in the utilization of community resources.

Community organization also has its roots in the settlement house movement. While the COS movement was concerned with efficiency and the elimination of fraud, the settlement houses focused on *social action* oriented toward promoting legislation to achieve change and eliminate problems that stemmed from environmental causes. Child labor laws, legislation improving the treatment of institutionalized persons with mental illness, and workers' compensation laws are all attributable in part to the actions of the settlement house movement.

The reformist aspect of community practice was kept alive during the 1920s and 1930s by the labor movement and a few experiments of state and local governments. One notable experiment was the Chicago Area Project, begun in 1934 as an attempt to organize residents of slum areas in a juvenile delinquency prevention program (Kobrin, 1959). This was generally regarded as the period of the ascendancy of psychoanalytic concepts and the preeminence of social *casework* practice. Shortly before World War II, however, the Lane report to the National Conference of Social Work identified community organization as a method of social work practice. Another movement at this time was that of emphasizing expertise or technical skills—that is, a time of developing professionalization (Brager, Specht, & Torczyner, 1987). World War II also gave impetus to massive attempts at community organization when community councils, neighborhood associations, and block committees were established by the thousands in order to support the war effort.

Another landmark in community organization practice was the Back of the Yards movement in Chicago, organized by Saul Alinsky in the early years of World War II.

Although not a professional social worker himself, Alinsky did much to change the direction of community organization practice by developing a model of community change built around a strategy of conflict. Alinsky was a proponent of conflict-oriented "People's Organizations," which did not achieve popularity in the profession for another twenty-five years (Alinsky, 1946). Alinsky's ideology was socialistic and class-directed, but he generally soft-pedaled ideological principles in favor of success in organizing and bargaining for power. According to Alinsky's last published book (1971), an organizer "does not have a fixed truth—truth to him is relative and changing; *everything* to him is relative and changing" (p. 11). His ideas helped shape much of the profession's orientation to the civil rights movement of the 1960s.

The civil rights movement, which began in the middle 1950s, ushered in a dramatically altered model of community organization practice. Examples include the 1954 Supreme Court decision ending legal school segregation; the 1955 Montgomery, Alabama bus boycott; and growth of organizations such as the Southern Christian Leadership Conference, Congress of Racial Equality, Student Non-Violent Coordinating Committee, Mississippi Freedom Democratic Party, Black Panther Party, and the National Association for the Advancement of Colored People (Garvin & Cox, 1995).

In addition to civil rights issues, there were other catalysts in this changing form of practice. The 1954 amendments to the Housing Act of 1949 stimulated additional changes in community organization. This legislation required *citizen participation* in the planning of community programs. This trend continued through the mandate of "maximum feasible participation" of those affected by the programs contained in the Economic Opportunity Act of 1964, a major component of the War on Poverty. Urban renewal (sometimes pejoratively referred to as "Negro removal") also caused neighbors to band together to fight displacement from their neighborhoods.

All these events gave renewed vigor to grass-roots community organizing efforts. Citizen participation was also mandated in planning services in the areas of aging, education, mental health, and health care. Drawing directly from Alinsky's conflict tactics, groups such as the National Welfare Rights Organization and the National Tenants Organization actively opposed a welfare state that was perceived as an agent of social control (Kramer, 1969). In this era, concerns existed regarding the effectiveness of the New Deal, and society became positioned to later address the already emerging crises of racism, unemployment, and inadequate housing.

By 1962, community organization was recognized as a separate field of specialization for graduate study by the Council on Social Work Education. It became an increasingly popular course of study during the grass-roots movements in civil rights, poverty, and housing of the 1960s. Its popularity was also indisputably enhanced by the controversial war in Vietnam. Within a decade, however, the picture radically changed. The civil rights movement had achieved a considerable measure of success with passage of legislation on such issues as voting rights, educational and occupational opportunities, and housing. American troops were withdrawn from Vietnam, and the War on Poverty fell from the limelight. As student protest and populist activism diminished, the regard for community organization as a field of practice waned.

During the mid-1970s community organization, both as a graduate curriculum and a field of professional practice, reflected societal changes regarding organizing as an approach to social change. This is not to suggest the complete elimination of such content, but, as usual, social work education reflected societal trends. Jobs for community organizers disappeared, and many schools formally merged community organization and administration specializations into macropractice tracks. Perhaps one clear indication of the changing status of community organization practice is the fact that the 1987 edition of the *Encyclopedia of Social Work* did not carry it as a separate entry: It is listed as "Social Planning and Community Organization" (Gilbert & Specht, 1987). Nevertheless, in the most recent edition of the *Encyclopedia of Social Work,* Si Kahn (1995) authored a separate article on community organization in which he states, "Community organizing is a tool that is used in all cultures and societies to redress the classic imbalance between the powerless and the powerful." He goes on to say that there is "force in numbers—of many people thinking, working, and acting together..." (p. 569). Community organization in social work education programs went from being a separate sequence in the curriculum to being merged with macropractice paradigms. Sadly, except for the minimal content required by the Commission on Accreditation (see Chapter 2), community organization has all but disappeared in some MSW programs. It has suffered much the same fate as radical social work (see Chapters 3 and 5).

Community Organization Models

Typologies of community organization practice are usually based on some combination of the following elements: (1) the character of the action system, (2) the size of the locality, (3) the substance of the problems to be considered, (4) the nature of the target system to be changed, (5) the types of issues (conflict-generating versus consensus-producing), (6) the organizational structures used, (7) the role of the social worker, and (8) the auspices of the project.

The *community development* model involves mobilizing individuals who are directly affected by the problem and organizing them to take actions to resolve it. Process goals of this model might include strengthening bonds among residents of lower socioeconomic areas plagued by lack of sanitation, and training and enabling them to assume leadership positions in working with city government concerning garbage collection. Moreover, the community organizer would help to increase communications among these organized residents and coalesce action among allies in other parts of the city. The *social planning* model refers to "efforts to integrate and coordinate the work of agencies and organizations of the community" (Kramer & Specht, 1983, p. 16). Its action system consists primarily of representatives of organizations. Activities include the development of both intra- and interorganizational communication and planning systems, the utilization of administrative and political leadership, and the development of mechanisms of citizen participation and interagency coordination. A planner must be able to interact confidently and speak authoritatively with administrators and political leaders. Skill in handling budgets and knowledge of the laws and administrative regulations governing agencies in the action system are also requisites for this type of work.

BOX 4-3   Community Organization Example (Social Action)

Organizer: Do you live over there in the slummy building?

Answer: Yeah. What about it?

Organizer: What the hell do you live there for?

Answer: What do you mean, what do I live there for? Where else am I going to live?

Organizer: Oh, you mean you pay rent in that place?

Answer: Come on, is this a put-on? Very funny! You know where you can live for free?

Organizer: Hmm. That place looks like it's crawling with rats and bugs.

Answer: It sure is.

Organizer: Did you ever try to get that landlord to do anything about it?

Answer: Try to get him to do anything about anything! If you don't like it, get out. That's all he has to say. There are plenty more waiting.

Organizer: What if you don't pay your rent?

Answer: They'd throw you out in ten minutes.

Organizer: Hmm. What if nobody in that building paid their rent?

Answer: Well, they'd start to throw . . . Hey, you know, they'd have trouble throwing everybody out, wouldn't they?

Organizer: Yeah, I guess they would.

Answer: Hey, you know, maybe you got something—say, I'd like you to meet some of my friends. How about a drink?

Source: Saul Alinsky, *Rules for Radicals,* New York: Random House, 1991, pp. 103–104, © 1971 by Saul D. Alinsky. Reprinted with permission of Random House, Inc.

The ==social action== model is much closer to the community development model than the social planning model, but it places more emphasis on making basic changes in major social institutions and on the redistribution of power, resources, and authority in community decision making. Social action was the method for bringing about radical social changes during the era of the civil rights movement, student movements, and the Vietnam war. Radical social change includes those citizens willing to take risks against the "acceptable" social order. Many individuals who protested the Vietnam war were arrested for civil disobedience. Today, protestors concerned about nuclear sites and other environmental concerns and those protesting about abortion rights sometimes also break the law to direct attention to their causes. An example of the social action model of community organization is illustrated in Box 4-3.

Summary

Social casework, group work, and community organization practice are still recognizable areas of practice. However, these traditional practice areas have been reconfigured into the generalist model. The generalist approach to social work practice has brought a unifying force into the profession. Rather than identify themselves as specialists in one or more of the three methods, social workers today are more likely to identify themselves as generalist practitioners with micro, mezzo, and macro skills. Therefore, the skills used are those necessary to address the specific needs of a client system.

Suggested Readings

Compton, B., & Galaway, B. (1994). *Social work processes*. Monterey, CA: Brooks/Cole.

Kahn, S. (1994). *How people get power* (rev. ed.). Washington, DC: NASW Press.

Toseland, R., & Rivas, R. (1996). *An introduction to group work practices*. (2nd ed.) Boston: Allyn & Bacon.

5

Contemporary Social Work Methods: Beyond Direct Practice

Photo courtesy of Robert Harbison

The original chapter from the first edition of this book has been revised by STEPHEN P. WERNET, School of Social Work, St. Louis University.

Five years ago we warned students that despite their intentions to serve clients through a direct or clinical practice career, a substantial portion of social work graduates would move into macropractice positions within a relatively short time of graduation. That no longer seems to be the case, however. According to a 1985 study of NASW membership, at least 30 percent of all members worked in a position that was primarily administrative (National Association of Social Workers [NASW], 1985). By 1991 the total percentage of NASW members who listed "macro" practice as a primary function had declined to only 18.4 percent (Gibelman & Schervish, 1993).

Macropractice content remains one of the hallmarks of social work education and the social work profession, even though social work students do not ordinarily seek out many additional courses in macropractice voluntarily. The curriculum leading to a bachelor's degree in social work is not intended to prepare specialists in macropractice. The intent of this chapter is to introduce students to this complementary, and frequently influential, area of social work practice.

Emergence of Macropractice Methods

One of the puzzles in the history of the social work profession is the parallel development of community organization, policy planning, administration, and social research as practice methods. There are obvious areas of overlap among the four methods. All four are concerned with solving and preventing social problems at a level that is broader than the individual or group. All four methods are concerned with social change, program planning, program implementation, and impact. In recent years there have been serious attempts to combine community organization, administration, and policy practice into an integrated macromethod. Some social work educators see this as a logical outgrowth of a generalist social work practice. One possible rationale for maintaining their distinction is to preserve their differences in intent and focus. Those who practice community organization perceive themselves as agents of change focused on structural change, whereas social work administrators perceive themselves as managers or implementers of social programs.

History of Macropractice in Social Work

There is a long-standing and extensive involvement of social workers in macropractice. Almost from the beginning of the profession in the United States, social workers have recognized administration as a method of social work practice. Despite the ascendency of social casework as the major practice method in the early years, there were those who argued against making social work coterminous with social casework.

Some early, distinguished professional leaders, such as Jane Addams, Mary Richmond, Harry Hopkins, and Julia Lathrop, carried out their responsibilities without the benefit of an organized body of knowledge appropriate to social welfare administration (Patti, 1983). Even though the situation has changed somewhat, training and experience in direct services are still generally accepted as a necessary and perhaps sufficient background for assuming a managerial role in a social service agency.

Edith Abbott (1931) assessed the situation in 1927 when she criticized the profession for having to turn to the law, economics, or the ranks of universities in order to find persons "trained in the science of social welfare" (p. 37). Her argument was not against social casework as a central professional function, but against assuming that preparation for a direct service career was also an adequate foundation for a later transition to social welfare administration. James Hagerty (1931) wrote at about the same time that "the education of the leaders, the organizers, and the administrators" was the *most* important task for social work education (p. 99).

In 1929 the Milford conference provided a forum for leaders in the profession to define the nature of social work. Although the conferees paid lip service to administration by calling for professional training in this area and by recognizing the organizational context as critical to effective service delivery, little was said about the specific administrative skills that were needed (American Association of Social Workers, [AASW], 1929). That same year the first *Social Work Yearbook* was published, and it did not contain a single article on the topic of administration (Dunham, 1939). By 1930 social casework had become established as the dominant method in social work and, according to Arthur Dunham, was assumed to be the foundation for all forms of professional practice. "Administration was not ordinarily distinguished from direct practice, nor thought of as a separate function" (p. 16).

The Great Depression had as profound an effect on professional social work practice as it did on the delivery of services. Shortly after the creation of the Federal Emergency Relief Administration (FERA) in 1934, grants were made available through schools of social work to support short-term courses of study that would prepare personnel to work in public relief agencies. Schools of social work were asked to analyze casework and group work skills and suggest how they might be adapted to administrative tasks in public welfare agencies (Brown, 1940).

It was also during the Great Depression that the field of public administration began to emerge as a distinct discipline. Theories concerning such matters as span of control, specialization of function, and general management principles evolved during this period (Patti, 1983). This body of literature, adapted for social agency management, provided inspiration to those practitioners and educators who believed in the need for social work administration as a separate course of study.

The Great Depression also gave birth to the radical social work movement in the United States. Radical social workers believed that the federal government's response was inadequate and the New Deal programs could not significantly affect the rate of unemployment (Fisher, 1980). Most radical social workers during the Great Depression were affiliated with rank-and-file movements whose ideology and organizational structure were strongly influenced by Marxist-Leninist thought. The Depression itself was attributed to the imminent collapse of the capitalist order, and radical social workers were committed to the complete dissolution of capitalism and its replacement by socialism (Fisher, 1980). Radical social workers were responsible for starting discussion groups, helping to create unions, and publishing a journal,

Social Work Today. At the height of the movement in 1935 there were 48 local organizations of radical social workers in 23 cities (Burghardt & Fabricant, 1987).

Following World War II, macropractice shifted away from social change efforts and emphasized program administration. World War II and the subsequent McCarthy era made radical social work relatively unpopular. In 1940 textbooks such as *Problems of Administration in Social Work* had been written (Atwater, 1940). By the early 1950s administration had gained a strong enough foothold for a major study of social work education to be critical of the profession's lack of concern with preparing social workers for administrative practice (Hollis & Taylor, 1951). Resistance to specialized training for social work administrators, however, was still strong. The dominant pattern in graduate programs throughout the 1950s was to offer one introductory course in administration in a curriculum otherwise oriented toward preparation for direct practice.

During the 1960s several events coalesced to renew the profession's interest in the range of macropractice methods. First, the National Conference on Social Welfare featured a number of papers on administration, one of which challenged the idea that casework training and experience were the essential prerequisites for social welfare administration (Thompson, 1961). Shortly afterward Eveline Burns (1961), a leading social work educator, presented a paper to the Council on Social Work Education criticizing our professional schools for neglecting administration and policy content. By 1963 there was sufficient interest in administration to bring about the establishment of the Council on Social Work Administration within NASW (Trecker, 1977).

Second, as community action programs became established institutions, the community organizers who had won approval for those programs became their managers in the 1970s. Community organization and administrative practice came to resemble each other. More administrative expertise was needed in order to manage multimillion-dollar budgets that supported service programs in both nonprofit and public agencies.

Third, radical social workers shifted their focus away from economic oppression toward problems of discrimination. The economy experienced significant growth during the 1960s, obviating many of the earlier arguments that had been effectively used during the Depression. However, there were demands for the expansion of the welfare state as a means of addressing the grievances of disadvantaged minorities. Civil rights and African-American liberation movements, and the riots that occurred in Detroit, Newark, Watts, and other urban areas created a new climate favoring social reform. By the late 1960s many radical social workers were involved with such client organizations as the National Welfare Rights Organization and the National Tenants Organization.

Specific objectives of these radical practitioners were to increase services or benefit levels, equalize power between the client and the bureaucracy, and increase access to entitlements. At the same time, however, radicals were accusing the government of using welfare benefits as a means of increasing its control over the poor (Piven & Cloward, 1971). These radical movements were also concerned with limiting the influence and control of the welfare state.

During the 1980s radical practitioners returned to union organizing and became concerned with new social issues such as hunger, homelessness, gay rights, sexism, ageism, and domestic violence. In dealing with these problems they frequently turned to direct political action such as organizing and getting out the vote (Fisher, 1984). Piven and Cloward (1988) led a movement in 1983, called the Human Serve Campaign, to register social service clients to vote at the agencies in which they received services. Proponents assumed that agency heads would actively oppose or resist this effort which, in turn, would lead to increased radical activity. The resistance never occurred. Instead, the heads of major social welfare organizations strongly supported the campaign.

Administrative Education

The first curricular changes came slowly. By 1969 only seven schools had developed a full two-year specialization in administration; two years later only 2 percent of graduate social work students were enrolled in such programs (Sarri, 1973). By the mid-1970s, partly in response to this perceived threat of loss of status, jobs, and influence over social programs, and partly because of the stimulating effect of federal training grants to develop administrative curricula, specialized administrative training became available in at least thirty-five schools (Dumpson, Mullen, & First, 1978).

Administrative curricula were structured in one of three patterns: (1) administration as a distinct two-year concentration; (2) administration as a subspecialty within a combined policy, planning, and administration concentration; and (3) administration as a second-year concentration following specialization in either service delivery or social planning and community organization (Gummer, 1975).

The actual number of students choosing administration remained rather small. Many programs enrolled barely enough students to justify offering classes in administration. Enrollments in administrative specializations peaked around 1975, with about 9 percent of total graduate enrollment. That proportion dropped to 3 percent in 1983 (Sarri, 1987). Enrollments in administrative specializations have continued to plummet, with many schools either drastically altering their offerings or dropping the specialization altogether. (See Chapter 2.) Today only about 9 percent of all graduate students are enrolled in any type of macro specialization, including community organization (Lennon, 1995).

In the social work curriculum, policy content has usually been subsumed under either community organization or administration. A smaller parallel development occurred within social work, with a few schools experimenting with curricula that would allow students in their second year of an administration, planning, or community organization track to specialize in social policy practice methods. As late as 1983, only one graduate program allowed a specialization in policy methods alone; others allowed it in combination with administration, community organization, or planning. It is difficult to determine exactly how many students in any given year are policy majors, but it is unlikely ever to have been more than 1 percent of total graduate enrollment (Council on Social Work Education, 1983).

The number of policy studies programs outside social work mushroomed during the 1970s. In 1978 the Institute of Public Policy Studies at the University of Michigan listed 106 programs in public affairs and administration in U.S. universities. There were 7 special programs in public policy and 89 schools of public administration and public policy (Institute of Public Policy Studies, 1978). Just as in the field of administration, the movement toward a specialization in policy within graduate social work programs lagged behind other disciplines, such as political science and public administration.

Whatever the final outcome may be in this continuing debate over the preparation of social welfare administrators, the interest in macropractice specializations has generated enormous scholarly attention. There are more articles in professional journals (such as *Administration in Social Work* and *Administration in Mental Health*), more textbooks, and a richer literature to be found in both the theoretical and practical aspects of administration. This is also the case in other disciplines such as public administration, in which "administration" actually includes both administration and policy analysis. Journals with such names as *Public Policy, Policy Sciences,* and *Policy Analysis* have been established, signaling the emergence of policy studies as a separate activity from the study of administration. Scholars on both sides recognize the overlap in these areas, but still most seem to favor this increasing specialization.

Unifying Links among Macropractice Methods

Whereas micropractice methods focus on change at the personal or individual level, macropractice methods focus on change at the formal or structural level of society. Macropractice methods aim to influence the extrapersonal or societal level of human interactions through either programmatic operations, organizational operations, or legislative operations. Furthermore, macropractice methods may focus on either formal or informal interactions of individuals within formal societal structures. Although they differ in other ways, this focus on extrapersonal, formal societal structures is the common link among the macropractice methods.

Each macropractice method, however, attempts to influence societal structures through slightly different means. The macropractice methods divide into two approaches to their spheres of operation. Social work administration, policy practice, and research practice focus on operation and change *within* an organizational structure or sphere of influence. Radical social work, like community practice (discussed in Chapter 4), focuses on change most often from *outside* the system.

Each macropractice method also uses different theoretical frameworks for defining its practice techniques. Social work administration has the most extensive theoretical framework. It draws on a long history of theory and empirical work in organizational psychology, organizational sociology, and business administration. Policy practice and research practice draw on equally extensive lines of theory and empirical work in sociology, economics, psychology, and social science. Radical social work draws on a long practice tradition in political social work as well as theoretical and empirical work in political science and political sociology.

It follows that social work administration has the most extensive cluster of practice techniques. These range from interpersonal and interactional skills, similar to casework and group work techniques, to financial analysis and budgeting skills, similar to business administration. Policy practice and research practice draw on techniques typically associated with classic, empirical social science research and econometric analyses. Radical social work uses practice techniques most closely associated with community practice, labor organizing, or the political organizing of disenfranchised people.

Finally, each macropractice method focuses on different clientele within its work. As with micropractice intervention, macropractice methods are frequently aimed simultaneously at multiple clients. The combination of clients is frequently complex and interconnected across levels of social organization. Social work administration is often attempting to influence direct service workers, program managers, boards of directors, and individuals charged with legislative oversight simultaneously. Policy practice and research practice are frequently attempting to influence legislators, state agency decision makers, social scientists, and voters. Radical social work, like community practice, attempts to influence legislators, state agency decision makers, and participants or consumers—anyone who may help effect social change.

The common link among the macropractice methods is their focus on influencing the societal structures within which social workers work. Macropractice methods focus on the means for delivery of social work services and their impact on clientele. To introduce you to each area of practice, we will now discuss the macropractice methods individually.

Social Work Administration

Theoretical Foundations of Social Work Administration

Just as general administrative theorists have borrowed heavily from disciplines such as sociology, psychology, social psychology, business administration, and political science, so has social welfare administration theory borrowed extensively from these and other fields. The contemporary literature on social welfare administration is highly eclectic and is based on many different models of organizational behavior. As the understanding about organizations and social structures has changed, the literature on social work administration has also evolved to reflect these changes. Theories of administrative practice differ on whether they emphasize an internal, organizational focus or an external, environmental focus. There has been a steady evolution away from focusing on the internal operation of an organization to understanding the influence of the external environment on the organization, which parallels the general development of knowledge about and understanding of the interaction between an organism and its environment. This evolution has expanded to include the concept of organizational networks and interorganizational relations. As we have moved from a general understanding about the single organism to appreciating the complex interrelationships among organisms, we have moved from trying to understand a single organization as a logical, controllable entity to understanding organizations as operating in complex, multidimensional networks of similar and dissimilar organizations.

Scientific Management

Ever since Max Weber first defined the characteristics of bureaucracy and linked them to organizational performance and social change, people have attempted to delineate those principles of management that would lead to more efficient and effective use of organizational resources. Theorists focusing on the private sector have been interested in the application of scientific management principles that will maximize organizational profits; public sector theorists more often speak of efficiency in goal attainment. In addition to the disciplines mentioned earlier, the scientific management school drew much of its strength and its literature from industrial engineering.

Frederick W. Taylor (1911), regarded by many as the father of scientific management, is remembered for suggesting that efficiency could be increased by the proper division of labor and by careful use of time. He advocated getting away from the "single gang boss" or military type of organization and moving toward functional management. This means dividing the work so that each employee, from the top down, performs as few functions as necessary.

Scientific management theorists focus on *formal* patterns of structure, communication, responsibility, and authority. They tend to disregard the informal aspects of an organization's operations. Scientific management asks such questions as, "How can work be best organized in order to maximize organizational output?" or "What is the most efficient division of labor?" Although interest in scientific management waned for a number of years, recent emphasis on the relationship between technology and productivity has created a resurgence (Sarri, 1973).

Human Relations

The human relations school is dated to the famous Hawthorne experiments in which studies of Western Electric employees revealed that meeting employees' social and psychological needs are just as effective as motivators as economic rewards. Elton Mayo, the author of the Hawthorne experiments, is frequently called the father of the human relations school (Fulmer, 1978).

Other assumptions of the human relations approach to management are that the norms of work groups have a strong influence on organizational performance, and that leadership and communication styles are critical influences on workers' behavior. Douglas McGregor (1960) suggested in *The Human Side of Enterprise* a number of management principles based on these assumptions. His Theory Y organization is one with a democratic work climate in which input from the workers is supported and encouraged. Professional employees, such as social workers, seem to thrive and be more productive in this type of organization.

Human relations theories have had a special appeal to administrators of human service organizations. These theories emphasize the interpersonal relationships and informal aspects of the organization. Questions from managers using this approach might include "How can the staff best be involved in planning agency policy?" or "How do we best meet the self-actualization needs of our staff?"

Structuralist Theories

The largest number of organizational theorists can probably be classified as structuralists. As such, they are particularly interested in the effect of structure on organization behavior. Herbert Simon (1976), one of the early structuralists, focused on decision-making processes that addressed both the rational and nonrational aspects of behavior.

Structuralists who emphasize rationality call attention to the importance of planned organizational design (Hickson, Hinings, Lee, Schneck & Pennings, 1971). Of particular interest are the effects of planned change on social relationships within the organization. Will it improve morale or increase productivity? Another important question concerns the effect of technological change on organizational variables (Lawrence & Lorsch, 1967). Will the introduction of a new (or different) treatment be compatible with current organizational structure?

The rational structuralists were also responsible for directing attention to *matrix* structures (Galbraith, 1973). In a matrix organization, subdivisions or departments of an organization or program operate in a traditional hierarchical manner, but specialists from each of these parallel units are assigned to functional teams to work on a common task.

Simon and his students and colleagues have attempted to bridge the human relations models of organizational behavior (March & Simon, 1958). They attempt to make sense of the seemingly illogical behavior of organizations. Rather than trying to achieve rationality in the economic sense—that is, maximizing benefits or realizing the best return on the least investment—organizations sacrifice and suboptimize. In other words, they look for a course of action that is good enough to meet certain minimal requirements. Organizations are incapable of processing the limited amounts of information they do have, and subsequently it is impossible to achieve complete rationality. Decisions are described as being rationally bounded.

Cohen, March, and Olsen have focused on the nonrational elements in organization behavior and decision making. In this circle, organizations are described as a "garbage can" containing a repertoire of responses to problems. If a proposed solution to a problem appears to be satisfactory or appropriate, it is applied to the problem. This model suggests that the organization also contains many of the problems, as well as the solutions, and that decision makers do not perceive that a decision needs to be made until a problem appears that matches one they have already experienced. If a situation does not match a known repertoire, the decision makers are not capable of recognizing it as a problem.

Other structuralists, such as Hasenfeld (1992), have been concerned more with the political economy of social welfare organizations. They direct their attention to the processes through which power and legitimacy are acquired and distributed both within an organization and between the organization and its environment. Behavior that otherwise seems nonrational may be completely rational when viewed within the political context. For example, an organization may choose to sacrifice short-term benefits, such as a preferred policy outcome, in order to win a long-term advantage, such as leadership in that particular policy arena.

Systems Theories

In many ways systems theories (see Chapter 3) represent an attempt to synthesize the structuralist and human relations approaches. They begin with the assumption that any organization is a social system consisting of several subsystems that are capable of performing such functions as maintenance, production, and adaptation (Katz & Kahn, 1978). The organization is viewed as analogous to a biological system, an organic whole consisting of interdependent, interrelated parts. There is usually an emphasis on the *openness* of the system, environmental constraints, and interorganizational exchanges.

Administrative Roles and Functions

The various organization theories differ in the implication each has for the role of administrators or managers. The leadership dimension of their role will differ, depending on whether a controlling and directing role of the administrator is emphasized or, at the other end of the dimension, a facilitating and coordinating role is emphasized. Leadership is closely related to and intertwined with theoretical focus. As the theoretical focus emphasizes the internal operations of an organization, the leadership dimension emphasizes the controlling and directing role of the administrator. As the theoretical focus emphasizes the external and interorganizational relationships of an organization, the leadership dimension emphasizes the facilitating and coordinating role.

An additional aspect to leadership is frequently overlooked and rarely discussed in the administrative practice literature—the level of responsibility. Although the literature rarely distinguishes between operational and executive leadership responsibilities and functions, there is a fundamental difference between these two spheres of responsibility. At the *operational* level, leadership is frequently referred to as operational management. Within social work administration, the operational level is referred to as program management or supervision. Within social work practice, supervision is often thought of as an educational function. Supervision is frequently provided by a social worker with a master's degree who is licensed at the independent practitioner level, and/or is certified by the Academy of Certified Social Workers (ACSW). However, the role of supervision is broader than education. In practice, the educational function is a minor aspect of supervision. The major responsibility of leadership in the supervisory or program management role is to ensure the integrity of the organization's program services. The supervisor is concerned with the practices of the program operations and ensuring that the policies are implemented according to the original intent. The supervisor provides an assurance to the quality of services being delivered by line social workers. In order to provide this quality assurance, supervisors should possess skills in research design and case record sampling, case record or document analysis, and quantitative analysis. The supervisor must also possess skills in interpersonal relations and personnel administration. Therefore, the supervisor, middle, or program manager as leader must possess a range of skills that includes both technical and interpersonal competencies.

The other level of responsibilities and functions is *executive* leadership. Organization literature on management and leadership implies that the leader is operating at the executive level of responsibility. This leadership level is different from the program manager or supervisory level of leadership. Executive leadership can be compared to the narrow center of an hourglass. In one compartment, it focuses on the internal operation of the organization. The executive leader is responsible for the totality of the organization's policies and practices. He or she must ensure (1) that an organization has policies that guide its operations, and (2) that all program practices are implemented according to the operating policies of the organization. In the other compartment, the executive leader focuses on the external relationships of the organization. He or she must ensure that the organization is involved with and connected to every constituent or major stakeholder that could influence the viability and success of the organization. It is within this sphere of operation that the executive leader must possess skills of network building and interpersonal relationships that are broader than relationships with other social work and human service professionals. The executive leader must be knowledgeable about politics, fund raising, policy development, and lobbying, as well as service needs and program operations. The executive leader must be as comfortable with budgeting and program service as with lobbying and public speaking.

An additional distinction that is frequently overlooked and rarely discussed in social work literature is the leader's sphere of operation. The literature ignores the operational differences between leadership of public organizations and nonprofit organizations. In the public sector, the social work administrator is responsible to a group of elected officials. The role of the administrator as leader is to implement policy and aid the governing board of elected officials in developing policy. The public sector administrator generally develops policy by incremental change.

In the private, nonprofit sector, however, the role of the administrator as policymaker is very different from the public sector administrator. In the nonprofit sector, the social work administrator is responsible to a self-perpetuating board of directors and will implement the policies as established by them. Unlike the public sector administrator, the social work administrator in the nonprofit sector may also have a major role in policy development. Therefore, the role of the social work administrator in the nonprofit sector may be more extensive and inclusive of the range of leadership roles than in the public sector.

Although some social workers see differences between the terms "management" and "administration," most contemporary scholars use them interchangeably (Patti, 1983). An early scholar on social welfare administration defined administration as "the totality of activities in a social welfare organization that are necessary for transforming social policy into social services (Kidneigh, 1950, p. 58). Sarri's (1973) definition specifies the following components:

1. Formulation of policy and its translation into operative goals
2. Program design and implementation
3. Funding and resource allocation
4. Management of internal and interorganizational operations
5. Personnel direction and supervision
6. Organizational representation and public relations
7. Community education
8. Monitoring, evaluation, and innovation to improve organizational productivity (pp. 29–30)

These components roughly coincide with what Patti (1983) calls the "principal tasks of social welfare administration" (p. 34). In an earlier study of social welfare managers, Patti (1977) also identified a number of activities that managers considered to be most significant in the performance of their jobs:

1. *Planning.* This set of activities included determining goals, policies, and courses of action. Planning activities also included strategy setting and work scheduling for major units.

2. *Information processing.* Communicating, report writing, paperwork, dictation, and filling out and signing forms were all forms of information processing.

3. *Controlling.* These activities consisted of collecting and analyzing information concerning the total operation of the agency, such as studying reports, preparing reports, and sharing information with subordinates and superiors. It was also called "keeping on top of the job." Not surprisingly, the managers in the study ranked this as their *most important* activity.

4. *Coordinating.* The time spent exchanging information with persons other than the managers' superiors or subordinates in order to provide information on programs or to adjust programs was classified as coordinating.

5. *Evaluating.* Research-related activities as well as the assessment of individual program performance were included in this category.

6. *Negotiating.* Negotiating included activities intended to reach an agreement with another party. Examples were contract negotiations with a labor union, handling employee grievances, or developing contractual agreements with a vendor.

7. *Representing.* Speeches to external groups, press conferences, and other contacts with individuals outside the agency intended to advance the interests of the agency belonged in this group of activities.

8. *Staffing.* Staffing included recruitment, screening, and interviewing prospective employees, as well as placing, promoting, transferring, or terminating employees.

9. *Supervising.* This category included leading, directing, training, and reviewing the work of subordinates. This was ranked by the managers as the second most important activity, and they also reported that it was the single most time-consuming of all of their management activities.

BOX 5-1   Managing a Woman's Shelter

Joyce is the executive director of a small, private shelter for battered women. This is a new agency with very limited financial means. It was begun at the suggestion of a group of local ministers, and its funding comes from the churches, United Way, and private contributions. The agency lives a hand-to-mouth existence, and Joyce spends much of her time seeking additional funding.

Her day begins around 7:30 a.m., looking over her schedule and planning activities. She sees her secretary at 8:00 a.m. to sign letters and pay bills. There is a twice-weekly staff meeting at 10:30. Since she only employs one other trained social worker, Joyce usually sees one or two clients in the morning and several others in the afternoon. In a typical week she has at least three luncheon meetings for fund-raising or public relations purposes. She also speaks to at least two groups per week during the evenings.

In her spare time Joyce has been looking for a larger facility. Her client population has quadrupled in the past year. The problem is that any new facility will have to be obtained at a below market rental rate, since the prospect of additional funding is quite dim. She has just learned of a new federal grant program that might be available, however, and she is also busy preparing the grant application. The annual United Way funding process has also just begun, and she needs to block out two or three days next week to prepare the budget for her agency.

Like most social workers, Joyce went through the direct practice track in her graduate program and has very little training in administrative matters. She is learning on the job and considering taking a course in grant writing and fiscal management next year.

"Joyce"

---

10. *Supplying.* This was the time spent in securing noncash resources for the agency, such as space, equipment, and supplies.

11. *Extracurricular.* These activities were not ordinarily considered part of the employees' formal job descriptions, yet they were considered to be important responsibilities of agency managers. They included such things as partisan political activity, union organizing, attending classes or receiving other training, and representing the profession.

12. *Direct service.* Many administrators, especially in smaller voluntary agencies, were involved in the provision of direct services to clients.

13. *Budgeting.* This included the time spent planning expenditures and allocating resources among items and programs in the budget. The amount of time devoted to this function generally increased as employees moved up the hierarchy (pp. 5–18).

Patti's research suggests that the activities associated with controlling, planning, supervising, and coordinating are the most important administrative tasks performed in social welfare organizations as judged by agency managers in terms of both the amount of time consumed by them and the significance attached to them. A management position in a small, private agency is described in Box 5-1 by a recent MSW graduate.

Policy as a Practice Method

An NASW (1984) study of the membership reported that only 1 percent of current members identified their primary practice setting as "social policy." By 1991 that number had declined to 0.5 percent (Gibbelman & Schervish, 1993). All social workers have some responsibility for the development and implementation of social policy. Not realizing that a large part of what they do in their jobs really is social policy may be due to a failure of the educational system to bridge the gap between social change and the kinds of interpersonal helping that most social workers do on a daily basis.

There are positions for social workers to specialize in social welfare policy, such as program planner and evaluator, legislative committee staff or policy analyst in the governor's (or mayor's) office, in public interest groups, advocacy groups, and client organizations. Policy practice may never represent a large segment of social work employment. If the profession does not train people for these roles, other disciplines and professions will, and social work may once more find that it has become the handmaiden of other professions.

There is an endless array of definitions of policy. As used in this chapter, policy always means *public* policy, and the simplest and most straightforward definition we have found is "anything a government chooses to do, or not to do, that affects the quality of life of its people" (DiNitto, 1995, p. 2).

According to DiNitto (1995), policy-making involves a combination of processes. Although not always clear cut and distinguishable in the real world, for purposes of our analysis we can identify the following:

Identifying policy problems: the identification of policy problems through publicized demands for government action.

Formulating policy alternatives: the formulation of policy proposals through political channels by policy-planning organizations, interest groups, government bureaucracies, and the president and Congress.

Legitimizing public policy: public statements or actions by the president, Congress, or courts, including executive orders and budgets, laws and appropriations, rules and regulations, and decisions and interpretations, which have the effect of setting policy directions.

Implementing public policy: the implementation of public policy through the activities of public bureaucracies and expenditure of public funds.

Evaluating policy: the evaluation of policies by government agencies, by outside consultants, by interest groups, by the mass media, and by the public (see Jones, 1978; DiNitto, p. 12).

Milan Dluhy (1981) has identified three roles for the policy practitioner: the *technician,* the *pragmatist,* and the *dramatist.* The technician uses methods that are primarily intellectual, collecting and analyzing data to support different policy options or researching and writing policy documents. The pragmatist uses more interpersonal

---

BOX 5-2   Policy Planning

Rick is a program planner in a large state public welfare agency. His particular unit is responsible for planning child welfare programs. He spends a great deal of his time collecting data. When he started this job five years ago, no one really knew what kinds of programs were needed in order to serve the children of this state. He now has a fairly reliable database from which he can predict needs for such services as foster homes, juvenile detention, and teenage parent programs.

He works directly with the personnel who operate these programs in proposing budgetary requests to the state legislature. Although public employees in this state are technically prohibited from lobbying, he spends much of his time during the legislative session testifying before the House and Senate subcommittees on children's services. He also has lunch with friendly legisla-

tors, and he makes a point of attending many social functions with other legislators, hoping for opportunities to "make points" for his agency's program proposals. Rick is well acquainted with all of the state's major human services lobbies, and he has worked hard to influence their agendas. During the legislative session he has twice-weekly meetings with the executive director of NASW, the president of the League for Human Services, the director of the local Urban League, and officials of several other small organizations. He has been very active in the state NASW chapter, serving in several elective positions. This has given him an opportunity to help determine its agenda.

Although his position is called "program planner," a more accurate description is "policy analyst/developer."

"Rick"

---

skills in doing much the same work as politicians in looking after the process of policy-making, mending fences, assuaging feelings, and seeing that the proper steps are taken. The dramatist, or policy advocate, uses a mixture of interpersonal and analytical skills in orchestrating policy to serve particular ends. Mitch Snyder (an advocate for the homeless), Ralph Nader (a consumer advocate), and Dorothea Dix (an advocate for the mentally ill) are examples of the latter. A social worker's role in policy planning in a large public agency is described in Box 5-2 by a recent Ph.D. graduate.

Radical Social Work Practice

Radical social work practice is frequently perceived as community organization practice with a Marxist ideology. Radical social workers generally distinguish themselves from other professional social workers by (1) their primary focus on political and economic variables as explanations for social problems, (2) their reliance on political (especially organizing) skills as opposed to technical knowledge in direct practice or clinical methods, (3) their definition of the arena of struggle as outside the social welfare agency and within the larger social environment, and (4) their ties to larger social movements. Radical social workers view most of professional social work practice as being underpinned by erroneous assumptions concerning both the nature of social problems and appropriate strategies for their resolution. They perceive most nonradical social workers as relying on a single methodological skill (such as

---

BOX 5-3   Tenets for Radical Action

First, we have to break with the professional doctrine that the institutions in which social workers are employed have benign motives.

We must free ourselves from the doctrine that what is good for the agency is good for the client.

We have to break with the professional doctrine that ascribes most of the problems that clients experience to defects in personality development and family relationships.

We must become aware of the ways in which professional knowledge and technique are used to legitimate our bureaucratic power over clients. There is no basis for the belief that we who have masters of social work degrees are better able to discern and deal with our clients' problems than *they* are (Cloward & Piven, 1976).

---

casework or group work) which *incorrectly* identifies variables *within* the client as the focus of problem resolution.

Radical social work practice, or *progressive* social work, as it is now frequently called, begins with the premise that the problems of at-risk populations can be traced to political or economic relationships that exist in the larger social system (Longres, 1996). Therefore, the problems of individual clients are defined in terms of the social forces that shape their circumstances. An alcoholic client may have become debilitated after turning to this drug as a way of coping with the frustration and sense of hopelessness that often accompany intergenerational poverty. In the case of certain groups, their dysfunction may be perceived as having been thrust upon them *purposely* as a way of reinforcing the power of a dominant group within the political system. Piven and Cloward (1971) contend that welfare benefits are used by the state in order to increase the dependence of the poor and to control their behavior (see Box 5-3).

Research and Evaluation Practice

Research and evaluation are two of the newest and smallest practice methods in the profession of social work. The modest growth of professional interest in these areas is indirectly due to the popular philosophies of accountability and responsibility that prospered in the late 1960s and early 1970s. Public programs funded with public tax dollars were expected to prove their worth and justify their existence. For a while there were requirements in certain program areas, such as community mental health, that a minimum percentage of the local agency's budget be spent in evaluating services. Human services that were funded through state and local governments on a contractual basis were expected to furnish similar evidence of their impact (Tripodi, Fellin, & Myer, 1983). The need for additional personnel capable of conducting research and evaluating programs was eventually recognized by the professional schools that train social workers.

According to Tripodi et al. (1983), research is "the application of systematic procedures for the purposes of developing, modifying, and expanding knowledge that can be communicated and verified by independent investigators" (p. 1). Program evaluation is also research, but it is research with a more immediate and practical application. It involves "the use of social research strategies and methods for determining the extent to which programs are implemented, effective, and efficient" (p. 128). Program evaluation attempts to provide answers to such questions as, "Is incentive probation or a group home placement a more effective method of delivering services to delinquent youth?" and "Is group therapy for drug abusers a more cost-efficient method of treatment than individual therapy?"

The professional foundation content in research usually prepares students "to evaluate their own practice and contribute to the generation of knowledge for practice" (CSWE, 1984, p. 127). The thrust of this effort recently has been directed primarily at such techniques as the use of single subject designs (Reid, 1995). This type of research is most useful in the evaluation of one's own practice, but does not often lead to "the generation of knowledge" (Bloom & Fischer, 1982).

Relatively few schools have developed a concentration in research at the MSW level; it has been somewhat more common to find specialized training in "program evaluation" (often in conjunction with program *planning*) within a master's degree program. Concentrations in other types of research are generally found only in doctoral programs.

Another type of research, *policy* research, seeks to "use methods of social research to generate knowledge that informs the formulation, implementation, and/or evaluation of social policies" (Tripodi et al., 1983, p. 152). Policy research seeks to answer questions such as, "Is there a need for funding additional foster homes within the state?" and "What impact would a guaranteed annual income have on work incentives?"

Despite the modest growth in these different types of research in recent years, professional social work employment in research as a *primary function* is still quite small. In an NASW survey of 25,761 members in 1987, only 0.3 percent of the respondents were engaged primarily in research. By 1991 that number had grown to 0.6 percent (Gibelman & Schervish, 1993). The real importance of research is in the professional's recognition of it as a *practice method* to be used by social workers in all areas of social work practice.

Summary

The social work practice methods described in this chapter are very different from the ones covered in Chapter 4. Macro social workers have a number of skills that most other social workers do not have. Just as important, they may lack some of the practice skills that other social workers believe are at the heart of the profession. There are many similarities between radical practice and community organization practice, but there is a world of difference between doing casework with individual clients and supervising program services provided by caseworkers. One must wonder whether the generalists' search for a practice perspective sufficiently broad to incorporate the entire range of social work activities has adequately considered the extreme degrees of specialization that are taking place within the profession. Commonalities among social workers sometimes seem to be mostly ideological (except for radical practice), while divisions are based on function, technology, and the difficulty of keeping pace in training and education with the rapid expansion of knowledge.

Suggested Readings

Dluhy, M. (1981). *Changing the system.* Beverly Hills, CA: Sage.

Patti, R. J. (1983). *Social welfare administration: Managing social programs in a developmental context.* Englewood Cliffs, NJ: Prentice-Hall.

Perlmutter, R. D., & Slavin, S. (Eds.). (1980). *Leadership in social administration, perspectives for the 1980s.* Philadelphia: Temple University.

Sarri, R. C., & Hasenfeld, Y. (Eds.). (1978). *The management of human services.* New York: Columbia University.

Skidmore, R. A. (1983). *Social work administration: Dynamic management and human relationships.* Englewood Cliffs, NJ: Prentice-Hall.

Tripodi, T., Fellin, P., & Myer, H. (1978). *Differential social program evaluation.* Itasca, IL: Peacock.

6

Social Work's Response to Mental Illness

The original chapter from the first edition of this book has been revised by ARA LEWELLEN, Social Work Program, East Texas State University, and CATHELEEN JORDAN, School of Social Work, University of Texas at Arlington.

Photo courtesy of Mary Ellen Lernika

The field of mental health involves everything from divorce adjustment services to the treatment of depression and schizophrenia. Treatment for alcoholism and other forms of drug abuse sometimes falls under the umbrella of mental health services; however, we address problems of alcohol and drug abuse in the next chapter of this text. Social workers offer mental health services to clients in inpatient and outpatient settings and through public, private nonprofit (voluntary), and for-profit (proprietary) organizations. The number of social workers in mental health practice has grown dramatically in the last few decades. Thirty-three percent of NASW members now identify mental health as their primary practice area and 28 percent as their secondary practice area (Ginsberg, 1995). No other single practice area is identified by as many NASW members.

History of Mental Health Services

In early Greek writings, some argued that those with a mental illness were morally corrupt or possessed by the devil, while others believed that the seat of mental illness was physical decay of the body. By the nineteenth century treatment of mentally ill persons reflected both moralistic and biological forms of treatment. In an effort to improve the care of people with mental illness, French physician Phillipe Pinel introduced "moral treatment," a kind and considerate approach that encouraged clients to discuss personal problems and lead an active life (Mechanic, 1989). This humane approach to treating mental illness was not offered to most mental health patients, however, as many of those who were homeless, poor, or members of racial or ethnic minorities were confined to asylums, jails, or prisons. Dorothea Dix, a social reformer during the mid-1800s, sought to improve the plights of severely mistreated inmates with mental illness by encouraging their separation from criminals and other populations. Dix also succeeded in improving conditions within mental institutions, but as increasing numbers of persons were labeled mentally ill, institutions grew larger and less able to help the many patients (Mechanic, 1989).

During the early part of this century, social workers and other professionals in the mental health field were influenced by the work of Sigmund Freud (see Austin, 1986). Prominent social worker Mary Jarrett presented a paper at the 1919 National Conference of Social Work that discussed the relationship between social casework and Freudian concepts such as the "inner self," the "unconscious," and "infantile sexual desires." Freud's influence led many social workers away from their efforts at social reform and consideration of external, environmental factors in case assessment toward a greater consideration of intrapsychic factors and the need for personal adjustment and change by clients. Freud's work also reinforced the medical model as the desired form of practice with mental health patients (also see Macarov, 1978). The medical model focused on isolating either a physical or mental cause of bizarre behaviors, thoughts, and feelings and largely ignored "person in environment" considerations.

The Industrial Revolution in the United States contributed to a number of social problems, including mental illness (see Mechanic, 1989). People came to the cities seeking jobs and wealth and instead found overcrowding, joblessness, and other miseries. Those migrating to the cities from rural areas, often without the support of family and friends, found coping with urban problems difficult. Immigrants from other countries also flocked to the cities, and those who did not acculturate quickly into American society were often considered deviant or mentally ill (Grob, 1966). City dwellers, overwhelmed with problems, had little tolerance for what they considered to be deviations from normal behavior. This increased the number of persons sent to mental health institutions.

Apart from public institutions, there were few programs or social policies aimed at helping people with mental illness. Following Dix's efforts to reform mental institutions, Clifford Beers was responsible for introducing the mental hygiene movement in the early twentieth century. Beers knew well the dehumanizing conditions of mental institutions; he himself had been a patient. Beers's efforts to expose conditions in these institutions, like Dix's, resulted in better care, but the custodial and institutional philosophies of mental health treatment continued (see Mechanic, 1989).

Beginning in the 1930s and 1940s two schools of thought shaped formal training for social workers in mental health settings; their influence is seen today. The diagnostic school, based in New York, emphasized internal psychological processes as the primary focus of intervention for mental disorders. Categorical diagnosis of mental disorders led to treatment through long-term social casework. On the other hand, the functional or Rankian school, based in Pennsylvania, focused on the current problems of those with a mental disorder. This approach was characterized by a time-limited, task-oriented intervention based on an assessment of functional or daily living needs. Social workers trained in the functional school facilitated access to community resources; social workers trained in the diagnostic model tried to fix the mental disorder. While debate over the appropriate approach to treatment continues today, most persons with a severe and chronic mental illness are treated by social workers trained to integrate the roles of counselor, case manager, family educator, and multidisciplinary treatment team member.

During World War II, the routine psychiatric screening of potential recruits revealed alarming numbers of young men rejected as unfit for military service due to psychiatric reasons (see Mechanic, 1989). Although the accuracy and methods of these psychiatric screening procedures have been criticized, the identification of so many young men with mental health problems brought renewed attention to the field of mental health. This concern was reflected in the passage of the Mental Health Act of 1946 that established the National Institute of Mental Health (NIMH). NIMH remains the federal government's primary agency concerned with mental health training, education, and research.

The 1950s heralded the discovery of new psychotherapeutic drugs, an important development in mental health treatment. These drugs reduced many of the symptoms of mental health patients, such as hallucinations and aggressive behavior, and allowed hospital staff to eliminate many restrictions on patients' freedom (see Mechanic, 1989). They also made patients more acceptable to the community. Although controversy remains over the appropriate use of drug therapies, these drugs have played an important part in preventing and reducing the length of hospitalizations for many patients.

Psychotherapeutic drugs helped lay some of the groundwork for the passage of the Community Mental Health Act of 1963. As part of an emerging community mental health movement, the act emphasized increased community-based care and greater federal involvement in this care, a reduction in state hospital treatment, better coordination between community services and hospitals, improved services to those with chronic mental illness, more education and prevention services, and greater utilization of paraprofessional staff. The act provided for the establishment and staffing of community mental health centers (CMHCs) throughout the nation. Initial funding for CMHCs came primarily from the federal government with some state and local support, as well as from the generally modest fees paid by clients. While the burden of public funding for mental health care has shifted to the states, clients with very low incomes continue to pay little or no fees for the services they receive.

President Jimmy Carter and his wife Rosalyn expressed a special concern for people with mental health problems. In 1977 Carter appointed the President's Commission on Mental Health. Following many of the recommendations made by the commission, Congress passed the Mental Health Systems Act in 1980. It extended many provisions of the Community Mental Health Act and added special provisions for people with chronic (now called serious) mental illness, severely disturbed children and adolescents, and other unserved and underserved groups such as the elderly and ethnic minorities.

In 1981 President Reagan proposed to Congress the Alcohol, Drug Abuse, and Mental Health Block Grant that superseded the Mental Health Systems Act and cut mental health funding by over 25 percent (Health program spending cut, 1981). With reductions in federal funds, community mental health centers increasingly looked to Medicaid, Medicare, and private insurance companies to pay for mental health services. However, insurance policies usually excluded major mental illnesses or provided only limited coverage.

In 1992 the federal government reorganized the Alcohol, Drug Abuse, and Mental Health Administration into the Substance Abuse and Mental Health Services Administration (SAMHSA) but kept it within the U.S. Department of Health and Human Services. SAMHSA has three centers: the Center for Mental Health Services, Center for Substance Abuse Prevention, and Center for Substance Abuse Treatment. In addition, SAMHSA created an Office on AIDS, an Office of Applied Studies, and an Office for Women's Services. The restructuring of alcohol, drug, and mental health service programs at the federal level has not changed the responsibilities and program offerings of state mental health agencies. These state agencies remain responsible for provision of mental health and substance abuse services; however, the type and quality of service delivery continues to vary widely from state to state. In addition, in some states, mental health services are provided under a single administrative authority, but in others, they are combined with alcohol and drug services. And while some states operate their own community mental health centers, others contract with local agencies to provide these services.

In 1993 President Clinton established the White House Task Force on National Health Care Reform to develop a national health care plan. A major debate emerged over the nature and extent of mental health care coverage. The National Alliance for the Mentally Ill (NAMI) argued for an emphasis on coverage for serious mental illness (Barbour, 1995), while others urged that a national plan be comprehensive, including coverage for less disabling mental health problems. Tipper Gore, wife of Vice President Albert Gore, chaired the President's Mental Health/Substance Abuse (MH/SA) Working Group Cluster of the President's Task Force on National Health Care Reform. Group members recommended providing comprehensive mental health and substance abuse services within a managed care framework. The model consisted of a broad network of services integrating both private and public MH/SA providers. Many provider networks have already been established today. Unfortunately, health and mental health care reform stalled when President Clinton came to loggerheads with a new, Republican-controlled Congress in 1994.

The Scope of Mental Health Problems

One reason so many social workers practice in the mental health field is that a large number of people in the United States experience these problems. However, the definitions of "mental disorder," "mental illness," and "mental health" vary according to cultural norms, values, and research criteria. The authors of the *Diagnostic and Statistical Manual of Mental Disorders* (DSM-IV) have tried to reduce definitional problems by specifying biopsychosocial criteria for each mental disorder (American Psychiartic Association [APA], 1994). Furthermore, the APA states that a diagnosis of "mental disorder" requires the significant criterion, ". . . causes clinically significant distress or impairment in social, occupational, or other important areas of functioning" (p. 7). Some mental disorders, such as depression related to a personal loss, are temporary. Other mental disorders, such as schizophrenia, are termed serious because they are long-term rather than acute problems. These more serious problems are considered diseases of the mind, referring to abnormal pathology of the brain. They are often referred to as mental illnesses. Mental health, on the other hand, can be thought of as a healthy mind and body.

Social workers in public mental health settings work primarily with those who have a serious mental illness (SMI). The population of people with SMI such as schizophrenia or bipolar illness have chronic or persistent conditions with no known cure. Many of these people, however, lead normal lives for long periods of time. Medications called neuroleptics or psychotropic drugs help to control psychiatric symptoms. Even when patients take medication as directed, however, relapse is a concern. Current studies suggest that when family support and rehabilitation services are combined with medication management, relapses may decrease significantly. Today, most people with SMI live in communities rather than in hospitals or institutions. Social workers often serve as brokers between this population and community providers, and they also provide therapy for clients and their families.

People diagnosed with a mental disorder may also have substance abuse problems. Mental health professionals refer to those with both mental and substance abuse disorders as dually diagnosed or comorbid. Some people use alcohol and other drugs in an attempt to self-treat uncomfortable psychiatric symptoms such as hallucinations or depression. But nonprescribed drugs can cause mental illness-like symptoms, such as flashbacks, hallucinations, and panic reactions. It often takes detoxification from alcohol or drugs before professionals can accurately make a diagnosis of mental illness, substance abuse, or both problems. The treatment recommended for people with serious mental illness and a substance abuse problem generally differs from what is offered by most chemical dependency programs, particularly in the way persons are taught to deal with medications. Clients with mental illness are encouraged to comply with a regimen of prescribed medications. When chemical dependence is the major diagnosis, however, treatment traditionally includes abstinence from all psychoactive substances, including medications.

How many people experience mental health and substance abuse problems? The National Institute of Mental Health estimates that 28.1 percent of the U. S. population has mental or addictive disorders but that only 12.5 percent receive inpatient or ambulatory (outpatient) mental health or addiction services in one year (Manderscheid & Sonnenschein, 1994, p. 24). Many of these people are seen in a combination of medical and human service settings, including voluntary support networks such as Emotions Anonymous and Alcoholics Anonymous. People with schizophrenia have one of the highest rates of service utilization. Service use has increased for those with dual diagnoses of mental and addictive disorders. Of over 3.9 million persons seen for an addiction-related reason, 60 percent also had a mental disorder.

The problems faced by people with serious mental illnesses are compounded when they are also homeless. The largest groups of homeless people are those with alcohol, drug, and serious mental disorders (Berlin & McAllister, 1992; Interagency Council on the Homeless, 1992). The deinstitutionalization of patients with mental illness gained momentum in the 1970s. Its motive—to prevent unnecessary confinement of patients—was humane. Unfortunately, the resources to allow all these people to live with adequate means in the community never followed. Life on the streets aggravates existing mental illness, and conversely, people forced onto the street may be more prone to developing mental disorders (Burt, 1992).

Community Mental Health Services

The Community Mental Health Act of 1963 mandated that CMHCs provide five essential services: (1) inpatient care, (2) outpatient care, (3) emergency services, (4) partial hospitalization, and (5) consultation and education. In 1975 amendments to the act mandated more essential services, including special programs for children and the elderly, aftercare and halfway house services for patients discharged from mental health hospitals, and services to courts and related agencies to screen those who might need treatment. In 1977, NIMH began the Community Support Program, which established federal-state partnerships to encourage long-term care for persons with a serious mental illness. But in 1980 community mental health centers no longer had to provide all the essential services in order to qualify for federal funding. Instead, each state must now develop a discretionary State Comprehensive Mental Health Services Plan. These three-year plans are submitted to NIMH regarding services for people with serious mental illness, homeless people with mental illness, and children with severe disturbances. NIMH recommends one or more of the following services for these priority populations: residential services, client and family support, psychosocial rehabilitation programs, and case management (League of Women Voters, 1988).

Residential services require a range of living arrangements with varying degrees of structure and medical or clinical supervision. Crisis stabilization units are highly supervised twenty-four-hour residential services for people in a psychiatric crisis who, without short-term support, might require longer term hospitalization. If a crisis service is not available, mental health authorities contract with a local general or private psychiatric hospital to provide short-term stabilization services. In addition, residential services that provide supported housing options are available in some areas. Currently, many community mental health centers also provide mobile crisis intervention units, crisis walk-in services, and intensive in-home services for children and adolescents.

Client and family support are outpatient programs designed to enable individuals and families to obtain twenty-four-hour emergency screening and assessment, general family education and support, and medication-related services. Education about psychotropic medications and their benefits and side effects, and maintenance programs to help mental health consumers and their families to develop specific coping strategies to use during times of stress, are included. Many mental health centers also provide counseling to allow clients and families to grieve the loss of "normal lives" and to provide emotional support.

Psychosocial habilitation or rehabilitation programs encourage people with severe psychiatric disabilities to develop vocational skills, social skills, and independent living skills. Based on physical rehabilitation models, these programs help people develop or restore daily living functions and gain or regain participation in their communities.

Case management makes other services work. Case managers recognize that every individual has specific biopsychosocial needs. Functions of case management include active outreach to clients in a crisis, coordination of services, resource brokering, and ongoing support. In some models mental health professionals work cooperatively as a team of case managers. Case management models are closely related to social work values. Both assume that people with mental illness have strengths to be developed, that self-determination is a client's right, that stress precipitates illness, and that the community has a responsibility to its most vulnerable citizens.

Leadership for mental health programs continues to shift from the federal government to states and communities. Although many states provide innovative and comprehensive services, others have serious problems with inadequate facilities, lack of qualified mental health professionals, no housing for clients discharged from state hospitals, and few rehabilitation programs. Many mental health professionals fear that care for people with a severe mental illness will revert to premoral treatment practices. In fact, jails and prisons are full of people with serious psychiatric disturbances. Others point to real reforms in publicly funded care which stress quality services, humane conditions, and ethical standards consistent with recognition of the rights of all individuals needing and wanting help.

Looking ahead to the year 2000 and beyond, social workers will remain primary caregivers and advocates for people with mental illness. In 1989 NIMH formed a national task force of leading social workers to evaluate current social work research and to develop a strategic plan for new directions in social work research in mental health. To date, four Centers for Social Work Research Development have been funded by NIMH at Washington University in St. Louis, the University of Tennessee-Knoxville, the University of Michigan, and Portland State University.

Social work research focuses primarily on the psychosocial problems experienced by clients and the effectiveness of services provided to clients (see, for example, Bergin & Garfield, 1994). Recent research by social workers on children's mental health has focused on special problems of children and risk assessment. In the areas of adult and family services, social work studies of clinical outcomes of couple and family intervention show some positive results. Couple therapies are effective, especially if both partners participate in treatment, but no single approach has been shown to be superior over others. Family therapy interventions have shown less positive results with the exception of psychoeducational approaches with families with a schizophrenic or substance-abusing member. These interventions, while consistently shown to be effective with middle-class, white families, have not been effectively developed or tested with ethnic minority or poor families (Jordan, Vandiver, & Lewellen, 1994).

Social Workers and Mental Health Practice

Social workers work in many capacities in the mental health field to insure that clients receive the services they need, as the examples in Box 6-1 illustrate. The most common direct services that social workers provide fall into two categories: psychoeducation and case management.

Family Psychoeducation

Family psychoeducation is a social work intervention for families with a member who has a mental illness. Family psychoeducation has been used extensively in addressing schizophrenia. It is an important intervention because families' levels of expressed emotion (EE) or degree of criticism, hostility, and overinvolvement is related to the schizophrenic member's relapse rate, with lower relapse rates associated with lower EE. From this knowledge of the effects of EE, family psychoeducational interventions have been developed combining education, social skills training, and behavioral family therapy (see, for example, Jordan et al., 1994). Family psychoeducation has four phases:

BOX 6-1   Social Work Practice in the Mental Health Field

Social workers work at three different levels in the mental health field: micro, mezzo, and macro, as these examples indicate.

Mary Yu is a social worker employed at the micro level in a private inpatient mental health program that serves adolescents and their families. Mary has five years post-BSW experience and is currently enrolled in a part-time MSW program. When Mary arrives at the center each morning she reviews the charts to see how many new clients have arrived and consults with the nursing staff about the clients' situations. Mary does brief intake interviews with all the new clients, then conducts a peer support group with clients before lunch. The group may discuss problems with family members or teachers, concerns about hospitalization, or difficulties in getting along with peers at the center. After lunch Mary meets with clinical staff to discuss clients' treatment and discharge plans. She may arrange for referrals to a group foster home, intensive inpatient treatment, or outpatient treatment at a family service agency following the recommendations of each client's clinical treatment team. One night a week, the center has a family night when Mary provides clients' families with information on adolescent development, parenting or communication skills, or referrals to community resources. Mary also does some community education at schools and churches.

Joyce Powers is the executive director of a community mental health center. Joyce's job is considered social work practice at the mezzo level. She is responsible for a staff of sixty employees, including six supervisors who report directly to her. Four of the supervisors are responsible for clinical services, one is responsi-

ble for all support staff activities including clerical and accounting functions, and one is responsible for building maintenance. Joyce has a master's degree in social work and fifteen years' experience in mental health services. She no longer treats clients. Today most of her time is spent working on grant proposals to support the center's programs, meeting with city and county commissioners to encourage their continued financial support, and meeting with supervisors to ensure that client services are being delivered in accordance with program standards.

John Velasquez is the Assistant Deputy Commissioner for Mental Health Services in a northeastern state. He has an MSW and a Ph.D. in social work. John practices macrolevel social work. His job involves making policy recommendations and planning decisions for the entire state. The staff in John's office monitors the expenditures of public funds that support services for mental health clients. Staff from his office conduct annual reviews of the programs it funds to determine whether they are in compliance with state and federal regulations. Periodically, John's staff conducts studies of services to clients. Two staff members recently completed a study of adolescents discharged from state mental health hospitals to determine what happened to these clients following discharge. A major finding of the study was that there are inadequate community-based programs to assist adolescents when they leave the state hospital. As a result, 30 percent returned to the state hospital within six months of discharge. This study has been forwarded to the state legislature in the hope that it will appropriate more money for adolescent mental health treatment during its next session.

- Phase 1: Connection involves joining with the family to form a therapeutic alliance. Offering support and suggestions for coping are important in the first phase.
- Phase 2: Survival skills workshops are the information or educational phase of the treatment. Families learn about their relative's illness and stress reduction techniques.

- Phase 3: Reentry and application focuses on increasing skills in areas such as family communication and problem solving.
- Phase 4: Maintenance aims to reintegrate the patient into the community with the family. Sessions may become less frequent at this phase (Anderson, Reiss, & Hogarty, 1986 cited in Jordan et al., 1994).

Reviews of family psychoeducational interventions conclude that (1) these interventions reduce, but do not prevent, relapse; (2) behavioral interventions are superior to other treatment modalities or education only; (3) long-term intervention is necessary; and (4) lowering family members' EE promotes decreased relapse (Bergin & Garfield, 1994).

Case Management

Today many social workers whose highest degree is a baccalaureate are providing case management services. According to one model "case management [now often called care management] is defined as a system in which a single accountable individual performs activities in the service of the client, ensuring to the maximum extent possible that the client has access to, and receives, all resources and services which can help the client reach and maintain his/her optimal level of functioning" (Texas Department of Mental Health and Mental Retardation [TDMHMR], 1984). Case management is designed to:

1. Enhance the natural support system and provide continuity of care, continuing service responsibility, overall program coordination, and links to the services of other agencies for persons with mental illness or mental retardation.
2. Establish responsibility and accountability for identified individuals in the service delivery system.
3. Provide clients with a single point of accountability in the service delivery system (TDMHMR).

Case management is being used extensively with clients "whose social, emotional, or developmental disabilities are so serious and persistent that without continuing special support . . . [they are] . . . unable to maintain a stable adjustment to community life. This group includes not only those clients with long histories of mental impairment, substance abuse, and institutionalization, but also younger clients whose history and clinical picture suggest a chronic course" (TDMHMR). Case management services may also be needed by clients "whose behavior is dysfunctional, perhaps similar in appearance to . . . chronic dysfunctional [behavior], as a result of specific crisis experiences. In conditions of crisis, whether developmental or situational in origin, normal behavioral patterns are ineffective and the person's level of functioning is significantly decreased. Without intervention the possibility of institutionalization . . . [may be] imminent" (TDMHMR).

In order to carry out their responsibilities, the job duties of case managers may read like this:

- Actively reaches out to each client in the environment and establishes a relationship in which the client views the case manager as a positive helper.
- Performs a comprehensive life needs assessment taking into account needs as viewed by the client, case manager, significant others, and present service providers.
- Develops a comprehensive service plan to address clients' needs.
- Implements all necessary service referrals.
- Coordinates activities of all service providers so the individual client experiences an integrated service system.
- Maintains regular contact with each assigned client to monitor response to services and identify problem areas.
- Provides informal counseling to assigned clients as needed, including supportive friendly conversation related to daily living problems, use of resources, and basic coping strategies.
- Participates in scheduled rotation of night/weekend/holiday coverage to ensure that all clients experience twenty-four-hour available support from staff familiar with their needs and informs other rotation staff of pending problems that may surface during off-duty hours.
- Assists in accessing transportation services.
- Documents services provided according to current recording policy and procedures (TDMHMR, 1984).

Clearly, case management has been designed to prevent many problems that occur in mental health service delivery systems. These include situations in which the client may get lost in the system, fall through the cracks, or fail to get all needed services. The philosophy of case management and the skills needed to be an effective case manager have long been an integral part of social work education and reflect a systems perspective on social work practice (see Chapter 3). The social work prototypes of the Charity Organization Society performed the first types of case management.

Mental Health and the Competing Professions

Social workers are only one professional group of many who provide care for individuals with mental health and chemical dependency problems. Psychiatrists, psychologists, and psychiatric nurses also have long traditions as mental health service providers. As the definition of mental health care has expanded to include marital and family counseling and an array of preventive services, other professionals have joined the ranks of mental health service providers. They include marriage and family counselors and others with baccalaureate and graduate degrees who often refer to themselves as "counselors" or "therapists."

When clients seek mental health services at a public or nonprofit CMHC, child guidance center, or similar program, they often have little opportunity to select the mental health professionals who will screen and treat them. Clinic procedures and staffing patterns usually determine the assignment of cases. For example, in some CMHCs, staff take turns on intake duty, and staff members retain on their caseloads most clients they interview during intake. Another method is to assign clients on the basis of their age. Certain staff may specialize in the treatment of children or adolescents, others in treating older clients. In other CMHCs, the type of problem the client presents may be the basis for selection of the client's caseworker. For example, one staff member may carry a caseload of clients with schizophrenia, while another specializes in working with substance abusers. State-operated hospitals for people with mental illness assign cases in similar ways.

In the private sector, however, the selection of treatment professionals can be quite different. Individuals seeking outpatient therapeutic services often have many choices. An array of private practitioners representing various helping professions may all offer similar services. Clients seeking private inpatient treatment may also have a number of options. As competition for patients has increased, private providers are likely to advertise their services in newspapers and magazines and on radio and television.

Often the decision of which professional to see or program to enter is contingent on insurance coverage. People covered by group health insurance plans through their employers, or those with individual coverage, may be restricted to certain providers if they wish to receive full or partial reimbursement for services. The cost of treatment, especially private treatment, is quite high. For example, a thirty-day stay in a psychiatric or substance abuse program usually costs several thousand dollars. Many insurance plans, including health maintenance organizations and other managed care programs, cover only thirty days of inpatient psychiatric care a year, and they may also limit the number of covered outpatient visits. Because the costs are so high, most people cannot afford private treatment unless their insurance covers most of the bill. In the private practice arena, psychiatrists and psychologists are the professionals most likely to be covered under insurance plans offering mental health services, although social workers have made substantial progress in obtaining third-party reimbursement for their services (see Chapter 2).

Although social workers probably continue to outnumber other professionals in the mental health field, psychiatrist David Upton (1983) notes "that no single professional group by itself can meet the treatment needs of all persons suffering mental illness/emotional problems" (p. 85). Although services of the mental health professions overlap, each profession has important contributions to make. Psychiatrists are licensed physicians who can prescribe medication; psychologists receive education in conducting and interpreting psychometric tests to assess mental health problems; the education of social workers emphasizes a systems perspective by incorporating family members in the treatment process and utilizing a variety of community resources to promote client functioning. All these professionals receive training in counseling and other therapeutic modalities. Many community-based inpatient and outpatient mental health programs use treatment teams composed of social workers, psychiatrists, psychologists, nurses, and vocational, occupational, and recreational therapists. The philosophy behind the team concept is that each professional is important in the client's rehabilitation. The goal of the team is to cooperate in order to provide the client with *all* the services needed for recovery. However, it is also true that job competition in the mental health field has increased in this era of cost containment, especially among private practitioners.

When selecting a mental health practitioner, the public should be confident that the professional is qualified. Psychiatrists and psychologists must be licensed by the state in which they practice. All states now license, certify, or otherwise regulate social workers (see Chapter 2). The National Association of Social Workers also maintains a clinical register of qualified social workers. Consumers of mental health services are encouraged to check credentials before selecting a mental health practitioner.

Private Practice

A growing number of social workers are opening private practices. Wallace (1982) suggests that social workers enter private practice for a number of reasons, including lack of stable funding in public and private agencies, lack of autonomy and restrictiveness of employment in agency settings, and agency pressures to move out of clinical practice and into administrative positions in order to gain salary increases. Jayaratne and his colleagues (1991) found that the "personal well-being" of social workers in private practice was better than those in agency settings. These factors make private practice sound like an attractive option, but the flight of social workers into private practice has caused consternation among many social workers who believe their colleagues are abandoning the profession's commitment to serving people who cannot afford private treatment. Those who support the increased interest in private practice argue that social workers, like members of other helping professions, have a right to be paid competitive fees for their services. In addition, social workers in private practice may charge lower fees than psychiatrists and psychologists, making their services a more economical and more accessible alternative.

Another concern about social workers' interest in private practice is that the profession is losing sight of its involvement in social policy and social change in favor of individual client treatment. Criticism has extended to the use of the *Diagnostic and Statistical Manual of Mental Disorders* (DSM) with its emphasis on labeling clients in order to obtain third-party payments, regardless of whether labeling is in the best interest of clients or practitioners (see, for example, Kirk & Kutchins, 1992). Some critics of the DSM believe that clients can be successfully treated without labels and that diagnoses such as schizophrenia, bipolar disorder, or adjustment disorder in a client's records can be misused. These labels may negatively influence the way others view and treat the client. Other critics believe that the primary purpose of the DSM is to increase payments for treatment services rather than to improve client care.

The majority of students pursuing master's degrees in social work are choosing concentrations in direct client services (see Chapter 2). In 1984 Rubin and Johnson published a study of 257 new master's students entering direct practice concentrations and found that "86 percent ... wanted to enter private practice, and 82 percent ... wanted to do so within five years after graduation" (p. 10). Schools of social work usually discourage new graduates from engaging in private practice until they have had considerable supervised social work experience, and some states have laws restricting which social workers can engage in private practice. These laws may include required course work, a number of years of practice experience, and prior supervision.

Self-Help and Voluntary Associations

Another set of players in mental health services are the self-help groups. These are important adjuncts to the services provided by social workers and other professionals. One self-help group for people with mental illness is Emotions Anonymous (EA). Their program is patterned after the Alcoholics Anonymous (AA) program (1976). (See Chapter 7.) A major emphasis of mental health consumer groups such as EA is client empowerment and mutual support and help. Like other similar groups, they recognize the spirituality of all persons. In consumer support groups, members share problems and receive help from others with mental illness (Sands, 1991, p. 249).

Some support groups for people with mental illness are co-led by a recovering mental health services consumer and a professional mental health service provider. For example, Good Chemistry groups were designed for people with dual diagnoses of mental illness and substance abuse and are co-led by a professional and an individual recovering from dual diagnoses (Webb, 1995). One reason special support groups like these are needed for people with mental illnesses is that some traditional members of other self-help groups such as AA and Narcotics Anonymous (NA) do not understand the nature and treatment of mental illnesses, especially the use of psychotropic medications (see DiNitto & Webb, 1994).

There are also some well-known voluntary associations in the mental health field. Among the most prominent is the Mental Health Association (MHA). "The mission of the Mental Health Association is to promote mental health; to work for improved prevention, research, detection, and diagnosis of mental illness; and to advocate for improved care and treatment of persons with mental illness" (MHA, 1985). The MHA helps to develop support groups for individuals with mental health problems and their families and friends. It also helps develop community residences for people with mental illnesses. Another important voluntary association is the National Alliance for the Mentally Ill (NAMI), a grass-roots advocacy organization that brings together families and friends of people with mental illnesses. The mission of NAMI is "to eradicate mental illness and to improve the quality of life for those who suffer from these no-fault brain diseases" (NAMI, 1995). Most professionals have abandoned the idea that serious mental illness is "caused" by families. Today, family members are recognized for the important contributions they can make in assisting a mentally ill member to recover. NAMI has educational and support groups in communities nationwide.

Ethnic Minorities, Women, and Mental Health Care

Throughout this book we address the concerns of women and men, members of various ethnic groups, and other populations. Although it is impossible to do justice in this chapter to each population group and the mental health issues they may face, we touch on a few issues and encourage readers to pursue additional information on these topics (more information on ethnic minorities is found in Chapter 15 and on women in Chapter 17).

Racism and sexism affect mental health services to ethnic minorities and women (Sue, Sue, & Sue, 1994). Professional bias is seen in overuse of severe diagnostic categories with African American and Hispanic groups (Loring & Powell, 1988). For example, white male and female psychiatrists are more likely to give a diagnosis of paranoid schizophrenia to black male clients than to white clients. Escobar (1987) reports that somatic complaints common among some Hispanic groups are often interpreted as symptoms of depressive and schizophrenic illnesses. He challenges whether the scope of the symptoms justifies a diagnosis of mental illness. And contrary to beliefs that many ethnic minorities are resistant to treatment, Karno and Morales (1976) have stated that Mexican American clients "respond at least as well as their Anglo counterparts when they are offered professionally expert treatment in a context of cultural and linguistic familiarity and acceptance" (p. 240; also see Gonzalez-Ramos, 1990).

Growing populations in the United States are from East Asia (Japan, China, Korea), South Asia (Pakistan, India, Sri Lanka), Southeast Asia (Indonesia, Vietnam, Cambodia, Laos, Thailand, the Philippines, Burma), and Pacific-Asian areas (Guam, Samoa, and Tonga). These groups, which resided primarily on the West Coast and in Hawaii, are now living across the country (Kitano, 1987). Many people of Asian descent fled their homelands to escape political upheavals and the scourges of war and famine. The added struggle to start a new way of life in this country makes them vulnerable to mental health problems. Paradoxically, their utilization of mental health resources remains low. Crystal (1989) finds that behaviors of Asian Americans such as "diligence" and strong work ethics, coupled with relatively high educational levels and median incomes, are viewed by many Americans as indicators of successful adaptation. These views may prevent Asian Americans from being referred to mental health services. In addition, the culturally motivated desire to "save face" may prevent Asians from seeking mental health services.

Reports of high incomes among Asian Americans obscure other issues, such as jobs that are not in keeping with their previous training and the prevalence of two wage earners in families (Crystal, 1989). Among all ethnic groups, however, the prevalence of mental illness is highest in low-socioeconomic groups. Poverty and lack of education affect rates of mental illness regardless of race. When researchers control for socioeconomic status, rates of mental illness are comparable across the races (Williams, 1986).

A current trend in social services is to promote awareness of ethnic-related biases through diversity training (Smith, 1990). Diversity training recognizes that behaviors that may appear abnormal to white Europeans may be culturally appropriate behaviors for certain populations. For example, white mental health professionals may misinterpret blacks' emotional expressions as "lacking in normal affect or blunted," one of the symptoms of schizophrenia. However, this behavior may be appropriate for clients who have experienced racism and accompanying unfair treatment in other institutional settings.

There is comparably little information on women's mental and physical health concerns because most research has been performed with male subjects. But "everywhere women's high risk status is reflected in their greater likelihood to suffer from severe depression..." (Wetzel, 1994, p. 232). Biological differences between men and women seem insufficient to explain women's greater incidence of depression. Societal factors suggest that women's depression is related to their low status in society, labeling, and masculine-based assumptions of healthy behavior. Some studies suggest that women may be diagnosed as mentally ill as a result of socialized behaviors, such as submissiveness, dependency, unaggressiveness, and conceit about appearance. These results indicate a double standard of what constitutes mental health for males and females (Tarvis, 1991). If this is true, more education and training about women's gender roles is critical to avoid gender stereotyping in the mental health field.

Both racism and sexism remain major barriers in the accurate assessment, treatment, and long-term management of mental health problems. Social workers would do well to examine the values of U.S. society and how they may affect the roles of mental health professionals. Understanding how society's biases influence social workers and their clients is a crucial step in helping to reduce the significant mental health problems of minority groups.

The Rights of Clients with Mental Illness

Sometimes treatment cannot be provided to people with mental health problems on an outpatient basis or in community facilities. Community mental health programs may not be equipped to assist those whose mental health problems are very severe, or specialized facilities may not exist in a community. Treatment in an inpatient mental health facility may be necessary. This type of treatment restricts an individual from moving about in the community. Only recently have mental health consumers gained substantial recognition of their civil rights in order to protect them from inappropriate institutionalization. The federal and state governments are responsible for protecting these rights (see Mechanic, 1989). Patients must be informed of their rights to obtain and refuse treatment, and those who are not able to read must have this information explained to them.

There is no lack of controversy over the appropriate use of hospitalization and institutionalization. Some people believe that mental health providers, particularly in the private sector, are too quick to opt for hospitalization. In fact, recent Congressional investigations have uncovered practices such as finder's fees for patient referrals and other abuses of inpatient mental health care. On the other hand, public facilities often come under attack for failing to provide hospitalization when family and community members think it is needed (see Krauthammer, 1985). The line between protection of patients and community members and the civil rights of people with mental illness is often difficult to draw.

When people are admitted to psychiatric facilities, a number of obstacles may prevent them from receiving the best treatment. Patients should always be treated in a way that respects their individual dignity, but this manner of treatment is contingent on the quality of the treatment facility and its staff. Facilities are often crowded and caseloads high. Some are located in remote areas where there may be an inadequate number of persons trained to provide mental health services. Thus, qualified staff may be difficult to recruit and retain. Yet the decisions about a patient's day-to-day activities are largely staff decisions. The patient may have little influence in choosing these activities, short of refusing to participate. Moreover, when patients refuse to participate in activities, they are often considered to be uncooperative and resistant to treatment. This may serve to prolong their stay in the mental hospital.

Patients have the right to know the reasons for their admission and what must happen before release can be granted. They must be provided access to mental health laws and legal assistance. Patients should be afforded privacy when they have visitors, and visits should not be denied unless there is reason to believe that this might be harmful to the patient or others. Unfortunately, when hospitals are located far from the patient's home, it is more difficult for family members to visit or for the patient to visit them on short leaves of absence from the hospital. Policies relating to the care of people with mental illness are not always implemented to serve the best interests of clients.

Social workers should be aware that most consumers of mental health services have the same rights as other citizens. However, some of those rights may be compromised if the individual is declared incompetent by a judge. In these cases a legal guardian is assigned to handle the individual's affairs, such as financial management. Many guardianship programs lack oversight, so there is potential for exploitation of people judged incompetent. A number of states have adopted a bill of rights for all mental health consumers, including:

the right to appropriate treatment and an understanding of what it includes
the right to an individualized treatment plan
the right to refuse treatment
the right to freedom from restraint and seclusion
the right to confidentiality of records
the right to see one's records
the right to file a grievance (see Sands, 1991, p. 249)

Social workers often serve as advocates for consumers of mental health services and help to safeguard their rights.

Future of Social Work in the Mental Health Fields

The themes of this book have important implications for social work practice in the mental health field. On the one hand, social workers have long been educated to work with mental health clients. Their expertise in providing case management services and family psychoeducation makes them well equipped to work with these clients, especially those with serious mental illness who have been targeted through federal legislation to receive community-based services. On the other hand, the encroachment of new helping professionals, also claiming expertise in the treatment of mental health problems, has made for more competition in a job market that has tightened due to funding constraints. As social workers compete for jobs in mental health care, they are reminded of the problems of defining social work practice and distinguishing social work from other professions. This concern is further complicated because the newer helping professionals have borrowed heavily from social workers in this area of practice. The lines of demarcation among the mental health professions have become fuzzier.

Another important concern involves the value base of the profession that mandates social workers to seek all avenues of help for clients. Social workers are alarmed at the number of persons who need services but who receive inadequate care or no care at all. They frequently try to assist clients but have nowhere to refer them. At other times social workers must face the situation of those who are seemingly in need but reject offers of assistance. People who are homeless and mentally ill are an example of these value dilemmas. Considering the limits on the availability of publicly funded services and the high cost of private services, it is not surprising that many needy persons do not receive appropriate care.

Can social workers remain responsible to and for clients when services are grossly inadequate to meet needs? Clients and social workers must often settle for less than optimum services. The influx of social workers into the private arena may further threaten the ability to provide optimum services to the neediest of clients. However, since governments are contracting with the private sector more than ever, and since social workers are unlikely to abandon the private arena, the more pertinent question is how to make services universally available to all in need. In Chapter 14 we explore the benefits of a particular type of mental health practice—employee assistance practice—designed to help people obtain assistance before their problems become so severe that they result in unemployment and homelessness.

Many people with a serious mental illness are now living in communities, making meaningful contributions to their families, friends, schools, and the workplace. Some do have the benefits of decent affordable housing, medical and dental care, employment, and supportive safety networks. To see that more people with serious mental illness receive these benefits, social workers need to keep pace with knowledge of the kinds of services that best help individuals and families. Social workers are needed on a micro level to provide consumers a renewed sense of dignity and self-regard, to emphasize hope through building on individual strengths, and to promote the value of self-determination, a core social work value. On the mezzo level, social workers have the challenge of making communities aware that every person can make a contribution. And on the macro level, social workers must advocate for the range and quality of services necessary to maximize a national network of support and caring for all who live with a mental illness and their loved ones.

Summary

There is much satisfaction to be gained from helping clients overcome mental health problems. Trends in social work practice and education indicate that social workers' interest in mental health practice will continue to grow. The challenge to social workers is to expand the number, types, and quality of services to prevent and treat mental health problems among all segments of the population.

Suggested Readings

NIMH Quarterly Journal

Psychiatric Services (formerly *Hospital and Community Psychiatry*)

Schizophrenia Bulletin

Sands, R. G. (1991). *Clinical social work practice in community mental health*. New York: Merrill.

Sue, D., Sue, D., & Sue, S. (1994). *Understanding abnormal behavior* (4th ed.). Princeton NJ: Houghton Mifflin.

7

New Directions in Social Work's Response to Alcohol and Other Drug Abuse

Photo courtesy of C. Aaron McNeece

The original chapter from the first edition of this book has been revised by MARY S. JACKSON, School of Social Work, East Carolina University.

Stories of the use and abuse of alcohol and other drugs continue to make media headlines, and while more and more users and sellers are jailed and imprisoned, many clients remain on waiting lists to receive alcohol and other drug abuse (AODA) treatment services. This chapter considers some of the challenges that the social work profession faces in light of the continuing problems with alcohol and other drug abuse occurring in the United States and other parts of the world. Now more than ever, social workers in almost all areas of practice need to collaborate with other professionals concerned about substance abuse in order to provide quality intervention and prevention strategies at micro, mezzo, and macro levels.

Sin, Crime, or Disease?

Alcohol and other drug abuse has been a public health issue in U.S. history as long as this country has existed, but more often than not, it has been treated as a sin or crime. During the colonial period, alcohol use was common, but "habitual drunkenness was [considered] a problem of individual responsibility, morality, and religion" (Paredes, 1976, p. 15). Abusers were often subjected to public humiliation by being placed in stocks or in jail, or they were subjected to religious censure (Paredes, 1976). Early in the nineteenth century, the focus remained on the person who drank too much, as drunkenness was considered a violation of a social ritual (Sournia, 1990). Thus, jailing continued to be the major social response to the problem. By the 1820s the temperance movement was born. It eventually moved from a position of moderation in alcohol use to abstinence (Paredes). In addition to jails, alcoholics often ended up confined to mental institutions.

The medical profession was the first discipline to show professional interest in people with AODA problems, specifically with alcoholism. The Swedish doctor Magnus Huss coined the term "alcoholism" and identified its signs and physical and mental symptoms and the effects that alcohol has on the human body. In 1849 he published his holistic approach to alcoholism entitled *Alcoholismus Chronicus* (see Sournia, 1990).

But early in the twentieth century in the United States, the criminalization of alcohol and other drug abuse continued. The Harrison Narcotics Act of 1914, the Volstead Act (alcohol prohibition) of 1917, and the Marijuana Tax Act of 1937 attached further sanctions to the distribution, possession, and use of mind-altering substances.

A significant advance in addressing alcoholism that was more consistent with the needs of the alcoholic came in 1935 when Alcoholics Anonymous (AA) was founded by two men trying to overcome the devastation that alcoholism had caused them (Alcoholics Anonymous, 1976). Many recovering alcoholics have viewed this program as their salvation, and for many years, it was the only help available to most alcoholics short of institutionalization or incarceration. Although not everyone espouses the approach used by AA and similar self-help groups such as Narcotics Anonymous and Cocaine Anonymous, social workers owe it to themselves and their clients to become familiar with these options.

In the late 1940s corporations began to address the problems of alcohol abuse in the workplace by establishing occupational alcohol programs that were often staffed by recovering alcoholics (see Chapter 14). In the 1950s the World Health Organization (WHO) devoted a great deal of attention to defining alcoholism, and both WHO and the American Medical Association recognized the need for treatment of people suffering from this problem. The concept of alcoholism as a disease or illness gained greater acceptance (Jellinek, 1960). While we continue to debate this conceptualization, it did reduce the stigma attached to the diagnosis of alcoholism and opened the doors to more humane treatment for many people with alcoholism problems (also see Pattison, Sobell, & Sobell, 1977).

In 1970 the federal government took a greater role in addressing AODA problems when it passed the Comprehensive Alcohol Abuse and Alcoholism Prevention, Treatment, and Rehabilitation Act. The act established the National Institute on Alcohol Abuse and Alcoholism (NIAAA). Shortly after, the National Institute on Drug Abuse (NIDA) was established. These are important events in the federal government's approach to AODA problems. Some states decriminalized public intoxication in an effort to direct chronic alcoholics away from jails for drying out and into community detoxification centers with the hope that this would promote longer-term rehabilitation.

Until the last few decades, however, social workers and other helping professionals rarely took an active role in the prevention and treatment of AODA problems. The social work profession did recognize the role alcoholism played in family disruption. Accordingly, social work interventions were largely directed at helping families of alcoholics (see Jackson, 1954). There were probably several reasons for social workers' lack of attention to alcoholics and addicts. The social work field was strongly influenced by religious values (Kohns, 1966), and those with AODA problems were considered immoral and weak willed. The thinking was that alcoholics could stop drinking and become sober if they were determined to do so. Wechsler & Rohman (1985) attribute this negative response from social workers to a lack of skills and knowledge in working with alcoholics and addicts, which fostered a sense of professional insecurity, and also to the poor prognosis social workers saw for these clients. Alcoholics and addicts were deemed to be difficult and resistive and to have very low success rates. As with their counterparts in the criminal and juvenile justice systems, little was done to improve social work practice techniques with AODA clients (Barber, 1994).

AODA Problems and Social Work Practice

Alcohol and other drug abuse remain insidious problems, but many people who need help are added to waiting lists for services, leaving them and professionals such as social workers frustrated. Clients who do receive services generally discover that the services are short term and growing shorter all the time. Typical thirty-day treatment programs have been scaled back, even when substance abuse professionals and clients see the need for more treatment, not less. And when clients do "succeed" in drug treatment programs (success is frequently measured by the client's ability to complete the program offered to them), there is often no aftercare component to assist with stabilization as they attempt to adjust to a new life of sobriety (without alcohol and drugs) in the community.

The social work profession faces additional problems in the AODA field. For example, although social workers agree that there is an AODA problem, they do not necessarily agree on a definition of the problem, causes of the problem, or what methodologies to use in working with clients to resolve the problem (see McNeece & DiNitto, 1994). There is evidence of genetic and other biological risk factors, environmental (social) risk factors, and psychological risk factors for alcoholism (see National Institute on Alcohol Abuse and Alcoholism [NIAAA], 1993; Chapters 3 and 6). However, some social workers and substance abuse practitioners believe that alcoholics and other drug abusers should take more responsibility for their actions, that substance abuse is a learned behavior, or that substance abusers can be taught to control their use of drugs.

Another area of contention is whether alcohol and other drug abuse should fall under the auspices of mental health services. Some professionals view AODA problems as mental illness while others do not. Some mental health programs offer AODA services, but others have decided to maintain separate services. The separation of services is a dilemma for the many individuals who have diagnoses of both substance abuse or dependence and mental illness, because the philosophies of AODA treatment and treatment for serious mental illness are often contradictory (DiNitto & Webb, 1994; also see Chapter 6). Clients with dual diagnoses often have difficulty getting services because neither mental health professionals nor AODA professionals see them as within their purview.

The social work profession continues to struggle with (1) its purpose (should it work primarily to eliminate poverty? [Garrett, 1994]); (2) its identity (are social workers professionals who work with individuals and families or should they be concerned with changing larger systems?); and (3) its future direction (should the profession prepare students for generalist practice or should it focus on preparing independent, licensed, specialist practitioners?). The widespread abuse of alcohol and other drugs adds to these struggles as social work tries to define these problems and to develop an adequate practice response.

Unlike poverty, drugs have touched virtually every segment of the American population. Yet only a small percentage of clients receive AODA services from social workers. We can summarize reasons for this under three broad categories:

1. The interprofessional competition between social workers and substance abuse counselors
2. The lack of a mandate from the Council on Social Work Education (CSWE) to include AODA content in social work curricula
3. Limited funds to try new directions in treatment

Interprofessional Competition

In the late 1980s, substance abuse or chemical dependency counselors developed their own credentialing bodies. Initially these bodies consisted primarily of recovering alcoholics and addicts whose treatment philosophies came from the tenets of AA, which are rooted in religion. Dembo (1994) believes that one method of measuring the maturity of a field of study is its increased theoretical incisiveness in developing paradigms for practice. Although the primary theoretical underpinning in the AODA field is the disease model, contemporary substance abuse counselors are moving to consider other theoretical conceptualizations as legitimate. For example, social learning theory may be considered a valid response to AODA treatment when clients can be taught how to control or moderate their use of drugs. This is contrary to the disease model and to the AA program's commitment to total abstinence. The National Association of Alcohol and Drug Abuse Counselors and state credentialing boards for substance abuse counselors generally adhere to the disease model. Many social workers, on the other hand, are skeptical that one theory is acceptable for working with diverse populations and believe that practitioners should be well versed in many theoretical frameworks. In fact, social work education at the undergraduate level focuses on the generalist, not specialist, practice model.

Both the social worker and the substance abuse counselor's goal is to assist clients in their struggle to stop using drugs. Though their goal is the same, their approaches to treatment may vary. The substance abuse counselor is likely to focus on the drinking or drug-taking behavior, while the social worker is likely to use a systems perspective that takes into account other areas of life functioning, such as family and social relations and employment. Although many people achieve long-term recovery from AODA problems, the other reality is that relapse rates remain high. The best predictors of treatment success are client characteristics—higher socioeconomic status and stability in a marital relationship, in psychological functioning, and in employment—regardless of the type, length, or intensity of the treatment modality used (see Emrick & Hansen, 1983; Nathan, 1986; NIAAA, 1990). While professionals have yet to develop treatment approaches that are effective for the many diverse clients with AODA problems, social workers may be on the right track, since the biopsychosocial and ecological perspectives (see Chapter 3) are concerned with more than just the client's drinking or drug-taking behavior.

Most states allow both social workers and substance abuse counselors to work with AODA clients. Some social workers are also certified or licensed as substance abuse counselors. In fact, insurance companies and substance abuse funding sources are moving in the direction of requiring, or strongly recommending, chemical dependency certification or licensure of almost all health care professionals (e.g., medical doctors, psychologists, psychiatrists) who work with AODA clients. Conversely, the moves toward professionalism and private practice in the substance abuse field have also encouraged substance abuse counselors, many of whom are recovering themselves, to earn degrees in social work and the other helping professions. In 1994, only 4 percent of NASW members defined their primary practice area as substance abuse, although 10 percent defined it as their secondary practice area (Ginsberg, 1995), but it is difficult to imagine a social worker who doesn't encounter people with AODA problems in his or her practice.

Education in Substance Abuse

To date the Council on Social Work Education (CSWE) has not mandated the inclusion of AODA content in the curricula of social work education programs. Since so many clients have AODA-related problems, some community agencies that supervise field placement are concerned about the preparedness of social work students who have never taken a substance abuse course. CSWE could take a more proactive approach on this issue as it did concerning content on diversity (content on diversity is now a specific evaluation standard by which all social work programs are evaluated in order to receive accreditation status; see Chapter 2). Some social workers believe that CSWE should also adopt a standard that requires social work education programs to provide substance abuse content. In 1995, the Substance Abuse and Mental Health Services Administration published *Curriculum Modules on Alcohol and Other Drug Problems for Schools of Social Work.* The modules were developed by social work educators and practitioners from around the country for incorporation in a variety of courses taught in social work education programs.

Limited Funding

There are limited funds to try new directions in substance abuse treatment as the pendulum has swung back to a crime-control model. Policy direction from the federal government leans more toward punishment than prevention while placing even more limits on funds provided for substance abuse treatment services. As a result of recent crime legislation passed by Congress, approximately $150 billion will be funneled through the criminal justice system between 1995 and 2000. The primary provisions of the crime bill focus on the "supply" side of the drug problem by hiring more law enforcement officers and imposing harsher sanctions for certain offenders. Although the legislation attempts to divert first-time and nonviolent drug offenders into drug courts that offer rehabilitation and intensive supervision, there is less emphasis on prevention and treatment of AODA problems that might reduce the "demand" for drugs. In January of 1996, President Clinton appointed an army general as his antidrug policy advisor (see Box 7-1). The combination of more funds directed at crime control and the looming federal budget crisis means that federal AODA agencies such as NIAAA, NIDA, and the newly created Center for Substance Abuse Treatment (CSAT) may face sharper decreases in their budgets. With this may come more decreases in community services for people with AODA-related problems.

Casualties of the War on Drugs

Substance abusers have always faced substantial stigma. Women with AODA problems face even greater stigma than men because of social norms suggesting that drunkenness and drug use are less acceptable for women (see Davis & DiNitto, 1994, for a review of this literature). Much of the substance abuse research has been conducted on white men, and much of the treatment has focused on their needs. Only recently have gender and ethnicity been considered significant factors in treatment planning (see McNeece & DiNitto, 1994). But as we shall see, politics may undo the progress that has been made in these areas.

Women and Children Last

According to Hoffman (1995), since 1987, nineteen states as well as the District of Columbia have instituted criminal proceedings against females who use drugs while pregnant. Since public policy places the interests of the pregnant woman over that of the fetus, these attempts at prosecution have been largely unsuccessful. However, once a child is delivered, there may be grounds for removal if the mother cannot adequately care for the child. At least eight states include in utero drug exposure under their abuse and neglect laws (Hoffman). Although these "get tough" policies are aimed at reducing AODA problems and enhancing child protection, they may be creating more problems. The Crime Bill, signed on September 14, 1994 by President Clinton, has not only created harsher sanctions for some drug abusers, but some of it may create more victims of the so called war on drugs. For example, women incarcerated for repeated drug offenses, some of whom are HIV infected, are unlikely to get adequate substance abuse or medical treatment in jail. In addition, some will deliver babies who are also crack addicted or HIV infected, leading to the expansion of a lost generation of children.

The issue of crack babies is controversial because experts disagree on cocaine's effect on the fetus. Some researchers believe that taking cocaine while pregnant can create devastating psychological and physical problems for these children, while others report either no major difference or limited differences between control babies and crack- or cocaine-exposed babies (Schwartzberg, 1995).

More research has been conducted on the effects of prenatal exposure to alcohol. Fetal alcohol syndrome (FAS) and fetal alcohol effects (FAE) are now referred to as alcohol-related birth defects. Babies born to some alcoholic mothers experience similar symptoms as babies born to mothers who use crack: growth deficiency, developmental delay, and motor dysfunctioning (Rivers, 1994). There is less debate about the effects of alcohol on the fetus than illicit drugs because there has been more longitudinal research on children exposed to alcohol prenatally. Crack babies came to our attention in the 1980s, and most have not matured enough to provide needed data on this population. Ongoing intensive research should accomplish the goal of clarifying the effects of crack on the fetus. Gustavsson (1991) and Schwartz-

---

BOX 7-1   New Advisor on Drug Policy Appointed

Getting Serious about the "War"?

Army Gen. Barry McCaffrey, an expert on narcotics trafficking, has been chosen as President Clinton's anti-drugs policy advisor. The 31-year Army veteran is the head of the U.S. military's Southern Command based in Panama. The four-star general has guided U.S. military cooperation with Latin American and Caribbean nations in drug intelligence and interdiction efforts for two years. He replaces Lee Brown, who resigned the post to teach at Rice University in Houston.

Reuters News Service (1/24/96)

berg (1995) concluded that many of the earlier studies that attributed children's psychological and physical problems to the mothers' prenatal use of crack or other forms of cocaine failed to consider variables such as poverty, living arrangements and other environmental factors, and poly drug abuse. There is little debate by social workers, however, on the need to focus on prevention of prenatal drug exposure and to provide services to children and adolescents who have drug-related birth defects.

Children of drug addicts pose other challenges for social workers. Many social workers who work in child protective service agencies are the primary investigators in alleged cases of child abuse and neglect (see Chapter 10). They have to determine whether neglect or abuse has occurred and whether the child or children should be removed from the home (Hoffman, 1992). Many social workers are not properly prepared to deal with their findings in these cases because many have not received substance abuse education. They may handle such cases by trial and error unless the agency provides training in substance abuse. As social workers continue to deal with more and more cases of neglect and abuse, they will need more sophisticated knowledge about AODA problems.

AODA problems among adolescents in the general population are considered substantial. After peaks in the 1970s and early 1980s, illicit drug use declined as the 1980s progressed; however, drug use is again on the rise (Johnston, O'Malley, & Bachman, 1995; Thomas, 1995). Schlaadt (1992) estimates that only about 10 percent of the total number of adolescents who use drugs in the United States receive alcohol and other drug abuse treatment, while the vast majority go untreated by social workers and substance abuse counselors. This may be due primarily to practitioners' inability to recognize early signs and symptoms of drug abuse and to a lack of referrals among, and coordination between, social agencies. In addition, many families of children who go untreated simply cannot afford private treatment services. Although many public programs assess fees on a sliding scale, families may still not be able to afford the services, or they may wait a long time before a treatment slot becomes available. Box 7-2 describes the many types of individuals with substance abuse problems and the range of knowledge that is needed to practice in this field.

Forgotten Older People

The understudied populations generally identified in the literature with respect to substance abuse are women, gay men and lesbians (see Chapter 16), homeless people, and children of alcoholics. Seldom are the elderly included on this list, but they are a group that has long been ignored in the field of substance abuse treatment. However, they too suffer from substance abuse.

A decade ago Raffoul (1986) warned social work practitioners of the need to heighten their knowledge and working skills in order to deal effectively with alcohol and other drug abuse among the elderly population. Barnea and Teichman (1994) describe three primary patterns of abuse among older Americans, beginning with the most common and dangerous for this population: (1) improper use of prescription

---

BOX 7-2   Thursday Was Tough! A Day in the Life of an AWARE Staff Member

Where can you go when your world starts to crash? If your reason is alcohol or other drug use, or if you are caught up in someone else's addiction, AWARE can help.

These are the highlights from one day on a counselor's log at AWARE.

8:45 Opened up and found 8 urgent calls on the answer machine.

8:48 Returned call to a woman who is threatening suicide if she isn't seen today. She is AIDS antibody positive and a cocaine addict. Appointment set for 11:00 am.

9:15 Shared messages with other staff and interns. Phone continues to ring.

9:30 Received call from another suicidal woman who needs immediate counseling. I reassured her and set an appointment for today with another staff member.

9:47 Answered call from a recently married man who is hurt, angry and very concerned about his wife. He says she drinks and uses drugs. I encouraged him to seek long term counseling for both him and his wife and referred him to Al-Anon and other resources. I explained that his wife must call personally before we can make an appointment for her here.

10:18 Spoke with a very distressed San Antonio mother seeking help for her alcoholic, self-mutilating lesbian daughter. Referred her to Al-Anon and other San Antonio centers.

11:00 Met for 1½ hours with a client who called earlier threatening suicide. She is AIDS antibody positive and a cocaine addict. Her problems are complex. Besides needing treatment she has little money and no place to stay having just left her junkie boyfriend. All treat-ment centers with free beds are full but there may be an opening at Oak Springs in a few days. The Salvation Army can shelter her until we can find a residential treatment center. I recommended Al-Anon and also set an appointment with The Care Unit, which focuses on AIDS and substance abuse counseling. Before she left I praised her efforts to change and had her sign a no suicide pact. Finding places for clients who need free beds is difficult.

12:30–2:45 Phone very busy.

3:00 Saw a wife who wants to stop her husband's use of alcohol, pot and coke. She needs a lot of education about co-dependency and related family problems. I told her how she can take care of herself through counseling and support groups such as Al-Anon. I praised her for having the courage to seek help and sent her to Child and Family Services for long term counseling. Their waiting list is over six weeks but they are one of the few agencies with fees on a sliding scale.

5:00 Spoke with a San Marcos counselor who was trying to find a treatment center for a young battered chemically dependent lesbian for whom he is an advocate. I referred him to the Alcoholism Center for Women in Los Angeles, the only center of its kind in the country. (AWARE acts as a national resource on alcoholism and often advises out of state callers.)

5:15 Turned on the message machine as I left to run a class.

Where would these callers have gone if AWARE had not been there? This log represented only one day and one counselor. The need is there, and unfortunately it is growing.

Source: Newsletter of the University YWCA, Austin, TX, (512-472-9246) Spring 1989, p. 3. Reprinted by permission.

and over-the-counter medications that leads unwittingly to a situation of drug abuse; (2) abuse of alcohol; (3) abuse of illegal drugs.

The elderly may become victims of drug abuse if prescribed psychoactive medications such as sleeping pills or tranquillizers. Quite often patients do not follow dosage instructions and eventually overmedicate themselves. In some instances lack of appropriate medical monitoring is a contributing factor to abuse of prescribed medications as doctors seem to rely on medications as the preferred treatment modality (Schlaadt, 1992).

Over-the-counter (OTC) drugs—drugs that do not require a doctor's prescription—are usually purchased by the elderly or by their family members. Due to factors such as expense, lack of transportation, or fear of medical environments, older people may not go to a doctor and thus may simply purchase familiar OTC drugs to treat their ailments. Unknowingly, this may create more problems for them. For example, the most common OTC drug used by the elderly is aspirin (Schaie & Willis, 1991) or some of its name brand derivatives, such as BC or Stanback. Aspirin is supposed to relieve or reduce inflammation and pain (Schlaadt, 1992), but doctors disagree about its long-term side effects if taken in abundance. One side effect is said to be anticlotting action, which could lead to internal bleeding, irritation of the stomach lining, or ringing in the ears (Schlaadt).

Alcohol abuse and dependence in the elderly can also be devastating because of the physiological changes associated with the aging process. It is well known that prolonged, frequent use of alcohol can cause numerous and serious health problems (e.g., cirrhosis of the liver); however, some elderly people attribute their "good" health to medicinal alcohol use. In fact, some recent evidence does indicate that modest amounts of alcohol may be helpful over the course of a lifetime, and other research indicates that moderate drinking among the elderly produces a less isolated, less hopeless, less depressed, and more sociable person (Schaie & Willis, 1991). The benefits and problems of alcohol use will continue to be a topic of considerable interest. In the illustration of Mrs. O in Box 7-3, a social worker helps an older woman who is experiencing some negative effects of alcohol abuse. Her problems are compounded by her son's drinking problems.

The elderly population is sometimes caught indirectly in the illicit drug scene. They may observe drug deals and the associated violence and deterioration in their neighborhoods and experience feelings of helplessness, frustration, and fear. Illicit drug use among the elderly themselves appears to be rare but may be underestimated, as limited data are available on this population. And although heavy drinking and illicit drug use seem to remit with age, as the baby boomers (and subsequent generations who have also had substantial exposure to illicit drugs) mature, there may be an increased incidence of these problems.

Serious consideration should be given to developing drug abuse treatment strategies specifically for the elderly population. In any event, no drug should be taken unmonitored or considered safe enough to be harmless. Currently there is limited social work practice information on elderly drug abuse. Graduate social work programs with specializations in gerontology seldom include much drug abuse content in their curricula; therefore, students are rarely taught intervention techniques with this population. These gaps in education and services might compel social workers and society in general to think now about preparing to meet the substance abuse service needs of this population; if not, future ramifications could be substantial.

BOX 7-3 The Social Worker and Mrs. O.

Mrs. O, an Irish Catholic woman in her early seventies, was referred by a housing manager to a worker at a public assistance agency for help with some concrete needs such as a hearing aid and new glasses and for an evaluation regarding preventive intervention. The manager who had referred her to the agency was concerned about a drinking problem, her relationship with her son, and about possible problems in her perception of reality. The manager reported that Mrs. O had one son who was an alcoholic and who came to see her, demanding money which she gave him even though she had very little. Mrs. O had been separated from her husband for a number of years; he had died three months before the referral. She also had another son and a daughter with whom she had contact and a sister who visited occasionally. The rest of the family would become angry with her when she aided the alcoholic son, however, and during these times would decrease their contact with her.

Contact

When Mrs. O was first introduced to the worker at the housing project by the manager, she agreed to an appointment but stated that she was going out and would let them know when she returned. She did not do so, but the worker happened to see her return. The worker, therefore, went to her apartment, but the woman said she could not see the worker at that time because she had a drink at dinner and had to sleep it off. They made an appointment for the following week, and the woman did not avoid the worker this time. In fact, when the worker explained that Mrs. O did not have to see her if she did not want to, the woman indicated a desire to speak with the worker. The woman's greatest concern centered around a buzzing in her ears which bothered her to such an extent that she did not feel like seeing anyone. She was reluctant to cook for herself since she had found roaches in her apartment. She was also concerned about her alcoholic son and her own drinking.

The son would encourage her to drink when he came, and she would do so and then feel sick. This, plus his requests for money and his disturbances when he arrived at the apartment drunk, made her angry with him; and yet she felt that she needed to take care of him. She also shared some bizarre thoughts about events that she thought caused her difficulties, even though in reality they had no connection with her problems. The worker located a hot-meal program, which the client considered; she encouraged her to put a telephone in her apartment and attempted to enable her to visit a medical clinic (with home service) in her apartment building. Within a few weeks, she seemed to improve considerably.

After regular contact of a few months she was able to go out and enjoy people more; she was drinking less and was less bothered by the buzzing in her ears. Shortly thereafter she could take action in relation to her alcoholic son by obtaining a restraining order keeping him out of the building when he was drunk. The worker was also able to help her obtain a television set to keep her company and help her remain oriented to reality. Although she was frightened of it at first, she grew to like it, and it did help with keeping her mind off the buzzing in her ears and other unpleasant and unrealistic thoughts.

She admitted that loneliness was her main problem. Although this was intensified by her hearing problem, she could not accept a hearing aid. When her family discovered that she was no longer subject to unexpected visits from her alcoholic son when he was drinking, they began to visit her more often. After a few months of contact, the client did follow through on an appointment with an outpatient facility for a medical investigation of her hearing problem. She had a considerable amount of wax taken out of one ear and this stopped the buzzing and improved her hearing somewhat. She also finally followed through on an appointment to a hospital eye clinic and was able to obtain new glasses.

By the end of the contact, she functioned at a much better level. She had obtained concrete help and achieved a more frequent and meaningful contact with her family, and she was able to participate in the social activities in the housing project. The worker remained in touch with the housing manager and spoke on Mrs. O's behalf to him, pointing out to him Mrs. O's progress and urging him to look after her from time to time.

Discussion of the Illustration

The case illustrates the way in which an elderly person is to be perceived as a unique individual with the right to her own self-determination in a dignified manner. The worker recognizes this by allowing her to decide which services she wishes to accept and at what pace. At the same time, the worker reaches out in order to help her accept the service offered without being frightened. The worker draws on the client's strengths in connection with her relationship with her family, her common sense and her desire to feel more comfortable. The worker then uses these strengths to help the client achieve a restored equilibrium through ameliorating some of her debilitating conditions and through helping her to provide satisfying and growth enhancing experiences that promote self-actualization and prevent further deterioration.

The worker performs mainly the role of broker between the client, her family, and health-care agencies. In the role of enabler, an essential part of the enabling function centered on using the relationship between the worker and the client and by being a consistent, caring listener who eventually could help the client sort out the realities of her situation. The degree of improvement is striking and so is the client's ability to maintain this improvement and to operate more independently by the end of the contact. The worker worked as an advocate vis-a-vis the housing manager, though the enabler and broker roles were more evident in this situation.

Source: Reprinted by permission of Waveland Press, Inc. from Lowy, L. *Social work with the aging: The challenge and promise of the later years* (2nd ed.). (Prospect Heights, IL; Waveland Press, Inc., 1985 [reissued 1991]) All rights reserved.

Future Directions

Social work practice is facing the enormous task of moving beyond the point of simply acknowledging drug use as a problem to a point of doing something to help bring about change. Just as Dorothea Dix led the battle for the humane treatment of people with mental illness and mental retardation (see Chapter 6); as Mary Richmond led the battle for casework (see Chapters 2 and 4); as Helen Northern (1969) led the battle for group work; and Molefi Asante (1988) led the battle for Afrocentrism in treatment, so might social workers think about taking a more prominent role in substance abuse prevention and treatment strategies.

The literature is full of discussions of the roles of social workers. As the political atmosphere changes, it affects what social workers do and how they do it. For example, with more emphasis on law enforcement strategies in substance abuse, one idea is to place social workers in nontraditional settings, such as police substations. As we move into the twenty-first century, role changes like this may become a necessity.

While volumes of data on drug-using clients accumulate, social workers have produced few of the intervention techniques with AODA populations. Substance abuse counselors are flooding the book market with their techniques, which for the most part focus on the use of the medical model. They consider the client to be ill and advocate the AA program as the primary supplement to treatment. Although this may be effective for many clients, substantial numbers are not helped with these approaches (Jackson, 1995). Social workers might give more serious consideration to ways they can use their holistic perspective to create innovative interventions with this population. Though the philosophy of the profession may be seen as increasingly unpopular in this time of attacks on social service funding, social workers have been successful in the past in supporting the causes of oppressed groups (e.g., women, ethnic minorities, the poor). Social work practice is dedicated to a code of ethics that specifies respect for human dignity and the right of self-determination. Work with people with AODA problems to improve their overall quality of life is wholly consistent with these principles. This idea steps beyond the simplistic notion of abstinence to help clients enter or reenter a life of sobriety. Collaboration with substance abuse counselors may prove a worthy strategy in this practice role, as the magnitude of the problem is too great to tackle alone.

Langton (1991) asks why more college textbooks don't include information on AODA research. Another issue to ponder is why more social work education programs do not require students to become knowledgeable and skilled in identifying and treating AODA clients? And why hasn't CSWE taken a more proactive role in mandating inclusion of alcohol and other drug content in preparing students for professional practice?

Summary

This chapter considers the place of social workers in the field of alcohol and other drug abuse prevention and treatment. This is an important area of practice but not one in which most social work students receive adequate preparation, and not one in which many social workers have taken the lead in developing models of intervention. Given the number of people affected by alcohol and drug abuse problems, it is inevitable that social workers will encounter these problems regardless of the area in which they work. Social workers must therefore prepare themselves to respond to clients with these problems. Social workers can also play a role in contributing to the knowledge base, since there is still much to be learned about the causes of substance abuse and effective strategies for prevention and intervention.

Suggested Reading

Alcoholics Anonymous World Services. (1976). *Alcoholics Anonymous* (3rd ed.). New York: Alcoholics Anonymous World Services.

Barber, J. G. (1995). *Social work with addictions*. Basingstoke: Macmillan.

Kinney, J., & Leaton, G. (1995). *Loosening the grip: A handbook of alcohol information* (5th ed.). St. Louis: C. V. Mosby.

McNeece, C. A., & DiNitto, D. M. (1994). *Chemical dependency: A systems approach*. Englewood Cliffs, NJ: Prentice-Hall.

National Institute on Alcohol Abuse and Alcoholism. (1993). *Eighth special report to the U.S. Congress on alcohol and health*. Rockville, MD: U.S. Department of Health and Human Services.

8

Meeting the Crisis in Health Care

Photo courtesy of C. Aaron McNeece

The original chapter from the first edition of this book has been revised by CYNTHIA MONIZ and STEPHEN GORIN, Social Work Program, Plymouth State College.

Until recently the locus of medical care was the hospital and nursing home. This was largely due to advances in technology, which were best used on a highly centralized basis. Social work practice in hospitals dates from the turn of the century, when Dr. Richard Cabot established a social services network at Boston's Massachusetts General Hospital (Reynolds, 1963). Along with Ida Cannon, a social work graduate of Simmons College, Cabot laid the foundation for hospital social work (Poole, 1995). By the 1960s, hospital social workers had established themselves as key players within both the profession and the larger medical community (Ross, 1995).

Social work in health care settings is now the third largest field of practice for professional social workers, after mental health practice and practice with children, according to one NASW study. In 1991 about 13 percent of all NASW members worked in hospitals and medical clinics. Hospitals and medical clinics also ranked second and third, respectively, as the primary physical settings for social work practitioners (Gibelman & Schervish, 1993). Considering that social workers in many other settings (corrections, mental health, child welfare, aging) may also perform health care functions for clients, the number of social workers employed in health care is staggering. Employment in this area more than doubled between the 1960s and early 1980s (NASW, 1983).

Early social work in health care settings existed almost entirely within hospitals. The arrangement with Massachusetts General Hospital was developed in 1905 in order "to meet patients' needs—economic, mental, or moral" (Cabot, 1919). The American Association of Hospital Social Workers, one of the earliest organizations of professional social workers, was founded in 1918. The first specialized course for medical social workers was developed at Simmons College in 1912 (Kerson, 1982). By the 1980s, approximately half of all schools of social work had a health care concentration (CSWE, 1985).

Social workers are still very much involved in hospital social work, but they also plan health care programs; teach medical students; consult with doctors, nurses, and other medical personnel; conduct research on access to and utilization of health care programs; evaluate the outcomes of public health projects; link patients and their families to community services; advocate for victims of abuse and rape; and provide an almost endless array of other services in the health field (Bracht, 1978). They will continue to play an active role as the U.S. health care system undergoes major restructuring. There is a tendency to identify these kinds of social work practice as "hospital" or "medical" social work, but the currently preferred terminology seems to be social work practice in health care, social work in health settings, or simply *health social work* (Carlton, 1984).

Basic Premises and Goals of Social Work in Health Care

The five basic premises of health social work described here are well established in the research literature and provide a framework and a strong argument for the utilization of social workers in the delivery of health care programs (Bracht, 1978).

- *Premise 1*　Health status, illness prevention, and recovery from illness are affected by far more than what is narrowly defined as medical treatment. Social, economic, and cultural conditions have a profound impact on health. For example, people in poverty are more prone to disability and are less likely to receive preventive health care. Social workers therefore often secure appointments for people at health clinics.
- *Premise 2*　Illness conditions are frequently exacerbated by the effects of institutionalization, and illness-related behaviors may disrupt personal or family equilibrium and coping behaviors. Social workers may help alleviate these side effects of hospitalization, or they may help family members adjust to the death or disability of other family members.
- *Premise 3*　Medical treatment alone, without accompanying social services, is often incomplete. Medical treatment is sometimes possible only when accompanied by such services. For example, social workers help people overcome fear about cancer treatment so they can take advantage of it, or they help a single parent secure child care while receiving treatment.
- *Premise 4*　Problems of access and utilization of health care services are endemic to the health care delivery system and require concerted community action in order to establish appropriate links between providers and consumers. For example, many communities have family planning programs that are not being appropriately utilized by sexually active teenagers.
- *Premise 5*　Interdisciplinary health team collaboration on community health problems is an effective approach to solving complex sociomedical problems. Social workers have participated in planning needle and syringe exchange programs in order to stem the spread of AIDS and other contagious diseases.

As part of a health care team, social workers collaborate with physicians, nurses, physical therapists, public health officials, vocational rehabilitation counselors, and other health care experts in order to promote the quality of clients' health. It is generally agreed that the specific objectives of social work in the field of health care are the following:

1. To assess psychosocial and environmental stresses encountered by physically ill persons and their families
2. To provide direct therapeutic help
3. To help patients and their families make optimal use of health care programs
4. To make appropriate health care programs available and accessible to all persons in need
5. To humanize institutional programs in the interest of patients' needs
6. To facilitate the comprehensive treatment of the patient in collaboration with the physician and other medical personnel
7. To contribute to the analysis and improvement of social health care policy and program development

8. To provide leadership in educating consumers about health care programs
9. To effectively administer and evaluate the delivery of health care programs (Berkman, 1987)

Knowledge, Skills, and Values

The accomplishment of such a wide range of objectives requires a holistic approach. Health care social workers bring the same generic knowledge and practice to bear on problems as other social workers, but they must also understand the psychological, social, and physiological factors relevant to the etiology of disease and the care of the patient. They must comprehend the health implications of different ethnic and cultural backgrounds and have a thorough knowledge of family systems and dynamics (also see chapter 15). Especially important is the ability to work in a collaborative, multidisciplinary setting and to appreciate the different professions' knowledge and value systems in treating a client. The social worker in a medical setting frequently will be a member of an interdisciplinary team, along with doctors, nurses, psychologists, and other medical personnel. It is not uncommon for the conflicts and divisions that characterize organizational units of the hospital, as well as the professions, to spill over into the team's activities. A systems theory framework is essential to understanding social work in a health care setting.

One of the most compelling arguments for social work practice in health care settings is that minorities and the poor suffer disproportionately from acute and chronic illnesses and die earlier than those in better economic circumstances. Any analysis of U.S. health problems should take into account the special and unmet needs of these disadvantaged groups (Schlesinger, 1985). Social work's particular concern with the problems of people of color and poor people makes it a natural profession in health care settings. In the 1950s the death rate from tuberculosis reached epidemic proportions among Native Americans in Alaska. The Indian Health Service was established in the mid-1950s. Using social workers and paraprofessionals to assist other medical professionals, the reduction in both tuberculosis and infant death rates within the next few years was extraordinary. The Indian Health Service currently provides a wide range of services, including child protection, mental health, substance abuse treatment and prevention, and many other social services (Mohatt, McDiarmid, & Montoya, 1988). Meeting the health care needs of America's homeless is another natural activity for social workers in the health care field.

Health Care Policy

According to a prominent political scientist, there is no better illustration of the dilemmas of rational policy-making than in the field of health care (Dye, 1987). The primary obstacle to rationality is that good health is more strongly associated with factors that are rarely considered in the public debates on health care policy. Rather than implementing policies focused on *good health,* U.S. health care policies are more often directed at improving *medical care.*

BOX 8-1   A Social Worker Assists a Client with AIDS

Robert Hancock was admitted to Metropolis Memorial Hospital over the weekend with problems related to his AIDS-related dementia. He had been diagnosed with AIDS almost two years earlier, and had done very well at first. In the last year, however, he had several admissions with seizures, episodes of confusion, weight loss, and drug-resistant tuberculosis. With his deteriorating cognitive and physical status, he had become a seriously-ill patient with poor prognosis. This was his fourth admission.

On Monday morning, Margaret Cannon, the social worker for the AIDS Unit at Metropolis Memorial Hospital, stood at the nurse's station, picking up the new referrals and screening the patients' charts in order to identify other patients who might be in need of social work intervention. Relying on referrals from the medical team sometimes had resulted in missed opportunities in providing counseling, information, and other psychosocial support, so chart review was a routine part of her activities. Developing closer relationships and conducting in-service education sessions with the nursing and medical staff had led her to a better understanding of what social work could provide, but she had found that it was best to take a proactive position in case finding in order to fully meet the needs of patients on her unit in the hospital.

Initially, the social worker had been called in to assist with financial assistance, since Mr. Hancock had lost his job and medical insurance just prior to his first admission. He had worked for a large retail store as an appliance salesperson, with a good salary, but had only a small savings account. During the initial stages of the illness he had still been engaged in a good deal of denial about the expected course of the disease, and had made no plans for any changes in his situation. As a middle-class, independent man who had never had any contact with the human service system before, it was difficult for him to accept help from a social worker.

Her activities with him on the first admission consisted primarily of providing information and conducting a limited psychosocial assessment to identify immediate problems in his situation. He preferred to keep their communications on a task-centered basis, discussing appeals procedures for his medial insurance reinstatement, examples of similar cases that had been successfully fought, sources of other financial assistance when his slim savings were exhausted, etc. On subsequent admissions, he had become more comfortable with disclosing how this condition had changed his life and how he had been trying to cope with it. This expanded therapeutic relationship also enabled her to establish contacts with family members, with his consent, who eventually were called on to provide more assistance as his condition deteriorated. Since he had become too confused to live alone and had exhausted his savings, Mr. Hancock had moved in with a married sister in recent months.

A few days after his fourth admission, the weekly neurology team meeting was held, at which representatives of several disciplines met to staff cases. The physician gave an update on Mr. Hancock's current medical status and outlined plans for treatment, pointing out areas for different team members to address. Because of his weight loss and debilitation, a nutritionist had been involved in Mr. Hancock's care, counseling him about his nutritional needs and learning more about his lifestyle and food preferences. This enabled her to make more individualized recommendations about preparation and types of food that would be more enjoyable and likely to be incorporated in his regular diet. However, with his poor cognitive functioning and behavior problems, it was necessary to place him on hyper-alimentation, a liquid form of nourishment. The physical therapist and occupational therapist had also worked with Mr. Hancock and his sister to increase his ability to manage independently, with specific exercises and adaptations of the home environment. At this point, however, he was no longer cooperative with physical therapy and had become com-

continued

bative on occasion with family members and staff.

At this meeting, the team discussed Mr. Hancock's new status. His sister had expressed to nursing staff on admission that she simply could no longer manage him at home and that she was ready to place him in a nursing home. It was decided that the social worker, Ms. Cannon, would meet with her and assess the home situation and the ability of the family to continue caring for Mr. Hancock. With additional emotional support, behavioral management techniques, and changes in his medication, it was possible that nursing home placement could be deferred. Ms. Cannon found that many families were unaware of the resources available to them, including home health services, hospice care, respite services, disability income, and sup-

port groups. In this case, she had found the sister's family to be very caring and highly motivated to adapt their family life to meet the needs of this seriously ill man. She planned to set up a meeting with them to discuss the situation as soon as possible. Securing disability income and related benefits, as well as receiving emotional support, in-home services, and behavioral strategies for dealing with his complex problems might enable them to better meet his needs in a home setting. If this should not prove to be feasible or acceptable, Ms. Cannon would begin the process of nursing home placement, including financial aspects, locating a facility that would accept him, working with the family to foster a continuing relationship with Mr. Hancock, and assisting the patient himself with his transition.

Good Health and Medical Care: The Missing Link

One of the essential things to understand about good health is that it is strongly associated with a number of factors over which doctors, nurses, medical social workers, and hospitals have little or no control. Good health is correlated with heredity, income, lifestyle (drinking alcohol, smoking, drug use, exercise, anxiety, and so forth), and the physical environment (sewage disposal, air and water quality, working conditions, and so forth). Most ill health is beyond the reach of doctors, hospitals, and medical programs. In the long run, sickness, life span, and infant mortality are affected very little by the quality of medical care (Evans, Morris & Marmor, 1994). If you want to be healthy and live a long life, it helps to start off with parents who have lived long, healthy lives. Then you should do all of those things your mother told you: don't drink, smoke, worry, or overeat, and get plenty of rest and exercise!

Most of the reductions in infant mortality and increases in life span have been due to improvements in public health and sanitation—including immunization against diseases such as smallpox and polio, upgrading of the quality of public water supplies, improved sanitation and sewage disposal, and a better diet. Nevertheless, health care policy in the United States focuses mostly on the questionable notion that better medical care necessarily means better health (Dye, 1987).

Health Care for the Poor and Minorities

Social workers should feel a special concern for providing health care to blacks and the poor. Death rates for these groups, although declining, remain considerably higher than death rates for affluent white people (National Center for Health Statistics, 1994). Infant mortality rates have also been considerably higher for blacks than for whites, although the rate for both races has declined significantly during the past few decades. It is clear that people of color and poor people do not enjoy the same level of health as the nonpoor, but is this a product of inadequate medical care or differences in lifestyle, nutrition, environment, and other nonmedical factors? Or is it both?

The introduction of Medicare and Medicaid in 1965 broadened access to health care in the United States. Today, low-income people actually see their doctors more often than people with higher incomes. (This is largely because low-income people are less healthy than others.) Overall, despite improving *access* to health care, low-income people remain in poorer health and face greater difficulty in getting care than others (Wolfe, 1994).

Health Care as Welfare: The Case of Medicaid

Before 1965 medical care for poor people was primarily a responsibility of state and local governments and private charities, despite the fact that health insurance bills had been introduced in the U.S. Congress every year since 1935. Although a significant progressive element was strongly interested in providing better health care for poor people, powerful lobbies such as the American Medical Association (AMA) succeeded in delaying federally subsidized health programs by calling them "socialized medicine." The first major breakthrough came in 1950 when Congress authorized the states to use public assistance funds (under the Old Age Assistance, Aid to the Blind, Aid to the Permanently and Totally Disabled, and Aid to Families with Dependent Children programs) for medical services. In 1957 another federal-state matching program was developed under the Kerr-Mills Act to fund hospital care for poor and elderly people.

The Medicaid program finally passed in 1965 under Title XIX of the Social Security Act, replacing earlier medical assistance features of the Kerr-Mills Act. Medicaid is now the nation's largest welfare program. In 1993, Medicaid covered 32.1 million people, or more than 10 percent of the population, at a cost of $125.1 billion (Kaiser Family Foundation, 1995). Low-income people with Medicaid have greater access to medical care than those without it (DeLew, 1995).

Medicaid is a means-tested program run by the states within federal guidelines. States receive between 50 and 80 percent of the costs of Medicaid from the federal government, depending on their per capita income. States are required to cover recipients of Aid to Families with Dependent Children (AFDC); poor, first-time pregnant women if they would qualify for AFDC on the birth of the child; pregnant women in two-parent families in which the primary breadwinner is unemployed; poor children; and most recipients of Supplemental Security Income (SSI). Currently, pregnant women and children with incomes up to 133 percent of poverty are also eligible, and thirty states have extended coverage to pregnant women and infants in families with incomes up to 185 percent of poverty.

Most states extend eligibility to other low-income, so-called medically needy, individuals who do not qualify for public assistance. This group includes individuals with very high medical expenses that would reduce their incomes to a level that qualifies them for Medicaid. In addition, some states extend Medicaid benefits to families headed by an individual receiving unemployment compensation.

Adults and children in low-income families make up almost 75 percent of the Medicaid population. More than a quarter of children and adolescents with health insurance have it through Medicaid (Flint, Yodkowsky, & Tang, 1995). Despite this, children account for only 15 percent of Medicaid spending (DeLew, 1995). On the other hand, while older adults and people with disabilities make up only 27 percent of the Medicaid population, they account for 59 percent of Medicaid spending (Kaiser Family Foundation, 1995). Medicaid finances half the nation's nursing home bill and about a quarter of home health care expenditures. In recent years, many middle-class people, particularly older adults in need of long-term care, have divested themselves of property to meet Medicaid's stringent qualifications. This reflects the growing inability of even people with middle-class backgrounds to obtain medical care without government assistance. This problem will become more acute as the population—especially the baby boom generation—ages.

In recent years, concern has grown about the cost of Medicaid. Much of the increase has been due to more people in need of long-term care, as well as waivers in the law that enabled states to expend Medicaid funds for persons above the poverty level. Although Medicaid spending has leveled off, concern about the program's costs remains widespread, particularly among state officials (DeLew, 1995). In response, the federal government and the states are using a number of approaches to reduce costs. Most states have received federal waivers (exemptions from the regular rules) that allow them to require Medicaid recipients to enroll in managed care programs; a smaller number have received waivers allowing them to revise eligibility requirements and alter benefits.

Health Care for the Elderly: Medicare

Medicare was enacted along with Medicaid in 1965 as an amendment to the Social Security Act. Unlike Medicaid, however, Medicare is a social *insurance* program. Elderly people are the largest group of beneficiaries, making up 90 percent of the program; the remaining 10 percent are other Social Security recipients who have disabilities or are renal dialysis patients. Medicare provides prepaid hospital insurance and voluntary medical insurance, administered by the federal government. Hospital Insurance (HI), or Part A of Medicare, is a compulsory health insurance plan for hospital care and is financed from a payroll tax collected through the Social Security system. Supplemental Medical Insurance (SMI), or Part B of Medicare, is a voluntary supplemental insurance plan for outpatient medical care. It is financed in part by premiums paid by the beneficiaries and in part by general tax revenues. The premiums for Part B are less expensive than private health insurance, and nearly all Medicare recipients participate. In 1995, Part A included a $716 hospital deductible (the first $716 of hospital bills are paid by the beneficiary). Part B included a $100 medical deductible and a monthly premium of $46.10 (DeLew, 1995).

From its rather modest $3.4 billion cost during the first year of operation, Medicare costs for its 37 million clients grew to $142.2 billion in 1993 (DeLew, 1995). Congress has enacted several measures to hold down the costs of medical care, including, in 1983, the DRGs (diagnostic related groups), in which the federal government specifies *in advance* what it will pay for the treatment of 468 different illnesses. Although the DRGs succeeded in reducing the average length of hospital stays, critics argued that they resulted in the premature discharge of patients. In 1989, Medicare adopted a resource-based relative value scale (RBRVS), which revised payments to physicians, increasing reimbursement for primary care providers and reducing it for specialists. Between 1984 and 1991, spending for Medicare and Medicaid increased at a slower rate than spending in the private sector (DeLew, 1995). At the same time, surveys show that most Medicare beneficiaries are satisfied with their care (Health Care Finance Administration, 1995).

Despite Medicare's achievements, critics point to crucial gaps in the program. First, Medicare generally does not pay for nursing home or other long-term care, which can easily cost $40,000 a year. In order to obtain long-term assistance, individuals must meet stringent income standards. Medicare also does not pay for prescription drugs or eyeglasses. Moreover, as a result of copays and deductibles, older adults today spend 14 percent of their disposable incomes on health care, a higher proportion than *before* the enactment of Medicare (Vladick, 1995). Many Medicare beneficiaries purchase supplemental private insurance, sometimes called Medi-Gap insurance.

Health Care Reform

Although approximately 84 percent of the total U.S. population is covered either by Medicare, Medicaid, or private insurance, significant problems of access and coverage remain. In 1993, 16 percent of the U.S. population, or 41 million people, had *no* coverage (Wiatrowski, 1995). In addition, approximately 50 million people are *underinsured*. Underinsurance refers to breaks in continuous coverage or serious limitations in coverage (e.g., exclusions due to preexisting conditions), either of which can lead to high out-of-pocket expenses for consumers.

During the early 1990s, pressure for health care reform grew in the United States. The National Association of Social Workers (NASW) advocated a single-payer system, modeled on the Canadian system, which provides universal coverage and limits increases in the cost of health care. Reform played a major role in the presidential election of 1992. According to one survey of voters on election day, 67 percent of Clinton's supporters ranked health care among the two most important issues facing the nation (American Political Network, 1992). In 1993, Clinton appointed a task force, headed by Hillary Rodham Clinton, to analyze the problem and propose a solution. This resulted in the Health Security Act, which Clinton presented to a joint session of Congress on September 22, 1993.

The Health Security Act would have provided universal coverage and a comprehensive benefit package and controlled the rate of increase in insurance premiums.

The act would also have provided support services, such as transportation, translation, and child care, to people in underserved inner city and rural areas. It also would have promoted the development of managed care, in which networks or groups of providers meet the total health care needs of individuals in exchange for premium payments.

Managed care differs from traditional fee for service, in which consumers pay for each individual service. The purpose of managed care is to control costs by reducing unnecessary treatment and expanding preventive service. The chief and most cost-efficient form of managed care seems to be a staff-model health maintenance organization (HMO), such as Kaiser-Permanente in California. Under this system, providers no longer work for themselves but receive a salary from the HMO and deliver care to members for a fixed, prepaid fee.

Clinton's plan faced criticism from many sides. To the disappointment of many single-payer supporters, including many in NASW, the bill preserved the private health insurance industry. On the other hand, conservatives argued that it relied too heavily on government intervention and amounted to socialized medicine. On another front, several observers challenged claims that managed care would contain health care costs (Enthoven, 1993; Newhouse, 1993, 1995). Others argued that managed care focuses more on cost containment than the needs of patients and may reduce the quality of care (Magner, 1996). Finally, the Health Security Act faced opposition from small businesspeople (who felt they would be asked to contribute too much) and even some Democrats. In the end, the act's opponents succeeded in confusing the public, and support for the act quickly dissipated.

The election in 1994 of a Republican Congress completely altered the health care equation. For social workers and other health care advocates the issue is no longer promoting universal coverage but protecting existing programs, particularly Medicare and Medicaid. The Republicans proposed replacing Title XIX of the Social Security Act, Medicaid, with a new Title XXI, which would create "Medigrants," or block grants to the states. To balance the federal budget by 2002, the Republicans have proposed cutting Medicare by $270 billion and Medicaid by $182 billion (Dewar, 1995). Although Congressional leaders contend these are not cuts but merely reductions in rates of growth, this argument seems disingenuous. Current projections call for spending on these programs to increase by 10 percent a year (Toner, 1995).

The Republican proposals would cap per capita growth for Medicaid at 1.2 percent annually and for Medicare at 3.9 percent (*American Health Security News,* 1995). In contrast, private insurance rates will increase by 7.1 percent a year.

In response to concerns about these spending reductions, Republicans have identified managed care as a way to reduce costs without cutting services. This is ironic, since a year ago they criticized President Clinton for relying on managed care, which they claimed would limit consumer's choices. The Health Security Act included mechanisms to protect consumers; the Republican proposals do not. As mentioned earlier, it also remains unclear whether managed care really limits cost increases. The evidence thus far suggests that managed care will yield only modest savings in Medicare and Medicaid (*American Health Security News,* 1995).

The proposed spending reductions could dramatically alter the health care system in the United States. First, they would make it more difficult for hospitals to serve uninsured people. To the extent that hospitals continue to do this, they would need to shift these costs to the private sector. This would result in higher premiums and less coverage. Although managed care would limit cost shifting, it would also make it more difficult for hospitals to treat the uninsured (Toner, 1995).

Second, the spending reductions would shred the long-term care safety net. Since Medicare does not pay for most long-term care, those in need of care who cannot afford it must rely on Medicaid. The Long Term Care Campaign (1995) predicts that by 2002 the proposed reductions in Medicaid could cause more than three million people to lose long-term care services.

Third, the reductions could make it more difficult for older adults, low-income people, and others, to obtain care. As Medicaid and Medicare reduce levels of reimbursement, many providers refuse to see recipients. Finally, the reductions would increase out-of-pocket costs for Medicare recipients, 78 percent of whom have incomes below $25,000 (Toner, 1995).

Social Work in Health Care Settings

The primary purpose of social work practice in hospitals and nursing homes is to help individuals deal with the physical and psychological crises associated with ill health. This may involve assisting individuals in enhancing coping skills, obtaining social supports, and working with family members. In realizing these purposes, social workers engage in the following activities: screening and case finding; crisis intervention; psychosocial assessment and intervention planning; brief counseling; bereavement services; discharge planning; post discharge follow-up and outreach; and group work.

Traditionally, social work services in hospitals have fallen into three major areas: preadmission, inpatient care, and discharge planning/aftercare (Bracht, 1978). The original purpose of hospital social work was to assist in post discharge planning to help patients sustain improved health. Increasingly, social work moved into counseling services, and the discharge planning function was relegated to less experienced workers. It was assumed that this function required less skill than counseling (Germain, 1984). Today, however, discharge planning is recognized as a central component of patient care.

Preadmission

Preadmission services include participation in communitywide planning efforts, outreach planning with families, health education, and preventive work. Special outreach programs linking the hospital with poor and underserved groups are also important.

Inpatient Services

The largest array of social work interventions in a hospital setting fall under inpatient services. They include screening and intake, patient advocacy, patient and staff

education, and counseling for patients and their families. Some of the earliest providers of inpatient services were the lady almoners in English hospitals. They served
in a number of voluntary capacities, conducting social investigations, deciding
whether the hospital should provide free care to indigent patients, and referring patients to charity organizations. Today these inpatient services have broadened to include pre- and postoperative counseling, alcohol and drug counseling, workshops
on parenting skills, seminars for medical and nursing students, and counseling for
the terminally ill and their families.

Discharge Planning

Discharge planning for the patient's return home or his or her transfer to another
facility, has a long history in medical social work. In late nineteenth-century England
it was recognized that discharged patients of mental hospitals needed aftercare in
order to avoid recurrence of their illness. About the same time, social workers from
the Henry Street Settlement House in New York began to visit the homes of sick people who could not pay for medical treatment. Some hospitals suspected that these
home visits improved the outcomes of medical treatment and began sending nurses
from the hospital to provide aftercare services (Friedlander & Apte, 1980). Discharge
planning also includes referrals to homemaking services, rehabilitation programs, or
other community services, and arranges transportation and visiting nurses services.
As hospitals are pressured into early release of patients, great care should be exercised to ensure that the patient is able to function appropriately outside the hospital.
Premature release could put the patient at unnecessary risk.

Future of Health Social Work

Despite the failure of large-scale health care reform, the U.S. health care system has
undergone fundamental changes in recent years. These include a rapid growth in for-
profit health care, the takeover by large corporations of previously independent hospitals and institutions, and the development of corporate networks and systems (Sherrill, 1995). The "corporatization of health care" (Eckholm, 1994) has encouraged the
spread of managed care. Two thirds of workers with insurance belong to managed
care plans, and three fourths of physicians are now associated with managed care networks (Eckholm). By the year 2000, a relative handful of networks could dominate
the entire system (Weil, 1994; Rosenberg, 1994; Southwick, 1994). These trends have
placed immense pressure on providers to affiliate with the emerging systems.

This transition in health care delivery has also resulted in a shift in incentives.
Under managed care, providers have an incentive to prevent people from getting
sick and keep them healthy. This will place new emphasis on strategies for long-
term health and provide new opportunities for social workers in health promotion
and education (Rosenberg, 1994). The new system will emphasize primary care and
a continuum of care. With networks assuming responsibility for individuals throughout their lifetimes, demand for case management and care coordination will also

grow (Southwick, 1994). Providers will increasingly function as members of teams and follow patients through the various phases of treatment and care. While these developments should increase demand for social workers in these areas, they will also intensify competition with nurses, nurse practitioners, and physicians' assistants, who will also seek to fill these roles.

The new system already focuses less on inpatient hospital care and more on treatment in outpatient, ambulatory, and community settings (Rosenberg, 1994). In recent years, hospital admissions have fallen dramatically, and this trend seems likely to accelerate in the years ahead. This will reduce demand for social workers in traditional hospital settings but increase demand for social workers in outpatient and community settings. The aging of the population will accelerate these trends by increasing the demand for long-term care. Social worker's roles in nursing homes, home support programs, and rehabilitative services will expand (Rosenberg).

Future of the Public's Health

While the United States clearly needs universal health coverage, medical care itself plays a limited role in promoting health (Frank & Mustard, 1994). The crucial factor in national health seems to be distribution of income, with countries having the greatest income equality enjoying the longest life expectancy (Wilkinson, 1994). Most important, within nations, even small differences in income levels result in marked differences in health status and mortality. While people from middle-income groups are in better health than those from low-income groups, they are in worse health than people with higher incomes (Evans et al., 1994; Marmot et al., 1994).

Inequality also lies at the root of many health problems in the United States. Many problems linked with inequality and poverty—such as, alcohol and drug abuse, gambling, violence, and motor vehicle accidents—are mistakenly treated as medical problems (Schwartz, 1994). To improve the general health of a population, a nation must make investments not only in the health care system but other areas as well, including the environment. Society should be making greater investments in prevention programs and services that strengthen families, encourage children to say in school, and increase the general well-being of the community. In short, social workers must continue to address these fundamental issues of inequality and poverty.

Summary

Social workers are involved in the entire range of organizations, programs, and services dealing with the delivery of medical or health care services, including hospitals, clinics, nursing homes, hospices, public health or welfare departments, community planning organizations, health maintenance organizations, and rehabilitation programs. The social worker is a key link between health care delivery systems and the client. Social work involvement ranges from the planning and development of prevention programs that may affect millions of people to the provision of direct services.

Suggested Readings

Bracht, N. (1978). *Social work in health care: A guide to professional practice*. New York: Haworth Press.

Cabot, R. C. (1915). *Social service and the art of healing*. New York: Moffat, Yard.

Germain, C. B. (1984). *Social work practice in health care: An ecological perspective*. New York: Free Press.

Henk, M. (Ed.). (1989). *Social work in primary care*. Newbury Park, CA: Sage.

Holosko, M., and Taylor, P. A. (Eds.). (1992). *Social work practice in health care settings*. Toronto: Canadian Scholars Press.

Kerson, T. S. (1982). *Social work in health settings: Practice in context*. New York: Longman.

Miller, R., & Rehr, H. (1983). *Social work issues in health care*. Englewood Cliffs, NJ: Prentice-Hall.

Rosenberg, G., & Rehr, H. (Eds.). (1983). *Advancing social work practice in the health care field*. New York: Haworth Press.

9

Developmental Disabilities: Striving toward Inclusion

Photo courtesy of Robert Harbison

The original chapter from the first edition of this book has been revised by KEVIN L. DeWEAVER, School of Social Work, University of Georgia.

What Are Developmental Disabilities?

Many people are uncertain about what the term "developmental disabilities" (DD) means. For years people thought of this field of social work practice primarily as work with clients with mental retardation, but this condition is just one of the developmental disabilities. Since its inception in 1970, the definition of DD in federal legislation has broadened. The current definition is found in the Developmental Disabilities Assistance and Bill of Rights Act Amendments of 1994 (PL 103-230). We give you the essentials here.

Developmental disability means a severe, chronic disability of an individual five years of age or older that:

1. *is attributable to a mental or physical impairment or combination of mental and physical impairments;*
2. *is manifested before the individual attains age twenty-two;*
3. *is likely to continue indefinitely;*
4. *results in substantial functional limitations in three or more of the following areas of major life activity:*

   a. *self-care;*
   b. *receptive and expressive language;*
   c. *learning;*
   d. *mobility;*
   e. *self-direction;*
   f. *capacity for independent living;*
   g. *economic self-sufficiency; and*

5. *reflects the individual's need for a combination and sequence of special, interdisciplinary, or generic services, supports, or other assistance that is of lifelong or extended duration and is individually planned and coordinated; except that such term, when applied to infants and young children means individuals from birth to age five, inclusive, who have substantial developmental delay or specific congenital or acquired conditions with a high probability of resulting in developmental disabilities if services are not provided.*

Some disabilities included in this definition are mental retardation, cerebral palsy, epilepsy, autism, dyslexia (or developmental reading disorder), and orthopedic problems (e.g., spina bifida). One reason that social workers and other professionals are generally pleased with the expanded definition is that it does not limit federally funded services to people who fit only these specific diagnoses. DeWeaver (1995) has stated that, "the definition of DD is . . . functional, focusing on what the person can do and what skill development steps are needed" to improve the individual's functioning (p. 713). It is these skill development steps and links to appropriate services that are the focus of most social workers' efforts to assist clients with DD.[1] However, there is concern that the definition leaves out a number of people with less severe disabilities (e.g., many children with mild mental retardation) who need, but cannot afford, services that could improve the quality of their lives (McDonald-Wikler, 1987). Others believe that the definition is now so all-encompassing that it has lost much of its meaning. In addition, an argument could be made that age twenty-two is an arbitrary cutoff adopted more for administrative expediency than for developing a rational definition (Summers, 1981). The eight most common developmentally disabling conditions are described in Box 9-1.

[1]Social workers also assist others with physical and mental disabilities whose conditions are not developmental. See Chapter 6 on mental health, Chapter 7 on substance abuse, and Chapter 8 on health care.

BOX 9-1   The Eight Most Prevalent Developmentally Disabling Conditions

Mental Retardation

The American Association on Mental Retardation says that "*mental retardation* refers to substantial limitations in present functioning. It is characterized by significantly subaverage intellectual functioning, existing concurrently with related limitations in two or more of the following applicable adaptive skill areas: communication, self-care, home living, social skills, community use, self-direction, health and safety, functional academics, leisure and work. Mental retardation manifests before age 18."[1] There are many possible causes of mental retardation; among them are chromosomal abnormalities, environmental factors such as psychosocial disadvantages, alcohol consumption by the mother during pregnancy, and brain disease. An individual with mental retardation is unable to perform age appropriate cognitive and adaptive tasks. For example, a child with mental retardation is unable to perform tasks in school that children of the same age are expected to perform. The Wechsler Scale of Intelligence classifications of mental retardation fall within these approximate ranges: mild with an IQ of 50–70; moderate with an IQ of 35–50; severe with an IQ of 20–35; profound with an IQ of 0–20.

Cerebral Palsy

Cerebral palsy is caused by pre- or postnatal brain damage. It is characterized by lack of muscle control. There are three types. The spastic type involves stiffness and difficulty in moving; athetoid results in involuntary, uncontrollable movements; ataxic results in distortions of balance and depth perception. Cerebral palsy ranges from mild to severe, and specific problems are determined by the amount and location of brain damage. In addition to the difficulties already mentioned, other manifestations may be mental retardation; sight, hearing, and speech problems; tremors; spasms; and seizures.

Autism

Although the etiology of autism is not known, it is defined as a cluster of symptoms affecting several areas of functioning that manifest themselves before age three. Some of the symptoms are cognitive impairment; an autistic child seems to progress normally but later regresses and exhibits uneven cognitive development across various types of intellectual development. The child may continuously repeat particular motions. Sensory distortions are also typical; the child may fail to report pain or become fixated on listening

[1]American Association on Mental Retardation (1992). *Mental retardation: Definition, classification, and systems of supports, workbook.* Washington, DC: Author, p. iii.

continued

to nonmeaningful sounds or watching flickering lights. Serious language deficits, including not speaking at all or echoing what others have said, are common. Autistic children fail to bond with their caretakers. Although the incidence of autism is rare, this disability is so severe that children are often placed in residential treatment facilities.

Orthopedic Problems

These are physical impairments of the bones, muscles, or joints. To be considered a developmental disability the problem must be present from birth and interfere with three major life activities. Examples of orthopedic problems are spina bifida, bone diseases and deformities, and missing limbs.

Hearing Problems

Like many other developmental disabilities, the problem of hearing loss may vary from mild to profound (deafness). A serious hearing loss can severely impede a child's language and speech development.

Epilepsy

Epilepsy is the result of excessive discharges of electrical energy in the brain called seizures. There are two types of seizures, petit mal and grand mal. Petit mal may be difficult to detect because the individual may simply appear to be daydreaming and these seizures may last only a few seconds, but an individual may experience many in a single day. Grand mal, also called convulsions, are easily detected because they cause the entire body to shake violently. Grand mal seizures last a few minutes followed by a deep sleep or unconsciousness.

Learning Disabilities

This category includes visual-perceptual and visual motor handicaps, minimal brain dysfunction, and dyslexia (but it does not include learning problems that are primarily due to mental retardation; emotional problems; environmental deficits; and visual, hearing, or motor impairments). Learning disabilities are disorders in the psychological processes needed to use and understand language which result in difficulties in listening, thinking, speaking, reading, writing, spelling, or doing mathematics.

Multiple Disabilities

For some individuals brain damage results in more than one disability. For example, a person with mental retardation may also have epilepsy and cerebral palsy. Approximately twenty-eight percent of people with developmental disabilities have two or more such diagnoses.

Adapted from Lynn McDonald-Wikler, "Disabilities: Developmental," in A. Minahan (Ed.), *Encyclopedia of Social Work,* 18th ed., Vol. 1, 1987, pp. 424–425. Silver Spring, MD: NASW. Copyright 1990, National Association of Social Workers, Inc.

More Terminology

Like other areas of social work practice, DD has its own terminology. Of special importance to social workers are the terms deinstitutionalization, mainstreaming, and normalization.

Deinstitutionalization gained impetus in the 1970s with a shift from "warehousing" clients in institutional settings, such as state hospitals and state schools, to returning them to the community or helping them remain in the community. Advocates of deinstitutionalization believe that people should be able to live in the "least restrictive" environment possible. Social workers and others who support the rights of people with DD believe that it is inappropriate to institutionalize an individual who can live in a community setting. In 1972 the Fifth U.S. Circuit Court of Appeals upheld this principle in the case of *Wyatt v. Stickney* (344 F. Supp. 387 [M.D. Ala 1972]) with its decision that, "No persons shall be admitted to the institution unless prior determination shall have been made that residence in the institution is the least restrictive habilitation setting."

In theory, deinstitutionalization is an accepted practice. Many people with developmental disabilities were transferred from institutions to communities in the 1970s, but unfortunately, funding for services did not necessarily go with them. Many had no suitable community residences to which to return, and few community services were provided for them. Begab (1983) captured the dilemma posed by deinstitutionalization by weighing the social work value of client self-determination against the client's need for protection: "[A] zealous concern about human rights . . . has sometimes displaced concern about human needs and protections. Many mentally retarded people caught up in the fervor to close institutions are being exploited, exposed to stresses with which they cannot cope, subjected to repeated failures and rejection, and led down the garden path—but with their "rights intact" (p. 38).

Today most states, with federal approval, have eliminated the institutional bias in Medicaid by allowing funds to be used for services in community-based settings. However, not everyone supported the decision. Parents whose children had lived in institutions for many years feared that their sons and daughters would not be able to adapt to a new environment. Unions representing institutional workers also opposed the move, claiming that jobs would needlessly be lost by those who for years had provided excellent care to clients. But many institutions have closed. For example, Vermont became the second state in the nation to shut down all its intermediate care facilities (ICFs) when it permanently closed the institution called the Brandon Training School.

Mainstreaming has become a common word in public school systems throughout the country. According to this concept, children should be placed in regular public schools and taught in regular classes whenever possible rather than in separate schools or separate classes. The concept of mainstreaming is embodied in the Education for All Handicapped Children Act of 1975. Like deinstitutionalization, mainstreaming is embraced as a sensible and humane policy, but it is not without problems. There is always the possibility that appropriate individual educational programs mandated by the act will not be made or carried through for students, either because parents do not participate fully or because of a lack of time and resources on the part of public school administrators and teachers.

The concept of *normalization* originated in Sweden in the 1960s. Normalization is defined as access to "patterns of life and conditions of everyday living which are as close as possible to the regular circumstances and ways of life of society" (Nirje, 1976, p. 231). Social workers believe that regardless of the severity of an individual's disability, he or she should have the opportunity to live as much like other citizens as possible. For example, people with DD should be afforded opportunities for participation in normal, everyday, age-appropriate life activities, such as shopping and attending recreational events, to the full extent of their capabilities (Wolfensberger, 1972). In addition, their homes should be located in regular residential communities and should resemble other homes in the community.

Social workers sometimes find themselves in the middle of community zoning battles, defending their clients' rights to live in any section of town they choose, just like other citizens. Restrictive zoning ordinances are often used to prevent the location of community residences (formerly called group homes) in residential neighborhoods. Residents fear declining property values or harm from clients, but studies indicate that group homes do not affect property values and that "clients are more often the *victims* rather than suspects in criminal investigations" (Harbolt, 1981, p. 14). In 1985 a social worker successfully protested the use of restrictive zoning practices against people with mental retardation in *City of Cleburne, Texas v. Cleburne Living Center* (473 U.S. 432, 105 S. Ct. 3249,87 L. Ed. 2d 313), a case heard by the U.S. Supreme Court.

Social Concern and Mental Retardation

Although mental retardation is just one condition subsumed under the label of DD, it offers a long history of social concern. We discuss the history of this field of practice as one example of how today's services for people with developmental disabilities have emerged.[2]

Before 1800 only a few organized efforts existed to shelter, protect, or educate people with mental retardation (also see DeWeaver, 1995). Most ancient civilizations mistreated those with mental retardation through incarceration and punishment. By the seventeenth and eighteenth centuries people with mental retardation who were not cared for by their parents were usually placed in institutions where their treatment was generally abominable. However, several pioneers during this period tried to bring a more enlightened attitude toward mental retardation. St. Vincent de Paul of France cared for those with mental retardation and contended that mental diseases were no different than physical diseases. Philipe Pinel, another Frenchman, is known for striking the chains from institutionalized patients and providing them with "moral" treatment that involved kindness and care, a calm environment, and participation in regular life activities. William Tuke, an Englishman, was another important figure in the history of mental retardation services. He established the Retreat at York that was known for its excellent care of people with mental illness and people with mental retardation. In the mid-1700s, the idea of special education for children with disabilities also began to develop. An important stride came in 1760 when the first public school for deaf children was established in Paris. In 1784 a school for blind children was founded.

During the 1800s significant advancements were made in understanding mental retardation. A number of syndromes and diseases, such as Tay-Sachs, which is associated with mental retardation, were identified. Several schemes for categorizing levels of mental retardation were also developed. Edouard Seguin of France, the father of special education for people with mental retardation, opened a private school. He

[2] This section relies on Sheerenberger, R. C. (1983). *A history of mental retardation*. Baltimore: Paul H. Brookes Publishing Co. Reprinted with permission.

later immigrated to the United States and organized a group of superintendents of schools for people with mental retardation that became the American Association on Mental Deficiency (now called the American Association on Mental Retardation). Seguin was among the first to believe that children with mental retardation could be trained or educated. He used educational techniques that are still popular today, including positive reinforcement and modeling. Seguin believed that once educated, these children should return home from institutions. When children could not return home, he advocated special institutions that were to be small and located in the community. He believed that these institutions should also assist children with mental retardation who were living with their parents.

Among others interested in educating children with mental retardation was Maria Montessori, the first Italian female physician. Montessori's work began with children with mental retardation and expanded to include general childhood education. (Schools bearing her name are found today in the United States and abroad.) During this period mental retardation, known as "feeblemindness," was distinguished from mental illness.

At first people with mental retardation in the United States who could not work received "outdoor relief" (assistance in their own homes), but if considered to be a nuisance, they were incarcerated. In 1766 the first institution specifically for people with mental illness and people with mental retardation was established in Virginia Colony, and others followed. Inadequate institutional care was the norm during the nineteenth century because outdoor relief was considered too costly (today, studies indicate that community rather than inpatient care is usually *more* cost efficient). Benjamin Rush contributed to some improvements in the treatment of patients and wrote a text on "diseases of the mind." Dorothea Dix and others protested the terrible treatment of those with mental illnesses and mental retardation in institutions. Samuel Gridley Howe also helped to improve services for children who were blind and those labeled mentally retarded. Dix and Howe were able to influence a number of legislative decisions that promoted better treatment of these individuals.

Ironically, as U.S. physicians' interest and the literature on mental retardation grew during the later half of the nineteenth century, public attitudes toward people with mental retardation deteriorated. They were considered undesirables and criticized as being paupers, prostitutes, and criminals. Immigrants, the poor, people with epilepsy, and people with mental retardation were accused of producing offspring with mental retardation. In rural areas and in immigrant ghettos in the cities, many people with mental retardation worked hard at menial jobs. For others, almshouses, incarceration, and other punitive measures were frequently used. Many institutions went from small and homelike to "large, overcrowded, and underfinanced" (Scheerenberger, 1983, p. 123). These institutions turned out to be warehouses to "protect" society from people with mental retardation; they usually did not provide humane treatment and education for them.

There were some advancements during this period. Notable figures such as Hervey B. Wilbur and J. B. Richards pioneered improved education for children with mental retardation. Another advancement was the concept of the "colony plan" that divided residents of institutions into groups based on age and other characteristics.

Some public school programs for children with mental retardation were developed, but many children with retardation and other disabilities were excluded. Some officials and educators believed that public school education was supposed to prepare children with mental retardation for institutional life, while others thought it was to prepare them for independent living. Many debates ensued about what, how, and where to teach children with retardation.

During the Progressive Era in the United States (1900 to 1920), some additional progress was made. In 1909 President Theodore Roosevelt called the first White House Conference on Children, and in 1912 the Children's Bureau was established. Both contributed to assisting those with mental retardation. Advances were made in the measurement of intelligence, including the development of the well-known Stanford-Binet Test of Intelligence and Fred Kuhlmann's application of the normal curve to intelligence quotients.

Interest in hereditary causes of mental retardation burgeoned and included Henry Goddard's famous but notoriously spurious study of the Kallikak family in which he claimed mental retardation was hereditary. A negative effect of these studies was that they encouraged many professionals to advocate institutionalization, prohibition of marriage, and sterilization of people with mental retardation. Other professionals, such as Charles Bernstein, advocated just as strongly for community rehabilitation programs. Bernstein promoted colony programs that were the forerunners of today's community living arrangements for people with developmentally disabling conditions. During this time, half the public institutions in the United States had colony programs.

Support for community programs in the U.S. eventually increased for eight reasons:

1. They were cost efficient.
2. Many parents did not want to institutionalize their children.
3. Institutions failed to serve people with mental retardation adequately.
4. Services provided by public schools were improving.
5. Many citizens with mental retardation were living successfully in the community.
6. Studies showed that people with mental retardation were not disruptive to the community.
7. Beliefs about institutions were changing, and they were considered inappropriate for many who could function in less restrictive settings.
8. Many men with retardation served admirably in World War I.

During this period special education clearly emerged as a responsibility of the *state*. In spite of the progress, services for clients with mental retardation remained fragmented, and the debate on what constituted appropriate services continued. In 1922 the Council for Exceptional Children was established; it continues to emphasize educational opportunities for children with disabilities.

Although the Great Depression and World War II thwarted some potential developments in the field, the Social Security Act of 1935 brought increased assistance for children with disabilities. Improvements in intelligence testing were also made, including the assessment of human behavior. Most notable was Edgar Doll's Vineland Social Maturity Scale. Advances were also made in understanding the etiology of mental retardation, despite a number of studies that were later discredited. Although heredity had been considered the primary cause of mental retardation, the effects of *environment* were being demonstrated. Treatment of offenders with retardation aroused considerable concern.

But discrimination against people with mental retardation continued. People from other countries considered to be undesirables, including those who were "feeble-minded," were prohibited from immigrating to the United States. Laws prohibiting people with mental retardation from marrying proved unenforceable, but interest in sterilization continued, despite the protests of those who considered the practice improper or unconstitutional. Conditions in institutions remained abysmal and staff turnover was very high. During the Hoover administration a committee was appointed to study the well-being of children; it advanced the first bill of rights for "handicapped children" as well as components of desirable programs for these children. During this period, the use of family care, foster homes, and boarding homes was promoted.

During the 1940s and 1950s concern with the definition and classification of mental retardation continued. In 1940 another White House Conference on Children pointed out deficiencies in services to people with mental retardation and emphasized the need for community services. In the early 1950s Parents and Friends of Mentally Retarded Children was formed. Later the organization was called the Association for Retarded Citizens of the United States. Today it is simply referred to as ARC, eliminating the word *retarded* altogether. More educational advancements were made. Children with moderate mental retardation—referred to as "trainable"—and children with mild mental retardation—referred to as "educable"—were accepted by the public schools. But professionals still encouraged many parents to institutionalize children with mental retardation. As a result, the population of institutions increased, but the quality of care did not improve. By the 1950s no one disputed the need for institutional reform. A movement to adopt standards for institutions developed, and in 1971 the Accreditation Council for Facilities for the Mentally Retarded was formed. Standards developed by the council were adopted by the federal government. The idea of deinstitutionalization gained momentum in the 1950s but was not officially adopted by the federal government until the 1970s.

In 1961 President Kennedy, who had a sister with mental retardation, helped pave the way for expanded services by establishing the President's Panel on Mental Retardation. Recommendations of the panel were influential in broadening legislation. There were also developments on the international scene. In 1968 the International League of Societies for the Mentally Handicapped made a "Declaration of General and Special Rights of the Mentally Retarded," which was adopted in 1971 by the United Nations General Assembly. The concept of normalization was advanced. Studies showed that students with mental retardation enrolled in special education classes were not making greater gains than those educated in regular classrooms. There was concern that special education classes might not encourage children to strive to reach their highest potential and might also have a negative effect on self-esteem. The contemporary movement for mainstreaming had begun. In 1962 the Joseph P. Kennedy Foundation presented its first awards for significant achievement in the field of mental retardation. The stage was set for further advancements.

Contemporary Social Policy and Developmental Disabilities

The 1960s heralded an important public policy period for people with DD. Among the most prominent pieces of legislation were the Mental Retardation Facilities and Community Mental Health Centers Construction Act of 1963, the Maternal and Child Health and Mental Retardation Planning Amendments of 1963, the Elementary and Secondary Education Act of 1965, and the Vocational Rehabilitation Amendments of 1965 and 1973. In the 1970s there were also the Developmental Disabilities Services and Facilities and Construction Amendments of 1970, the Education for All Handicapped Children Act of 1975, the Developmentally Disabled and Bill of Rights Act of 1975, and subsequently the Rehabilitation, Comprehensive Services and Developmental Disabilities Amendments of 1978 with additions in 1984, 1987, and 1990. The latter amendments called for attention to members of racial and ethnic minority groups with DD.

Under the Bill of Rights Act each state operates a DD program and receives federal funds to ensure that clients receive habilitation and other necessary services. The DD programs are intended to "improve the quality of services through comprehensive planning, coordination of resources and developing programs to fill gaps in services" (Office of Information, 1983, p. 1). Since each state develops its own plans under federal guidelines, state programs differ. Clients moving from one state to another are sometimes surprised to find that they are either entitled to more or fewer services in their new place of residence. People with DD and their families are cautioned to research the availability of services carefully before making a move that might limit their access to specific social services.

Other laws specifically bar discrimination against people with disabilities. Especially important is Title V of the Rehabilitation Act of 1973 that requires the following:

- Federal agencies and all businesses, universities, foundations, and other institutions holding contracts with the U.S. government must have affirmative action programs to hire and promote qualified people with disabilities. (Too often people with disabilities who are capable of work are denied jobs or advancement because they are perceived to be incapable of handling the position. There are provisions for redress, but pursuing a case through legal channels is usually not easy.)
- All buildings constructed in whole or in part with federal funds, as well as buildings owned or leased by federal agencies, must have ramps, elevators, or other barrier-free access for people who are blind, deaf, in wheelchairs, or have other disabilities. Provisions now also include removing communications barriers. (People with disabilities are stymied when the principle of normalization cannot be practiced due to lack of access to buildings where meetings, recreational activities, and other events are held. Those using wheelchairs who want to attend public events or go to a restaurant or club know to call ahead for assurance that there are no obstructions such as curbs and steps and that the bathrooms are accessible.)

- Discrimination against qualified people with disabilities (employees, students, and receivers of health care and other services) in all public and private institutions receiving federal assistance is prohibited. (Some people may hesitate to accept clients with DD into social, educational, and recreational programs because even professionals lack knowledge about these disabilities!)

The Rehabilitation Act of 1973 was the first to provide specific protections to people with disabilities in programs receiving federal funding. "Even though the Act was passed in 1973, implementing regulations were not issued until 1977—and then only after extensive demonstrations by people with disabilities throughout the country" (World Institute on Disability, 1992, p. 9). Offices of civil rights in the U.S. Department of Education and the U.S. Department of Health and Human Services are responsible for enforcing federal laws that prohibit discrimination against people with disabilities.

In 1990 federal legislation was further enriched with passage of the Americans with Disabilities Act (ADA). The act broadened concern from DD to disabilities in general. The definition of disability in this bill is the same as that in parts of the Rehabilitation Act and in amendments to the Fair Housing Act: A person with a disability is one who has "a physical or mental impairment that substantially limits one or more major life activities, a record of such an impairment, or being regarded as having such an impairment." The act goes much further than previous legislation in requiring that the private sector (restaurants, hotels, theaters, etc.) provide accommodations for people with disabilities. The act also broadened prohibitions on employment discrimination. These provisions pertain to businesses with fifteen or more employees (including Congress but not federal agencies!), requiring them to make "reasonable accommodations" for those with disabilities unless this would cause the business "undue hardship." Kingson and Berkowitz (1993), who have written extensively on social welfare policy, complained, however, that the ADA is "legislation on the cheap, mandating new responsibilities for private employers without offering any new financial assistance either to the employers or to the disabled people themselves" (p. 148).

Telecommunications provisions of the ADA require that telephone companies provide relay services for customers with hearing and speech impairments. In the area of transportation, all new buses and trains must be made accessible to wheelchair users. Amtrak, the federally subsidized rail system, had already taken steps to assure that all new cars have facilities for passengers with disabilities. Airlines are not included in the ADA because they are covered under the 1986 Air Carrier Access Act, which prohibits airlines from discriminating against travelers with disabilities. While it may still be too early to assess the effects of the ADA, implementation has not proceeded fast enough for many. As a result, the disability rights movement has become increasingly strident. A series of lawsuits are aimed at promoting compliance by businesses, universities, and other facilities, and demonstrations have taken place at public and private facilities. Finally, the 1990 and 1994 amendments to the DD Assistance and Bill of Rights Act (P. L. 101-496 and P. L. 103-230, respectively) renewed funds to basic service programs, again broadened the definition of DD, and emphasized the goals of maximizing potential and inclusion of all citizens with DD.

Case Management: Knowledge, Skills, and Values

The practice of social work in the DD field includes many different activities. Some social workers provide direct services. The techniques they use range from non-aversive methods to reduce self-injurious behaviors among nonverbal clients in institutions (Underwood & Thyer, 1990) to various forms of psychotherapy with clients who can benefit from discussion of the problems they face (Selan, 1976). After a number of years in the field, social workers may move to indirect services, such as middle-level or program management, high-level administration, or policy practice such as lobbying. But many social workers employed in the DD field, including most beginning social workers with a bachelor's degree, do case management.

Case management developed largely in the DD field. The need for case management stems from the multiple needs and fragmented nature of services to those with DD. These clients often require a combination of medical, social, and financial services (such as Supplemental Security Income discussed in Chapter 12) that are provided by different agencies. Weil and Karls (1985) define case management as "a set of logical steps and a process of interaction within a service network which assure that a client receives needed services in a supportive, effective, efficient, and cost-effective manner" (p. 2). The major purpose of case management for people with DD is "to enable them to participate in the normal processes of life in the least restrictive environment possible" (Caires & Weil, 1985, p. 248). The Rehabilitation, Comprehensive Services and Developmental Disabilities Amendments of 1978 mandated the provision of case management services to DD clients. Under this law, case management is defined as "services to people with developmental disabilities as will assist them in gaining access to needed social, medical, educational, and other services."

The knowledge base for case management in the DD field is very broad. NASW helped define this knowledge by issuing *Standards for Social Work in Developmental Disabilities* in 1987 and *Standards for Social Work Case Management* in 1992. Social workers need knowledge of clients' legal rights, pharmacology (since many clients take medications and some may abuse alcohol and other drugs), interagency policy, self-help group utilization, and principles of crisis intervention (DeWeaver & Johnson, 1983).

Regarding skills, breadth is the keyword. Levy (1995) says that social workers must be able to work on a team, be able to do social work assessments that include the client and the family, and be versed in several practice modalities. Discussing requisite skills, DeWeaver and Johnson (1983) summarized that case managers need to be persuasive and flexible, be able to mediate and arbitrate, be confident speaking in public, be assertive, write clear behavioral objectives, motivate others, empower the client and/or the client's family to assert their wants and needs to others, assess client functioning from many perspectives, assess strengths and pressures in the local neighborhood, enlist natural helpers from the folk support system to be part of the caregiving team, and be comfortable in working outside office and clinic settings (p. 27). Since all these skills cannot be acquired fully in school, a great deal of learning continues once a social worker accepts a case management job in the DD field.

Values are generally more abstract than knowledge or skills and are thus more difficult to identify for case management practice. Hanley and Parkinson (1994) stress that the following applications of values are useful in the DD field: focus on individual dignity and self-determination; make "securing human rights" for clients a central value; foster acceptance and public awareness of people with DD (pp. 428–429). Regarding values and case management in the DD field, DeWeaver and Johnson (1983) stress the importance of the following client rights: the right to co-plan treatment; the right to access to services; the right to services in the least restrictive environment; the right to advocacy (p. 28).

The term case management may be replaced in the future because there is resistance to labeling people as "cases" and then "managing" them. In P. L. 101–496 in 1990, case management was renamed "systems coordination and community education." However, the practice world has been slow to adopt these newer terms, especially when it comes to position titles. Hence, many employers still advertise for "case managers."

Aged People with Mental Retardation

An important and growing aspect of practice in the DD field is with adult clients, especially aged people with mental retardation. Emphasis has been on serving children with mental retardation, but like the general population, people with mental retardation are living longer. Health and human service professionals are beginning to recognize that specific services are needed to assist this growing group of clients throughout adulthood.

Thus far, concerns are that these people have "often [been] denied assistance by both the aging services network and by the traditional network of programs and services that provides assistance to younger developmentally disabled people" (Kaufman, DeWeaver, & Glicken, 1989, p. 94). Unfortunately, when a client falls under two or more service categories (in this case services for older people and services for those with developmentally disabling conditions), they may have more difficulty obtaining assistance, because professionals in each field may believe that the client should be served by the other. Kaufman, DeWeaver and Glicken have studied the problems of aged people with mental retardation and have developed a case management model for these clients. They recommend that social work services be based on whether the client lives in an institution, an agency-sponsored community residence, or in a family setting. Table 9-1 depicts their case management model by specifying the social workers' roles and activities for clients in each setting. This model can be adapted for use with clients of all age groups who have developmental disabilities.

Working with Families

Families of children with DD, especially children with mental retardation, have been a strong force in the movement to expand and improve services. In the 1950s these parents banded together to form what is now the ARC. There is an affiliate chapter

TABLE 9-1 **Case Management Models for Social Work Practice with People Who Are Mentally Retarded and Aged (m. r. aged)**

Practice Roles	Model A Institutionalized M. R. Aged	Model B Deinstitutionalized M. R. Aged	Model C M. R. Aged Living in a Family Unit
Outreach Worker	Identify frail aged & determine if unmet needs exist. Determine if institutional care is necessary	Identify m. r. aged in community who are at risk because they lack needed supervision and care.	Identify families caring for m. r. aged that require supportive services. Identify situations of actual or potential neglect or abuse.
Advocate	Ensure clients are receiving needed care and services. Ensure rights are not violated.	Ensure client has access to needed services. Identify service gaps in the community & work to fill them.	Assist family unit to overcome obstacles in securing needed services.
Teacher	Educate staff, volunteers, and family members about aging process & its impact on m. r. persons.	Educate general community about m. r. aged & work to eliminate stereotypes & discrimination.	Help family members learn about aging & m. r. Increase family's knowledge of available services & resources.
Therapist	Monitor client's emotional & behavioral functioning. Develop interventions as needed.	Monitor client's emotional & behavioral functioning. Develop interventions as needed.	Focus on functioning of all members of family unit. Assist elderly caregivers of m. r. clients to cope with their own aging issues.
Enabler/ Facilitator	Help client maximize independent functioning & avoid the development of increased dependency.	Help client maximize independent functioning & avoid the development of increased dependency.	Help client maximize independent functioning within family unit. Support efforts of family to keep older m. r. person at home.
Broker/ Coordinator	Develop & implement individualized program plan. Link client to needed institutional & community-based services & monitor their provision.	Develop & implement individualized program plan. Link client to needed community services & monitor their provision.	Develop and implement individualized program plan. Link client to needed community services & monitor their provision. Involve family in developing & monitoring program plan.

Source: Allan V. Kaufman, Kevin DeWeaver, and Morley Glickman, (1989). "The Mentally Retarded Aged: Implications for Social Work Practice," *Journal of Gerontological Social Work, 14*(1/2), 93–110. Reprinted with permission of the Haworth Press, Inc., 10 Alice Street, Binghamton, NY 13904.

of the ARC in every state. ARC works to educate the public and to promote national and state legislation that will improve the treatment of people with DD.

Working with families is an integral part of social work with people with DD. As soon as a diagnosis of one or more developmentally disabling conditions is made, families generally need information and support to help them cope with the situation. Not so long ago, parents of children with DD were encouraged by professionals to institutionalize their children and move on with their own lives. Many parents experienced severe guilt by doing this, but accepted the advice of medical professionals. Today there is much more support for parents who wish to keep their children at home, but parents generally need assistance whether their child lives with them or elsewhere.

Just as social workers need particular knowledge and skills to serve people with DD, they need preparation for working with family members. In a well-known article in *Social Casework,* Simon Olshansky (1962) described what he called "chronic sorrow" among the parents of children with mental retardation, regardless of whether the child remained with the family or was institutionalized. He encouraged professionals to recognize that this sorrow is natural, not neurotic. In 1956 Letha Patterson, a parent of a child with mental retardation, offered suggestions to increase the sensitivity of professionals working with families of children with mental retardation. They remain useful today. For example, she recommended meeting with both parents, selecting words carefully, and never putting parents on the defensive.

Social Workers in the Developmental Disability Field

Horejsi (1979) notes that the field of mental retardation practice and the profession of social work developed separately and that it was not until the 1960s that the two intersected due to deinstitutionalization and other public policy movements that affected services to people with DD. With this convergence, many social workers accepted employment in direct services, social planning, policy-making activities, community organization, and administration in the DD field, an area of practice new to the profession (DeWeaver, 1995).

The seeming reluctance of social work and other professions to enter the DD field (DeWeaver, 1982), especially with clients who have severe disabilities, may have had several reasons. Research indicates that professionals prefer to work with clients who are verbal, intelligent, attractive, and similar to themselves (Hall, Ford, Moss, & Dineen, 1986). This may mean that professionals find it more difficult to work with clients who cannot communicate verbally and who have severe physical deformities. Human service professionals may also avoid working in institutions where clients with disabilities reside, because they assume their skills can be better used in less restrictive settings with less severely disabled clients. Some professionals are unaware of the treatment possibilities for clients with developmentally disabling conditions. For example, several authors have elaborated on the use of psychotherapy with people with mental retardation (see, for example, Selan, 1976). Clients with developmentally disabling conditions are often very responsive to professionals (Selan, 1976), which is not always the case with other client groups.

In addition to institutions and other traditional public programs, there are many career opportunities for social workers in innovative community programs. The nonprofit sector has increased its involvement in the DD field. A number of states now contract with nonprofit corporations to provide many of the residential and social services the state once provided. Job opportunities include case management and various middle- and upper-level positions in management and administration. The job market in this field looks especially good for those with undergraduate social work degrees, since entry-level positions in case management appear plentiful. Although placing clients with DD in competitive employment has been a major focus of federally funded services, a newer emphasis is on serving very young individuals (from birth to three years) and aged people. Although serving people of all ages is important, shifts in client groups to be given priority by the federal government have made long-range planning at the service-delivery level difficult.

There are no comprehensive figures on the numbers of social workers in the DD field, but surveys of NASW members indicate only a small percentage are employed in this field. A 1972 survey of the NASW membership indicated that slightly less than 2 percent worked with people with mental retardation (Membership survey, 1983). In 1988, 3 percent of members defined "mental-developmental disabilities" as their primary practice area (Gibelman & Schervish, 1993, p. 79). In 1991, this figure dropped to 2.7 percent, but it represented 7.1 percent of all NASW members whose highest degree was a bachelor's, 2.8 percent whose highest degree was a master's, and 2.1 percent of those with a doctorate (Gibelman & Schervish, p. 80). In addition, 2.1 percent of NASW members defined "mental-developmental disabilities" as their secondary area of practice in 1988, but only 1.2 percent did so in 1991 (Gibelman & Schervish, p. 88). There were about 700 members of the Social Work Division of the American Association on Mental Retardation (AAMR) in 1994 (DeWeaver, 1995). The National Association of Social Workers increased its participation in this field when it collaborated with AAMR's Social Work Division on a set of standards for social work practice with clients with DD that were approved in 1982 and revised in 1987.

Despite the need for professionals in this field, a survey of incoming master's students in social work indicated that developmental disabilities ranked twelfth among sixteen service areas in which these students wanted to work (Rubin, Johnson, & DeWeaver, 1986). In addition, there has been a lack of preparation for the DD field in social work education programs (DeWeaver & Kropf, 1992). Although the number of graduate social work programs offering course work in this field tripled during the 1970s (Wikler, 1981), a survey of social work professionals in the DD field indicated that 80 percent had never taken a course on mental retardation (DeWeaver, 1980). Some graduate social work programs do offer a specialization in mental retardation, and some undergraduate programs offer substantial elective offerings on disabilities (e.g., Staten Island College). Of particular interest are those associated with university-affiliated programs (UAPs) funded through the Maternal and Child Health Services Block Grant and the Administration on Developmental Disabilities (part of the U.S. Department of Health and Human Services), but UAPs have been targeted for funding reductions as attempts to balance the federal budget continue.

Employment Settings

Social workers in the DD field work in many types of settings. We consider these from the most to the least restrictive client settings. The most restrictive environments are institutions, often called state schools or training centers, but now technically known as *intermediate care facilities*. Every state has operated these institutions, but two have phased them out in favor of assisting clients in smaller community facilities. Social workers are also employed in private institutions.

Many clients who remain in institutions are severely disabled and often have multiple physical disabilities and/or severe behavioral problems. In residential facilities, teamwork and networking are essential skills. Social workers are members of interdisciplinary teams that include health care professionals, various types of therapists, social service personnel, and other professionals. Social workers are often the case managers who do the networking between direct care providers and officials within and outside the institution to ensure high-quality client treatment. They are also the major link between the institutionalized client and the client's family.

Cluster homes and similar residential facilities are also settings in which social workers play an important role. Clients in these facilities may have severe disabilities, but they live in residential communities. Social workers provide case management, advocacy, networking, and other types of services to clients based on the client's level of functioning.

Community residences (the term group home is now thought to be demeaning and paternalistic) are still another setting in which social workers assist clients with DD. A social worker may be responsible for developing the individual program plans for clients in one or more residences. Client plans may involve everything from self-care activities to participation in a sheltered workshop or a job in the community. Social workers also assist these clients with social and recreational activities to maximize normalization. Still other social workers carry caseloads of clients who are living with their families or independently in the community.

Sheltered workshops and *adult training centers* provide another work setting for social workers. Clients in sheltered workshops usually live in community residences, with their families, or independently. In addition to concern for the client's progress in learning a job skill, the social worker may also be responsible for a broad range of case management services. In recent years there has been considerable emphasis on preparing clients for competitive employment, although social workers have warned that additional services are needed to help clients cope with the stress of the job market (Hall, Ford, Moss, & Dineen, 1986; Rusch & Hughes, 1989). One response to this is "supported employment" in which clients receive services such as "job coaches" to help them remain on the job.

Public schools are another work setting for social workers interested in DD. School social workers work with children with developmental disabilities and their families. They participate in formulating the individual education programs that are supposed to be developed for each child under the Education for All Handicapped Children Act, and they work with the children's parents. Social workers are also found in many *medical settings* that provide services to children with disabilities.

Organizations concerned with the *prevention* of DD also employ social workers (Levy, 1995). DD is strongly associated with poverty. Many developmentally disabling conditions could be prevented if all pregnant women had access to proper prenatal care; and proper infant and child health care and safe environmental conditions are equally important. Social workers in public health clinics, health care programs for indigent people, and other medical settings play an important role in educating parents-to-be and new parents about disabilities that are preventable. Some philanthropic organizations, such as the March of Dimes, are also involved in preventing DD. Concern about the use of alcohol and other drugs during pregnancy and their influence on DD is growing (see Chapter 7). For example, alcohol use by pregnant women is a major, but preventable, cause of mental retardation among children.

Another specialty area of practice that has attracted some social workers is *genetic counseling* (Rauch & Black, 1995). Social workers in this area assist couples who are considering having a child but know they carry a gene for a hereditary condition such as hemophilia. They also assist parents who have had a child with a disabling condition due to genetic factors, and those who learn that a current pregnancy will result in a child with a genetic deformity. Social workers may educate the couple about the disabling condition, provide support in accepting the situation and coping with it, and help clients decide whether to pursue or terminate a pregnancy.

Advocacy is another area of social work, and professionals particularly interested in this aspect of policy practice are likely to seek employment with voluntary agencies such as the national, state, and local offices of the ARC. Other policy and administrative practice positions are with the Developmental Disabilities Administration at the federal level and with offices that plan, monitor, and provide services for people with developmentally disabling conditions at the state level.

Another alternative for DD specialists is in *private practice*. Private DD practitioners have been around since the 1970s and are usually found only in urban areas. These social workers are often quite experienced in the field and most do this on a part-time basis to augment their income and broaden their service experience. Often these social workers counsel clients, parents, or other family members; identify needed services; and provide necessary and often forgotten follow-up services (DeWeaver, 1995).

Future Trends and Directions

Social workers are adopting a family orientation to DD practice with an emphasis on family support, especially now that institutions are closing (DeWeaver, 1983). Some of the special needs of siblings of children with disabilities were identified years ago (Trevino, 1979). For example, siblings must learn how to cope with having a sister or brother who has a disability. Although the child with a disability needs added attention, parents must give all of their children the attention they deserve. Today, as people with developmental disabilities live longer, concerns extend to adult siblings and other family members who may one day provide the primary supports for people with disabilities. Prevention also deserves increased attention, and this includes preventing disabilities themselves as well as potential problems that may occur after disabilities are discovered (Levy, 1995).

Self-help groups, also known as the self-advocacy movement in this field (Longhurst, 1994), are useful approaches in assisting both people with DD and their family members to resolve problems through sharing information and providing emotional support. Independent living centers (ILCs), which are "private non-profit self-help organization[s] that provide a range of basic services that help people with disabilities live independently in the community" (World Institute on Disability, 1992, p. 9), and similar self-help efforts continue to gain strength. Finally, a concern for cultural diversity issues (Kropf & DeWeaver, in press) and women's issues (Hanley & Parkinson, 1994) has recently developed in this field. Social workers can draw on their long history of concerns and contributions in both areas to participate in these movements.

In social work education programs, more awareness of DD and of what future social workers need to know about this area is needed. This awareness usually develops when a faculty member or a small team have an interest in this area; unfortunately, there are not interested faculty in every social work education program. One way to alleviate this problem is to hire part-time faculty who are knowledgeable about DD. The educational technique of curriculum infusion is an appropriate strategy to use when separate DD courses are not possible (DeWeaver & Kropf, 1992). Continuing education is needed in this field due to the lack of course offerings in degree programs. Even when people with DD are not the primary clientele, social workers may encounter clients with various developmental disabilities in their practice. A model for continuing education workshops and training sessions on mental retardation has been suggested by Monfils (1984), but more updated frameworks need to be developed, delivered, and evaluated. Finally, social workers have contributed to DD research. Lately there has been an increase in social work doctoral dissertations on DD; however, many more areas need empirical investigations to improve practice.

Summary

The federal definition of developmentally disabling conditions has expanded, as has the role of social workers in the DD field. The advent of deinstitutionalization and normalization has heightened the need for social workers in this field. Today there are many community-based practice settings for social workers in the DD field, and social workers who choose this area must be adept at working with clients with DD as well as clients' families. Case management models are used extensively by social workers and are particularly needed by clients with developmentally disabling conditions, because these clients often have multiple needs and the services available to them have historically been fragmented. As states move more clients out of institutions and refuse to admit additional clients, concern about the availability of an adequate number of community living arrangements increases. Social workers are also active with groups, such as ARC, that educate people about mental retardation and promote more and better services and increased funding to improve the lives of people with developmentally disabling conditions.

Suggested Readings

DeWeaver, K. L. (1995). Developmental disabilities: Definitions and policies. In R. L. Edwards (Ed.), *Encyclopedia of social work* (19th ed., Vol. 1, pp. 712–720). Washington, DC: NASW Press.

Freedman, R. I. (1995). Developmental disabilities: Direct practice. In R. L. Edwards (Ed.). *Encyclopedia of social work* (pp. 721–729). Washington, DC: NASW Press.

Thyer, B. A., & Kropf, N. P. (Eds.). (1995). *Developmental disabilities*. Cambridge, MA: Brookline Books.

10

Services to Vulnerable Children and Their Families

Photo courtesy of Robert Harbison

The original chapter from the first edition of this book has been revised by DORINDA N. NOBLE, School of Social Work, Louisiana State University.

Social work has a long and close relationship to children. In 1991, 16.3 percent of members of the National Association of Social Workers reported working primarily with children; another 11.3 percent reported dealing principally with families, and 4.7 percent identified school social work as their primary practice field (Gibelman & Schervish, 1993). Many of the youngsters these social workers help have serious medical, emotional, or educational problems; and many have been traumatized by the violence experienced in their young lives. Children also need care when their parents need help: parents may be too young to act as competent child rearers; parents may be addicted to drugs or alcohol; they may be in prison or in the hospital; they may not have adequate income or shelter to nurture their children; they may be ill or disturbed; they may not have adequate child care; they may be single and struggling; or parents may be breaking up and fighting over custody of children.

Children do not live in a vacuum; what happens to children's families happens to them. But "family" can refer to radically different rules, roles, and configurations. Are families those people who are *structurally* related by blood, marriage, or adoption, or those who *functionally* live in relationships marked by acceptance and caring (Zimmerman, 1992)? Courts, legislatures, and the public battle over this question in determining child custody, inheritance, health coverage, housing arrangements, and welfare. Box 10-1 illustrates the outcome of one such battle. The debates are driven by the many different and deeply emotional cultural ideas, local habits, religious beliefs, political pressures, and economic realities that shape society's view of families and children.

The Need for a System

Let's consider in more detail some of the reasons that children and adolescents need social work interventions. Over half of teenagers have experienced sex by age eighteen (Hofferth & Hayes, 1987); over a million become pregnant each year. Ninety percent of white and 97 percent of black teens who carry these pregnancies to term

---

BOX 10-1   A Battle over Child Custody Ends

Baby Jessica spent last Monday morning visiting her pediatrician and playing in the park with her parents. When they got home, her dad started packing her toys and clothes...into a red van.... At 2:00, the toddler's small world exploded. Jan and Roberta DeBoer tried through their tears to explain that they still loved her, that none of this was her fault. Then they shook with grief as the child was carried screaming from the house and placed in the van to leave them forever...the awful scene marked the culmination of a two-year dispute between the DeBoers [the adoptive parents] and Jessica's biological parents, Dan and Cara Schmidt. A hearing had established that staying with the DeBoers was in Jessica's best interest, but the courts said her interests didn't count. In effect, she was property, and the Schmidts were the rightful owners.

keep their babies, even though they do not have adequate resources to raise them (Ladner, 1987).

In 1992 more than half of mothers with infants less than one year old were employed outside the home (Lindsey, 1994); they worked because they needed the money or wanted the sense of achievement that work affords. One reason they have to work is that marriage is not a safe haven for parents; almost half of all marriages end in divorce (Lindsey). After divorce, the average standard of living of the mother and children falls by 73 percent, while the father's increases by 42 percent (Weitzman, 1985), partially because of women's lower earning power in U.S. society. Though mothers do most of the child rearing and household activities in addition to working outside the home, they often cannot count on child support: only 61 percent of children living with lone mothers are covered by court-awarded child support; less than half these children ever receive the full amount, and 30 percent receive nothing (Garfinkel & McLanahan, 1986). Because of the cost and frequent unavailability of child care facilities, approximately 2.1 million children under thirteen are left without adult supervision for part of the day (Lindsey).

These factors combine to make children, particularly those under six, the poorest group in the nation. Without the vote, children wield limited political clout. The federal government spends approximately one dollar per child for every eleven dollars spent per elderly citizen (Ozawa, 1993). The values at the core of U.S. society—freedom, private property, and minimal government intervention—lead to a laissez-faire approach to families; an attitude that government is best when it governs least and hence is not a source of support for families (Zimmerman, 1992). Most services available to children in the United States are "residual"—that is, available only to those in financial need; public education is the major exception.

Child protective service caseloads reflect the fact that poor children are requiring more and more of the available resources: physical abuse is four times more frequent, and neglect is seven times more frequent for children from families earning less than $15,000 per year (Sedlak, 1991). What was traditionally called *child welfare* services to (*strengthen* families and *protect* children from abuse or neglect) have increasingly become *child protective* services: the investigation, evaluation, and action taken when children are reported as physically or sexually abused. Because of declining public monies to fund child welfare, services are increasingly organized around abuse investigation and risk assessment rather than treatment; many families in which allegations are not substantiated receive no help regardless of how troubled the children and families may be (Kamerman & Kahn, 1990).

Because of these factors, policies that directly relate to children and families are a patchy, inconsistent, nonsystem that leaves many gaps through which children fall. The American Humane Association (Fact Sheet No. 8, 1995) pinpoints more of the grave situations children in the United States face:

- In 1994 an estimated 1,271 children suffered from abuse or neglect. Another 18,000 were permanently disabled because of near-fatal abuse or neglect.
- In 1994 76 percent of states reported that substance abuse was one of the top two problems facing families reported for abuse or neglect.

- In 1992 7.1 percent of infants born in the United States were low-birth-weight babies, ranking the United States twentieth behind countries such as Bulgaria, Portugal, and Costa Rica.
- During 1993 an estimated 462,000 U.S. children lived apart from their families in residential or foster care, representing a 70 percent increase since 1982.
- In 1988 as many as 450,700 children were classified as runaways.
- Every day, 13 children are killed and 30 are wounded by guns in the United States.
- Children are the poorest citizens of the United States. Approximately 1 of 5 children under age eighteen, and 1 of 4 children under age six live in poverty. Every night, about 100,000 children go to sleep homeless in this country.

Development of Children's Services

Since colonial times, the state could remove a child from a family with a court order. However, such action was generally taken only when families were poor, fatherless, or unable to control or educate children—in other words, children were removed because of issues that reflected the community's moral judgments and its self-interests. Children were not seen as different from adults, except in size and the fact that they had virtually no rights. That children were in dangerous or exploitative situations did not generally result in any state intervention.

Services for needy children in this country have vacillated between in-home care and out-of-home care (Davidson, 1994). Early American villages often gave assistance (called "outdoor relief" because it was given outside an institution) to poor people in their own homes. In colonial America, when labor was scarce and religion glorified hard work, families valued children as workers. Consequently, orphans, children from fatherless families (single mothers were generally considered unable or unfit to raise children), and children of the destitute were often indentured—an apprenticeship which amounted to involuntary servitude. By the early 1800s, slavery had become well-established as a way to alleviate labor shortages (Cohen, 1992). The trend reversed when waves of immigrants increased both the cheap labor supply and the numbers of indigent children. Industrialization, mechanization, and the shift from an agrarian economy to town commercialism put both child and adult laborers out of work. As the numbers of poor grew, so did the expense of caring for them. Societies became more intolerant and punitive toward paupers. Communities responded by building institutional living arrangements for the poor outside their homes.

From Almshouses to Support of Children in Their Homes

Almshouses

America became dotted with almshouses, congregate facilities maintained at public expense for people who were poor, sick, mentally ill, alcoholics, and criminals. In many of these facilities, the majority of "inmates" were women with children. Because of the crowded, filthy conditions in these almshouses, child mortality rates were high. Between 1880 and 1920, over 75,000 children resided in almshouses nationwide, sometimes kept in locked cells and cared for by criminals (Davidson, 1994).

Orphanages

By the mid-1800s the deplorable conditions of children in almshouses angered many citizens. They supported the rise of another congregate facility: the orphanage. Although the first orphanage in the nation was established by the Ursuline Convent in New Orleans in 1727, the Civil War, which left many children orphaned and destitute, contributed to the growth of orphanages. Many state Boards of Charity removed children from almshouses to orphanages in the latter half of the 1800s. These institutions were typically large and regimented, with children sleeping and eating in large halls and having virtually no family contact. Most of these children were not orphans, but were fatherless, or "half orphans" (Davidson, 1994). Some orphanages soon began to resemble dirty, crowded almshouses, providing children little opportunity to develop independent skills.

A few orphanages, notably those formed and supported by Quakers, served black children. However, these needy children were served primarily by black families who took in children and by black women's religious and community societies (Cohen, 1992; Davidson, 1994).

Adoption

Also in the mid- to late 1800s, people began to move toward the use of more home-like settings for children in need of care: adoption and foster care. Adoption is an ancient process; for example, Moses was adopted by the Egyptian Pharaoh's daughter. However, adoption in antiquity was often a way to insure inheritance of family wealth (Noble, 1994). After 1851, when Massachusetts passed the first adoption law, adoption increasingly became a mechanism by which adults provided a home for a homeless child and added to their family.

Foster Care

In 1850, when New York City's population was 500,000, about 10,000 children lived on the streets (Morris, 1995). Immigrants poured into the cities, where extreme poverty and epidemics of smallpox and tuberculosis resulted in thousands of orphans and abandoned children. Charles Loring Brace founded the Children's Aid Society in 1853 and began gathering poor children from the streets, putting them on "orphan trains" and transporting them across the Midwest and South, where farm families would take them home to work. Other agencies repeated the pattern, relocating many thousands of children (Morris). Some of these placements resembled adoption, but many of them were identical to indenturing. Not all of the children placed were orphans; some were separated from their poverty-stricken parents and siblings. Because these parents often never knew where their children were placed, and because children's names were frequently changed, family members that were separated often lost track of each other forever.

By the end of the nineteenth century, state Boards of Charity and other advocates demanded that foster homes be screened for suitability, and the Catholic

Church brought pressure to stop placing Catholic immigrant children in Protestant homes (Davidson, 1994). These advocates of more protection for children found, in 1874, a case which was to become famous in the history of child welfare: Mary Ellen, a child whom neighbors knew was piteously mistreated. A New York woman turned to the director of the Society for the Prevention of Cruelty to Animals to stop the abusive treatment of the child. The publicity of this case led to the organization of the New York Society for the Prevention of Cruelty to Children in 1874.

Support of Children in Their Own Homes

The Charity Organization Society, although originally opposed to providing money to relieve destitution, eventually realized that many children were poor, not because of parental sloth, but because of environmental conditions such as unemployment. Their philosophy gradually merged with that of the settlement house movement to provide support for day care centers, family life education programs, and other developmental services for children.

By 1909, at the first White House Conference on the Care of Dependent Children, President Theodore Roosevelt urged that children not be removed from their homes and their mothers for reasons of poverty alone. During the late nineteenth and early twentieth centuries, legislatures and courts began to award custody of fatherless children to mothers. The highly influential ideas of Freud that mothers and children had an elemental emotional relationship, and growing political power among women, added to this shift (Noble, 1983). Women were pivotal in the passage of child labor legislation, which protected youngsters from exploitation in the labor market, and in the creation of the U.S. Children's Bureau, which marked the first time the federal government entered the field of social services (as distinguished from public health and education) and clarified its compelling interest in the children of the nation (Cohen, 1992). A private organization, the Child Welfare League of America, formed in 1920, focused interests of private groups on children's welfare.

Child Welfare Activities Expand

It took the Great Depression to provide impetus for the watershed federal legislation in child welfare: the Social Security Act of 1935. Title IV provided child welfare services and sharply reduced the rates of fatherless children entering out-of-home care by establishing Aid to Dependent Children (later Aid to Families with Dependent Children, AFDC). AFDC legitimized the idea of giving pensions to mothers. Title V (later known as Title IV-B) provided grants to states to establish and extend public services to children through a single state agency, and set standards for program administration. Today, Title IV-E provides federal funds for foster care for children who are eligible for AFDC, while Title XIX, Medicaid (added in 1965), provides medical services for foster children.

While the federal government shared in the responsibility for child welfare, control remained at the state level as outlined in the Social Security Act. States (beginning with Alabama) developed child welfare systems. By the 1950s, child welfare agencies had become professional state public entities, providing foster care, adoption, and other services (Lindsey, 1994).

Child welfare agencies had much work to do. The 1962 work of Walter Kempe and associates defined the "battered child syndrome" as a medical condition; this event was extremely influential in propelling the child welfare system toward a child protective system (Kempe, Silverman, Steele, Droegmueller, & Silver, 1962). Using the ammunition provided by this ground-breaking work, advocates successfully lobbied for laws that would help to identify alleged cases of abuse. By the late 1960s, all states had enacted mandatory reporting laws, in which physicians, social workers, and other professionals were required to report suspected abuse to authorities; the federal government mandated reporting in the Child Abuse Prevention and Treatment Act of 1974 (PL 93-247). The federal definition of abuse, however, was much broader than Kempe and associates had outlined.

Consequently, the level of reporting rose dramatically. However, funding for handling child welfare cases did not and agencies increasingly became child protective agencies, serving only the most dramatic cases of physical and sexual abuse. They found themselves financially unable to provide services to the many children who suffered chronic neglect, or to attack the causes of neglect and abuse. Because the battered child syndrome was based on the conception of disease and pathology (a medical model), it also tended to lock in the notion that parents of abused children were pathological; authorities tended to ignore family stresses, family strengths, and family support as they focused on rooting out abuse.

Deinstitutionalization and Privatization

Child welfare activities, particularly foster care, came under attack as society emphasized desegregation, deinstitutionalization, and civil rights. Research data pointed out negative aspects of foster care. In 1959 Maas and Engler described foster care "drift," in which children drifted from temporary foster home to temporary foster home, almost randomly, for years. Bowlby (1962) criticized foster care for depriving children of their mothers, while Fanshel and Shinn (1978) noted that the system did not properly monitor placements and used foster care unnecessarily for children of color. *Beyond the Best Interest of the Child* (Goldstein, Freud, & Solnit, 1973) was an influential work arguing that a child must have a psychological parent and that separation from that parent is so harmful that it should not be undertaken except in extraordinary cases.

Partially as a result of these studies, and because society was concerned about civil rights, several federal laws were passed which spoke to children's needs. In 1975, the Education of All Handicapped Children Act (PL 94-142) mandated that states locate and offer full education to all children with disabilities in the least restrictive environment, with emphasis on mainstreaming the child into regular classrooms. Individual educational plans were to be devised for each child, and intelligence testing mechanisms that do not discriminate racially or culturally were to be used. In 1986, PL 94-142 was amended with Part H, providing services to children disabled from birth. One group of children, Native Americans, was targeted specifically in the Indian Child Welfare Act of 1978 (PL 95-608), which gave tribal governments much greater voice in overseeing the services offered to their children.

Title XX of the Social Security Act, passed in 1975, greatly altered the structure of child protective services, by allowing government agencies to "purchase services" (such as family counseling, transportation, play therapy, etc.) from private providers. As a result, government could avoid the costs of administering programs. Many voluntary agencies secured purchase-of-service contracts, becoming, in effect, subcontractors of social services (Karger & Stoesz, 1994). Services for which government has responsibility (such as protective services for children) are now provided by a mix of public and private agencies.

This partnership of public and private services may expand if the current trend toward managed care in children's services continues to develop. Similar to managed care in physical and mental health services, these systems arrange for delivery of services to private providers, giving rigorous attention to quality and appropriateness of services. Providers are reimbursed for those services. The aim of managed care in children's (and other) services is to reduce the overall costs of service delivery and ensure the quality of services delivered (Emenhiser, Barker, & DeWoody, 1995). Such private managed care systems in child welfare already operate in localities in Arkansas, Arizona, and other states.

Permanency Planning

The legislation that most altered child welfare practice was the Adoption Assistance and Child Welfare Act of 1980 (PL 96-272). This law emphasizes *permanency planning*, the concept that children need long-term homes and that shifts in care are damaging to a child's development. Under this legislation, states must demonstrate that they make "reasonable" efforts to prevent removing children from their homes and "reasonable" efforts to reunify families from which children have been removed. The act specifies that reuniting a child with his or her own family is the most desirable option, followed by adoption for those who cannot be reunited. A third option is guardianship or long-term foster care for those who can neither be reunited or adopted, and the final option is, residential care.

Funding streams from federal to state governments support activities aimed at prevention, reunification, and adoption (particularly of children with special needs). The act also ensures that families are notified of and included in hearings every six months to review their children's cases. Case plans developed at these hearings must center on the child's best interests and provide the least restrictive (most homelike) living situation possible to meet the child's needs. Under this law, states are also required to monitor and gather information on the status, demographics, and goals of all child welfare cases.

The emphasis on keeping children with their families has continued. In 1993, Congress passed the Family Preservation and Support Services legislation (part of the Omnibus Reconciliation Act, PL 103-66), which provides monies to states to establish, expand, or operate family preservation services. These services are comprehensive but time-limited efforts to improve family relations and keep families together. However, the impact of this and other children's services legislation is in doubt because of the current move in Congress to include such services in block grants to states. Block grants would move responsibility for programs from the federal to state governments, with fewer restrictions to avoid comingling block grant monies with other funds and fewer demands to keep records (National Association of Social

Workers, 1995). Social workers generally fear that this would cause the content and quality of programs to vary considerably from state to state, and programs would be more vulnerable to funding and eligibility restrictions. Comingling also makes accountability for proper use of the funds much more difficult.

Children's Mental Health

Many child-serving components of the community, such as education, juvenile justice, child protective units, and family counseling groups, recognize that children's mental health needs are pressing but often unmet. In 1984, the National Institute of Mental Health (with federal monies) developed the Child and Adolescent Service System Program (CASSP), through which states can apply for grants to develop local community-based continuums of care for children with severe emotional disturbances (Stein, 1995). The Mental Health Act of 1989 (PL 99-660) required states to develop and implement plans for comprehensive community-based care systems for disturbed children and their families.

Challenges of Current Services

Between 1983 and 1993, reports of child abuse and neglect nearly doubled, and foster care caseloads grew by two thirds. While foster care funding has increased dramatically at all levels of government, federal funding for services has lagged, so that some states have already more than tripled their expenditures in this area (General Accounting Office, 1995). Costs of caring for vulnerable children is increasing because these children present greater medical, emotional, and behavioral difficulties. In one study, over half the preschool-age foster children had developmental delays, low birth weight, prenatal drug exposure, heart problems, and HIV-disease (General Accounting Office).

Children's services also tend to target minority children. In 1990, 40 percent of children in foster care were black, 11 percent were Hispanic, and 39 percent were white; further, black and Hispanic children tend to stay in foster care longer than white children (General Accounting Office). Contrast this with the fact that only 12 percent of the total population is black and about 9 percent is Hispanic. To some extent, this overrepresentation of minorities in children's services reflects the residual nature of those services. Services are targeted toward the poor—and about 42 percent of nonwhite children live in poverty (Lindsey, 1994). But these figures also suggest the continuing influences of institutional racism in the child welfare system in which white social workers may remove children from their homes or fail to place them with relatives when these homes do not reflect the social worker's perceptions of suitability.

Policy and Service Development Summary

Services for vulnerable children have been marked by several realities:

- Historically, services have tended to be judgmental toward children of immigrants and children of ethnic, racial, and cultural minorities.
- Society has connected child welfare with poverty and formulated services to meet family needs only after the family has been determined to be very needy

or unlucky. Such residual services, offered only after children meet certain criteria (such as delinquent behavior or allegations of abuse), carry heavy social stigmas.

- Funding has emphasized child rescue over family support, and treatment over prevention. Consequently, society often focuses on parental pathology and blame, rather than sustained efforts to alleviate family stresses and shore up family strengths. Given that children's problems are increasingly serious and financial resources to deal with them are contracting, children in grave situations receive a disproportionate share of child welfare resources, to the detriment of children who are not in immediate danger but in situations more amenable to change.

Current Services to Children

Family Preservation

The family preservation, or home-based, model reflects the belief that a child is best served by remaining in her or his own home, even though the family struggles with major difficulties. As opposed to a pathological view of the family in crisis, family preservation employs a holistic, ecological view that recognizes that family troubles are exacerbated by societal and community issues, such as high unemployment or lack of affordable child care. Beyond this philosophical stance, however, the family preservation movement is also driven by economic and practical motivations: adequate alternatives to family care (such as foster or residential care) are hard to find and expensive to finance. Family preservation programs, through providing short-term, intensive services, aim to help families improve their functioning and child-rearing skills at lower cost.

These services vary widely. They may include education and help in locating needed resources. For families in identifiable trouble, services may include more targeted marriage and family or drug and alcohol counseling, training in child-rearing and homemaking skills, practical services such as transportation, housing, or job training and employment assistance. For a family in crisis and at risk for having a child removed (or whose child has been removed but may return home), services may be much more focused. Social workers may spend up to eight hours a week or more for four to twelve weeks in the family's home (Pecora, Whittaker, & Maluccio, 1992). One innovative residential center moved mother-headed families (who were nearly homeless and at risk of having children removed) onto a residential campus and provided family-based services there (Gibson & Noble, 1991; Noble & Gibson, 1994). Because this work is labor intensive, social workers carry small caseloads (in some instances as few as two cases at a time) and are more immediately available to families to resolve crisis situations, such as disagreements that threaten to turn violent.

The median cost of family preservation services is $4,500 per family or $3,000 per child; this compares with a median annual cost of $17,500 to support one child in foster care, or a range of $10,000–$100,000 annually to support a child in residential care (American Humane Association, Fact Sheet No. 11, 1995) depending on the array of services provided. At first blush, then, family preservation appears to be cost effective. However, assessing the costs of family preservation services is complex, because the collateral services (such as special education programs, welfare and nutrition benefits, transportation, housing and home improvement programs, and home health and medical services) that help stabilize the troubled family can amount to substantial sums.

Are these services effective? One of the primary outcomes that family preservation aims to achieve is preventing out-of-home placements. Current evidence shows that the majority of families receiving intensive home-based services avoided foster care placements for one year after service, but at least 20 percent of the children who stayed at home through these efforts were later placed in out-of-home care (Barth & Berry, 1994). Because services are short term, they may be inadequate to maintain stability of families with long-term, intractable problems that remain once the family preservation services have run their course. Families with high motivation to avoid placement and to resolve family difficulties are the best candidates to use family preservation effectively. Box 10-2 tells of one successful family preservation effort.

A paramount concern of family preservation workers is to help parents deal, early and often, with their anger and frustration in ways that do not compromise the safety of children. However, abuse of spouses or partners (the overwhelming number of victims being women) is closely related to child abuse (Grinspoon, 1993). Thus workers in domestic violence programs have questioned whether the emphasis on keeping families together puts abused wives at particular risk, pressuring them to stay in unsafe environments for the sake of family preservation. Advocates of family preservation respond that 80 percent of families served remain safely together (American Humane Association, Fact Sheet No. 11, 1995).

The more diverse and entrenched a family's problems, the more costly and difficult is reunification. Services that may help the family cope with their complex problems often do not exist or are scarce and costly. Determining when and how to

---

BOX 10-2 Keeping a Family Together

At eight years of age, Mickey was a bright, energetic child. By nine, however, he had become withdrawn, his grades in school had fallen, and he showed signs of depression. In the intervening year his mother, who was single and earned a meager living as a waitress, faced serious difficulties. She was the victim of a brutal assault and rape, leaving her with permanent nerve damage. She had no health insurance and was unable to continue working. With bills mounting, and suffering from chronic pain and psychic misery, Mickey's mother began abusing pain-killers and neglecting Mickey. Family preservation workers identified Mickey as being at high risk of needing out-of-home placement. They worked with Mickey's mother to secure Supplemental Security Income based on her permanent disability, and they helped her to find housekeeping assistance and transportation help for Mickey. Through a family service agency, Mickey's mother received counseling to overcome the trauma of her attack; she also attended parenting classes at the agency. She obtained drug abuse counseling at a local mental health center. Workers also negotiated with Mickey's teachers to provide extra outside help with school work. Ultimately, workers helped Mickey's mother make plans to move back to her hometown, where she would have family support. Mickey remained at home with his mother.

return a child to the home requires a mixture of judgment, skill, and luck; the outcomes can mean life or death to a child. Because of the potential danger to children, many localities have stiffened their criteria for making reunification decisions (Tatara, 1994).

Child Care

During World War II, when women were desperately needed in war industries, the federal government gave generous subsidies for day care facilities. Upon the return of fighting men, however, day care subsidies were discontinued because society assumed that women would stop working. Although many women did leave the paid work force, their daughters and granddaughters have moved back with a vengeance. To maintain family integrity and provide a safe environment for their children, working parents need reliable child care, particularly for children younger than school age.

Public entities, including the federal government, have made few accommodations to the need for child care. Under Title XX of the Social Security Act, states were able to purchase day care for poor families, but few appropriated sufficient funds to take advantage of this provision (Karger & Stoesz, 1994). Another governmental accommodation is the dependent care tax credit, which allows parents to deduct between 20 and 30 percent of the first $2,400 they spend annually for child care. This deduction benefits middle- and upper-class families most because they earn more than poor families, and it requires that child care expenses be paid up front and partially refunded later—and many poor persons do not have the cash flow to pay for child care (Karger & Stoesz).

Another accommodation to changing child care needs is the Family and Medical Leave Act, twice vetoed by President Bush but finally signed into law by President Clinton in 1993. This act provides up to twelve weeks of unpaid leave in a twelve-month period for workers who have been employed for at least one year and worked 1,250 hours. It can be used upon the birth or adoption of a child; to provide foster care for a child; to care for a son, daughter, spouse, or biological parent with a serious health condition; or to recuperate from a personal, serious health condition. However, companies with fewer than fifty employees are exempt, and employers may deny leave to the highest paid 10 percent of employees if it would cause "substantial and grievous injury" to the business.

The public's lack of support for child care is particularly puzzling in the case of single mothers. On the one hand, many in society tell single mothers that they should devote themselves to the care and development of their children; on the other hand, they urge single mothers to be self-supporting (Lindsey, 1994). In fact, AFDC rules that require beneficiaries to find and take employment have the effect of mandating that single mothers leave their children in alternate care.

The quality of that alternate care varies widely. The cost of licensed, reputable child care is about $3,000 per year (McWhirter, McWhirter, McWhirter, & McWhirter, 1993), part of which is due to the cost of liability insurance for child care centers. Child care is a growth industry, even though typical wages and job benefits are very low, and worker turnover is high (Davies, 1994). Some large corporations, including the military, have created on-site child care centers for the benefit of employees, but two thirds of American workers must get their child care from private individuals whose ability to provide a safe, nurturing environment is not verified by any official entity. Only one in four children under the age of five receive care in an organized day/group care center or nursery school/preschool facility (Bureau of the Census, 1992, p. 374).

Despite a great deal of rhetoric about "family values," the lack of quality child care in the midst of so many employed parents highlights how far U.S. society has to go in committing the necessary resources to prove that the care and nurturing of children is a high priority. The issue is of particular importance to social workers who, though not involved in the delivery of child care services in great numbers, deal with many clients who need these services. The social work labor force also has a vested interest in child care because many social workers are women responsible for the care of their own children.

Mental Health Services

Estimates are that at least 11.8 percent of children in the nation need mental health care (Silver, 1988), but many do not receive the care they need. In many communities securing adequate services for children is difficult due to low funding. Mental health problems of children are, in many respects, unlike those of adults and are much more difficult to identify (Dougherty, Saxe, Cross, & Silverman, 1987). Social workers are involved in many aspects of mental health services for children, including drug and alcohol treatment, suicide prevention programs, respite care and advocacy for families of emotionally disturbed children, and both in-patient and out-patient mental health treatment of children.

Physical Health Services

Ten million American children lack any kind of health insurance (American Humane Association Fact Sheet No. 8, 1995). A growing number of children are born needing long-term care; modern medicine's ability to save premature babies, children born addicted to drugs, and children born with congenital and genetic disorders far outstrips our society's efforts or willingness to support families by providing children with basic health care or care for compromising medical or mental conditions. Trends suggest that use of both tobacco and alcohol is beginning at increasingly early ages and affecting substantial numbers of teens (McWhirter et al., 1993). Rates of sexually transmitted diseases, including HIV-disease, are also escalating among teens (McWhirter et al.).

Social workers are involved in all aspects of physical health care, including genetic screening and counseling, prenatal counseling, and early childhood development programs. They work in neonatal units and pediatric wards of hospitals, in programs helping children and their families deal with catastrophic children's diseases, respite care and other supports for families of seriously ill children, and programs dealing with pregnant teens and teens with sexually transmitted diseases.

Education Services

Another vital aspect of children's lives is the school, where children spend a substantial part of their developing years. With the passage of the Education for All Handicapped Children Act in 1975, social work became more integral to schools. School social workers prepare social or developmental histories on children with disabilities, conduct group and individual counseling with children and families, address problems in the child's environment that affect school performance, and mobilize school and community resources to enhance the child's educational experience (Anderson & Staudt, 1990).

Immigrant children are particularly vulnerable in U.S. schools. Conservative politicians in California, Texas, and other areas, are attempting to deny immigrant children equal educational opportunities. These children are also sometimes pressured to stop speaking their native tongues. Social workers working with immigrant and refugee children face particular tasks in helping them cope with the disruption in their lives and the hostility they may face in the United States.

Child Protective Services

The catalogue of ways to abuse, neglect, reject, abandon, and exploit children is endless (see Box 10-3). *Neglect* is an act of omission; it is the failure of adults to perform essential physical child-rearing tasks or to provide the emotional, mental, or social atmosphere necessary for a child's development. It results in cumulative, often long-term harm and can hinder virtually every aspect of the child's progress. Because current child welfare resources are channeled into assessing the risk of imminent harm to a child and acting on the most serious cases, neglect, which is considered lower risk than abuse, often receives limited attention. Yet neglect cases are the most likely to be re-referred (English, interview, 1994). What constitutes neglect is debated both in agencies and in courts; for instance, does neglect exist when a family denies traditional medical care to a child based on the parents' religious beliefs, or when children are left at home unsupervised?

Abuse is nonaccidental injury inflicted on a child by a caregiver. *Physical abuse* includes violence against a child that results in physical damage. Some cases of violence clearly violate society's standards, but in other cases (such as corporal punishment in the schools), society has trouble distinguishing legitimate discipline from excessive, inappropriate violence. *Psychological abuse* is found in all other kinds of abuse, and it is likely to have longer-lasting effects than either physical or sexual abuse alone. Behaviors such as consistently ignoring, rejecting, isolating, terrorizing, degrading, or corrupting a child qualify as psychological abuse. *Sexual abuse* of a child can include sexual intercourse, oral-genital contact, fondling, incest, exploitation (including pornography), and exposure. However, like physical abuse, there is controversy about the definition and boundaries of abusive sexuality, which is not surprising in a society that permits pervasive marketing of sex while limiting sex education for its youngsters.

What triggers neglectful and abusive behavior toward children is complex and often unclear. Consequently, treatment responses must be flexible and multidimensional.

BOX 10-3   A Case of Child Abuse

NEW YORK—Wednesday, Elisa Izquierdo, 6, was buried, one more fatally abused child. Each year, such children die at a rate of more than one a week in New York City. Elisa was No. 58. Elisa's story is remarkable not because of her suffering but because so many knew so much yet did so little...By her own admission, [the mother] mopped the floor with her daughter's head and punished her in other unspeakable ways. Neighbors in the housing project heard shouts and cries. "We thought it was their way of disciplining the kids," said [a neighbor]. On the Monday before Thanksgiving, police say Lopez [the child's mother] smacked Elisa into the wall, bursting blood vessels in the child's brain. Lopez has been jailed without bail on murder charges. A city supposedly beyond outrage was enraged.

Rick Hampson, *The Associated Press,* November 30, 1995.

Parents may need education about how and when children reach developmental milestones, or they may benefit from learning new techniques of handling children's emotions and demands. In some areas, homemaker services are available, in which a homemaker or home health aide comes to the home to perform and model needed housekeeping and child care tasks. Eliminating environmental stresses, such as lack of housing or child care or health care, may relieve pressures on the parents, and thus on the children. Parents may benefit by joining support groups of other parents who deal with similar situations (such as parents of children born with cystic fibrosis). Frequently families need to learn better ways of communicating with each other. Children may be able to work out their feelings through play therapy. Parents may find individual or marital counseling helpful; they may need drug or alcohol treatment; in some cases, an abused wife must be supported in removing herself and her children from the abuser's reach.

Social workers dealing with abusive and neglectful families must be able to use a variety of these approaches. Not only must they be thoroughly familiar with community resources, but they must also be creative in developing resources—particularly in rural areas. They are frequently active in constructing and lobbying for laws that are more responsive to the needs of troubled families and children. And social workers must know about legal constraints in these cases. Work with neglectful and abusive families is quite demanding: by the time these family problems come to the attention of social workers, they are long standing and intractable, and families who are at risk of or have experienced public intervention in their families can be very resistant to that intervention.

Services to Children Outside Their Homes

Emergency Care

Sometimes the techniques we have discussed are not delivered often enough, well enough, or soon enough to protect children (see Box 10-4). States encourage citi-

---

BOX 10-4   Multidimensional Treatment for a Troubled Teen

Thirteen-year-old Jill lived with her family in a small, poorly kept shack. Her father, a carpenter, was often unable to work; he had been diagnosed as mentally ill for some years, periodically asserting that he was Jesus Christ, a CIA agent, or the president. Jill's mother, who lacked education or job training, supplemented the family income by prostitution and drug dealing. The father, as well as several of the mother's clients, had sexually and physically abused Jill and her two older sisters, both of whom had borne babies who also lived in the home. When she was nine, Jill was referred to child protection authorities by the school nurse, who detected many bruises on Jill. The agency had been involved with Jill's family before and secured, through the court, temporary custody of Jill to get medical attention. Physicians confirmed that she was malnourished, possibly anorexic, and in poor shape. Jill went home while staff worked with her family to get more consistent mental health treatment for the father and to secure financial aid so that Jill's mother would not be driven to dealing with clients who molested her child. However, Jill's behavior indicated deep levels of rage; she attacked her mother with a carving knife and periodically destroyed family possessions. Ultimately, the court placed Jill in a residential treatment center, where she slowly began to deal with her deep depression and anger. Attempts to place Jill back home after a year of treatment were unsuccessful; she ran away from home and was on the streets for some months. After a stay in a psychiatric ward, Jill was placed in a group home for troubled teens.

---

zens and require professionals to report suspected cases of child abuse; such reports can be anonymous and do not carry legal liability if offered in good faith. States have two sets of laws regarding child abuse and neglect: criminal and civil. Under civil statutes, the state may, through its public children's protective agency, request an immediate judicial hearing to secure authority to remove a child who is in imminent danger of harm. Deciding when a child is in imminent danger requires skilled judgment, and agencies develop specialized investigation or emergency response units to respond to reports of children in these situations. Agencies also develop emergency shelters or family homes to accept abused children who have been suddenly removed from their homes, often under traumatic circumstances. (Shelters for abused women may also shelter children, but in those cases, the mother voluntarily seeks shelter.) Typically, these emergency shelters house a child for about a month while the agencies and courts further assess the family and disposition of the case.

Removing a child raises questions of the civil rights of both parents and children. Child protective workers have broad rights to investigate claims of child abuse, such as interviewing third parties (Saltzman & Proch, 1990). Children can also be removed from the home because of potential harm without giving parents notice or opportunity to be heard, though strict standards exist to give parents notice and a prompt opportunity to make their case soon after removal. Children are also assigned a guardian ad litem to speak for their interests in court proceedings (Saltzman & Proch). If the child cannot be returned home, he or she typically becomes a ward of the court.

The state may choose to prosecute the alleged abuser under the criminal code of the state. Social workers may be called upon to testify in these cases; certainly, they must help the children cope with the effects of a criminal trial and possible incarceration of the abuser.

Foster Care

While rehabilitation of the family and reunion with the child is the preferred scenario, agencies maintain foster homes to care for children who cannot yet go home and who are not free for adoption because parental rights have not been severed. Foster homes receive very modest payment for these services. In such cases, the court must periodically and regularly review the child's case to ensure that reasonable efforts are being made to develop a permanent plan for the child; a court hearing must be held no later than eighteen months after the original placement.

Foster families receive training and licensure from the state agency before they can begin caring for foster children. Usually one to six youngsters are placed in a home. Unfortunately, screening and training of foster families may be inadequate to prepare them for the emotionally scarred children they receive, and children may be subject to mistreatment by poorly trained, stressed-out, or even unpleasant foster parents. Because so many women work outside the home, and because many families are unwilling to cope with distressed children, child protective agencies frequently face a shortage of appropriate foster homes (Barth, Courtney, Berrick, & Albert, 1994). These facts, coupled with the difficulties which many foster children present, contribute to frequent breakdowns in placement, with the result that foster children are shuffled from one home to another, or are prematurely placed back in a home environment that is still unsafe. Though the average length of stay in foster care is less than a year (Tatara, 1994), for some children, foster care becomes an odyssey of many years and numerous placements.

For those children who suffer compromising medical problems or difficult behavior problems, agencies are developing *specialized* or *therapeutic* foster homes (Barth et al., 1994). These homes may serve fewer children at a time, and they receive higher rates of reimbursement and training in how to deal with particularly challenging children.

Kinship Care and Guardianship

One placement alternative that allows a child to maintain family ties is kinship care—placement with a relative. Because it is not always in the child's best interests to maintain family ties if family problems continue to be acute, placements with relatives must be carefully evaluated to determine the impact on the child and the family. In particular, the likelihood that the child can be protected from an abusive parent or parents must be assured. When returning the child home is not feasible, some relatives or foster parents may wish to petition the court for guardianship of the child. This is a useful alternative when the child is twelve years old or older and does not want the legal relationship with his or her parents severed, and the caretakers do not wish to adopt the child but are willing to assume decision-making roles (Barth & Berry, 1994). Guardianship is not as widely used as it could be, possibly because guardians do not receive the financial assistance that foster parents do.

Residental Care

Some children have difficulty living in family settings, or they need services that cannot be provided in a home. Residential care may be particularly appropriate for children who have been through numerous foster care placements and who no longer have the emotional energy to fit into the constraints of a family. Large sibling groups that have close emotional ties with one another may also be good candidates for residential care. *Group homes* care for about four to ten children, and they are operated by foster parents (single people or married couples), or by paid child care staff working in shifts. Group homes may serve such clients as older adolescents who need a transitional home between regular foster care and independent living, or children with behavior disorders for whom regular foster homes are difficult to secure. Professional personnel, such as social workers, psychiatrists, and psychologists, are frequently involved with the child care staff in a team treatment approach. The facility strives to fit into the community, participating in school, church, and social activities (Stein, 1995).

Institutional care is provided in one or more buildings specially designed to house fifteen or more children who cannot live in families. Though some of these facilities serve children of normal behavior and development, most are designed to meet special needs. Professionally trained staff admit, discharge, handle crises, and provide therapy for children, and, when possible, parents. They coordinate educational, social, and developmental activities for the children.

States are responsible for licensing residential care facilities, though the rigor of licensing regulations varies from state to state. Because many children in residential care are in the custody of the state, states find residential care to be the most expensive form of care—costs for supervision, maintenance, laundry, food service, insurance, administration, and therapy can range from $22,000 to $92,000 a year per child (Stein, 1995). Those costs, coupled with the prevailing policy emphasis on family preservation, have led to a sharp drop in the numbers of children housed in residential facilities over the past few years. Nonetheless, a proposal contained in the recent Republican "Contract with America" called for denying welfare benefits to unmarried mothers under age eighteen, allowing states to use that money instead to build group homes or "orphanages" for poor children (Morris, 1995). Other political leaders and child protective authorities have suggested that expanding institutional care for children is a better alternative than the disruption children experience moving from home to several foster placements and back home again, often several times over.

Adoption

Adoption, like marriage, is a legal pathway to build a family. Only state courts, and in some instances Indian tribal courts, are authorized to grant adoptions (Hollinger,

1993). To be available for adoption, a child must be legally severed from her or his parents, either voluntarily by the parents, or because the parents have forfeited their rights due to failure to perform parental duties. Adoptive parents (who, by law in all fifty states, may be single) must undergo a home study and then petition the court to adopt; if the court grants the petition, adoptive parents assume all the rights and responsibilities of parents as if that child had been born into the family. Traditionally, the child's birth certificate is altered to reflect the adoptive family's name. After a period of supervision, the adoption is consummated. An adoption decree is irrevocable except in cases of fraud or some fundamental irregularity, such as failure to secure termination of rights from the biological father (which was the issue in the Baby Jessica case cited at the beginning of this chapter). Because adoption, like other family matters, is subject to state rather than federal control, there is no uniform adoption law, and adoption statutes and practices vary from state to state.

In the United States, one compelling feature of all adoption practice is that it is to be a gratuitous rather than a commercial transaction (Hollinger, 1993). That is not to say that money does not change hands; adoptive parents may pay fees to agencies that charge for adoption-related, professional services—and those services may cost tens of thousand of dollars. In addition, fees may be paid to private attorneys who handle adoptions. Adoption is also historically rooted in the concept of confidentiality and anonymity. In recent years, however, *open adoption,* in which birth parents, adoptive parents, and the child have knowledge of and even contact with each other, has gained popularity. Further, states are establishing and refining processes by which adult adoptees and biological parents can register to reestablish contact with each other. In many cases, of course, adoptions cannot be confidential because the child is old enough to have memories and connections with the biological family.

About five million adoptees are now thought to live in the United States; at least 100,000 adoptions are granted each year (Hollinger, 1993). Half or more of these are stepparent or relative adoptions, the least regulated but often most contentious types of adoptions. Feelings may run higher when there are conflicts, disputes, hostilities, and so forth, among relatives regarding the welfare of children.

Older child placement and placement of children with special needs (medical, mental, or emotional) are usually the province of public agencies, while most infant adoptions are handled primarily through private agencies or independent (nonagency) means. Because the number of healthy white infants available for adoption is limited, infant adoption is highly competitive. To encourage the adoption of children with special needs, changes are slowly being made. Because foster care was supposed to be temporary, foster care parents were formerly discouraged from considering the adoption of a child placed with them. But today many adoptive parents of special needs children have first been foster parents to that child. The Adoption Assistance and Child Welfare Act of 1980 provides for adoption subsidies for special needs children. Unfortunately, in many states those subsidies are lower than foster care rates, often making it financially impossible for many foster parents to adopt children with special needs. In the next few years, one group of special children in the adoption arena will increase: children whose mothers have died of AIDS and who may themselves be infected with HIV.

A growing area of adoption is international adoption, in which adoptive parents must negotiate both the laws of the nation where the child was born, and U.S. immigration laws, which do not recognize a foreign adoption decree nor grant automatic citizenship to a child upon adoption by U.S. citizens (Schulman & Behrman, 1993). Another area of adoption that has generated substantial controversy is transracial and transcultural adoption, particularly the adoption of minority children by white families (McRoy, 1989). The Indian Child Welfare Act of 1978 lowered rates of adoption of Native American children by whites (Schulman & Behrman), while agency policies and practices advocated by the National Association of Black Social Workers slowed the placement of black children with whites. Adoption agencies have tried, with varying levels of success, to recruit minority families to adopt minority children. Some blame the problems in recruitment on unfair screening practices such as requirements that the family have certain financial resources or a separate room for a child. However, given the fact that tens of thousands of adoptable children are waiting for a permanent home, and because of growing concerns about the legality of denying adoption placements based solely on race, the federal Multiethnic Placement Act of 1994 stipulates that any agency receiving federal assistance may not categorically deny or delay adoption based on race, color, or national origin of the child or adoptive parents involved. The law resulted from some highly publicized cases in which white foster parents were denied adoption priviledges after a black or Hispanic child had lived with them for some time.

Members of the adoptive triad—adopted child, adoptive parents, and biological parents—all have special needs. The child and biological parents must cope with feelings of rejection and loss, and all have feelings of being "different" from others (Noble, 1994). These issues, in addition to the fact that adopted children often bring scarred memories into adoption, create a demand for periodic counseling, particularly at transition points in life (such as adolescence or marriage). Social workers, consequently, are involved not only at the early stages of adoption, but frequently work with members of the adoptive triad in many different life situations on issues surrounding adoption. Despite these issues, the prevailing evidence is that adoption is an excellent choice for parentless children. Even in widely differing types of adoption, there is a remarkable consistency of favorable outcomes (Schulman & Behrman, 1993). Though research studies primarily deal with infant adoptions, the preponderance of evidence shows that adopted children achieve well in school and suffer very low levels of abuse in adoptive homes (Barth & Berry, 1994). The majority of adopted children ultimately adapt successfully both psychologically and academically (Brodzinsky, 1987).

Custody Disputes

Social workers are often involved in helping courts sort out the allegations and the facts of child custody disputes (Noble, 1983). Although parents generally want the best for their children, when engaged in bitter disputes they may falsely accuse each other of misdeeds. Workers conduct home studies, interview children, and testify in court on custody issues. They are also involved in working with children—the objects of the disputed custody—to help them cope with the uncomfortable process and the decisions that are made. Social workers are frequently assigned to supervise a placement or parental visitation and report back to the court. A small but growing number of social workers provide mediation in disputed custody cases, in which the worker facilitates communication between the arguing parties to assist them in developing solutions, compromises, and resolutions to their disputes. Mediators do not act as lawyers, therapists, or decision makers with their clients, but courts are increasingly relying on mediators in these difficult situations (Severson & Bankston, 1995).

Summary

There are many stresses in working with children and families in an age when family troubles are legion. One statewide study of child protective workers in a southern state described those workers' most pressing concerns about their jobs: while they were somewhat satisfied with the pay and benefits, they believed they should get hazard pay for working in unsafe neighborhoods with angry and violent people; they were concerned about the lack of promotional opportunities; they felt the disdain of a public that is uninformed about and highly critical of children's protective services; they were sometimes housed in uncomfortable, unpleasant work situations; the caseload levels were high, with heavy paperwork and accountability requirements; and they believed themselves to be legally vulnerable should they make mistakes in case decisions (Midgley, Ellett, Nobel, & Bennett, 1995). Similar problems have been noted in just about every other state.

Notwithstanding these job concerns, workers also reported being very committed to their work. Comments such as, "I just love working with those little kids," or "the children make it all worthwhile," and "maybe what I do doesn't make a hell of a lot of difference in these kids' lives, but at least they know that I'm there and that I genuinely care about them!" were common (Midgley et al., 1995). The sense of mission that children's workers feel inspires confidence that, despite the nearly overwhelming problems that troubled families face, and despite the lack of a consistent national policy to deal with those problems, social workers will continue to search for more innovative, effective ways to meet the needs of vulnerable children and their families.

Suggested Readings

Costin, L., Karger, H., & Stoesz, D. (1996). *The politics of child abuse in America*. New York: Oxford University Press.

Costin, L., & Rapp, C. (1984). *Child welfare: Policies and practice*. New York: McGraw-Hill.

Gustavsson, N., & Segal, E. (1994). *Critical issues in child welfare*. Thousand Oaks, CA: Sage.

Kadushin, A., & Martin, J. (1988). *Child welfare services* (4th ed.). New York: Collier Macmillan.

11

Social Work Faces the Graying of America

The original chapter from the first edition of this book has been revised by ALLAN V. KAUFMAN, School of Social Work, University of Alabama.

Our chapter on gerontology and social work begins with a definition of gerontology as the "science and study of aging, including biological, psychological, and sociological processes" (Brown & Onzuka-Anderson, 1985, p. 254). But what should social workers call the clients to whom they provide gerontological services—"the elderly," "older adults," "older Americans," "seniors," "senior citizens," "golden agers," or would another term be more appropriate? One factor to consider in selecting an appropriate term is that the life span has increased substantially; what once was considered old or elderly may no longer apply. Furthermore, in providing services to this segment of the population, the minimum age for eligibility may be fifty-five, sixty, sixty-five, or older, depending on the specific program.

The U.S. Bureau of the Census uses the term "older" to describe those fifty-five years and older, "elderly" for those sixty-five and over, "aged" for those seventy-five and older, and "very old" for those eighty-five and older. Another term used to distinguish a subgroup of the older population is the "frail elderly"— those seventy-five years and older "whose general condition interferes with functioning, as well as those over sixty who suffer chronic conditions of an incapacitating nature" (Silverstone & Burack-Weiss, 1984, p. xiii). Others use the terms "young-old" and "old-old" to describe individuals at the ends of the continuum of older Americans, but it is often quite difficult to distinguish these groups by their level of activity. Many elderly remain active well into their seventies and eighties, while others begin to limit their activities much earlier, in their fifties or sixties, due to poor physical health, depression, or other problems.

The Faces of Older Americans

Although it may be difficult to decide on terminology, we can consider some of the characteristics of older Americans. This group is the fastest growing segment of the population. Today nearly 13 percent (over 33 million people) of the population is sixty-five years of age or older (see Treas, 1995). By the year 2030 it is expected that about one fifth of the population will be sixty-five years or older.[1] The U.S. population age sixty-five and older has grown quite rapidly; in the last few decades this group grew twice as fast as the rest of the population, and the segment eighty-five years and older is growing even faster. The primary reason the elderly now constitute such a large part of the population is the increase in the birth rate prior to 1920. Increased longevity is a second cause of growth among this population segment. Improvements in health care, including strides in reducing mortality rates, and recent declines in the birth rate have also contributed to the increasing portion of the U.S. population that is older.

Approximately 85 percent of the elderly population is non-Hispanic white.[2] Blacks are the largest group of minority elderly, making up 8 percent of the elderly population, followed by Hispanics at 5 percent, Asians and Pacific Islanders at 2 per-

---

[1]The remainder of this paragraph relies on Taeuber, C. M. (1983, September). America in transition: An aging society. *Current Population Reports,* Series P23, No.128, Bureau of the Census.

[2]This paragraph relies on Treas, J. (1995). Older Americans in the 1990s and beyond. *Population Bulletin 50* (1). Washington, DC: Population Reference Bureau.

cent, and Native Americans at 0.4 percent. Life span has increased dramatically since the turn of the century. Life expectancy for persons born in 1900 was 47.3; the average life expectancy for those born in 1993 is 75.5 years. Life expectancies continue to be significantly longer for women than for men and longer for whites than for many ethnic minorities. The projected life expectancy for men born in 1993 is 72.1 years compared with 78.9 years for women. For white males it is 73.0 years and for black males, 64.7 years. The figure for white women is 79.5 years and for black women, 73.7 years. Since women live longer, they constitute a greater percentage of the elderly population than men. Along with increased longevity, older Americans are feeling better than ever. Seventy-two percent of those sixty-five and over rate their health as "excellent," "very good," or "good" (Adams & Benson, 1991, p. 112).

Other facts about the elderly are also of concern to social workers. For example, although poverty among the elderly has decreased considerably in the last quarter century, it remains a concern. Approximately 12 percent of persons age sixty-five and older are poor (Bureau of the Census, 1995). Women and minorities are disproportionately represented among the poor. Poverty among elderly women is almost twice as high as for men. Poverty is also a more serious problem for ethnic minorities than for the white elderly of both genders. Poverty figures are highest among ethnic minority women; about 44 percent of all elderly black women have incomes below the poverty level. Since women outlive men, they are also more likely to be widowed and live alone. This presents special challenges to the elderly and to social service providers. For example, elderly women often find their incomes reduced considerably upon the death of their spouses, and living alone may also mean that they are less likely to enjoy the social and emotional supports they once had. As people age, their needs for health care and social services may increase, and as more people live alone, either by choice or circumstance, they are likely to require the assistance of professional social service providers in their later years.

The United States has made important strides in meeting the health and social service needs of the elderly. One reason for this is that the elderly are a very vocal group. The growing portion of the elderly population, combined with older Americans' willingness to go to the polls, have made them a powerful voting bloc. Since their numbers will continue to swell with the graying of the baby boom generation after the turn of the century, older Americans will become an even more powerful force—a group healthier, wealthier, and more vital and active than ever. America's youth-oriented culture is going to have a much different appearance.

Some Old Myths

Some people are apprehensive about growing old because of the many myths associated with aging.[3] These myths are generally easy to identify: All older people become senile and suffer from brain deterioration; older people have difficulty learning;

---

[3]This section is reprinted by permission of Waveland Press, Inc. from Lowy, L. *Social work with the aging: The challenge and promise of the later years* (2nd ed.). (Prospect Heights, IL; Waveland Press, Inc., 1985 [reissued 1991]) All rights reserved; and is based on Saul, S. (1974). *Aging—An album of people growing old*, pp. 20–25. New York: Wiley.

old age means becoming unproductive; old people lose interest in sexual activity; debilitating physical illnesses are inevitable in old age; older people are lonely; it's useless to provide therapy to older people because they can't benefit from it. Unfortunately, perpetuation of these and other myths has also contributed to age prejudice and age discrimination, and to a general devaluation of older persons in U.S. society.

Research on the realities of aging contradicts these myths. For example, although changes in the brain do take place as we grow older, severe deterioration of mental functioning is not inevitable. Most elderly people remain mentally alert throughout their lives. Likewise, most older people are in good health. Many older adults take on new activities after retirement, learning new skills and making significant contributions to their communities; others never completely retire from work. Although physical problems are more likely to occur with advancing age, severe physical deterioration is not necessarily an outcome of old age, and most physical and mental problems are treatable if they do occur. Many mental health problems associated with old age, such as depression, respond well to treatment. Sexual desire and ability do not disappear with aging. Most persons maintain sexual interest and are able to engage in satisfying sexual activity well into old age. There is no need for older people to deny their sexuality or to withdraw from sexual activity of which they are capable. In fact, should physical or emotional conditions negatively affect sexual activity, they also often respond to treatment.

Of course, an individual's psychological and physical well-being are closely related. A physically healthy individual is probably less susceptible to emotional and psychological problems, and a psychologically healthy person is probably less susceptible to physical deterioration and better able to cope with physical problems if they do occur. The number of older adults who are aging successfully continues to grow. We can go almost anywhere and see Americans with full agendas in their later years. Ronald Reagan served as president of the United States well into his seventies. Claude Pepper served as a U.S. senator into his late eighties, championing the causes of the elderly, especially through Social Security legislation. Maggie Kuhn, another older American, was dauntless in her leadership of the Gray Panthers, an organization composed largely of older social activists. Jessica Tandy won an Academy Award in her eighties, and George Burns continued his comedy career into his late nineties. As the fiscal and physical health of the elderly has improved, people have begun to look forward to their later years to fulfill many of their life's ambitions.

Services for Older Americans

Although social workers provide a number of services to the elderly, they are only one of the major providers of services to this growing segment of the population. Social workers who specialize in gerontology are generally familiar with the range of these professionals and the services and programs available to older Americans. In this section we survey these major programs and services, including social insurance, public assistance, health care, nutrition, and social services, as well as services provided through churches and private organizations, and the most important source of support of all—the family.

Social Insurance

The major social insurance programs for the elderly are Social Security retirement benefits and Medicare. In order to qualify for most social insurance benefits, recipients must have contributed to the program through taxes on their salaries or wages. Those who have not held paying jobs may qualify on the basis of taxes paid on their spouses' salaries or wages. The Social Security retirement program was the cornerstone of the Social Security Act of 1935 (also see Chapter 12). Social Security retirement benefits pay workers a sum of money each month after retirement from their jobs at age sixty-two or later. Payments are modest—usually a few hundred dollars a month—and are based on previous earnings. Those who retire at ages sixty-two to sixty-four receive lower benefits than those who retire at age sixty-five or older. For workers born in 1938 or later, the Social Security Act has been amended so that full benefits will not be available until after their sixty-fifth birthday. This change will be phased in gradually. By 2027 the retirement age will be sixty-seven for those who wish to collect full benefits.

The Social Security Act allows retirees, under certain circumstances, to receive employment earnings while still collecting full retirement benefits. In 1996, retirees sixty-two to sixty-four years of age could earn up to $8,280 and those sixty-five to sixty-nine years of age up to $11,520 without reduction of their benefits. For retirees seventy years or older, there are no earnings restrictions.

For many years, no income taxes were levied on Social Security benefits, but today, half of an individual's or couple's Social Security benefits are taxed if their gross annual income plus one half of their Social Security benefits fall between $25,000 and $34,000 for single persons or between $32,000 and $44,000 for married couples. If annual incomes for either single or married beneficiaries are above these amounts, they may be required to pay taxes on up to 85 percent of their Social Security benefits.

Social Security retirement benefits are an important source of income for many older Americans, but these payments were never intended to fully support retirees. Although steps have been taken to ensure that the Social Security program remains financially solvent into the twenty-first century, few workers today feel secure about the program. Many employees are now also covered by pension programs through their employers, and many who can afford it are also planning for retirement through optional plans at work, individual retirement accounts (IRAs), or other investments in order to insure a decent standard of living in retirement.

Many issues remain unresolved about the Social Security retirement program. Intergenerational equity is an important concern. What is a fair burden to place on current workers to support retirees? The dependency ratio—the ratio of beneficiaries to workers—is growing rapidly and will be especially burdensome when the baby boom generation (those born between 1946 and 1964) reaches retirement. Although Social Security payments to retirees now far exceed what retirees paid into the system, rates of return are being slowed so that the program will remain stable.

Another important issue is the benefits now being paid to women. When the Social Security program was established, the roles of men and women were quite different than they are today. Women were less likely to work outside the home and divorce was less common. Women were considered dependents of their spouses. Social Security is the sole or major source of income for most older women, but payments are often not sufficient to prevent poverty. Women have not been treated fairly by the Social Security system for several reasons: (1) women's wages remain lower than men's wages, resulting in lower benefits paid to women when they retire; (2) women may spend less time in the work force than men because they are more likely to carry the major responsibilities for home and children; (3) divorced women are entitled to only one half of their former husband's benefits, and only if they were married at least ten years; (4) widows generally do not qualify for benefits unless they are sixty years or older or have minor children in the home; (5) homemakers are not covered on their own unless they have been employed in a job covered by Social Security (U.S. Department of Health, Education and Welfare, 1979). The solvency and equity of the Social Security program will be reckoned with for years to come, but as more women work outside the home, and as the salaries of women increase, some gender inequities will be reduced.

In addition to gender inequities in Social Security, private pension plans have also come under criticism for sexist practices. Although men and women were paying the same rates during their working years, women's benefits at retirement were lower because of their longer life expectancies. Challenges to this practice have resulted in equalizing payments for women and men at retirement.

Medicare is also a social insurance program (see Chapter 8). It was established in 1965 under Title XVIII of the Social Security Act in order to cover many of the health care costs of older Americans. A portion of Social Security taxes are earmarked for Medicare. Under Medicare the elderly seek physician and other medical services of their choice that are paid for in large part through Medicare funds. The Medicare program makes up a large portion of the federal government's health care budget. Although Medicare pays a substantial amount of the hospital and physician costs of older Americans, it has some serious shortcomings, known as "medigaps." For example, Medicare generally does not pay for prescription drugs, for custodial nursing home care, or for eyeglasses and hearing aids. Even with Medicare coverage, many older Americans with low incomes have difficulty paying for needed medical care because of the increasing deductibles, copayments, and premiums required from program participants. Current pressures on Congress to balance the budget are likely to result in more out-of-pocket costs for Medicare recipients.

Public Assistance

Most elderly manage on their own assets and Social Security, but some are unable to do so. Those with little or no income from employment, savings, investments, or Social Security may qualify for public assistance under the Supplemental Security Income (SSI) program or through General Assistance (also see Chapter 12). SSI, primarily a federal social welfare program, is financed through general tax revenues paid by citizens to the federal government. In addition, most states supplement federal SSI payments. A person need not have paid Social Security taxes in order to receive monthly SSI checks. Elderly persons who believe they may qualify can apply at their local Social Security offices.

In some states and communities poor elderly persons may qualify for General Assistance, which is funded by state and/or local governments with no federal government involvement. The state and local governments that choose to operate a program determine eligibility requirements and payments. There are hundreds of different General Assistance programs throughout the country, but some states and many communities do not have the program (also see Chapter 12).

Medicaid, Title XIX of the Social Security Act, another public assistance program, helps poor people obtain medical care (also see Chapter 8). It was established along with Medicare in 1965; however, Medicaid is considerably different from Medicare. Medicare is totally administered and funded through the federal government, whereas state governments administer Medicaid under guidelines established by the federal government, and both the federal and state governments finance the program. Under Medicaid, states are required to provide certain medical services with some latitude in determining what additional services will be provided and who qualifies for the program. Medicare serves virtually all those age sixty-five and over regardless of income, whereas Medicaid serves people of all ages but only if they meet the means (income and asset) test and other eligibility criteria, which are generally quite stringent. A substantial portion of Medicaid funds go to the elderly. For example, in 1993, 35 percent of all Medicaid payments went to pay for nursing home care and home health care (see Serafini, 1995), much of which was used by older persons.

There may come a time in the life of an older person when custodial care is necessary. While Medicaid provides funds for long-term care, it has an institutional bias—it primarily funds nursing home care for the poor rather than home care services. In order to receive Medicaid assistance, many older persons are forced to enter nursing homes. However, most states are experimenting with waiver programs that allow Medicaid funds to be used to purchase long-term home care. These types of initiatives help maximize choices and preserve the dignity of the elderly by allowing them to reside in the least restrictive environment. Although home care does not necessarily result in cost savings over the long run, most older Americans, their families, and policymakers favor this alternative (Weissert, Cready, & Pawelak, 1988).

Nutrition

Other social welfare programs are directed at meeting the nutritional needs of the elderly. They include the Food Stamp Program (also see Chapter 12), Meals-on-Wheels, and congregate meal programs. The Food Stamp Program is a public assistance program because people must be poor or near the poverty line to qualify. Because it is federally administered, participation requirements and payment levels are the same throughout most of the country. The program provides food coupons to needy people of all ages that can be used like money in regular grocery stores and supermarkets. Most retail food stores accept food stamps. Elderly people may also use their food stamps to purchase meals in participating restaurants, a benefit not available to younger recipients. Interestingly, many eligible older people do not receive food stamps (see Committee on Ways and Means, 1994) because they think they do not qualify (Hollonbeck & Ohls, 1984). According to the General Accounting Office (cited in Ohls & Beebout, 1993, pp. 58–60), there are also administrative barriers to participation, such as difficulty getting to Food Stamp offices to apply and lengthy application procedures; it can also be embarrassing to use food stamps at the grocery store. Electronic benefit transfer (EBT) is now making it easier and less stigmatizing to participate in the Food Stamp Program. EBT makes use of a plastic card that works like a bank debit card. Once these cards are used nationwide, the Food Stamp Program will need a new name.

Under the Meals-on-Wheels program, prepared meals are brought to the home-bound or other elderly who have difficulty cooking. The program began in 1972 as part of a federal effort to improve the nutrition of the elderly. States receive federal funding for the program, and local agencies take responsibility for preparing and de-livering meals. Meals can be paid for with food stamps, and a donation is suggested for those who can afford to pay something for their meals. In addition to improved nutrition, the program has other important benefits. There is personal contact with staff or volunteers who deliver the meals, and this can provide an opportunity for identification of other social service or medical needs of elderly people.

Congregate meal programs are located at one or more sites in a community, of-ten senior citizen centers or churches. Senior citizen centers offer many activities, but meals are the major attraction for many older people. Similar to Meals-on-Wheels, congregate meal programs provide social contact and can help identify other needs of participants. Donations are also requested from those who can afford the nominal costs of the meals. A major source of funds for these nutrition programs is the Older Americans Act along with assistance from the U.S. Department of Agriculture. The Older Americans Act also provides supportive services such as shopping assistance and nutrition education.

Social Services

In addition to financial, medical, and nutritional programs, a number of other services are available to the elderly. Many of these services are supported at least in part through the Older Americans Act (OAA), originally passed in 1965. The act has ten goals:

1. an adequate income in retirement in accordance with the U.S. standard of living;
2. the best possible physical and mental health that science can make available without regard to economic status;
3. suitable housing that is independently selected, designed, and located, with ref-erence to special needs and available at costs older citizens can afford;
4. full restorative services for those who require institutional care;
5. opportunity for employment with no discriminatory personnel practices because of age;
6. retirement in health, honor, and dignity—after years of contribution to the econ-omy;
7. pursuit of meaningful activity within the widest range of civic, cultural, and rec-reational opportunities;
8. efficient community services, including access to low-cost transportation, which provide a choice in supported living arrangements and social assistance;

9. immediate benefit from proven research knowledge that can sustain and improve health and happiness;
10. freedom, independence, and the free exercise of individual initiative in planning and managing one's own life.

These are lofty intentions that the United States has only begun to meet. In order to qualify for services under the OAA, a person must be at least sixty years old. Income is not always the criterion for eligibility, but the poor are of special concern.

The OAA created an "aging network" to express the concerns of older Americans.[4] The network operates at the federal, regional, state, and local levels. At the federal level is the Administration on Aging (AoA), which is part of the Department of Health and Human Services. In addition to its advocacy function for older Americans, the AoA coordinates all federally operated programs for the aged. It also provides technical assistance to state and local governments to help them develop and implement services for elderly persons, conducts evaluations of programs and research on aging, and acts as a national clearinghouse on information about the elderly. To assist in its efforts, the AoA has ten regional offices across the United States. Another important federal entity is The National Institute on Aging, with its focus on gerontological research.

At the state level, the aging network is generally found in the state's human services or welfare department, under an aging program office. The state offices assist in implementing federal policies and act as advocates for elderly citizens. They make the needs and problems of the aged known to the AoA and also to their own state legislatures, which make decisions on the funding and administration of state aging programs.

Most social services for the elderly are provided at the local level. Approximately 700 Area Agencies on Aging (AAAs) are located in communities throughout the country. Each AAA is guided by an advisory council composed primarily of older persons. The AAAs perform their advocacy function by assessing the needs of the elderly in their communities and making these needs known to the community at large. AAAs also distribute funds to community agencies that deliver services directly to the aged. Among the services provided are nutrition programs, senior centers, information and referral, transportation, homemaker and chore services, legal counseling, escort services, home repair and renovation, home health aid, shopping assistance, friendly visitation, and telephone assurance to check on the well-being of elderly individuals.

The OAA and the aging network are important adjuncts to the major cash, medical, and nutritional programs for America's elderly. These social services provide important links for the elderly with the community in order to meet the OAA's goals of increasing independence and integrating older individuals in mainstream American life. In addition to these federal, state, and local entities, there are other components

---

[4]The remainder of this section relies on Getze, L. H. (1981, March). Need Help? What the aging network can do for you. *Modern Maturity*, 33–36. Also see Torres-Gil, F. M. (1992). *The new aging: Politics and change in America* (Chapter 2). New York: Auburn House.

of the aging services network. The AoA oversees four national centers on long-term care. The centers have broad concerns that include the development of better models of service for older people as well as the provision of technical assistance and training for service providers.

The National Association of State Units on Aging (NASUA) provides technical assistance and training to state aging authorities, and the National Association of Area Agencies on Aging (N4A) provides technical assistance and training to the AAAs. These organizations are also concerned with social policy, advocacy, and research. Figure 11-1 provides a diagram of the relationships among the organizations dedicated to improving the lives of older people. In order to improve the policies and programs for older Americans, there have been White House Conferences on Aging in 1961, 1971, 1981, and 1995.

Private Agencies

Many of the services discussed thus far are provided by public and private nonprofit (voluntary) agencies. Other groups, such as churches and church-affiliated social services agencies, also provide services to the elderly, and the private for-profit (proprietary) sector offers assistance at market rates to those who can afford to pay. Proprietary agencies have long been in the business of providing services such as nursing home care. The advent of Medicaid and Medicare increased the number of people who could purchase services from proprietary organizations. As a result, the number of health care providers, including nursing homes, has risen substantially.

Among the services for senior citizens that can be purchased from voluntary and proprietary organizations are day care, respite care, and case management. Senior day care is supervised activity during the day for elderly people who reside with their families, in foster care, in boarding homes, or in group homes. Activities generally include socialization, recreation, orientation, and reminiscence groups. Respite care allows caretaker families to leave the elderly member under supervision for an hour or longer as the need arises. This allows caretakers to go shopping, take a vacation, or pursue other activities. Case management or care management services are growing in importance to the frail elderly and their families. Social workers act as case managers to assess personal care and other service needs and to ensure that their frail elderly clients receive these services as effectively and efficiently as possible. Case management is also helpful to adult children whose other responsibilities or distance from their parents prevent them from assisting with medical appointments and other activities.

Services Provided by Families

The missing link in diagrams of the aging services network is the family. The major source of help for the elderly, including the frail elderly, is family members. Less than 5 percent of the elderly population resides in nursing homes at any given time (Price, Rimkunas, & O'Shaughnessy, 1990, cited in Committee on Ways and Means, 1994, p. 889). The vast majority of elderly people live alone or with other family members.

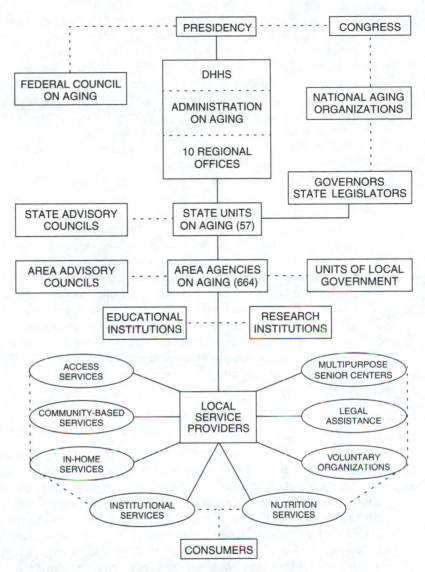

FIGURE 11-1   Older Americans Act Network

Source: F. Torres-Gil, THE NEW AGING (Auburn House, an imprint of Greenwood Publishing Group, Inc., Westport, CT, 1991), p. 56. Copyright © 1991 by Fernando M. Torres-Gil. Reprinted with permission.

Illustration prepared by Brian Louis Lipshy, based on the National Association of State Units on Aging, 1985.

Most home care for the elderly (perhaps more than 70 percent) is provided by family, friends, and other unpaid caregivers (Committee on Ways and Means, 1993; Oster-kamp, 1988). About 75 percent of informal caregivers are wives and daughters of the person in need, and 35 percent are elderly themselves (Committee on Ways and

Means, 1993; Pepper Commission, 1990; Stone, Cafferata, & Sangl, 1987). But caregivers "may reduce their work hours, take time off without pay, or quit jobs because of elder care responsibilities" (Pepper Commission, p. 94).

Social workers are quite aware of the important role families play in the lives of elderly members, and they work to increase the availability of services that supplement and support the efforts of these natural helping networks. Respite services can be especially important in helping families care for older members, as can personal care services such as helping the older person bathe.

Social workers also help older people and their families in deciding whether the older family member should be cared for at home or in a retirement community, a nursing home, or other facility. These decisions are often difficult ones, and family members may benefit from professional assistance in weighing the benefits and burdens of the alternatives.

An increasing number of families are becoming part of the "sandwich generation." This term refers to those who are providing care to their children and to their own parents. For example, a couple in their forties or fifties may be raising teenage children, providing assistance to their own parents who are in their seventies or eighties, and holding down jobs. In other cases the children of the elderly are elderly themselves. As the life span has increased, it is not unusual to see individuals in their sixties or seventies concerned about their own health and future and also concerned about parents in their eighties or nineties. The stress can be substantial, and the need to provide relief to both the elderly and their caretaker children is becoming apparent to many more people.

Models of Service

Tobin and Toseland (1990) state that the types of services each elderly client needs depend on the client's level of impairment and the amount of help already available.[5] Two elderly clients with similar levels of impairment may require different types of services depending on existing resources. One may be placed in a nursing home because no family member is willing or able to care for the individual at home, while the other who lives with family members may require the services of a home health aide a few times a week to assist with bathing and other personal care. Although there is no single way to classify services for the elderly, the schema shown in Table 11-1 suggest that services should be based on both the degree of impairment and the setting in which the service is offered. Generally, the social worker's job is to determine the resources already available to the elderly client and then to identify the least restrictive types of services that will address the client's current needs.

Tobin and Toseland also discuss a number of policy issues to be addressed in designing comprehensive service models for the older population. They begin by asking three questions:

[5]This section from *Handbook of Gerontological Services,* 2nd edition by Abraham Monk. Copyright © 1990 by Columbia University Press. Reprinted with permission of the publisher.

**TABLE 11-1   A Classification of Services for Older Persons
(Focus of Service Delivery)**

Degree of Impairment	Community-Based	Home-Based	Congregate Residential and Institutional Based
Minimal	Adult education Senior centers Voluntary organizations Congregate dining programs Individual and family information and referral, advice, and counseling	Home repair services Home equity conversion Share-a-home Transportation Telephone reassurance	Retirement communities Senior housing Congregate residential Housing with meals
Moderate	Multipurpose senior centers Community mental health centers Outpatient health services Case management systems (social/health maintenance organizations, etc.)	Foster family care Homemaker Meals-on-Wheels Case management for family caregivers and elderly impaired members	Group homes Sheltered residential facilities Board and care (domiciliary care) facilities Respite care
Severe	Medical day care Psychiatric day care Alzheimers family groups	Home health care Protective services Hospital care at home	Acute hospitals Mental hospitals Intermediate (health related) nursing facilities Skilled nursing facilities Hospice care in a facility

Source: From *Handbook of Gerontological Services,* 2nd edition by Abraham Monk. Copyright © 1990 by Columbia University Press. Reprinted with permission of the publisher.

- For whom should the services be designed?
- What services should be offered?
- How should services be delivered?

For Whom Should Services Be Designed?

Many programs have eligibility requirements based on age. This seemed reasonable at the time they were established because poverty statistics indicated that the elderly were an especially disadvantaged group. For example, in 1959, 35 percent of those sixty-five years and older met official poverty guidelines. However, the picture in 1994 was considerably different; 12 percent of individuals in this age bracket met official poverty guidelines—a 66 percent reduction in poverty among this age group. This change has led to recommendations that financial need (means testing) rather than age be a primary eligibility criterion in social service programs. There are arguments on both sides of the issue. An age-based policy may be easier to administer because age is easier to determine than financial eligibility, and it would provide a more universal approach that reduces stigma. On the other hand, a means test would be more efficient in reaching those in greatest financial need of assistance. In using a means test, a determination must be made concerning the types of income and assets to consider in assessing eligibility. Another concern about using financial need criteria is how to focus attention on preventing problems among potentially vulnerable elderly who may later develop serious problems. These issues only touch the surface of policymakers' problems as they try to decide for whom services should be designed.

What Services Should Be Offered?

Theoretically the list of services is endless, but given limited resources, some system of rationing or deciding which services and how much of these services to provide is necessary. Estimates must be made to determine which services are needed by a large number of people and which are needed by smaller numbers of people. For example, the capacity of meal programs should probably be larger than the capacity of nursing homes, because nutrition services are likely to be needed by a larger segment of the elderly population than residential care.

How Should Services Be Delivered?

Case or care management (also discussed in Chapters 6 and 9) is one approach to the comprehensive delivery of services, but Tobin and Toseland argue that no community-based case management system can control the services provided by institutions or other providers, since they are often administered under different auspices from the case management system. A truly comprehensive and integrated service delivery system for older Americans would be nearly impossible to achieve given the current fragmented nature of the service delivery system.

The Graying Concerns of Social Work

Gerontology is among the fastest growing areas of social work practice, but it is difficult to ascertain the number of social workers who practice in this area. According to the National Association of Social Workers (NASW), 4.6 percent of members responding to its 1994 membership survey reported aging services as their primary practice area and 5.3 percent as their secondary practice area (Ginsberg, 1995, p. 368). Although these figures may seem small, many social workers who do not identify themselves as gerontological social workers are employed in practice settings that provide considerable amounts of service to older persons and their families. For example, 18.9 percent of respondents to the 1994 NASW membership survey reported hospitals as their primary practice setting, and 16.7 percent reported medical clinics as their primary practice setting (Ginsberg, p. 368). Both of these settings typically provide services to many older adults.

Social work educators are also attempting to meet the needs of the growing elderly population. The Council on Social Work Education (CSWE) has conducted studies of the gerontological content of baccalaureate, master's, and doctoral social work education programs and has published several reports on gerontological education (see Greene, 1988; Levine, 1984; Nelson & Schneider, 1984; Schneider, 1984; Schneider & Kropf, 1989a & b). In 1981 CSWE formed the National Committee for Gerontology in Social Work Education. In 1983, CSWE received a grant from the AoA to "expand and strengthen the capabilities of social work faculty and programs to prepare students at the baccalaureate and master's levels for practice with an increasingly large aged population" (Nelson & Schneider, 1984, p. 1). In 1994, 44 percent of the MSW programs accredited by the CSWE (1995) offered a concentration or specialization in gerontology.

Principles of Social Work Practice with the Elderly

The following guidelines are adapted from an article by Abraham Monk that appeared in a special volume of *Social Work* on conceptual frameworks for social work practice.[6] Consistent with the values of the profession, Monk articulated the following goals, principles, and objectives of social work practice with older people.

1. *Help people enlarge their competence and increase their problem-solving and coping abilities.*

   a. Old age is a distinct phase of the life cycle with its own intrinsic value.
   b. Each older person is an individual with his or her own set of coping skills and his or her own potentials to be realized.
   c. The strengths of the older person should be maximized at every opportunity, regardless of the severity of the individual's condition.
   d. Treatment objectives should realistically reflect the abilities of the individual, recognizing that all improvements, large or small, are important.
   e. Personal integrity should always be maximized.

2. *Help people obtain resources.*

   a. Do everything possible to help clients obtain services while preserving the client's pride and dignity.
   b. Utilize case management skills to assure that the client receives all needed services for as long as necessary in the most effective and efficient manner.
   c. Guard against becoming overprotective of clients by maximizing the client's independence through preservation of his or her lifestyle and preferences.

3. *Make organizations responsive to people and influence interactions between organizations and institutions.*

[6]Monk, A. (1981). Social work with the aged: Principles of practice. *Social Work 26*(1), 61–68. Copyright 1981, National Association of Social Workers, Inc. Reprinted with permission. Italicized information is taken verbatim and other information is paraphrased from the author's work.

a. As the number of older people increases, social workers must assume more responsibility for assuring that agency services are designed to address their problems, such as personal losses, mental and physical limitations, and obstacles in utilizing services.

b. Services will be most helpful to elderly individuals if they are designed to reduce stress and feelings of helplessness.

c. Clients' sense of mastery should be maximized by providing service options that are easily accessed, for example, through the geographic centralization of services.

d. Clients' options can be maximized by providing services in both age-integrated and age-segregated settings and allowing the client to choose between them. When service options are limited, social workers should take care to prepare the client for what is to transpire.

4. *Facilitate interaction between older persons and others in their environment.*

a. Because older persons are likely to experience more deaths of friends and associates, social workers should be particularly sensitive to helping them cope with losses.

b. Social workers should be adept at helping clients socialize and resocialize as a means of coping with bereavement.

c. Social workers should facilitate mutually beneficial interactions between members of different generations.

d. As changes in family composition occur, social workers can help clients redefine family life in meaningful ways.

e. Social workers can strive to help clients live in their environment of choice as long as possible by providing services that support this goal; and if this goal can no longer be achieved, social workers should make all efforts to prepare the client for the transition to residential care.

5. *Influence social and environmental policy.*

a. The increased availability of services for the aged should not delude us into thinking that they are adequate. Services must be continually reassessed so that they remain relevant to older Americans.

b. Programs must be critically examined to ensure that they reflect the intent of legislation, and social workers are responsible for reassessing problems and recommending better initiatives.

c. Social workers should determine the appropriate balance of cash and in-kind provisions to best serve the needs of older persons.

d. Social workers should promote government and family responsibility by encouraging programs to help families assist their elder members. Social workers can also support self-sufficiency by promoting job opportunities and alternative living arrangements for older persons.

As you read and analyze the case of Anne Freeman in Box 11-1, think about how these principles can be applied.

BOX 11-1 Anne Freeman Was 76, Sick, and Alone

"I don't know, Mary. I suppose some people would say I wasn't accepting this real well. But—not even able to get out of bed! Me, of all people! Why, I can't even control..." Miss Freeman's voice trailed off, and she lay quietly, looking out of the window of her stone cabin in the California hills. Miss Anne Freeman was seventy-six and for the last twenty-five years she had lived alone in this modest cabin, without hot water, without a refrigerator, washing machine, or even a telephone. She had had a spectacular view, her painting and her needlework, and most important, she had had her privacy. Now her own body was revolting against her. She was about to lose everything, the cabin, the hills, and her privacy.

Ms. Mary Sanders, the woman to whom Miss Freeman had been talking, was a social worker with almost forty years of professional experience. From their first meeting, Miss Freeman had insisted on calling her "Mary"; she seemed to pretend that "Mary's" visits were completely social and had nothing to do with her professional capacity. Ms. Sanders certainly hadn't objected; many of her clients called her by her first name, and Ms. Sanders was close enough to Miss Freeman's age that she could imagine some of what she was going through.

Besides, in at least one way, her visits no longer had much to do with her professional capacity. Ms. Sanders worked for the Regional Domiciliary Care Service, and for thirty-three years she had tried to do everything she could to make it possible for elderly people to stay in their homes. That was why she had originally come to see Miss Freeman. But this time it would have to be a losing effort. Miss Freeman needed too much care; the family couldn't provide it, and she had only a small pension coming in. She would be forced to go into a home, and she would see that for herself before much longer. When the time came, Ms. Sanders knew, the problem wouldn't be in convincing her to go but in helping her to maintain her pride and her dignity.

Ms. Sanders had noted that Miss Freeman hadn't been able to finish her last sentence. She hadn't been able to say out loud that she was losing control of her own bowels. Her chronic diarrhea and the loss of control were being caused by a fisula, for which nothing could be done. She also suffered urinary incontinence because of a vesicovaginal fistula. In the past two months, she had required three transfusions to treat her anemia. All of these problems were related to a cancer of the uterus which had been originally diagnosed six years before. Miss Freeman had received radiotherapy then, and the doctors were not now sure of the state of the cancer, but Miss Freeman realized that the prognosis for the long term couldn't be good. She was ready—perhaps too ready—to die, but this wasn't the death she would have chosen. She could endure the pain, which would be considerable, but this was so debilitating, so humiliating, and it made her so utterly dependent on others.

When Ms. Sanders had first met her, Miss Freeman hadn't wanted to depend on anyone. She had asked her niece to contact the Domiciliary Care Service because she was having trouble getting on and off the toilet and in and out of chairs by herself. She had heard that the service could provide, as she put it, "some sort of chair blocks and toilet raisers, or something—sounds like block and tackles, or something to lift furniture to me—but if it'll help me to get around my place, I'll take 'em!" Ms. Sanders had made sure that Miss Freeman got what she needed, and, at the time, that kind of help with the cottage had been all she had needed.

Soon, however, Miss Freeman was receiving other help. She reluctantly agreed, at the urging of her niece, to accept Meals-on-Wheels. "I can cook well enough, I suppose," she had said, "but it is kind of hard when you don't have a refrigerator. I can't walk into town to shop every day, like I used to." She often ended up feeding the meals to the birds—they were "tasteless"

continued

she said—and living off of the pastries and cookies her niece brought her, along with some fresh fruit.

This niece, Mrs. Joanna Perry, had been Miss Freeman's primary emotional support for some time. She had visited her daily for years, and her sons helped with chores. Since Miss Freeman's last series of medical setbacks, Mrs. Perry had been forced to do more and more for her aunt. When Miss Freeman finally reached a point where she could no longer get herself out of bed in the mornings, she refused an offer from a volunteer nursing agency to send someone to help her every morning; she insisted that her niece drive out from town each morning, get her up for the day, and cook her breakfast, all before she had to return home to get her four sons off to school and herself off to work. Mrs. Perry had also begun to do all of her aunt's washing.

Despite all her niece did for her, Miss Freeman showed little affection toward her. She seemed to view the help her niece offered as her "due"; she had raised her niece's father and their other three younger brothers after their parents had died when she was fifteen. She had stayed at home and not gone to art school. To her, her niece's help was like having a loan paid back.

In fact, Miss Freeman hadn't generally shown much affection toward anyone. Throughout her life, she had demonstrated an independence that bordered on rudeness. There had been an unpleasant situation when Miss Freeman had decided that a Meals-on-Wheels volunteer was "prying into her private affairs." Miss Freeman had always enjoyed the remoteness of her cottage; she had few friends, and she didn't want any more than she had. Besides her niece and Ms. Sanders, the only person who had visited the cottage in years was the woman who had come up from the local craft store to collect Miss Freeman's paintings and quilts to sell. She hadn't come in months, and Miss Freeman had stopped mentioning her.

Yet despite Miss Freeman's aloofness and general independence, there were signs that she became overly demanding and overly dependent once she lost control of a situation. Ms. Sanders discovered, while talking to Mrs. Perry, that six years before, when Miss Freeman's cancer was first diagnosed, she had been given a colostomy. She was very depressed about that condition and refused to eat unless she was hand-fed by her niece. The stoma had abscessed and needed multiple dressings daily, but Miss Freeman would allow no one but her niece to do that, either.

After the colostomy had closed, Miss Freeman had resumed her normal, independent life, living in her cottage in the hills, painting and staying away from people. But now it was all coming back, the disease, the depression, the revulsion with her own body, even the growing dependence on her niece. This time it was going to be much worse. She was going to need constant care, and her niece couldn't possibly leave her job. A nursing home seemed to be the only option, and Miss Freeman seemed to be beginning to see that. Only three months ago she had refused to consider it. Two months ago she had been willing to talk about it. Last month she had applied to a local Methodist home.

"Oh, Anne will go all right," Ms. Sanders thought as she looked at the thin figure on the bed. "She won't have much choice, will she? But how do I make her feel all right about it? How do I make a woman like her see that it's okay to let other people help you? And how, in the little time that's left, do I help her to accept what's happening to her body?"

And, as Mary Sanders got up to leave, she looked at Anne Freeman once more and realized there was one more question she needed to start asking herself. "How do I deal with myself when I find out I can't make it all right for her?"

Source: This material first appeared in Schmidt, M. G., & Kinzey, R. (1984). Anne Freeman was seventy-six, sick and alone. In R. L. Schneider (Ed.) with T. Decker, J. Freeman, & C. Syran. *The integration of gerontology into social work educational curricula* (pp. 39–41). Washington, DC: Council on Social Work Education, 1984. Reprinted with the permission of the Council on Social Work Education.

Dilemmas in Working with Older Clients

Whether you are a social work student or a social worker with years of experience, questions and concerns about professional practice always arise. In the case described in Box 11-1, a seasoned social worker struggles with her ability to help an older client. If you were the social worker, how might you assess and respond to this situation? After reading the case, appraise it, using the guidelines presented in Table 11-2.

TABLE 11-2   Suggested Tasks in Analyzing Case Vignettes of Gerontological Social Work

Directions	Questions to Ask Yourself
Identify the important elements of the vignette	What are the important facts? What is happening to whom? Is all relevant information accessible?
Specify the major issues	Who is responsible for making decisions? What decisions need to be determined? What issues and consequences need to be considered?
Evaluate constraints and resources	Which forces support and oppose which actions? What are the major barriers? Which resources are available for plans/actions?
Determine objectives and goals to be achieved	Which results are possible? Which are desirable? Which objectives are most important to whom?
Evaluate the behavior of professionals and clients	Does the social worker exhibit leadership? Is the client involved in the decision making?
Assess the conflicts or professional dilemmas	Of what do the conflicts or dilemmas consist? Can conflicting plans be reconciled? Can dilemmas be resolved?
Identify alternative plans or programs	Are there plans, ideas, or programs that have not been identified? Are the alternatives mutually exclusive?
Assess the consequences of possible decisions and actions	What outcomes are likely to result from the decisions made? What are the short- and long-term consequences for the individuals and the profession? What unintended consequences might evolve?
Review appropriate strategies	What are the most effective ways of achieving the goals sought? What recommended actions seem appropriate now?

Source: Schneider, R. L. (Ed.) with T. Decker, J. Freeman, and C. Syran, (1984). *The integration of gerontology into social work educational curricula,* (p. 157). Washington, DC: Council on Social Work Education. This material was first published by the Council on Social Work Education and is reprinted here with permission.

The Makings of a Gerontological Social Worker

Lowy has identified four broad and growing areas of knowledge that social workers must master in order to be effective gerontological practitioners: biological and physiological; psychological; sociological; political-economic.[7] These areas indicate the amount and diversity of knowledge needed by social workers; they also point to the fact that gerontology is a multidisciplinary field requiring cooperation and coordination among a variety of health care and social service professionals.

Biological and physiological knowledge includes learning about the skeletal, muscular, circulatory, endocrine, respiratory, digestive, and reproductive systems as well as the senses, sexuality, and chronic illness and how all are affected by the processes of aging. This also includes learning about cognitive-sensory processes such as possible changes in vision, hearing, taste, and perception.

Psychological knowledge includes psychomotor performance and information about feelings, affect, emotions, and learning throughout the life cycle. Knowledge of personality theories, such as disengagement theory, activity theory, life satisfaction theory, and developmental theory, are particularly relevant. Each of these theories contributes to understanding the psychological adjustments that people may make as they grow older.

Developmental theories have been extensively applied in social work practice. These theories posit that tasks to be mastered change throughout the life cycle, that individuals may take different approaches to mastering life tasks, and that some individuals age more successfully than others. For example, the task of facing death is approached differently by individuals; some face their later years with a more positive outlook than others.

Other important aspects of psychological knowledge include psychiatric disorders, psychophysiological (psychosomatic) disorders, the possibility of suicide, brain syndromes, and dementias including Alzheimer's disease. Alzheimer's is "a brain disease in which cell loss is prominent; it is the most common cause of organic mental impairment in the elderly" (Brown & Onzuka-Anderson, 1985, p. 251).

Sociological knowledge presents yet another challenge. Of special significance is social role theory. Older persons often have particular concerns about their roles as spouses or as widows or widowers. They also may have concerns about their sexuality. In addition, they may find themselves depending more on their children or other relatives. Accepting the role of retiree may be difficult for some and welcomed by others. And some choose never to retire from their work. Some begin or increase participation in hobbies and volunteer activities, while others become socially withdrawn. The education of social workers can be especially helpful in assisting older persons in making role transitions and adjustments.

Political and economic knowledge is also important. Older persons are a significant voting bloc in the United States. They are especially vocal when proposals emerge to limit social insurance benefits. The American Association of Retired Per-

---

[7]Reprinted by permission of Waveland Press, Inc. This section relies on Lowy, L. (1985). *Social work with the aging: The challenge and promise of the later years,* (2nd ed., Chapter 8). (Prospect Heights, IL; Waveland Press, Inc., 1985 [reissued 1991]) All rights reserved.

sons (AARP) is a large membership organization of 33 million individuals age fifty and older who support efforts to improve the lives of senior citizens. The annual membership fee of eight dollars provides subscriptions to a magazine and a newspaper, as well as other membership benefits such as access to prescription medications at reduced cost and information on leisure, consumer affairs, and other topics of interest to members. The organization is politically active and closely follows legislation affecting members. The Gray Panthers, an advocacy organization composed of many older adults with a membership of about 45,000, has local chapters throughout the country. It has a particular concern for intergenerational issues. There are many issues on the public policy agenda for older Americans; among the most prominent are health care issues, including long-term care. Social workers are helping to address these concerns by applying their policy and advocacy skills.

Armed with all this knowledge, social workers still might not be equipped to work with older clients. Perhaps a fifth category of knowledge, called attitudinal, should be added here. This category encompasses more than knowledge; it also includes a deep appreciation of the later stages of life. Monk (1981) has commented that, "For social work practitioners, no matter how young, providing services to older people means glimpsing images and therefore anticipating their own final destiny" (p. 61).[8] He adds that while social workers often help clients with problems such as chemical dependency or unwanted pregnancies, they may never confront these problems in their own lives; aging, however, affects everyone. We expect to live long enough to experience aging, and most of us will see our parents grow old. Given our own concerns about aging, work with older people can raise feelings of discomfort and may prevent social workers from entering this area of practice. Monk also comments that work with the elderly is complicated by the fact that younger social workers may have never had a close personal relationship with an older person. America's youth-oriented society inhibits the full integration of the generations and promotes "gerontophobia." This fear results in many stereotypical beliefs about aging. Social workers, like other professionals, may harbor beliefs that the elderly are unlikely to respond to therapeutic interventions. While some aspects of practice, such as obtaining basic social history information, may be accomplished by most human service professionals, developing effective social work interventions must include a true appreciation of the later phases of life.

Assessing the Older Client

In addition to what social workers must know to assess clients in most agency settings, they also need information specific to particular client groups such as the elderly. Rosalie Kane offers some helpful information about assessing the older client.[9] Taking a social history can be complex because older persons have accumulated many life experiences and their current functioning is influenced by the interaction of numerous physical, mental, and social factors. Other difficulties are posed by com-

---

[8]The remainder of this paragraph relies on Monk, A. (1981). Social work with the aged: Principles of practice. *Social Work, 26*(1), p. 61. Copyright © 1981, National Association of Social Workers, Inc.
[9]From *Handbook of Gerontological Services,* 2nd edition by Abraham Monk. Copyright © 1990 by Columbia University Press. Reprinted with permission of the publisher.

munication problems such as hearing loss. The generation gap between social worker and client might also pose a problem. Social service assessment is made increasingly difficult when accurate medical or psychiatric diagnoses of the client are not available and when the elderly client lacks access to medical and mental health services.

Kane describes a multidimensional assessment for older clients that includes the following components: physical, emotional, environmental, self-care capacity, preferences, cognitive, social, services received, and burden on support system (see Figure 11-2). The social worker may begin by obtaining information from clients and their families about the client's physical history. During this process the worker may recognize signs that further medical evaluation is needed. For example, if the client has not seen a physician recently but is taking several prescription or nonprescription drugs and has several diagnoses, further medical assessment may be indicated.

Emotional factors are equally important. Signs of depression such as poor appetite, insomnia, and diminished sexual interest may be difficult to identify or are overlooked or dismissed because of misconceptions that these occurrences are normal in older persons. Standardized instruments may be used to help assess depression, psychological well-being, and the life satisfaction of elderly persons. In the area of cognition, assessment of intellectual and memory impairment should include the use of diagnostic instruments and social history information such as a description of the onset of the impairment and the client's usual level of functioning. Social factors include the client's contact with family, friends, and others, and the client's level of social activity. Since there is no optimum level of social contacts and activities, their adequacy should be based on what the client is used to and what contributes to the client's general satisfaction.

Environment is very important but often difficult to assess, especially by the inexperienced social worker, because few standardized approaches are available for conducting environmental assessments. Some factors to consider are the individual's feeling of safety at home and access to shopping, medical attention, social activities, and other activities necessary and important to the individual, such as church. Not to be overlooked is whether the elderly person may be the victim of physical or emotional neglect or abuse. Although some cases may be readily identified, others can be difficult to discern. For example, inadequate nutrition may be blamed on the client's depression, although there may be an alternative explanation, such as the caretaker's failure to provide adequate meals. Many states now provide a criminal penalty for failing to report elder abuse, similar to cases of child abuse.

Self-care can be assessed by considering activities of daily living (ADL) and instrumental activities of daily living (IADL). ADL are the more basic skills that include ambulation, feeding, dressing, bathing, and continence. Also considered is whether the individual can accomplish these tasks alone or requires assistance; for example, an older person may be able to feed him- or herself but may need help cutting meat. The speed with which an activity is completed should also be considered. IADL are more complex activities which support independent living and include cooking, cleaning, using the telephone and transportation, and managing money. The ability to carry out some of these activities is made easier by washing machines and clothes dryers, but some elderly lack even the basic conveniences such as indoor plumbing

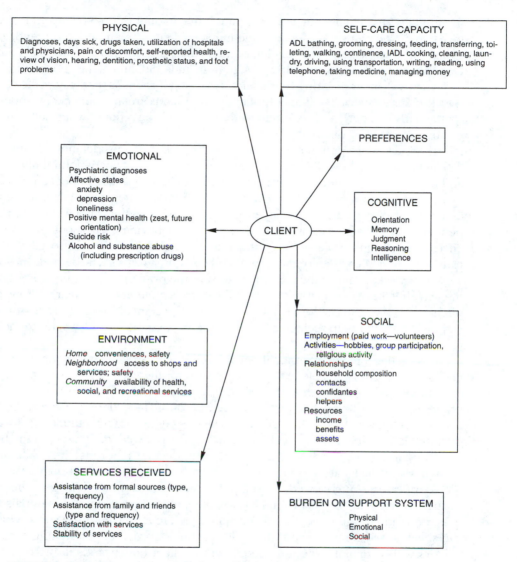

FIGURE 11-2   Components of a Multidimensional Assessment

Source: From *Handbook of Gerontological Services,* 2nd edition by Abraham Monk. Copyright © 1990 by Columbia University Press. Reprinted with permission of the publisher.

and heating. Another factor to be considered is whether the person has a history of doing the activity. A widower may have had little experience cooking or washing clothes; a widow may have never written a check.

The social worker also considers assistance the client is currently receiving on a no-charge basis from social agencies, services paid for directly by the client or through third-party insurance, services provided on a voluntary basis by family and friends, services actually needed or required, the amount of time family and friends invest in providing needed services, the number of family members and friends providing these services, and the likelihood that family and friends can and will continue to assist. Burdens on the support system include difficulties the spouse or other caretaker may incur in caring for the elderly person. Problems that may make caring for the elderly especially difficult for family and friends are incontinence, wandering (particularly at night), and refusal to move from one's own home when self-care capacities are severely diminished.

The individual's preferences are the last factor in our consideration of client assessment, but as Kane (1990) reminds us, preferences are of "paramount importance and may be the most neglected aspect of a multidimensional assessment" (p. 79). Of course, preferences of the elderly vary. For example, some prefer increased safety and security over greater independence in living, while others choose greater independence at the expense of security. However, in planning decisions, the preferences of family and professionals rather than the client often prevail. Social workers can help all involved determine how the client's preferences can be met. In doing so, social workers must take care to make sure their own preferences do not get in the way. If it is not reasonable to pursue the client's preferences in their entirety, and often this is the case by the time a social worker gets involved, the social worker's responsibility is to help seek creative ways for meeting the client's wishes to the extent possible.

In selecting a multidimensional or comprehensive assessment tool, Kane stresses choosing one that is reliable, valid, and practical for the client and assessor. In addition, the assessment tool should be suited to the population, since the elderly, like other segments of the population, are a diverse group. The Older Americans Resource and Service Center at Duke University has developed the OARS methodology to conduct multidimensional assessments of clients. OARS is a well-known tool in the field.

Good interviewing skills are important in conducting a thorough assessment. Although some clients are too impaired to provide the necessary information, when an older person is interviewed, several points should be kept in mind: gear the pace of the interview to the client's abilities; make sure the print on any materials that must be read is large enough; select a quiet, private area where the social worker can speak loudly if necessary and the client's embarrassment at discussing personal matters will be diminished; and make sure the client understands the terminology used during the interview. Depending on the client's stamina, more than one assessment session may be needed.

Primary, Secondary, and Tertiary Intervention

Beaver and Miller present social work with the elderly as involving three levels of prevention or intervention—primary, secondary, and tertiary.[10] These three levels are borrowed from the health professions. Primary intervention is synonymous with

---

[10]This section relies on Beaver, M. L., & Miller, D. (1992). *Clinical social work practice with the elderly* (2nd ed.). Belmont, CA: Wadsworth.

preventing a negative condition from occurring. Examples are promoting good dietary habits and regular health care to prevent illness, and retirement planning to prevent financial problems during the later years.

Gerontological social workers are concerned about a number of primary interventions. Information and referral services, for example, can help avert problems or help elderly people obtain assistance at the first sign of a problem. The media can be especially helpful in disseminating primary prevention information to elderly people. But in some cases, individual, personal contacts are the best method. The rural elderly are of particular concern when disseminating information because they are often more isolated and poorer than the urban elderly. Other primary prevention efforts include health promotion programs often provided at senior citizen centers and health clinics or at work; public service announcements and T.V. documentaries are also good tools for disseminating information.[11] Health problems such as diabetes, high blood pressure, alcoholism, smoking, and breast cancer have been highlighted in the media because these problems can be prevented, identified early, and/or controlled.

Crime prevention is another area of special concern to the elderly, who may virtually become trapped in their homes because they fear victimization. Although it is unclear if the elderly are more frequent targets of crime, they are aware of their susceptibility. Whether it is violent crime—being mugged for one's Social Security check—or white-collar crime—being sold worthless insurance policies or placebos to cure illnesses—the potential for victimization is real. Crime prevention projects teach elderly individuals how to defend their person and how to spot scams. Neighborhood watch programs can also add to the security of older people.

Transportation also falls under the rubric of primary prevention. It is a good feeling to know that one can get up and go to the store, to visit family, to church, to a favorite park, to the library, or elsewhere. Yet many communities, especially rural communities, lack transportation that is easily accessible to people who are older or disabled. Older drivers often find it difficult to give up the keys to the car. Some drive longer than they should, perhaps because they are not aware of their sight or hearing impairments or because there are no good alternatives to their own car.

Adequate housing is another item in the category of primary prevention. Although most older people own their own homes, the housing is not always adequate to meet their needs. A home without plumbing, heating, cooling, and hot water or one that is rodent infested is a problem for anyone, especially to the very old who are most vulnerable to illness. Safety equipment—grips in the shower and tub and rails on staircases—are also important in maintaining independence and security. There are many opportunities for meeting the primary prevention needs of older adults.

Primary intervention roles of the social worker are consultant, educator, and advocate. The social worker may provide education and consultation directly to older adults or to service providers to help them better assist older clients. In the role of

---

[11]For additional information on health, crime prevention, and other programs for the elderly, also see Gelfand, D. E. (1993). *The aging network: Programs and services.* (4th ed.). New York: Springer.

advocate, social workers may practice case advocacy, for example, by preventing a client from being evicted from his or her apartment. Social workers may also practice class advocacy, for example, by working with legislators to pass a bill expanding transportation services for older persons.

Secondary prevention is synonymous with remedial interventions aimed at preventing or stopping an existing condition from becoming worse. Optimally, these efforts occur at the earliest possible opportunity, but these services are often not sought until the problem has progressed. Marriage counseling, for example, could be helpful early in a problem relationship, but it is generally not sought until a couple has experienced significant marital problems. Beaver and Miller cite examples of bereavement that may require secondary prevention. The death of a spouse is generally followed by a grieving process. Although it may take time, most people make a satisfactory adjustment to this loss. However, when an individual remains depressed over a long period, mental health services may be the appropriate secondary intervention to relieve the problem.

Secondary intervention roles of social workers are clinician, broker, advocate, enabler, and outreach worker. Clinicians work with individuals, families, and small groups. Clinical work with individuals includes casework or therapy to relieve problems such as depression, isolation, or fear. Work with families may be directed at improving strained relationships between older adults and other family members or helping the family decide whether to care for an older member at home or make a residential placement. Group work may serve therapeutic functions such as helping isolated widows and widowers adjust to their new roles through increased socialization.

As brokers, social workers link clients with needed services. Older adults may require assistance, but not know of available services. Social workers' knowledge of community resources allows them to fill the role of broker.

In the role of advocate, social workers ensure that the rights of the elderly are upheld and not violated and that their needs are met. Ombudsmen in nursing homes are examples of advocates. Older adults may need advocacy services to help them cut through the bureaucracy in obtaining social insurance, public assistance, and other benefits.

The enabler also helps clients get needed services or work through problems. But the methods of the enabler differ from those of the advocate. The advocate obtains the service or other desired result for clients, while the enabler helps clients obtain these outcomes themselves. For example, an older person who is having a conflict with a caretaker may discuss the problem with a social worker acting in the role of enabler, explore alternatives for improving the relationship, and then approach the caretaker on his or her own to resolve the difficulty. This differs from the social worker acting as advocate who intervenes on behalf of the client and talks directly with the caretaker. The role used depends on the client's abilities, the urgency of the situation, and other factors such as the likelihood that one approach may produce a better result.

Outreach workers are usually not found at their desks because they are in the community identifying people in need, following up on calls about people in need, and using their brokering and advocacy skills to see that the needs of older adults are met. There is no lack of calls to adult protective services units of state welfare departments from concerned family, friends, neighbors, and service providers who report that an elderly person they know needs assistance. Some elderly people need assistance because they are abused or neglected by their caretaker or other person. Others are suffering from self-neglect because they are no longer willing or able to care for themselves. Outreach workers investigate these cases. Outreach workers may also be employed by other types of agencies, such as family services agencies. The job of outreach workers is often difficult because they are sent to help older adults who may not want their services or who may be incapable of making rational decisions about their need for care.

Tertiary prevention is also called rehabilitative intervention. These services are needed when a significant deterioration in the client's condition has occurred and the client cannot be restored to optimum functioning. A chronic alcoholic may have such severe brain and liver damage that little reversal of these conditions can be expected (although sobriety may prevent further deterioration). In this case, social workers' efforts may be aimed at assisting the client in maintaining sobriety and using his or her faculties to the fullest extent possible. Or a client who has recently had a stroke may regain at least partial functioning through various rehabilitation services. Since tertiary interventions address the needs that arise when disability limits effective functioning, they also often include the provision of long-term care in the older person's home, in the home of a relative, or in an institution such as a nursing home. Tertiary intervention roles of the social worker are similar to secondary intervention roles, but tertiary services are applied to more severe situations.

Social workers attempt to prevent as many problems as possible, but not all problems are preventable. We cannot stop the aging process, nor do we currently know enough about diseases such as Alzheimer's to prevent them. Many times social workers become aware of a problem only after it has reached serious proportions, as in the case of an older person who is the victim of long-term abuse or neglect by a caretaker. Beaver and Miller's discussion of primary, secondary, and tertiary intervention roles provides an opportunity for social workers to think about service delivery models that encourage intervention at the earliest possible moment and promote effective responses even in the most serious cases.

Summary

This discussion of gerontological social work has led us to consider direct practice, policy, and administrative issues that arise in serving the older population. We are not certain how many social workers currently practice in this field, but we are relatively certain that the growing numbers of elderly will bring more social workers into this specialty. The events we are now seeing in social, political, and economic systems, combined with continuing demographic shifts in the U.S. population, will have important implications for future cohorts of older persons. As we look to the future, it is likely that gerontological social workers will face a changing set of issues and challenges. For instance, the American family, as an institution, is undergoing a number of transitions in structure, composition, and functioning that have implications for the older population. The increasing number of women in the paid labor force, the trend among young adults to delay the age at which they first marry, the declining size of families, the high rate of divorce, the growing number of single-parent families, serial marriages, and blended families, all raise questions about the family's ability to continue its role as the primary care provider for the frail elderly. This concern is especially critical when we consider that the fastest growing segment of the population is those age eighty-five and older, who are most likely to need long-term care.

Another concern centers on the growing debate in the United States over the organization and financing of the health care and income maintenance systems. Congress and the state legislatures across the country are considering a variety of proposals for drastically redesigning those systems. Some of these proposals, targeted at programs such as the Social Security retirement system, Supplemental Security Income, Medicaid, Medicare, and food stamps, if implemented, will significantly affect how well a large percentage of the older population as well as the younger population will be able to satisfy health care and income needs.

Finally, another set of issues concerns changes in the older population itself. Besides the growth in numbers, future cohorts of older persons are likely to be healthier and better educated, and have higher incomes than today's older population. Even as the age to receive full Social Security retirement benefits increases, many people will continue to choose to retire at an earlier age, causing increased concern about quality of life issues among older people. Such concern will undoubtedly focus on the development of new roles for these young and healthy retirees to meet their needs as they approach many years of retirement. As the overall population also continues to grow, our society is challenged to find the economic and human resources necessary for all Americans, young and old, to enjoy a decent standard of living. To meet this challenge, our society will need to make better use of the energy, knowledge, and skills of older persons than it has in the past. We anticipate that social workers will play important roles in this process.

Suggested Readings

Atchley, R. C. (1994). *Social forces and aging* (7th ed.). Belmont, CA: Wadsworth.

Beaver, M. L., & Miller, D. (1992). *Clinical social work practice with the elderly* (2nd ed.). Belmont, CA: Wadsworth.

Gelfand, D. E. (1993). *The aging network: Programs and services* (4th ed.). New York: Springer.

Hooyman, N., & Kiyak, H. A. (1996). *Social gerontology: A multidisciplinary perspective* (4th ed.). Boston: Allyn & Bacon.

Lowy, L. (1985). *Social work with the aging: The challenge and promise of the later years* (2nd ed.). New York: Longman.

Monk, A. (1981). Social work with the aged: Principles of practice. *Social Work, 26*(1), 61–68.

Monk, A. (Ed.). (1990). *Handbook of gerontological services* (2nd ed.). New York: Columbia University.

Schneider, R. L., & Kropf, N. P. (Eds.). (1992). *Gerontological social work: Knowledge, service settings, and special populations*. Chicago: Nelson-Hall.

Torres-Gil, F. M. (1992). *The new aging: Politics and change in America*. New York: Auburn House.

12

Poverty: Improving the Quality of Life for America's Poor

Photo courtesy of Robert Harbison

The original chapter from the first edition of this book has been revised by GAYLE T. WYKLE, Social Work Program, University of Alabama at Birmingham.

Social Work with the Poor: Are Professional Skills Needed?

Social work's roots and history tell of a long tradition of concern with poor and disadvantaged groups. Today, this focus on the poor requires reinforcement because of the weakening concern within our profession in recent years with the poor *as the poor.*

Evidence of this decreased concern for the poor is all around us. Most introductory textbooks in social work do not consider working with the poor, or social work in public assistance, public welfare, income maintenance, and so forth, as a separate field of practice. Therefore, some people might question the inclusion of a chapter on poverty in this text. Other indicators of what we feel to be an unfortunate trend in the profession are found in studies which show that few members of the National Association of Social Workers (NASW)—0.6 percent in a 1992 report by Teare and Sheafor (cited in Gibelman & Schervish, p. 15), and 1.2 percent in a 1987 NASW study (pp. 7–9)—classified themselves as working in public assistance. When stacked against over 40 percent in both studies who said they worked in the combined medical and mental health fields, we have a dramatic reflection of social workers' priorities and values. Both studies also show that many social workers in public assistance are not NASW members. Perhaps something about professional identification through NASW membership works against a desire to work with the poor themselves.

Another disturbing trend has been the declassification of social work positions in programs that deal primarily with the problems of poverty. One state after another has eliminated requirements for formal social work education as a prerequisite for employment in public welfare programs such as AFDC, the Food Stamp Program, and General Assistance. Although declassification has also been a problem in other fields, such as mental health and child welfare, public welfare has been particularly hard hit in many states (NASW, Florida Chapter, 1984). There have been many contributing factors, including the separation of services from income maintenance programs, the financial crisis in public welfare, and the gradual movement of professionally trained social workers into more prestigious areas of practice. The bottom line is that finding a social worker with legitimate social work education credentials in a public welfare agency is becoming increasingly difficult. In many public welfare agencies almost any type of college degree is acceptable as appropriate education for entry-level social work positions. In still others, educational qualifications range from a high school diploma to one or two years of college.

Many of the entry-level positions for BSW graduates in poverty programs such as public assistance are not very attractive. Low pay, high caseloads, limited opportunities for using professional skills, and restricted career opportunities combine to push baccalaureate social workers into other areas of employment—or into graduate school. There may be more interesting positions in poverty programs in the private sector, but salaries are probably no better.

Some have argued that there is simply no role for the professional social worker in public assistance programs (Hoshino, 1972), but others maintain that the function and professional identification of public assistance personnel should be that of social work (Wyers, 1980). Since the 1988 Family Support Act added the requirement that public assistance departments reduce the number of people receiving AFDC and food stamps, it is more difficult to maintain that the public assistance worker's job could be defined simply as a clerical function of completing applications quickly and accurately (Lindsey, 1993, p. 37). Eligibility workers must now have skills necessary to identify whether clients are ready for work or will need training or education.

Eligibility workers are not case managers, but they do need relationship, listening, and empathy skills. Their job is to identify obstacles to using services, to make appropriate referrals, and to motivate clients to follow through with their plans. In Georgia, where interpersonal skills instruction has been included in training new workers, "supervisors and newly hired caseworkers had surprisingly positive attitudes about the relevance of casework skills for the public assistance interview" (Lindsey, p. 41). They also found clients to be extremely positive when asked about their newly trained workers' conduct of interviews.

The skills needed to perform such intervention to the client's benefit cannot be learned on the job. With the proliferation of baccalaureate social work degree programs throughout the nation, we now have an opportunity to establish a link between the profession and the income maintenance function.

Emerging Dilemma: Individual versus System Level of Intervention

The traditional concern of social work with the problems of poverty in the United States dates back at least to the beginnings of the Charity Organization Society (COS) movement in the nineteenth century. These societies developed at a time when rapid industrialization and urbanization brought great upheaval and many significant changes to our way of life. Most European immigrants settled in the cities but were unable to find jobs. Unemployment was also a problem for many persons who migrated from rural to urban areas. As a result poverty became rampant in many American cities.

In order to conserve and to distribute efficiently the badly strained resources of local government and private agencies, the COS developed a plan for investigating requests for assistance, maintaining files to avoid duplication of services, and referring the poor to appropriate agencies for help. In most cases after an evaluation was conducted by a COS staff member, a volunteer was assigned as a "friendly visitor" to the family applying for aid. This system exhorted the poor to become better parents, to improve their moral standards, and to shift their aspirations to conform to middle-class norms. There has always been some uneasiness within the profession because of the condescending, sometimes punitive, nature of these early efforts. As early as 1893, Robert Treat Paine wrote the following critique of the COS movement:

> *Has not the new charity organization movement too long been content to aim at . . . single cases without asking if there are not . . .[systemic] causes permanently at work to create want, vice, crime, disease and death . . .?*
>
> *If such [systemic] causes of pauperism exist, how vain to waste our energies on single cases of relief. . .(cited in Pumphrey and Pumphrey, 1969, p. 230).*

Despite its moralizing and patronizing approach, the emerging COS of the late nineteenth century clearly established a social work tradition of working with the poor, and there was a strong feeling among some early social workers that social system reform, not casework with individuals, was the key to alleviating poverty. In contemporary terms, the debate would be framed as whether to intervene at the individual versus the system level to eliminate the causes of poverty. Consequently, Congress continues to wrestle with the same question of blaming the system or individuals for their poverty. Social workers employed in public assistance have a responsibility not only to administer existing policies, but also to use social work skills to inform legislators and assist clients through individual advocacy, community organizing, and political activity. To begin with, social workers need to make clear what life circumstances the poor can realistically be expected to control in order to get out of poverty and what conditions the system presents that individuals cannot control. Blaming individuals for what they cannot control serves no productive purpose.

In 1899 the first treatise on working with the poor, *Friendly Visiting among the Poor,* was published by COS worker Mary Richmond (NASW, 1987, p. 937). Eighteen years later she published the first textbook on social casework. This text, *Social Diagnosis,* used Freudian theory as its model of human behavior, and it became the cornerstone of family welfare practice in the early twentieth century. By this time, the profession's concern with working with the poor as a dominant field of practice was firmly in place.

Challenge to Social Work: Meeting Financial Needs of the Poor

The economic crash of 1929 proved to almost everyone that local governments and private charities could not handle the demands for relief (Wenocur & Reisch, 1989, pp. 156–164). The Social Security Act of 1935 contained two major provisions: social insurance and public assistance. The social insurance provisions were intended to prevent poverty by providing certain programs for workers and their dependents. These programs do indeed affect large numbers of poor persons, but we will not consider them here because they were not designed primarily to deal with the *consequences* of poverty. The public assistance provisions were directed at those who had no stable employment and included three major income maintenance programs: Old Age Assistance (OAA), Aid to the Blind (AB), and Aid to Dependent Children (ADC). Each of these programs was administered by state governments through a federal grant-in-aid to state welfare departments. Because the states, not the federal government, administered income assistance to the poor in these three federally authorized programs, eligibility requirements and payment levels were considerably different from state to state. A person or family who qualified for assistance in one state might be declared ineligible in another state.

In 1950, the Aid to the Permanently and Totally Disabled (APTD) program was added to the other public assistance categories. In 1972, OAA, AB, and APTD were merged by the *federal* government to form Supplemental Security Income (SSI). SSI, a federal program, now provides a basic income to poor persons who are aged, blind, or otherwise disabled, regardless of their geographic residence. Though distinctly separate from the other Social Security programs, SSI is administered by the Social Security Administration. States may supplement the federal SSI payments if they wish. The name of the Aid to Dependent Children program was changed to Aid to Families with Dependent Children in 1962. Known as AFDC, it continues to be financed by both the federal and state governments and administered by the states. Rather than having one AFDC program, there are really fifty AFDC programs—one for each state.

Voucher programs such as food stamps, school lunch/breakfast, and Medicaid have been added to the list of public assistance programs. Although these programs do not provide direct cash assistance to the poor, they are a form of income maintenance. Medicaid, with expenditures exceeding all other public assistance programs, is legitimately viewed as a "poverty program," but it is considered in Chapter 8, because it overlaps with other health care programs. Table 12-1 compares the major public assistance programs. For a profile of who these programs help, see Box 12-1.

Because some poor people do not meet the criteria for AFDC, SSI, or any other major federal-state welfare program, some states or communities have established another category of aid called General Assistance. It may be called "county aid" or "county welfare" in some communities. The rules of eligibility and administration vary greatly from one state or community to the next, but General Assistance is often available only for emergency or short-term relief.

Despite the massive intervention of the federal-state income maintenance programs, private charities continue to provide emergency relief to poor families, especially to those who fall between the cracks of public assistance programs. In addition to housing programs, which are discussed later in this chapter, AFDC, SSI, the Food Stamp Program, General Assistance, and private relief efforts are the major programs available within the context of social work with the poor.

TABLE 12-1   Major Public Assistance Programs, Expenditures, and Beneficiaries, 1992

Program	Expenditures (Billions)	Beneficiaries (Millions)
AFDC	$24.9	13.7
SSI	22.8	5.6
Food Stamps	24.9	26.9
General Assistance	3.3	1.2
Medicaid	90.8	30.9
School Lunch/Breakfast	4.1	24.5

Note. Adapted from Table No. 577, in U.S. Bureau of the Census, 1994, *Statistical abstract of the United States 1994* (114th ed.), p. 373.

BOX 12-1   Who Are the Poor?

Both poverty and homelessness are episodic, not permanent, states for most people, with half of all poverty spells lasting about four months (Wagner, 1994, p. 720). About 36.9 million people experienced poverty in 1992 (Bureau of the Census, 1993). Approximately 23 percent of the population used one of the major government aid programs. Although poverty is episodic, children and the elderly who fell into poverty were much less likely than others to climb out of those circumstances (Masumura & Ryscavage, 1994, p. 25; Shea, 1995, p. 2). Children under age eighteen were almost 22 percent of the poor in 1992, and persons over sixty-five were about 13 percent of the poor. One third of the poor were black; 29 percent were Hispanic, and just under 12 percent were white. Female-headed households were more than five times as likely to be poor as married couples and their children. Over 40 percent of the poor in 1992 worked, and 9.2 percent worked in year-round, full-time jobs (Bureau of the Census, 1993).

AFDC: Helping Poor Families Stay Together

Americans lack a national consensus about the objectives of the AFDC program. AFDC was preceded by state programs designed to assist children whose fathers were deceased. Gradually some states added provisions to aid children whose fathers were disabled or absent because of divorce or desertion (DiNitto, 1995, pp. 168–169). Most of these early programs were known as "mothers' pensions" or "mothers' aid." The federal ADC program was originally conceived as a short-term method of assisting financially needy children. Families that had an able-bodied father residing at home were not eligible for these benefits, even if the father was unemployed or underemployed. This rule led to quite a bit of criticism that the program contributed to the desertion of fathers from families. In 1961 a new component, called the Unemployed Parent (UP) provision, was added to the program. This provision made it possible for families to receive assistance if an *able-bodied unemployed* father resided at home. Unfortunately, only half the states adopted the UP provision, and in those states strict eligibility requirements kept the number of unemployed fathers receiving aid quite small. The Family Support Act of 1988 now requires all states to provide AFDC payments to two-parent families for at least six months a year, but the number of fathers in the program remains small.

Americans' strong attachment to the work ethic and our concern with the morality of welfare recipients were reflected in "man-in-the-house rules" for AFDC eligibility. The possibility of welfare mothers allowing able-bodied men who were *not* their husbands to reside with them and their children led a number of states to conduct midnight raids. Any able-bodied adult male found residing with the family was considered to be responsible for their support, and the family's AFDC benefits were terminated. In 1968 the U.S. Supreme Court decided that midnight raids and man-in-the-house rules could not be used to "flatly deny" public assistance benefits to children.

The emphasis has since shifted to making children's legal fathers and mothers contribute to their financial support. Federal law was amended in 1974 to allow the enforcement of child support obligations by absent parents by locating parents (primarily fathers), establishing paternity, and obtaining support payments. Support for child support enforcement was so strong in Congress that in 1984 tough new measures that make it more difficult for parents to avoid paying support passed both the House and Senate unanimously. Even so, the *majority* of absent parents still are not contributing to their children's financial support. This may be due partly to the rising number of children dependent on AFDC born to parents who are not legally married. Establishing paternity is one of the greatest obstacles to obtaining child support.

In 1962 amendments were added to AFDC and other public assistance programs as a means of "rehabilitating" the poor. These amendments provided services such as counseling, vocational training, child-management training, and family planning services. Because there were not enough trained social workers to provide these services, Congress also provided generous funding to universities to train social workers. During the mid-1960s, stipends for graduate social work training were relatively easy to obtain. Professional organizations such as NASW convinced Congress that by training enough professional social workers, the welfare rolls could be reduced. By the late 1960s it became obvious that both the number of trained social workers and the number of welfare clients were increasing, and most of the training funds were withdrawn.

As enthusiasm for the rehabilitation approach waned, new amendments added in 1967 contained both carrot-and-stick approaches to reducing the number of welfare clients (Lynn, 1977, p. 74). The Work Incentive Now (WIN) program was established to train AFDC parents for work and to help them locate employment. WIN was originally called the Work Incentive Program, but its acronym, WIP, made it the butt of many jokes and unkind remarks. Under the 1967 amendments the federal government could deny matching funds to states that paid benefits to able-bodied recipients who refused to work or take advantage of job training.

Also in 1967 Congress apparently recognized that not all poor families need rehabilitative social services. Until that time the AFDC caseworker was responsible for ensuring that the family received both its benefit check and its social services. The 1967 amendments resulted in the separation of payments and services. One worker would be responsible for all matters related to the distribution of assistance checks, and another would be responsible for obtaining social services for the family. This amendment was directed at a common feeling among AFDC families that they must accept many services as a condition of receiving financial assistance. It was also a recognition that services had done nothing to reduce the welfare rolls. It was no surprise that the number of clients who continued to request services after 1967 fell dramatically in some communities (Piliavin & Gross, 1977).

The WIN program survived for over two decades, until the Reagan administration attempted to replace it with "workfare"—mandatory employment in return for welfare assistance. Federal law allowed the states to operate workfare programs, but few had done more than test workfare on an experimental basis. Some believe that this approach will reduce the numbers of clients and the costs of welfare by improving job skills and discouraging malingering. Opponents point out that the number of malingerers is already negligible, and that welfare recipients who can, would gladly take decent jobs if they were available (Goodwin, 1981). One of the strongest disincentives for AFDC clients taking low-paying jobs is the possible loss of medical benefits under Medicaid, for which all AFDC recipients automatically qualify. Taking a minimum-wage job with no fringe benefits is simply not an incentive for an AFDC recipient whose total income from AFDC, food stamps, Medicaid, and subsidized housing may far exceed any potential earnings from full-time employment. Since 1990, the Family Support Act of 1988 has allowed AFDC families to retain their Medicaid coverage and child care assistance for up to one year after going to work. However, it also requires mandatory training and community service programs for AFDC families, prompting some of its critics to call the new provisions "slavefare" rather than "workfare" (Welfare law altered, 1988).

Designing Programs to Make Housing Affordable to the Poor

Ask most people to list what they believe to be our most basic human needs, and the top three items are likely to be food, clothing, and shelter (Maslow, 1962). Indeed, income and housing are inextricably related. In the Housing Act of 1949, the U.S. Congress acknowledged the need for a "decent home and suitable living environment for every American family." The 1990 Cranston-Gonzalez National Affordable Housing Act reaffirmed the goal that "every American be able to afford a decent home in a suitable environment" (U.S. Department of Housing and Urban Development [HUD], 1994c, p. 1). Despite this promise, almost 30 percent of all households in 1991 had housing problems. Housing problems were much more likely to be experienced by renters than owners, and the lower the income the greater the likelihood of problems. In 1994, in addition to the 98.7 million households who had a place to live in one of the nation's 111 million housing units, the most careful counts placed the number of homeless between a quarter and three quarters of a million (Callis, 1995, p. 6; Grall, 1994, p. 2; HUD, 1994c, pp. 3, 41).

According to the American Housing Survey (AHS), there were 13.2 million very low income renters eligible for federal rental assistance programs in 1991. However, only one quarter of this population lived in public or assisted housing. Another 8.5 million faced crowded or physically inadequate housing or paid a significant portion of their income for rent and utilities (HUD, 1994c, Foreword). The Center on Budget and Policy Priorities reports that "46 percent of poor renter households nationwide spent at least 70 percent of income on housing in 1987" (Hou & Lazere, 1991, p. xiii) and that in thirty-nine of forty-four metropolitan areas studied, housing costs exceeded the entire grant received by AFDC families (Gugliotta, 1992, p. A7).

Household income did not keep pace with the 9 percent increase in average rents between 1989 and 1991 (HUD, 1994c, p. ii). The "official" recession, of July 1990 to March 1991 resulted in 2.8 million more people leaving than entering jobs. For men, those who did find another full-time job took about a $5,500 annual pay cut in jobs that either required them to pay for their own health insurance or provided no health insurance at all (Masumura & Ryscavage, 1994, p. 2). Social workers should not forget how difficult it is for the poor to compete for decent housing in a predominantly private market, especially when there is a definite middle-class bias in federal housing policy. It is much easier for middle-class Americans to secure a government-guaranteed FHA loan than for low-income persons to obtain public housing or a housing subsidy. In 1992, of the total number of FHA insured loans granted, 82 percent went to white families while only 8 percent went to black families (HUD, 1992, p. 4). Home owners receive an additional subsidy through the income tax laws; the interest on a home mortgage is deductible from their gross income.

Low-income families are much more likely to be renters, but in competition for rental units, very low income families may not find affordable housing, according to the Urban Institute. The institute considered a unit affordable for very low income families if the rent was less than 30 percent of their income. Using 1990 data, they found that the number of affordable rental units for very low income families fell short in every region of the United States, and the shortfall was 20 percent nationwide. There are houses just out of reach for many low-income families that could become affordable with Section 8 or housing voucher assistance (Bogdon, Silver, & Turner, 1993, pp. 51–53).

Another major problem is the displacement of low-income families resulting from urban renewal (sometimes called "Negro removal" by its critics) and from state and federal highway projects. In one community after another the poor have been displaced from urban renewal areas so that the cleared land could be used for middle-class housing, parks, or industrial development. Many larger cities have experienced a phenomenon called *gentrification*—in which poor minority families are pushed out by affluent, white professionals who frequently are subsidized by the city's "urban homestead" program. They often purchase an older home in the central city for a nominal cost in return for their promise to renovate the property and "bring it up to code." Federal requirements for relocation planning did little good. Communities could frequently certify that "adequate housing" was available for displaced families and individuals even though the available housing was expensive and located in white neighborhoods, and the displaced families were generally low income and either black or Hispanic (McNeece, 1966).

In 1979 HUD identified about 15 percent of the nation's public housing units as "troubled" (HUD, 1979), and by 1995 the Government Accounting Office estimated vacant and uninhabitable units to be close to 22 percent of the total (1995, p. 1). In 1995 Congress finally considered waivers to the rule that require a one-for-one replacement of any dilapidated public housing units that are demolished or sold, thus providing greater incentives for new housing construction in the inner city. These units are located primarily in crime-ridden neighborhoods in urban areas. HUD authorized grants to be awarded for services to families in public housing to combat crime and drugs, and to provide recreation for youths, child care, job training, computer classes, and counseling (HUD, 1994a; HUD 1994b; HUD, 1995). At the same time HUD Secretary Henry Cisneros stated that "Public housing should be a starting point, not a permanent destination, for families working toward self-sufficiency" (HUD, 1995, p. 1). Social workers can provide services to families in housing projects as well as help housing agencies identify and obtain funds to provide needed services.

Another housing problem that receives somewhat less attention today is the difficulty of establishing group homes for people who are mentally ill or retarded, juvenile and adult offenders, and people in drug and alcohol treatment programs. It is not uncommon for pressure groups such as neighborhood and business associations to besiege city councils and demand changes in local zoning ordinances in order to prohibit the establishment of such group homes. Citizens' fears of increased crime, reduced safety, and lowered property values are usually unwarranted (see, for example, Harbolt, 1981), but they frequently win out over the need for providing care in the least restrictive environment.

A number of other housing problems also relate to the special situation of the elderly poor, especially those living alone. Many of them also have impaired health and require a wide range of services, such as home health care, homemaker services, and transportation, in order to continue living independently. While there are many lovely retirement centers for those who can afford them, the poor elderly may wait years to obtain a modest apartment in a publicly subsidized project.

Social workers have found a niche in the housing field within community organizations that advocate for better and more low-income housing. Some public housing projects employ social workers to deal with all of the problems that residents of low-income housing encounter. Although indications are that large housing projects do not seem to not work well, the continued efforts of social workers and other concerned individuals are needed to bring about major change in the direction of housing policy.

Service Needs of People Who Are Homeless

Social workers are perhaps more aware of the plight of the nation's homeless citizens than they are of other housing problems we have mentioned. In 1990, the Bureau of the Census reported that there were 178,828 homeless people in 11,000 shelters, and 49,793 on the streets—228,621 total on a given day. Other more recent counts or estimates put the total number at a million or more homeless (Ginsberg, 1995, pp. 348–349; HUD, 1994c, p. 41; Seltser & Miller, 1993, p. 135). Discrepancies in the count of homeless hinge mostly on whether the count is of people homeless on one given day or people who were homeless any time in the past twelve months. However, undercounts also occur because some homeless may be "doubling up" for a night by sleeping on a friend or relative's floor, "hotbedding" (sleeping in shifts in the same beds), or are otherwise hard to find. Social workers recognize that funding for services is tied to accurate documentation of numbers of persons in need, and they are well positioned to sharpen the accuracy of the demographic picture of the homeless because they serve considerable numbers of this (see Box 12-2). It is reassuring that HUD has launched an effort to tie services to the provision of shelter. The 1987 McKinney Homeless Assistance Act allotted $25.8 million in grants that requires grantees to provide $50 million in matching funds, with 45 percent of the money being spent on supportive social services and 25 percent on community action to remedy homelessness. The goal of the Shelter Plus Care program is "homeless recovery," demonstrated by securing permanent or stable housing (The Urban Institute, 1994, pp. iii, 2.4).

The Urban Institute found that the largest single problem—presented by 46 percent of the homeless who needed services in addition to shelter—was domestic

---

BOX 12-2   Helping the Homeless

Jim is a social worker for a church organization's social service program in central Florida. He works out of an office in a local church, primarily assisting the homeless. Twenty years ago most of his clients were older, transient, single males who tended to abuse alcohol. Today at least half of his caseload consists of women, women and their children, or entire families, and most of the clients are citizens from the immediate area, not transients.

Peggy is a forty-three-year-old divorced white female who graduated from the local high school. After her husband disappeared several years ago, Peggy worked as a waitress for a short time to support her two children. The diner where she worked went out of business, and she has been employed sporadically since then. She was on AFDC for a while, but because of a serious alcohol problem, the court awarded custody of her children to her parents, and she lost her benefits. She is estranged from her parents, and they will not assist her. She has been "on the street" for three years, spending an occasional night, mostly during the winter, in a shelter. Living this way presents enormous difficulties in attending to personal hygiene. Peggy still looks for work most days, but with most of her front teeth missing, dirty clothes, and very noticeable body odor, most employers will not hire her. Jim is trying to get her a one-week voucher for a local motel so that she can clean up. He has arranged an interview for her with the janitorial service used by his church, and he has arranged for one of his personal friends to take her to daily AA meetings. There is still much to be done.

The *Thompson* family arrived here about six months ago after Mr. Thompson was laid off his job in a factory in Ohio. This is where their money and their gas ran out. They have three school-age children who weren't allowed to enroll for the first two months they were here. Jim had to intercede with the schools and get the children seen at the local public health department for inoculations before they could enroll. A private physician could have taken care of this immediately, but there was no money. One of the children also suffers from asthma, and Jim has taken her to the public health department several times for treatment.

They are currently living in a tent in a state park just outside of town. Mr. Thompson walks into town every day at 6:00 a.m. and goes to the labor pool. He averages about $35 a day on those days when he works, just enough to feed his family and pay the $12 camping fee at the park. (The Thompsons recently took in a homeless teenager who is also sleeping in their tent, and they say he is a "big eater.") Jim has made an appointment for Mrs. Thompson to apply for food stamps next week. They would have done this earlier, but the Thompsons have been very reluctant to accept any kind of "welfare."

The cost of moving into a modest apartment here is about $1,200 including the security deposit, first month's rent, and utility turn-on fees. Jim has referred the Thompsons to another church organization that makes loans (up to $1,000) to homeless families in order to secure housing. He is looking for another $200 or $300 to provide the Thompsons with the minimum move-in fees. Florida has no General Assistance program. Mr. Thompson makes "too much money" to qualify for AFDC. He also owns a five-year-old automobile (which no longer runs) that he would have to sell in order to be eligible. He has hopes of eventually repairing it and using it to look for a better job.

violence (p. x). Most of these clients were women with children. They were referred to residential agencies whose locations are kept confidential to protect them from the perpetrators. Although estimates vary, about 68,000 children and youths age sixteen and younger are homeless, and many are not attending school (Seltser & Miller, 1993, pp. 135–136; Ginsberg, 1995, p. 349). Poverty puts people at risk of becoming homeless.

In response to the growing number of children and youths with multiple problems, some with no desire to return to their families, a national twenty-four-hour hotline, the Runaway Switchboard, 1–800/621–4000, was established by a private nonprofit organization in Chicago (U.S. Department of Health and Human Services, 1994, p. 19). Many young adults who become homeless "street people" are educated, talented people who have left home where they were neglected, emotionally abused, or at odds with family and community because of mild psychiatric symptoms. One college-educated young man who simply left home one day on his bicycle commented to a researcher: "Who would have thought I'd be eating in soup kitchens . . . ? But I became independent, grew up." A young, homeless, college graduate from a wealthy southern family and recently discharged from a psychiatric facility commented that she "finally learned not to keep going to my family for a vision of a relationship I never had" (Wagner, 1993, p. 54).

Some young adults choose the street and the road because they are disaffected with the country's economic and political systems. This category of homeless is not new and has been known in other eras as bohemians, beatniks, and hippies. Now, some claim the title New Age people. As part of "dropping out of society," they eschew ongoing nine-to-five professional jobs in favor of making and selling crafts, performing as street musicians, or working at temporary jobs. Many have "straight" families and friends to whom they can turn, and they consider themselves different from the sick, the destitute, and criminals who are homeless. When they apply for food stamps or other services, social workers are perplexed by their seeming sloth and unwillingness to seek "recovery" from homelessness and joblessness. This is especially true as Congress increasingly presses welfare recipients to learn work skills, seek work, or be employed in order to be eligible for aid.

Homelessness accelerated rapidly in the early 1970s when mental hospitals began to release patients as a result of the increased effectiveness of psychotropic medications, decreased funding for institutional programs, and the strengthening of patients' rights movements. Social workers were involved in the initial stages of discharge planning for this mass deinstitutionalization and have become the case managers for patients who need continued treatment and support in their communities. Unfortunately, many people with mental illness do not have family, friends, or a supportive network, and they become part of the homeless population. Estimates put the proportion of homeless with some psychiatric symptoms or illness at 29 percent. When those with drug and alcohol problems are added, the proportion is well over half of all the homeless—with an estimated 10 percent having dual or multiple problems (Ginsberg, 1995, pp. 348–349; The Urban Institute, 1994, p. x).

The fastest growing group of homeless persons, however, are families who can't locate affordable housing (Ginsberg, 1995, p. 349; Seltser & Miller, 1993, pp. 7–15).

The number of middle-class individuals with no history of mental illness who are becoming homeless is rapidly increasing, and rural poverty is also growing (First, Rife, and Toomey, 1994). Farm foreclosures, auto industry layoffs, and the uncertainties of oil economics have made the futures of middle-class families much less secure. Many are made homeless by some type of catastrophe such as the death of a spouse with inadequate life insurance, or a serious or prolonged illness (because the United States has no national health insurance program to protect against large medical expenses).

Some scholars who have studied homelessness argue that it makes little difference why people are homeless: Their primary need is shelter, and why they are living on the streets is irrelevant to their need for shelter (Seltser & Miller, 1993, p. 114; Proch & Taber, 1987). On the other hand, their reasons for being on the streets might make a considerable difference regarding the type of housing they need. Some people with mental illness who are homeless may require a structured environment with much supervision. Homeless persons who are frail and elderly may need several different types of health and social services in order to live in a noninstitutional setting. Homeless young couples with children have still other housing needs, including access to schools and child care.

It is obvious from these data that the conventional concept of the typical homeless person as a skid-row alcoholic is no longer valid. The homeless are a heterogeneous group of people. Typically mentioned in government recommendations for assisting the homeless are expanded employment opportunities, higher income maintenance payments, more social services, the development of more long-term care facilities for people with mental illness, and more low-cost housing. (Of course, such improvements would eliminate most of our other social problems as well!)

Summary

Many entry-level positions for social workers in poverty programs are unattractive because of low pay, high caseloads, and inadequate opportunity for the use of professional skills. A growing bias within social work seems to prevent many students from even considering employment in income maintenance or housing programs. However, Congress's determination to "get people off the dole" by funding innovative programs to enable people to be self-sufficient, combined with the heterogeneous population of the poor, the homeless, and street people, mean that social work skills are needed at many levels.

Opportunities for working with the homeless and other poor people are found with private foundations such as the Salvation Army, Travelers Aid Society, and the Committee for Creative Non-Violence in Washington, D.C. Other opportunities are available in many state public welfare offices, church-sponsored social service organizations, and city-operated emergency shelters.

Interested students might also consider careers in *policy-related* positions in fields such as income maintenance, housing, and food programs. Many schools are preparing social workers at the baccalaureate level to provide services to the poor and to advocate or mobilize low-income communities. Graduate schools prepare social workers for careers in policy analysis, policy development, and policy evaluation. Poverty is an excellent area for utilizing the community organization skills covered in Chapter 4 and the macrolevel interventions discussed in Chapter 5.

Suggested Readings

DiNitto, D. M. (1995). *Social welfare: Politics and public policy,* (4th ed.). Boston: Allyn & Bacon.

Gilder, G. (1981). *Wealth and poverty.* New York: Bantam Books.

Harrington, M. (1984). *The new American poverty.* New York: Holt, Rinehart, & Winston.

Harrington, M. (1962). *The other America: Poverty in the United States.* New York: Macmillan.

Murray, C. (1984). *Losing ground: American social policy, 1950–1980.* New York: Basic Books.

Piven, F. F., & Cloward, R. (1982). *The new class war.* New York: Pantheon.

Piven, F. F., & Cloward, R. (1977). *Poor people's movements: Why they succeed, how they fail.* New York: Vintage Books.

Wagner, D. (1993). *Checkerboard square.* Boulder, CO: Westview Press.

13

Seeking Justice for Clients in the Legal System

Photo courtesy of C. Aaron McNeece

The original chapter from the first edition of this book has been revised by JOSE B. ASHFORD, School of Social Work, Arizona State University.

Social Workers in the Justice System

Almost three of every hundred Americans is under some form of correctional supervision (Bureau of Justice Statistics [BJS], 1995a). More than three quarters of this population is being supervised in the community on probation or parole. The other quarter (1.5 million) is in either jail or prison. The U.S. correctional population exceeded 5 million in 1995 (BJS, 1995b). Yet only about 1.2 percent of social workers identify their primary field of practice as corrections (Ginsberg, 1995). With so many individuals in the correctional system, one might well ask why more social workers aren't employed in criminal justice. One might also ask why more social workers do not seem to be more interested in employment in the field of corrections. These are only two of the many questions that we will attempt to answer in this chapter.

Every seventeen seconds a violent crime is committed in the United States (Federal Bureau of Investigation [FBI], 1995). Yet the rate of violent crime witnessed a small decrease between 1992 and 1993. An exception to these statistics is the category of juvenile gang killings, which has steadily increased since 1980 to 371 percent (FBI, 1994). This increase finally triggered an alarm in our society about serious juvenile crime. Policy reforms are under way that are intended to convey disapproval of this behavior and to provide increased protection for citizens. Society must disapprove of acts of crime and delinquency. How it shows this disapproval explains why the justice system needs social workers. Social workers seek to provide a more humanistic response to the treatment of criminal offenders.

The impact of the justice system on our lives seems even more profound when we consider that as many as one out of ten juveniles comes under the jurisdiction of the juvenile court (McNeece, 1996), and that 3 percent to 5 percent of males born in the United States today are likely to serve a sentence in an adult prison at some time during their lives (BJS, 1986a). About 25 percent of males from large cities in our country will be arrested for a serious violent or property crime (Gabor, 1994). Given the generally negative perceptions of the correctional system in this country, we should be concerned not only with the harm from crime but also with the potential harm that could be done to so many people who are incarcerated.

Social workers have some special problems in assisting clients in the justice system. The major difficulty is that these clients are in the system involuntarily. Coercion is a way of life for them. Anyone employed by the system is likely to be viewed as an agent of control, not as a helper. Nevertheless, the social worker must often perform certain services for the client, whether or not the client desires them. Keep in mind the social worker's traditional attachment to the client's right of self-determination, but remember that among these clients there are rapists, murderers, and other persons whose behavior *must* be controlled. They are in the justice system because of behavior that society, through its official legal institutions, has condemned.

On the other hand, social workers in the juvenile justice system have frequently worked with clients who were guilty of absolutely no criminal behavior. These clients' worst problems were rebelling against parents, skipping school, or being sexually promiscuous. Fortunately, we have come a long way in removing this type of client from the justice system, but we still have a long way to go.

Social workers have roles in both juvenile and adult probation and parole (often called aftercare), juvenile and adult institutions, court clinics, group homes, and halfway houses. In addition, many social workers are employed in juvenile delinquency prevention and diversion programs. In many communities there are social workers who attempt to link correctional services with other social services, and who plan correctional programs for both juveniles and adults. There is also a new breed of social workers who serve as expert witnesses in capital murder cases and other sentencing matters in which an offender's life history is examined to determine mitigating circumstances. A relatively new phenomenon is the employment of social workers in law enforcement agencies and public defenders' offices to assist witnesses and victims of crimes. This includes various forms of trauma debriefing for families of murder victims and officers involved in critical incidents.

Crime: As American as Apple Pie?

In order to understand the justice system, we should first look at a few facts about crime in the United States. For example, Chicago has more burglaries than the entire nation of Japan, Miami has more homicides than the Republic of Ireland, and Los Angeles has more drug addiction than all of Western Europe (Saney, 1986). The Bureau of Justice Statistics (1993a) reported that 5 percent of all American households experienced violent crime in 1992. Another 22 million of the nation's almost 100 million households were affected by crime in that same year (BJS, 1993b). This was down from a high of 32 percent in 1975 (BJS, 1986a). But this still means that almost one out of every four households is a victim of some form of crime (BJS, 1993b).

Victims of violent crime are more likely to be African American or Hispanic, young, and have relatively low incomes (BJS, 1986a). The risk of homicide is much greater for African Americans. In fact, murder is the leading cause of death among young African American males (National Association of Social Workers [NASW], 1987). Crimes of violence and theft are both higher in central cities than in the suburbs or rural areas. They are also most likely to take place in the West and least likely in the Northeast. Cities with populations over 500,000 have the highest theft rates, and households with incomes under $15,000 are at the highest risk of becoming a victim of burglary (BJS, 1993b).

The nation's adult probation population grew by 5.9 percent in 1990 to 2,670,234 (DOJ, 1994), but increased by 10 percent in 1994 to almost 3,000,000 (BJS, 1995a). Texas had the largest number of persons on probation, 503,000, followed by California with 370,000 (BJS, 1995a). The number of parolees was up 16.3 percent to almost 700,000, and the nation's population of offenders held in jails grew by 6.7 percent, to 490,442 (BJS, 1995b). Jail populations in twenty-one states have more than doubled between 1983 and 1993 (BJS, 1995b). Jails and prisons are generally overcrowded.

The inmate population has a number of interesting characteristics. For example, blacks represent only 12 percent of the national population, but they represent approximately 46 percent of all prison inmates. Overall, almost two thirds of prison inmates belong to racial or ethnic minorities (BJS, 1993a). White defendants are more likely to get probation; minorities are incarcerated.

Another interesting fact is that one third of all inmates reported that they drank alcohol heavily just before they committed the offense for which they were convicted, and 20 percent reported drinking heavily every day of the year before their arrest. Another one third were under the influence of an illegal drug at the time of their offense. Thirty percent of the inmates were addicted to heroin, compared with 2 percent of the general population (DOJ, 1983).

Nearly two thirds of all crimes are not reported to the police, with motor vehicle theft the most likely to be reported, and larceny the least likely. The overall crime rate, including violent crime, has declined since its peak in 1981. Blacks are more likely than whites to be the victims of violent crime. Males also have higher rates of victimization than women. Most victims are victimized by offenders of the same race (DOJ, 1993b).

The crime rate for women is still much lower than for men, but it is increasing at a more rapid rate. Women represented only 19.4 percent of total arrests in 1994, but that was up 5 percent since 1989 (FBI, 1994). Women are more likely to participate in economic crime, such as forgery, fraud, counterfeiting, larceny, or prostitution (FBI, 1983). One ready explanation for the increase in this type of crime by women is the feminization of poverty. Women are simply more likely than men to be poor. Another explanation offered by some criminologists is that judges may be treating women more harshly than in the past.

This is a rather grim picture of crime in the United States. Even though there have been some downward trends in certain types of crime, we are still one of the most crime-ridden societies in the world. A great number of our citizens, especially urban dwellers, members of disenfranchised groups, persons of color, and the elderly, live under the constant threat of victimization. A disproportionate number of incarcerated individuals are disadvantaged people of color, who frequently lived in overcrowded conditions with little hope of any meaningful life.

The Justice System

It is something of a misnomer to say that there is actually a justice system in the United States because of its amorphous and highly decentralized nature. To the extent that it is a system, its major components are law enforcement, the courts, and corrections. In 1993 there were approximately 746,000 employees in law enforcement—over 225,000 in the courts, and almost 557,000 in corrections (DOJ, 1994).

Law Enforcement

For most clients in the justice system, law enforcement agencies are the gatekeepers. Of the 746,736 law enforcement personnel employed in 1993, almost 614,000 were employed by city or county governments (DOJ, 1994). City police departments are the largest component in the criminal justice system. Over three fourths of the total funds expended by municipal governments are allocated to police departments, so Americans apparently believe this to be a very important function (Humphrey &

Milakovich, 1981). Law enforcement is not the only goal of police departments. According to Wilson (1968), only 10 percent of a police officer's time is devoted to actual law enforcement, while 30 percent is spent maintaining order, and 60 percent is allocated to gathering information and performing public services. In the early 1900s, policewomen were commonly assigned to providing social services, primarily to women and juveniles. By 1930 there were 509 policewomen in 200 police departments across the country. As early as 1924, there were recommendations for social workers to enter police departments to work with juveniles and plan delinquency prevention programs (Winkle, 1924).

Police social work has never been a large or popular area of employment. Social workers don't always find police departments to be hospitable organizations, since police officers frequently view law enforcement goals and social work goals to be basically antithetical. Today the small number of social workers employed by law enforcement agencies are still using their time working with women and juveniles, doing community relations work, or working in victim assistance programs. One state that has abolished the bail bond system, Kentucky, uses social workers to determine whether to release a person charged with a criminal offense prior to trial. In a few communities social workers are being recruited to serve as officers in community policing programs.

In most states, criminal sentences of less than one year are likely to be served in a county jail, prison, or county prison farm, under the supervision of the county judge or sheriff. Many of the larger counties employ social workers who provide services to inmates within these settings, as in the case described in Box 13-1.

BOX 13-1 Realistic Goals in County Jail

R. is a twenty-one-year-old, single, Caucasian male prisoner who had failed on probation several times. He came from a middle-class home, the only child of both parents' second marriage, but with several half-siblings from his parents' previous marriages. His mother is alcoholic, and his father has little contact with him.

He was diagnosed as hyperactive and placed on Ritalin as a child. He was a problem student and was placed in special education classes. Barely literate, he was able to read paperback mystery stories with some difficulty, but he could hardly write more than his name. R. had no work history of any significance. He had a minor juvenile offense record, but he had several arrests after the age of eighteen for forging checks, possession of stolen property, simple assault, and violation of probation.

R. was sentenced to a one-year term for his last offense. Originally sent to the "honor farm,"

he was referred for counseling because his behavior at the farm did not conform to the rules, resulting in his transfer to the county jail disciplinary unit. He was very confrontational, hostile, and argumentative and viewed the jail, its staff, and the judge as responsible for his current status.

Treatment focused on allowing him to vent without supporting his views, but providing him with support and advice concerning how to cope with the demands and stress of being in jail. He needed to know what he could do to alter his interactions with staff, as he clearly had no power to demand changes from them. Tapping his stress and coaching him in managing his side of these interactions finally resulted in his being transferred from the disciplinary unit into less restrictive housing.

Rolf Lamar

Types of Courts

Most alleged offenders in the United States, both adult and juvenile, have their cases heard in county or state courts. Many states have special courts for hearing juvenile cases. They may be called juvenile courts, family courts, domestic relations courts, or some other name. States with no divisions between juvenile and adult courts have special laws for trying juveniles. Thus, even in a state where a juvenile case is heard by a district judge, the judge uses juvenile law and sits as a juvenile judge in hearing the case. In some states the probation personnel are employed by the court or the county; in others they are members of a centralized state probation or probation and parole agency. Some courts or state agencies hire only social workers or other trained human services staff such as probation officers; others hire persons with no specific training for this job.

Juveniles are more likely to have their cases heard in a court of limited jurisdiction, such as a juvenile or family court, while adult offenders are generally tried in a court of general jurisdiction, also called a major trial court (BJS, 1980). There are approximately 3,700 courts of general jurisdiction and 1,200 juvenile courts in the United States (BJS, 1980). While adult trial courts are likely to be part of a state court system, juvenile courts are much more frequently organized independently at the local (county, municipal, or township) level.

Juvenile Courts and Civil Rights

Before the creation of separate juvenile courts in the United States in the early part of this century, juvenile court functions were still handled by courts of chancery or equity. While statutory power is limited by the Constitution, chancery power of parens patriae has historically been limited only by the desires of the judge.

Under the English common law it was recognized that the care of infants was lodged in the king, and this care was delegated to the court of Chancery (Sussman, 1968). The fundamental rule of parens patriae, "that the exercise of the jurisdiction depends upon the sound and enlightened discretion of the court, and has for its sole object the highest well-being of the infant" (Pomeroy, 1883, p. 1308), has withstood those pressures that have resulted in comprehensive due process guarantees for adults. Many believe that this philosophy has been in the best interests of juvenile clients, while others feel that it has been detrimental.

The reformers, who had argued for the creation of special courts for children, wanted much more than simply separating the processing of adult and juvenile clients. They wanted the juvenile court to adopt a new philosophy of case processing, one not based on the legal concepts of justice and retribution, but one that viewed the client as an unfortunate victim of societal inequities. These clients, still thought to be malleable to proper socialization, were to be rehabilitated rather than punished. Herein lies the paradox of the contemporary juvenile court.

A fundamental issue is whether the courts are the paramount protectors of the state's interests and therefore have an inherent right to control the care and custody of its children. The proponents of the juvenile court movement were willing to trade certain constitutional guarantees for promises of rehabilitation and treatment. Some state statutes were drawn so broadly that juvenile courts had virtually all of the power that courts of chancery had under English common law (*Foy v. Foy,* 1938; *Orr v. State,* 1919).

During the early history of the juvenile court, the alleged trade of constitutional rights for rehabilitation and treatment perhaps worked to the disadvantage of youth on both counts, because neither the provision of treatment nor the improvement of conditions in juvenile institutions were widespread. While advances in treatment have proceeded rather slowly and undramatically, recent changes in the constitutional rights of juveniles are generally regarded as "wide-sweeping" and "drastic" (Fox, 1970). In recent years the Supreme Court has decided that juveniles must be afforded some due process guarantees: notice of charges, right to counsel, right to confront and cross-examine witnesses, and protection against self-incrimination (*Kent v. United States,* 1966). But it has stopped short of granting children the same constitutional guarantees as adults. For example, juvenile offenders still do not have the right to a jury trial, unless that protection is afforded to them by the state (*McKeiver v. Pennsylvania,* 1971). Whereas the police must have "probable cause" for conducting a search regarding an adult, the Supreme Court has held that "reasonable cause" is sufficient justification for searching a juvenile's school locker, car, or person (*New Jersey v. T. L. O.,* 1985).

The more vocal critics of the juvenile court claim not only that children received a "raw deal" in trading rights for rehabilitation, but that the juvenile court itself has been responsible for creating entirely new categories of delinquent behavior (Platt, 1969). Behavior that was once treated as a normal part of growing up, according to these critics, is now labeled as deviant (e.g., sexual promiscuity, truancy, running away from home, "in need of supervision," and so forth) and treated by the court. At one time Indiana made "playing on the railroad tracks" an offense covered by the court's jurisdiction.

At the opposite end of this philosophical continuum are those who feel that juveniles should be brought under the court's delinquency jurisdiction only when they have broken the law—exactly the same as for adult offenders. Otherwise the court should restrain itself and practice "nonintervention" (Empey, 1978). A strong argument could be made that unnecessary judicial intervention may increase the risk of stigmatization and further involvement of the juvenile in the justice system.

Today the institution of the juvenile court is under attack. For instance, Hirschi and Gottfredson (1993) contend that the meaning of crime is the same regardless of the perpetrator's stage of development. This suggests that there is no real justification for having separate courts. In their view, the same causes influence crimes committed by adults as juveniles. This is why they have recommended that one justice system is better than two. They do not believe that most of the assumptions underlying the need for a separate system are valid. Regardless of the sanctions, crime peaks around the age of seventeen and declines sharply thereafter. But the rate of decline is about the same between the ages of nineteen and twenty-four as between the twenty-nine and thirty-four age group. These findings suggest that the impact of juvenile sanctions will not change the overall rate of crime in society. The rates of crime will stay the same regardless of whether youths receive adult or juvenile sanctions (Hirschi & Gottfredson).

The Courts and Probation

The great majority of adult and juvenile offenders under correctional supervision are maintained in the community through probation or parole. In 1995, three fourths of all adult offenders were on probation or parole status (BJS, 1995a). About 3 million offenders were on probation, and another 690,000 were on parole (BJS, 1995a).

Probation is an arrangement whereby an adult who has been convicted of a criminal offense or a juvenile who has been adjudicated delinquent is allowed to remain in the community under the supervision of a probation officer. This practice was developed in the United States during the nineteenth century as an outgrowth of the concern of a Boston cobbler, John Augustus. He visited the Boston jails as a volunteer and asked local judges to release the younger, less serious offenders into his custody pending final disposition of their cases (NASW, 1987). With the development of the juvenile court movement at the turn of the century, the role of probation officer rapidly spread and became institutionalized. Courts of general jurisdiction soon adopted probation for adult offenders.

Today adult probation is the exclusive responsibility of state-level agencies in a majority of states. In the others, state and local governments generally share this responsibility, but it is still strictly a local function in a few states (Champion, 1990). Juvenile probation is the exclusive function of a state-level agency in only twenty states. In fourteen states, responsibility is shared between state and local governments, and sixteen states place the responsibility solely on the local judiciary (Ezell, 1996). Probation functions often performed by social workers include intake screening and preadjudication services, psychological and psychosocial assessment, court investigations, courtroom testimony, probation supervision, and provision of social services (Needleman, 1996). However, most probation officers are *not* trained social workers (Eskridge, 1979).

Intake/Preadjudication

It is common in many jurisdictions for more than half of all referrals of juvenile clients to be screened out at intake. Children may be referred to court for reasons that frequently seem trivial. A parent may bring in a child and tell the court, "I just can't handle him/her anymore." A neighbor may file a complaint because a youth is walking across a corner of his yard on the way to or from school. A merchant may complain that a youth is "hanging out" too much around the cash register. If there is no factual basis for a court referral, the case may go no further than the intake officer.

Even when a child has technically violated the law, if the offense is minor and the child has not come to the court's attention before, the intake officer may attempt to settle the matter at intake through an informal adjustment. The complainant may agree that a stern lecture by the intake officer will be sufficient punishment, or that restitution for damaged property along with an apology is a better alternative than official processing.

At this stage a child, or occasionally an adult, who is felt to be in need of services rather than official sanctions may be referred to a diversion program. During the late 1960s and early 1970s the federal Law Enforcement Assistance Administration (LEAA) provided funding for thousands of diversion programs throughout the nation (Mc-Neece, 1996). Unfortunately some evidence indicates that these diversion programs may have had the unintended consequence of widening the net and labeling and stigmatizing more youth than ever before. Critics of diversion argue that less harm might have been done by keeping the clients within the official justice system (Blomberg, Heald, & Ezell, 1986). As long as the funding continued, however, many social workers found employment in diversion programs that existed primarily on court referrals.

Intake probation officers play an important role in the court's relationships with community agencies such as schools, police departments, and social services. They may establish policies and procedures that govern referrals, provide information to agencies concerning the outcomes of cases, work on joint projects to prevent delinquency, counsel members of the client's family at intake, and so forth.

Juveniles are more likely to be referred to court for noncriminal (*status*) offenses than for criminal (*delinquency*) offenses. Examples of status offenses would be truancy, running away, failing to obey parents, or sexual promiscuity (Creekmore, 1976). Adults are not as likely to have their cases adjusted at intake. They are always referred to a criminal court because of alleged criminal behavior, so this leaves little room for nonadjudicatory adjustment of charges against adult offenders. When it does happen, it is likely to involve a minor crime, for example, a first-time stolen check offense.

Assessment/Investigation

In addition to providing the court with an assessment of the client's emotional condition or level of psychological functioning, the probation officer usually investigates the client's moral character, neighborhood environment, family situation, school performance, and peer relationships. Ideally this social investigation should not be conducted until after the adjudicatory hearing. Theoretically, this information is not used in making a judgment about a client's guilt or innocence, but only in deciding the disposition of a case after a finding of guilt (or delinquency). The purpose of this information is to help the court act in the best interests of the client. In practice, however, it is strongly suspected that this kind of information, especially in juvenile cases, may prejudice the court's adjudicatory decision.

Courtroom Testimony

Frequently probation officers will be called upon to testify either as expert witnesses or as witnesses with direct knowledge of a case. This is particularly true in cases of repeat offenders who have been before the court several times. In such cases a probation officer is likely to have as much knowledge of a case as anyone else. The probation officer may have already worked with the client or supervised the client's probation for months, or even years. This function is likely to cause the social worker some role conflict, because of prior commitments to the client (Needleman, 1996).

It is difficult for a probation officer to act both as a social worker and a law enforcement officer. One of the dilemmas involves the confidentiality that should exist between the social worker and the client. Subsequent violations of the law by a client could lead to incarceration. Can the client confide problems involving criminal behavior to a probation officer who is an officer of the court, sworn to uphold the law?

Probation Supervision

For those offenders who are found guilty or adjudicated delinquent, the most common disposition is probation supervision (Champion, 1990). In most cases the judge will specify certain conditions of probation that must be met: regular school attendance, community service, participation in a drug or alcohol counseling program, maintaining only "healthy" peer associations, and so forth. The client is also asked, of course, to stay out of any further trouble. Violations of any of the conditions could be cause for revocation of probation and the imposition of a more harsh disposition, such as incarceration.

The client will be assigned to meet on a regular basis with a probation officer. These meetings serve not only as a technique of social control, but also as an opportunity for the client to receive some additional counseling and casework services. Unfortunately, the caseloads of most probation officers are too large to permit the kind of intensive services that are often needed. Even more unfortunately, the overworked probation officer will often resort to short-cut methods of checking on clients that are demeaning and stigmatizing, such as unannounced visits to the school or work site.

Social Services

Many social workers come into contact with probationers because they work in agencies to which the court assigns social workers for services. A state human services or public welfare department may actually be assigned to provide supervision (Ezell, 1996). Other agencies may be requested to provide mental health or drug counseling, family therapy, or other services. Courts will frequently maintain contracts with external public or private agencies to provide services for their clients for a fixed fee.

Parole

Parole is a status attached to an offender who is conditionally released from a correctional institution prior to the expiration of the sentence imposed by the court. In almost every case, the released offender is placed under the supervision of a parole officer. The term aftercare is used in many states when referring to the conditional release of juveniles. Parole services are frequently combined within the same agency as probation services, but when parole services are organized independently, they are usually provided by a state rather than a local agency (Champion, 1990).

In any given year at least a half million adults are under parole supervision (DOJ, 1995a). The number has fallen somewhat in recent years because of longer sentences and because some states no longer use parole. In most states, however, an adult offender is not expected to serve the full sentence imposed by the court, and most offenders are released on parole. The median sentence imposed by courts in 1982 was 51 months, while the median time served was 16 months (BJS, 1986a). By 1991 the median sentence imposed was 108 months. Of all inmates incarcerated in 1991, half expected to serve 37 months or less before their release. Overall the mean time expected to be served was 5.5 years (BJS, 1993c).

In most states and for most offenders, the judge imposes an indeterminate sentence on an adult offender. This means that the judge determines the type of sentence (such as incarceration) and places upper and lower bounds on the length of the sentence, within statutory limits. The actual time served by the inmate is determined by a parole board or authority. The primary factors that influence the parole board's decision concerning a release date are (1) the inmate's behavior, and (2) the degree of overcrowding within the prison system (McNeece & DiNitto, 1982). Inmate behavior is logically related to release from prison, but most experts do not think that using prison overcrowding is well suited to a "justice" model of corrections. Approximately 84 percent of adult prisoners in 1992 were released under some form of parole supervision (BJS, 1995a).

By 1990, most states had either abolished parole and established a determinate sentencing policy or adopted mandatory minimum sentences for various types of crimes. Under determinate sentencing the judge sets a sentence length, and the parole board may not release prisoners before the expiration date—except for "good time," which is earned by inmates. In fact, many parole boards have been abolished. Mandatory minimum sentences are used more often in crimes involving the use of firearms and in drug crimes. In the federal system possession of five grams of crack cocaine calls for a mandatory five-year prison term, even for a first offender (U.S. Sentencing Commission, 1990).

There are at least 50,000 juveniles on aftercare status on any given day in the United States (BJS, 1994). These juveniles are placed in an institution for an average of five months (BJS, 1986a). Juvenile parole or aftercare is more likely to be housed with juvenile probation than with adult parole. While there may be little difference between juvenile probationers and parolees, most probation and parole workers seem to think that there are enormous differences between juvenile and adult parolees. Mixing the caseloads in a combined agency, therefore, does not seem to be a good practice. The trend in juvenile aftercare is to make it more of a social services function than a correctional function and to maintain indeterminate sentences (Ashford & LeCroy, 1993). Washington state is the only jurisdiction with purely determinate sentences for juvenile offenders (Ashford & LeCroy).

Other Correctional Programs

Adult Incarceration: America Leads the World

After probation, the disposition most likely for adult offenders is incarceration. In 1995, there were over one million persons in prison in the United States (BJS, 1995a). We have the dubious distinction of incarcerating more offenders than any other

Western nation. From 1988 to 1992, admissions to state prisons increased about 36 percent, with the rate of increase for African Americans (42 percent) being twice the rate of increase for whites (BJS, 1993c). The proportion of the American population incarcerated in 1992 was approximately 330 per 100,000. This is about ten times that of the Netherlands and four times that of the United Kingdom. The highest rate of incarceration was in the District of Columbia, 1,125 per 100,000 (DOJ, 1994). Almost three quarters of the new admissions to state prisons has been for nonviolent offenses. Twenty-four percent of the women entering U.S. prisons for the first time were from substance-related offenses (BJS, 1993b). The propensity for incarceration is so great that many states must release inmates early because of overcrowding. Half of the states are currently operating one or more adult penal facilities under a federal court order because of the extent of overcrowding (BJS, 1993d).

Social Work in Prisons

It is generally agreed that there is an "uneasy partnership" between social work and correctional institutions (Handler, 1975). However, a social worker might practice several useful skills in a prison setting. The controversy concerns whether those skills can and should be used solely on the client's behalf, or whether the exercise of those skills is likely to result only in the strengthening of institutional control over the client.

Social workers are trained to see clients as part of a larger system that contributes both to the problem and the solution. Advocacy on behalf of the client, within the prison and within the community to which he or she will inevitably be released, is a major function of the social worker. Prison environments are almost always "violent, depressing, regimented, boring, and dehumanizing" (Netherland, 1987, p. 358). An obvious possibility for assisting the clients is helping them to serve their terms in this kind of negative environment without losing hope—or their sanity. The social worker may directly provide support and assist the inmate in developing other sources of emotional and social support within the prison.

Advocating for change within the prison is another major role. One does not have to look far to discover that improvements in living arrangements, meals, recreation, medical care, race relations, and treatment are almost universally needed. An advocate for these causes must proceed cautiously. Such institutions will tolerate just so many demands for change before attempting to eliminate the sources of unrest.

Finally, we cannot deny that many inmates have a substantial need for change in their behavior, behavior which may be directly responsible for their incarceration. Casework and group work skills may be used toward such goals as helping the client learn to take responsibility for his or her behavior rather than assigning blame elsewhere. In many prisons, social workers provide alcohol and drug counseling to inmates. This is an important service, since a great many inmates have a substance abuse problem (DOJ, 1983a). (See Chapter 7.) In a few prisons social workers provide marriage counseling and family therapy to the inmate, the spouse, and the family (Showalter & Hunsinger, 1996). This is a particularly important function, since research has shown that inmates with strong support from their families have a much better chance of completing probation successfully (Holt & Miller, 1972).

Alternatives to Incarceration

In recent years a number of alternative programs have gained popularity. These include such arrangements as restitution, work/educational release, and community service. These programs may be used in combination with probation or parole. Technology also now makes it possible for a court or law enforcement agency to use electronic transmitters to monitor offenders who are remanded to their homes.

While these alternatives are undoubtedly more humane than prisons, there is little evidence to indicate that they are any more or less effective in achieving correctional objectives (Austin & Krisberg, 1982). Many of these alternatives are even more costly than traditional forms of incarceration (BJS, 1983).

Juveniles: Diversion from the System

Diversion, decriminalization, and deinstitutionalization have been major trends in juvenile corrections during the past two decades (McNeece, 1996). Juvenile justice philosophy is based on the assumption that juvenile clients are susceptible to rehabilitative efforts, and that society has an obligation to provide treatment to those in need. The juvenile codes of the states clearly reflect the belief that the primary purpose of bringing a child into the juvenile justice system is to provide diagnosis and treatment, not to mete out punishment (Levin & Sarri, 1974). "Progressive" juvenile codes have not necessarily served the best interests of children. As we mentioned earlier, since the creation of the juvenile court system in the United States, many kinds of noncriminal behaviors have been defined as appropriate matters of concern for the court. As early as 1967 there were strong pressures to redefine such behavior and remove it from the court's delinquency jurisdiction. The President's Commission on Law Enforcement and the Administration of Justice (1967) recommended the complete elimination of the court's power over children for noncriminal conduct.

For at least twenty years, there has been concern that the indiscriminate labeling and mixing of status offenders with other juvenile offenders might result in unwarranted stigmatization of children who were not accused of criminal activity. Pressures for change finally resulted in the passage of the Juvenile Justice and Delinquency Prevention Act of 1974, which threatened to cut off federal funds to juvenile offender programs that placed status offenders in detention or incarcerated them along with juvenile delinquents. Unfortunately, there is some evidence that certain states have resorted to "name games," such as simply changing the labels under which offenders are processed, in order to route them into legally acceptable disposition alternatives (McNeece, 1980; Hylton, 1982).

Some critics of formal court processing for juveniles argue that (1) the court consistently fails to protect the legal rights of juvenile clients, (2) any official court processing has a stigmatizing effect on juveniles, and (3) legal sanction is ineffective in compelling treatment (Schur, 1973). One answer to these problems, they say, is diversion from formal court processing. On the other hand, proponents of formal court processing argue that the diversion of a client from the court is a denial of the client's right to help from the court. Some feel that the court would be abdicating its responsibility if it did not "support parents with its authority" (Martin & Snyder, 1972 p. 45).

The present state of this debate would indicate that most scholars and practitioners of juvenile justice believe that serious juvenile offenders should continue to be routed to the juvenile court for formal handling, while diversion is more appropriate for first offenders and those accused of trivial offenses. Beyond that, there is little agreement on the matter of diversion, including an acceptable definition. To some it means that the police and the courts should adopt a hands-off policy, leaving children alone whenever possible. To others it means that children should not only be diverted *from* formal handling, but also *to* agencies that provide appropriate services (Cressey & McDermott, 1973).

The custody rate in juvenile facilities in 1993 was 221 per 100,000 (BJS, 1994). The Juvenile Justice and Delinquency Prevention Act of 1974 was directed at reducing the populations of juvenile institutions by diverting juveniles from the traditional juvenile justice system and providing critically needed alternatives to institutionalization. The results have been mixed and somewhat difficult to interpret. Although there have been dramatic decreases in incarceration in some states, there have been offsetting increases in others. And though there has been a substantial decrease in the institutionalization of females, the group most likely to fall into the "status offender" category, there has been a substantial increase in institutionalized males (BJS, 1988). Rather than reflecting a change in levels of delinquency, it appears that changes within the overall rate of incarceration reflect shifts in judicial and institutional practices. In 1991, there were 57,543 juveniles held in public facilities (BJS, 1994).

Perhaps the most comprehensive effort to deinstitutionalize was the closing of juvenile facilities in Massachusetts. Led by Jerome Miller, proponents of reform managed to push through a program that closed all public juvenile institutions within a two-month period. Even more surprising, this rapid deinstitutionalization did not lead to an appreciable increase in crime, even though other resources for caring for this population were not readily available in the state (Romig, 1978).

Community-based diversion and treatment programs that have been developed in recent years are committed to intervention in the least restrictive setting possible. The goal is to allow the client to function in a social environment that is as close as possible to "normal." These programs vary in duration, treatment approach, quality of staff, and relationship to the community and to the network of other services (Coates, Miller, & Ohlin, 1978). The most common approaches used to treat juveniles within the community include individual, family, and group counseling; guided group interaction (a type of group work with more direction from the group leader); and behavior modification (Romig, 1978).

Despite the fact that the evaluations of alternative treatment and diversion programs have consistently shown that they are no more effective than traditional methods of case handling (that is, formal court processing and incarceration), they are undoubtedly more humane and result in less social control over the clients (Spergel, Reamer, & Lynch, 1981). Despite periodic calls for harsher punishment and extended incarceration, the move toward community-based programming is likely to continue. If recidivism is no greater than before with community- based services, and if costs remain less than for institutional care, then we are not likely to return to programs of large-scale incarceration.

One other form of juvenile "diversion" deserves our attention. An alarming trend is to certify or waive juveniles for processing in adult criminal courts. Between 1985 and 1989 the number of juveniles tried as adults more than doubled. The number of nonwhite males charged with drug offenses who were waived to adult courts grew by 850 percent (McNeece, 1994). Waiver tends to single out minority children for harsher punishment, especially when drugs are involved.

Issues in Corrections

For social workers, major issues in the corrections field can be grouped into professional concerns, such as confidentiality and coercion, and social policy issues, such as social control, determinate sentencing, and the quality of care.

Confidentiality

In most adult and juvenile correctional programs, it is rare to find a social worker who can honestly promise a client that all communications will be held in confidence. Most social workers in the justice system are bound by both law and agency policy to reveal information concerning infractions of the rules, probation violations, illegal behavior, and so forth. Any social worker has a duty to warn the appropriate authorities about plans for a prison escape or to injure or kill another inmate. The social worker should inform the client at the beginning of the relationship that such information cannot be held in confidence. By doing this, however, the inmate will certainly not be able to trust the social worker to the same degree as when confidentiality is guaranteed. This may be one of the major obstacles to establishing a therapeutic relationship with a client in the correctional system (Showalter & Hunsinger, 1996). This dilemma is illustrated in Box 13-2.

In many instances in noninstitutional correctional programs, such as probation or parole, the social worker may turn a blind eye to minor infractions of the rules. In such cases, however, parolees must live with the ever present possibility that their parole status might be revoked at any time. If a social worker chooses to selectively enforce the rules, it might do more damage to the relationship than strict adherence. In the situation described in Box 13-2, the client at least knows where he or she stands.

Coercion

Few people would seriously object to the notion that coercion is required in dealing with dangerous criminal behavior. Social workers have trouble dealing with the fact

BOX 13-2   Dilemma in a Correctional Field Placement

Sue was a second-year graduate student who was assigned to a prison for her final field placement. Her supervisor was an MSW who had worked in the correctional system for over twenty years. On the first day of her placement Sue's supervisor explained to her that confidentiality in this system could not be guaranteed. As employees of the correctional system, he and all other employees (as well as student interns) were morally and legally obligated to report violations of criminal law and infractions of the inmate code of conduct.

Halfway through the semester one of the inmates, Doug, confided to Sue that he was being sexually abused by another inmate almost daily. He asked her not to tell anyone, though, because his life had been threatened. Sue knew by this time that an inmate who "finked" on another was likely to be killed. Doug had told Sue about

this situation only because he wanted to enlist her assistance in getting transferred to another cell block where he might escape this sexual abuse.

As a graduate intern, all Sue could do was to make a request through the case manager, her supervisor. Inmates could be transferred within the prison only for a compelling reason, and she must be prepared to provide a reason for this request. She felt that if she gave her supervisor the real reason, she would be violating Doug's confidentiality, possibly putting him in danger. She could have lied about the reason for the request, but that was also a violation of professional ethics. She could also tell Doug that she simply could not help him unless she was allowed to provide the case manager with a truthful explanation.

What would you do?

---

that the treatment of offenders is often conducted under the threat of imposing sanctions. This could be one of the major reasons that only 1.2 percent of a recent sample of NASW members were employed in the field of corrections (Ginsberg, 1995). Coerced treatment directly contradicts the client's right of self-determination as expressed in the NASW Code of Ethics (Section II. G.).

"Treatment" is a relatively new philosophy in corrections, and one that is still struggling to prove its worth. Its proponents contend that the behavior of individuals can often be changed by providing treatment, even if it is against their will. By providing treatment, so the argument goes, social workers enable clients to be better prepared to make choices about their lives after their release.

Not everyone is convinced of the merits of coerced treatment. Most of the pros and cons have been popularized in such works as *A Clockwork Orange* (a 1972 movie by Stanley Kubrick). In his book *The Right to Be Different,* Nicholas N. Kittrie (1973) compares the treatment model with the punishment (or retribution) model and claims that in some ways the former is less humane than the latter. Francis Allen (1964) argued over thirty years ago that the treatment ideology has imparted a misleading impression of beneficence and hides the harsher realities of punishment that still dominate correctional programs. In most other situations in which an individual is diagnosed as "sick," the option is available of not choosing treatment. This has become much less an option for the client of a correctional system.

Does coerced treatment work? Although the reports are quite mixed, the evidence for all types of correctional programs (both juvenile and adult) seems to indicate that most approaches are equally ineffective, whether or not a treatment component is present (Wilks & Martinson, 1976). Given this knowledge, social workers will continue to be skeptical of the value of coerced treatment.

Determinate versus Indeterminate Sentencing

The introduction of indeterminate sentences was originally seen as a progressive movement toward more humane and therapeutic policies. An inmate who was "rehabilitated" after serving two years of a "one year to life" sentence should not have to serve additional time. Thus a parole board could monitor and analyze inmates' progress in the prison and determine an appropriate time for release.

Late in the 1960s a new reform movement decried the coercive nature of indeterminate sentences. After all, the all-consuming goal of an inmate is to get out of prison. Pursuant to that goal, most inmates seem to do whatever they believe is necessary in order to convince the authorities to release them (DOJ, 1978). The therapeutic value of the many prison rehabilitative programs was felt to be minimal, since inmates enrolled in everything from alcohol and drug counseling to arts and crafts in order to convince parole boards that they had been appropriately rehabilitated. Today most states have either abolished parole and returned to determinate sentencing or have severely restricted the practice of parole (Champion, 1990).

There is evidence that the majority of inmates in both state and federal correctional institutions would prefer to serve determinate sentences, even if they are longer, than to suffer the uncertainties of indeterminate sentences, followed by parole (McNeece & Lusk, 1979). Of course, we don't allow inmates to set correctional policies, but we would be wise to consider how they feel about these issues. Determinate sentencing also reduces some of the great discrepancies in sentences set by judges in the same state.

Quality of Care

Partly because of longer determinate sentences, partly because of new mandatory and presumptive sentencing policies (which require prison sentences of a specified length in certain cases), and partly because of increased crime and arrest rates, prisons have become even more crowded in recent years. As mentioned earlier, half of the states are operating their prisons under federal court orders because of overcrowding, and state and federal prisons operate at an average of 110 percent of capacity (Sherman & Hawkins, 1981). At one time conditions were so overcrowded in Florida that the State Department of Corrections resorted to housing up to 10 percent of the male inmates in tents (Inmates, 1988)! (Within a few years so many additional prisons had been built that not all were needed. Some had not opened their doors years after completion.)

In addition to overcrowding, prisons have a host of other problems. Several states have also been placed under federal court orders because of the poor quality of food and medical care. Even in those states that are not under a federal judge's mandate to improve conditions, the quality of care is seldom anything to boast about.

Summary

Social workers in the legal system face a special problem in dealing with clients who are in the system involuntarily. The client is in a coercive system and is likely to view everyone who is part of that system as an enemy. Most professional social workers are not attracted to working in an authoritarian system with unmotivated, involuntary clients. This situation is further exacerbated by the movement of state, local, and federal correctional agencies away from rehabilitation and toward control. Occasionally there are efforts to build therapeutic components, such as therapeutic communities and other drug rehabilitation programs, into correctional programs. Still, the correctional system is generally not perceived as a therapeutic, helping, caring system.

Suggested Readings

Gottfredson, M. R., & Hirschi, T. (1990). *A general theory of crime*. Stanford, CA: Stanford University.

Keve, P. W. (1995). *Crime control and justice in America: Searching for facts and answers*. Chicago: American Library Association.

Platt, A. (1969). *The child savers: The invention of delinquency*. Chicago: University of Chicago.

Roberts, A. R. (1996). *Social work in juvenile and criminal justice settings* (2nd ed.). Springfield, IL: Charles C. Thomas.

Schur, E. M. (1973). *Radical nonintervention: Rethinking the delinquency problem*. Englewood Cliffs, NJ: Prentice-Hall.

Sherman, M., & Hawkins, G. E. (1981). *Imprisonment in America: Choosing the future*. Chicago: University of Chicago.

Von Hirsch, A. (1976). *Doing justice: The choice of punishments*. New York: Hill and Wang.

Wilson, J. Q. (1975). *Thinking about crime*. New York: Basic Books.

14

Social Work and the Occupational Arena

The original chapter from the first edition of this book has been revised by MICHAEL L. SMITH and ORREN DALE, Walter H. Richter Institute of Social Work, Southwest Texas State University.

Most social workers work in agencies such as mental health centers, health clinics, welfare departments, halfway houses for alcoholics and drug abusers, and centers for battered women. However, a growing number of social workers are employed by such diverse organizations as high-tech firms, telephone companies, and manufacturing plants—and virtually every other type of business you might name. The primary job of many of these social workers is to help employees deal with the various types of personal problems that interfere with work performance, including substance abuse, illness and disability, marital and other family problems, and mental illnesses.

Of course, not all productivity problems in the workplace can be traced to personal difficulties of employees. Sometimes the workplace does not encourage productivity and worker satisfaction. Jobs are often routine and dull. Workers are given orders, but they do not necessarily take part in important decisions affecting their jobs. Friction or poor communication between departments can result in low productivity, as can friction between individual workers. Occupational social workers are concerned about these issues as well. It is common to see social workers employed in personnel departments of companies doing various types of jobs.

Social workers also act as consultants to business and industry. For example, some social workers are concerned with the structure of work. They help businesses and organizations explore innovations such as job sharing, in which two people, often working mothers, share a full-time position. Still other social workers offer training to improve communication and cohesion (team building) within the workplace or help in goal setting and planning. Social workers are broadly educated in "people skills," and this can prove to be quite useful in the work world.

Although the public may have a rather narrow view of what social workers do, it would take many pages to list the variety of jobs held by professional social workers. The skills taught in social work education programs—interviewing and other communication skills, advocacy, clinical interventions, and so forth—may well be described as versatile because they can be put to use in many ways in many different work settings.

History of Social Workers in the Workplace

Social work in the workplace has had a number of promising starts, followed by an almost equal number of disappointing setbacks (also see Masi, 1982). Occupational social work, like so many other forms of social work, can be traced to the social reform movements of the nineteenth century. Early union activists who sought to organize labor to resist management exploitation and abuse often made common cause with poverty workers, children's advocates, and other early social workers. There was a particular affinity between union advocates and social workers in the settlement house movement in large cities (also see Chapter 4). These reformers were generally adversarial toward management, a position historically more comfortable for the reform wing of the social work profession. While their approaches differed from the more clinical orientation common today, they formed part of the historical foundation for occupational social work.

During the early twentieth century, a number of companies employed "welfare secretaries," whose function was partly to assist employees and partly to monitor activities in the workplace (Masi, 1982; Popple, 1981). The uneasy compromise in serving the interests of both workers and management was a theme of the early occupational efforts. As the nature of the workplace evolved, sometimes rapidly, the demands on occupational social workers changed. World War I prompted the hiring of more women, the placement of women in higher positions in the workplace, and some relaxation in racial discrimination in employment. These changes in turn prompted the hiring of more trained social workers to help address new workplace issues (see Masi). The Progressive Era, dating from the turn of the century to about 1919, was characterized by aggressive welfare reform and social change. Labor reform, child labor laws, union organizing, and workplace safety were all high on the social agenda. Social workers in the workplace were active in this era, but this activity died out quickly in the postwar years (also see Masi). Professional infatuation with Freudian analysis, the quest to unify the profession, and the continued pressure for professionalism in social work drained energy from the function of the profession in the workplace.

The Depression Era was marked by large-scale unemployment, social unrest, and class divisions. The focus of the profession shifted naturally to the unemployed rather than to the comparatively minor needs of the employed. The bitterness of the Hoover years was followed by the birth of activist social programs spawned by the New Deal. Events combined to make government rather than industry the focus of social work's professional attention. Nonetheless, some progress could be noted in the occupational arena.

Mary Parker Follet is credited with fostering an emphasis on the importance of human relationships in the workplace during this period. Although not a social worker, she brought insights about the importance of social relationships into management discourse (Szilagyi & Wallace, 1980; Weinbach, 1994). This management approach, quite congenial to social workers, was termed the "Human Relations School" (Argyris, 1957; Perrow, 1972). The human relations management school developed much of its early impetus in this period, competing against the sometimes repressive "scientific management" models of work efficiency advanced by Frederick Taylor and the early industrial engineers (Hellreigel, Slocum, & Woodman, 1976; Weinbach, 1994).

World War II produced changes of landslide proportions in the workplace (see Masi, 1982). The military draft disrupted work and family life and brought financial hardship and home-front rationing. Women moved into the workplace in huge numbers. Punishing work schedules combined with other factors to create a workplace fraught with ambiguity and tension that produced a resurgence of social work interest in the workplace. Labor unions, management, and government programs were created to address new workplace demands. The American Red Cross, and later the branches of the armed forces themselves, created social work programs to assist uniformed personnel. These services were later expanded to cover military dependents. The government also extended the use of "employee relations specialists" to assist civilian employees. While these services were by no means the exclusive domain of social workers, there was a consistent and important social work presence in their development.

After World War II, there was another lull in occupational social work services (Masi, 1982). New Deal programs that survived the war became major employers of social workers, but the postwar period of high employment, increasing wages, and unparalleled economic expansion overshadowed the stresses that were building in the workplace. Union activity was oriented primarily toward improving wages and working conditions, with little attention to the more personal needs of workers (Perlis, 1978). The split between social workers and labor unions began in the 1930s when some family agencies denied services to striking workers (Masi). As social workers drifted away from the workplace and social reform and became more clinical, the profession lost influence in the labor movement.

New issues were emerging in the workplace. For example, as management became concerned about the effects of alcoholism on productivity, new programs called "occupational alcohol programs" were created. Many staff for these programs were alcoholics recovering through Alcoholics Anonymous, which began in 1935 (Strachan, 1982). By the late 1940s, a number of companies and government departments had followed the lead of the DuPont Corporation in establishing occupational alcohol programs.

During the 1950s, new psychotropic drugs allowed many patients to return home from remote state mental hospitals. Community-based mental health services, new approaches to counseling and psychotherapy, and coverage for mental health services by insurance companies increased public awareness and acceptance of mental health services. As treatment for mental illness emerged from the shadows, there was more demand for mental health services in the workplace. Social workers were again encouraged to put more emphasis on therapeutic approaches and less on organizing and social reform.

During the 1960s, community mental health programs expanded dramatically; the social programs of the Great Society proliferated; illicit drug use flourished; and racial and class conflict culminated in both riots and new civil rights legislation. Employers had to learn to deal with a more assertive work force, a more culturally diverse workplace, and a social climate that said, "challenge authority." Along with a resurgence of interest in the social work profession came another struggle to determine whether the clinical or social activist wing of the profession would set the agenda.

By the early 1970s, a number of companies and government agencies were developing new programs to assist employees. It was a time of experimentation and innovation fueled by the federal government's creation of the National Institute on Alcohol Abuse and Alcoholism and, shortly after, the National Institute on Drug Abuse. The issue of substance abuse, with its known productivity costs and problems, remained a selling point in getting business and industry to adopt these programs. Social workers found themselves in the awkward position of competing with recovering alcoholics and addicts for leadership in this segment of the movement.

The 1980s brought a more comprehensive, professional approach to employee services. Termed the "broad brush" approach, this emphasis was nurtured at schools such as Columbia University, Boston University, the University of Utah, and Hunter College. The skills social workers had developed in individual and family counseling, in mediation, in resource development and referral, and in consultation with management created a more comprehensive service. These programs went well beyond the services of the occupational alcohol programs typified by the Association of Labor-Management Administrators and Consultants, the forerunner to the current Employee Assistance Professionals Association. By 1982, more than fifty social work schools had students in occupational social work field placements (Masi, 1982). The National Association of Social Workers and the Council on Social Work Education sanctioned efforts to expand and define the field of occupational social work.

Although social workers are still active in social reform, the 1980s and 1990s are most notable for the expansion of the clinical wing of the profession into the private practice arena. The entrepreneurial approach to social services is a model familiar to human resource managers in industry. Social workers like private practice because it offers them flexible work opportunities and professionalism. Business and industry find hiring social workers attractive because they often offer their services at lower costs than other mental health professionals. These factors have propelled social workers into a prominent position in providing human services in occupational settings even though they continue to debate whether this is the best use of social workers' energies. Social work in the workplace may cause further abandonment of the traditional commitment to assisting the poor and oppressed (Specht & Courtney, 1994), but social work practice continues to expand in occupational settings.

Occupational Social Work Today

As we continue to explore social work in the workplace, clarification of terminology is necessary. Social work in the workplace is also referred to as industrial social work, occupational social work, and work in employee assistance programs. Googins and Godfrey (1987) define occupational social work as "a field of practice in which social workers attend to the human and social needs of the work community by designing and executing appropriate interventions to insure healthier individuals and environments" (p. 5). Kurzman (1987) uses both the terms industrial and occupational social work and offers another definition of the field:

> *In the United States, industrial (or occupational) social work generally is defined as programs and services, under the auspices of labor or management, that utilize professional social workers to serve members or employees and the legitimate social welfare needs of the labor or industrial organization. It also includes the use, by a voluntary or proprietary social agency, of trained social workers to provide social welfare services or consultation to a trade union or employing organization under a specific contractual agreement.*

*The employing organizations are not only labor unions and corporations,
but often government agencies and not-for-profit organizations (p. 899).*

De Silva (1988) sees occupational social work as "the application of social work
knowledge and skill in responding to the personal, organizational, and community
needs and problems of organizational employees, customers, and relevant publics
in their interactions with organizations" (p. 283).

While these definitions vary in their particulars, the following shared themes
suggest the essential characteristics of social work in the workplace:

- Professionalism: Social work brings a body of knowledge, skills, and values to
  the occupational setting which are consistent with practice throughout the social
  work profession.
- Auspices: Occupational social work services are offered through the world of
  work and on behalf of the various groups that compose this arena.
- Social context: The concerns of occupational social workers include but go beyond individual behavior. The organizational context within which individual
  behavior occurs is generally a more critical element of occupational practice
  than of other areas of social work practice (Smith & Gould, 1993).

Occupational social work includes many activities, and like other areas of social
work practice, these activities seem limited only by the services that social workers
can create and "sell" to others to improve the quality of life. They include the following:

- Assessment: Evaluating the client-system's level of social functioning, taking into
  account traditional factors such as mental and physical health and financial circumstances in addition to assessment of workplace factors which may contribute
  to employee distress
- Counseling: Problem-solving activities with troubled employees to help them
  solve personal problems and maintain their productivity
- Brokering: Linking the employee (client) to appropriate community resources
  and services
- Training: Preparing front-line personnel (union representatives, foremen, line
  supervisors) to (1) identify when changes in job performance warrant referral to
  a social service unit, and (2) carry out an appropriate approach that will result
  in the employee's referral
- Planning: Developing strategies for needs assessment, future programs, and
  staffing
- Consultation: Advising management on human resource issues, on specific cases,
  and on training needs
- Record keeping: Developing and providing oversight of management information systems that retain essential client information, protect confidentiality, and
  provide databases for case assessment and program evaluation

- Initiating: Starting community health, welfare, recreational, or educational programs for employees; planning new ventures; participating in employee benefits administration; providing advice on corporate donations to social service programs; and suggesting organizational positions on pending social welfare legislation
- Evaluating: Assessing the effectiveness of individual case interventions, of the outside provider network, of the overall program, and of the ongoing issues in the organization as a whole (Akabas & Kurzman, 1982; Kurzman, 1987)

Kurzman (1987) notes that an important characteristic of human services in the workplace is universalism. Universal services are available to everyone, and this characteristic makes human services in the workplace especially useful to workers and especially congruent with social work values. Universal services tend to be preventive in nature. For example, employees whose alcohol abuse is diagnosed early, while they are still working, can receive treatment and keep their jobs. This is far more beneficial than ignoring the problem until it becomes so severe that employees face job termination and must resort to residual services such as public assistance to support their families. Preventive services offered before problems become chronic are also less costly than treatment for chronic conditions. Indeed, this is a key advantage of early intervention arising from the workplace.

There are obvious advantages to offering social services in the workplace. However, there have long been questions about the motives of employers in offering these services. Vinet and Jones (1983) asked occupational social workers to identify the reasons businesses and unions provided human services in the workplace. The reasons or motivations fell into three broad categories: existence of social problems at work, legal or social mandates, and concern for employees.

The first category included the desire to avoid violence, strikes, and high turnover and the need to increase productivity. Another reason in this category was that a key management figure had benefited from human services such as alcoholism treatment. Legal or social mandates included factors such as the desire to avoid lawsuits and other problems stemming from discriminatory hiring practices, workplace safety concerns, mandatory drug screening for employees in certain categories (airline pilots, truck drivers, ship's captains, etc.), work grievances, and legal or regulatory requirements of outside agencies.

The third (and perhaps most important) factor that social workers believed influenced the provision of human services at work was employers' positive regard for workers. This was reflected in statements such as, "Employees are the company's most valuable asset" and "Workers' advice should be sought in decision making because they have to carry out the day-to-day operations."

Employers offer social services to employees for reasons ranging from humanitarian concerns for workers to a "bottom line" focus on costs and productivity. The motives are contributing factors in the various forms that occupational social work programs take. In the following section, we discuss the variations in service philosophy and focus.

A Framework for Understanding Occupational Social Work

Occupational social work has several distinct practice traditions. In part, these traditions spring from the three different populations with which organizations relate—employees, customers, and communities (de Silva, Biasucci, Keegan, & Wijnberg, 1982; de Silva, 1988; Shank, 1985). This realization led de Silva and his associates to distinguish between employee assistance, customer assistance, and corporate public involvement traditions or models within occupational social work. Straussner (1990) added two additional elements: the "employer/work organization service model" and the "work-related public policy model." We will discuss each of these models.

Employee Assistance Program Model

The most familiar context for occupational social work practice is in the Employee Assistance Program, or EAP. More than 95 percent of the Fortune 500 companies have an EAP (Bilik & Pasco, 1993, p. 15). Government agencies, universities, many religious organizations, and the military have developed variations on EAPs. Most commonly, the core of the EAP is composed of various forms of clinical services offered to employees and their family members. Substance abuse treatment, personal counseling, family therapy, and financial counseling services are the most commonly offered services (Lanier, 1991). As the EAP field has grown, a variety of different ways of organizing and staffing these programs has emerged. In this section, we discuss the organization of EAPs and the roles played by professional social workers in this field of specialty practice.

There are several different models of EAPs, but they fall into two broad categories: the internal (or in-house) model, and the external contractor model (see Fleisher & Kaplan, 1988). Internal EAPs are often located in personnel or medical departments of larger companies. The organization employs one or more EAP staff, usually depending on the size of the work force. Consultants may be called in to set up the program and do the initial training of work supervisors and EAP staff. The EAP staff is usually responsible for the ongoing training of supervisors in the EAP-related policies and procedures of the company. In almost all such programs, employees seeking services are assessed by the EAP staff. Depending on the size and philosophy of the program, the employee may then be offered appropriate services directly by the EAP or be referred to outside service providers.

Some companies prefer that all clinical intervention be done by outside providers. Others, particularly organizations with large numbers of employees, may provide a range of services within the EAP itself. Consider the case of a woman who is performing poorly at work. She may be referred to the internal EAP, where the reason for her poor work performance is assessed as grief over the death of her husband. If the internal EAP services include bereavement counseling, she may be treated by an EAP staff member. If not, she may be referred to a service provider in the community, with the EAP staff offering case management services in following her progress. Since EAP professionals cannot be experts in providing all types of services, almost all internal EAPs, regardless of size, refer some cases to qualified providers outside the organization. Cases that require intensive inpatient hospitalization for mental health or substance abuse treatment, or cases in which minor dependents of employees require residential treatment, are almost always referred to outside services. Increasingly, a function of the EAP is to "triage" cases, referring employees to the type and level of service best suited to their problems. The use of external providers may also allay employees' concerns about keeping information about their personal lives confidential.

There are several reasons that the employer may choose an external contractor. Often a small company wishes to provide EAP services but finds it is not cost efficient or practical to operate its own EAP. A large company may contract for this service rather than provide it directly because it prefers not to be in the business of operating treatment services. Other large companies prefer this model because their work forces are decentralized and multiple service locations are needed to assist employees. Decentralized companies may select different EAP contractors for each of their geographical locations, or they may contract with an EAP provider that offers services nationwide. Traditional social service agencies such as Family Services of America offer such programs. Increasingly, facilities such as hospitals, mental health centers, and private clinical counseling groups are offering EAP services as part of their programming. In recent years, a number of regional or national private organizations have emerged whose sole business is provision of contract EAP services to companies with multiple locations or specialized needs.

Health maintenance organizations sometimes operate EAPs, typically offering a limited number of outpatient clinical visits as part of the benefit package. Yet another format is for a number of small businesses to contract jointly with an EAP provider for services that would be too expensive or inefficient if offered by a single small employer.

EAP Referrals

Employee assistance programs generally permit two types of referrals—self and supervisory. Many organizations encourage self-referral, in which the employee voluntarily seeks EAP services in response to some personal need. Self-referrals can help employees deal with personal problems before they interfere with job performance. When an employee is self-referred, the supervisor is generally not informed of the situation unless the employee chooses to tell the supervisor. EAPs that publicize their services and encourage employees to contact them directly are likely to have large numbers of self-referrals (Winkelpleck & Smith, 1988). A second type of voluntary or self-referral occurs when the employee has the option of bypassing the EAP staff and obtaining services directly from a treatment provider whose services will be paid for by the employing organization. This option is similar to the use of private insurance that the employee may use to obtain services. It permits the employee greater confidentiality; however, it is more difficult for the EAP staff to monitor patterns of service utilization and to ensure that services are being used efficiently (Winkelpleck & Smith).

Supervisory referrals may be handled on a formal or informal basis. On an informal basis, a supervisor and an employee may talk about personal problems. For example, an employee whose job performance is quite satisfactory may mention to his supervisor during a lunchtime conversation that he and his ex-wife are having difficulty working out the visitation arrangements for their child. The supervisor may recommend the services of the EAP counselor. Since there is no job deterioration, the supervisor suggests this option on an informal basis. The employee is, of course, free to take the advice or not. This case is virtually indistinguishable from a self-referral.

Another type of informal supervisory referral may occur when a supervisor begins to notice deterioration in an employee's job performance. Many supervisors are hesitant to discuss or confront employees about poor job performance. This is one reason that proper training of supervisors is essential for an effective EAP. Supervisors may prefer to soft-pedal their initial discussions about poor work performance and may recommend the use of the EAP before they feel forced to make a formal referral, as illustrated in Box 14-1.

A formal supervisory referral usually occurs after a supervisor has documented an employee's repeated job performance problems and has discussed the problems with the employee on several occasions. Supervisors are generally taught to recognize job performance problems, which according to Cohen may include any of the following: "increased absenteeism; unexpected vacation requests; sporadic productivity and erratic performance; missed deadlines; increased tardiness; increased strife with coworkers; loss of enthusiasm for work; unpredictable behavior; increased conflicts with the boss; increased complaining and moodiness; an above average rate of accidents at work; costly errors; difficulty remembering and following instructions; difficulty getting along with coworkers; outright defiance" (Cohen, 1985, p. 184). In most programs, supervisors are specifically advised to avoid trying to diagnose employee problems. Referrals should be based on unreasonable employee requests or on observed problems in objective work performance deficiencies (Winkelpleck & Smith, 1988). These should be documented and then discussed with the employee. The EAP referral is then made as one way of addressing the work deficiencies. It is important that employees be advised that merely keeping an appointment with an EAP counselor is not sufficient to resolve the situation. By stressing that the employee must make needed changes in work performance, a clear goal is established which is shared by the worker, the supervisor, and the EAP professional (Winkelpleck & Smith). It is precisely this concrete focus on outcome that gives the EAP significant advantages over other helping approaches.

Social Work Roles

In their initial contact with employees, social workers begin by conducting an assessment. The purpose of this assessment is to explore with the employee problems and issues to be addressed and to identify possible solutions. The problem may be an unreasonable supervisor, dissatisfaction with the job itself, or problems at home. Many times the problem is a personal one.

BOX 14-1   A Troubled Employee and a Reluctant Supervisor

Joanne Hemphill has been employed as an account clerk in a public utility department for three years. She is a generally pleasant individual who is helpful to customers and gets along well with coworkers. Over the last four months her supervisor, Anna Ortiz, has become concerned about changes in Joanne's job performance. Joanne has come to work late on several occasions, although she always calls to say she will be late. She has also spent an increasing amount of time on the phone speaking with family members, and has recently used the majority of her sick leave. The turnaround on processing her accounts has become slower. Anna has just received a reminder notice from the personnel office that Joanne's annual performance evaluation is due at the end of the month.

Anna is sitting at her desk looking at the reminder. She is never comfortable doing annual evaluations, and she especially hates to do them when the employee's performance has been poor. Anna puts the reminder on a pile on her desk. She'll worry about it later.

During the next two weeks Joanne calls in three times saying she needs the day off. She seems near tears. When Anna asks if something is wrong, Joanne just says, "family problems." Anna receives another notice saying that Joanne's personnel evaluation is due. Anna finally sits down to fill out the form and schedules an appointment with Joanne to discuss it. Anna carefully weighs each item on the employee evaluation form. She always takes these evaluations seriously. She likes Joanne and surmises that something must be seriously wrong for her performance to change so much, but she also believes that she should respond honestly to the questions on the evaluation form.

At the time of their meeting, Anna has copies of Joanne's previous evaluations. She reviews with Joanne her perceptions of Joanne's current performance and compares these with her past evaluations. She tells Joanne that she is con-cerned that something is wrong and asks if she might be able to help.

At this point, Joanne breaks into tears. She tells Anna that her fifteen-year-old son James has been sniffing glue and paint. She is also afraid he is using other drugs. She has missed work because she has been afraid to leave James alone and because she has gone out looking for him when he hasn't come home at night.

Anna feels nothing but sorrow for Joanne. She, too, has teenage children and worries about their exposure to drugs. Anna asks Joanne if she has gotten James any help, but Joanne says she has been embarrassed to talk with anyone except her sister and that James refuses to talk with anyone. Anna recommends talking with the EAP counselor, but Joanne is reluctant. Anna suggests she think about it.

The situation worsens. James is staying away from home more and Joanne has missed work three days in a row. Anna is getting ready to talk with Joanne again, when Joanne comes in to ask if she can take an hour to talk with the EAP counselor. Anna is relieved and glad to oblige.

Joanne, at her wit's end, describes the problem in detail to the social worker. Recognizing the severity of the situation, the social worker makes an emergency referral to a local program for chemically dependent adolescents. This case ends on a positive note. The staff at the chemical dependency program help Joanne and her family conduct a family intervention with James. James enters the program and appears to be responding to treatment.

Meanwhile, the social worker at the EAP is glad she could help Joanne, but wonders why it took so long for her to come for assistance. Perhaps it is time for some additional supervisory training and for more outreach to employees.

The information and names contained in this case are fictitious.

Following the assessment phase, the steps that can be taken to resolve the problem are determined. Family members or other significant individuals may be asked to participate with the employee's permission. The social worker identifies the services needed and helps the employee obtain these services. The social worker also monitors the employee's progress. The supervisor continues to assess the employee's work performance. If the worker's performance improves, the case may be closed. In some cases, employees find it beneficial to continue to see the EAP social worker at their own request, even after the job problem that prompted the referral is resolved.

When job performance does not improve, management may take some sort of action. Workers may be reassigned, transferred, demoted, or even terminated. The threat of possible job loss or loss of income introduces a coercive element to the employee assistance process. Although referrals are ostensibly voluntary, it is obvious that the potential for subtle coercion exists. It is possible that the worker may feel that a friendly referral is in fact mandatory. Care must be taken that referrals are clearly explained to employees, and the employee's right to refuse service must be emphasized. This right of refusal must also be made clear to management. When the only alternative is some sort of change of employee status (termination, suspension, or demotion), then the EAP referral may be seen as punitive. In such cases, the prospects for desirable outcomes are much reduced (Atkinson & Kunkel, 1992).

Ethics in Employee Assistance Practice

Many aspects of social work practice are fraught with ethical dilemmas. Social workers in the workplace face a special set of ethical concerns similar to those faced by social workers in the criminal justice and child protection systems. Two of them are discussed here. The first is, to whom are social workers accountable—employees, employers, or some combination of the two? The second is the issue of client confidentiality when assisting workers.

Who Is the Client?   Social workers who are employed by some type of organization—hospital, mental health center, association of citizens with mental retardation, or business—are responsible to their employing organization for their actions. Etzioni (1969) calls these workers "semiprofessionals" since their activities are carried out within the context of a sponsoring organization. A review of the NASW Code of Ethics reminds us, however, that the first responsibility of the social worker is to the client. At times social workers' responsibilities to clients may conflict with their responsibilities to their employers. For example, a mental health center may see its role as providing short-term therapy to clients, yet a social worker may see clients who need long-term treatment in order to minimize the need for repeated psychiatric hospitalizations. Does the social worker follow the mandate of the agency or address the needs of the client? As Kurzman (1988) has pointedly asked, "Whose agent are we?" (p. 21). Many times the occupational social worker faces similar conundrums. For example, what is the social worker's role in deciding whether an employee who is seriously depressed and unproductive at work should be terminated? If the social worker believes that the employee may be able to return to work in six months with proper treatment, can that information be ethically divulged? Is it ethical to withhold from the employer an opinion that an employee is unlikely to return to productive employment? If two employees are in chronic conflict at work and the company asks which of the two should be terminated, can the social worker who has seen both employees as clients take part in that decision?

Social workers who work in EAPs or other programs within business, industry, and government also face dilemmas at the organizational level. For example, what is the appropriate response of the social worker when a company layoff is pending? Is it to encourage the company to seek alternatives to laying off employees, whether or not administration has asked for such suggestions? Is it the role of the social worker to organize employees to fight the layoffs, or is it the social worker's responsibility to provide services to those about to be laid off in order to help them deal with the stress and to locate new jobs? In discussing these dilemmas, Briar and Vinet (1985; Briar, 1983a) comment that social workers are rarely in a position to stop company layoffs, but they can help employees accept a layoff and initiate actions to locate new employment, obtain compensation, change careers, and so forth. However, if management has not made efforts to consider constructive alternatives such as job-sharing or to provide adequate transition services to these employees, the social worker may face an ethical dilemma. The NASW Code of Ethics offers guidance in the matter, not only in terms of what is right for clients, but also to determine whether it is possible to uphold the ethics of the profession while remaining in the employ of the work organization. Kurzman (1988) provides some advice for social workers concerned about ethical practice in the workplace:

> *What becomes most important, from the outset, is the nature of the contract with the employer in labor and industrial settings. If occupational social workers suggest that they may bring greater productivity or profit to the company, for example, people (employees) will quickly become a means, not an end. If one defines the social work function, however, as helping the corporation fulfill its social obligations and its commitment to improving the quality of life for its work force, the practitioner's role is more likely to become an ethical one. Occupational social work expertise is not in promoting profit maximization but in helping organizations meet the needs of individuals, groups, and communities in the world of work—and, reciprocally, in recognizing unions' and managements' obligation and vested interest in doing so (p. 21).*

The key question is whether the demands of the employer and the needs of employees can be ethically reconciled. If they cannot, as Sherwood (1981) and Keith-Lucas (1985) believe, the choice is to resign or openly refuse to accede to the demands of the employer.

Confidentiality.　The everyday work of social workers involves maintaining client confidentiality. Many of the principles governing the practice of confidentiality among social workers apply across work settings. For instance, it is usually considered unethical to release information about clients without their consent. Exceptions occur when clients pose a danger to themselves or others. Some aspects of confidentiality apply to specific work settings. For example, agencies that provide mental health services to minors may be unable to do so without the formal consent of the child's parents even if the child requests services on his or her own. In occupational social work there are certain principles and guidelines that most practitioners believe should govern professional practice.

Starr has written about confidentiality in EAPs by responding to six questions commonly asked about confidentiality in workplace employee assistance programs.

1. What issues arise with regard to confidentiality in employee assistance programs?

   - Disclosure of information should be subject to written agreements between service providers and management.
   - When employees self-refer, no information should be disclosed.
   - When employees are referred by management for job deficiencies, the employer may be informed of EAP participation if the client signs appropriate release forms.

2. What about records that are kept on employees?

   - These records are confidential and may not be disclosed unless authorized by the employee/client.
   - These records must be secured from unauthorized access.

3. When can information be released without an employee's consent?

   - Among the most common situations are cases of child abuse or when an employee poses a danger to self or others.
   - Family may be notified of a bona fide medical emergency.
   - Information may be disclosed for legitimate research purposes, management audits, financial audits, or program evaluations so long as it does not permit identification of individual clients.
   - Court orders may mandate disclosure which is otherwise prohibited, so long as it is confined to data needed to fulfill the purposes of the order.

4. What is considered an employee's consent and what should a written release include?

   - Consent must be written, stipulating the person to whom disclosure is to be made, the client's name, and the reasons for disclosure.
   - Date or conditions under which consent to disclose will expire must be specified.
   - Employees must be informed of the right to revoke a consent for disclosure (but revocation may not be retroactive).
   - Disclosure consents must be signed by the employee and dated.

5. Is it better to have an on-site or off-site program because of confidentiality?

- Off-site locations protect against accidental disclosure.
- Programs with a reputation for confidentiality will be used without regard to location.

6. How will information from third-party providers be handled?

- Information from third-party providers is protected as confidential.
- Third parties should have a release to share information with EAPs.
- Additional information on confidentiality is found in federal statutes and federal regulations.[1]

Kurzman (1987) also underscores the importance of confidentiality in the workplace "because a breach of confidentiality could mean the loss of a worker's job or a stigma that could affect the worker's advancement in a job..." (p. 906). Although breaches appear to be rare, employees are often especially concerned about this aspect of EAPs (Kurzman). Care should be taken to ensure that everyone involved fully understands the principle of confidentiality and the procedures for service providers to maintain confidentiality. Moreover, the subtle or implicit pressure to release information to the employer when an employee feels threatened by job loss must be recognized. A well-publicized policy on confidentiality of services is imperative in creating a credible employee assistance program.

Employer/Organizational Service Model

Increasingly, occupational social workers are involved in practice in which the primary client of intervention is the work organization itself rather than employees or members. This model of social work in the workplace is oriented toward promoting broad policies and services sensitive to the interests or needs of the workforce (Googins & Davidson, 1993; Straussner, 1990). This approach "conceptualizes individual problems in the context of the environment and perceives organizational and environmental variables as being central to the development, maintenance, and treatment of individual problems" (Googins & Davidson, p. 479). This model has been more extensively used in Europe than in the United States, but there are quite a few American examples. Smith and Gould (1993) list some possibilities for this model:

- Consultation on corporate or union-sponsored day care programs for workers' dependents (McCroskey, 1988)
- Negotiation and design of benefits packages (Antoniades & Bellinger, 1983; Kamerman & Kahn, 1987; Kurzman & Akabas, 1981)

[1]Condensed from Starr, A. (1987). Establishing a foundation for effective employee assistance programs. Alexandria, VA: American Society for Personnel Administration, pp. 13–14. Used with permission of The Society for Human Resource Management. Some of this work is based on Carnahan, W. A. (1984). Legal issues affecting employee assistance programs. Arlington, VA: Association of Labor-Management Administrators and Consultants on Alcoholism, Inc., pp. 7–17.

- Examination of shiftwork schedules with an eye to stressors that affect workers' families (Meadow, 1988)
- Development of company relocation policies and services (Gaylord & Symons, 1986; Gullotta & Donohue, 1981; McGehee, 1985; Siegel, 1988)
- Design and operation of equal employment and affirmative action systems (Akabas, Fine, & Yasser, 1982; Wilk, 1988)
- Development of policies relating to employees who have HIV-related disorders (Finch & Ell, 1988; Ryan, 1986) or other life-threatening illnesses
- Development of preretirement, partial retirement, and retirement policies and programs (Habib & Gutwill, 1985; Wilks, Rowen, Hosang, & Knoepler, 1988)
- Promotion of occupational safety and health (Lewis, 1989; Shanker, 1983)

Practitioners' roles most common in this form of occupational social work include consultant, evaluator/analyst, trainer, program developer, and negotiator (Smith, 1988).

Customer Assistance Model

Historically, occupational social workers have been primarily concerned with members of the work force and their families. However, a number of industrial organizations have begun to respond to special needs of customers by developing a wide range of social work services unique to their businesses (de Silva, 1988). Occupational social work interventions are well suited for those organizations whose clients, customers, or consumers include vulnerable or at-risk populations (Smith, 1988). Utility companies, bank trust departments, and funeral homes are among the businesses offering professional social work services to their customers.

Social services offered through Customer Assistance Programs (CAPs) include consumer education, assistance with paying bills for the company's services or products, short-term counseling, liaison, and referral (de Silva, 1988). Practitioners' roles frequently employed in this model include counselor, program planner, consultant, and advocate (Straussner, 1990).

Community Assistance Model

The community assistance model refers to social work practice that helps businesses make contributions to the economic and social well-being of the communities in which they operate (de Silva et al., 1982). This model also addresses the impact of the business on the community and its residents and involves concerns such as local tax rates; employment opportunities; housing costs; demands for educational, social, cultural, and recreational services; and police and fire protection (Smith, 1988).

Among the most common ways that business and social workers have addressed these issues is through the United Way, with businesses providing much of the leadership and incentives during fund-raising drives and social workers providing technical expertise as well as administering and staffing participating agencies (Burke, 1987, 1988). More recently, a number of social workers have been hired to direct corporate contributions to civic and humanitarian concerns (Brilliant & Rice, 1988). Social workers also provide training, supervision, and evaluation services to companies engaged in specific community improvement projects (Masi, 1982; Smith, 1988). Practitioners' roles for this model include community analyst and planner, budget allocator, program developer, broker, advocate, and negotiator (Straussner, 1990).

Work-Related Public Policy Model

The work-related public policy model involves the formulation, identification, analysis, and advocacy of public policies, programs, and services affecting the world of work (Straussner, 1990). For example, both the Americans with Disabilities Act of 1990 and the Family and Medical Leave Act of 1993 have profound effects on the workplace specifically, and on residents of the nation generally (Akabas, 1995). Unemployment is a major problem with serious psychological and social costs (Briar, 1983b; Briar, 1987; Keefe, 1984). Social work activities that aim to shape employment or employment-related policies and program outcomes represent the core of this model of occupational social work. Policy planning and analysis, program development, advocacy, coalition building, and networking are key elements of this model (Foster & Schore, 1989; Sherraden, 1985).

Social Work in the Military

The Uniformed Services of the United States Military is the largest single employer in this country. Members of the Air Force, Army, Marine Corps, Navy, and Coast Guard, along with many of their family members, have access to social services through various military social work programs (also see Garber & McNelis, 1995). You may be surprised to know that the military is host to some of the most extensive and comprehensive programs within all of occupational social work.

This extensive array of programming exists largely due to the unique stressors that military members and their families face. Whitworth (1984) identifies eight such stressors: (1) high mobility, (2) recurring separations, (3) periodic absence of parents, (4) special challenges in the adjustment of children, (5) overseas assignments, (6) high-risk and high-stress jobs, (7) conflicts between needs of military families and needs of the military organization, and (8) authoritarian command requirements. In response to these stressors, the military pioneered some of the most comprehensive family-oriented programs to be found anywhere in occupational social work (Masi, 1982).

Social workers in the military are either commissioned officers or civilian employees. They work in a variety of practice settings, including combat units, mental health facilities, substance abuse treatment programs, hospitals, community service agencies, research facilities, and as commanders' staffs in major military headquarters. Given the range of services available, social work in the military has the potential to be more holistic than other EAP services, and social workers also have the opportunity to influence policies that affect many aspects of military life including housing, relocation, and education (Vinet, personal communication, 1988).

Social work in the military may not appeal to many social workers because they may frequently be critical of military actions. In addition, some social workers may find it difficult to work in a military environment. It is true that social work practice in the military can pose special dilemmas for social workers (also see Masi, 1982). For example, military social work officers can find themselves juggling the simultaneous demands of two distinct professions. According to Smith (1985):

> *This issue is framed by two conflicting questions: is the individual a professional social worker (who happens to be a member of a military organization) primarily oriented to the values, ethics, roles, and mission of a specific helping profession? Or is the individual a military officer oriented primarily to the values, ethics, roles, and mission of the country's armed forces? The answer for hundreds of social workers to both of these questions is yes. Many military social workers define themselves as both full-time, fully committed social workers and full-time, fully committed military officers. Which identity they emphasize and the situations in which they do so become the key issues in adjusting to the inevitable role conflicts they face (p. 52).*

Confidentiality is a special concern since the military social worker cannot assure absolute confidentiality to clients. In fact, chaplains are the only professionals that carry this privilege. Though a military social worker may rarely be required to reveal confidential information, the possibility may affect the client's willingness to entrust the social worker with sensitive information. Social workers versed in the NASW Code of Ethics may feel that military rules governing confidentiality jeopardize their ability to practice as professionals. Of course, many states also do not recognize privileged communication for social workers, and social work records and social workers may be subject to subpoena by the courts. The military does, however, have broader discretion with regard to requiring the release of information about its personnel.

Role conflict, role ambiguity, and concerns about confidentiality are common in most areas of social work practice. Although these issues create tensions and the need for flexibility and creativity, they do not necessarily prevent the ethical and professional application of social work knowledge, values, and skills.

Current Issues in Occupational Social Work

Among the major issues affecting workers in all types of workplaces are those in the following discussions.

Substance Abuse

As mentioned earlier, the modern EAP movement was founded in large part on the need for services related to substance abuse. The widespread nature of substance abuse in U.S. society, the tendency of abusers to deny the problem, and the complex web of problems which ensue from substance abuse make it a prime concern for employers. In recent years, substance abuse has become a greater concern due to the prevalence of illegal drugs (also see Chapter 7 on substance abuse).

Many employers now screen job applicants for illegal drugs. And many use "for cause" testing, in which employees may be required to undergo testing if they appear to be under the influence, if they have been involved in an accident, or if there is evidence of drug paraphernalia. In some cases, drug screening programs are mandated by legislation. Since screening measures involve intrusive procedures such as collection of body fluids, and since the consequences could include job termination, drug screening has become a controversial topic. One concern is that some drugs, such as marijuana, can be detected long after they are used. Since these drugs may have been consumed away from work, the question arises about whether drug testing violates the privacy rights of employees. And while alcohol presents the most problems for employers, its consumption is legal. Furthermore, alcohol is metabolized rather quickly, making it more difficult to detect through screening. Drug testing has created friction between management and the work force, particularly in unionized industries. For many social workers routine testing raises privacy and other civil rights issues.

Education on drug effects, training of supervisors in recognizing and detecting symptoms of abuse, assessment and intervention with abusing employees, counseling and family therapy during treatment, and continuing care and relapse prevention programs during recovery are commonly provided by occupational social workers. Referral to outside service providers is the norm for intensive treatment, although the spiraling costs of substance abuse treatment have caused employers, insurance companies, and treatment providers to substitute less costly alternatives for hospital-based treatment.

Managed Care

The use of managed mental health care programs, most of which are external to the companies they serve, resulted from the desire to contain rising costs. These programs were also seen as a way to direct employees to the type of services best suited to the employee's particular needs. In the days before managed mental health care, most mental health benefits required that services be provided by psychiatrists, and many covered only inpatient treatment in hospitals. This often inappropriate and expensive utilization pattern led to efforts to create more flexible and appropriate types of service.

Occupational social work and employee assistance programs to address these needs proliferated in the 1980s. Paradoxically, at the same time that many of these programs were instituted to control costs, improved mental health benefits in many companies drove up utilization rates for these services. The cost of mental health benefits rose to about 15 percent of the total health benefit cost of employers, despite the fact that about only about 5 percent of the employees used employee assistance programs (Bergmark, Parker, Dell, & Polich, 1991).

During the 1980s, many occupational social workers served as case managers directing employees to service providers. Companies that managed mental health and substance abuse benefits initially worked parallel to the occupational social workers in EAP programs, though the functions of the occupational social worker sometimes overlapped with those of managed care providers. However, the triage function of the managed care companies tended to be less important than the cost containment function, often resulting in friction between occupational social workers and managed mental health programs.

There is every reason to expect that more efforts will be made to control benefit costs. Occupational social workers will continue to balance the desire to obtain necessary services for employees with cost sensitivity in this era of managed health care. Fully integrating occupational social work and managed care functions may result in a better coordinated, comprehensive continuum of care (McMichael, 1994), although social workers generally prefer the client advocate function to financial monitoring.

Sexual Harassment

The increasing numbers of women in the workplace raises additional issues of importance in occupational social work practice. One of the most obvious is sexual harassment, usually defined as unwanted, uninvited sexual advances. Often these advances come from employees who have administrative influence over the worker, thus placing tremendous pressure on the individual subjected to the advances. While the advances are most commonly made toward female workers by male peers or superiors, sexual harassment may also occur when women approach men and between people of the same gender.

Sexual harassment, under provisions of the 1991 Civil Rights Act, is a legal issue. Both civil and criminal actions have resulted from sexual harassment allegations in the workplace, although by far the most common type of legal action is a civil suit. The suit may be brought against the perpetrator, the company, or in some cases against particular individuals who did not use proper remedies in dealing with allegations of sexual harassment.

Sexual harassment is also a significant mental health issue. A recent study indicated that more than 80 percent of the victims of sexual harassment reported symptoms of significant psychological distress (Johnston, 1994, p. 14). Only about 12 percent of sexual harassment victims are believed to seek professional therapeutic help (Johnston, p. 13), and only about one half ever tell anybody at all (Bravo & Cassidy, 1992). Studies of the incidence of sexual harassment in the workplace vary widely; estimates are that 42 percent to 90 percent of women in the workplace will experience some form of sexual harassment (Johnston, p. 13). The degree and type of harassment also vary widely (Houden & Demarest, 1993).

It is clear that many old ways of communicating and interacting present problems and can contribute to what is called a "hostile workplace environment." Overt harassment, in which sexual compliance is required in return for continuing employment or advancement, still occurs. However, more subtle forms of harassment now command professional attention. Social work roles in this important issue take various forms:

- Legal: The development of sexual harassment policies often requires that occupational social workers be knowledgeable about the law, about definitions of proscribed behavior, and about proper procedures for handling complaints. While social workers cannot and should not offer legal opinions, they may be called as witnesses in legal actions alleging sexual harassment.
- Education: Another role is in education programs to alert workers and management to the problem and to inform them of remedies and the personal assistance available. This also serves the purpose of informing potential perpetrators of the importance of this issue and of the possible ramifications.
- Therapy: Social workers also provide therapeutic services to those who have been harassed and sometimes to their families. Family impact is often noted, much as it is in rape cases. For most victims, the required period of therapy is brief. Less commonly, occupational social work programs provide therapeutic services to perpetrators.
- Consultation: Another social work function is consultation with managers and workers as part of the follow-up to sexual harassment complaints, especially if such complaints become public knowledge. This function is part education, part preventive intervention, and part stress reduction.
- Advocacy: Those who have been harassed often manifest symptoms such as depression, absenteeism, reduced motivation, and marital problems. These problems may result in decreased work productivity, which may unwittingly prompt management action against the employee who has already been victimized. In such cases, the employee may benefit from the assistance of a social worker who takes the role of client advocate.
- Evaluation: A crucial function is evaluation of both preventive and therapeutic interventions to determine the effectiveness of services and to suggest needed modification in services. The development of clear, well-communicated policies, prompt investigative action on complaints, provision of support and therapeutic services, and attention to the work situation in which the harassment occurred are all important factors and are consistent with a holistic social work practice approach.

The continuing evolution of gender roles in society, the increasing concern about civil rights protections for gay men and lesbians, and the movement of women into the full range of occupational roles are likely to produce continuing tension over sexual behavior at work. The role of social workers in addressing this issue can be expected to change. More emphasis on prevention, education, and early intervention is already evident in progressive programs.

Workplace Stress

Like sexual harassment, stress in the workplace has taken on increased prominence as the relationship between workers and jobs continues to evolve and as employees become more sophisticated consumers of mental health and social services. Stress is one of the most widespread mental health concerns of recent years. Originally, this term was used to describe any condition that taxed the ability of a bodily system to make adjustments. Early studies on stress and its effects on health focused on physical factors such as noise, heat, and exertion. Over time, this term has come to be identified with psychological stress of the type studied in landmark work by Hans Selye (1978). In this usage, stress is defined as a nonspecific physiological and psychological response to a perceived threat (stressor).

The term stressors now refers to a wide range of phenomena. Some of the most studied job stressors are geographic mobility, in which an individual must make frequent work-related moves (such as in the military); overpromotion, in which an individual takes a position for which he or she does not have the appropriate skills or training; underpromotion, in which frustration results because the employee works at jobs below his or her capabilities; too much work to accomplish; role ambiguity, in which the objectives or requirements of a job are poorly defined; and role conflict (Klarreich, 1985). This last stressor encompasses several problems, including conflicting demands about what ought to be done on the job, doing jobs that the employee does not want to do or does not believe is part of his or her job, and poor relationships with supervisors (Klarreich). During periods of economic recession, stress due to potential job loss runs high. Lengthy recessions in particular industries and geographic areas add to workers' worries about potential employment and job advancement.

Women and ethnic minorities may be particularly susceptible to some job stressors. For example, in occupations that have only recently been available to women, African Americans, and Hispanics, it may take some time for these new workers to become assimilated into the informal and formal communication networks on the job. Since new employees are the "last hired," they also fear being the "first fired."

Individual worker's beliefs and behavioral habits can also contribute to stress. Klarreich (1985) has identified a number of beliefs that, when rigidly held by an employee, can result in considerable stress. For example, some employees feel they must always be perfect, or they may feel that they should never question supervisors. Holding unrealistic beliefs can lead to inappropriate behavioral responses by the individual, including aggressive behavior such as arguments with others at work; avoidance of other employees or meetings; and passivity that includes failure to respond to negative events at work such as accepting unfair assignments without questioning them (Klarreich).

Prolonged stress has been shown to predict serious illness and to contribute to drug abuse and clinical depression. In addition, stress is closely aligned with job burnout. Many companies have, for these reasons, embarked on stress management programs which have goals of employee "wellness." Others offer courses in coping with stress more effectively. Some offer treatment programs for those who are experiencing stress, and almost all have some sort of medical benefit that deals with the depression associated with late-stage stress.

The nonspecific nature of stress has also produced what many managers believe to be frivolous complaints about job stress. The use of the term by health profession-als, particularly psychiatrists, has given credence to the perceptions of many workers that the very nature of work produces debilitating symptoms for which they are en-titled to compensation or consideration.

No one, of course, can protect us from all stress—it is part of life. The current response of employers and occupational social workers is defining clearer roles in the prevention, management, and treatment of stress. As stress and stress disability have increasingly become matters of litigation as well as therapeutic attention, the social worker's tasks in addressing employee concerns have grown more complex. However, the intervention methods themselves are relatively straightforward and ef-fective. With the popularity of stress management at work, social work roles have broadened. Management consultation on work design, mediation in work disputes, promotion of healthier lifestyles, and many other approaches are being advanced as more effective ways to prevent, manage, and treat work stress.

Workplace Violence

One growing source of stress is the threat of violence in the workplace. By some cal-culations, homicide is the nation's third leading cause of work-related death (Barnett-Queen & Bergman, 1993). Violence in the workplace is both more common and more lethal than in the past. The interplay of job insecurity, drug use, serious mental illness, availability of weapons, and ease of opportunity make the epidemic of violence a se-rious concern in many vocational settings.

Social workers, many of whom have had long experience with domestic vio-lence, recognize that there are patterns to most violent behavior. In most cases, prior warnings of dangerous potential can be noted. Threats, past episodes, and escalating severity of violence are common. Factors such as marital problems, substance abuse, illness, threats of job loss, or conflicts with fellow workers (especially supervisors) form a basis of concern.

Many programs are now under way in which social workers and employee as-sistance programs cooperate with law enforcement and security services to develop clear policies on violence, patrol volatile workplaces, and monitor threatening em-ployees. Potential violence can also be defused through professional intervention with employees who pose concerns.

Social work roles in relation to workplace violence consist of:

- Screening: This involves the identification of employees, even at the time of hir-ing, who conform to a profile that may suggest violent potential. In this role, care must be taken not to infringe on the employment rights of an individual merely because of something he or she *might* do.

- Early identification: Most violence prevention programs stress early identification of patterns of behavior that may escalate to violence. Baron (1993), among others, identifies three levels of violence, the first of which may be evident long before there is injury or death.
- Preventive intervention: Social workers offer counseling, family assistance, referral to outside resources, and mediation between workers and supervisors when a threat is identified.
- Debriefing: When violence does occur, the critical period following the event can be very difficult for employees. For example, after the terrorist bombing in Oklahoma City in 1995, social workers and other mental health professionals volunteered hundreds of hours to do *critical incident stress debriefing,* which is designed to prevent or ameliorate later problems such as post-traumatic stress disorder.

The threat of violence in the workplace requires close cooperation between social workers, management, unions, law enforcement, and security forces, and may involve medical professionals as well. Social workers are increasingly being trained in management of hostile and aggressive behavior, threat recognition, and response. For the foreseeable future, social work will likely continue to be a front-line profession regarding this issue.

A Changing, Aging Work Force

Changes in the legal and demographic landscapes of American society promise significant changes in the workplace as well. Millions of people previously denied work are expected to find employment over the next several decades thanks largely to the protections against discrimination afforded by legislation such as the Americans with Disabilities Act of 1990 (Tucker, 1990). Age discrimination laws allow many people to work as long as they are able to perform satisfactorily. Employment opportunities for older people and those with physical disabilities have also increased as a result of reduced physical demands due to new industrial technologies. This is an especially important dynamic as baby boomers of the post-World War II generation approach their elder years (Wilks, et al., 1988; Dychtwald & Flower, 1989). As Smith and Gould (1993) point out, it is important that social workers "provide leadership in promulgating policies and programs that offer older persons opportunities for growth, productivity, and meaning, remembering that the most appropriate *care* that society can provide for many older individuals is meaningful work" (p. 18).

Women, African Americans, Hispanic Americans, and new immigrants are growing mainstays of the workplace, with women constituting as much as two thirds of new entrants to the work force (Smith & Gould, 1993). Many new workers, particularly those from disadvantaged backgrounds and those with little education or few job skills, are likely to be assigned to the most menial and unstable work. Occupational social workers will need to advocate for the least well-prepared employees to ensure that they receive adequate training and gain access to viable career paths. In addition, social workers in the workplace will likely be active in adapting human resource policies and benefits packages, job designs, retirement (including pre-retirement and partial retirement) policies, employee training programs, and other organizational features to the demands of a changing work force.

Dependent Care

Day care and other related services for employees' children and elderly parents are becoming more important and more common features of the workplace (Burud, Aschbacher, & McCroskey, 1984; McCroskey, 1984, 1988). Since child care responsibilities continue to fall mostly on women, raising a family poses a significant barrier to their participation in the work force. An increasing number of employers are attempting to address this problem by fully or partially sponsoring or underwriting child care facilities that are accessible with respect to cost, location, and availability.

Increasingly, workers also face caring for their elderly parents. Few employers assist in providing elder care, although the Family and Medical Leave Act, signed by President Clinton in 1993, requires many employers to provide unpaid leave when younger or older family members need care. Responsibility for elder care also falls primarily on women. Ninety percent of care given to older parents is provided by middle-aged women—women who are typically members of the work force (Dychtwald & Flower, 1989). Today, the average woman can expect to spend more time providing care to her parents than she does to her children (Trading places, 1990)!

Occupational social workers can provide leadership in clarifying the advantages and disadvantages of various models of corporate support of child care and elder care services. Social workers can help shape benefit packages that address dependent care issues, especially for single-parent households. They can also help develop community coalitions to improve child care and elder care services.

Summary

We have considered the varied types of work that social workers do in the occupational arena, from directly intervening in substance abuse and mental health problems to consulting on job design and employee benefit packages. We have also discussed the many settings that employ occupational social workers, from large industrial corporations to small private practices that offer mental health counseling or consultation services. And we have addressed issues of concern to these practitioners, ranging from confidentiality and drug testing to the dual roles of these social workers in serving both employees and employers. Many additional opportunities for practice in the workplace are emerging due to factors as different as increased workplace violence and the changing demographics of the workplace, which will be composed of more women, older workers, and people from a variety of ethnic backgrounds. Given the importance of work in the lives of Americans, this field has a great deal of growth potential. Social workers continue to be optimistic about the future of occupational social work because it allows them to use their knowledge and creativity to improve the lives of many.

Suggested Readings

Googins, B., & Godfrey, J. (1987). *Occupational social work*. Englewood Cliffs, NJ: Prentice-Hall.

Gould, G. M., & Smith M. L. (Eds.). (1988). *Social work in the workplace: Practice and principles*. New York: Springer.

Klarreich, S. H., Francek, J. L., & Moore, C. E. (Eds.). (1985). *The human resources management handbook: Principles and practice of employee assistance programs*. New York: Praeger.

Kurzman, P. A., & Akabas, S. H. (Eds.). (1993). *Work and well-being: The occupational social work advantage*. Washington, DC: NASW Press.

Masi, D. A. (1984). *Designing employee assistance programs*. New York: American Management Associations.

15

Toward Cultural Competence: Social Work, Ethnicity, and Culture

Photo courtesy of Robert Harbison

The original chapter from the first edition of this book has been revised by BRENDA JARMON and GLORIA DURAN AGUILAR, School of Social Work, Florida State University.

Why Social Workers Need to Be Culturally Competent

Imagine that you are the traditional college student—young and living on campus. Think about your first day at college. It was all about leaving home and entering a new world. You arrived at college and, at least metaphorically, unloaded the old family station wagon. You carried all of your family's biases directly to your dorm room. You brought in your whole past—what you believed as well as what your parents believed. With you went your religion, social class, parents' prejudices, and personal prejudices about people of color. All that baggage you brought with you was your self-definition. Those biases and beliefs formed the basis of how you looked at and judged the world (Schuman and Olufs, 1995). Now begin to make a list of words that come to mind when you think of Mexican, African, Chinese, Japanese, and Native Americans. What does this list reveal to you about your perceptions of ethnic minority groups? How will your value system affect you as a social work practitioner? What knowledge, skills, and values will you need to be culturally competent?

Since many cultural groups within the population of the United States have grown during the last two decades and will continue to grow over the next several decades, most social workers feel an obligation to improve their cultural competence. Members of the helping professions and educators continue to move toward developing cultural competence in delivering services and developing public policy proposals. Cross, Bazron, Dennis, and Issacs (1989, cited in Rounds, Weil, & Bishop, 1994) outline five essential elements that contribute to cultural competence at the system, agency, program, and practitioner level (pp. 6–7):

1. Acknowledge and value diversity in terms of understanding how race, culture, and ethnicity contribute to the uniqueness of the individual, family, and community; and recognize the differences among and within ethnic, cultural, and racial groups.
2. Conduct a cultural self-assessment in terms of an awareness of your own culture and how it shapes your personal and professional beliefs and behaviors (see Box 15-1).
3. Recognize and understand the dynamics of difference in terms of the client's and practitioner's behavioral expectations, their interactions, their degrees of self-disclosure, the client's collective orientation (extended family and community), and issues of racism, rapport, and trust levels.
4. Acquire cultural knowledge in terms of client background (socioeconomic status, education, family history, ethnic group identification, and immigration), and cultural knowledge of the community (informal social networks, help-seeking and helping norms, and perceptions of agency accessibility and roles).
5. Adapt social work skills (assessment of problems and relevant interventions) to the needs and styles of the client's culture.

You might say, all that sounds interesting, but why not just apply the basic social work principle that all people should be treated with respect and dignity regardless of their individual characteristics? Certainly this principle should be foremost in the

---

BOX 15-1 Cross-Cultural Exercise

Shared Pride

Break into groups of two to share your ethnic/cultural experiences. Use these questions as a guide for your discussion session. Answer them in order. You may prompt your partner with the questions, helping to keep her or him moving through the list in the time allotted (fifteen minutes total).

- Pick a group that you are a part of.
- What is hard and what is great about being in that group?
- What are you proud of about your group membership?
- Have you always felt proud of your membership in that group?
- What got in the way of feeling completely proud of your membership?

Source: Kathy Castania, Cornell University, 1996.

minds of social workers and other human service professionals, but applying it is not as simple as it may seem.

Ethnicity and culture can influence what clients and social workers *perceive* to be respectful treatment. For example, when a client fails to make direct eye contact with the social worker, this may be misinterpreted by a social worker unfamiliar with the client's cultural experience. For many Hispanics and Native Americans, not making direct eye contact with an older individual or an individual in authority may be a sign of respect, yet the worker may think the client is disinterested or uncooperative.

Treating clients with respect and dignity requires social workers to have more than a passing knowledge of cultural and ethnic groups. It also means that social workers understand the *importance* of culture and ethnicity to their clients. When social workers are familiar with culture and ethnicity, they can say and do things that let clients know that they respect them. Equally important, social workers can consider cultural and ethnic factors that may have a bearing on the client's perception of his or her problems and acceptable ways of handling these problems.

Social work students often ask whether professionals are better or more successful in working with clients when they share the clients' ethnic identity, and whether clients prefer professionals with the same ethnic identity. The professional literature addresses these questions (see Green, 1995; Iglehart & Becerra, 1995; Lum, 1996; Kadushin, 1972; Mizio, 1972; Morales & Sheafor, 1995; Popple & Leighninger, 1993; Schuman & Olufs, 1995). When individuals share similar characteristics it will likely be easier for them to find common ground on which to establish initial rapport, but because two people are black, white, or Mexican American does not ensure that this will happen. An ethnic minority client who has had repeated negative experiences with white professionals is likely to view other white professionals with suspicion and to prefer a worker of the same ethnicity. But two individuals of the same ethnic background may be very different. For example, a Mexican American client may be poor, have a limited education, may practice many traditional Mexican customs, and hold traditional values; while his or her Mexican American social worker may be middle class and highly acculturated, may hold a master's degree, and espouse many values and customs that could be termed Anglo in orientation. It may take consider-able effort for this client and social worker to find the ground on which to establish a working relationship.

Iglehart and Becerra (1995) believe that "ambivalence is reflected in discussions of the best person to work with whom...There is an implication that the *preferred* worker is the trained worker of the same ethnic group as the client" (p. 282). Al-though ethnic minority clients may express a preference for seeing professionals of the same ethnic group, research shows that they often regard their own social worker as highly capable even if he or she is from a different ethnic group (Backner, 1970; Barret & Perlmutter, 1972). In some cases it may be obvious that a professional of the same ethnic background is preferable. For example, a militant African American client may refuse to see anyone but an African American social worker.

Sometimes it is not possible to honor a client's request for a worker of the same ethnic background, because the characteristics of clients may not match the charac-teristics of available staff. In such cases, we recommend that a culturally sensitive worker of another racial or ethnic group be assigned. And sometimes it is not pref-erable to match clients with workers of the same ethnicity. For example, assigning all black clients to black workers and all white clients to white workers is likely to be defined as racist because it discourages associations between members of differ-ent ethnic groups. In most circumstances the critical variables in establishing a sound relationship with a client are the social worker's concern for the client and knowl-edge of good social work practice, including knowledge of the client's ethnicity and culture.

Lum (1996) offers the *metacultural perspective* as a way to further develop a cul-turally competent practice by addressing "the commonalities of people of color in terms of cultural values, beliefs, and behavior" (p. 81). In this context, meta means "between" or "among." The metacultural perspective then is concerned with com-parisons between and among cultures. For example, a worker who adopts a meta-cultural perspective "is concerned with the common cultural linkages that bind the major ethnic groups" (p. 81). While this framework acknowledges differences, it af-firms common cultural themes among people of various ethnicities and reinforces the fact that shared cultures bring about a better understanding of each other's lan-guage and dialect, nonverbal communications, perspectives and world views, be-havioral styles and nuances, methods of reasoning and validating knowledge, and cultural identification.

Terminology for Culturally Sensitive Practice

Social workers frequently confront cultural and ethnic issues in their professional practice. In order to prepare social workers for this aspect of their work, we discuss terminology useful for developing a culturally sensitive knowledge base. The con-cepts we examine are culture, culturally diverse practice, cultural competence, social class, underclass, race, minority, and ethnicity.

According to Schlesinger and Devore (1995), "*culture* is variously defined. It often refers to the fact that human groups differ in how they structure their behavior, their world view, their perspectives on the rhythms and patterns of life, and their concept of the essential nature of the human condition" (p. 903). In an effort to develop a culturally sensitive practice, social workers must recognize and respect the various ideas, customs, skills, and belief (value) systems of people of color. Some definitions of culture focus on behavior while others emphasize shared knowledge. Green (1982) suggests "that in cross-cultural relationships, culture can be thought of as those elements of a people's history, tradition, values, and social organization that become implicitly or explicitly meaningful to the participants during an encounter" (p. 7). As highlighted in this chapter, culture is more than "race" and "ethnicity."

Lum (1996) defines *culturally diverse practice* as "recognizing and respecting the importance of difference and variety in people and the crucial role of culture in the helping relationship" (p. 12). He adds that the primary groups to consider when developing a culturally diverse practice are African Americans, Latino Americans, Asian Americans, and Native Americans. We devote our discussions to these four major ethnic groups. Our intent is to focus on the strengths of these groups' cultural beliefs and practices in assisting students to develop a culturally diverse practice as well as cultural competence in social work practice. As Lum (1996) suggests, social workers should *not* treat people of color as "separate and different" groups; social workers "need to see them as individuals in collective associations: entities in family and community cohorts" (p. 13).

Cultural competence refers to a set of congruent behaviors, attitudes, and policies that come together in a system, agency, or among professionals and enable that system, agency, or those professionals to work effectively in cross-cultural situations (Cross, 1988, p. 1). This produces positive outcomes which enhance the functioning of the client and worker (and ultimately the system, agency, or organization) in terms of their own goals and in future exchanges with members of other cultures. Achieving cultural competence is a *process* not a *product*. It leads to an "ethnic-sensitive practice" that relies on adapting social work principles and skills and takes into account ethnicity and culture. The NASW Code of Ethics embraces diversity and recognizes the pluralistic society in which we live. Developing cultural competence, then, is a step in the right direction in practicing social work.

Social class is often used synonymously with the terms social stratification and socioeconomic status. According to Gordon (1964), "social class phenomena refer to hierarchical arrangements of persons in a society based on differences in economic power, political power, or social status" (p. 40). Hollingshead and Redlick (1958) used three factors to determine social class: "place of residence, occupation of the head of the household, and number of years of education completed." There may also be a psychological component to social class. For example, many Americans probably *think* of themselves as middle class even though they may fall into the lower or upper class of a particular index used to determine class status. Social class is often divided into three categories—lower, middle, and upper, but additional gradations such as lower-lower and lower-middle are often used as well. The term *underclass* refers to those who fall into the bottom end of the lower-class strata and includes many of the homeless and those who have limited opportunity for a better future. Individuals in the underclass may experience chronic unemployment and receive public assistance on a long-term basis. More recently the term underclass has been used in a narrower sense to describe blacks concentrated in ghetto communities (Devore & Schlesinger, 1987). Sociologist William Julius Wilson (1987) suggests that the phrase "socially isolated" is more descriptive of people in these circumstances.

A common dictionary definition of *race* is "a division of the human species characterized by a more or less distinctive combination of physical traits that are transmitted in descent" (Stein, 1978, p. 735). Green is critical of the term race, calling it "the least useful" of the concepts that "describe and account for the difference among human beings" (Green, 1982, p. 6).

> *"Race" as such has no standing as a scientific or analytical category . . . "Races" exist only to the degree that phenotypic characteristics of individuals, such as skin color or hair form, are given prominence as criteria for allocating or withholding social and economic benefits. In nature there are no "races," only populations of organisms which can be described in terms of such natural forces as selection, genetic change, and reproductive characteristics. Race is really a social concept, not a biological one, and it serves no purpose other than to make and justify invidious distinctions between groups of people (Green, 1995, p. 6).*

Green makes it clear that myths and stereotypes based on racial characteristics serve as the basis for discriminatory practices. Some of these practices are defined as individual racism while others are so ingrained in our culture that the term *institutional racism* is used to describe them (Knowles & Prewitt, 1969). A teacher who gives less attention to black students than to white, whether or not he or she consciously does so, commits an act of individual racism. A state judicial system that has a record of handing longer sentences to Hispanics convicted of crimes than to whites is an example of institutional racism.

Although race may not be a scientific concept, people are forced to deal with it daily. Employers may be asked to account for the numbers of African Americans and other racial groups in the work force; public schools must account for racial balance among students. People are commonly described in terms of whether they are black, brown, or white. Social workers often use the phrase "people of color" to identify groups of historically oppressed people who are identified by racial characteristics.

There is considerable debate about the meaning of the term *minority.* It has been used to identify groups that can be distinguished by their cultures and those that have faced political and economic disadvantages. Hopps (1982) commented that the term minority now includes numerous groups, including

> *immigrants, all those with Spanish surnames, women, the physically handicapped, gay men and lesbians, former mental patients, and the elderly . . . Society has now generated and accepted so many definitions that the term,*

the related problems, and the proposed solutions have lost all meaning. As a profession committed to including, not excluding, and to serving groups at risk, social work must recognize and respect the fact that many groups have valid needs and grievances. However, the blurring of the nature and degree of their oppression serves neither their respective causes nor social justice. So- cial work needs to focus on the nuances, subtleties, and specifics of different forms of oppression. It must focus on what is unique as well as what is com- mon. (p. 3)

De La Cancela, Jenkins, and Chin (1993) make the following argument about the word minority:

Minority, used as a label to refer to populations of color, ignores the reality that it is the Caucasian race which is in a numerical minority globally. It also acknowledges what group is in a political majority (i.e., power elite) in the United States and generalizes this to the entire world. We see in this term op- pressive connotations of disempoweredness and poverty that are inappropri- ate and offensive in the context of African, Latino, indigenous, and Asian ethnic groups who are becoming increasingly numerous, economically strong, and sociopolitically organized. (p. 7)

We also believe that the term minority reflects the oppressive nature of U.S. society. While the debate rages, you will be called on to be clear about your value system and where you stand on issues of cultural importance. As both providers and users of social services, we are influenced by certain values, norms, beliefs, and traditions. As social workers strive for an ethnic-sensitive practice, we encourage you to move toward cultural competence by knowing your value system and becoming familiar with the current terminology and trends in the field.

Ethnicity is yet another term with many definitions. McAdoo (1987) writes that the term *ethnic* has traditionally been reserved to describe those of European origin (Italian, Irish, Polish, and so forth) "which indicates the acceptance of the cultural di- versity of [these] more favored groups" (p. 195). On the other hand, the terms race and minority have been reserved for people of color as a means of denying the va- lidity of their culture and ethnicity. As a result, many now prefer to use the terms eth- nicity and culture rather than race and minority to describe these groups (McAdoo; Schlesinger & Devore, 1995). Green (1982) identifies three elements found in most contemporary definitions of ethnicity: (1) There is "a sense of a shared past and sim- ilar origins;" (2) "members of an ethnic group believe themselves to be distinctive from others in some significant way;" (3) "ethnicity is most important at those times when members of differing groups are in contact" (p. 9). Lum (1992) also emphasizes the importance of the term when he states that "ethnicity is a powerful unifying force that gives one a sense of belonging based on commonality" (p. 58).

Our review of the terms culture, culturally sensitive practice, cultural compe- tence, class, ethnicity, minority, and race demonstrates that there is considerable overlap among them and disagreement about how best to define them. In addition, "individuals may act in accordance with their perceived class interests in some situations and in accordance with their cultural preferences or minority identity in others" (Green, 1982, p. 8; also see Devore & Schlesinger, 1987, p. 29). There are also combinations of these concepts. For example, Gordon (1964) coined the term *ethclass* as the combination or intersection of ethnicity and social class, because ethnicity may be used to explain differences among individuals who belong to the same social class group, and social class may be used to explain differences among individuals who belong to the same ethnic group. Despite the confusion among some definitions, social workers constantly encounter the realities and ramifications of these concepts. In this chapter we rely primarily on the terms ethnicity and culture. They are more acceptable because they offer richer descriptions of people than race and minority and therefore better serve the purposes of social workers.

Ethnic-Sensitive Practice

In order to improve social work practice, several authors have developed models that can be used to conceptualize and address ethnic and cultural issues. This section presents one of these approaches.

Schlesinger and Devore (1995) define *ethnic-sensitive practice* as "the view that practice must be attuned to the values and dispositions related to clients' ethnic group membership and social-class position" (p. 903).[1] According to this model, the social worker's primary role is to address the client's problem while keeping in mind the client's ethnic identity and history. Ethnicity has a significant influence on the development of the individual's identity, and ethnic experiences provide a sense of belonging and historical continuity essential to healthy psychological development. An individual with a secure ethnic identity is more likely to achieve personal success.

Schlesinger and Devore identify the components of ethnic-sensitive practice as: (1) "layers of understanding"; (2) a series of assumptions; and (3) prevailing practice principles, skills, and strategies (p. 904). These components assist the social work practitioner in becoming attuned to the special dispositions of each ethnic group.

Layers of understanding incorporate the "values, knowledge, and skills that are the essential ingredients of professional practice in social work. They include social work values, knowledge of human behavior, knowledge of social welfare policies and services, self-awareness, and knowledge of the impact of ethnic reality" (Schlesinger & Devore, pp. 904–905).

Four assumptions underlie ethnic-sensitive practice:

1. Individual and collective history have a bearing on problem generation and solution.
2. The present is more important.

---

[1]This section is based on Schlesinger, E. G., & Devore, W. (1995). Ethnic-sensitive practice. In *Encyclopedia of social work* (19th ed., Vol. 1, pp. 902–908). Washington, DC: NASW Press. Copyright 1995, National Association of Social Workers, Inc.; also see Devore, W., & Schlesinger, E. G. (1987). Ethnic-sensitive social work practice (2nd ed.). Columbus, Ohio: Merrill.

3. Ethnicity has a significant influence on individual identity formation.
4. Ethnicity is a source of cohesion, identity, and strength as well as a source of strain, discord, and strife (p. 905).

An important concept for social workers to understand is that one of the most powerful influences on ethnic group identity is the group's historical experience of oppression and its attempts to ameliorate these problems through culture, language, and religion. Celebrations of political, religious, and family holidays help preserve an ethnic group's feelings of solidarity and dignity. Another critical factor is the group's interaction with mainstream cultures through immigration (such as the case of Haitians and Cubans immigrating to the United States) or through being conquered (as has been Native Americans' and blacks' experiences with whites). These historical events and their transmission from generation to generation affect an individual's perception of life problems and the way in which she or he is likely to seek solutions to these problems. For example, the historical experiences of slavery and discrimination have taught many blacks to remain wary of whites in social interactions until a degree of trust has been established. Ethnic-sensitive practice means paying attention to the systematic sources of oppression that would deny people access to the goods, services, work, and esteem that are consonant with professional social work values.

There are many important cultural institutions that simultaneously serve as sources of cohesion and strength and as sources of strain and discord for members of ethnic groups. The ethnic family is one of these institutions. Devore and Schlesinger (1987) indicate that "the value placed on the family and the extent of commitment to solution of diverse family problems varies by ethnicity and social class" (p. 157). Ethnic and parochial schools, as well as rituals, celebrations, and other traditions also serve as sources of cohesion, but they can cause stress when younger members react differently, especially negatively, to participation in these institutions and activities. Language can also be a source of cohesion and conflict. There are those who wish to maintain their native language, those who prefer to speak only English, and those who use English or their native language depending on the situation. Children may not appreciate their parents' insistence that they speak the family's native language at home when everyone knows English.

According to Schlesinger and Devore (1995), the practice models most consonant with the principles of ethnic-sensitive practice are the problem-solving models (Perlman, 1957; 1986); the structural model (Wood & Middleman, 1989); select segments of task-centered practice (Reid, 1978; Reid & Epstein, 1972); ecological models (Germain & Gitterman, 1980; 1986); and institutional change models (Netting, Kettner, & McMurtry, 1993; Rivera & Erlich, 1992). Ethnic-sensitive practice involves adapting the cognitive, affective, and behavioral skills of social work in keeping with an understanding of clients' ethnic realities.

At the *cognitive* level, ethnic-sensitive practice involves knowledge of the rationale behind the stages of the helping process. The preparatory work involves identifying the characteristics of the community, the agency context, and the nature of the ethnic populations who tend to be served. It is equally important to know how to adapt strategies, such as launching the interaction process and displaying warmth, empathy, and genuineness, in keeping with the client's ethnic reality. Social work practitioners should learn about indigenous helping networks, the use of formally organized helping systems, and the ways in which members of various ethnic groups are likely to define and cope with problems.

Affective skills involve an effort to respond to the client's sense of self and the fact that some members of minority groups (e.g., Native Americans) usually do not seek services voluntarily. Developing cultural competence in this area requires that social workers respect the uniqueness of cultures and acknowledge culture as a dominant force in shaping behaviors, attitudes, and values.

Behavioral skills involve the capacity to move with each client at a pace and in a direction determined by the client's perception of the problem, understanding that that perception is likely to be affected by the client's ethnicity. Social workers must often adapt to the client's environment. For example, the process may involve giving up one's cherished notions about how to treat a client and submitting to the ministrations of elder spokespersons in some groups (e.g., Native Americans and Asian Americans). The social worker must learn to respect the view of many Native Americans, Asian Americans, and people from Eastern Europe that their elders' point of view is the best medicine for them. The elders capacity to smooth troubled family situations or to alleviate symptoms that do not respond to conventional medical treatment may be the only treatment these groups will consider.

Ethnic competence also includes the ability to be a systematic, client-oriented learner as well as a professional or expert.[2] Social workers have much to learn from clients. Ethnically competent social workers view clients as sources of knowledge in defining their own problems and in devising strategies to alleviate these problems. These social workers are also adept at utilizing cultural resources and natural helping networks, as well as the formal agency referrals that social workers and other helping professionals are most often taught to utilize. Finally, ethnically competent social workers recognize *ethnic integrity*. They view other cultures as "whole" or "intact," not "problematic" and in need of intervention by the majority culture.

Cultural and Ethnic Groups in the United States

There are far too many cultural and ethnic groups in the United States to discuss in a single chapter or even a single book. We therefore limit our discussion to Native Americans, black Americans, Hispanic Americans, and Asian (Chinese and Japanese) Americans. Even this limit precludes us from relaying as much useful information as we would like for social work practice, since none of these groups is homogeneous. The ethnic diversity of black Americans is probably least appreciated despite the adversities they faced as slaves and the many different communities they established throughout the old South (Green, 1995). There are hundreds of Native American

---

[2]This paragraph relies on Green, J. W. (1982). *Cultural awareness in the human services* (Chapter 2). Englewood Cliffs, NJ: Prentice-Hall. Copyright © 1982 by Allyn and Bacon. Reprinted/adapted with permission.

tribes, each of which differs in its values, culture, and norms. Hispanics constitute the fastest growing ethnic group in the United States today, but the term Hispanic is so broad that it includes those whose heritages are Mexican, Spanish, Cuban, and Puerto Rican as well as those from Central and South America. There are similarities among these groups, but there are also considerable differences. It is also incorrect to assume that all individuals who are members of a particular Native American tribe or all those from Mexico think and act alike. These factors make it difficult to discuss ethnic and cultural groups in this chapter, and by discussing only a few groups, we will likely disappoint or even offend many people. However, we devote the next sections of this chapter to a presentation of illustrative information that can add to an understanding of social work with clients from various cultural and ethnic backgrounds.

Native Americans

It seems logical to start by discussing Native Americans, since there were an estimated two to three million Native Americans living here when Columbus "discovered" America (Green, 1982). One generalization that we will make is that in population surveys, Native Americans are often reported to have the highest indices of social problems in the country, including poor physical and mental health, economic depression, substandard housing, high crime rates, high accident rates, and low levels of education (Carpenter, 1980; Graves, 1967; Chadwick & Strauss, 1975; Walz & Askerooth, 1973; Wilkinson, 1980). Today it seems astonishing that Native Americans were not accorded citizenship until 1924, that some remained slaves until 1935, and that in New Mexico they did not have the right to vote until 1940 (Wilkinson, 1980).

According to the 1990 census, nearly two million people identify themselves as Native Americans (a 65 percent increase from the 1980 census), including Eskimos and Aleuts (Green, 1995). There are 546 federally recognized tribes (personal communication with staff of the Bureau of Indian Affairs, 1995). Many more groups would like to gain federal recognition in order to increase their access to health, education, and welfare benefits, but federal recognition is increasingly difficult to obtain. From 1977 to 1987, only 13 of 118 applicant groups successfully gained federal recognition (Cook, Masterson, & Trahant, 1987a).

Native American Families

The concept of family is important in all cultures, as it is with Native Americans, but their concept of the extended family is quite different from the Western concept. "American Indian family networks... are structurally open and assume a village-type characteristic. Their extension is inclusive of several households representing significant relatives along both vertical and horizontal lines," including parents, children, grandparents, aunts, uncles, and cousins (Red Horse, Lewis, Feit, & Decker, 1978, p. 68; also see Lewis, 1983; Red Horse, 1980; Wilkinson, 1980). In small reservation communities these households may be in close proximity, but family ties may extend over several states, and these kinship bonds may also be seen in urban areas (Red Horse). It follows that, "[a] tribe is a collection of families in which everyone has accepted duties and obligations to different people..." (Wilkinson, p. 451).

In keeping with social work's tradition of identifying the strengths of people, Lewis (1983) describes the strong points of many Native American families. First, in spite of the high incidence of social problems, Native American families help each other. Social workers are encouraged to look to these natural helping networks. A second source of strength for Native Americans is their religion or spirituality. Rather than identification with a particular religion, this spiritual quality can be described as "seeking peace with nature and with your fellow beings and creator. There is a spirit of cooperation, not competition; a spirit of being in tune and rhythm with the earth" (Lewis, p. 10). Native Americans are actually not "pessimistic and stoical" as sometimes thought; instead, "in the midst of abject poverty and sorrow comes 'the courage to be,' to face life as it is and yet maintain a spiritual optimism" (Lewis, p. 10). A third strength is the intensity and respect found in personal relationships. This includes respect for the creator, for older and younger people, and all other forms of life. One example of the respect for children is that corporal punishment is not condoned. Children comply with their parents' requests out of mutual respect for one another.

Oppression of Native Americans

The long history of white exploitation of Native Americans includes many forms of degradation, from depriving them of their land and mineral rights to removing children from their families and tribes. It is ironic that the government that created many of these social problems faced by Native Americans is now attempting to mitigate them. And the consensus is that federal and state governments continue to do this in ways that fly in the face of what has been advocated as culturally sensitive. Social service delivery systems are poorly equipped to assist Native Americans. As Wilkinson (1980) points out, the social service delivery system is fragmented; one agency handles health problems, another child welfare concerns, and another welfare payments. This is antithetical to the life view of many Native American people. Among Native Americans, the institutions of the family, government, and religion are not separate but parts of a whole (Wilkinson).

Many Native American communities are actually run by the Bureau of Indian Affairs (BIA), a federal agency established in 1824 under the War Department. Although many BIA employees are Native Americans, the agency has long been criticized for its authoritarian attitude toward the Native American people. According to Walz and Askerooth (1973), "the BIA takes care of Indians' money, land, children, water, roads, etc., with authority complete as that of a prison" (p. 25). The intrusion of the BIA has destroyed many of the roles and much of the mutual interdependence that form the heart of Native American families and tribes. In October 1987 Senator Daniel Inouye, a Democrat from Hawaii and chairperson of the Senate Select Committee on Indian Affairs, called for full investigative hearings after a series of articles appeared in the *Arizona Republic* claiming "widespread fraud, mismanagement and waste in the almost $3 billion-a-year federal Indian programs (Cook, 1987, pp. A1, 5). Other claims were that oil companies with government assistance bilked Native Americans out of billions of dollars from oil and gas reserves (Cook, Masterson, & Trahant, 1987b).

The agency responsible for many of the health care needs of Native Americans is the Indian Health Service (IHS); it has also been the target of criticism, including charges of inadequate and incompetent treatment of patients. Although once part of the BIA, the IHS is now under the U.S. Department of Health and Human Services. According to Cook, Masterson, and Trahant (1987c), "the IHS...considers itself a secondary health care provider for Indians, [and] is openly striving to curtail its responsibility for health care among the nation's...Indians" (p. A18).

Other concerns involve the treatment of Native American children. One of the worst degradations has been the removal of children from their families and tribes to be raised by others. This practice was rationalized by welfare workers who viewed Native American child rearing practices as overly harsh. The Indian Child Welfare Act of 1978 was designed to remedy problems concerning the placement of Native American children by restoring greater control over child placement to the tribes. Priority for placement of Native American children is now given to members of the child's own tribe rather than to non-Native American families (see Miller, Hoffman, & Turner, 1980).

In addition, a sizeable number of Native American children were not educated in their home communities and instead were sent to boarding schools where they were not permitted to speak their own language or practice tribal customs. Day schools have also come under attack. Other charges made against some schools for Native American children were maltreatment, including sexual abuse, health and safety violations, inadequate buildings, and lack of attention to the educational needs of students (Cook, Masterson, & Trahant, 1987d, e; Hall & Shaffer, 1987). Native American children drop out of school at a much higher rate than the national average. Children raised in traditional homes sometimes have difficulty in school because their cultural norms differ from those of teachers and school administrators. In the home children may be taught that competition and correcting others are not appropriate. If a Native American child is called on in school to correct another child's answer, he or she may fail to do so out of respect for a classmate rather than an inability to answer the question correctly. Teachers, however, may assume that the child is not paying attention, does not know the answer, or does not care.

The Indian Self-Determination and Education Assistance Act of 1975 emphasized tribal self-government and the establishment of independent health, education, and welfare services for Native Americans, but it seems clear that such legislation has not led to dramatic changes in their lives. In order to improve the situation of Native Americans, Carpenter (1980) calls for a clarification of their legal status, greater accountability on the part of the BIA, and greater use of educational programs by Native Americans; but most important, he calls for a hands-off policy by non-Native Americans and a return of responsibility for planning to Native Americans themselves.

Black Americans

In keeping with Devore and Schlesinger's (1987) "assumptions for ethnic-sensitive practice," we first consider some historical events that have influenced black Americans. No experience has been so profound as that of slavery. Every school child knows of the capture of blacks from Africa, their enslavement in this country, and the vestiges of these experiences in the forms of segregation and discrimination. After slavery was abolished, the Freedmen's Bureau—the first social welfare program to assist blacks—was established; it survived until 1872. "Yet despite the efforts of that agency, for most of the nineteenth century, black Americans were almost totally excluded from social service institutions" (Leigh & Green, 1982, p. 94). The Charity Organization Society largely ignored blacks, but the settlement house workers of the 1880s opened their doors to blacks and were active in the establishment of the National Association for the Advancement of Colored People (NAACP) and the National Urban League (Leigh & Green). The general pattern of segregation of blacks in all sectors of society, including social welfare, persisted well into the twentieth century.

It was not until the 1950s that public policy began to address squarely the issue of racial inequality in America. Until then the segregation of students in public schools was condoned, as was segregation in other public facilities such as buses. The Fourteenth Amendment to the Constitution guarantees all citizens equal protection under the law, but in the 1896 case of *Plessy v. Ferguson* the U.S. Supreme Court decided that facilities for blacks and whites could be *separate* as long as they were *equal*. In 1954 a growing dissatisfaction among blacks with this separate but equal doctrine resulted in a U.S. Supreme Court ruling that marked the official recognition of racial inequality in America. Schools in Topeka, Kansas were segregated but considered equal in terms of physical conditions and quality of education. However, in the case of *Brown v. the Board of Education of Topeka, Kansas,* the Court ruled that separate was not equal. In its decision the Court took the position that "the policy of separating the races is usually interpreted as denoting the inferiority of the Negro Group." The civil rights movement of the 1950s and 1960s and the welfare rights movement of the 1960s and 1970s continued to focus attention on the effects of oppression on blacks and poor people. Demonstrations and protests ranged from peaceful to violent. The Civil Rights Act of 1964 further addressed the issue of racial inequality, but civil rights riots continued into the late 1960s. The 1964 act prohibits racial discrimination in voting and in establishments such as restaurants and theaters. It prohibits discrimination by all programs receiving federal funds, and it bars discrimination on the basis of race and color (as well as religion, sex, and national origin) by all employers and unions with more than twenty-five employees.

However, the effects of discrimination remain. Although workplaces and public accommodations are far more integrated than they were in the 1950s, many universities and colleges continue to struggle with minority recruitment, admissions, and retention, and segregation is still prominent in most residential neighborhoods.

The Black Family

The black family—its strengths and weaknesses—has been a subject of heated debate. One of the most striking characteristics of African society was the strong helping tradition of nuclear families, clans, and tribes or communities. The extended family served as the basis for this mutual aid that was characterized by cooperative relationships between men and women and among those of different class groups (see Martin & Martin, 1985). Although enslavement severely altered blacks' self-help efforts, these traditions continue to influence relationships in black families and communities today.

What we often read in the literature constitutes a weakness or "deficit" model of the black family. Leigh and Green (1982) are critical of this deficit image that "has included notions of poverty, of family and community disorganization, and of deviance from what is assumed to be the accepted cultural patterns of mainstream American life" (p. 105).[3] The stereotypical notion of the black family has been of a single woman with children receiving welfare. While it is true that black women are over-represented in the Aid to Families with Dependent Children program, the diversity among black families has been ignored. One of the most frequently cited publications on the deficit model of black families is the Moynihan Report published in 1965. Moynihan (1965) concluded that, "at the heart of the deterioration of the fabric of Negro society is the deterioration of the Negro family. It is the fundamental source of the weakness of the Negro community at the present time" (p. 1). Other authors have pointed to the fallacies and misconceptions in Moynihan's arguments. Billingsley (1968), in particular, has criticized Moynihan's interpretations, and Hill (1971) identified five major themes that take us away from a pathological view of black families and emphasize their strengths. These five themes are strong kinship bonds, strong work orientation, adaptability of family roles, high achievement orientation, and religious orientation.

Leigh and Green (1982) comment on these five strengths. Evidence of strong kinship bonds is seen in the informal adoption of children and in the roles that older members play in family decision making. Family ties are also reinforced through work. In many families, husband and wife are equal breadwinners, and adult children and adolescents may be expected to help out financially when there is a need for additional income. Flexible family roles are noted in the egalitarian relationships between many husbands and wives, demonstrated not only by spouses' being equal wage earners, but also by sharing in household tasks and decision making. Many single-parent households in the black community benefit from the values of black families, since they can often look to relatives for assistance with finances, child rearing, and other concerns. According to Leigh and Green, "it is this model of interconnected, extended-family households, not the imagery of broken, female-dominated units, that is essential to understanding black family relationships" (p. 111). These relationships are complex, and exchanges between family members are very important, including expectations about what each member should share and contribute in terms of material resources and services.

There is also a strong identification with churches in the black community. Churches reinforce the roles of black families and provide many social services to parishioners. In addition to meeting spiritual needs, churches provide a means of releasing tension and are a source of social activities.

---

[3]Much of this section relies on Leigh, J. W., & Green, J. W. (1982). The structure of the black community. In J. W. Green, *Cultural awareness in the human services* (pp. 94–121). Englewood Cliffs, NJ: Prentice-Hall. Copyright © 1982 by Allyn and Bacon. Reprinted/adapted by permission.

The black population is currently 33 million (12.6 percent of the U.S. population) and is projected to reach 48 million (14.2 percent) by the year 2025 (Bureau of the Census, 1995, p. 14). This population has grown faster than either the total or white population since the 1980 decennial census (Bureau of the Census, 1993). This growth underscores the need for continued ethnic sensitivity in social work practice.

Hispanic Americans

Within the Spanish-speaking population in the United States, there is considerable cultural, racial, ethnic, and national diversity. This makes it difficult, if not impossible, to speak of Hispanics as a "consolidated minority" (Green, 1982). This group generally refers to people "of Mexican, Puerto Rican, Cuban, Central or South American, or other Spanish culture or origin, regardless of race" (Federal Register, 1978, cited in Green, 1995, p. 243). Marin and Marin (1991) suggest that when using labels for a population this diverse, primary attention ought to be given to people's own affirmations of their ancestry and their preference for whatever cultural features they choose to emphasize. Therefore, social workers should follow this general rule: Preferences vary, so when in doubt, ask.

Although most white Americans tend to think of all Spanish-speaking people as immigrants, huge areas of what is now the United States were explored and settled by Spaniards. Mexico once included all of the Southwest, from Texas to California, and extended as far north as Colorado, Utah, Nevada, and Wyoming. In the middle to late 1880s, the vast amount of land Mexico owned was seized by white settlers through both legal and extralegal means. People of Mexican ancestry residing in Texas and the Southwest suffered overt economic, political, and social subordination as white Americans began descending on the territory. As the territory grew in population, white establishments posted "No Mexicans Allowed," "No Mexicans Served," "Whites Only," and similar signs to keep Mexican or Mexican-American clientele out (Iglehart & Becerra, 1995, p. 54).

Currently about 27 million people of Hispanic origin live in the United States—approximately 10.2 percent of the population (Bureau of the Census, 1995, p. 14). Mexican Americans are the largest group of Spanish speakers, with people from Central and South American countries being the second largest group (Campbell, 1994). Puerto Ricans are the third largest group, and Cubans are the smallest group. At the current rate of growth, Hispanics will soon become the largest ethnic minority group in the country. By the year 2025, they are expected to number 57 million, or 16.8 percent of the population (Bureau of the Census, p. 14). Demographically, Hispanics are relatively young, due to immigration by younger people seeking work and to their high fertility rate. The Hispanic population averages eight years younger than the white population and two years younger than the black population, with one third of Hispanics under the age of fifteen. Nearly 90 percent of all Hispanics live in urban areas (Campbell, 1994). The Hispanic population is an important cultural force in the United States, and its rapid growth warrants close attention by social service providers.

Familia

The Spanish word for family is *familia*. According to Aragon de Valdez and Gallegos (1982), "Familia is . . . a primary socializing force, based on traditionalism through language, custom, and social role" (p. 200). Familia is a powerful force in Hispanic families, and it can also be very powerful in Hispanic American families. One component of familialism is authority, especially that of the father (Juarez, 1985). Stereotypes of "machismo" usually suggest domination, but Hispanic male authority in the family is more appropriately economic and moral leadership, protection of women and children, personal and family honor and honorableness, and quiet persistence in overcoming obstacles (Juarez). Values held by Hispanic women include obedience to the husband and nurturance and respect for children. Children, in turn, are expected to defer to siblings who are older. Thus traditional Hispanic values are hierarchical, not egalitarian; this hierarchy is associated with unity and especially strength (Juarez).

A value common to many white Americans as well as Hispanics is that of individualism. For whites individualism means being first or the best in a field of like-minded competitors. But the Hispanic idea of individualism suggests distinctiveness, true difference, and implies participation rather than separateness, in the sense that differences give each of us something unique to offer and something for which we can be respected (Green, 1982). Finally, the Catholic church is an important adjunct to the Hispanic community. Hispanic Americans may seek solace in the church and assistance from clergy when serious problems occur.

Asian Americans

The major Asian ethnic groups in the United States are Chinese and Japanese.[4] The first Chinese to immigrate to the United States came in the 1800s as a result of floods and famine and the ensuing social disorganization in their homeland. Most were men who were prohibited from bringing their families and who planned on returning to China. As the numbers of Chinese immigrants grew, many Americans became alarmed and fearful of their presence, and Chinese immigrants became the targets of hostility. This resulted in the passage of the Chinese Exclusion Act of 1882 and other legislation that severely curtailed the immigration of Chinese to the United States. The relaxation of immigration laws in more recent decades has prompted more Chinese to immigrate to the United States.

Confucianism and Buddhism play strong roles in the lives of the Chinese and Japanese people. Confucianism places great value on maintaining harmony within the world by paying close attention to interpersonal relationships. Buddhism is also concerned with personal relationships, since the well-being of others is considered to be more important than the individual's personal concerns. Individuals are expected to be compassionate, respect life, and be moderate in their behavior.

[4]This section relies on Ishisaka, H. A., & Takagi, C. Y. (1982). Social work with Asian and Pacific Americans. In J. W. Green, *Cultural awareness in the human services* (pp. 122–156). Englewood Cliffs, NJ: Prentice-Hall. Copyright © 1982 by Allyn and Bacon. Reprinted/adapted by permission.

Family life is of paramount importance to the Chinese. Children are taught to show great love and respect for their parents and other family elders. This regard for parents is known as "filial piety." Marriages are the concern of all family members and are carefully negotiated to ensure that these unions will be good for the entire family. Children are part of most family activities and care is taken to socialize them in the ways of proper family conduct. Family relationships are clearly primary, while friendships are secondary. These are some ideals of the Chinese way of life, but acculturation has certainly affected Chinese Americans. Today, there is more emphasis on the nuclear family in many Chinese American households. Social relationships may still be of great concern, but the goal of financial independence from one's family has become more apparent. Chinese Americans are still likely to marry within their own ethnic group, and although cross-ethnic marriages have become more frequent, divorce remains rare.

Many of today's Japanese Americans are not newly arrived but are the relatives of earlier immigrants to the United States. Japanese Americans are often identified by generation. The first generation, those who immigrated from Japan between 1885 and 1924, are called "Issei." The second generation (the children of the Issei born in the United States) are called "Nisei," and the third generation are called "Sansei." The Issei were usually well educated as a result of the emphasis placed on literacy and moral education in Japan. Although Japanese immigrants were at first well received, the majority population eventually became concerned that they might pose a threat to the labor force. Many Japanese immigrants were employed in agriculture, and a number of them eventually captured a large share of the retail vegetable and fruit market on the west coast. Japanese were also quite successful in their self-help ventures, such as mutual aid societies that assisted new arrivals and educated members about discriminatory laws. In addition Japanese immigrants developed their own form of lending institutions that helped many to establish businesses.

Of major importance in the history of Japanese immigrants to the United States is their internment in "relocation" camps after Japan bombed Pearl Harbor in 1941 and World War II erupted. President Franklin D. Roosevelt and others rationalized that internment was necessary because Japanese immigrants and Japanese Americans might threaten the security of the United States, and they needed protection from possible attacks by Americans angered by Japan's actions (Brieland, Costin, & Atherton, 1980). Japanese Americans were forced to give up their jobs and their possessions. Even in the face of these degradations, many volunteered to serve in the armed forces in order to show their allegiance to the United States. It was not until 1987 that Congress officially approved an apology to Japanese Americans for these actions, and in 1988 it approved financial retribution to those who were interned.

Language is of considerable importance to the Japanese people. In fact, they have four types of language—honorific, polite, ordinary, and humble. Each is used to show a different degree of respect. The family line is called the "ie" and represents all the descendants of a particular ancestor. The head of the ie is treated with great respect. Men in traditional Japanese households hold positions superior to women. Of ultimate importance are the respect and loyalty of children to their parents. Respect must also be shown by subordinates in all relationships with superiors. Like the Chinese, the Japanese believe in the common good over individual self-interest. The goal in relationships is to reduce conflict and promote harmony. Individuals are responsible for not bringing shame to themselves or their families.

Cultural Contrasts in Families

As you can see, one of the most important concepts in all cultures is the family. To summarize the differences among the primary ethnic groups, Table 15-1 provides brief statements that contrast some family structural characteristics and values among white Americans, Native Americans, black Americans, Hispanic Americans, and Asian Americans.

The Profession's Response

Social workers have expressed their concerns about policies and services in the larger society that affect ethnic and cultural groups. They have also established special organizations and committees and adopted policies that affect culturally sensitive social work practice and social work education.

Professional Organizations

Several organizations represent the interests of social workers of particular ethnic backgrounds. Williams (1987) comments that "the presence of ethnic and racial special interest organizations is primarily the result of efforts both within and outside the profession to combat racism and discrimination in social work" (p. 343). For example, the National Association of Black Social Workers (NABSW) was established in 1968 to respond to "problems of the black community that had not been sufficiently addressed by mainstream social work" (Williams, p. 344). Its headquarters is in New York City. The NABSW has been concerned with many policy and practice issues, such as the inclusion of more blacks in the profession and improving services to black clients (see McAdoo, 1987, p. 204). The organization holds an annual conference and publishes a journal called *Black Caucus*.

The National Association of Puerto Rican/Hispanic Social Workers is particularly concerned with policies that affect Latinos (Hispanics) and professional opportunities for Latino social service providers (Tourse, 1995). The National Indian Social Workers Association was founded in 1970 to encourage Native Americans and Alaskan Natives to pursue careers in social work (Tourse; Williams, 1987). It also offers consultation to those who provide social services to Native Americans and Alaskan Natives, and promotes legislation that will better the lives of these ethnic groups. Although no national association of Asian American social workers is currently active, state and local organizations concerned with particular Asian cultural and ethnic groups may be operating.

The National Association of Social Workers (NASW) is also concerned about ethnic and cultural issues. In the 1960s it responded to concerns of social workers from

TABLE 15-1 Cultural Contrasts for Knowledge Base Development

White American	Native American	Black American	Hispanic American	Asian American
The single-household "nuclear" family is the preferred form, although numerous variations occur and the perceived strengths and/or weaknesses of these variations are topics of discussion and sometimes controversy.	Family structure is varied from tribe to tribe and rural to urban areas but extended units in various forms are common.	Flexibility in family forms is considered normal; the word "family" sometimes refers to a household unit, and sometimes to a network of households containing affiliated kin.	Family matters command the individual's loyalty. Other institutions or activities are clearly of secondary importance. Families are thought of in an extended sense and include not only kin but sometimes fictive kin (friends of the family).	Strong mutual support, including cooperation, interdependence, and harmony are expected within the family and community.
Extended families in regular contact are believed to be uncommon although they occur in many communities. Individuals linked by kinship have limited obligations to one another and are expected to show loyalty to members of their own household first.	Children often have multiple caregivers and live with various relatives as is convenient.	Extended family networks are common, usually centered on a "base" household with specific links to satellite households. Satellites may be newly married couples, single adults with children, or individuals living alone. The term "family" often includes these units.	Personalism in relations with others is a culturally recognized style and individuals are judged in terms of their behavior with family and friends, and less on their roles or position in formal institutions. Strong personal commitment to others and a warm feeling in relationships are favored.	A strongly hierarchial, stable pattern of family and community relations is the setting for mutual support, expressed through a strong sense of obligation and duty to others. This duty overrides individual preferences.
Relations with those outside the family are a matter of individual preference and limited family control.	Cooperation and sharing are highly valued; individualism, assertiveness, and impulse are discouraged.	One individual in the base household commonly takes on a leadership role on behalf of all members of the family and their households. This individual is often an older woman, occasionally an older man. She may make day-to-day decisions affecting the welfare of others in the family network, and that leadership provides centrality and stability to the family as an extended unit.	Individualism is valued in the same sense that the uniqueness and specialness of persons is in what they specifically do and are in their relationships with others, for example, as someone's mother, father, brother, or child. Individualism in this sense is an aspect of one's personality.	Relations with those outside the family are an extension of family interests expressed most pointedly in family influence in the choice of friends or a mate.
Assertive (but not aggressive) speech and behavioral styles are favored. Leadership and individual achievement are honored.	Noninterference and respect for the rights and choices of others are highly valued. Confrontation is rarely appropriate.	A mutual aid system is typical of extended family networks, and the welfare of others in the network is a primary obligation.	Respect for hierarchy and authority is important, especially when it is seen as an extension of family relations and values. By contrast,	Problems are solved within the family and a code of family pride and honor limits the degree to which internal problems should

White American	Native American	Black American	Hispanic American	Asian American
		Mutual aid is strongly linked to person-centered (in contrast to object-centered) values and to a diffuse sense of humanitarianism, assistance, and sharing.	authoritarianism in extrafamilial contexts is subject to challenge and negotiation, especially if it conflicts with family values of hierarchy and clear role structure.	be known outside the family or shared with professional helpers such as counselors.
Although men's and women's roles traditionally have been defined as separate and distinct, role clarity is sometimes difficult to maintain as economic expectations lead to two-career families.	Pacing activities to the needs and expectations of others is more important than observing clock time and abstract schedules.	Flexibility of roles is highly valued. Wives may work, older children may supervise younger ones, and children may be informally adopted as the needs of households vary. Relations between men and women are ideally egalitarian. Flexibility is viewed as critical to the survival of households and families.	*Machismo* refers to male leadership (and female complementarity) as an extension of hierarchy and authority. Machismo is most properly associated with concepts of honor, trustworthiness, moral courage, and responsibility, and only secondarily with sexual prowess. The honor of women for whom a man is responsible—wife, daughters, sisters, mother—is particularly important.	There is great family pressure to succeed, especially through education. Failure is a failure of obligation to one's family.
Older persons often retain their separateness and independence from households of their adult children. They sometimes worry about "becoming a burden" on others and are expected to maintain their independence as long as possible.	Elders have important ceremonial and sometimes political roles; their views count.	Older persons are often held in high esteem. Their experience in surviving in a hostile world is viewed as evidence of skill and wisdom. A strong religious orientation is sometimes associated with aging and authority. Deference to elders is sometimes demanded.	Some Hispanic individuals and families exhibit a philosophy of fatalism, not as a negative or passive view of the world, but as an appreciation of human frailty and limitations. Wisdom is in recognizing limitations but also in the courage to cope with and endure them. Religious belief may support this sense of struggle as a normal part of the human condition.	Ambiguity in social relations is a source of anxiety.
Religious and ritual practice is a matter of personal preference with little stigma attached to either participation or avoidance.	Religious values and ritual practices infuse life and are critical components in preserving identity and promoting healing.			

Source: Green, J. W. (1995). *Cultural awareness in the human services*. Boston: Allyn and Bacon. Copyright © 1995 by Allyn and Bacon. Reprinted/adapted by permission.

many ethnic groups for additional attention to the pressing issues of civil rights and welfare rights (Williams, 1987). "In 1969, the Delegate Assembly created new policy directions by establishing an overriding priority—the elimination of poverty and racism..." (Battle, 1987, p. 335). NASW's National Committee on Racial and Ethnic Diversity (formerly the National Committee on Minority Affairs) is concerned with policies and programs for ethnic groups including affirmative action within the organization and the larger society. "NASW Standards for Social Work Personnel Practices" also contains nondiscrimination and affirmative action policies for agencies employing social workers (NASW, 1975).

Social Work Education in Cultural Diversity

In 1971 the Council on Social Work Education (CSWE) developed a curriculum policy statement that recognized racial and cultural factors as essential components in social work education. CSWE's most recent standards state that "each program is required to include content about population groups that are particularly relevant to the program's mission ... [and] the curriculum must provide content about people of color, women, and gay and lesbian people ..." (CSWE, 1994, pp. 101, and 140).

CSWE also has standards on the admission of students to social work education programs and employment of faculty to promote cultural and ethnic diversity. These standards not only address nondiscrimination and affirmative action, but they also imply that the student body should reflect the ethnic makeup of the area or region served by the program. Some social work education programs define their primary mission as education for practice with specific ethnic groups. These programs generally have substantial numbers of ethnic minority students.

Many schools attempt to increase enrollments of ethnic and culturally diverse students but are hampered by factors such as inadequate student financial support or perceptions that the college or university is not a welcoming environment. Data compiled by CSWE show that 27 percent of all juniors and seniors enrolled full-time in social work education programs in the 1993–94 academic year were ethnic minorities and that almost two thirds of these students are African American (Lennon, 1995). Ethnic minorities were 21 percent of full-time and 23 percent of part-time master's degree students and 22 percent of full-time doctoral students (Lennon).

Recruitment of ethnically and culturally diverse faculty is another issue faced by social work education programs. Are there many or any faculty from ethnic minority groups in the social work education program you are attending? These faculty are at a premium. Those who have recently received doctorates or who are nearing completion of their dissertations are heavily recruited. The lack of financial support has made it more difficult to return to school for a doctorate. In addition, social workers in high-level agency positions or in private practice may not believe it is reasonable to seek a doctorate when they are currently being paid higher salaries than they could make as assistant or even associate professors.

The content on ethnicity and cultural diversity included in each social work education program may be largely influenced by the program's ethnic minority faculty. While all faculty have an obligation to teach content on ethnicity and cultural diversity, courses with a major focus on this content often fall to faculty from particular ethnic groups. Ethnic minority students often seek out faculty of similar backgrounds for academic counseling and professional advice. These faculty may also play an important role in recruiting students from culturally diverse backgrounds.

CSWE statistics show that ethnic minorities are 27 percent of all faculty teaching in baccalaureate programs and 23 percent teaching in graduate and joint programs (Lennon, 1995). African Americans make up 70 percent of all ethnic minority faculty in baccalaureate programs and 61 percent in graduate and joint programs. If we examine faculty by ethnicity and highest earned degree, at least half of all baccalaureate faculty in each ethnic category except Asian American have a master's degree in social work as their highest degree, while 48 percent of Mexican Americans, 33 percent of African Americans and 38 percent of whites who teach at the baccalaureate level hold a doctorate. In baccalaureate programs, 31 percent of white faculty and 29 percent of black faculty are assistant professors, and 38 percent of white faculty and 32 percent of black faculty held the rank of associate professor or professor (Lennon). In graduate and joint programs, 36 percent of white faculty are associate or full professors compared to 38 percent of black faculty, 51 percent of Asian American faculty, and 30 percent of Mexican American faculty (Lennon).

Retention of ethnically and culturally diverse faculty is an important issue. At most institutions the emphasis on publishing as a requirement for tenure has increased. When senior faculty fail to assist "junior" faculty with establishing a record of research and publications, and when deans and directors give especially heavy teaching loads and committee assignments to assistant professors, it becomes more difficult to weather tenure decisions successfully. Ethnic minority faculty are called on to fill many roles, and because their numbers in academic institutions are usually small, university administrators may stretch these faculty thin by including them on many committees and projects to improve ethnic representation. Frequent appointments are to affirmative action and faculty and student recruitment committees, as advisors to ethnic student organizations, and as mentors to ethnic minority students. While these are laudable and necessary activities, they can distract new faculty from research and teaching activities on which tenure decisions are heavily based. Ethnic minority faculty are also frequently called upon by community agencies and organizations as consultants and board members. These faculty are under considerable pressure to meet all the demands for university and community involvement while meeting requirements for tenure.

The small number of culturally diverse faculty in some social work education programs raises interesting questions, such as whether it is possible to receive a thorough, professional, social work education if there are no or very few ethnic minority faculty—especially if a student expects to practice in a community with a high percentage of culturally diverse clients. In addition, what is the effect on students' education if there are few ethnic minority students in the program or if students do not have ethnic minority clients or other assignments concerned with ethnicity and culture during their field placements? Of course, as the population of particular ethnic groups grows in the United States, we can hope to recruit more African, Hispanic, Asian, and Native Americans to the profession.

Summary

Developing cultural competence and an ethnic-sensitive social work practice is the major theme of this chapter. We live in a multicultural world and nation. Recognizing that culture is a dominant force in shaping behaviors, attitudes, and values, the profession should place a high priority on developing culturally competent practitioners and ethnically sensitive practices. A culturally competent practitioner accepts and respects cultural differences, pays careful attention to the dynamics of those differences, and continually assesses his or her approach regarding culture. Such a practitioner seeks to expand cultural knowledge and resources and adapts services to better meet the needs of clients, whatever their culture. Further, these social workers seek to hire unbiased employees of varied ethnicities and races who are capable of negotiating a multicultural world. Finally, they provide support for staff to become comfortable working in cross-cultural situations. Social workers must be prepared to work with and for clients of diverse cultural and ethnic groups at the appropriate levels of intervention.

Suggested Readings

Boyd-Franklin, N. (1989). *Black families in therapy: A multisystems approach.* New York: The Guilford Press.

Burgest, D. R. (1989). *Social work practice with minorities.* Metuchen, NJ: Scarecrow Press.

Cose, E. (1993). *The rage of the privileged class.* New York: HarperCollins.

Gonzales, J. L., Jr. (1993). *Racial and ethnic groups in America.* Dubuque, IA: Kendall/Hunt.

Green, J. W. (1995). *Cultural awareness in the human services: A multi-ethnic approach.* Boston: Allyn & Bacon.

Greenbaum, S. (1991). What's in a label? Identity problems of Southern tribes. *Journal of Ethnic Studies, 19*(19), 107–126.

Lomawaima, K. T. (1993). Domesticity in the federal Indian school: The power of authority over mind and body. *American Ethnologist, 20,* 227–240.

Lum, D. (1996). *Social work practice and people of color: A process-stage approach* (3rd ed.). Pacific Grove, CA: Brooks/Cole.

Marin, G., & Marin, B. (1991). *Research with Hispanic populations.* Newbury Park, CA: Sage.

McMahon, A., & Allen-Meares, P. (1992). Is social work racist? A content analysis of recent literature. *Social Work, 35,* 533–539.

Saleebey, D. (1992). Introduction: Power in the people. In D. Saleebey (Ed.), *The strengths perspective in social work practice.* New York: Longman.

Staples, R. (1994). *The black family: Essays and studies.* Belmont, CA: Wadsworth.

Ulba, L. (1994). *Asian Americans: Personality patterns, identity, and mental health.* New York: Guilford Press.

Wilson, T. P. (1992). Blood quantum: Native American mixed bloods. In M. P. P. Root (Ed.), *Racially mixed people in America.* Newbury Park, CA: Sage.

16

Lesbians, Gay Men, Bisexuals, and Social Work Practice

Photo courtesy of Robert Cohen. Reprinted with permission. The 1987 Cactus Yearbook, The University of Texas at Austin.

The original chapter from the first edition of this book has been revised by LACEY SLOAN, School of Social Work, State University of New York at Buffalo.

Homosexuality and Bisexuality

Homosexuality is a complex concept but it may be understood initially by considering an individual's sexual orientation.

> *Sexual orientation concerns the individual's preference for partners of the same sex, opposite sex, or both sexes for sexual and affectional relations. Although many people believe that sexual attraction is the only determinant of sexual orientation, the desire to share affection or become life partners also plays a role. A gay man, then, is one who is attracted primarily to other men to satisfy sexual and affectional needs (Berger, 1987, p. 796).*

Likewise, a lesbian is attracted primarily to other women to satisfy these needs, and bisexuals may meet these needs through persons of either gender (also see Moses & Hawkins, 1982, pp. 43–44). However, sexual orientation is not identical to gender identity or gender role. "*Gender identity* is the individual's perception of himself or herself as male or female and is established early in life" (Berger, p. 796). Although the concept of *gender role* has been widely attacked, it "...refers to the set of role behaviors generally expected of males and females..." (Berger, p. 796).

Homosexual is sometimes confused with the terms transvestite and transsexual (Clark, 1987, p. 141). *Transvestites* are individuals who dress and behave like members of the opposite sex; they may be heterosexual, homosexual, or bisexual in their sexual orientation. *Transsexuals* (also referred to as transgendered) are "individuals whose subjective perception of their gender identity differs from their physical characteristics..." (Gochros, Gochros, & Fischer, 1986, p. 18). They may have undergone surgery or other medical procedures to help create a match between their gender identity and appearance. Transvestites and transsexuals are frequently affiliated with the lesbian, gay, and bisexual community.

Although sexual orientation is defined as a preference for sexual and affectional partners of the same or opposite gender, sexual orientation is a *relative* rather than an *absolute* concept. Research such as the well-known work of Kinsey and his colleagues indicates that an individual's sexual orientation falls along a continuum, from totally heterosexual to totally homosexual (Kinsey, Pomeroy, & Martin, 1948). In addition, others have shown that sexual orientation may change during the course of an individual's life, from heterosexual to bisexual to homosexual, or vice versa (see Berger, 1984). There is disagreement about the incidence of homosexuality in the general population. The most widely held estimate is 10 percent, although research indicates that a higher percentage of individuals have had some homosexual experience (Kinsey et al., 1948; Bell & Weinberg, 1978). However, recent research on male sexuality challenges the 10 percent figure as too high (Billy, Tanfer, Grady, & Klepinger, 1993).

Until 1973 homosexuality was defined as a mental illness in the American Psychiatric Association's *Diagnostic and Statistical Manual of Mental Disorders* (DSM). Professionals attempted to help homosexual individuals to understand the causes of their homosexuality or to learn new behaviors in order to encourage them to become heterosexual. This "treatment" often occurred whether or not individuals *wanted* to change their sexual orientation. The decision to remove homosexuality from the DSM was hailed as an important achievement by gay rights groups and others who had fought for its removal.

Negative attitudes toward lesbians, gays, and bisexuals have been blamed on a lack of accurate information about homosexuality, on homophobia, and on heterosexism. *Homophobia* is a fear of homosexuality which is sometimes manifested in expressions of hatred toward lesbians and gay men. *Heterosexism* is "a set of values and structures that assumes heterosexuality to be the only natural form of sexual and emotional expression" (Zimmerman, 1992, p. 342). The inclusion of a chapter on lesbians, gay men, and bisexuals in this text does not imply that these individuals by virtue of their sexual orientation require the assistance of social workers. It does imply that some lesbians, gay men, or bisexuals may need the assistance of social workers because they are members of an oppressed group, and because they may encounter the types of problems of concern to social workers that people from all walks of life face.

Diversity in the Gay Community

The rainbow flag symbolizes the great diversity in the gay community. Lesbians, gay men, and bisexuals may be of any ethnicity, socioeconomic status, age, religion, or political persuasion. Although lesbians, gay men, and bisexuals share many experiences of oppression and discrimination, it is important to acknowledge the additional issues faced by women and people of color due to their gender or ethnicity.

Lesbians and bisexual women face additional oppression and discrimination due to sexism. Many lesbians have felt that gay liberation was insensitive to them as women who rejected the patriarchal ideas embedded in heterosexuality (Bristow & Wilson, 1993). Lesbians and bisexual women have worked to expand the objectives of the gay rights movement to include women's issues, and to expand the objectives of the women's movement to include lesbian issues. For some, lesbianism is an important component of feminism's response to sexism because it challenges the idea that women must be in subservient (hetero)sexual roles with men (feminism is also discussed in Chapter 17).

Lesbian, gay, and bisexual people of color also face many challenges that are compounded by their membership in particular ethnic groups. "Growing up in a racist, sexist, and homophobic society, [they] must deal not only with their sexual identity but with their racial or ethnic identity as well" (Hunter & Schaecher, 1995, p. 1057). By "coming out" as gay or bisexual, people of color may be rejected by members of their own ethnic group and also face racism within the gay community. In recent years, lesbian, gay, and bisexual people of color have been breaking their silence by organizing and by affirming their sexual orientation (see Angelou, 1970; Anzaldua, 1992; Lorde, 1983).

The stigma facing bisexual women and men results in considerable rejection by the straight and gay communities. For example, bisexual men have been labeled as the carriers of acquired immune deficiency syndrome (AIDS) from the gay population to the heterosexual population. In the past, bisexual women and men were often excluded from lesbian and gay organizations. Some lesbian groups are still critical of women who identify as bisexual, accusing them of refusing to give up their heterosexual privilege. When bisexuals date or marry those of the opposite sex, their inclusion in the gay community may become even more suspect. Fortunately, many lesbian and gay organizations now include bisexual and transgendered people in their activities and membership.

Intimate Relationships

Sexual orientation is not synonymous with sexual lifestyle. In other words, people who identify as heterosexual, lesbian, gay, or bisexual may be single or with a partner; celibate, monogamous, or polygamous; and they may or may not practice safe sex. Although much of the attention around AIDS has focused on gay men, it is not homosexual behavior that spreads AIDS, it is unsafe sex practices. Sexual orientation is not a sufficient indicator of lifestyle choices.

For most people—whether they are gay, "bi," or straight—one of their most important concerns is their love relationships. But for the lesbian, gay, and bisexual population, social opportunities for meeting potential partners are more limited. Lesbian or gay bars or bath houses were once about the only places for doing so, but most bath houses have closed in response to the AIDS pandemic. Although bars are still common meeting places for gay and straight singles, there is a growing awareness in both communities that there are better ways to meet people. Bars, where drinking alcohol is the focus, are not necessarily healthy places to make friends and establish satisfying, long-term relationships.

A significant number of lesbians and gay men live as couples. Couples who choose to keep their sexual orientation a secret from their families and others usually suffer considerable stress. A common difficulty is explaining a single bedroom. "Keeping up the front" may also mean spending holidays with family but not being able to bring one's lover along. Because lesbians and gay men have few models on which to base their relationships (Berzon, 1992), special problems can arise and the "rules" of the relationship may need to be clarified (Berger, 1986). Many gay couples struggle to work out their own approaches; in doing so they may confront and consider what they believe to be the ideal relationship (Toder, 1979).

While some relationship issues are unique to lesbian or gay couples, many are similar to those faced by heterosexual couples (Berger, 1986; also see Toder, 1979). An important similarity is the concern for satisfying interpersonal relationships. But many couples, regardless of sexual orientation, experience a lack of intimacy and trust in their relationships, and most do not seek help for their relationship problems even when it is readily available (Berger, 1986).

Lesbians, Gay Men, and Bisexuals Married to Heterosexuals

Many lesbians, gay men, and bisexuals are in marital or intimate relationships with heterosexual partners.[1] Some choose not to tell their heterosexual partners of their feelings for or relationships with members of the same sex. This places everyone involved in a difficult situation. The lesbian, gay, or bisexual individual is either forced to live two lives or to suppress her or his feelings for persons of the same sex, and the heterosexual partner lacks the information needed to understand problems in the relationship. The heterosexual individual may suspect that her or his partner is bisexual or gay but deny or fail to confront the issue. If either partner decides to have extramarital relationships, the problem is further complicated by the possibility of transmitting AIDS and other sexually transmitted diseases, even if precautions are taken.

An increasing number of lesbians, gay men, and bisexuals are choosing to tell their spouses of their sexual orientation. The straight spouse may feel betrayed or used or simply may not wish to continue a relationship with a lesbian, gay, or bisexual partner. The result may be separation or divorce. Other couples may decide to remain in the marriage; they are likely to have strong positive feelings for each other after many years together or they may remain together "for the children." Remaining together may mean working out a mutually agreeable arrangement for extramarital relationships, although the health and emotional risks are apparent. There is no single method for resolving these issues, and one role of social workers is to assist couples in sorting through the possibilities.

Lesbian, Gay, and Bisexual Parents

A number of lesbians, gay men, and bisexuals are parents, and the question arises as to what, if anything, to tell children about the parent's sexual identity (see Berger, 1986; Dolce, 1983). Some parents keep the information from the children because they fear that it will upset them or subject them to ridicule. However, some research indicates that the more open gay parents are about their sexual orientation, the better adjusted the child (Polikoff, 1990). And other research shows that concerns about children of lesbian and gay parents being harassed or teased more frequently than children of heterosexual parents are unwarranted (Patterson, 1992; Polikoff). Many lesbian, gay, and bisexual parents are choosing to tell their children about their sexual orientation so that they do not have to live a lie in their own homes.

Today, lesbians, gay men, and bisexuals are more likely to assert their desires or rights to be parents, but they may still have a difficult time convincing courts of their suitability for parenting, especially when they are seeking custody (Dolce, 1983). Berger (1986) points to the lack of evidence about harm to children who are raised by homosexual parents when he states, "that despite media propaganda to

---

[1]This section relies on Berger, R. M. (1986). Gay men. In H. L. Gochros, J. S. Gochros, & J. Fischer. *Helping the sexually oppressed* (pp. 162–180). Englewood Cliffs, NJ: Prentice-Hall. Copyright © 1986 by Allyn & Bacon. Reprinted/adapted by permission.

the contrary, most children, especially younger ones, are more accepting of a parent's homosexuality than are adults (p. 176). Maddox (1982) concluded that gay parents are no more likely to have homosexual children than heterosexual parents and that the rate of emotional or psychological disturbance is no higher among the children of homosexuals.

There are more options now for parenting among lesbians, gay men, and bisexuals. For example, some lesbian couples are making decisions to have children and are seeking the services of sperm banks or other donors (sometimes a friend or relative of the partner who will not be impregnated). In many states, lesbian and gay parents have used existing adoption laws to allow their same-sex partner to execute a second parent adoption, thereby guaranteeing their child and their partner the legal protection and benefits afforded by adoption (Association of the Bar in the City of New York, 1992; Child Welfare League of America, 1995). Although still controversial and not widely practiced, in some areas lesbians and gay men have been approved as both foster and adoptive parents, especially for hard-to-place children such as youths who identify as gay (Berger, 1986; Maddox, 1982) or children with disabilities.

Coming Out

Coming out is an important process for lesbians, gay men, and bisexuals. Although many hide their sexual orientation from most of the people with whom they associate, more and more are coming out—acknowledging their homosexuality or bisexuality to others in their environment such as family, friends, and coworkers as well as to themselves. Moses and Hawkins (1982) say that "coming out of the closet, that is, identifying or labeling oneself as gay, is one of the most difficult and potentially traumatic experiences a gay person undertakes" (p. 80).[2] An understanding of coming out is useful for social workers since they are likely to encounter clients in many areas of social work practice who are going through this process. Social workers in schools, health centers, counseling programs, and elsewhere who are sensitive to the coming out process can make this period easier for their clients who are looking for an accepting adult with whom to share this information.

Coming out is a lifelong process. Moses and Hawkins describe it as involving four stages: coming out to oneself; identifying oneself to others who are gay; identifying oneself to nongay people; and going public. The process of labeling oneself gay or lesbian is called *signification.* There are a number of different reactions to signification. "One person may be relieved to have a name given to the feeling of being different, another may be devastated by the thought of being 'queer' or 'sick,' and a third person may be confused about what it means" (Moses & Hawkins, p. 80).

Once an adult accepts a homosexual or bisexual identity, the first person with whom she or he shares this signification is usually another lesbian or gay person in

[2]Most of this section relies on Moses, A. E., & Hawkins, R. O., Jr. (1982). *Counseling lesbian women and gay men.* St. Louis: C. V. Mosby. Terminology has been updated to include bisexuality.

a close relationship. The next step is to identify her- or himself to others in the gay community, often by socializing with other lesbians, gays, or bisexuals.

Coming out to nongays is another matter, and lesbians, gay men, and bisexuals do it because "being in the closet is depressing, exhausting, anxiety provoking, and time consuming" (Moses & Hawkins, p. 90). But Moses and Hawkins recommend that before making decisions to come out to specific individuals, lesbians, gays, and bisexuals consider what is to be gained and why they wish to come out, because coming out does not necessarily improve relationships with heterosexuals. Poor relationships with others may be the result of conflict or behaviors that are not related to sexual orientation.

It is usually most difficult to come out to parents. If a lesbian, gay, or bisexual individual decides to do so, he or she should be warned that parents' initial reactions may be negative but to remain calm, keep the lines of communication open, and be patient. Parents are also encouraged to keep the lines of communication open, learn all they can about homosexuality or bisexuality, and not try to "change" their child. If the relationship has been good, there is hope that it will continue to thrive. In some cases one parent accepts the information much more positively than the other parent. When telling parents, Moses and Hawkins recommend giving them reading material addressed to parents of lesbian, gay, and bisexual children (examples are Bernstein, 1995; Borhek, 1983; Clark, 1987; Fairchild, 1992). Helping professionals can also assist parents and siblings by providing accurate information, discussing family members' feelings, helping them to decide how best to respond to questions from others, and deciding with whom to share their daughter or son's sexual identity. Referrals to support groups can also be helpful. For example, Parents and Friends of Lesbians and Gays (PFLAG) has chapters in every state.

Some different aspects of coming out for adolescents warrant attention. Many lesbian, gay, and bisexual people realize their sexual orientation before they are twenty, and many, especially young men, do so before they are fifteen. Adolescents are, however, frequently given the message that it is *not* all right to discuss this subject; consequently these young people are left without factual information and emotional support and are likely to develop negative self-images. Helping professionals should not dissuade adolescents from perceiving themselves as lesbian, gay, or bisexual. Instead, they should help to educate their clients about sexuality, help them explore their feelings about sexuality, and help them develop behaviors with which they are comfortable (for additional information on assisting gay, lesbian, and bisexual youth, see Ashkinazy, 1984; DeCrescenzo, 1992). Moses and Hawkins believe that most adolescents should be *discouraged* from coming out to others until they have reached adulthood, because many parents have a negative response which may lead to punishment and attempts to "cure" the child. According to George Ayala, a human-services professional who serves gay and lesbian adolescents, "more than a quarter of all gay and lesbian youth who come out to their parents are actually ejected from their homes" (see Bernstein, 1995, p. 9). Peers may also be unaccepting. Adolescence is a time when conformity is stressed, and lesbian, gay, or bisexual youths may find little solace from coming out to heterosexual peers. If the client has already identified to others or wants to do so, the professional can educate parents and help the adolescent and her or his family work things out as well as possible. Support groups and agencies are springing up across the country to help lesbian, gay, or bisexual adolescents, including youths who are questioning their sexual orientation.

The coming out stories of adolescents are as varied as the many young women and men who have identified themselves as lesbian, gay, or bisexual. The story of Sara reprinted in Box 16-1 is just one illustration of what coming out is like for a young person.

BOX 16-1 Sara's Coming Out Story

My name is Sara and I am a thirty-three-year-old social worker. I have been an out lesbian for fifteen years. I came out my freshman year of college when I was eighteen. Up to that point, I had not been consciously aware of being a lesbian. I dated boys during high school, had two different marriage proposals my senior year, and lived with a boyfriend my first semester of college. Prior to going to college, I had, to the best of my knowledge, not even known anyone who was gay. I grew up in a conservative family, and we lived in a rural farming community in the Northeast. Like most kids, I had heard and used the sarcastic terms designed to insult—fag, queer, homo, lesie—without awareness of their actual meanings. It was clear, however, that being gay was not okay. I remember having crushes on a few female TV characters from *The Brady Bunch, Family,* and *Charlie's Angels* but not on anyone that was real or in my life. It had never occurred to me that I was gay.

During my first semester at college, I volunteered to work at a hotline that had a large number of gay and lesbian volunteers. I found myself intrigued and freaked out. There was a strong emphasis placed on volunteers being accepting and nonjudgmental—this was a real challenge for me. I became best friends with one of the hotline staff, Devon, a sophomore who was also living with her boyfriend. She told me that she had been in a lesbian relationship once, but other than that, all her dating partners had been men. She felt very positive about her lesbian experience but was committed to her boyfriend to whom she was engaged to be married. Devon and I had become the closest of friends. I felt

more deeply connected to her than any human being I had ever known and it seemed mutual. There was, however, something about this feeling that terrified me. Over time I became aware that I had fallen in love with Devon.

I was totally unprepared for the realization of being in love with Devon. I felt scared and anxious. I had reached the point of it being OK for other people to be gay but not me. The situation was intensified by the fact that Devon and I had each ended our relationships with our boyfriends in the preceding few months. Technically we were both available, which made my feelings all the more unacceptable to me. I paced around my apartment telling myself I was not gay. I could not even say the word lesbian, it felt too graphic and ugly. I felt betrayed by my feelings and yet every moment with Devon was more wonderful than anything I had ever known. I felt extremely confused and overwhelmed. I was too afraid to tell Devon how I felt. I was afraid that she would either reject me or encourage me; neither scenario quieted my distress. I decided to keep my feelings to myself, and I hoped they would dissipate.

A month later, I went to a dance, got extremely drunk and kissed Leslie, a lesbian friend of mine. I had noticed myself watching her whenever she was around. Immediately after kissing Leslie I became embarrassed. I apologized profusely. I emphasized to her that I was straight and had not meant to lead her on. Leslie graciously took me home, put me to bed, and slept on the couch. The panic began again. I was shocked by what I had done. I had kissed a woman. I was incredibly upset and sought solace from Devon. She felt like I was overreacting. I felt very alone and did not know what to make of my experience. I decided it would be best if I avoided going to anymore dances where lesbians would be.

Devon talked me into going to a dance with her two months later and I drank excessively to cope with my anxiety. I ended up kissing Jamie, another lesbian that I had met once before. Again I was mortified by my actions. I told Devon what I had done and in my drunken state, confessed to her that I was in love with her. For weeks afterward we talked about our feelings but decided not to act on them. This was a tremendous relief for me. I clearly was not ready for a lesbian relationship. In fact, I was inclined to think that I was really not gay, I just happened to have fallen in love with a woman. It was a comforting thought. Kissing Leslie and Jamie was the result of excessive drinking, not an indication that I was a lesbian. I needed to avoid dances and dramatically reduce my alcohol intake.

To my surprise, Jamie sent me a very sweet card and asked me out on a date. I found myself feeling very excited by the invitation but nervous. I decided that I needed to see what it would be like to go out on a date with a gay woman. Perhaps on a date I could clarify this straight or gay question that had invaded my psyche. To evaluate the issue fairly, I had to stay sober. After all, I had only kissed women under the influence. We went to a friend's house for dinner and had a very fun evening. I had been nervous; people usually are nervous on first dates but I did not need to drink to get through it. Jamie and I continued to date for six months and then we moved in together.

The most difficult part of my coming out experience was self-acceptance. My sense of self was significantly altered by coming out, as was my view of the future. I loved Jamie very much but I also had to grieve the loss of an envisioned heterosexual life. Although happy, I had to think about what I might lose by coming out to important people in my life. I wanted to share my excitement and joy with those closest to me, but it was very risky. For me, being in the closet did not feel like an option. I have been more fortunate than most in that I have received a great deal of support and acceptance. I am out with all of my family, including both sets of grandparents. One of my sisters was enthusiastically supportive for years, but after becoming a fundamentalist born-again Christian, she disowned me. We have not spoken in three years. It has been the biggest loss and I never would have predicted it. I have chosen to work in settings where I can be openly out; it is a luxury not everyone can afford.

Jamie and I were together for eight years and have remained close friends. My current partner Liz and I have been together seven years and are talking about having a baby. I know if we become parents we will encounter a whole new layer of coming out. I know we are up for whatever challenges that might entail.

Important Issues for Lesbians, Gay Men, and Bisexuals

Lesbians, gay men, and bisexuals suffer many forms of prejudice, discrimination, and oppression. Both individuals and the state have perpetrated violence against them (Herek & Berrill, 1992).[3] This hatred may result in a myriad of problems for lesbians, gay men, and bisexuals, including loss of employment, hate crimes, and poor treatment by heterosexist health and mental health services. In addition, those who internalize these negative messages into self-hatred may participate in self-destructive behavior such as alcohol and drug abuse and even suicide. The following sections

---

[3]In addition to state atrocities such as those that occurred in Nazi war camps, in early America, sodomy was punishable by death or castration. In some states it is still punishable by imprisonment.

discuss some problems facing lesbians, gay men, and bisexuals. Problems such as hate crimes and discrimination have specific implications for the gay community, and although problems such as AIDS and violent relationships occur in all segments of our society, they are also addressed here. The social worker is likely to encounter these issues in various practice settings, and interventions may be needed at the micro, mezzo, and macro levels.

Discrimination

Few states have laws protecting lesbians, gay men, and bisexuals from discrimination based on their sexual orientation.[4] This means that they may be discriminated against in employment, housing, education, and other activities with the sanction of law. Benefits that most heterosexuals take for granted are denied to lesbians, gay men, and bisexuals. For example, same-sex partners cannot legally marry in any state in the United States. Sex between consenting adults of the same gender is illegal in over half of the states. Lesbian and gay parents have lost custody of their children when their sexual orientation became known. Unless a power of attorney provides authorization, or relatives permit it, same-sex partners may not make medical decisions or even funeral arrangements for each other.

Lesbian and gay groups have worked to change and overturn laws and policies that have negatively affected them. For example, laws prohibiting sodomy and other sexual acts between people of the same gender have been repealed or overturned in many states. Some companies and municipalities have extended health insurance benefits to the same-sex partners of employees (also known as domestic partnerships). Lesbians and gay men are asserting their right to marry through religious or private, noncivil ceremonies. However, there are still many negative stereotypes and attitudes that must be overcome before lesbians, gay men, and bisexuals are able to enjoy the full benefits of our society.

Hate Crimes

As U.S. Representative John Conyers, Jr. has said:

> *Whether based on sexual orientation, race, religion, or ethnicity, bigotry and the violence it inspires pose a grave threat to the peace and harmony of our communities. . . . We need especially to educate our youth about tolerance and about appreciating the benefits that we enjoy as a result of our culture's rich diversity of people, beliefs and ways of living (cited in Herek & Berrill, 1992, p. xv).*

Hate crimes are perpetrated against others because of their sexual orientation, race, ethnicity, or religion. These crimes take many forms, including harassment, vandal-

---

[4]This section relies on Herek, G. M., & Berrill, K. T. (1992). *Hate crimes: Confronting violence against lesbians and gay men.* Newbury Park, CA: Sage.

ism, arson, terrorism, assault, sexual assault, and murder. In some states, laws have been passed to enhance the penalties for crimes motivated by hate. In a study conducted by the National Gay and Lesbian Task Force (NGLTF, 1984), 19 percent of respondents reported that they had been assaulted ("punched, hit, kicked, or beaten") at least once because of their sexual orientation, 44 percent had been "threatened with physical violence...[and] 94 percent had experienced some type of victimization" (p. 20). Hate crimes are generally perpetrated by male adolescents or young adults, who are strangers to the victim, and who frequently attack in groups (NGLTF). Many believe that hate crimes are socially condoned in U.S. society because laws allow discrimination against homosexuals and criminalization of homosexual acts.

Health Care

Health care is an important issue because of the poor attitudes and insensitivity of many health care professionals toward gay men, lesbians, and bisexuals. The National Gay Health Coalition and the National Lesbian and Gay Health Foundation are two organizations concerned with the health care needs and treatment of these groups. Janne Dooley (1986) asserts that, "the health care system serves as an agent of social control in reinforcing the sexism and homophobia that exists in all areas of the society" (p. 181). When a new patient goes to a doctor's office or health clinic, the usual procedure is to complete a questionnaire about one's medical history or to be interviewed about this information. But these questionnaires and interviews are usually geared toward heterosexuals (Dooley). For example, a lesbian may be asked questions about the use of birth control without ever addressing her sexual orientation.

AIDS

Gay and bisexual men have been disproportionately affected by AIDS. Approximately 50 pecent of those with AIDS are men who had sex with men (Center for Disease Control, 1995). Although the percentage of new AIDS cases contracted this way is leveling off, most gay and bisexual men have experienced the deaths of friends or loved ones as a result of AIDS, and most have friends who are living with HIV or AIDS. Helping professionals must be aware of the implications of this disease for the gay community, but AIDS affects *all* segments of the population. It is not a "gay disease"; it is a disease transmitted through high-risk behaviors (also see Chapter 8 on health care).

Although some health care professionals have been unwilling to treat people with AIDS, most have responded to it as they have to other serious communicable diseases—by taking necessary precautions when treating patients. Social workers are concerned with the many needs of people with AIDS, such as helping them obtain medical care and fighting discrimination. They may assist with social supports because of the loneliness and isolation that can pervade the final stages of life for those who do not have caring family and friends. Social workers may also provide support to the friends and loved ones of people with AIDS. From education to hospice services, social workers have been an integral part of prevention and treatment in the AIDS pandemic.

Before leaving the subject of AIDS, it is important to address a possible misconception that lesbian women are also highly susceptible to AIDS. Although it is possible for a woman to transmit AIDS to another woman through sexual contact, the incidence of transmission of AIDS between women appears rare (Dressner, 1987). In general, lesbian women have a lower incidence of sexually transmitted diseases than heterosexual women (Dooley, 1986).

Chemical Dependency

Substance abuse problems also occur in all segments of the population, although it is unclear whether gay, lesbian, and bisexual people are at greater risk for alcohol and drug problems. Initial research indicated that homosexuals, especially lesbians, were at higher risk for excessive drinking, drug use, and alcohol-related problems than the general population (see, for example, Fifield, 1975, cited in Kus, 1988, and Hawkins, 1976; Saghir, Robins, Walbran, & Gentry, 1970a, b), but these studies suffer from many design flaws, such as the use of small, convenience samples (see McNeece & DiNitto, 1994, Chapter 12, for a review of this literature; also see Bloomfield, 1993). While more recent and better designed studies show that differences in heavy drinking among lesbians and gay men compared to heterosexuals may be considerably smaller than once thought (McKirnan & Peterson, 1989; Stall & Wiley, 1988; Saulnier, in review, Drug and alcohol problems), some studies show that lesbians and gay men are less likely to be abstainers (McKirnan & Peterson; Skinner, 1994), and lesbians and gay men report more alcohol-related problems than heterosexuals (McKirnan & Peterson). However, research also suggests that lesbians may have a higher awareness of and sensitivity to alcohol problems than the general population, which may result in higher reports of alcohol problems (Hall, 1993).

Considerable debate exists as to whether separate alcohol and drug treatment programs are needed for lesbians, gay men, and bisexuals. Individual client characteristics and preferences should be taken into account when making referrals (see Vourakis, 1983, for a discussion of these treatment issues). Clients should not necessarily be in the same group just because they are gay or lesbian, and in some areas it is difficult to identify enough clients at one time to form a gay or lesbian group (Vourakis). Although the dilemma of whether separate programs and groups are preferable is not easily resolved, social workers are mindful of the principle of self-determination. From this perspective, the social worker's responsibility is to discuss all treatment options with the client; the client may then select from among the available options.

Although twelve-step programs such as Alcoholics Anonymous have been touted as important resources for those recovering from chemical dependency, some people have challenged the appropriateness of this model with oppressed groups such as women and gays (Saulnier, 1994). While many groups welcome members regardless of their sexual orientation, not all members are immune to stereotypical beliefs about homosexuality. In an effort to avoid prejudices experienced in some of these groups and to help people explore aspects of chemical dependency specific to them, self-help groups for gays and lesbians have emerged. Gay Alcoholics Anonymous is the best known. Social workers and other chemical dependency professionals usually keep an ample supply of meeting schedules available for clients, but not every community has these specialized meetings.

Suicide

Suicide is a serious problem, especially among lesbian, gay, and bisexual adolescents. Estimates are that approximately 30 percent of gay youths attempt suicide, which is five times higher than their heterosexual peers (Hunter & Schaecher, 1995). Suicide may be the leading cause of death for gay youths (Gibson, 1989). Regardless of gender and ethnicity, the risk of suicide is higher for people who are gay, but white lesbians are most likely to attempt suicide (Bell & Weinberg, 1978). The risk for suicide decreases with adulthood, perhaps due to greater ability to connect with the gay community (Hunter & Schaecher, 1995).

Oppression, stigma, and isolation are generally considered to be reasons that lesbian and gay youths are more likely to attempt suicide than heterosexual youths. Research also suggests that youths who have been violently assaulted are at higher risk to attempt suicide (Hunter & Schaecher, 1990). Social workers can help reduce the risk of suicide for lesbian, gay, and bisexual youths by working to end the oppression and discrimination they face. In addition, social workers can help lesbians, gays, and bisexuals connect with other lesbians, gays, or bisexuals, and gay-friendly people. It is also important that lesbian and gay youths have positive gay role models so that they can receive support and validation and learn how to adopt a healthy identity (Saulnier, in review, Suicide).

Violence in Relationships

We know that violence can occur in both heterosexual and homosexual relationships. It is discussed in this chapter because it is an issue that has been inadequately addressed in lesbian, gay, and bisexual communities. Relationships are marred by domestic violence, and that violence can result in life-threatening injuries. Many studies suggest the same incidence of violence in gay and lesbian relationships as in heterosexual relationships (Renzetti, 1989; also see Island & Letellier, 1991). In addition, the type of violence experienced in gay and straight relationships is thought to be similar. For example, approximately one third of battered lesbians and one third of battered heterosexual women are sexually assaulted by their partners (see Renzetti, 1988; Texas Department of Human Services, 1991; Waterman, Dawson, & Bologna, 1989).

Lesbians, gay men, and bisexuals face barriers in addition to the ones typically encountered by heterosexual women in overcoming violent relationships. Violence in same-sex relationships may not be recognized as such due to lack of role models for healthy relationships. Closeted battered lesbians and gay men may be threatened with outing either by their abusive partner or by coming forward to report the abuse. Due to homophobia and heterosexism among staff and clients, services designed for battered women may not be supportive of battered lesbians. Battered women's shelters may not openly advertise their services for battered lesbians for fear that they will lose funding or community support. In response to increased awareness of the problem, specific services have been developed in some cities to assist battered lesbians and gay men.[5] There are also antiviolence task groups that address the problem of battering in lesbian and gay relationships, including the Lesbian and Gay Anti-Violence Project in New York City, and the Lesbian Intervention Project of the National Coalition Against Domestic Violence.

Guidelines for Working with Lesbian, Gay, and Bisexual Clients

Helping professionals are likely to encounter gay, lesbian, and bisexual clients regardless of the setting in which they work. Therefore, it is important that services be *accessible* to these clients—this means not only physically, but emotionally and culturally. Although lesbians, gay men, and bisexuals experience many of the same stressors in their lives as heterosexual clients, they face additional stressors of oppression and stigma that social workers can help them address. It has been hypothesized that when lesbians, gay men, and bisexuals present with common clinical complaints such as depression or anxiety, those complaints are the direct result of the negative valued placed on their sexual orientation by the dominant culture in this country" (Bernstein & Miller, 1996, p. 128).[6] The following guidelines provide suggestions to help you meet the needs of lesbian, gay, and bisexual clients in health care, mental health care, and other types of practice settings.

1. *Create nonheterosexist and nonhomophobic services and office space*. All forms and brochures should be written in nonheterosexist language (see Bernstein, 1992). "For example, ask whom to notify in an emergency rather than next of kin. It is also important for all staff to use nonheterosexist language" (Bernstein, 1993, p. 39). This means that you should not assume the sexual orientation of the client. Select reading material for the waiting room that is not offensive to or exclusive of lesbians, gay men, and bisexuals.

2. *Become comfortable with your own sexual orientation and your feelings about lesbians, gay men, and bisexuals.* This is important regardless of your own sexual orientation; if you are uncomfortable with your sexual feelings you will inevitably communicate this to your clients even if you try not to do so (see Clark, 1987, p. 233).

3. *Ask "questions about sexual orientation and sexual activity...[as] part of every thorough assessment.* One of the reasons lesbians and gays do not identify them-

---

[5]Men Overcoming Violence (MOVE) is a program serving both battered gay men and men who batter. As is typical with most domestic violence treatment, couples treatment is not recommended until the violent behavior is stopped. For more information, contact MOVE, 52 Mint St., Suite 300, San Francisco, CA 94103.

[6]Bernstein (1993) actually considers the foundation of clinical issues for lesbians and gay men to be different from heterosexuals and bisexuals. Although her article is thoughtful, we feel that bisexuals experience oppression similar to lesbians and gay men.

selves to their therapist is that they are not asked the right questions. . . . Ask whether people consider themselves to be exclusively heterosexual, mostly heterosexual, bisexual, mostly gay or lesbian, or exclusively lesbian or gay. Separate questions about sexual activity are also important. Some people have a primary identity but occasionally are sexually active with members of the nonpreferred gender. Some people are in transition" (Bernstein, 1993, p. 37).

4. *Recognize the diversity among lesbian, gay, and bisexual people.* Lesbians, gay men, and bisexuals come from all socioeconomic and ethnic backgrounds, and can be of any age, religion, political affiliation, and appearance. Acknowledge and learn about cultural differences—do not ignore them—because they make the person who she or he is.

5. *Appreciate that "all gay people have experienced some form of oppression related to their being gay."* You must work to understand both the subtle and overt oppression that lesbians, gay men, and bisexuals have encountered and continue to face. They may have tried to bury their feelings about these experiences. The helping professional's responsibility is to assist the client in reaffirming his or her own self-worth (Clark, 1987, pp. 234–235).

6. *Understand that being lesbian, gay, or bisexual does not necessarily change someone's emotional reactions to traumatic or crisis situations.* It may, however, add to the stress and limit the options and support available to the person. For example, the critical illness of a life partner will result in similar emotional reactions for anyone who experiences this crisis. However, lesbians, gays, and bisexuals may have to deal with additional stressors and dilemmas if they are not out to their families.

7. *If you are working with a heterosexual woman or man who feels attracted to people of the same gender, validate their feelings.* Do not assume it is just a stage. Instead, tell her or him that these feelings may or may not continue and that such feelings are normal and healthy. It is your job to provide information and help clients explore their options (Howell, R., Working with lesbian clients, National Coalition Against Sexual Assault Workshop, date unknown).

8. *Help your clients identify negative stereotypes of lesbian, gay, and bisexual people that they may have incorporated into their belief system (internalized oppression) and challenge these.* You can help clients by encouraging them to discuss these negative stereotypes. It is common for gay, lesbian, and bisexual people to internalize at least some of these stereotypes because they are so widespread in society. They may express these negative ideas about themselves or about other lesbians, gay men, and bisexuals in subtle or overt ways, but therapists or other helping professionals should not gloss over them with simple intellectualizations about the inaccuracies of such ideas (Clark, 1987, pp. 235–236).

9. *"While working toward expanding the range and depth of awareness of feelings, be particularly alert to facilitate identification and expression of anger, constructively channeled, and affection, openly given."* Like members of other oppressed groups, gay men, lesbians, and bisexuals have learned to hide or repress their feelings. You can assure clients that it is all right to express all feelings, including affection and anger, and you can help them identify acceptable ways of expressing these emotions (Clark, 1987, pp. 236–237).

10. *"Encourage your clients to establish a . . . support system . . . [of] gay people with mutual personal caring and respect for each other."* Lesbians, gay men, and bisexuals frequently experience loneliness during adolescence and adulthood. Encourage clients who do not have a support network of gay friends to develop one. Members of the support system can provide validation for being homosexual or bisexual, and they can serve as a means of reality testing for gay people (Clark, 1987, pp. 239–240).

11. *Encourage clients to educate themselves and to become involved with lesbian, gay, and bisexual communities and issues.* For lesbians, gay men, and bisexuals, just being with others of the same sexual orientation can be an important reminder that they are not as different as they may think. These groups help gays, lesbians, and bisexual individuals realize the universality of their thoughts and feelings. Other means of achieving greater consciousness are reading pro-gay material and working on projects or issues in the gay community (Clark, 1987, pp. 240–241).

12. *"Encourage your client[s] to question basic assumptions about being gay and to develop a personally relevant value system as a basis for self-assessment. Point out the dangers of relying on society's value system for self-validation."* Clients can list their values and assumptions, review them with you, and consider which are worth keeping and which are not. All of us have learned things from our families, schools, and churches that may be more harmful than helpful, but gay men, lesbians, and bisexuals have often been harmed more by these traditional assumptions. By reviewing these assumptions, each person can determine which are useful guides for living fulfilling lives and which are not (Clark, 1987, p. 242).

13. *"Approve homosexual thoughts, behavior, and feelings when reported by your client. This is important to counteract experience with disapproval by authority figures."* Sensitive members of the helping professions can counter the messages of those who believe that homosexuality or bisexuality is not good. Professionals can do this verbally and nonverbally with appropriate touches, smiles, or other approving facial expressions when lesbian, gay, and bisexual clients are mutually expressing affection for one another (Clark, 1987, pp. 243–244).

Organizations for the Gay Community

Lesbian, gay, and bisexual clients who come to see social workers often need opportunities to interact with other lesbian, gay, and bisexual individuals. The number of organizations that provide these opportunities has grown, although they are more limited for gays in rural communities due to ". . . small size, lack of diversity, and extreme secretiveness of the gay community" (Moses & Hawkins, 1982). Berger (1986) identifies five types of organizations that may be of interest to gay people: political, religious, social, professional, and volunteer.[7]

The best known of the political organizations are the National Gay and Lesbian Task Force and the Human Rights Lobby, both located in Washington, D.C. There

---

[7]Much of this section relies on Berger, R. (1986). Gay men. In H. L. Gochros, J. S. Gochros, & J. Fischer. *Helping the sexually oppressed* (pp. 173–174). Englewood Cliffs, NJ: Prenctice-Hall. Copyright © 1986 by Allyn and Bacon. Reprinted/adapted by permission.

are also a number of state and local groups that are concerned with issues such as prevention of discrimination in employment and housing, extension of health insurance benefits to domestic partners, and the repeal of laws prohibiting sexual acts between people of the same gender. But the interests of these and other politically oriented groups are quite broad and also include involvement ". . . in women's issues, in marriage laws, and in any law that attempts to limit personal freedom of sexual, relational, and affectional lifestyles" (LeBaugh, 1979, p. 199). In addition to local, state, and federal legislation, these groups are also concerned with the presentation of gay men, lesbians, and bisexuals in the media and the representation of gay concerns in social service agencies and on human rights boards.

Religious organizations include Dignity for Catholics, Integrity for Episcopalians, and the Metropolitan Community Synagogue for Jews (see Berzon, 1992). These religious organizations were modeled after the Metropolitan Community Church (MCC). MCC began in the 1960s as part of a movement that recognized the need for ". . . a nondenominational church for gays and lesbians who were not welcome or comfortable in traditional churches" (Berger, 1986, p. 176). The Unity Church also welcomes members regardless of sexual orientation. Although a discussion of the opinions of various churches on homosexuality is beyond the scope of this chapter, the organizations mentioned here are concerned that the spiritual needs of lesbians, gay men, and bisexuals be met.

While everyone does not have a desire to join political or religious organizations, everyone needs social contacts. Almost all individuals have at least some informal network of friends. Social groups for lesbians, gay men, and bisexuals are often found on college campuses, or they may be an offshoot of a community political organization. A host of social, sports, and recreational activities and organizations have sprung up around the country. Many post notices of their meetings in the newspapers. They may use the Greek word *lambda* in their names or other symbols, such as the pink or black triangle or the rainbow flag. The rainbow flag, also known as the freedom flag, has become a popular symbol for the gay community in the 1990s. The pink triangle was a symbol used in Hilter's Germany to identify gay men, and the black triangle was used to identify lesbians (as well as gypsies)—all groups Hitler considered undesirable. Today these symbols are used by some lesbian, gay, and bisexual groups to show their strength in spite of adversity.

Professional organizations have also multiplied rapidly. Among them are groups as diverse as the Association of Gay and Lesbian Psychiatrists, Gay Pilots Association, and the Association for Gay Seminarians and Clergy (see Berzon, 1992).

Volunteer organizations include community centers for gays. Some centers are small, receive little funding, and may rely solely on volunteers; others are larger and have paid staff. These organizations often operate an information and referral line, and they may handle crisis calls as well as offer support groups and reading materials. Some communities have more specialized social service agencies for lesbians, gay men, and bisexuals which also offer professional counseling services. Many gay men are now active in AIDS information and support groups. Separate social service agencies for lesbians and gay men developed because traditional agencies and helping professionals have generally been unresponsive to gay, lesbian, and bisexual clients and have often been more harmful than helpful to them.

Although publications for the gay community advertise many of these activities and services, people who are just beginning to explore their lesbian, gay, or bisexual identity may be unaware of the names of local or national publications and where to obtain them (DeCrescenzo & Fifield, 1979). Examples of these publications are the *Advocate, Lesbian Connection,* and *Deneuve Magazine.* The *Gayellow Pages, Gaia's Guide,* and *Places of Interest to Women* are also useful directories.

In rural areas where organized social opportunities for the gay community are often limited, lesbians may participate in organizations such as women's social action groups (DeCrescenzo & Fifield, 1979). We do not intend to convey the impression that lesbians, gay men, and bisexuals are never interested in socializing with heterosexuals. Many do so quite comfortably. It is important, however, to emphasize the ways in which lesbians, gay men, and bisexuals are likely to meet their needs for socialization with other gay and bisexual people.

Social Work and the Gay Community

Some social workers have noted that the profession has hardly been at the forefront of advocacy for lesbians, gay men, and bisexuals. For example, the eighteenth edition of the *Encyclopedia of Social Work,* published in 1987, contains the first separate articles (Berger, 1987; Woodman, 1987) that the National Association of Social Workers (NASW) published on gays and lesbians in its encyclopedia. The nineteenth edition, published in 1995, contains more articles, such as "Gay and Lesbian Adolescents," "Bisexuals," "Gay Men and Parenting," and "Lesbians and Parenting." In recent years the profession has taken a number of actions to affirm its commitment to gay, lesbian, and bisexual individuals. The current NASW Code of Ethics (1980) contains the following statement:

> *The social worker should not practice, condone, facilitate or collaborate with any form of discrimination on the basis of race, color, sexual orientation, age, religion, national origin, marital status, political belief, mental or physical handicap, or any other preference or personal characteristic, condition or status (p. 4).*

Another acknowledgment of the profession's concern includes the NASW policy statements on gay and lesbian issues of 1977, 1987, and 1993. The 1993 policy states that the association "affirms its commitment to work toward full social and legal acceptance and recognition of lesbian and gay people" (NASW, 1994, p. 163). In 1982 NASW established the National Task Force on Lesbian and Gay Issues. Social workers can promote better treatment of lesbians, gay men, and bisexuals by mainstreaming services for them in traditional social service agencies (Grace & Fergal, 1984; Balint, 1985). Mainstreaming allows greater access to a variety of community services.

Some social workers, because of their religious affiliation or other personal values, are unaccepting of gay men, lesbians, and bisexuals. These social workers must face the question of what to do when they have knowledge that a client is lesbian, gay, or bisexual. Another concern arises for the social worker who believes that non-discrimination should be practiced with regard to sexual orientation but is uncomfortable working with clients who are not heterosexual. Social workers faced with these issues may be encouraged to seek assistance to help overcome their concerns, but some social workers do not want to confront or change their beliefs and feelings. These social workers can assume professional responsibility by transferring or referring lesbian, gay, and bisexual clients to colleagues who are accepting of homosexuality and bisexuality.

The Council on Social Work Education (CSWE) has acknowledged its concern for gay, lesbian, and bisexual individuals through its Commission on Gay Men and Lesbian Women. CSWE's curriculum policy statement defines one of the purposes of social work as a commitment to the "enhancement of human well-being and to the alleviation of poverty and oppression" (Commission on Accreditation, 1994, pp. 97, 135). The curriculum policy also states,

> *Each [baccalaureate and master's] program is required to include content about population groups that are particularly relevant to the program's mission. These include, but are not limited to, groups distinguished by race, ethnicity, culture, class, gender, sexual orientation, religion, physical or mental ability, age, and national origin (Commission on Accreditation, pp. 84, 122).*

CSWE's *Handbook of Accreditation Standards and Procedures* also contains specific references to sexual orientation. The evaluative criteria for baccalaureate and master's programs include a requirement that "policies and procedures support the organization and implementation of the program without discrimination on the basis of race, color, gender, age, creed, ethnic or national origin, disability, or political or sexual orientation" (Commission on Accreditation, 1994, pp. 106, 148). Although most colleges and universities also have a written affirmative action policy governing the entire institution, neither federal law nor CSWE standards require that the policy include nondiscrimination based on sexual orientation. However, some state legislatures have adopted such a provision. At this time there are questions about whether CSWE can or should require social work education programs to comply with prohibitions against discrimination based on sexual orientation. The issue is currently under debate (see Van Soest, 1996). CSWE published an extensive bibliography on homosexuality in 1983 (Task Force on Lesbian and Gay Issues, 1983). Also of interest to social workers are journals such as the *Journal of Homosexuality* and the *Journal of Gay and Lesbian Social Services*.

Summary

Our discussion of homosexuality and bisexuality has led to a consideration of a number of topics, including what it means to be lesbian, gay, or bisexual. We have offered information in an attempt to correct a number of myths and misconceptions about homosexual and bisexual individuals and to provide an appreciation of the covert and overt forms of prejudice, discrimination, and oppression directed at lesbians, gays, and bisexuals. Social workers can help gay, lesbian, and bisexual individuals with a number of life issues. These include assisting them with the coming out process and with developing and maintaining healthy personal relationships. Social workers can assist in promoting social, recreational, and political activities within the gay community. They can also work to end oppression and discrimination against lesbians, gay men, and bisexuals. Although social work may not have been at the forefront of the gay rights movement, the profession has clearly moved toward a position in support of the rights of lesbians, gay men, and bisexuals.

Suggested Readings

Bernstein, R. A. (1995). *Straight parents, gay children*. New York: Thunder's Mouth Press.

Berzon, B. (Ed.). (1992). *Positively gay: New approaches to gay and lesbian life*. Berkeley: Celestial Arts.

Borhek, M. (1983). *Coming out to parents*. New York: The Pilgrim Press.

Clark, D. (1987). *The new loving someone gay*. Berkeley: Celestial Arts.

Gochros, H. L., Gochros, J. S., & Fischer, J. (Eds.). (1986). *Helping the sexually oppressed*. Englewood Cliffs, NJ: Prentice-Hall.

Moses, A. E., & Hawkins, R. O., Jr. (1982). *Counseling lesbian women and gay men: A lifestyles approach*. St. Louis: C. V. Mosby.

17

A Feminist Perspective on Social Work

The original chapter from the first edition of this book has been revised by BEVERLY BLACK, School of Social Work, Wayne State University.

Social work is an exciting and challenging profession, but along with teaching and nursing, it has traditionally been thought of as a woman's profession, characterized by low salaries and little prestige. Over three quarters of the 150,000 members of the National Association of Social Workers are women. Given the large numbers of women in social work, and given the concern of many social workers with women's equality, it is no surprise that the profession has a strong interest in women's issues. The term "women's issues" is a misnomer, however, because the issues that affect women affect all of society. A feminist perspective on social work provides a much broader view than would be addressed under "women's issues" because feminism is a frame of reference, including a political perspective, which advocates changes to existing economic and social structures (Van Den Bergh & Cooper, 1986). This framework is useful for studying social issues and problems that are relevant to women and other disenfrancised groups of people.

Our study of a feminist perspective on social work takes us on two tracks. One track explores some of the problems and issues especially facing women in society —poverty, low wages, sexual assault, domestic violence—and social work's response to these problems. The other track considers some of these issues within the profession itself. Concerns within the social work profession focus on job discrimination, sexual harassment, and status due to the large number of women in the profession.

The Feminization of Poverty

The phrase "feminization of poverty" is relatively new, but the concept is not. Among the local and state welfare programs that developed during the early part of the twentieth century were mother's aid and mother's pensions designed to help poor children and their mothers when the father was deceased or had deserted the family. Later, with the passage of the Social Security Act of 1935, the federal government stepped in to help the states with the Aid to Dependent Children program, now called Aid to Families with Dependent Children (AFDC). As discussed in Chapters 10 and 12, most AFDC recipients are children and their mothers. Poor families in which the father is the sole caretaker of the children or in which there are two parents, but one parent is disabled and requires care or is unemployed, may also qualify. The Family Support Act passed in 1988 attempted to decrease dependency by putting parents (primarily mothers) receiving public assistance to work. The legislation requires more recipients to sign up for work programs and provides additional federal dollars for education, job training, and child care (O'Donnell, 1993).

Women have been more likely to become the recipients of public assistance for several reasons. Earlier in this century, fewer women worked outside the home because the appropriate roles of women were thought to be homemaking and child care. Single mothers often had few alternatives to welfare. Another reason for women's poverty is that education and employment opportunities for women have been more limited, and the "pink-collar" jobs in which many women are employed are often low paying. Many women escape poverty or leave the welfare rolls by remarrying; others do so when higher-paying jobs become available; and others leave the welfare rolls when their children grow older (see Committee on Ways and Means, 1993, pp. 724–725). But while they are receiving public assistance, life is generally a continuous struggle to make ends meet.

The astounding poverty figures for women and children in the United States reveal the inability of the current social welfare system to reduce poverty. The United States has one of the highest percentages of children living in poverty among industrialized nations. The overall poverty rate for children is over 21 percent, compared with 9.3 percent for Canada and 2.8 percent for Germany (Danziger & Danziger, 1993). Poverty rates in the United States vary greatly by race; about 15 percent of white children, 44 percent of black children, and 38 percent of Hispanic children live in poverty (Danziger & Danziger). Over 50 percent of children living in single-parent families live in poverty (Jones, 1995), and the number of single-parent families continues to rise. Today, 27 percent of families are classified as single-parent (Jones).

There is a general misconception among the public that the majority of families receiving AFDC remain on the rolls for years, if not for generations. Research confirms that most families remain on welfare for only a short time—about one third stay on welfare more than two years (Abramovitz & Newdom, 1994). However, at any point in time 38 percent of recipients will have received AFDC for more than eight years (Pavetti, 1993, cited in Committee on Ways and Means, 1993, pp. 715–716).

Another misconception relates to the belief that mothers receiving AFDC bear more children in order to receive additional money. There is no research to substantiate this claim. In states where AFDC benefits increase when the number of children increases, "births for mothers receiving public assistance are no more frequent and no greater in number than in states with flat or falling AFDC payments" (Jones, 1995, p. 501).

Most experiences with workfare programs have failed to get parents off AFDC due to the low-wage job assignments they receive. Many recipients are unable to earn sufficient wages to afford child care and health care in addition to general living expenses. Currently, even a modest amount of earnings can result in denial of most public assistance benefits to poor families. Social welfare policy might be more rational if policymakers recognize that some families need public support in addition to work effort on their part (Spalter-Roth, Hartmann, & Andrews, 1992). The editorial by Ellen Goodman in Box 17-1 addresses the dilemmas in a policy that expects mothers to work when child care is not available.

In addition to changes in policies related to public assistance, child care, health care, alimony, and child support to reduce poverty, we could adopt more dramatic solutions. We could pay a wage to parents who stay at home full time to raise their children rather than work outside the home. Although this suggestion has not gained much support in the United States, almost everyone would agree that raising children and keeping house is work. This policy would acknowledge that child rearing has a value similar to the value given to other forms of work. We could also offer all families an adequate guaranteed income to ensure that no American lives in poverty. Another alternative is a policy used in European countries that provides children's allowances—payments to all children to ensure a minimum level of care, regardless of the family's income.

BOX 17-1   Working Mothers and Child Care

Who Will Take Care of the Kids?

BOSTON—In the rush to overhaul welfare, we must have missed the eulogy hidden in all the rhetoric. After all, this policy-making isn't just about ending welfare as we know it. It marks the end of a long cultural debate about motherhood as we know it.

Democrats and Republicans, Senate and House, left and right, are wrangling over the details. But they have already arrived at a consensus as radical as it is unacknowledged. It's a consensus that says: A mother's place is in the work force.

The Democrats called their plan "Work First." They labeled the Republicans' plan "Home Alone." But no one in this rancorous session argued that poor mothers should be at home with their children. Rather, they were arguing about child care funds, about whether anyone would be with those children.

To consider how profound a shift this is, just look back to the origins of welfare. Over half a century ago, the program was deliberately set up to enable widows to care for their children. It purposely discouraged them from going to work. People assumed that children should be with their mothers and that it was pound-foolish to pay others to care for these young. Mothers knew best.

Fast forward to the 1950s when the cultural pressures were overwhelmingly in favor of full-time motherhood. Fast forward to the late 1960s when the women's movement first broke through those domestic boundaries. Even then, feminists deliberately insisted that they were in favor of choice: a woman's choice to stay home or go to work.

Fast forward again, through the 1970s and 1980s when a tidal wave of mothers went to work, not to exercise their choice, but because they had no choice. They entered a work world that remains to this day resolutely hostile to family life.

In a world of working mothers, we have arrived at a point where there is virtually no support for AFDC. Indeed the women struggling hardest at the lowest-paying jobs are often the most angry at paying taxes for others to stay at home. This anger is the real "mommy war" in America.

The ideal of motherhood—the images and the emotions wrapped up in the age-old portrait of mother and child—makes this a tender subject, too tender to be dismissed in public corridors. It's never explicitly said that children are not better off with their mothers.

Indeed in the welfare debate, it is remarkable how rarely the word "mother" is heard unless it is preceded by the phrase "teen-age" or "unwed." The preferred phrase is "people on welfare" and occasionally "able-bodied recipients"—as if AFDC had suddenly become an equal opportunity program.

"I want a comprehensive welfare bill," said Phil Gramm, "that asks the people riding in the wagon to get out of the wagon and help the rest of us pull."

So much for that old button that read "Every mother is a working mother."

The message about what constitutes good motherhood in 1995 is clear. Massachusetts Gov. Bill Weld, waxing poetic about welfare reform, talked about the proud look in a child's eyes when his mother went off to her first job. Was that child 15 or 2? Does it still matter?

So too, Bill Clinton, who initiated the movement to "end welfare as we know it," talks regularly about "parental responsibility." But "parental responsibility" for a poor mother now includes a job.

We continue to praise middle-class women who leave the work force for child-raising. But we insist that poor women leave their children for work.

Rather than acknowledging any conflict in these messages, we divide the two groups of unemployed mothers—not by class or by fate or by a husband's paycheck—into moral categories. The one virtuous, the other promiscuous, lazy, maybe neglectful. We would rather not know how many of today's AFDC mothers were yesterday's married mothers.

There's no doubt that we need to reform welfare. And I see no way out of this mess except through work.

But as a working mother nearly all my life I know how hard it is. I know how laughable the supports are that Congress proposes as part of the package to overhaul the lives of families on welfare. And as someone who has watched the vast transformation in American society, I see the old ideas of motherhood finally crashing to the ground with hardly a wince.

We have come through a great change of mind about mothering. And yet we still haven't answered the question: "Who will take care of the children?"

Poverty is not just a problem of younger women and their children. It is also a problem of older women. Increased Social Security payments in the 1970s and 1980s led to a general decline in poverty among the elderly; however, older women are more likely to be poor than older men. In addition, the likelihood of poverty increases with age, and this is an especially serious problem for women since they tend to live longer than men. In 1993, 15 percent of women and 8 percent of men over age sixty-five were living in poverty (American Association of Retired Persons, 1994). Social welfare programs assisting low-income older Americans include Social Security, Supplemental Security Income, food stamps, Meals-on-Wheels, Medicare, and Medicaid (also see Chapters 11 and 12). Policymakers must carefully plan strategies that will alleviate poverty among all segments of society. The expertise of social workers can be used to do more than provide casework services to women on welfare. Social workers can advocate for policies to prevent and reduce poverty.

Equal Rights

Some of the issues women face, such as poverty and low pay, might be addressed if citizens of the United States added an amendment to the Constitution giving women equal protection under the law. Women gained the right to vote in the United States in 1920; immediately thereafter, an Equal Rights Amendment (ERA) was introduced in Congress. Fifty-two years later Congress passed the following Equal Rights Amendment and sent it to the states for ratification:

Section 1: Equality of rights under the law shall not be denied or abridged by the United States or by any state on account of sex.

Section 2: Congress shall have the power to enforce by appropriate legislation the provisions of this article.

Section 3: This amendment shall take effect two years after the date of ratification.

Thirty-five states, three short of the thirty-eight necessary to ratify the amendment, did so by the 1982 deadline. Therefore, today, no constitutional law guarantees equal rights for women. Although many states adopted their own ERA during the 1970s, no states have done so since the 1982 defeat of the federal ERA. In the last ten years, voters in Vermont and Iowa defeated ERAs in state referendums.

Opponents of the ERA believed the amendment was unnecessary because equal rights for women are guaranteed in various federal, state, and local laws, including the 1964 Civil Rights Act. Additionally, opponents argued that passage of an ERA might lead to an extension of a military registration which could then include a draft and combat duty for women. As you can see by reading the amendment, it did not specifically address the role of women in the armed services or other issues such as marriage, divorce, child custody, and inheritance. Some believed that the vagueness of the amendment left too much interpretation to the courts.

Many polls (e.g., *Washington Post*-ABC News and Gallup) conducted in the early 1980s found that 61 percent to 71 percent of Americans supported equal rights (National Organization for Women [NOW], 1981). To many ERA supporters, it seemed only logical that women should be protected from gender discrimination. Supporters insisted on the necessity of a constitutional amendment rather than a patchwork quilt of laws subject to repeal and modification by Congress or state and local governments. Many supporters of the ERA also believed that it was important for women to have access to the training and opportunities available to men in the military and that military assignments for women should be based on performance and capability as they are for men. These struggles continue today as women press for entrance into the Citadel and other all-male institutions.

Many social workers supported the Equal Rights Amendment and worked hard for its ratification. The National Association of Social Workers endorsed the legislation, believing that the amendment reflected the basic social work values of nondiscrimination and equality. Currently, supporters of an ERA discuss and debate a variety of versions. Many supporters believe an ERA should be broader than the one originally passed by Congress and include the elimination of discrimination based on gender, race, sexual orientation, marital status, and indigence. Some supporters believe that a renewed push for passage of an ERA should not occur until the makeup of the state legislatures across the country suggest a strong likelihood of ratification. Given recent wins by many conservatives, this may take a while.

Pay Equity

The wage gap between men and women narrowed by about ten percentage points in the past ten years. Some of this narrowing is a result of a decrease in men's earnings, and some is a result of an increase in women's earnings. However, women continue to earn less than men, even in the same professions. White women earn an average of 71 cents for every dollar earned by white men, black women earn an average of 64 cents for every dollar earned by black men, and Hispanic women earn an average of 54 cents for every dollar earned by Hispanic men (National Committee on Pay Equity, 1995). Some people note that salary differences occur because women often have less work experience than men and because they spend more time out of the work force having children and caring for their families. Although this is sometimes the case, it also means that women are penalized for performing necessary roles in society.

Various pieces of federal, state, and local legislation prohibit pay discrimination. The Equal Pay Act of 1963 prohibits unequal pay for equal or "substantially equal" work performed by men and women. Title VII of the Civil Rights Act of 1964 prohibits wage discrimination on the basis of race, color, sex, religion, or national origin. In 1981, a Supreme Court decision in *Gunther v. County of Washington, Oregon* made it evident that Title VII prohibits wage discrimination even when the jobs are not identical (National Committee on Pay Equity, 1995). Wage discrimination laws are generally poorly enforced; however, the Equal Employment Opportunity Commission (EEOC) and the Office of Federal Contract Compliance are available to address individual cases of discrimination. Class action suits address pay discrimination when groups of women are affected. These suits are most often very difficult to prove and to win. Although the law seems clear on the subject of equal pay for equal work, stronger legislation and legal redress are needed to ease the burden of those filing discrimination claims and to ensure that employers fulfill their obligations not only concerning pay but in hiring, firing, and promotion decisions.

What about equal pay for different types of work that have similar worth because they require similar skills, effort, responsibility, and working conditions? This issue is known as pay equity (also called comparable worth), and it is a means of eliminating gender and race discrimination in the wage-setting system. Proponents of pay equity base their arguments on the clear gender segregation of occupations and the existence of a dual career ladder which tracks men into certain jobs and women into different jobs. Sixty-one percent of all women workers hold clerical positions or jobs in the service sector (National Committee on Pay Equity, 1995). The major problem with tracking women and men into different jobs is that men are tracked into higher paying jobs than women. For example, many noncollege-educated women are tracked into low-paying jobs as secretaries, retail sales clerks, child care workers, and bank tellers. Noncollege men are tracked into higher paying jobs as auto mechanics, electricians, plumbers, and truck drivers (Queralt, 1996). Thus, the salary differentials between men and women are not addressed fully by the Equal Pay Act.

Pay equity requires that jobs be evaluated according to factors such as the amount of education, years of experience, and level of skill and risk needed to perform each job satisfactorily. The federal government and a majority of firms already use some form of job evaluation. Jobs that require the same levels of these factors are placed on the same pay scale. For example, an executive secretary and a master mechanic would be paid the same if a job evaluation indicated that the same levels of skill, responsibility, and working conditions are needed to perform both jobs, even though the jobs are different.

Opponents of pay equity point to the difficulty and enormity of classifying jobs. They insist that labor markets should be left to operate freely without government interference and that the best determinant of salary is what the market will bear. Others contend that even if the ideas of pay equity and comparable worth have merit, they are impractical, because they are too costly to implement. Salaries for the majority of women would have to be raised, as it would be unlikely that the salaries of men would be reduced.

Supporters of pay equity laws counter this concern by suggesting that the economy would be strengthened if the purchasing power of women was increased. Pay equity would allow many women to become self-sufficient and reduce their reliance on public assistance programs. Several states have successfully implemented pay equity legislation over a period of several years without destroying the state's budget. For example, implementation of pay equity legislation over a four-year period cost Minnesota less than 1 percent of the budget each year (National Committee on Pay Equity, 1995).

The courts have responded to the issue of pay equity by supporting salary differences that appear to arise from labor force competition. In one case, nursing faculty at the University of Washington filed suit, stating they were paid less than male faculty in other departments. The Ninth Circuit Court ruled against the nurses, stating that under Title VII of the Civil Rights Act, suits cannot be brought if salary inequities are due to labor-market conditions.

It is interesting to think about what pay scales for social workers might be if the concept of pay equity were applied and social workers were paid commensurate with their levels of skill and responsibility. Although there is not widespread acceptance of pay equity, as of December 1994, forty-two states had collected data on pay equity, twenty-four states had completed a pay equity study, twenty states had begun making pay equity adjustments, and seven states had fully implemented pay equity (National Committee on Pay Equity, 1995).

Affirmative Action

Affirmative action is one approach that has been used to promote more equitable treatment of women and members of particular ethnic groups. It is a set of public policies adopted, first under President Johnson in 1965, to help eliminate discrimination in employment based on race, color, religion, gender, or national origin. Affirmative action encompasses measures to correct or compensate for past or present discrimination or to prevent discrimination from recurring in the future. It is based on the principle that women and members of minority groups should be admitted, hired, and promoted in proportion to their representation in the population.

Nondiscrimination means that preferential treatment will not be given to particular groups (and that other groups will not be excluded from employment or admissions), but affirmative action implies something quite different. Affirmative action means that organizations and programs will actively promote the hiring and admission of women and members of particular ethnic groups, especially where they are not represented with respect to their numbers in the population. However, affirmative action also relies on the premise that those benefiting have relevant and valid job or educational qualifications.

The National Association of Social Workers (NASW) has long been a supporter of affirmative action. Many social workers' strong belief in equality leads them to support measures to compensate for past discrimination and to prevent future discrimination. In 1975, NASW (p. 13) outlined components necessary for an affirmative action program in human service agencies that can apply to other types of employment as well:

1. The agency should have a strong policy and commitment to implementing it.
2. Responsibility and authority for the program should be assigned to a top agency administrator.
3. The present work force should be analyzed to identify sections or occupations in which minorities, women, or men are underutilized.
4. Specific, measurable, and attainable hiring and promotion goals should be set, with target dates for each area of underutilization.
5. In large agencies, each section manager should be responsible and accountable for helping to meet the goals.
6. Job descriptions, hiring criteria, and job classifications should be reviewed to assure that they reflect actual job needs.
7. The agency should actively search for minorities and women who qualify or can become qualified.
8. All personnel and employment procedures should be reviewed and revised to assure that they do not have a discriminatory effect and that they help attain goals.
9. Procedures or a system to monitor and measure progress regularly should be developed.

Beginning in the late 1960s, the use of affirmative action plans to assist women and ethnic minorities grew. However, since the 1980s, critics of affirmative action programs have increased. In 1995, Pete Wilson, the governor of California, signed an executive order abolishing the state's affirmative action programs. The Board of Regents for the state of California also repealed its affirmative action program for admission of students and hiring of faculty and staff. In 1996 the Fifth U.S. Circuit Court of Appeals ruled that the University of Texas could not use race as a factor in admitting students. Many other efforts at the state and federal level are under way to repeal gender- and race-based affirmative action programs. Opposition to affirmative action is usually based on the grounds of reverse discrimination and unwarranted preferences. But others believe that without these policies there will be an erosion of the gains that women and particular ethnic groups have made.

Abortion: A Woman's Right?

Abortions became illegal in the United States around the middle to late 1800s. Few states permitted abortions except when the mother's life was in danger. In 1973 the U.S. Supreme Court fundamentally changed abortion policy in the United States. In the important *Roe v. Wade* decision, the court ruled that the right to privacy extends to the decision of a woman, in consultation with her physician, to terminate her pregnancy. Thus, state laws prohibiting abortions were invalidated. The Supreme Court also declared that the Fifth and Fourteenth amendments to the Constitution, which guarantee all persons "life, liberty and property," did not include the life of the unborn fetus. The Supreme Court decision established the "trimester" framework for determining when and what restrictions by states were permissible: (1) during the first three months of pregnancy the states cannot restrict the mother's decision for an abortion; (2) from the fourth to sixth months of pregnancy the states cannot restrict abortions, but they can protect the health of the mother by setting standards for how and when abortions can be performed; (3) during the last three months of pregnancy the states can regulate or prohibit all abortions except those to protect the mother's life and health. Increasing numbers of women sought abortions following the *Roe v. Wade* decision; however, over the last ten years, the number of abortions has remained largely constant. Over 90 percent of abortions are performed within the first twelve weeks of pregnancy, and over half of all women seeking abortions did so because their birth control method failed (NOW, 1992).

Regulations and restrictions on abortions have increased since the *Roe v Wade* decision. Initially, poor pregnant women were able to obtain federally funded abortions under the Medicaid program. But in 1977 antiabortion groups successfully supported the passage of the Hyde Amendment, which prohibited the federal government from paying for abortions except in cases endangering the mother's life. Some states decided to use their own funds to provide abortions under their Medicaid programs. In 1993 Congress passed a law allowing federal Medicaid dollars to be used for abortions in cases of rape or incest. In 1993 the average monthly AFDC benefit of $367 (Abramovitz & Newdom, 1994) barely covered the approximately $250 to $325 it takes to obtain a first trimester abortion. Recent additional regulations on abortion, such as mandatory waiting periods, also may disproportionately affect poor women because they may result in increased transportation and lodging expenses when women have to travel to obtain an abortion. In some states and in nonmetropolitan areas, access to abortions can be difficult because there are few abortion providers.

In 1989 the U.S. Supreme Court placed additional regulations on abortion. In a Missouri case, *Webster v. Reproductive Health Services,* the court ruled that states could prohibit the use of public funds, facilities, and personnel for abortions, and could use viability testing to determine whether abortions should be performed. In the 1991 *Rust v. Sullivan* case, the court also upheld a regulation allowing the government to withhold Title X family planning funds from federally funded family planning clinics that perform abortions or provide information on abortion as an option. The regulations prohibited nurses and social workers from discussing abortions and assisting women with abortion referrals, even if asked. This prohibition, supported by the Reagan and Bush administrations, became known as the "gag rule," but President Clinton rescinded it two days after taking office. In 1992, the U.S. Supreme Court upheld many restrictions on abortion in *Planned Parenthood of Southeastern Pennsylvania v. Casey,* including a twenty-four-hour waiting period for most women seeking an abortion and consent of one parent for women under age eighteen with a judicial bypass provision if the young woman can convince a judge to give permission in lieu of her parents.

Opponents of abortion usually refer to themselves as "pro-life." They believe that abortion is tantamount to taking a human life. Based on religious, moral, or biological grounds, they believe that life begins at conception, and thus, the life should be constitutionally protected. Pro-life groups demonstrate annually in Washington on the anniversary of the *Roe v. Wade* decision and picket weekly at health clinics across the country that perform abortions. Recently, opponents of abortion rights have escalated their efforts to stop abortions with more frequent and violent actions. Over 1,730 violent acts have been reported against abortion clinics and providers (Ames, 1995). These acts include gas attacks, fire-bombings, vandalism, threats, assaults, and murder. Protesters also picket the homes and threaten the families of doctors who perform abortions.

Supporters of abortion rights often call themselves "pro-choice." They believe in the fundamental right of a woman to make decisions about her own body, including the decision to terminate an unwanted pregnancy. Without recourse to safe, legal abortions, they fear that women will return to the unsafe procedures that once made illegal abortion a leading cause of maternal death (Perlmutter, 1994).

What is the position of social workers with respect to abortion? Many social workers believe in a woman's right to an abortion based on their belief in a person's right to self-determination (NASW, 1994, p. 3). Some social workers openly advocate for the protection of abortion rights and participate in groups such as the National Abortion Rights Action League, Planned Parenthood (a family planning organization), and Catholics for a Free Choice. Other social workers' personal beliefs do not permit them to condone abortion. In some employment settings, such as Catholic Charities, social workers are not permitted to recommend abortion to clients due to the strong opposition of the Catholic Church to abortion. But social workers are supposed to uphold the client's right to self-determination. This means that a social worker who does not condone abortion, or who works in an agency that does not condone abortion, is obligated to refer clients requesting abortion services or in need of information concerning abortion to an agency (such as Planned Parenthood) that can advise them (NASW, 1994, p. 3). Social workers are often staff members of Planned Parenthood and other family planning organizations, and others work in abortion clinics. The NASW Code of Ethics (see NASW, 1994, pp. 277–283) implies that social workers should carefully consider their own views toward abortion and their responses to clients who seek abortion services.

Violence against Women

The renaming of violent acts against women in recent decades has generalized the phenomenon away from the primary victims who are women. Wife beating and wife battering became spouse abuse, domestic violence, and family violence. Rape became sexual assault. This section addresses two types of violence against women: domestic or intimate violence against adult women, and sexual assault of adult women (child abuse is addressed in Chapter 10; abuse of the elderly is discussed in Chapter 11). The provision of services to battered women and survivors of sexual assault has been a growing area of social work practice during the last twenty-five years.

Domestic Violence

Domestic violence occurs among all racial, class, and ethnic groups. Avis (1992) estimates that 18 percent to 36 percent of women are physically abused by a male partner at some point in their lives. Yet many incidents of abuse go unreported. Severe, repeated violence occurs in one of fourteen marriages, with an average of thirty-five violent incidents before it is reported (Avis). When family violence erupts, law enforcement officers are likely to be called to the scene; however, they respond less quickly and are less likely to take a report when the victim knows the offender (Bachman, 1994). Law enforcement officers are leery of domestic calls for several reasons: there is a high risk of officers being injured while investigating calls; laws about legal intervention in cases involving husbands and wives are unclear; wives often return to abusive husbands, only to call law enforcement when the abuse occurs again; there are insufficient numbers of services available to assist husbands and wives in violent relationships.

Although women return to battering situations for many reasons, research indicates that over half of battered women do so because they feel they cannot support themselves and their children (Sullivan, Basta, Tan, & Davidson, 1992). Psychological abuse generally accompanies physical abuse. Over a long period of time, the battered woman begins to believe she is at fault and has little value. Many battered women also fear that leaving will further enrage their partners and bring more harm to them and their children.

The women's movement of the 1960s and 1970s strongly influenced the battered women's movement. Women began speaking out about battering, and they pushed for better remedies, including more legal protection. By the late 1970s, some states officially recognized that battered women were not receiving adequate legal protection. Today all states have some type of legislation to protect battered women, but provisions among states vary. Although there is no uniform federal legislation for legal intervention in cases of abuse, Congress did pass the Violence Against Women Act in 1994 as part of a larger crime bill. The act establishes new penalties for offenders and grants for programs to reduce domestic violence and other crimes against women, but the illustration in Box 17-2 shows that not everyone is enamored of some of these strategies. What do you think about them? As social workers how can we better defend the interventions we use?

BOX 17-2   One Perspective on Government's Response to Crime against Women

Paperwork Won't Stop Violence against Women

By Anita K. Blair
Special to the American-Statesman

If you were a woman living in fear of violent crime, whom would you rather call: a police officer or a court gender-bias trainer?

If you were a victim of violent crime hoping to bring your attacker to justice, which would suit you better: a speedy trial by experienced prosecutors in your local court or a long wait for a trial date on a federal docket crowded with drug-trafficking cases?

If you were a victim of domestic violence awaiting your ex-boyfriend's sentencing, which would you rather see applied: a federal rule that allows abusers to get off with "treatment" and parole, or a state rule that puts offenders in prison and abolishes parole?

If you were a battered wife, which would help you more: a hometown volunteer group who could help you find a job and a new place for you and your kids to live, or a federally funded feminist who would educate you about the "truth" concerning domestic violence?

Recently, the House of Representative voted to appropriate $75 million for local law enforcement proposed under the Violence Against Women Act, part of the 1994 Crime Bill. The House sensibly concluded that returning money for local crime-fighting needs is the most effective thing the federal government can do to protect the safety of women in their homes and neighborhoods.

But there is another bill, this one to appropriate an additional $40 million as part of the Labor/Health and Human Services appropriations bill for activities envisioned by the act. Unlike the $75 million for law enforcement, this additional $40 million won't prevent or punish violent crime against women. Instead, it will support a massive victimhood industry, whose primary interest is not to help crime victims but to perpetuate itself.

The hype surrounding the enactment of the act last year would lead anyone to believe that domestic violence is an airborne contagion liable to strike any family at any time. For example, the National Coalition Against Domestic Violence and other proponents of the act loudly proclaimed that violent crime strikes a woman in America every 15 seconds. Last March, an embarrassed White House publicly retracted the same statement by President Clinton, admitting it was completely unsubstantiated.

The facts are different. The 1985 National Family Violence Survey (a national sample of 6,000 men and women still regarded as the most authoritative study on this subject) showed that the incidence of severe domestic violence—that is, violence with a high probability of causing injury—by men against women is 34 per 1,000 population. Actual injury-producing domestic assaults by men against women occurred at the rate of 3.7 per 1,000, vs. 0.6 per 1,000 for assaults by women against men.

Although few in number, these people need our help, as do others who live under the threat of violence. What kind of help is most effective?

Experts say that when a woman is threatened or abused by the man she lives with, the key to preventing further injury is to separate them. If the woman can't or won't leave, she risks additional, and more serious, injury. Therefore, laws against domestic violence should aim at isolating and removing the offenders. Suitably long prison sentences and abolition of parole could effectively address this problem. Instead, the act provides for treatment and parole of domestic violence offenders—in other words, freedom to continue their violent behavior.

The Clinton administration seems to believe that, if forced to fill out forms and attend a lot of dull meetings, violent crime will go away. Violent crime—including that arising out of arguments between husbands and wives—can't be "managed" from Washington, D.C., but must be fought where it happens, in the streets and homes of America. To do this we need local police and prosecutors, not federal gender facilitators.

Blair is the executive vice president and general counsel of the Independent Women's Forum in Arlington, Va.

Source: Blair, A. K. (1995). Paperwork won't stop violence against women. *Austin American Statesman,* August 15, p. A9.

Battered women have two types of legal recourse: civil and criminal. Civil laws are used to "settle disputes between individuals and to compensate for injuries," and criminal laws are used to "punish acts which are disruptive of social order and to deter other similar acts" (Lerman, 1983, p. 29). In many communities today, the district attorney—not the victim—brings criminal charges against the alleged abuser.

Proponents of this practice believe that it prevents offenders from intimidating victims into dropping the charges once filed. Others believe that this type of policy may serve to reduce the number of calls to law enforcement agencies because women will be more hesitant to report if they know the perpetrator will be prosecuted.

Another type of remedy for domestic violence is social services. Most direct services for battered women have been developed at the community level. Over 2,000 domestic violence programs exist across the United States today, and most of these are shelters for battered women which are constantly filled to capacity (Sullivan & Rumptz, 1994). Staff often consists of social workers and other human service professionals. Many shelters are minimally funded and rely heavily on volunteers to help meet the increasing demand for services. Services include shelter (often on a relatively short-term basis because of the need to serve so many); counseling for the children who generally accompany their mothers to the shelters; counseling for the women to discuss many issues, including raising self-esteem; job placement; assistance in locating permanent housing; and assistance with other independent living skills such as budgeting. Shelters may provide education and counseling on alcohol and drug abuse due to its relationship to violent behavior. Many shelters also try to provide transitional housing for women, recognizing the length of time it takes for women to start a new life.

Today, the providers of services to victims of domestic violence must respond to the varying needs of a diverse clientele. Women of all races and ethnicities seek refuge in shelters; however, cultural values or legal issues may deter some women from seeking help. In some cultures, especially those that do not condone divorce, women have been taught to stand by their man even when the relationship is abusive. Particularly in border states, such as California, Florida, and Texas, women who have entered the country without appropriate documentation may be afraid to seek services for fear of deportation. Gay and lesbian domestic violence is increasingly being recognized and must also be addressed. Battering in lesbian relationships occurs on par with the frequency of abuse in heterosexual relationships, suggesting that abuse is unrelated to sexual orientation (also see Chapter 16). However, this phenomenon needs further study since women are generally less likely than men to engage in violent behavior. And, finally, victims of domestic violence include men as well as women. Service providers must be able to respond to male victims as the number identifying themselves increases.

Sexual Assault

Sexual assault may be defined as one adult forcing or attempting to force another adult to engage in any type of sexual activity, but the definitions of forcible sexual contact used in state and federal laws vary. Estimates suggest that a woman is raped in the United States every six minutes (National Institute of Justice Statistics, 1995). However, the actual incidence of sexual assault is unknown due to the fact that the majority of victims (perhaps as many as nine out of ten) never report that the assault took place (National Institute of Justice Statistics). Reasons women are reluctant to report a rape include embarrassment, fear of revenge from the rapist, concerns about poor treatment from the criminal justice system and others, and the effect it may have on a relationship with a husband or boyfriend. Date rapes are especially under-reported. Koss and her colleagues (1985) found that many victims of date rape did not identify the assault as rape. About half of all rapes are committed by someone known to the victim—an acquaintance, boyfriend, relative, or husband. But in some states the law does not permit a wife to file rape charges against her husband.

Burgess and Holmstrom (1974) recommend an understanding of the rape trauma syndrome and the use of crisis counseling techniques with those who have been sexually assaulted. Rape victims (or rape "survivors" as they are also called) often experience serious psychological effects. Burgess and Holmstrom identified this as the rape trauma syndrome after studying the reactions of 146 rape survivors in the Boston area. The syndrome consists of an acute disorganization phase and a long-term reorganization phase. The disorganization phase begins immediately after the rape, and the reorganization phase is likely to begin about three weeks after the incident.

Early in the disorganization phase, women's coping styles vary. Some exhibit anxiety, fear, and anger by crying, being restless, and even smiling. Others exhibit a controlled style. They appear calm and subdued, which may be surprising to casual observers. Physical symptoms accompany this disorganization phase. Physical trauma such as soreness and bruising may result from the physical attack. Throat irritation is prominent in those forced to engage in oral sex. Skeletal muscle tension includes sleep disturbances as well as excessive edginess. Gastrointestinal difficulties include stomach aches and nausea and are common among those who have been given medication to prevent pregnancy. Nausea may also occur from thinking about the rape. Survivors forced to engage in anal sex may also report rectal pain and bleeding. And today, infection with HIV is another serious concern.

Emotional symptoms that continue to mark the disorganization phase include fear, humiliation, embarrassment, anger, and a desire for revenge. Fears of physical violence and death are prominent. Self-blame is also common. Survivors often wonder if they did something that provoked the attack or if they could have done more to prevent the attack.

In the reorganization phase, there are nightmares, phobias, and difficulties with motor activities. In the area of motor activities, survivors are likely to change residences, take a trip (especially to see family), and change their telephone numbers (often to an unlisted number) because they fear the perpetrator will find them. Nightmares take two forms. At first the dreams may be ones in which the survivor feels threatened, but she wakens before she is able to act against the perpetrator. Later the dreams may change to those in which the survivor is able to defend herself against the attack.

Phobias experienced by rape survivors may be called "traumatophobias"—phobic reactions following a traumatic event (Rado, 1948). They may include fear of being indoors or fear of the outdoors, depending on where the rape occurred, and fear of being alone, because victims are usually alone when raped. Many survivors also develop fears of sex.

Like victims of domestic violence, sexual assault survivors have two legal routes to help them deal with their experiences. They may pursue legal remedies through criminal and civil courts; however, survivors often fear involvement with the legal system. Changes in the legal system have come about slowly, but many police departments now require special training of officers in dealing sensitively with survivors. In addition, in many states information cannot be presented in court about the woman's past sexual history.

Medical and social service providers can do a great deal to help survivors recover from sexual assault. But survivors often experience long waits to undergo the "sexual assault examination protocol" (the examination of the survivor to collect evidence of the assault). This exam is usually conducted in hospital emergency rooms, but survivors who are not in life-threatening situations may wait hours, either because a physician is unavailable or perhaps because the physician is reluctant to collect evidence and possibly be called to court to testify (Martin, DiNitto, Norton, & Maxwell, 1984). Some hospitals employ social workers to provide emotional support to survivors, calm family or friends, and arrange for transportation home and follow-up services.

Rape crisis centers share many similarities with shelters for battered women: they developed in the 1970s; social workers are often members of the staffs; they are frequently underfunded; and they rely heavily on volunteers. The typical rape crisis center operates a twenty-four-hour telephone line that survivors can call for help. The center's staff are trained to meet the survivor's needs and generally support her decision of whether or not to report the rape to law enforcement. Among the services provided by rape crisis center staff are (1) support at the hospital and explanation of the sexual assault examination protocol if the survivor decides to seek this service, (2) accompaniment to meetings with law enforcement officers and attorneys and to court if the case proceeds through any or all of these legal channels, (3) individual and group counseling to help cope with the aftermath of rape, (4) support of significant others who may have difficulty coping with the assault of a loved one, (5) education to the community about rape prevention and what help is available if an assault occurs, and (6) training of community professionals to improve services to sexual assault survivors. Rape survivors receive the best services when law enforcement officers, prosecutors, hospital staff, and rape crisis staff closely cooperate (Martin et al 1984). Social workers can use their planning, networking, and community-organizing skills to help promote this cooperation.

Feminism—Its Place in Social Work Practice

What is feminism? If you were to ask several people this question, you would most likely receive several different responses. The *Random House College Dictionary* (Urdang & Flexner, 1973, p. 486) defines feminism as "the doctrine advocating social and political rights for women equal to those of men." Many people are surprised by this definition and feel that although they support the definition, they do not consider themselves feminists. Feminism is not just being nonsexist. It is a conceptual framework—a way of thinking and behaving. Many social workers support the inclusion of a feminist perspective in social work education and social work practice.

Van Den Bergh (1995) stresses the value that can be gained from incorporating feminist principles into social work practice:

> *A practice informed by listening to many ways of knowing, centered and located within diverse client life experiences and co-created through relationships that are reflexive and intersubjective, can provide a context for caring, connecting, partnering, and community building. That, very simply, may be how we move out of the problem and into the solution (pp. xxxiv–xxxv).*

Several themes generally underlie the ideology of feminist social work practice. Bricker-Jenkins and Hooyman (1986) identified seven of them (see Table 17–1). First is the need to end patriarchy. "Patriarchy, as the institutionalized system of male domination and privilege, is the mechanism that ensures women's subordination" (Bricker-Jenkins & Hooyman, p. 9). Feminism supports and promotes an egalitarian society for all.

The second theme is empowerment. Feminists believe that they cannot stand by while others use their power in ways that are detrimental to women. Feminists have a different view of power than domination of one person or group over another. They perceive power as a resource without limits. Power is not something to be won or lost; it is to be shared. In feminist social work practice, the social worker and the client share power and experiences. The relationship between social worker and client is reciprocal, not authoritarian or hierarchical, and the social worker as well as the client is expected to be affected by the therapeutic exchange.

Third, feminists are as concerned with process (how one accomplishes a goal) as they are with product (the end result or goal attainment). Van Den Bergh and Cooper (1986) define the feminist vision of process and outcome as "based on an assumption that the merit of a goal is directly related to the way in which it is achieved. Goals achieved through bad processes must always be mistrusted. How one pursues an objective becomes a goal in and of itself" (p. 7).

A fourth theme is that the person is political. Feminists believe that "our feelings about ourselves and our conditions—our consciousness—are shaped by political forces" and that these forces have been controlled primarily by others (Bricker-Jenkins & Hooyman, 1986, p. 14). The concept of "personal is political" emanated from early consciousness-raising groups in which women recognized the commonalities of their lives. This awareness of the patterns of oppression women experienced led to an understanding of institutionalized patterns of oppression and the need for collective action (Van Den Bergh & Cooper). For feminists, collective action is directed toward eliminating the most debilitating conditions experienced by women, including inadequate food, housing, and health care. Feminist social workers assist clients in understanding the relationship between their own issues and problems and political issues.

The fifth theme is unity-diversity, and feminists appreciate both concepts. Feminists do more than strive together to eliminate all forms of oppression. They "affirm the need for diversity by actively reaching out to achieve it.... The use of noncompetitive working principles and noncoercive conflict resolution are [feminist] attempts to promote the presence of diversity" (Bricker-Jenkins & Hooyman, p. 15).

Validation of the nonrational is a sixth theme. In a patriarchal society emphasis is placed on what are termed scientific and rational approaches to defining and solving problems. In reality, however, there is no single way to define or solve a problem, despite the beliefs of those who assert that their definitions and solutions are right or correct. Labeling an idea rational can cause people to deny the emotional and spiritual aspects of their lives when, in fact, all these components lead individuals to their own valid views of life. Feminist practice embraces a holistic perspective, stressing the interconnectedness of the body, mind, and spirit.

Finally, a seventh aspect of feminist practice is consciousness raising and praxis. Consciousness raising is an interpersonal healing process in which women examine and share their own experiences, often in small groups. This interpersonal process is critical to appreciating and respecting others. It is a process by which women take responsibility for infusing feminist values into society. Its goal is *praxis,* that is, the development of a theory-practice dialectic through which reality can be understood and shaped.

More recently, these feminist principles have been combined with ethnic-sensitive practice (see Chapter 15) to produce culturally competent feminist practice. Suarez, Lewis, and Clark (1995, pp. 198–201) identify elements of culturally competent feminist practice:

1. relates the political and historical contexts of women to their economic status, ethnicity, and race;
2. recognizes the strengths of women of color, including their support systems and resources;
3. accesses and intervenes using a generalist, empowerment perspective;
4. requires self-assessment by the practitioner on how he or she personally benefits from discrimination that dominates the lives of the women with whom he or she works;
5. requires practitioners to acknowledge their own limitations, fears, and inconsistencies;
6. recognizes the effects of dichotomous thinking and monoculturalism in society and in work with women; and
7. focuses on the process and sharing the power within the working relationship.

Although most social workers would define themselves as nonsexist and support at least some of the feminist principles, many would not consider themselves feminists. However, the principles of social work often mirror the feminist premises explained here. For example, the NASW Code of Ethics stresses an action component to one's concern for human welfare, just as feminist principles stress action to raise consciousness about political issues. But it is evident that much of social work practice is not feminist. In many social service agencies, process is not valued over product. Most social service agencies are hierarchically structured, implying that the opinions and interests of all individuals are not equally valued within the organization. Those at higher levels of authority make the decisions that affect other members of the organization, often without considering the opinions of employees at various

TABLE 17-1   Feminist Ideological Themes

End to Patriarchy

Demystify and demythicize; reclaim history

Meet human needs; respect life

Transform personal and social relationships; end all systems of subordination and privilege

Value women's perspectives and experiences

Empowerment

"Power" reconceptualized is limitless, collective, and transactive

Implies individual responsibility, not individual property

Egalitarianism; no "power over"

Enabling, nonviolent problem solving

Inclusiveness; making common cause

Process

Process as product; ends in the means

Must be prefigurative, culture building, nonoppressive

Must educate, democratize, enable leadership and responsibility

"We're all in process"; nonjudgmental

Nonlinear, dynamic; consciousness and conditions are ever changing

Developmental; effectiveness, as well as efficiency

The Personal Is Political

Personal problems and conditions have historical, material, and cultural bases and dimensions

We are all connected; there are no personal (private) solutions

Failure to act is to act

Achieve personal growth through political action, "taking charge"

Change selves, change the world

Orientation to fundamental structural change

Unity-Diversity

None is free until all are free

Sisterhood, solidarity

Respect differences, preserve uniqueness; diversity as a source of strength and growth

Conflict is inevitable; peace is achievable

Elimination of false dichotomies-artificial separations

Synthesis and wholeness

Validation of the Nonrational

Healing

Spirituality

Nonlinear, multidimensional thinking

Reintegrating public and private spheres

Process of defining problems is recognized as subjective

Multiple competing definitions of problems; many "truths"

Consciousness Raising/Praxis

Renaming-recreating reality

Liberation through one's own actions; self-reliance

"Rugged collectivism"

Infusion of consciousness and values in material world

Revolution as process, not event

Source: Bricker-Jenkins, M., & Hooyman, N. R. (1986). A feminist world view: Ideological themes from the feminist movement. In M. Bricker-Jenkins & N. R. Hooyman (Eds.), *Not for women only: Social work practice for a feminist future* (pp. 10–11). Silver Spring, MD: NASW. Copyright 1986, National Association of Social Workers, Inc.

levels within the organization. As a reaction to these types of patriarchal organizations, feminists developed alternative human service organizations such as rape crisis centers, shelters for battered women, and health clinics in which the organizational structure and service delivery system were modeled more from a feminist perspective.

Feminism is a model that can be applied when working with particular population groups: women with substance abuse problems, homeless women, and women with AIDS (Van Den Bergh, 1995). Feminism can also be applied to all methods of social work practice: casework, group work, community organization, administration, research, and policy (see Van Den Bergh; Van Den Bergh & Cooper, 1986). For example, Chernesky (1995) compares feminist and nonfeminist styles of administration. A feminist leadership style would empower others in the organization, whereas a nonfeminist style would command and control; a feminist problem-solving style would be participative, whereas a nonfeminist style would be top down.

Sexual Discrimination and Harassment in Social Work

Before social workers point to the numerous examples of gender discrimination and sexual harassment in society, they should examine their own house. This section considers sexual discrimination and harassment within the profession. As social work educators, we continue to see older women in our classes amazed at younger female students who say they have never experienced discrimination. Older students believe their younger counterparts are naive to assume that such problems rarely occur today. They feel that discriminatory practices today may be more subtle, but that they continue to exist.

Sexual Discrimination

The sexual discrimination within social work which first became highly visible and debated twenty years ago is still apparent today. In a 1976 article Kravetz described how female social workers were paid less than male social workers. Dressel (1992) points out that the situation still exists today. Although about two thirds of social workers are women, males dominate the administrative positions, and women in social work continue to earn less than their male counterparts. Mean salaries for female social workers are 84 percent of the mean salaries for male social workers (Gibelman & Schervish, 1995). Landers (1992) reported that males in private practice had a median income of $57,273, whereas females in private practice had a median income of $47,000. Female social work educators still earn less than their male colleagues with comparable rank, degree, and experience (Gould & Bok-Lim, 1976; Sowers-Hoag & Harrison, 1991).

Social workers continue to debate the reasons for these differentials. Some argue that women prefer direct service to administrative work and that women educators don't publish as many articles as male educators. Others contend that women are not encouraged as much as men to exercise their administrative talents and that the work that female faculty often do is not valued as much as that of male faculty.

Sexual Harassment

Another problem for women in the workplace is sexual harassment. According to the EEOC:

Unwelcome sexual advances, requests for sexual favors, and other verbal or physical conduct of a sexual nature constitute sexual harassment when:

1. *submission to such conduct is made either explicitly or implicitly a term or condition of an individual's employment or admission to an academic program;*
2. *submission to or rejection of such conduct is used as the basis for decisions affecting an individual's employment status or academic standing; or*
3. *such conduct has the purpose or effect of substantially interfering with an individual's performance on the job or in the classroom, or creating an intimidating, hostile, or offensive work or study environment (Code of Federal Regulations, Vol. 29, Sec. 1604.11).*

The problem was exposed when Anita Hill accused Supreme Court nominee (now Supreme Court Justice) Clarence Thomas of sexual harassment that occurred when she worked for him. The number of sexual harassment charges compiled by the EEOC (1995) more than doubled between 1989 and 1993. Approximately one out of every three employed women reports having been sexually harassed (Akabas, 1995), and most remain silent out of fear of losing their jobs and ostracism and uncertainty about their rights and avenues for exposing the harassment.

Does sexual misconduct exist in the helping professions, including social work? Although the codes of ethics of both the American Psychological Association and the National Association of Social Workers expressly prohibit sexual contact between professionals and clients, surveys indicate that sexual contact occurs. Pope, Levenson, and Schover (1986) found that among psychologists, 12 percent of male psychotherapists and 3 percent of female psychotherapists reported sexual contact with clients. It is important to consider the potential issues involved when a sexual relationship develops between a person who is in a more powerful or superior position and another who is in a less powerful or subordinate position, especially when the person in the more powerful position is supposed to be providing therapeutic services.

A study of NASW members indicated that one third of female respondents and one seventh of male respondents had been subjected to some form of sexual harassment by other workers, supervisors, or clients (Maypole, 1986). Verbal harassment was most frequent, followed by touching, fondling, and kissing. In another study, undergraduate and master's social work students were asked to respond to questions about sexual harassment in the classroom and in field placement (McNeece, DiNitto, DeWeaver, & Johnson, 1987). Nearly 30 percent of the 264 respondents reported some form of harassment. Ninety percent of those who experienced harassment were female. Most of the harassment was perpetrated by males. Verbal harassment, including sexual innuendos, jokes, and suggestive remarks, was most common. There were no statistically significant differences in reports between undergraduate and master's students, nor between classroom and field experiences. The most extreme form of harassment reported in this study was demands for sex. Female students encountered this in field placement (2.4 percent) and in the classroom (2.9 percent), but no male students reported this problem. Three quarters of the students who were harassed reported only one instance of harassment. Male and female students typically dealt with the harassment by joking or ignoring it, but female students were more likely to avoid the harasser. Only 12.4 percent of the female students who were harassed confronted the harasser, and only 5.3 percent reported the incidents.

For another perspective on the subject, Singer (1989) surveyed deans of the graduate social work programs in the United States. Eighty-four percent responded, and 54 percent had received reports of sexual harassment during the previous five-year period. Average age of the victims was twenty-eight. Most of the accused harassers were senior faculty. Initial reports were more likely to be made to the dean by someone other than the victim. In nine cases victims filed formal grievances. The disposition was reported for seven of these cases. Recommendations were to dismiss charges in two cases, reprimand the faculty member in four, and dismiss the faculty member in one case.

We have discussed sexual discrimination and harassment in this chapter because they are phenomena that warrant professional concern. Although social work students and professional social workers may not expect to encounter these situations often, potential exists for experiencing both discrimination and harassment in the workplace and on campus. For those not aware of procedures for addressing gender discrimination (the same applies to racial discrimination) and sexual harassment within their own college, university, or place of employment, this may be the time to investigate them. More cases of sexual harassment are being reported at work and at school. Colleges, universities, and other employers may be held responsible if they fail to remedy cases of sexual harassment. Social work education programs should include information on sexual harassment in their printed material and in their orientation for new students, and reemphasize this before students enter field placements.

Professional Groups and Women's Issues

There are several groups of professional social workers whose primary goals are to focus attention on the special concerns of women and to improve the status of women both in the profession and within the larger society. These groups include the National Committee on Women's Issues (NCOWI), the Commission on the Role and Status of Women in Social Work Education (referred to as the Women's Commission), Association for Women in Social Work (AWSW), and the Women's Caucus of the International Association of Schools of Social Work.

The NCOWI is a committee of the National Association of Social Workers. Established in 1975, "the committee develops affirmative action initiatives and monitors plans and goals, [and] ensures that women's issues are addressed in NASW programs and policies . . . with the broad mission to promote women's leadership in the profession, to promote pay equity in the profession, and to combat discrimination in the profession and in society" (Van Den Bergh, 1995, p. vii). NCOWI has held national conferences and institutes on topics concerning women.

The Women's Commission of the Council on Social Work Education (CSWE) "is concerned with assuring affirmative action for women in all aspects of social work education and with promoting appropriate content on women's issues in social work curricula (*Affilia,* 1986, *1*(4), p. 65; also see Commission Annual Reports, 1995, pp. 8–9). The President of CSWE appoints the members of the commission. CSWE accreditation standards mandate the inclusion of content on women in the curricula of both undergraduate and master's social work programs (Commission on Accreditation, 1994), and the Women's Commission has been active in identifying models that can be used to ensure that sufficient content on women is provided. CSWE standards also address affirmative action in the hiring and promotion of female faculty and in the admission of female students to social work education programs. To assist women faculty, the commission has organized presentations at CSWE's Annual Program Meetings on successfully weathering promotion and tenure.

The AWSW was formed in 1984. The purposes of the association are as follows:

To further the development of feminist values, knowledge, assumptions, research, and behaviors; to promote their infusion into social work practice and education

To facilitate the formation of feminist networks, support, and work groups among social workers

To model and foster the development of learning and practice environments which reflect feminist values and concerns in their structures and processes

To promote in the membership the development of the knowledge and skill base required to protect women from the effects of oppression (including, but not limited to oppression on the basis of gender, race, class, age, disability, and sexual and affectional preference), and

To enable us to advance the interests of women in mainstream and alternative organizations

To promote the development and legitimation of policies, services, and political action to meet the special needs and concerns of women

To promote the infusion of feminist values, principles, priorities, and content within the standing organizations of the profession (*Affilia,* 1986, *1*(1), p. 66).

The national steering committee of the AWSW encourages the development of local groups that support the functions of the organization. The organization practices feminist values through its decentralized and nonhierarchical structure. Dues are based on each member's annual income. The AWSW publishes a newsletter and was instrumental in launching *Affilia: Journal of Women and Social Work,* a quarterly publication established in 1986. As articulated in its mission statement, "this journal is committed to the discussion and development of feminist values, theories, and knowledge as they relate to social work research, education, and practice" (*Affilia,* 1986, *1*(2), p. 2). Articles as well as poetry are accepted for publication in the journal.

In 1995 the Women's Caucus of the International Association of Schools of Social Work developed a resolution to address the epidemic of gender-based violence which "includes violence that is interpersonal, institutional, cultural, and structural."

The ten-point resolution was presented at the United Nations Fourth World Conference on Women held in Beijing, China:

1. Look to the women: listen to the women.
2. Require economic self-determination.
3. Free women from fear and domination.
4. Value all women's work.
5. Place women in decision-making positions.
6. Promote shared responsibilities in all forms of family and social partnerships.
7. Invest in health care and education.
8. Educate all women regarding their legal rights and other laws pertinent to them.
9. Promote positive perceptions of and by women.
10. Press for relevant gender-specific data collection and research.

Summary

Poverty, violence, and discrimination prevent women from full and equal participation in society. Social workers must be committed to the elimination of all forms of discrimination, including sexism, within their own profession and within the larger society. Social workers must also be aware of and take responsibility for their own attitudes and behaviors that contribute to sexism. Until the inequities that women face are fully addressed, the richness of women's, as well as men's, diverse contributions to the betterment of society cannot be fully realized.

As we move into the twenty-first century, most indicators suggest that the problems especially affecting women are not diminishing. Feminist social workers must continue to define and assess these problems in a holistic manner—as a complex interaction of biological, psychological, social, and environmental factors. Feminist social workers will continue to advocate for interventions that address these complex situations.

Suggested Readings

Affilia: Journal of Women and Social Work.

Bricker-Jenkins, M., & Hooyman, N. (1986). *Not for women only: Social work practice for a feminist future.* Silver Spring, MD: NASW.

Doninelli, L., & McLeod, E. (1989). *Feminist social work.* London: Macmillan.

Perlmutter, F. D. (1994). *Women & social change: Nonprofits and social policy.* Washington, DC: NASW Press.

Rodgers, H. R., Jr. (1990). *Poor women, poor families: The economic plight of America's female-headed households* (rev. ed.). Armonk, NY: M. E. Sharpe.

Signs: Journal of Women in Culture and Society.

Van Den Bergh, N. (Ed.). (1995). *Feminist practice in the 21st century.* Washington, DC: NASW Press.

Van Den Bergh, N., & Cooper, L. (Eds.). (1986). *Feminist visions for social work.* Washington, DC: NASW Press.

Women's Studies Quarterly.

18

Is There a Future for Social Work?

Photo courtesy of Robert Harbison

The original chapter from the first edition of this book has been revised by PAUL R. RAFFOUL, Graduate School of Social Work, University of Houston.

In 1981 the National Association of Social Workers organized a Professional Futures commission for the purpose of considering what social work practice will be in the twenty-first century. One of the most interesting conclusions was that what is good for social work and social agencies is not necessarily good for people (Beck, 1981, p. 37). One possible scenario, called "sweet transformationalism," envisioned a society in which the major organizational form shifts from the centralized, bureaucratic structure to arrangements for mutual aid, self-help, and consumer cooperatives. In such a system, social workers who have concentrated on the development of clinical skills will have a diminished role, and the profession might even gradually disappear.

Another equally plausible scenario envisions a postindustrial society characterized by a thriving service economy and an extremely high level of computer technology. With the exception of agricultural products, most goods would be produced in third-world nations. Social services would be directed toward those persons who are not able to adjust to the shift in the economy. Social work would emphasize narrow specialization, primarily in clinical and computer skills, and there would be a greater divergence between the leadership, who are concerned with social policy and social action, and the rank and file, who are concerned with direct practice. Training for social work practice might be at the doctoral level, and there would be a much diminished role for social philosophers (Beck, 1981, p. 368).

Not much has changed since 1981 to suggest a different set of scenarios for social work practice in the next century. Either of these scenarios, as well as many others, seem quite plausible on the basis of current trends. Significant changes have already occurred within the profession during the past few decades, and it appears certain that there are even more profound changes ahead. One of the most important questions is how the profession itself will shape its own future. A leading social work educator warned two decades ago that, "Unless the profession demonstrates that it can meet critical social needs and *provide leadership* [emphasis ours] in the design and delivery of social services, it will be relegated to roles as private practitioners and handmaidens to other professionals" (Sarri, 1973, pp. 31–32). Some educators have recently reminded us of social work's historical mission and suggested that a solution to this dilemma lies in clarifying the difference between social work and psychotherapy and asking not, "Does it feel good to *you?*" but rather, "Is it good for the *community?*" (Specht & Courtney, 1994, p. 175).

What do you think will be the future of the social work profession? We can make predictions within the context of current trends in the hope of making an informed answer to this question.

Trends in Education

As we noted in Chapter 2, there is little doubt that schools are preparing fewer people for roles in administration and management and are concentrating on the preparation of social workers for direct practice roles in working with individuals, families, and small groups. While social work educators have somewhat widened the generic base of the curriculum by the addition of a systems framework or ecological perspective, it still seems that the amount of effort devoted to training social workers in skills relevant to social administration, social action, and social policy is minimal. According to the latest statistics available from the Council on Social Work Education (CSWE, 1995), the vast majority of social work students are enrolled in micro rather than macro tracks. The problem is that while over 80 percent of students prepare for careers in direct practice, at least half of the MSW graduates are needed in macro-level positions (Sarri, 1986). The profession's failure to provide appropriate training for leaders in administration and policy-making means that other academic disciplines and other professions will, by default, assume those leadership roles.

Twenty years ago professional social work training was synonymous with the master of social work degree. Today there are almost as many social workers trained in baccalaureate programs as in master's degree programs (CSWE, 1995). While students are attending social work programs in greater numbers, they are not all attending as full-time *graduate* students. Currently part-time students make up fully one third of all master's program enrollments, and part-time students outnumbered full-time students in 16 of the 105 programs responding to the survey. Forty programs reported that at least 40 percent of their students were enrolled part-time (CSWE, p. 29).

While the number of accredited master's programs has increased slowly over the years, both bachelor's and doctoral programs have mushroomed. The rapid expansion of undergraduate programs since 1974 has created a growing demand for faculty for those programs, thus stimulating the growth in doctoral programs. Fifty-three doctoral programs in social work awarded 294 doctoral degrees in 1994 (CSWE, p. 31). With the rapid increase in specialized knowledge, it appears that there is a need to experiment with new forms of educational packaging for social work. For example, there have been occasional proposals to move to the Ph.D. or DSW as the terminal professional degree.

The decline in black and Hispanic enrollment in colleges and universities will have a profound impact on affirmative action, on the pool of qualified applicants for schools of social work education programs, and on the pool of trained social welfare administrators. This trend has occurred at a time of increased demand for ethnic minority social workers and administrators. Since 1990, however, CSWE has reported moderate increases in ethnic minority enrollments at both baccalaureate and graduate levels. For example, from 1990 to 1994 the percentage of ethnic minority BSW enrollment was 23.8, 24.6, 27.3, 26.9, 27.3; and for graduate students the percentages were 15.9, 16.7, 17.1, 17.6, and 19.2, respectively (CSWE, 1995, pp. 44–45).

CSWE (p. 28) reported the following ethnic breakdown for juniors and seniors enrolled full-time in baccalaureate programs on November 1, 1994: African American (16.9 percent), Mexican American (3.7 percent), Asian American (2.1 percent), Puerto Rican (2.0 percent), and other minorities (2.6 percent). For graduate students enrolled in master's programs the ethnic minority distribution is divided along full-time and part-time enrollment status, with almost always more ethnic minority students enrolled part-time than full-time. As of November 1, 1994, there were a total of 21.5 percent ethnic minorities enrolled full-time compared with 23.1 percent enrolled part-time in master's programs (CSWE, p. 33).

Recent trends in gender distribution indicate that the gender imbalance remains. In 1994, CSWE reported that there were 13.4 percent males and 86.6 percent females awarded baccalaureate degrees; compared with 18.1 percent males and 81.9 percent females awarded master's degrees; compared with 32 percent males and 68 percent females in doctoral programs awarded degrees (CSWE, p. 32).

As a way of coping with a serious decline in applications for MSW programs and the disappearance of financial aid for MSW students during the 1970s, a number of schools began offering at least part of the MSW curriculum on a part-time basis. Although many schools are reluctant to admit it, in some cases a majority of their graduate student enrollment consists of part-time students. Unless new methods of helping finance students (not only those in social work, but all students) are devised, this trend is likely to continue. Some schools have even launched experimental "weekend" MSW programs. Today's social work student is more likely to be older, "place-bound," and taking fewer credit hours than yesterday's student. Beginning in 1982, CSWE collected enrollment statistics on full-time and part-time graduate students. Since then the percentage of part-time to full-time master's students has steadily increased each year from 29 percent in 1982 to 35 percent in 1994. For example, in 1994, 21,622 master's students were enrolled full-time compared with 11,590 enrolled part-time (CSWE, p. 29).

More recently, MSW programs have begun to concentrate their advanced curricula (second year) to include a variety of fields of practice: both traditional fields, such as mental health, family and children, health care, gerontology, and not-so-traditional fields, such as political social work (see, for example, Fisher, 1995; and Haynes, 1996).

In addition to changes in the curriculum, there have been significant changes in instructional *methods* in social work education—as in most other academic units of colleges and universities. The most recent curriculum policy statement from CSWE has substantially increased the requirements for training in research at both the graduate and undergraduate levels. A specific mandate includes the foundation curricula requirement that students be prepared to systematically evaluate their practice. Many schools introduced a single-system design methods course along with a program evaluation course to address this mandate, although difficulties in evaluating the results of these designs has led to a tempering of enthusiasm (Downs & Rubin, 1994).

Another of the most common changes in social work classes has been the introduction of computers. Indeed, it is a rare graduate who is not forced to learn something about computer applications during the pursuit of a degree in social work. Also, expert systems are becoming more available to assist the clinician in diagnosing problems, developing treatment plans, and assessing outcomes for individual clients; and an array of "canned" computer programs are available for larger data sets. Personal computer software is now available to facilitate management decision making and improve service delivery. Cost-analysis studies as well as micro and macro evaluation programs have been made much easier with smaller, more powerful computer systems (see, for example, Nurius & Hudson, 1993).

There also has been a dramatic increase in social workers' participation in continuing education activities. Part of this trend may be due to a simple recognition by professional social workers that they must keep up with the rapid expansion of knowledge and the increasing sophistication of techniques in the field. Much of it is probably due to the fact that licensing and certification boards in many of the states require a minimum number of hours of continuing education activities in order to maintain professional standing. The social worker of the future should expect to spend a considerable amount of time keeping up with developments in the profession and "retooling" for career changes through continuing education programs.

At the same time, however, according to Gingerich & Green (1996), the future will provide technological innovations to facilitate the search for "self-help learning." With the increased development of

> *interactive TV, compact disc-interactive (CD-I), and other interactive multimedia technologies, a whole new set of psychosocial interactive intervention supports will be available. These interactive technologies will allow the participant to actively engage with the program they are "watching." For example, a person selecting a movie on interactive TV will control the level of violence, type of ending, gender of the lead, and otherwise directly shape the nature of the program he or she will watch. Likewise, self-help programs using CD-I technology will allow a parent to view a video scenario of a parent-child interaction, select a parenting response, and immediately view the effect of the choice on the child. Such tools will be accessible from home or from psychosocial support interactive technology centers.*
>
> *As multimedia self-help technology becomes more prevalent, a new social work role will emerge in which the social worker is the content specialist on the multimedia development team. However, the use of multimedia technology for self-help interventions will not be without problems. There will probably be a need for some type of "screening" system to make the more emotionally "powerful" interactive programs available only through licensed mental health practitioners. Further, legal issues of professional liability for interventions mediated through information technology have yet to be worked out (pp. 20–21).*

Trends in Practice

Social work practice has already gone through significant changes in its relatively short history. Until recently the practice of social work with individuals and families was guided primarily by psychodynamic perspectives derived from Freudian and neo-Freudian theories of human behavior. The dominance of these perspectives was eventually challenged and displaced by four developments. Beginning in the late 1940s systematic social and cultural perspectives from sociology, social psychology, and anthropology were reintroduced. Another challenge came from those critics who questioned whether the psychoanalytic perspective was adequate to encompass the psychosocial orientation needed in social work. The third challenge was the development of a body of research literature questioning the effectiveness of psychoanalytically oriented practice (Fischer, 1973). The last major challenge was the emergence of professional social work education at the undergraduate level, with its emphasis on the preparation of entry-level practitioners (Briar, 1987).

As the psychoanalytic model was displaced, social work practice experienced other major changes. One was the introduction of general systems theory and the ecological systems perspective that has brought an additional capacity to conceptualize person and environment interactions (Germain, 1979). Despite its tendency to be somewhat vague and abstract, it has helped to refocus attention on the "person-in-environment" approaches of earlier psychosocial models of practice. It also provides the basic framework for the generalist models used in many undergraduate programs.

Another major development has been the increased acceptance and use of behavioral approaches. Initially applied to practice with individuals, this model has been extended to use with groups (Rose, 1980), programs (Miller, 1978), and social change (Burgess & Bushell, 1969). Because of its emphasis on explicit, measurable objectives, the behavioral approach is more amenable than other approaches to research on its effectiveness.

Social workers in the future are more likely to use behavioral or cognitive-behavioral approaches in short-term programs, to be concerned with the effectiveness of their interventions, and to be trained to conduct limited research using single-subject or single-system research designs. Even if they were not so inclined, society's concern (some might say obsession) with accountability will require that social workers produce results quickly while rigorously evaluating their practice. Every social worker will be expected to incorporate evaluative feedback into his or her procedures in a way that improves practice.

Trends in Employment

There was a widespread fear among social workers at the beginning of the "Reagan Revolution" that both social services and social work positions would be greatly diminished. Despite all the talk about retrenchment and budget cutting, social work employment is still on the upswing. Except for entitlement programs, the states seem to have replaced most of the lost federal funding from the Reagan administration (Imershein, 1986). In 1991 the total social work labor force in the United States was approximately 603,000, and projections for employment during the next few years seem encouraging (Bureau of Labor Statistics, 1991). Just over half of all social workers appear to be employed in the practice areas of mental health and children and youth. If we add those working in "medical and health care" and "family services," these four areas account for about three fourths of all social work employment. Less than 2 percent are employed in public assistance and correctional programs (Gibelman & Schervish, 1993, p. 80). It certainly seems that the profession has moved away from some of the more traditional areas of practice. This reflects a dramatic change from 1961 when "52 percent of NASW members worked for federal, state, county, and municipal agencies" (Becker, 1961, p. 5). Among the reasons typically cited for this withdrawal of social workers from public service roles and positions are declassification, the unavailability of trained BSWs and MSWs to fill positions, the undifferentiated use of BSWs and MSWs, and the lowering of standards for hiring due to dwindling resources (Gibelman & Schervish, pp. 133–134).

It seems just as obvious, however, that there will be some shifts in the growth of new positions within the profession. The U.S. population is rapidly aging. As people live longer, they require more social and health care services. Within the Sunbelt states, there should be substantial increases in employment opportunities in programs serving the elderly. Unless there is a sudden and dramatic solution to the drug problem facing the nation, there should continue to be new social work positions in planning programs and providing services for drug abusers. Alcohol is still the most popular drug of choice, and approximately 18 million adults experience problems in functioning as a result of their drinking (U.S. Department of Health and Human Services, 1990). One of the major shifts in employment settings for social workers in the past decade has been the movement into private practice. Membership data from NASW indicated that 10.9 percent of its membership were employed in private practice in 1982, but that percentage had increased to 15.3 percent in 1987 (NASW, 1987). By 1994 there were an estimated 20,000 social workers primarily employed in private practice and another 45,000 secondarily engaged in private practice in addition to their primary social work jobs (Barker, 1995). As the number of social workers in private practice increases, a growing number of critics voice their fears that this is an indication of the gradual abandonment of the public sector by professional social workers. This concern is exacerbated by the fact that private practice is the fastest growing employment setting in the profession (Gibelman & Schervish, 1993). Indeed, there is a fear that social workers in private practice will be somewhat more conservative, at least on economic issues, than those in the public sector. There is a great deal of concern within the profession and within our graduate schools regarding privatization, as expressed in several recent publications (Specht & Courtney, 1994).

Demographic Trends

As a maturing society, increasing numbers of our elderly citizens require services of all types. There are also more children in need of care because of poverty, substance abuse, and other social problems. Both younger and older persons needing care are increasing in number at a time when the resources available to provide such care are dwindling. Additional demographic factors, including the increase in ethnic minority populations, single-parent families, and families in which both parents work full-time, have been less thoroughly analyzed, particularly in regard to the role that future demographic changes may play in determining the number of persons requiring assistance. As noted by Murdock and Michael (1996, p. 6):

> One of the reasons demographic factors often receive less attention than other dimensions is that they are not direct determinants of socioeconomic need. Rather, what effects demographic factors have on the demand for social

programs depends on the nature of relationships between demographic char-
acteristics and socioeconomic need. If need were equally distributed among
members of the population of the United States, then the growth in demand
for social welfare services would simply be a function of the overall increase
in the population ... Due to a variety of discriminatory, historical, and ac-
cess-related factors, poverty and accompanying need are disproportionately
experienced by minority populations and by the youngest and oldest and
those in certain household types in American society.

Murdock and Michael identify three demographic projections that will affect the demand for increased social welfare services in the future. First, population growth
(primarily by ethnic minority populations) will increase such that by 2050 more than
47 percent of the population would be composed of members of minority groups
(p. 10). Second, the population of immigrants to the United States will "account for
81.7 million additional persons by 2050 compared to what would have been in the
population if only natural increase had occurred between 1990 and 2050" (p. 10).
Third, dependent populations will grow more rapidly in the future. "Although the
percent of persons under eighteen will decline by 2 percent by 2050, the combination of young minority populations and older Anglo populations will result in an increase of 5.6 percent in the population in dependent ages ... Whereas those seventy-
five years of age or older accounted for 5.3 percent of the population or 13.2 million
persons in 1990, by 2050, persons seventy-five years of age or older would account
for 11.4 percent of the population or 43.6 million persons (p. 10).

We cannot help but predict that, given the demographic changes projected for
the United States in the coming years, the *need* for social services and social workers
will continue to grow. Whether we will be able to educate the social workers required and provide the social welfare services needed is quite another question.

Trends in Technology and Social Work

It is apparent that the personal computer has affected our society as a whole in many
ways. As Gingerich & Green (1996) note:

In the short fifty-year history of electronic computing, computers have moved
out of the research laboratories and universities and onto our office desks,
kitchen counters, and even our wrists. Computers now serve us when we go
to the bank to get cash, they draw three-dimensional pictures of vital human
organs, and they help to land the airplanes we fly. Computers advise auto
mechanics on what repairs to perform, and they help physicians decide
which patients can benefit most from scarce medical procedures. Computers
are so ubiquitous that they go largely unnoticed (p. 21).

Use of computers and other technological innovations by social work has lagged behind other professions, partially because social workers are more "high touch" than

"high tech," and also because until quite recently computers were not designed for most of the tasks performed routinely by social workers. Early users of information technology were "number crunchers" and data processors who could easily adapt to the new technology in terms of job efficiency and productivity.

> *The early adopters of information technology were found in industries such as banking, airlines, and retailing, whose tasks consisted largely of number crunching and data processing and were easily adapted to the new technology. Although social work has not adopted information technology in any significant way up to now (except for administrative functions), it will be impossible to avoid using information technology in the future. Information technology will permeate our homes and schools and, indeed, our workplaces (Gingerich & Green, 1996, pp. 21–24).*

For some in social work this technological revolution provides an opportunity to move more rapidly into the mainstream of modern computing. For those people who are positively oriented toward this technology it is an exciting time in the history of the profession. Future technological innovations will certainly affect social work practice in many ways, from automation of record keeping (including intake and assessment information entered directly by clients) to the development of treatment programs and the continuous monitoring of treatment progress using expert systems and clinical assessment programs (see Ingersoll-Dayton & Jayaratne, 1996).

Current observable trends toward cost containment, uniformity of clinical outcome criteria, and mandated case management services strongly suggest that future social workers will have to prepare themselves to take advantage of information technology in order to remain competitive and employable. Future social workers will have to be computer literate and familiar with the software programs that are available for single-system design research (Nurius & Hudson, 1993) and the inventory of rapid assessment instruments (Fischer & Corcoran, 1994). They must also have appropriate education in order to take advantage of these tools for determining practice efficacy.

However, some have already called the empirical practice movement of the past two decades a failure. "Deficiencies in the production, dissemination, and utilization of practice-relevant scientific information continue to undermine efforts to foster empirically based practice" (Howard & Lambert, 1996, p. 280). The need for this kind of knowledge (practice-relevant scientific information) for social work practice in the next century is seen as essential to ensure the profession's credibility, and more importantly, its survival.

For many in the profession of social work it is also a time of increasing concern and caution. The issues of access and secure control of information are of critical concern when ubiquitous computers could also mean everyone has access to personal and confidential information. Ensuring confidentiality may extend far beyond the social work offices and social welfare agencies of the future.

While the future of social work is not totally dependent on changes in computers and technology and their impact on society, they provide one opportunity to begin to move the profession into the next century with new vigor and energy. If social workers can take full advantage of one of the new products of technology, the personal computer, to help make their vision a reality and implement their mission, perhaps it can be the key to increased opportunity for the profession in the next century. As important (and wonderful) as this new technology is, however, the future of the social work profession will not be defined by its technological capabilities, but by its values and its ability to meet the needs of those in our society who deserve our most concentrated attention (Raffoul, 1996).

Suggested Readings

Raffoul, P. R., & McNeece, C. A. (1996). *Future issues for social work practice*. Boston: Allyn & Bacon.

References

Chapter 1

Abercrombie, N., Hill, S., & Turner, B. S. (1984). *Penguin Dictionary of Sociology.* New York: Penguin Books.

Addams, J. (1897). Social Settlements. *Proceedings: National Conference on Charities and Corrections, 339.*

Allen, H. E., Eskridge, C. W., Latessa, E. J., & Vito, G. F. (1985). *Probation and parole in America.* New York: Free Press.

Axinn, J., & Levin, H. (1982). *Social welfare: A history of the American response to need* (2nd ed.). New York: Harper & Row.

Bartlett, H. (1970). *The common base of social work practice.* New York: NASW Press.

Boehm, W. (1959). *Objectives of the social work education curriculum of the future* [Curriculum study]. New York: Council on Social Work Education.

Boehm, W. (1971). Education for social work. In R. Morris (Ed.), *Encyclopedia of social work* (16th ed., pp. 257–273). New York: NASW Press.

Compton, B. R., & Galaway B. (1975). *Social work processes.* Homewood, IL: Dorsey Press.

Council on Social Work Education. (1984). *Manual of accreditation standards.* New York: CSWE.

DiNitto, D. M. (1995). *Social welfare policy: Politics and public policy* (4th ed.). Englewood Cliffs, NJ: Prentice-Hall.

Dolgoff, R., & Feldstein, D. (1984). *Understanding social welfare.* (2nd ed.). New York: Longman.

Frumkin, M. L., & O'Connor, G. (1985). Where has the profession gone? Where is it going? Social work's search for identity. *The Urban and Social Change Review, 18*(1), 13–19.

Gilbert, N., & Specht, H. (1974). *Dimensions of social welfare policy.* Englewood Cliffs, NJ: Prentice-Hall.

Greenwood, E. (1957). Attributes of a profession. *Social Work, 2*(3), 44–55.

Hammond, L. H. (1922). *In the vanguard of a race.* New York: Council of Women for Home Missions.

Kidneigh, J. C. (1965). History of American social work. In H. L. Lurie (Ed.). *Encyclopedia of social work* (15th ed., pp. 3–19). New York: NASW Press.

Klein, P. (1971). *From philanthropy to social welfare*. San Francisco: Jossey-Bass.

Kropotkin, P. A. (1925). *Mutual aid: A factor of evolution*. New York: Knopf.

Lindsey, I. B. (1956). Some contributions to welfare services, 1865–1899. *Journal of Negro Education, 25,* 15–24.

Lubove, R. (1968). *The struggle for social security 1900–1935*. Cambridge, MA: Harvard Press.

Lubove, R. (1971). *The professional altruist*. New York: Atheneum.

Macarov, D. (1978). *The design of social welfare*. New York: Holt, Rinehart and Winston.

McNeece, C. A., DiNitto, D. M., & Johnson, P. (1984). Receptivity in the use of evaluation in community health centers. *Administration in Mental Health, 11*(3), 170–183.

Miller, J. (1995). Criminal justice: Social work roles. In R. L. Edwards (Ed.), *Encyclopedia of social work,* (19th ed., pp. 653–659). Washington, DC: NASW Press. Copyright 1995, National Association of Social Workers, Inc.

Morales, A., & Sheafor, B. (1986). *Social work: A profession of many faces* (4th ed.). Boston: Allyn & Bacon.

National Association of Social Workers. (1973). *Standards for social service manpower*. New York: NASW Press.

National Association of Social Workers. (1980, April). Summary of principles, *NASW News,* (19). Copyright 1993, National Association of Social Workers, Inc.

National Association of Social Workers. (1996, January). Proposed changes in code of ethics, *NASW News,* (41).

Noyes, A. P., & Kolb, L. C. (1961). *Modern clinical psychiatry*. Philadelphia: W. B. Saunders.

Pincus, A., & Minahan, A. (1973). *Social work practice: Model and method*. Itasca, IL: F. E. Peacock.

Popple, P. (1995). Social work profession: History. In R. L. Edwards (Ed.), *Encyclopedia of social work* (19th ed., pp. 2282–2292). Washington, DC: NASW Press. Copyright 1995, National Association of Social Workers, Inc.

Powell, A. C. (1923, January 14). The church in social work. *Opportunity, 15.*

Pumphrey, R. E., & Pumphrey, M. W. (1961). *The heritage of American social work*. New York: Columbia University Press.

Romanyshyn, J. M. (1971). *Social welfare: A charity to justice*. New York: Random House.

Sanders, D. S. (1973). *The impact of reform movements on social policy change: The case of social insurance*. Fair Lawn, NJ: R. R. Burdick.

Silverman, R. A. (1972). *Psychology*. Englewood Cliffs, NJ: Prentice-Hall.

Specht, H. (1972). The professionalization of social work. *Social Work, 17*(2), 3–15.

Specht, H., & Courtney, M. (1994). *Unfaithful angels: How social work has abandoned it's mission*. New York: Free Press.

Timms, N., & Timms, R. (1982). *Dictionary of social welfare*. London: Routledge and Kegan Paul.

Urdang, L. (1983). *Mosby's medical and nursing dictionary*. St. Louis: C. V. Mosby.

Chapter 2

Abell, N., & McDonnell, J. (1990, Winter). Preparing for practice: Motivations, expectations and aspirations of the MSW class of 1990. *Journal of Social Work Education, 26*(1), 57–64.

Ansberry, C. (1987, January 5). Desperate straits. *The Wall Street Journal,* pp. 1, 10.

Barker, R. L. (1992). Social work in private practice. Washington, DC: NASW Press.

Biggerstaff, M. A. (1995). Licensing, regulation, and certification. In R. L. Edwards (Ed.), *Encyclopedia of social work* (19th ed., pp. 1616–1624). Washington, DC: NASW Press. Copyright 1995, National Association of Social Workers, Inc.

Booz-Allen & Hamilton. (1987). *The Maryland social work services job analysis and personnel qualifications study.* Annapolis, MD: Maryland Department of Human Resources.

Butler, A. (1990, Winter). A reevaluation of social work students' career interests: Grounds for optimism. *Journal of Social Work Education, 26*(1), 47–56.

Butler, A. (1992, Winter). The attractions of private practice. *Journal of Social Work Education, 28*(1), 47–60.

Commission on Accreditation. (1994). *Handbook of accreditation standards and procedures* (4th ed.). Alexandria, VA: Council on Social Work Education.

Eisenberg, S. (1956). *Supervision in the changing field of social work.* Philadelphia: The Jewish Family Service of Philadelphia.

Ewalt, P. (Ed.). (1980). *Toward a definition of clinical social work.* Washington, DC: NASW.

Fischer, J. (1973, January). Is casework effective? A review. *Social Work, 18,* 5–20.

Germain, C. (1970). Casework and science: A historical encounter. In R. Roberts & R. Nee (Eds.), *Theories of social casework* (pp. 5–32). Chicago: University of Chicago Press.

Gibelman, M., & Schervish, P. H. (1993a). *Who we are: The social work labor force as reflected in the NASW membership.* Washington, DC: NASW Press. Copyright 1993, National Association of Social Workers, Inc.

Gibelman, M., & Schervish, P. H. (1993b). *What we earn: 1993 salary survey.* Washington, DC: NASW Press. Copyright 1993, National Association of Social Workers, Inc.

Gilder, G. (1981). *Wealth and poverty.* New York: Bantam Books.

Goldstein, H. (1990). The knowledge base of social work practice: Theory, wisdom, analogue, or art? *Families in Society, 70*(1), 32–43.

Goldstein, S., & Beebe, L. (1995). National Association of Social Workers. In R. L. Edwards (Ed.), *Encyclopedia of social work.* (19th ed., Vol. 2, pp. 1747–1764). Washington, DC: NASW Press. Copyright 1995, National Association of Social Workers, Inc.

Gradler, G., & Schrammel, K. (1994, Spring). The 1992–2005 job outlook in brief. *Occupational Outlook Quarterly,* 2–47.

Hardcastle, D. (1987). *The social work labor force.* Austin: The University of Texas at Austin, School of Social Work.

Harrington, M. (1962). *The other America: Poverty in the United States.* New York: Macmillan.

Heineman, M. (1981, September). The obsolete scientific imperative in social work practice. *Social Service Review, 55*(3), 371–397.

Hopps, J., & Collins, P. (1995). Social work profession overview. In R. L. Edwards (Ed.), *Encyclopedia of social work* (19th ed., Vol. 3, pp. 2267–2282). Washington, DC: NASW Press. Copyright 1995, National Association of Social Workers, Inc.

Imre, R. (1984). The nature of knowledge in social work. *Social Work, 29*(1), 41–45.

Karger, H. (1983). Science, research, and social work: Who controls the profession? *Social Work, 28*(3), 200–205.

Lennon, T. (1995). *Statistics on social work education in the United States: 1994*. Alexandria, VA: Council on Social Work Education.

Middleman, R. R. (1984, March-April). How competent is social work's approach to the assessment of competence? *Social Work, 29*(2), 146–153.

Murray, C. (1984). *Losing ground: American social policy, 1950–1980*. New York: Basic Books.

National Association of Social Workers. (1994). *Social work speaks: NASW policy statements* (3rd ed.). Washington, DC: NASW Press.

Parloff, M. (1982, June). Psychotherapy research evidence and reimbursement decisions: Bambi meets Godzilla. *American Journal of Psychiatry, 139*(6), 718–727.

Piven, F., & Cloward, R. (1971). *Regulating the poor: The functions of public welfare*. New York: Random House.

Saleeby, D. (1979, Winter). The tension between research and practice: Assumptions for the experimental paradigm. *Clinical Social Work Journal, 7*, 269–284.

Shank, B. (1993, October). *The relationship between the generalist curriculum and tasks performed by BSW practitioners*. Paper presented at the 11th annual BPD conference, Baltimore, MD.

Sheafor, B. W., & Shank, B. W. (1986, Spring). *Undergraduate social work education: A survivor in a changing profession*. Austin: The University of Texas at Austin, School of Social Work.

Specht, H., & Courtney, M. (1994). *Unfaithful angels: How social work has abandoned its mission*. New York: Free Press.

Tambour, M. (1995). Unions. In R. L. Edwards (Ed.), *Encyclopedia of social work* (19th ed., Vol. 3, pp. 2418–2426). Washington, DC: NASW Press. Copyright 1995, National Association of Social Workers, Inc.

Chapter 3

Alinsky, S. (1946). *Reveille for radicals*. New York: Vintage Books.

Ashcraft, M. H. (1989). *Human memory and cognition*. Glenview, IL: Scott, Foresman.

Babbie, E. (1985). *The practice of social research* (4th ed.). Belmont, CA: Wadsworth.

Becvar, D. S., & Becvar, R. J. (1995). *Family therapy: A systemic integration* (3rd ed.). Boston: Allyn & Bacon.

Boulding, K. E. (1985). *The world as a total system*. Beverly Hills, CA: Sage.

Bruner, J. (1986). *Actual minds, possible worlds*. Cambridge, MA: Harvard University Press.

Burghardt, S. (1980). *The other side of organizing*. Cambridge, MA: Schenkman.

Burghardt, S., & Fabricant, M. (1987). Radical social work. In A. Minahan (Ed.), *Encyclopedia of social work* (18th ed., Vol. 2, pp. 455–462). Silver Spring, MD: NASW Press. Copyright 1990, National Association of Social Workers, Inc.

Cortes, F., Przeworski, A., & Sprague, J. (1974). *Systems analysis for social scientists*. New York: John Wiley & Sons.

Fook, J. (1993). *Radical casework: A theory of practice*. North Sydney, Australia: Allen & Unwin.

Franklin, C., & Streeter, C. (1992). Differential characteristics of high-achieving/high-income and low-achieving/low-income dropout youths: Considerations for treatment programs. *Social Work in Education, 14*(1), 42–55.

Franklin, C., & Warren, K. (in press). Ecological systems theory: A critical analysis. In C. Franklin and C. Jordan (Eds.), *Family practice for social workers: Interventions and integrations*. Belmont, CA: Brooks/Cole.

Galper, J. H. (1975). *The politics of social services*. Boston: Allyn & Bacon.

Germain, C. (1979). *Social work practice: People and environments: An ecological perspective*. New York: Columbia University Press.

Germain, C. B., & Gitterman, A. (1980). *The life model of social work practice*. New York: Columbia University Press.

Gibson, D. (1988). Which road for social work: The moral choices and ethical dilemmas. *Proceedings of the 10th International Symposium of the International Federation of Social Workers,* Stockholm, Sweden.

Gilder, G. (1981). *Wealth and poverty*. New York: Basic Books.

Greenwood, E. (1957). Attributes of a profession. *Social Work, 2*(3), 45–55.

Greif, G. L. (1986). The ecosystems perspective "meets the press." *Social Work, 31*(3), 225–226.

Hartman, A. (1970). To think about the unthinkable. *Social Casework, 51*(8), 467–474.

Hartman, A., & Laird, J. (1983). *Family centered social work practice*. New York: Free Press.

Harvey, D. L., & Reed, M. H. (1994). The evolution of dissipative social systems. *Journal of Social and Evolutionary Systems, 17*(4), 377–378.

Jordan, C., & Franklin, C. (1995). *Clinical assessment for social workers: Quantitative and qualitative methods*. Chicago: Lyceum/Nelson Hall.

Kaplan, A. (1963). *The conduct of inquiry*. New York: Harper & Row.

Kelly, G. (1955). *The psychology of personal constructs*. New York: Norton.

Kuhn, T. S. (1962). *The structure of scientific revolutions*. Chicago: University of Chicago Press.

Laszlo, E. (1972). *The systems view of the world: The natural philosophy of the new developments in the sciences*. New York: George Braziller.

Longres, J. (1996). Radical social work: Is there a future? In. P. Raffoul & C. McNeece (Eds.), *Future issues for social work practice* (pp. 229–238). Boston: Allyn & Bacon.

Macht, M. W., & Quam, J. K. (1986). *Social work: An introduction*. Columbus, OH: Charles E. Merrill.

Maluccio, A. N. (1981). Competence oriented social work practice: An ecological approach. In A. N. Maluccio (Ed.), *Promoting competence in clients: A new/old approach to social work practice*. New York: Free Press.

Martin, P. Y., & O'Connor, G. G. (1988). *The social environment: Open systems applications*. New York: Longman.

Mattaini, M. A. (1990). Contextual behavioral analysis in the assessment process. *Families in Society, 71*(4), 236–245.

Maturana, H., & Varela, F. (1980). *Autopoiesis and cognition: The realization of the living*. Dordrecht, Holland: D. Reidel.

Midgley, J. (1985). Models of welfare and social planning in third world countries. In B. Mohan (Ed.), *New horizons of social welfare and policy*. Cambridge, MA: Schenkman.

Miller, P. H. (1993). *Theories of developmental psychology*. New York: W. H. Freeman.

Minuchin, S. (1974). *Families and family therapy*. Cambridge, MA: Harvard University Press.

Morales, A., & Sheafor, B. (1980). *Social work: A profession of many faces* (2nd ed.). Boston: Allyn & Bacon.

Myerson, M., & Banfield, E. C. (1955). *Politics, planning, and the public interest*. New York: Free Press.

Pincus, A., & Minahan, A. (1973). *Social work practice*. Itasca, IL: F. E. Peacock.

Piven, F. F., & Cloward, R. (1971). *Regulating the poor*. New York: Pantheon Books.

Ryckman, R. M. (1994). *Theories of personality* (5th ed.). Belmont, CA: Brooks/Cole.

Saleeby, D. (1994). Culture, theory and narrative: The intersection of meanings in practice. *Social Work, 39*(4), 351–361.

Shapiro, F. (1989). Eye movement desensitization: A new treatment for post-traumatic stress disorder. *Journal of Behavior Therapy and Experimental Psychiatry, 23*, 269–275.

Thomas, R. M. (1992). *Comparing theories of child development*. Belmont CA: Wadsworth.

Webber, M. (1980). Abandoning illusions: The state and social change. *Catalyst, 6,* 41–66.

Chapter 4

Alinsky, S. (1946). *Reveille for radicals*. Chicago: University of Chicago Press.

Alinksy, S. (1971). *Rules for radicals*. New York: Random House.

Baer, B., & Federico, R. (Eds.). (1978–1979). *Educating the baccalaureate social worker*. Cambridge, MA: Ballinger.

Barker, R. L. (1995). *The social work dictionary* (3rd ed.). Washington, DC: NASW Press.

Brager, G., Specht, H., & Torczyner, J. L. (1987). *Community organizing* (2nd ed.). New York: Columbia University Press.

Commission on Accreditation. (1994). *Handbook of accreditation standards and procedures* (4th ed.). Alexandria, VA: Council on Social Work Education.

Compton, B., & Galaway, B. (1989). *Social work processes* (4th ed.). Belmont, CA: Wadsworth.

Epstein, L. (1980). *Helping people: The task-centered approach*. St. Louis: C. V. Mosby.

Gambrill, E. (1983). *Casework: A competency-based approach*. Englewood Cliffs, NJ: Prentice-Hall.

Garvin, C. D., & Cox, F. M. (1995). A history of community organizing since the Civil War with special reference to oppressed communities. In J. Rothman, J. L. Erlich, & J. E. Tropman (Eds.), *Strategies of community intervention* (pp. 64–99). Itasca, IL: F. E. Peacock.

Gilbert, N., & Specht, H. (1987). Social planning and community organization. In A. Minahan (Ed.), *Encyclopedia of social work*. (18th ed., Vol. 1, pp. 602–619). Silver Spring, MD: NASW Press. Copyright 1990, National Association of Social Workers, Inc.

Goldstein, H. (1982). Cognitive approaches to direct practice. *Social Service Review, 56*(4), 539–555.

Hamilton, G. (1940). *Theory and practice of social casework*. New York: Columbia University Press.

Hoffman, K., & Sallee, A. (1993). *Social work practice: Bridges to change*. Boston: Allyn & Bacon.

Johnson, L. (1986). *Social work practice: A generalist approach* (2nd ed.). Boston: Allyn & Bacon.

Kahn, S. (1995). Community organization. In R. L. Edwards (Ed.), *Encyclopedia of social work* (19th ed., pp. 569–576). Washington, DC: NASW Press. Copyright 1995, National Association of Social Workers, Inc.

Kirst-Ashman, K. K., & Hull, G. H., Jr. (1993). *Understanding generalist practice*. Chicago: Nelson-Hall.

Kunopka, G. (1963). *Social group work: A helping process*. Englewood Cliffs, NJ: Prentice-Hall, Inc.

Kobrin, S. (1959, March). The Chicago area project—A 25-year assessment. *The Annals of the American Academy of Political and Social Science, 233,* 19–29.

Kramer, R. M. (1969). *Participation of the poor*. Englewood Cliffs, NJ: Prentice-Hall.

Kramer, R. M., & Specht, H. (Eds.). (1983). *Readings in community organization practice* (3rd ed.). Englewood Cliffs, NJ: Prentice-Hall.

Macht, M. W., & Ashford, J. B. (1991). *Introduction to social work and social welfare*. New York: Macmillan.

Middleman, R. R., & Goldberg, G. (1987). Social work practice with groups. In A. Minahan (Ed.), *Encyclopedia of social work* (18th ed., Vol. 2, pp. 714–729). Silver Spring, MD: NASW Press. Copyright 1990, National Association of Social Workers, Inc.

O'Neil-McMahon, M. (1990). *The general method of social work practice: A problem solving approach* (2nd ed.). Englewood Cliffs, NJ: Prentice-Hall.

Papell, C. P., & Rothman, B. (1966, Fall). Social work practice with groups. *Journal of Education for Social Work, 2,* 66–77.

Perlman, H. H. (1957). *Social casework: a problem-solving process*. Chicago: University of Chicago Press.

Phillips, H. U. (1957). *Essentials of group work skills* (pp. 42–43). New York: NASW Press.

Quam, J. K. (1995). Biographies. In R. L. Edwards (Ed.), *Encyclopedia of social work* (19th ed., p. 2580). Washington, DC: NASW Press. Copyright 1995, National Association of Social Workers, Inc.

Reid, W. J. (1977). Task-centered treatment and trends in social work. In W. J. Reid & L. Epstein (Eds.), *Task-centered practice* (p. 2). New York: Columbia University Press.

Richmond, M. E. (1917). *Social diagnosis.* New York: Russell Sage Foundation.

Scheafor, B., Horejsi, C., & Horejsi, G. (1991). *Techniques and guidelines for social work practice* (2nd ed.). Boston: Allyn & Bacon.

Schopler, J. H. & Galinsky, M. J. (1995). Group practice overview. In R. L. Edwards (Ed.), *Encyclopedia of social work* (19th ed., pp. 1129–1142). Washington, DC: NASW Press. Copyright 1995, National Association of Social Workers, Inc.

Schwartz, W. (1961a). The social worker in the group. In *The social welfare forum* (pp. 146–171). New York: Columbia University Press.

Schwartz, W. (1961b). The social worker in the group. In *New perspectives on services to groups: Theory, organization, practice* (pp. 7–34). New York: NASW Press.

Smalley, R. (1967). *Theory for social work.* New York: Columbia University Press.

Thomas, E. J. (Ed.). (1967). *The socio-behavioral approach and applications to social work.* New York: Council on Social Work Education.

Thomas, E. J. (1973). Behavior modification: Selected operant techniques and principles. In J. Fischer (Ed.), *Interpersonal helping* (pp. 437–472). Springfield, IL: Charles C. Thomas.

Chapter 5

Abbott, E. (1931). *Social welfare and professional education.* Chicago: University of Chicago Press.

American Association of Social Workers. (1929). *Social casework: Generic and specific.* New York: American Association of Social Workers.

Atwater, P. (1940). *Problems of administration in social work.* Minneapolis: University of Minnesota Press.

Bloom, M., & Fischer, J. (1982). *Evaluating practice: Guidelines for the accountable professional.* Englewood Cliffs, NJ: Prentice-Hall.

Brown, J. C. (1940). *Public relief: 1929–1939.* New York: Henry Holt.

Burghardt, S., & Fabricant, M. (1987a). Radical social work. In A. Minahan (Ed.), *Encyclopedia of social work* (18th ed., Vol. 2, pp. 455–462). Silver Spring, MD: NASW Press. Copyright 1990, National Association of Social Workers, Inc.

Burghardt, S., & Fabricant, M. (1987b). *Working under the safety net: Politics and practice with the new American poor.* Beverly Hills, CA: Sage.

Burns, E. (1961). Social polity: Step-child of the curriculum. In *Education for social work.* Proceedings of the annual program meeting. New York: Council on Social Work Education.

Cloward, R., & Piven, F. F. (1976). Toward a radical social work. In R. Bailey & M. Brake (Eds.), *Radical social work* (pp. vii–xlvii). New York: Pantheon Books.

Council on Social Work Education. (1983). *Council on social work education: Summer information on master of social work programs.* New York: Council on Social Work Education.

Council on Social Work Education. (1984). Handbook of accrediation standards and procedures. New York: Author.

Dumpson, J. R., Mullen, E. J., & First, R. J. (1978). *Toward education for effective social welfare administrative practice*. New York: Council on Social Work Education.

DiNitto, D. M., (1995). *Social welfare: Politics and public policy* (4th ed.). Boston: Allyn & Bacon.

Dluhy, M. (1981). *Changing the system*. Beverly Hills, CA: Sage.

Dunham, A. (1939). The administration of social agencies. In *Social work yearbook*. New York: Russell Sage Foundation.

Dye, T. R. (1987). *Understanding public policy* (6th ed.). Englewood Cliffs, NJ: Prentice-Hall.

Fisher, J. (1980). *The response of social work to the depression*. Cambridge, MA: Schenkman.

Fisher, R. (1984). *Let the people decide*. Boston: G. K. Hall.

Fulmer, R. M. (1978). *The new management* (2nd ed.). New York: Macmillan.

Galbraith, J. (1973). *Designing complex organizations*. Reading, MA: Addison-Wesley.

Gibelman, M., & Schervish, P. (1993). *Who we are: The social work labor force as reflected in the NASW membership*. Washington, DC: NASW Press. Copyright 1993, National Association of Social Workers, Inc.

Gummer, B. (1975). Social planning and administration: Implications for curriculum development. *Journal of Education for Social Work, 11,* 71.

Hagarty, J. E. (1931). *The training of social workers*. New York: McGraw-Hill.

Hasenfeld, Y. (1992). The nature of human services organizations. In Y. Hasenfeld & R. English (Eds.), *Human services as complex organizations* (pp. 3–23). Newbury Park, CA: Sage.

Hickson D. J., Hinings, C. R., Lee, C. A., Schneck, R. E., & Pennings, J. M. (1971). A strategic contingencies theory of interorganizational power. *Administrative Science Quarterly, 16,* 216–229.

Hollis, E., & Taylor, A. (1951). *Social work education in the United States: The report of a study made for the national council on social work education*. New York: Columbia University Press.

Institute of public policy studies. (1978). *Directory*. Ann Arbor, MI: Unpublished.

Jones, C. O. (1978). *An introduction to the study of public policy*. North Scituate, MA: Duxbury Press.

Katz, D., & Kahn, R. (1978). *Social psychology of organizations* (rev. ed.). New York: Wiley.

Kidneigh, J. C. (1950). Social work administration: An area of social work practice. *Social Work Journal, 31*(2), 58.

Lawrence, P. R., & Lorsch, J. W. (1967). *Organizations and environment: Managing differentiation and integration*. Cambridge, MA: Harvard University Press.

Lennon, T. (1995). *Statistics on social work education in the United States: 1994*. Alexandria, VA: Council on Social Work Education.

Longres, J. (1996). Radical social work: Is there a future? In. P. Raffoul & C. McNeece (Eds.), *Future issues in social work practice* (pp. 229–239). Boston: Allyn & Bacon.

March, J., & Simon, H. (1958). *Organizations*. New York: John Wiley & Sons.

McGregor, G. (1960). *The human side of enterprise*. New York: McGraw-Hill.

National Association of Social Workers. (1984). *A study of attitudes of NASW members, lapsed members, and non-members*. Silver Spring, MD: NASW Press.

National Association of Social Workers. (1985). *NASW membership: National summary tables* (Report No. 1). Silver Spring, MD: NASW Press.

National Association of Social Workers. (1987). *Salaries in social work*. Silver Spring, MD: NASW Press.

Patti, R. J. (1977). Patterns of management activity in social welfare agencies. *Administration in Social Work, 1*(1), 5–18.

Patti, R. J. (1983). *Social welfare administration: Managing social programs in a developmental context*. Englewood Cliffs, NJ: Prentice-Hall.

Piven, F. F., & Cloward, R. (1971). *Regulating the poor*. New York: Pantheon Books.

Piven, F. F., & Cloward, R. (1988). *Why Americans don't vote*. New York: Pantheon Books.

Reid, W. (1995). Research overview. In R. L. Edwards (Ed.), *Encyclopedia of social work* (19th ed., pp. 2040–2050). Washington, DC: NASW Press. Copyright 1995, National Association of Social Workers, Inc.

Sarri, R. (1973). Effective social work intervention in administration and planning roles: Implications for education. In *Facing the challenge*. New York: Council on Social Work Education.

Sarri, R. (1987). Administration in social work. In A. Minahan (Ed.), *Encyclopedia of social work* (Vol. 1, 18th ed.). Silver Spring, MD: NASW Press. Copyright 1990, National Association of Social Workers, Inc.

Simon, H. A. (1976). *Administrative behavior* (3rd ed.). New York: Free Press.

Taylor, F. W. (1911). Shop management. In *Scientific management*. New York: Harper & Row.

Thompson, J. D. (1961). Common elements in administration. In E. Reed (Ed.), *Social welfare administration* (pp. 16–29). New York: Columbia University Press.

Tripodi, T., Fellin, P., & Myer, H. (1978). *Differential social program evaluation*. Itasca, IL: Peacock.

Tripodi, T., Fellin, P., & Myer, H. (1983). *The assessment of social research* (2nd ed.). Itasca, IL: Peacock.

Trecker, H. B. (1977). *Social work administration: Principles and practice* (rev. ed.). New York: Association Press.

Chapter 6

Alcoholics Anonymous World Services. (1976). *Alcoholics Anonymous* (3rd ed.). New York: Alcoholics Anonymous World Services.

American Psychiatric Association. (1994). *Diagnostic and statistical manual of mental disorders* (4th ed.). Washington, DC: American Psychiatric Association.

Anderson, C. M., Reiss, D. J., & Hogarty, G. (1986). *Schizophrenia and the family: A practitioner's guide to psychoeducation and management.* New York: Guilford Press.

Austin, D. M. (1986). *A history of social work education.* Austin: School of Social Work, University of Texas at Austin.

Barbour, W. (1995). *Mental illness: Opposing viewpoints.* San Diego: Greehaven.

Bergin, A., & Garfield, S. (1994). *Handbook of psychotherapy and behavior change* (4th ed.). New York: John Wiley & Sons.

Berlin, G., & McAllister, W. (1992). Homelessness. In H. J. Aaron & C. L. Shultze (Eds.), *Setting domestic priorities: What can government do?* (pp. 63–99). Washington, DC: Brookings Institution.

Burt, M. R. (1992). *Over the edge: The growth of homelessness in the 1980s.* New York: Russell Sage.

Crystal, D. (1989). Asian Americans and the myth of the model minority. *Social Casework, 70,* 405–413.

DiNitto, D. M., & Webb, D. K. (1994). Compounding the problem: Substance abuse and other disabilities. In C. A. McNeece & D. M. DiNitto (Eds.), *Chemical dependency: A systems approach* (pp. 312–348). Englewood Cliffs, NJ: Prentice-Hall.

Escobar, J. I. (1987). Cross-cultural aspects of the somatization trait. *Hospital and Community Psychiatry, 38,* 174–180.

Ginsberg, L. (1995). *Social work almanac* (2d ed.). Washington, DC: NASW Press.

Gonzalez-Ramos, G. (1990). Examining the myth of Hispanic families' resistance to treatment: Using the school as a site for services. *Social Work in Education, 12,* 261–274.

Grob, G. (1966). *The state and the mentally ill.* Chapel Hill, NC: University of North Carolina Press.

Health program spending cut by 25 percent. (1981). *Congressional Quarterly Almanac,* (Washington, DC), pp. 483–488.

Interagency Council on the Homeless and Federal Task Force on Homelessness and Severe Mental Illness. (1992). *Outcasts on Main Street* (Publication No. (ADM) 92–1904). Washington, DC: U.S. Department of Health and Human Services.

Jayaratne, S., Davis-Sacks, M. L., & Chess W. A. (1991). Private practice may be good for your health and well-being. *Social Work, 36*(3), 224–229.

Jordan, C., Vandiver, V., & Lewellen, A. (1994, November). A social work perspective of psychosocial rehabilitation: Psychoeducational models for minority families. *International Journal of Mental Health,* (November, pp. 27–43).

Karno, M., & Morales, A. (1976). A community mental health service for Mexican-Americans in a metropolis. In C. A. Hernandez, M. J. Hauz, & N. N. Wagner, *Chicanos: Social and psychological perspectives* (pp. 237–241). St. Louis: C. V. Mosby.

Kirk, S. A., & Kutchins, H. (1992). *The selling of DSM: The rhetoric of science in psychiatry.* New York: Aldine de Gruyter.

Kitano, H. H. L. (1987). Asian Americans. In A. Minahan (Ed.), *Encyclopedia of social work* (18th ed., Vol. 1, pp. 156–171). Silver Spring, MD: NASW Press. Copyright 1990, National Association of Social Workers, Inc.

Krauthammer, C. (1985, December 2). When liberty really means neglect. *Time*, pp. 103–104.

League of Women Voters of Texas. (1988). *Facts and issues: Services for the seriously mentally ill in Texas.* Austin: League of Women Voters Education Fund.

Loring, M., & Powell, B. (1988). Gender, race, and DSM-III: A study of the objectivity of psychiatric diagnostic behavior. *Journal of Health and Social Behavior, 29,* 1–22.

Macarov, D. (1978). *The design of social welfare.* New York: Holt, Rinehart and Winston.

Manderscheid, R. W., & Sonnenschein, M. A. (Eds.). *Mental health, United States, 1994* (DHHS Publication No. (SMA) 94-3000). Rockville, MD: Center for Mental Health Services and National Institute of Mental Health.

Mechanic, D. (1989). *Mental health and social policy* (3rd ed.). Englewood Cliffs, NJ: Prentice-Hall.

Mental Health Association in Texas. (1985). *Mental health association in Texas* [Mimeo]. Austin: Mental Health Association.

National Alliance for the Mentally Ill. (1995). *You are not alone: Finding help for people with mental illness and their families.* Arlington, VA: National Alliance for the Mentally Ill.

Rubin, A., & Johnson, P. J. (1984). Direct practice interests of entering MSW students. *Journal of Education for Social Work, 20*(2), 5–16.

Sands, R. G. (1991). *Clinical social work practice in community mental health.* New York: Merrill.

Smith, A. (1990). Social influence and antiprejudice training programs. In J. Edwards, R. S. Tindale, L. Heath, & E. J. Posavac (Eds.), *Social influence processes and prevention* (pp. 183–196). New York: Plenum Press.

Sue, D., Sue, D., & Sue, S. (1994). *Understanding abnormal behavior* (4th ed.). Princeton, NJ: Houghton Mifflin.

Tarvis, C. (1991). The measure of women: Paradoxes and perspectives in the study of gender. In J. D. Goodchilds (Ed.), *Psychological perspectives on human diversity in America* (pp. 91–136). Washington, DC: American Psychological Association.

Texas Department of Mental Health and Mental Retardation. (1984). *Case management system components by MH and MR authorities.* Texas Department of Mental Health and Mental Retardation.

Upton, D. (1983). *Mental health care and national health insurance.* New York: Plenum Press.

Wallace, M. E. (1982). Private practice: A nationwide study. *Social Work, 27*(3), 262–267.

Webb, D. K. (1995). *The good chemistry co-leaders manual.* Available from Deborah K. Webb, P.O. Box 3073, Austin, TX 78764.

Wetzel, J. W. (1994). Women of the world: The wonder class—A global perspective on women and mental health. In L. V. Davis (Ed.), *Building on women's strengths: A social work agenda for the 21st century* (pp. 229–243). New York: The Haworth Press.

Williams, D. H. (1986). The epidemiology of mental illness in Afro-Americans. *American Journal of Psychiatry, 142,* 798–805.

Chapter 7

Alcoholics Anonymous World Services. (1976). *Alcoholics Anonymous* (3rd ed). New York: Alcoholics Anonymous World Services.

Asante, M. (1988). *Afrocentricity*. Trenton, NJ: Africa World Press.

Barber, J. (1995). Alcohol addiction: Private trouble or social issue? *Social Service Review, 68*(4), 521–533.

Barnea, Z., & Teichman, M. (1994). Substance misuse and abuse among the elderly: Implications for social work intervention. *Journal of Gerontological Social Work, 21*(3), 133–148.

Davis, D. R., & DiNitto, D. M. (1994). Gender and drugs: Fact, fiction, and unanswered questions. In C. A. McNeece & D. M. DiNitto (Eds.), *Chemical dependency: A systems approach* (pp. 364–394). Englewood Cliffs, NJ: Prentice-Hall.

Dembo, R. (1994). Drugs & crime revisited: Introduction. *Journal of Drug Issues, 24*(1/2), 1.

DiNitto, D. M., & Webb, D. K. (1994). Compounding the problem: Substance abuse and other disabilities. In C. A. McNeece, & D. M. DiNitto (Eds.), *Chemical dependency: A systems approach* (pp. 312–348). Englewood Cliffs, NJ: Prentice-Hall.

Emrick, C. D., & Hansen, J. (1983, October). Assertions regarding effectiveness of treatment for alcoholism: Fact or fantasy? *American Psychologist*, 1078–1088.

Garrett, G. (1994, October). The professional base of social work. *Families in Society: The Journal of Contemporary Human Services*, 513–520.

Ginsberg, L. (1995). *The social work almanac* (2nd ed.). Washington, DC: NASW Press.

Gonet, M. M. (1994). *Counseling the adolescent substance abuser*. Thousand Oaks, CA: Sage.

Goshen, C. E. (1973). *Drinks, drugs, and do-gooders*. New York: Free Press.

Gustavsson, N. S. (1991). Pregnant chemically dependent women: The new criminals. *Affilia, 6*(2), 61–73.

Hoffman, J. (1995). Pregnant, addicted—and guilty? In E. Goode (Ed.), *Drugs, society, and behavior* (pp. 186–191). Guilford, CT: The Dushkin Publishing Group.

Jackson, J. (1954). The adjustment of the family to the crisis of alcoholism. *Quarterly Journal of Studies on Alcoholism, 15*(4), 562–568.

Jackson, M. S. (1995). Afrocentric treatment of African American women and their children in a residential chemical dependency program. *Journal of Black Studies, 26*(1), 17–30.

Jellinek, E. M. (1960). *The disease concept of alcoholism*. New Haven: Hillhouse Press.

Johnston, L., O'Malley, P., & Bachman, J. (1995). Smoking, drinking, and illicit drug use among American secondary school students, college students, and young adults, 1975–1992. In E. Goode (Ed.), *Drugs, society, and behavior* (pp. 83–89). Guilford, CT: The Dushkin Publishing Group.

Kohns, S. C. (1966). *The roots of social work*. New York: Association Press.

Langton, P. A. (1991). *Drug use and the alcohol dilemma*. Boston: Allyn & Bacon.

McNeece, C. A., & DiNitto, D. M. (1994). *Chemical dependency: A systems approach*. Englewood Cliffs, NJ: Prentice-Hall.

Musto, D. F. (1973). *The American disease*. Clinton, MA: The Colonial Press.

Nathan, P. E. (1986). Outcomes of treatment for alcoholism: Current data. *Annals of Behavioral Medicine, 8*(2–3), 40–46.

National Institute on Alcohol Abuse and Alcoholism. (1990). *Seventh special report to the U.S. Congress on alcohol and health*. Rockville, MD: U.S. Department of Health and Human Services.

National Institute on Alcohol Abuse and Alcoholism. (1993). *Eighth special report to the U.S. Congress on alcohol and health*. Rockville, MD: U.S. Department of Health and Human Services.

Northern, H. (1969). *Social work with groups*. New York: Columbia University Press.

Paredes, A. (1976). History of the concept of alcoholism. In R. E. Tarter & A. A. Sugerman, *Alcoholism: Interdisciplinary approaches to an enduring problem* (pp. 9–52). Reading, MA: Addison-Wesley.

Pattison, E. M., Sobell, M. B., & Sobell, L. C. (1977). *Emerging concepts of alcohol dependence*. New York: Springer.

Raffoul, P. (1986). Drug misuse among older people: Focus for interdisciplinary efforts. *Health & Social Work, 11,* 197–203.

Ratner, M. S. (1993). *Crack pipe as pimp*. New York: Lexington Books.

Rivers, P. C. (1994). *Alcohol and human behavior.* Englewood Cliffs, NJ: Prentice-Hall.

Schaie, K., & Willis, S. (1991). *Adult development and aging*. New York: Harper Collins.

Schlaadt, R. G. (1992). *Drugs, society, and behavior*. Guilford, CT: The Dushkin Publishing Group.

Schwartzberg, N. S. (1995). Cocaine effect on babies questioned. In E. Goode (Ed.), *Drugs, society, and behavior* (pp. 139–140). Guilford, CT: The Dushkin Publishing Group.

Sournia, J. (1990). *A history of alcoholism*. Cambridge, MA: T. J. Press.

Thomas, P. (1995, December 16). As more teen-agers use drugs, fewer see risks, survey finds. *Austin American-Statesman,* p. A17.

Wechsler, H., & Rohman, M. (1985). Future caregivers' views on alcoholism treatment: A poor prognosis. In E. M. Freeman (Ed.), *Social work practice with clients who have alcohol problems* (pp. 315–330). Springfield, IL: Thomas.

Chapter 8

American Health Security News (1995, June 14). Available from Congressman Jim McDermot, 1707 Longworth Building, Washington, DC 20515.

American Political Network, Inc. (1992, November 9). AETNA: Health care opinions on Eday [Poll update]. *American Health Line, 1,* 156.

Berkman, B. (1987). Healthcare specializations. In A. Minahan (Ed.), *Encyclopedia of social work* (18th ed., Vol. 1, pp. 711–714). Silver Spring, MD: NASW Press. Copyright 1990, National Association of Social Workers, Inc.

Bracht, N. F. (1978). *Social work in health care: A guide to professional practice*. New York: Haworth Press.

Cabot, R. (1919). *Social work essays on the meeting and growth of doctor and social worker.* New York: Houghton-Mifflin.

Carlton, T. O., et al. (1984). *Clinical social work in health settings:* Springer series on social work, (Vol. 4). New York: Springer.

Council on Social Work Education. (1985). *Statistics on social work education in the U.S.: 1984.* New York: Council on Social Work Education.

DeLew, N. (1995, July 19). The first 30 years of Medicare and Medicaid. *Journal of American Medical Association, 274*(3), 262–267.

Dewar, H. (1995, June 24). GOP pushes compromise on budget: Congress prepares for tax cut battles. *Washington Post,* A6.

Dye, T. (1987). *Understanding public policy* (6th ed.). Englewood Cliffs, NJ: Prentice-Hall.

Eckholm, E. (1994, December 18). While Congress remains silent, health care transforms itself. *The New York Times,* p. 1.

Enthoven, A. C. (1993). The history and principles of managed competition. *Health Affairs,* Supplement, 24–48.

Evans, R. G., Morris, B. L., & Marmor, T. R. (Eds.). (1994). *Why are some people healthy and others not? The determinants of health populations.* Hawthorne, NY: Aldine De Gruyter.

Flint, S., Yodkowsky, B., & Tang S. F. (1995). *Children's entitlement to Medicaid: What have we got to lose?* Unpublished article, American Academy of Pediatrics.

Frank, J. W., and Mustard, J. F. (1994). The determinants of health from a historical perspective. *Daedalus, 123*(4), 1–20.

Freudenhelm, M. (1996, April 2). Managed care empires in the making. *The New York Times,* D1.

Friedlander, W. A., & Apte, R. Z. (1980). *Introduction to social work* (5th ed.). Englewood Cliffs, NJ: Prentice-Hall.

Germain, C. B. (1984). *Social work practice in health care: An ecological perspective.* New York: Free Press.

Gibelman, M., & Schervish, P. (1993). *Who we are: The social work labor force as reflected in the NASW membership.* Washington, DC: NASW Press. Copyright 1993, National Association of Social Workers, Inc.

Health Care Finance Administration. (1995, July 7). HHS survey finds most beneficiaries satisfied with medicare [Press release].

Kaiser Family Foundation. (1995, February). *Medicaid facts.* Washington, DC: Kaiser Family Foundation.

Kerson, T. S. (1982). *Social work in health settings: Practice in context.* New York: Longman.

Long Term Care Campaign. (1995, May 15). *Some cuts never heal: National and state impacts of proposed budget cuts in long term care Medicaid.* Washington, DC.

Magner, G. (1996). Health care rationing. In P. Rafford & C. A. McNeece (Eds.), *Future issues for social work practice* (pp. 39–48). Boston: Allyn & Bacon.

Marmot, M. G., Smith, G. D., Stansfield, S., Patel, C., North, F., Head, J., White, I., Brunner, E., & Feeney, A. (1994). Health inequalities and social class. In P. R. Lee & C. L. Estes (Eds.), *The nation's health* (4th ed., pp. 34–40). Boston: Jones & Bartlett.

Mohatt, G., McDiarmid, W., & Montoya, V. (1988). Societies, families and change: The Alaskan example. In S. Manson and N. Dinges (Eds.), *Behavioral health issues among American Indians and Alaskan natives: Exploration on the frontiers of the behavioral sciences* (pp. 325–352). Denver, CO: National Center for American Indian and Alaska Native Mental Health Research, University of Colorado Health Sciences Center.

National Association of Social Workers. (1983). Membership survey shows practice shifts. *NASW News, 28* (10), 6–7.

National Center for Health Statistics. (1994). *Monthly Vital Statistics Report, 42*(13). Hyattsville, MD: National Center for Health Statistics.

Neil, A. (1988). *Health and healing.* Boston: Houghton Mifflin Co.

Newhouse, J. P. (1993). An inconoclastic view of health cost containment. *Health Affairs,* Supplement, 152–171.

Newhouse, J. P. (1995, Spring), Economists, policy entrepreneurs, and health care reform. *Health Affairs, 14,*(1), 182–198.

Poole, D. L. (1995). Health care: Direct practice. In R. L. Edwards (Ed.), *Encyclopedia of social work* (19th ed., Vol. 2, pp. 1156–1167). Washington, DC: NASW Press. Copyright 1995, National Association of Social Workers, Inc.

Reynolds, B. C. (1963). *Bertha C. Reynolds—An uncharted journey—Fifty years in social work by one of its great teachers.* Washington, DC: NASW Press.

Rosenberg, G. (1994). *The changing health care environment: Implications for social work services.* Paper presented at Social Work 1994, NASW's meeting of the profession, Nashville.

Ross, J. W. (1995). Hospital social work. In R. L. Edwards (Ed.), *Encyclopedia of social work* (19th ed., Vol. 2., pp. 1365–1377). Washington, DC: NASW Press. Copyright 1995, National Association of Social Workers, Inc.

Schlesinger, E. G. (1985). *Health care social work practice: Concepts & strategies.* St. Louis: Times Mirror/Mosby.

Schwartz, L. L. (1994, April). *The medicalization of social problems: America's special health care dilemma—Special report.* Washington, DC: American Health Systems Institute.

Sherrill, R. (1995). Dangerous to your health: The madness of the market. *The Nation, 2,* 45–72.

Southwick, K. (1994). Case study: Putting the pieces in place for regional integration. *Strategies for Healthcare Excellence, 1,* 1–7.

Toner, R. (1995, May 16). Medicare target could be elusive, many experts say. *The New York Times,* 1.

Vladeck, B. C. (1995, July 19). Medicare at 30 preparing for the future. *Journal of American Medical Association, 274*(3), 259–262.

Wiatrowski, W. J. (1995, June). Who really has access to employer-provided health benefits? *Monthly Labor Review.*

Wilkinson, R. G. (1994). The epidemiological transition: From material scarcity to social disadvantage? *Daedalus, 4,* 61–78.

Williamson, R. G. (1994). The epidemiological transition: From material scarcity to social disadvantage? *Daedalus, 123*(4), 61–77.

Wolfe, B. (1994). Reform of healthcare for nonelderly poor. In S. H. Danziger, G. D. Sardefur, & D. H. Weinberg (Eds.), *Confronting poverty-prescriptions for change* (pp. 253–288). New York: Russell Sage Foundation.

Chapter 9

Begab, M. J. (1983). Psychosocial aspects of mental retardation. In L. Wikler & M. P. Keenan (Eds.), *Developmental disabilities: No longer a private tragedy* (pp. 34–40). Washington, DC: National Association of Social Workers and American Association on Mental Deficiency.

Caires, K. B., & Weil, M. (1985). Developmentally disabled persons and their families. In M. Weil, J. M. Karls, & Associates (Eds.), *Case management in human service practice* (pp. 233–275). San Francisco: Jossey-Bass.

DeWeaver, K. L. (1980). An empirical analysis of social workers in the field of mental retardation. *Dissertation Abstracts International, 41,* 1214A–1215A. (University Microfilms No. 8020351.)

DeWeaver, K. L. (1982). Producing social workers trained for practice with the developmentally disabled. *Arete, 7*(1), 59–62.

DeWeaver, K. L. (1983). Deinstitutionalization of the developmentally disabled. *Social Work, 28,* 435–439.

DeWeaver, K. L. (1995). Developmental disabilities: Definitions and policies. In R. L. Edwards (Ed.), *Encyclopedia of social work* (19th ed., Vol.1, pp. 712–720). Washington, DC: NASW Press. Copyright 1995, National Association of Social Workers, Inc.

DeWeaver, K. L., & Johnson, P. J. (1983). Case management in rural areas for the developmentally disabled. *Human Services in the Rural Environment, 8*(4), 23–31.

DeWeaver, K. L., & Kropf, N. P. (1992). Persons with mental retardation: A forgotten minority in education. *Journal of Social Work Education, 28*(1), 36–46.

Gibelman, M., & Schervish, P. H. (1993). *Who we are: The social work labor force as reflected in the NASW membership.* Washington, DC: NASW Press. Copyright 1993, National Association of Social Workers, Inc.

Hall, J. A., Ford, L. H., Moss, J. W., & Dineen, J. P. (1986). Practice with mentally retarded adults as an adjunct to vocational training. *Social Work, 31*(2), 125–129.

Hanley, B., & Parkinson, C. B. (1994). Position paper on social work values: Practice with individuals who have developmental disabilities. *Mental Retardation, 32*(6), 426–431.

Harbolt, P. (1981). The fight against community programs. *Access, 4*(4), 14–18.

Horejsi, C. R. (1979). Developmental disabilities: Opportunities for social workers. *Social Work, 24,* 40–43.

Kaufman, A. V., DeWeaver, K., & Glicken, M. (1989). The mentally retarded aged: Implications for social work practice. *Journal of Gerontological Social Work, 14*(1/2), 93–110.

Kingson, E., & Berkowitz, E. D. (1993). *Social Security and Medicare: A policy primer.* Westport, CT: Auburn House.

Kropf, N. P., & DeWeaver, K. L. (in press). Social work and people with developmental disabilities. In J. Wodarski, D. Harrison, & B. Thyer (Eds.), *Cultural diversity and social work practice* (2nd ed.). Springfield, IL: Thomas.

Levy, J. M. (1995). Social work. In B. A. Thyer & N. P. Kropf (Eds.), *Developmental disabilities* (pp. 188–201). Cambridge, MA: Brookline Books.

Longhurst, N. A. (1994). *The self-advocacy movement by people with developmental disabilities: A demographic study and directory of self-advocacy groups in the United States.* Washington, DC: American Association on Mental Retardation.

McDonald-Wikler, L. (1987). Disabilities: Developmental. In A. Minahan (Ed.), *Encyclopedia of social work* (18th ed., Vol. 1, pp. 422–434). Silver Spring, MD: NASW Press. Copyright 1990, National Association of Social Workers, Inc.

Membership survey shows practice shifts. (1983, November). *NASW News, 6–7.*

Monfils, M. J. (1984). A pressing need: Continuing social work education in mental retardation. *Journal of Continuing Social Work Education, 2*(4), 3–7.

National Association of Social Workers. (1987). Standards for social work in developmental disabilities. In *NASW standards for social work in health care settings* (pp. 15–21). Silver Spring, MD: Author.

National Association of Social Workers. (1992). *NASW standards for social work case management.* Washington, DC: Author.

Nirje, B. (1976). The normalization principle. In R. B. Kugel & A. Sheerer (Eds.), *Changing patterns in residential services for the mentally retarded* (rev. ed., pp. 231–240). Washington, DC: President's Committee on Mental Retardation.

Office of Information and Resources for the Handicapped. (1983, September). *A pocket guide to federal help for the disabled person.* (Publication No. E-83-22002). Washington, DC: Department of Education.

Olshansky, S. (1962). Chronic sorrow: A response to having a mentally defective child. *Social Casework, 43,* 190–193.

Patterson L. L. (1956). Some pointers for professionals. *Children, 3*(1), 13–17.

Rauch, J. B., & Black, R. B. (1995). Genetics. In R. L. Edwards (Ed.), *Encyclopedia of social work* (19th ed., Vol. 2, pp. 1108–1117). Washington, DC: NASW Press. Copyright 1995, National Association of Social Workers, Inc.

Rubin, A., Johnson, P. J., & DeWeaver, K. L. (1986). Direct practice interests of MSW students: Changes from entry to graduation. *Journal of Social Work Education, 22*(2), 98–108.

Rusch, F. R., & Hughes, C. (1989). Overview of supported employment. *Journal of Applied Behavior Analysis, 22,* 351–363.

Scheerenberger, R. C. (1983). *A history of mental retardation.* Baltimore: Paul H. Brookes.

Selan, B. H. (1976). Psychotherapy with the developmentally disabled. *Health and Social Work, 1,* 73–85.

Summers, J. A. (1981). The definition of developmental disabilities: A concept in transition. *Mental Retardation, 19,* 259–265.

Trevino, F. (1979). Siblings of handicapped children: Identifying those at risk. *Social Casework, 60,* 488–493.

Underwood, L., & Thyer, B. A. (1990). Social work practice with the mentally retarded: Reducing self-injurious behaviors using non-aversive methods. *Arete, 15,* 14–23.

Weil, M., & Karls, J. M. (1985). Historical origins and recent developments. In M. Weil, J. M. Karls, & Associates (Eds.), *Case management in human service practice* (pp. 1–28). San Francisco: Jossey-Bass.

Wikler, L. (1981). Social work education and developmental disabilities. In J. A. Browne, B. A. Kirlin, & S. Watt (Eds.), *Rehabilitation services and the social work role: Challenge for change* (pp. 285–295). Baltimore: Williams & Wilkins.

Wolfensberger, W. (Ed.). (1972). *The principle of normalization in human services*. Toronto: National Institute on Mental Retardation.

World Institute on Disability. (1992). *Just like everyone else*. Oakland, CA: The Institute.

Chapter 10

American Humane Association. Fact Sheet No. 8. (1995). America's children: How are they doing? Englewood, CO: American Humane Association.

American Humane Association. Fact Sheet No. 11. (1995). Family preservation. Englewood, CO: American Humane Association.

Anderson, R., & Staudt, M. (1990). Social work in the schools. In H. W. Johnson, *The social services: An introduction* (3rd ed., pp. 151–170). Itasca, IL: Peacock.

Barth, R. P., & Berry, M. (1994). Implications of research on the welfare of children under permanency planning. In R. Barth, J. D. Berrick, & N. Gilbert (Eds.), *Child welfare research review,* (Vol. 1, pp. 323–369). New York: Columbia University Press.

Barth, R. P., Courtney, M., Berrick, J. D., & Albert, V. (1994). *From child abuse to permanency planning: Child welfare services pathways and placements*. New York: Aldine de Gruyter.

Bowlby, J. (1962). *Separation anxiety: A critical review of the literature*. New York: Child Welfare League of America.

Brodzinsky, D. M. (1987). Adjustment to adoption: A psychosocial perspective. *Clinical Psychology Review, 7,* 25–47.

Bureau of the Census, U.S. Department of Commerce. (1992). *Statistical abstract of the United States: 1992*. Washington, DC: U.S. Government Printing Office.

Cohen, N. A. (Ed.). (1992). *Child welfare: A multicultural focus*. Boston: Allyn & Bacon.

Cowley, G., Springen, K., Miller, S., Lewis, S. D., & Titunik, V. (1993, August 16). Who's looking after the interests of children? *Newsweek,* pp. 54–55.

Davidson, C. E. (1994). Dependent children and their families: A historical survey of United States policy. In F. H. Jacobs, & M. W. Davies, (Eds.), *More than kissing babies? Current child and family policy in the United States* (pp. 65–90). Westport, CT: Auburn.

Davies, M. W. (1994). Who's minding the baby? Reproductive work, productive work, and family policy in the United States. In F. H. Jacobs, & M. W. Davies, (Eds.), *More than kissing babies? Current child and family policy in the United States* (pp. 37–64). Westport, CT: Auburn.

Delgado, R. (1992). Generalist child welfare and Hispanic families. In N. A. Cohen (Ed.), *Child welfare: A multicultural focus* (pp. 130–156). Boston: Allyn & Bacon.

Dougherty, D. M., Saxe, L. M., Cross, T., & Silverman, N. (1987). *Children's mental health problems and services: A report by the Office of Technology Assessment.* Durham, NC: Duke University Press.

Emenhiser, D., Barker, R., & DeWoody, M. (1995). *Managed care: An agency guide to surviving and thriving.* Washington, DC: Child Welfare League of America.

Fanshel, D., & Shinn, E. (1978). *Children in foster care.* New York: Columbia University Press.

Garfinkel, I., & McLanahan, S. (1986). *Single mothers and their children: A new American dilemma.* Washington, DC: Urban Institute.

General Accounting Office. (1995, September). *Child welfare: Complex needs strain capacity to provide services.* Washington, DC: General Accounting Office.

Gibelman, M., & Schervish, P. H. (1993). *Who we are: The social work labor force as reflected in the NASW membership.* Washington, DC: NASW Press. Copyright 1993, National Association of Social Workers, Inc.

Gibson, D. L., & Noble, D. N. (1991, May-June). Creative permanency planning: Residential services for families. *Child Welfare, 70,* 371–382.

Goldstein, J., Freud, A., & Solnit, A. (1973). *Beyond the best interests of the child.* New York: Free Press.

Grinspoon, L. (Ed.). (1993, July). Child abuse—Parts I and II. *The Harvard Mental Health Letter.* Cambridge, MA: Harvard.

Hampson, R. (1995, November 30). Cinderella story takes a dark turn: Abuse robs NYC girl of hope, then life. *USA Today,* p. 3A.

Hofferth, S. L., & Hayes, C. D. (Eds.). (1987). *Risking the future* (Vol. 2). Washington, DC: National Academy Press.

Hollinger, J. H. (1993, Spring). Adoption law. *The Future of Children, 3,* 41–61.

Kamerman, S. B., & Kahn, A. J. (1990). Social services for children, youth and families in the United States. *Children and Youth Services Review, 12,* 1–84.

Karger, H. J., & Stoesz, D. (1994). *American social welfare policy: A pluralist approach* (2nd ed.). New York: Longman.

Kempe, C. H., Silverman, F., Steele, B., Droegmueller, W., & Silver, H. (1962). The battered-child syndrome. *Journal of American Medical Association, 181,* 17–24.

Ladner, J. A. (1987). Black teenage pregnancy: A challenge for educators. *Journal of Negro Education, 56,* 53–63.

Lindsey, D. (1994). *The welfare of children.* New York: Oxford.

Maas, S., & Engler, R. E. (1959). *Children in need of parents.* New York: Columbia University Press.

McRoy, R. G. (1989). An organizational dilemma: The case of transracial adoption. *Journal of Applied Behavioral Science 25*(2), 145–160.

McWhirter, J. J., McWhirter, B. T., McWhirter, A. M., & McWhirter, E. H. (1993). *At-risk youth: A comprehensive response.* Pacific Grove, CA: Brooks/Cole.

Midgley, J., Ellett, C., Noble, D. N., & Bennett, N. (1995). *Study of professional personnel needs for Office of Community Services*. Louisiana State University: Office of Research and Economic Development.

Morris, G. (1995, October 22). The orphan trains. *Baton Rouge Advocate,* pp. H1–2.

National Association of Social Workers. (1995). Position paper: Restructuring federal programs through the use of block grants. Washington, DC: NASW Press.

Noble, D. N. (1983). Custody contest: How to divide and reassemble a child. *Social Casework, 64,* 406–413.

Noble, D. N. (1994). Adoption and residential treatment: Where two service areas intersect. *Residential Treatment for Children and Youth, 11,* 63–79.

Noble, D. N., & Gibson, D. L. (1994, December). Family values in action: Family connectedness for children in substitute care. *Child and Youth Care Forum, 23*(5), 315–328.

Ozawa, M. N. (1993). America's future and her investment in children. *Child Welfare, 72,* 517–529.

Pecora, P. J., Whittaker, J. K., & Maluccio, A. N. (1992). *The child welfare challenge: Policy, practice, and research*. New York: Aldine de Gruyter.

Prater, G. S. (1992). Child welfare and African-American families. In N. A. Cohen, (Ed.), *Child welfare: A multicultural focus* (pp. 84–106). Boston: Allyn & Bacon.

Saltzman, A., & Proch, K. (1990). *Law in social work practice*. Chicago: Nelson-Hall.

Schulman, I., & Behrman, R. E. (1993, Spring). Adoption: Overview and major recommendations. *The Future of Children, 3.*

Sedlak, A. J. (1991). *Supplementary analyses of data on the national incidence of child abuse and neglect*. Rockville, MD: Westat.

Severson, M. M., & Bankston, T. V. (1995). Social work and the pursuit of justice through mediation. *Social Work, 40,* 683–691.

Silver, L. B. (1988). The scope of the problem in children and adolescents. In J. G. Looney, (Ed.), *Chronic mental illness in children and adolescents* (pp. 39–52). Washington, DC: American Psychiatric Press.

Stein, J. A. (1995). *Residential treatment of adolescents and children: Issues, principles, and techniques*. Chicago: Nelson-Hall.

Tatara, T. (1994). Some additional explanations for the recent rise in the U.S. child substitute care population: An analysis of national child substitute care flow data and future research questions. In R. Barth, J. D. Berrick, & N. Gilbert (Eds.), *Child welfare research review* (Vol. 1, pp. 126–145). New York: Columbia University Press.

Vodejda, B. (1995, January 22). Illinois orphanage offers model of what such places could be. *Baton Rouge Advocate,* p. 2E.

Weitzman, L. J. (1985). *The divorce revolution: The unexpected social and economic consequences for women and children in America*. New York: Free Press.

Zimmerman, S. L. (1992). *Family policies and family well-being: The role of political culture*. Newbury Park, CA: Sage.

Chapter 11

Adams, P. F., & Benson, V. (1991, December). Current estimates from the National Health Interview Survey, 1990. *Vital and Health Statistics, 10*(181). Hyattsville, MD: National Center for Health Statistics.

Brown, C., & Onzuka-Anderson, R. (1985). *Our aging parents: A practical guide to elder-care.* Honolulu: University of Hawaii Press.

Bureau of the Census. (1995). *Income, poverty, and valuation of noncash benefits: 1993* (Current Population Reports, Consumer Income, Series P60-188). Washington, DC: U.S. Government Printing Office.

Committee on Ways and Means, U.S. House of Representatives. (1993). *Overview of entitlement programs: 1993 green book.* Washington, DC: U.S. Government Printing Office.

Committee on Ways and Means, U.S. House of Representatives. (1994). *Overview of entitlement programs: 1994 green book.* Washington, DC: U.S. Government Printing Office.

Council on Social Work Education. (1995). *Summary information on master of social work programs, 1994–95.* Alexandria, VA: Council on Social Work Education.

Ginsberg, L. (1995). *Social work almanac* (2nd ed.). Washington, DC: NASW Press.

Greene, R. R. (1988). *Continuing education for gerontological careers.* Washington, DC: Council on Social Work Education.

Hollonbeck, D., & Ohls, J. C. (1984). Participation among the elderly in the Food Stamp Program. *The Gerontologist, 24*(6), 616–621.

Kane, R. (1990). Assessing the elderly client. In A. Monk (Ed.), *Handbook of gerontological services* (2nd ed., pp. 55–59). New York: Columbia University.

Levine, P. (1984). *A directory of gerontology study opportunities at graduate schools of social work.* Washington, DC: Council on Social Work Education.

Lowy, L. (1985). *Social work with the aging: The challenge and promise of the later years* (2nd ed.). New York: Longman.

Nelson, G. M., & Schneider, R. L. (1984). *The current status of gerontology in graduate social work education.* Washington, DC: Council on Social Work Education.

Ohls, J. C., & Beebout, H. (1993). *The Food Stamp Program: Design tradeoffs, policy, and impacts.* Washington, DC: Urban Institute.

Osterkamp, L. (1988). Family caregivers: America's primary long-term care resource. *Aging,* (358), 3–5.

Pepper Commission, U.S. Bipartisan Commission on Comprehensive Health Care. (1990, September). *A call for action, Final report.* Washington, DC: U.S. Government Printing Office.

Price, R., Rimkunas, R., & O'Shaughnessy, C. (1990, September 24). *Characteristics of nursing home residents and proposals for reforming coverage of nursing home care* (CRS Report for Congress, No. 90-471 EPW).Washington, DC Congressional Research Service, Library of Congress.

Schneider, R. L. (Ed.). (1984). *The integration of gerontology into social work educational curricula.* Washington, DC: Council on Social Work Education.

Schneider, R. L., & Kropf, N. P. (Eds.). (1989a). *Integrating gerontology into the BSW curriculum: Generalist practice, human behavior and the social environment, social policy, research, and field instruction.* Washington, DC: Council on Social Work Education and Richmond, VA: Virginia Commonwealth University, School of Social Work.

Schneider, R. L., & Kropf, N. P. (Eds.). (1989b). *Essential knowledge and skills for baccalaureate social work students in gerontology.* Washington, DC: Council on Social Work Education and Richmond, VA: Virginia Commonwealth University, School of Social Work.

Serafini, M. W. (1995, March 18). Plugging a big drain on Medicaid. *National Journal, 27*(11), 687.

Silverstone, B., & Burack-Weiss, A. (1984). *Social work practice with the frail elderly and their families: The auxiliary function model.* Springfield, IL: Charles Thomas.

Stone, R., Cafferata, G. L., & Sangl, J. (1987). Caregivers of the frail elderly: A national profile. *The Gerontologist, 27*(5), 616–626.

Tobin, S. S., & Toseland, R. (1990). Models of services for the elderly. In A. Monk (Ed.), *Handbook of gerontological services* (2nd ed., pp. 27–51). New York: Columbia University Press.

Treas, J. (1995). Older Americans in the 1990s and beyond. *Population Bulletin, 50*(1). Washington, DC: Population Reference Bureau.

U.S. Department of Health, Education and Welfare. (1979, February). *Social Security and the changing roles of men and women.* Washington, DC: U.S. Government Printing Office.

Weissert, W. G., Cready, C. M., & Pawelak, J. E. (1988). The past and future of home- and community-based long-term care. *The Milbank Quarterly, 66*(2), 309–386.

Chapter 12

Bogdon, A., Silver, J., & Turner, M. A. (1993). *National analysis of housing affordability, adequacy, and availability: A framework for local housing strategies—prepared by The Urban Institute for Housing and Urban Development Office of Policy Development and Research.* Washington, DC: U.S. Government Printing Office.

Bureau of the Census. (1981). *Annual housing survey: 1979.* Washington, DC: U.S. Government Printing Office.

Bureau of the Census. (1993). *Poverty in the United States: 1992.* Washington, DC: U.S. Government Printing Office.

Bureau of the Census. (1994). *Statistical abstract of the United States 1994* (114th ed.). Washington, DC: U.S. Government Printing Office.

Callis, R. R. (1995). *Housing vacancies and homeownership annual statistics: 1994* (Current Housing Reports Series H111/94A, Bureau of the Census Economics and Statistics Division). Washington, DC: U.S. Government Printing Office.

DiNitto, D. M. (1995). *Social welfare: Politics and public policy* (4th ed.). Boston: Allyn & Bacon.

First, R. J., Rife, J. C., & Toomey, B. G. (1994). Homelessness in rural areas: Causes, patterns, trends. *Social Work, 39,* 97–108.

Gibelman, M. & Schervish, P. H. (1993). *Who we are: The social work labor force as reflected in the NASW membership.* Washington, DC: NASW Press. Copyright 1993, National Association of Social Workers, Inc.

Ginsberg, L. H. (1983). *The practice of social work in public welfare.* New York: Free Press.

Ginsberg, L. H. (1995). *Social work almanac* (2nd ed.). Washington, DC: NASW Press.

Goodwin, L. (1981). Can workfare work? *Public Welfare, 39,* 19–25.

Government Accounting Office. (1995). *Public housing: Funding and other constraints limit housing authorities' ability to comply with one-for-one rule* (GAO B-259664 Report to Congressional Requesters). Washington, DC: U.S. Government Printing Office.

Grall, T. S. (1994). *Households at risk: Their housing situation* (Bureau of the Census Current Housing Reports, Series H121/94-2). Washington, DC: U.S. Government Printing Office.

Gugliotta, G. (1992, November 29). Study: Rent costs strain poor in cities. *Austin American-Statesman,* p. A7.

Harbolt, P. (1981, February-March). The fight against community programs. *Access: A Human Services Magazine, 4*(4), pp. 14–18. Tallahassee, FL: Florida Department of Health and Rehabilitative Services.

Hoshino, G. (1972). Separating maintenance from social services. *Public Welfare, 30,* 54–61.

Hou, J., & Lazere, E. B. (1991). A place to call home: The crisis in housing for the poor. Washington, DC: Center on Budget and Policy Priorities.

Lindsey, E. W. (1993). Training Georgia's eligibility workers: Staff are being taught to do their jobs differently. *Public Welfare, 51,* 35–41, 48.

Lynn, L. E., Jr. (1977). A decade of policy developments in the income-maintenance system. In R. H. Haveman (Ed.), *A decade of federal antipoverty programs: Achievements, failures, and lessons* (pp. 55–117). New York: Academic Press.

Masumura, W., & Ryscavage, P. (1994). *Dynamics of economic well-being: Labor force and income, 1990–1992* (Current Population Reports Series P-70, Bureau of the Census). Washington, DC: U.S. Government Printing Office.

Maslow, A. H. (1962). *Toward a psychology of being.* Princeton, NJ: Van Nostrand.

McNeece, C. A. (1966). *Family relocation in the Coronado Urban Renewal Project.* Unpublished master's thesis, Texas Technological University.

National Association of Social Workers. (1987). *Encyclopedia of social work* (18th ed., Vol. 2). Silver Spring, MD: NASW Press. Copyright 1990, National Association of Social Workers, Inc.

National Association of Social Workers, Florida Chapter. (1984). *Report and recommendations of the Florida Chapter National Association of Social Workers, Inc., Professional standards/classification ad hoc committee.* Tallahassee, FL: Author.

Piliavin, I., & Gross, A. E. (1977). The effects of separation of services and income maintenance on AFDC recipients. *Social Service Review, 51,* 389–406.

Proch, K., & Taber, M. A. (1987). Helping the homeless. *Public Welfare, 45,* 5–9.

Pumphrey, R. E., & Pumphrey, M. W. (1969). *The heritage of American social work.* New York: Columbia University Press.

Seltser, B. J., & Miller, D. E. (1993). *Homeless families: The struggle for dignity.* Urbana, IL: University of Illinois Press.

The Urban Institute. (1994). *Evaluation of the supplemental assistance for facilities to assist the homeless program* (HUD Office of Policy Development and Research Contract No. HC 5856). Washington, DC: U.S. Government Printing Office.

U.S. Department of Health and Human Services Administration on Children, Youth, and Families, Family and Youth Services Bureau. (1994). *Report to Congress on runaway homeless youth programs for FY 1992*. Washington, DC: U.S. Government Printing Office.

U.S. Department of Housing & Urban Development. (1979). *Problems affecting low rent public housing projects*. Washington, DC: U.S. Government Printing Office.

U.S. Department of Housing & Urban Development. (1992). *Annual civil rights data report to congress: HUD program applications and beneficiaries*. Washington, DC: U.S. Government Printing Office.

U.S. Department of Housing & Urban Development. (1994a). *News release: Cisneros awards $13.1 million to provide positive alternatives for youth living in public housing* (HUD No. 94-149). Washington, DC: U.S. Government Printing Office.

U.S. Department of Housing & Urban Development. (1994b). *News release: Cisneros awards $228.9 million to combat drug abuse in public housing nationwide* (HUD No. 94-149). Washington, DC: U.S. Government Printing Office.

U.S. Department of Housing & Urban Development. (1994c). *Worst case needs for housing assistance in the United States in 1990 and 1991: A report to Congress*. Washington, DC: U.S. Government Printing Office.

U.S. Department of Housing & Urban Development. (1995). *News release: HUD awards $67 million to help public housing residents obtain education and job opportunities* (HUD No. 95-02). Washington, DC: U.S. Government Printing Office.

Wagner, D. (1993). *Checkerboard square*. Boulder, CO: Westview Press.

Welfare law altered. (1988, November). *NASW News, 33,* 1–11.

Wenocur, S., & Reisch, M. (1989). *From charity to enterprise: The development of American social work in a market economy*. Urbana, IL: University of Illinois Press.

Wyers, N. L. (1980). Whatever happened to the income maintenance line worker? *Social Work, 25,* 259–263.

Chapter 13

Allen, F. (1964). *The borderland of criminal justice*. Chicago: University of Chicago Press.

Ashford, J. B., & LeCroy, C. W. (1993). Juvenile parole policy in the United States: Determinate versus indeterminate models. *Justice Quarterly, 10*(2), 179–195.

Austin, J., & Krisberg, B. (1982). The unmet promise of alternatives to incarceration. *Crime and Delinquency, 28*(2), 374–409.

Berkeley, J. (1978). *Determinate sentencing: Reform or regression?* Proceedings of the special conference. Washington, DC: National Institute of Law Enforcement and Criminal Justice.

Blomberg, T. B., Heald, G. R., & Ezell, M. (1986). Diversion and net-widening: A cost-savings assessment. *Evaluation Review, 10*(2), 45–64.

Bureau of Justice Statistics, U.S. Department of Justice. (1980). *Law enforcement agencies in the United States: Summary report, 1980*. Washington, DC: Author.

Bureau of Justice Statistics. (1983). *Justice expenditure and employment* (Publication No. NCJ 101776). Washington, DC: U.S. Government Printing office.

Bureau of Justice Statistics. (1985). *Criminal victimization, 1984* (Publication No. NCJ 98904). Washington, DC: U.S. Government Printing Office.

Bureau of Justice Statistics. (1986a). *Crime and justice facts* (Publication No. NCJ 100757). Washington, DC: U.S. Government Printing Office.

Bureau of Justice Statistics. (1986b). *Public juvenile facilities, 1985: Children in custody* (Publication No. NCJ 102457). Washington, DC: U.S. Government Printing Office.

Bureau of Justice Statistics. (1988). *Profile of state prison inmates, 1986* (Publication No. NCJ-109926). Washington, DC: U.S. Government Printing Office.

Bureau of Justice Statistics. (1993a). *Crimes affecting U.S. households reach new low.* Rockville, MD: Author.

Bureau of Justice Statistics. (1993b). *Highlights from 20 years of surveying crime victims: The national crime victimization survey, 1973–1992* (Publication No. NCJ-144525). Washington, DC: U.S. Government Printing Office.

Bureau of Justice Statistics. (1993c). *Survey of state prison inmates, 1991* (Publication No. NCJ-136949). Washington, DC: U.S. Government Printing Office.

Bureau of Justice Statistics. (1993d). *Correctional populations in the United States, 1991* (Publication No. NCJ-142729). Washington, DC: U.S. Government Printing Office.

Bureau of Justice Statistics. (1994). *Sourcebook of criminal justice statistics, 1993* (Publication No. NCJ 154591). Washington, DC: U.S. Department of Justice Office of Justice Programs.

Bureau of Justice Statistics. (1995a). *The nation's correctional population tops 5 million.* Washington, DC: Author.

Bureau of Justice Statistics. (1995b). *The nation's jails hold record 490,442 inmates.* Washington, DC: Author.

Champion, D. (1990). *Probation and parole in the United States.* New York: Macmillan.

Coates, R. B., Miller, A. D., & Ohlin, L. E. (1978). *Diversity in a youth correctional system: Handling delinquents in Massachusetts.* Cambridge, MA: Ballinger.

Creekmore, M. (1976). Case processing: Intake, adjudication, and disposition. In R. Sarri & Y. Hasenfeld (Eds.), *Brought to justice? Juveniles, the courts, and the law.* National assessment of juvenile corrections. Ann Arbor: University of Michigan.

Cressey, D. R., & McDermott, R. A. (1973). Diversion from the juvenile justice system. *National assessment of juvenile corrections.* Ann Arbor: University of Michigan.

Empey, L. T. (1978). *American delinquency: Its meaning and construction.* Homewood, IL: Dears Press.

Eskridge, C. W. (1979). Education and training of probation officers: A critical assessment. *Federal Probation, 43*(3), 41–48.

Ezell, M. (1996). The administration of juvenile justice. In C. McNeece & A. Roberts (Eds.), *Policy and practice in the justice system.* Chicago: Nelson-Hall.

Federal Bureau of Investigation. (1983). *Uniform crime report for the United States.* Washington, DC : Author.

Federal Bureau of Investigation. (1994). *Crime in the United States, 1993.* Washington, DC: Author.

Federal Bureau of Investigation. (1995). *Crime in the United States, 1994.* Washington, DC: Author.

Fox, S. J. (1970). Juvenile justice reform: An historical perspective. *Stanford Law Review, 22*(6), 1187–1239.

Foy v. Foy, 23 S.W.2d 543, 73 S.W.2d 618 (Cal. Ct. App. 1938).

Gabor, T. (1994). *Everybody does it: Crime by the public.* Toronto: University of Toronto Press.

Ginsberg, L. (1995). *Social work almanac* (2nd ed.). Washington, DC: NASW Press.

Handler, E. (1975). Social work and corrections: Comments on an uneasy partnership. *Criminology, 13*(2), 240–254.

Hirschi, T., & Gottfredson, M. (1993). Rethinking the juvenile justice system. *Crime & Delinquency, 39,* 262–271.

Holt, N., & Miller, D. (1972). *Explorations in inmate-family relationships* (Research report No. 46). California Department of Corrections.

Humphrey, J., & Milakovich, M. (1981). *The administration of justice.* New York: Human Sciences Press.

Hylton, J. H. (1982). Rhetoric and reality: A critical appraisal of community correctional programs. *Crime and delinquency, 28*(3), 341–373.

Inmates pitch tents. (1988, July 5). *Tallahassee Democrat,* p. B15.

Kent v. United States, 383 U.S. 541 (1966).

Kittrie, N. N. (1973). *The right to be different.* Baltimore: Penguin Books.

Levin, M. M., & Sarri, R. C. (1974). Juvenile delinquency: A comparative analysis of legal codes in the United States. *National assessment of juvenile corrections.* Ann Arbor: University of Michigan.

Martin, L. H., & Snyder, P. R. (1972). Jurisdiction over status offenders should not be removed from the juvenile curt. *Crime and Delinquency, 22,* 44–47.

McKeiver v. Pennsylvania, 403 U.S. 528 (1971).

McNeece, C. A. (1976). *Juvenile courts in the community environment.* Unpublished doctoral dissertation, University of Michigan.

McNeece, C. A. (1980). The deinstitutionalization of juvenile status offenders: New myths and old realities. *Journal of Sociology and Social Welfare, 7*(3), 236–245.

McNeece, C. A. (1994). National trends in offenses and case dispositions. In A. Roberts (Ed.), *Critical issues in crime and justice* (pp. 157–170). Thousand Oaks, CA: Sage.

McNeece, C. A. (1996). Juvenile justice policy. In A. R. Roberts (Ed.), *Social work in juvenile and criminal justice settings* (2nd ed.). Springfield, IL: Charles C. Thomas.

McNeece, C. A., & DiNitto, D. M. (1982, July). *Environmental influences on length of incarceration: Does overcrowding really matter?* Proceedings of the International Conference on Law and Psychology, Swansea, Wales.

McNeece, C. A., & Lusk, M. W. (1979). A consumer's view of correctional policy: Inmate attitudes regarding determinate sentencing. *Criminal Justice and Behavior, 6*(4), 383–389.

National Association of Social Workers. (1984, September). *A study of attitudes of NASW members, lapsed members and non-members*. Rockville, MD: Westat.

National Association of Social Workers. (1987). *Encyclopedia of social work* (18th ed., Vol. 1) Silver Spring, MD: NASW Press. Copyright 1990, National Association of Social Workers, Inc.

Needleman, C. (1996). Social work and probation in the juvenile court. In A. R. Roberts (Ed.), *Social work in juvenile and criminal justice settings* (2nd ed., pp. 165–179). Springfield, IL: Charles C. Thomas.

Netherland, W. (1987). Corrections system: Adult. In A. Minahan (Ed.), *Encyclopedia of social work* (18th ed., Vol. 1, p. 358). New York: NASW Press. Copyright 1990, National Association of Social Workers, Inc.

New Jersey v. T.L.O., 105 S. Ct. 733 (1985).

Orr v. State, 242 In.,123 N.E. 470 (1919).

Platt, A. (1969). *The child savers: The invention of delinquency*. Chicago: University of Chicago Press.

Pomeroy, J. N. (1883). *Pomeroy's equity jurisprudence* (Vol. III). San Franciso: Bancroft-Whitney.

President's commission on law enforcement and the administration of justice, task force report. (1967). *Juvenile delinquency and youth crime*. Washington, DC: U.S. Government Printing Office.

Romig, D. A. (1978). *Justice for our children: An examination of juvenile delinquent rehabilitation programs*. Lexington, MA: D.C. Heath.

Saney, P. (1986). *Crime and culture in America: A comparative perspective*. New York: Greenwood Press.

Schur, E. M. (1973). *Radical nonintervention: Rethinking the delinquency problem*. Englewood Cliffs, NJ: Prentice-Hall.

Sherman, M. E., & Hawkins, G. E. (1981). *Imprisonment in America: Choosing the future*. Chicago: University of Chicago Press.

Showalter, D., & Hunsinger, M. (1996). Social work within a maximum security setting. In A. R. Roberts (Ed.). *Social work in juvenile and criminal justice settings* (2nd ed., pp. 257–274). Springfield, IL: Charles C. Thomas.

Spergel, I. A., Reamer, F. G., & Lynch, J. P. (1981). Deinstitutionalization of status offenders: Individual outcome and system effects. *Journal of Research in Crime and Delinquency, 18*(1), 4–33.

Sussman, F. B. (1968). *Law of juvenile delinquency*. New York: Oceana.

U.S. Department of Justice. (1983). *Report to the nation on crime and justice* (NCO Publication No. 87068). Washington, DC: U.S. Government Printing Office.

U.S. Department of Justice. (1994). *National corrections reporting program, 1992* (Publication No. NCJ 145862). Washington, DC: Office of Justice Programs, Bureau of Justice Statistics.

U. S. Department of Justice, Law Enforcement Assistance Administration, National Criminal Justice Information and Statistics Service. (1978). *State and local probation and parole systems* (Report # SD-SB-6). Washington, DC: U.S. Government Printing Office.

U.S. Sentencing Commission. (1990). *Mandatory minimum penalties in the federal criminal justice system*. Washington, DC: Author.

Wilks, J., & Martinson. R. (1976). Is the treatment of criminal offenders really necessary. *Federal Probation, 40*(1), 3–9.

Wilson, J. Q. (1968). *Varieties of police behavior: The management of law and order in eight communities*. New York: Basic Books.

Winkle, M. (1924). The policewomen. *Proceedings of the fifty-first annual session of the National Conference of Social Work,* Toronto, Ontario. Chicago: University of Chicago Press.

Chapter 14

Akabas, S. H. (1995). Occupational social work. In R. L. Edwards (Ed.), *Encyclopedia of social work* (19th ed., pp. 1779–1786) Washington, DC: NASW Press. Copyright 1995, National Association of Social Workers, Inc.

Akabas, S. H., & Kurzman, P. A. (1982). The industrial social welfare specialist: What's so special? In S. H. Akabas & P. A. Kurzman (Eds.), *Work, workers, and work organizations: A view from social work* (pp. 197–235). Englewood Cliffs, NJ: Prentice-Hall.

Akabas, S. H., Fine, M., & Yasser, R. (1982). Putting secondary prevention to the test: A study of an early intervention strategy with disabled workers. *Journal of Primary Prevention, 3,* 165–187.

Antoniades, R., & Bellinger, S. (1983). Organized worksites: A help or a hindrance in the delivery of social work services in and to the workplace. In R. J. Thomlison (Ed.), *Perspectives on industrial social work practice* (pp. 29–38). Ottawa: Family Service Canada.

Argyris, C. (1957). *Personality and organization: The conflict between the system and the individual*. New York: Harper.

Atkinson, L., & Kunkel, O. (1992). Should social workers participate in treatment only if the client consents to such treatment freely and without coercion? In E. Gambrill & R. Pruger (Eds.), *Controversial issues in social work* (pp. 157–172). Boston: Allyn & Bacon.

Barnett-Queen, T., & Bergman, L. (1993, March). Coping after crises. *Employee Assistance: Solutions to the Problems, 5,* 6–34.

Baron, S. (1993). *Violence in the workplace: A prevention and management guide for business*. Ventura, CA: Pathfinder.

Bergmark, R., Parker, M., Dell, P., & Polich, C. (1991, July). EA programs: The challenge, the opportunity. *Employee Assistance: Solutions to the Problems, 3,* 9.

Bilik, S., & Pasco, T. (1993, September). EA and managed care: Facing the future together. *Employee Assistance: Solutions to the Problems, 6,* 14–15.

Bravo, E., & Cassidy, E. (1992). *The 9 to 5 guide to combating sexual harassment*. New York: John Wiley & Sons.

Briar, K. H. (1983a). Layoffs and social work intervention. *Urban and Social Change Review, 16*(2), 9–14.

Briar, K. H. (1983b). Unemployment: Toward a social work agenda. *Social Work, 28,* 211–216.

Briar, K. H. (1987). Unemployment and underemployment. In A. Minahan (Ed.), *Encyclopedia of social work* (18th ed., Vol. 2, pp. 778–788). Silver Spring, MD: NASW Press. Copyright 1990, National Association of Social Workers, Inc.

Briar, K. H., & Vinet, M. (1985). Ethical questions concerning an EAP: Who is the client? (Company or individual?). In S. H. Klarreich, J. L. Francek, & C. E. Moore (Eds.), *Human resources management handbook: Principles and practice of employee assistance programs* (pp. 342–359). New York: Praeger. Reproduced with permission of Greenwood Publishing Group, Inc., Westport, CT.

Brilliant, E. L., & Rice, K. A. (1988). Influencing corporate philanthropy. In G. M. Gould & M. L. Smith (Eds.), *Social work in the workplace: Practice and principles* (pp. 299–313). New York: Springer Publishing Company, Inc., New York 10012. Used by permission.

Burke, E. M. (1987). Corporate social responsibility. In A. Minahan (Ed.), *Encyclopedia of social work* (18th ed., Vol. 1, pp. 345–351). Silver Spring, MD: NASW Press. Copyright 1990, National Association of Social Workers, Inc.

Burke, E. M. (1988). Corporate community relations. In G. M. Gould & M. L. Smith (Eds.), *Social work in the workplace: Practice and principles* (pp. 314–327). New York: Springer Publishing Company, Inc., New York 10012. Used by permission.

Burud, S. L., Aschbacher, P. R., & McCroskey, J. (1984). *Employer-supported child care: Investing in human resources.* Dover, MA: Auburn House.

Cohen, M. (1985). EAP training to integrate performance appraisal, evaluation systems, and problem-solving skills. In S. H. Klarreich, J. L. Francek, & C. E. Moore (Eds.), *Human resources management handbook: Principles and practice of employee assistance programs* (pp. 183–188). New York: Praeger. Reproduced with permission of Greenwood Publishing Group, Inc., Westport, CT.

de Silva, E. G. (1988). Services to customers: Customer assistance programs. In G. M. Gould & M. L. Smith (Eds.), *Social work in the workplace: Practice and principles* (pp. 283–298). New York: Springer Publishing Company, Inc., New York 10012. Used by permission.

de Silva, E. G., Biasucci, P. A., Keegan, M., & Wijnberg, D. (1982). Promoting the future of social work education through labor and industry: A three-dimensional approach. Paper presented at the Annual Program Meeting of the Council on Social Work Education, New York.

Dychtwald, K., & Flower, J. (1989). *Age wave.* Los Angeles: Jeremy Tarcher.

Etzioni, A. (1969). *The semi-professions and their organization.* New York: Free Press.

Finch, W. A., Jr., & Ell, K. O. (1988). AIDS in the workplace. In G. M. Gould & M. L. Smith (Eds.), *Social work in the workplace: Practice and principles* (pp. 229–244). New York: Springer Publishing Company, Inc., New York 10012. Used by permission.

Fleisher, D., & Kaplan, B. H. (1988). Employee assistance/counseling typologies. In G. M. Gould & M. L. Smith (Eds.), *Social work in the workplace: Practice and principles.* (pp. 31–44). New York: Springer Publishing Company, Inc., New York 10012. Used by permission.

Foster, B., & Schore, L. (1989). Job loss and the occupational social worker. *Employee Assistance Quarterly, 5*(1), 77–97.

Garber, D. L., & McNelis, P. J. (1995). Military social work. In R. L. Edwards (Ed.), *Encyclopedia of social work* (19th ed., Vol. 2, pp. 1726–1736). Washington, DC: NASW Press. Copyright 1995, National Association of Social Workers, Inc.

Gaylord, M., & Symons, E. (1986). Relocation stress: A definition and need for services. *Employee Assistance Quarterly, 2*(1), 31–36.

Googins, B. (1987). Occupational social work: A developmental perspective. *Employee Assistance Quarterly, 2*(3), 37–54.

Googins, B., & Davidson, B. N. (1993). The organization as client: Broadening the concept of employee assistance programs. *Social Work, 38,* 477–484.

Googins, B., & Godfrey, J. (1985). The evolution of occupational social work. *Social Work, 30,* 396–402.

Googins, B., & Godfrey, J. (1987). *Occupational social work.* Englewood Cliffs, NJ: Prentice-Hall.

Gullotta, T. P., & Donahue, K. C. (1981). Corporate families: Implications for preventive intervention. *Social Casework, 62*(2), 109–114.

Habib, M., & Gutwill, S. (1985). The union setting: Working with retirees. *Journal of Gerontological Social Work, 8,* 247–255.

Hellreigel, D., Slocum, J., & Woodman, R. (1976). *Organizational behavior* (4th ed.). New York: West.

Houden, L., & Demarest, L. (1993, September). Stopping harassment before it erupts. *Employee Assistance: Solutions to the Problems, 6,* 26.

Johnston, J. (1994, July). Before it gets to court. *Employee Assistance: Solutions to the Problems, 6,* 77.

Kamerman, S. B., & Kahn, A. J. (1987). *The responsive workplace: Employers and a changing labor force.* New York: Columbia University Press.

Keefe, T. (1984). The stresses of unemployment. *Social Work, 29,* 264–268.

Keith-Lucas, A. (1985). *So you want to be a social worker.* St. Davids, PA: North American Association of Christians in Social Work.

Klarreich, S. H. (1985). Stress: An interpersonal approach. In S. H. Klarreich, J. L. Francek, & C. E. Moore (Eds.), *Human resources management handbook: Principles and practice of employee assistance programs* (pp. 304–318). New York: Praeger. Reproduced with permission of Greenwood Publishing Group, Inc., Westport, CT.

Kurzman, P. A. (1987). Industrial social work (occupational social work). In A. Minahan (Ed.), *Encyclopedia of social work* (18th ed., Vol. 1, pp. 899–910). Silver Spring, MD: NASW Press. Copyright 1990, National Association of Social Workers, Inc.

Kurzman, P. A. (1988). The ethical base for social work in the workplace. In G. M. Gould & M. L. Smith (Eds.), *Social work in the workplace: Practice and principles* (pp. 16–27). New York: Springer Publishing Company, Inc., New York 10012. Used by permission.

Kurzman, P. A., & Akabas, S. H. (1981). Industrial social work as an arena for practice. *Social Work, 26,* 52–60.

Lanier, D. (1991, May/June). New century, new challenges, new opportunities. *EAP Digest, 11,* 40–44.

Lewis, B. M. (1989). Social workers' role in promoting health and safety. *Employee Assistance Quarterly, 5*(1), 99–118.

Masi, D. (1982). *Human services in industry.* Lexington, MA: D. C. Heath.

McCroskey, J. (1984). In the wake of the subtle revolution—opportunities and challenges in child care. *Social Work Papers, 18,* 57–64.

McCroskey, J. (1988). Employer supported child care. In G. M. Gould & M. L. Smith (Eds.), *Social work in the workplace: Practice and principles* (pp. 170–184). New York: Springer Publishing Company, Inc., New York 10012. Used by permission.

McGehee, L. J. (1985). Executives, families, and the trauma of relocation. In S. H. Klarreich, J. L. Francek, & C. E. Moore (Eds.), *Human resources management handbook: Principles and practice of employee assistance programs* (pp. 281–290). New York: Praeger. Reproduced with permission of Greenwood Publishing Group, Inc., Westport, CT.

McMichael, C. (1994, September). The competitive edge. *Employee Assistance: Solutions to the Problems, 7,* 19.

Meadow, D. (1988). Managing shift work problems. In G. M. Gould & M. L. Smith (Eds.), *Social work in the workplace: Practice and principles* (pp. 152–169). New York: Springer Publishing company, Inc., New York 10012. Used by permission.

Perlis, L. (1978, May). Industrial social work—Problems and perspectives. *NASW News,* p. 3.

Perrow, C. (1972). *Complex organizations: A critical essay.* Glenview, IL: Scott-Foresman.

Popple, P. (1981). Social work practice in business and industry: 1875–1930. *Social Service Review, 55,* 257–269.

Ryan, C. (1986). AIDS in the workplace. Fullerton, CA: DaSak Associates.

Selye, H. (1978). *The stress of life.* New York: McGraw-Hill.

Shank, B. (1985). Considering a career in occupational social work? *EAP Digest, 5*(5), pp. 54–62.

Shanker, R. (1983). Occupational disease, workers' compensation and the social work advocate. *Social Work, 28*(1), 24–27.

Sherraden, M. W. (1985). Chronic unemployment: A social work perspective. *Social Work, 30*(5), 403–408.

Sherwood, D. (1981, Spring). Add to your faith virtue: The integration of Christian values and social work practice. *Social Work and Christianity, 8,* 41–54.

Siegel, D. I. (1988). Relocation counseling and services. In G. M. Gould & M. L. Smith (Eds.), *Social work in the workplace: Practice and principles* (pp. 109–122). New York: Springer Publishing Company, Inc., New York 10012. Used by permission.

Smith, M. L. (1985). Social work in the military: An occupational social work perspective. *Social work papers, 19,* 46–55.

Smith, M. L. (1988). Social work in the workplace: An overview. In G. M. Gould & M. L. Smith (Eds.), *Social work in the workplace: Practice and principles* (pp. 3–15). New York: Springer Publishing Company, Inc., New York 10012. Used by permission.

Smith, M. L., & Gould, G. M. (1993). A profession at the crossroads: Occupational social work—Present and future. In P. A. Kurzman & S. H. Akabas (Eds.), *Work and well-being: The occupational social work advantage* (pp. 7–25). Washington, D.C.: NASW Press. Copyright 1993, National Association of Social Workers, Inc.

Specht, H., & Courtney, M. (1994). *Unfaithful angels: How social work has abandoned its mission.* New York: Free Press.

Strachan, G. (1982). *Alcoholism: Treatable illness.* Vancouver, BC: Mitchell Press.

Straussner, S. L. A. (1990). Occupational social work today: An overview. In S. L. A. Straussner (Ed.), *Occupational social work today* (pp. 1–17). New York: Haworth Press.

Szilagyi, A., & Wallace, M. (1980). *Organizational behavior and performance* (2nd ed.). Santa Monica, CA: Goodyear.

Trading places. (1990, July 16). *Newsweek,* p. 49.

Tucker, B. P. (1990). The Americans with Disabilities Act: An overview. *University of Illinois Law Review, 1989,* 923–939.

Vinet, M., & Jones, C. (1983). *Social services and work: Initiation of social workers into labor and industry settings.* Silver Spring, MD: NASW Press.

Vinet, M., & Starr, A. (1988). Organizational change and its effects on EAP clients. Presented at the Conference of the Association of Labor-Management Administrators and Consultants on Alcoholism, Los Angeles, CA.

Wagman, J. B., & Schiff, J. (1990). Managed mental health care for employees: Roles for social workers. In S. L. A. Straussner (Ed.), *Occupational social work today* (pp. 53–66). New York: Haworth Press.

Weinbach, R. (1994). *The social worker as manager* (2nd ed.). Boston: Allyn & Bacon.

Whitworth, S. (1984). Testimony on military families. Hearings of the Select Committee on Children, Youth and Families, U.S. House of Representatives, 98th Congress, 2nd Session. Washington, DC: U.S. Government Printing Office.

Wilk, R. J. (1988). Assisting in affirmative action and equal employment opportunity. In G. M. Gould & M. L. Smith (Eds.), *Social work in the workplace: Practice and principles* (pp. 213–228). New York: Springer Publishing Company, Inc., New York 10012. Used by permission.

Wilks, C. S., Rowen, R. B., Hosang, M., & Knoepler, S. (1988). Human resource issues and aging. In G. M. Gould & M. L. Smith (Eds.), *Social work in the workplace: Practice and principles* (pp. 200–212). New York: Springer Publishing Company, Inc., New York 10012. Used by permission.

Winkelpleck, J., & Smith, M. L. (1988). Identifying and referring troubled employees to counseling. In G. M. Gould and M. L. Smith (Eds.), *Social work in the workplace: Practice and principles* (pp. 45–62). Springer Publishing Company, Inc., New York 10012. Used by permission.

Chapter 15

Aragon de Valdez, T., & Gallegos, J. (1982). The Chicano familia in social work. In J. W. Green, *Cultural awareness in the human services* (pp. 184–208). Englewood Cliffs, NJ: Prentice-Hall.

Backner, B. L. (1970). Counseling black students: Any place for whitey? *Journal of Higher Education, 41*(8), 630–637.

Barrett, F. T., & Perlmutter, F. (1972). Black clients and white workers: A report from the field. *Child Welfare, 50*(1), 19–24.

Battle, M. G. (1987). Professional associations: National Association of Social Workers. In A. Minahan (Ed.). *Encyclopedia of social work* (18th ed., Vol. 2, pp. 333–341). Silver Spring, MD: NASW Press. Copyright 1990, National Association of Social Workers, Inc.

Billingsley, A. (1968). Black families in white America. Englewood Cliffs, NJ: Prentice-Hall.

Brieland, D., Costin, L. B., & Atherton, C. R. (1980). *Contemporary social work: An introduction to social work and social welfare* (2nd ed.). New York: McGraw-Hill.

Bureau of the Census. (1993). *We the American blacks*. Washington, DC: U.S. Government Printing Office.

Bureau of the Census. (1995). *Statistical abstract of the United States: 1995*. Washington, DC: U.S. Government Printing Office.

Campbell, P. R. (1994). Population projections for states, by age, race, sex: 1993 to 2020 (U.S. Bureau of the Census, Current Population Reports, P25–1111). Washington, DC: U.S. Government Printing Office.

Carpenter, E. M. (1980). Social services, policies, and issues. *Social Casework, 61*(8), 455–461.

Chadwick, B. A., & Strauss, J. H. (1975). The assimilation of American Indians into urban society: The Seattle case. *Human Organization, 34*(4), 359–369.

Commission on Accreditation. (1994). *Handbook of accreditation standards and procedures*. Alexandria, VA: Council on Social Work Education.

Cook, C. (1987, October 16). BIA ordered to prepare for inquiry. *The Arizona Republic,* pp. A1, A5.

Cook, C., Masterson, M., & Trahant, M. N. (1987a, October 10). Issues of identity: Many seeking tribal status. *The Arizona Republic,* p. A24.

Cook, C., Masterson, M., & Trahant, M. N. (1987b, October 4). Indians are sold out by the U.S. *The Arizona Republic,* pp. A1, 18, 20.

Cook, C., Masterson, M., & Trahant, M. N. (1987c, October 7). Child's suffering is cry for reform. *The Arizona Republic,* p. A18.

Cook, C., Masterson, M., & Trahant, M. N. (1987d, October 11). Indian dropout 'stuck in bed of quicksand.' *The Arizona Republic,* p. A20.

Cook, C., Masterson, M., & Trahant, M. N. (1987e, October 11). Tribes' hope is education, but schools often terrible. *The Arizona Republic,* pp. A1, 21.

Cross, T. (1988). Services to minority populations: Cultural competence continuum. *Focal Point, 3*(1), 1–4.

Cross, T. L., Bazron, B. J., Dennis, K. W., & Isaacs, M. R. (1989). *Towards a culturally competent system of care: A monograph on effective services for minority children who are severely emotionally disturbed*. Washington, DC: Child and Adolescent Service System Program (CASSP), Technical Assistance Center, Georgetown University Child Development Center.

De La Cancela, V., Jenkins, Y. M., & Chin, J. L. (1993). Diversity in psychotherapy: Examination of racial, ethnic, gender, and political issues. In J. L. Chin, V. De La Cancela, & Y. M. Jenkins (Eds.), *Diversity in psychotherapy: The politics of race, ethnicity, and gender* (pp. 5–15). Westport, CT: Praeger.

Devore, W., & Schlesinger, E. G. (1987). *Ethnic-sensitive social work practice* (2nd ed.). Columbus: OH: Merrill.

Germain, C. B., & Gitterman, A. (1980). *The life model of social work practice*. New York: Columbia University Press.

Germain, C. B., & Gitterman, A. (1986). The life model approach to social work practice revisited. In J. Turner (Ed.), *Social work treatment* (3rd ed., pp. 618–644). New York: Free Press.

Gordon, M. (1964). *Assimilation in American life*. New York: Oxford University Press.

Graves, T. (1967). Acculturation, access and alcohol in a tri-ethnic community. *American Anthropologist, 69,* 306–321.

Green, J. W. (1982). *Cultural awareness in the human services*. Englewood Cliffs, NJ: Prentice-Hall. Copyright © 1982 by Allyn and Bacon. Reprinted/adapted by permission.

Green, J. W. (1995). *Cultural awareness in the human services: A multi-ethnic approach* (2nd ed.). Boston: Allyn & Bacon. Copyright © 1995 by Allyn and Bacon. Reprinted/adapted by permission.

Hall, A., & Shaffer, M. (1987, October 11). Child molesters attracted to jobs at Indian schools. *The Arizona Republic,* pp. A20, 22.

Hill, R. B. (1971). *The strengths of black families*. New York: Emerson Hall.

Hollingshead, A., & Redlick, F. (1958). *Social class and mental illness: A community study*. New York: John Wiley & Sons.

Hopps, J. (1982). Oppression based on color. *Social Work, 27*(1), 3.

Iglehart, A., & Becerra, R. (1995). *Social services and the ethnic community*. Boston: Allyn & Bacon.

Ishisaka, H. A., & Takagi, C. Y. (1982). Social work with Asian and Pacific Americans. In J. W. Green, *Cultural awareness in the human services* (pp. 122–156). Englewood Cliffs, NJ: Prentice-Hall.

Juarez, R. (1985). Core issues and psychotherapy with Hispanic children. *Psychotherapy, 22,* 441–448.

Kadushin, A. (1972). The racial factor in the interview. *Social Work, 17*(3), 88–98.

Knowles, L., & Prewitt, K. (1969). *Institutional racism in America*. Englewood Cliffs, NJ: Prentice-Hall.

Leigh, J. W., & Green, J. W. (1982). The structure of the black community. In J. W. Green, *Cultural awareness in the human services* (pp. 94–121). Englewood Cliffs, NJ: Prentice-Hall.

Lennon, T. M. (1995). *Statistics on social work education in the United States: 1994*. Alexandria, VA: Council on Social Work Education.

Lewis, R. (1983, February-March). Strengths of the American Indian family. *Human Development News,* p. 10.

Lum, D. (1992). *Social work practice and people of color: A process-stage approach* (2nd ed.). Pacific Grove, CA: Brooks/Cole.

Lum, D. (1996). *Social work practice and people of color: A process-stage approach* (3rd ed.). Pacific Grove, CA: Brooks/Cole.

Marin, G., & Marin, B. (1991). *Research with Hispanic populations*. Newbury Park, CA: Sage.

Martin, J. M., & Martin, E. P. (1985). *The helping tradition in the black family and community*. Silver Spring: MD: NASW Press.

McAdoo, H. P. (1987). Blacks. In A. Minahan (Ed.), *Encyclopedia of social work* (18th ed., Vol. 1, pp. 194–206). Silver Spring, MD: NASW Press. Copyright 1990, National Association of Social Workers, Inc.

Miller, D. L., Hoffman, F., & Turner, D. (1980). A perspective on the Indian Child Welfare Act. *Social Casework, 61*(8), 461–471.

Mizio, E. (1972). White worker-minority client. *Social Work, 17*(3), 82–86.

Morales, A. T., & Sheafor, B. W. (1995). *Social work: A profession of many faces* (7th ed.). Boston: Allyn & Bacon.

Moynihan, D. P. (1965). *The Negro family: The case for national action*. Washington, DC: U.S. Department of Labor.

National Association of Social Workers. (1975). NASW standards for social work personnel practices. Silver Spring, MD: NASW Press.

Netting, F. E., Kettner, P. M., & McMurtry, S. L. (1993). *Social work macro practice*. New York: Longman.

Perlman, H. H. (1957). *Social casework*. Chicago: University of Chicago Press.

Perlman, H. H. (1986). The problem solving model. In J. Turner (Ed.), *Social work treatment* (pp. 245–266). New York: Free Press.

Popple, P. R., & Leighninger, L. (1993). *Social work, social welfare, and American society* (2d ed.). Boston: Allyn & Bacon.

Red Horse, J. G. (1980). Family structure and value orientation in American Indians. *Social Casework, 61*(8), 462–467.

Red Horse, J. G., Lewis, R., Feit, M., & Decker, J. (1978). Family behavior of urban American Indians. *Social Casework, 59*(2), 67–72.

Reid, W. J. (1978). *The task centered system*. New York: Columbia University Press.

Reid, W. J., & Epstein, L. (1972). Task centered casework. New York: Columbia University Press.

Rivera, F. G., & Erlich, J. L. (1992). *Community organizing in a diverse society*. Boston: Allyn & Bacon.

Rounds, K. A., Weil, M., & Bishop, K. K. (1994). Practice with culturally diverse families of young children with disabilities. *Families in Society: The Journal of Contemporary Human Services, 75*(1), 3–15.

Schlesinger, E., & Devore, W. (1995). Ethnic sensitive practice. In R. L. Edwards (Ed.). *Encyclopedia of social work* (19th ed., Vol. 1, (pp. 902–908). Washington, DC: NASW Press. Copyright 1995, National Association of Social Workers, Inc.

Schuman, D., & Olufs, D. (1995). *Diversity on campus*. Boston: Allyn & Bacon.

Stein, J. (Ed.). (1978). *The Random House dictionary*. New York: Ballantine Books.

Tourse, R. W. C. (1995). Special-interest professional associations. In R. L. Edwards (Ed.), *Encyclopedia of social work* (19th ed., Vol. 3, pp. 2314–2319). Washington, DC: NASW Press. Copyright 1995, National Association of Social Workers, Inc.

Walz, T. H., & Askerooth, G. (1973). *The upside down welfare state*. Minneapolis: Elwood Printing.

Wilkinson, G. T. (1980). On assisting Indian people. *Social Casework, 61*(8), 451–454.

Williams, L. F. (1987). Professional associations: Special interest. In A. Minahan (Ed.). *Encyclopedia of social work,* (18th ed., Vol. 2, pp. 341–346). Silver Spring, MD: NASW Press. Copyright 1990, National Association of Social Workers, Inc.

Wilson, W. J. (1987). *The truly disadvantaged: The inner city, the underclass, and public policy*. Chicago: University of Chicago Press.

Wood, G. G., & Middleman, R. (1989). *The structural approach to direct practice in social work*. New York: Columbia University Press.

Chapter 16

Angelou, M. (1970). *I know why the caged bird sings*. New York: Random House.

Anzaldua, G. (1992). To(o) queer the writer—Loca, escritora y Chicana. In B. Warland (Ed). *Inversions: Writings by dykes, queers, and lesbians* (pp. 249–263). Vancouver: Press Gang Publishers.

Ashkinazy, S. (1984). Working with gay and lesbian youth. *Practice Digest, 7*(1) 9–12.

Association of the Bar of the City of New York. (1992). *Second-parent adoption in New York State*. New York: The Association.

Balint, R. (1985). Changing the traditional human service agency on behalf of lesbian and gay male clients. In H. Hidalgo, T. L. Peterson, & N. J. Woodman (Eds.), *Lesbian and gay issues: A resource manual for social workers* (pp. 119–122). Silver Spring, MD: NASW Press.

Bell, A. P., & Weinberg, M. S. (1978). *Homosexualities: A study of diversity among men and women*. New York: Simon and Schuster.

Berger, R. M. (1984). *Gay and gray: The older homosexual male*. Boston: Alyson Press.

Berger, R. (1986). Gay men. In H. L. Gochros, J. S. Gochros, & J. Fischer, *Helping the sexually oppressed* (pp. 162–180). Englewood Cliffs, NJ: Prentice-Hall. Copyright © 1986 by Allyn and Bacon. Reprinted/adapted by permission.

Berger, R. M. (1987). Homosexuality: Gay men. In A. Minahan (Ed.), *Encyclopedia of social work* (18th ed., Vol. 1, pp. 795–805). Silver Spring, MD: NASW Press. Copyright 1990, National Association of Social Workers, Inc.

Bernstein, G. S. (1992). How to avoid heterosexist language. *The Behavior Therapist, 15*(7), 161.

Bernstein, G. S. (1993). Assessment and goal selection with lesbian and gay clients. *The Behavior Therapist, 16*(2), 37–40. Copyright 1993 by the Association for Advancement of Behavior Therapy. Reprinted by permission of the publisher and the author.

Bernstein, G. S., & Miller, M. E. (1996). Behavior therapy with lesbian and gay individuals. In M. Hersen, R. Eisler, & P. M. Miller (Eds.), *Progress in behavior modification* (pp. 123–136). Pacific Grove, CA: Brooks/Cole.

Bernstein, R. A. (1995). *Straight parents, gay children.* New York: Thunder's Mouth Press.

Berzon, B. (Ed.). (1979). *Positively gay.* Los Angeles: Mediamix Associates.

Berzon B. (Ed.). (1992). *Positively gay: New approaches to gay and lesbian life.* Berkeley: Celestial Arts.

Billy, J. O. G., Tanfer, K., Grady, W. R., & Klepinger, D. H. (1993). The sexual behavior of men in the United States. *Family Planning Perspectives, 25*(2), 52–60.

Bloomfield, K. (1993). A comparison of alcohol consumption between lesbians and heterosexual women in an urban population. *Drug and Alcohol Dependence, 33,* 257–269.

Borhek, M. V. (1983). *Coming out to parents.* New York: The Pilgrim Press.

Bristow, J., & Wilson, A. R. (Eds.). (1993). *Activating theory: Lesbian, gay, bisexual politics.* London: Lawrence & Wishart.

Center for Disease Control. (1995). HIV/AIDS surveillance report. (Midyear edition, Vol. 7, No. 1).

Child Welfare League of America. (1995). *Issues in gay and lesbian adoption.* Conference proceedings of the Fourth Annual Peirce-Warwick Adoption Symposium, Washington, DC.

Clark, D. (1987). *New loving someone gay.* Berkeley: Celestial Arts. Excerpts from *New Loving Someone Gay,* copyright © 1987 by Don Clark. Reprinted by Celestial Arts, P.O. Box 7123, Berkeley, CA 94707.

Commission on Accreditation. (1994). *Handbook of accreditation standards and procedures.* Alexandria, VA: Council on Social Work Education.

DeCrescenzo, T. (1992). The brave new world of gay and lesbian youth. In B. Berzon (Ed.), *Positively gay: New approaches to gay and lesbian life* (pp. 275–287). Berkeley, CA: Celestial Arts.

DeCrescenzo, T., & Fifield, L. (1979). The changing lesbian social scene. In B. Berzon (Ed.), *Positively gay* (pp. 15–23). Los Angeles: Mediamix Associates.

Dolce, J. (1983, January 6). Gay daddies. *Advocate,* pp. 25–27.

Dooley, J. (1986). Lesbians. In H. L. Gochros, J. S. Gochros, & J. Fischer, *Helping the sexually oppressed* (pp. 181–190). Englewood Cliffs, NJ: Prentice-Hall. Copyright © 1986 by Allyn and Bacon. Reprinted/adapted by permission.

Dressner, F. (1987, August 31). Women and AIDS. *Newsletter of the Association for Women in Social Work, 1*(2), pp. 2–3.

Fairchild, B. (1992). For parents of lesbians and gays. In B. Berzon (Ed.), *Positively gay: New approaches to gay and lesbian life* (pp. 79–90). Berkeley, CA: Celestial Arts.

Fifield, L. (1975). On my way to nowhere: Alienated, isolated, drunk. Los Angeles: Gay Community Services Center & Department of Health Services.

Gibson, P. (1989). Gay male and lesbian youth suicide. *Report of the secretary's task force on youth suicide.* (Aicohol, Drug Abuse and Mental Health Administration, DHHS Publication Number [ADM] 89-1623, Volume 3: Prevention and interventions in youth suicide). Washington DC: U.S. Government Printing Office.

Gochros, H. L., Gochros, J. S., & Fischer, J. (1986). *Helping the sexually oppressed*. Englewood Cliffs, NJ: Prentice-Hall. Copyright © 1986 by Allyn & Bacon. Reprinted/adapted by permission.

Grace, J., & Fergal, J. (1984). On mainstreaming gay and lesbian services into traditional agencies. *Practice Digest, 7*(1), pp. 5–8.

Hall, J. M. (1993). Lesbians and alcohol: Patterns and paradoxes in medical notions and lesbians' beliefs. *Journal of Psychoactive Drugs, 25*, 109–119.

Hawkins, J. L. (1976). Lesbianism and alcoholism. In M. Greenblatt & M. A. Schuckit (Eds.), *Alcoholism problems in women and children* (pp. 137–153). New York: Grune & Stratton.

Herek, G. M., & Berrill, K. T. (1992). *Hate crimes: Confronting violence against lesbians and gay men*. Newbury Park, CA: Sage.

Hunter, J., & Schaecher, R. (1990). Violence against lesbian and gay male youths. *Journal of Interpersonal Violence, 5*, 295–300.

Hunter, J., & Schaecher, R. (1995). Gay and lesbian adolescents. In R. L. Edwards (Ed.), *Encyclopedia of social work* (19th ed., Vol. 2, pp. 1055–1063). Washington, DC: NASW Press. Copyright 1995, National Association of Social Workers, Inc.

Island, D., & Letellier, P. (1991). *Men who beat the men who love them*. Binghamton, NY: Haworth Press.

Kinsey, A. C., Pomeroy, W. B., & Martin, C. E. (1948). *Sexual behavior in the human male*. Philadelphia: W. B. Saunders.

Kus, R. J. (1988). Alcoholism and non-acceptance of gay self: The critical link. *Journal of Homosexuality, 15*(1–2), 25–41.

LeBaugh, R. A. (1979). Using your gay voting power. In B. Berzon (Ed.), *Positively gay* (pp. 199–208). Los Angeles: Mediamix Associates.

Lorde, A. (1983). The master's tools will never dismantle the master's house. In C. Moraga & G. Anzaldua (Eds.), *This bridge called my back: Writings by radical women of color* (pp. 98–101). New York: Kitchen Table: Women of Color Press.

Maddox, B. (1982, February). Homosexual parents. *Psychology Today, 16*(2), 62–69.

McKirnan, D. J., & Peterson, P. L. (1989). Alcohol and drug use among homosexual men and women: Epidemiology and population characteristics. *Addictive Behaviors, 14*, 545–553.

McNeece, C. A., & DiNitto, D. M. (1994). *Chemical dependency: A systems approach*. Englewood Cliffs: NJ: Prentice-Hall.

Moses, A. E., & Buckner, J. A. (1982). The special problems of rural gay clients. In A. E. Moses & R. O. Hawkins, *Counseling lesbian women and gay men*, (pp. 173–180).

Moses, A. E., & Hawkins, R. O., Jr. (1982). *Counseling lesbian women and gay men*. St. Louis: C.V. Mosby. Reprinted by permission of Prentice Hall, Upper Saddle River, New Jersey.

National Association of Social Workers. (1994). *Social work speaks: NASW policy statements*. Washington, DC: NASW Press. Copyright 1993, National Association of Social Workers, Inc.

National Gay and Lesbian Task Force (NGLTF). (1984). Anti-gay/lesbian victimization: A study by the National Gay and Lesbian Task Force in cooperation with gay and lesbian organizations in eight U.S. cities. Washington, DC: Author. (Available from NGLTF, 2320 17th Street, NW, Washington, DC 20009).

Patterson, C. (1992). Children of lesbian and gay parents. *Child Development, 63*(5), 1025–1042.

PFLAGpole. (1995, Summer). Newsletter of Parents, Families and Friends of Lesbians and Gays, p. 4. Available from PFLAG, 1101 14th Street, N.W., Washington, DC 20005.

Polikoff, N. D. (1990). This child does have two mothers: Redefining parenthood to meet the needs of children in lesbian-mother and other nontraditional families. *Georgetown Law Journal, 78*(3), 459–575.

Renzetti, C. M. (1988). Violence in lesbian relationships. *Journal of Interpersonal Violence, 3*, 381–399.

Renzetti, C. M. (1989). Building a second closet: Third party responses to victims of lesbian partner abuse. *Family Relations, 38*, 157–163.

Saghir, M. T., Robins, E., Walbran, B., & Gentry, K. A. (1970a). Homosexuality: III. Psychiatric disorders and disability in the male homosexual. *American Journal of Psychiatry, 126*(8), 1079–1086.

Saghir, M. T., Robins, E., Walbran, B., & Gentry, K. A. (1970b). Homosexuality: IV. Psychiatric disorders and disability in the female homosexual. *American Journal of Psychiatry, 127*(2), 147–154.

Saulnier, C. F. (1994). Twelve steps for everyone? Lesbians in Al-Anon. In T. J. Powell (Ed.). *Understanding the self-help organization* (pp. 247–271). Thousand Oaks, CA: Sage.

Saulnier, C. F. (in review). *Drug and alcohol problems: Heterosexuals compared to lesbian and bisexual women*. Available from Christine Flynn Saulnier, State University of New York at Buffalo, 359 Baldy Hall, Buffalo, NY 14260.

Saulnier, C. F. (in review). Suicide among lesbian and gay youth. Available from Christine Flynn Saulnier, State University of New York at Buffalo, 359 Baldy Hall, Buffalo, NY 14260.

Skinner, W. F. (1994). The prevalence and demographic predictors of illicit and licit drug use among lesbians and gay men. *American Journal of Public Health, 84*, 1307–1310.

Stall, R., & Wiley, J. (1988). A comparison of alcohol and drug use patterns of homosexual and heterosexual men: The San Francisco men's health study. *Drug and Alcohol Dependence, 22*, 63–73.

Task Force on Gay and Lesbian Issues. (1983). *An annotated bibliography of lesbian and gay readings,* (1st ed). New York: Council on Social Work Education.

Texas Department of Human Services. (1991). Types of abuse: Adult clients only. *Family Violence Program State Report* (Data source 2753, data item 23). Austin, TX: Author.

Toder, N. (1979). Lesbian couples: Special issues. In B. Berzon (Ed.), *Positively gay* (pp. 41–55). Los Angeles: Mediamix Associates.

Van Soest, D. (1996). The influence of competing ideologies about homosexuality on nondiscrimination policy: Implications for social work education. *Journal of Social Work Education, 32*(1), 53–64.

Vourakis, C. (1983). Homosexuals in substance abuse treatment. In G. Bennet, C. Vourakis, & D. S. Woolf (Eds.), *Substance abuse: Pharmacologic, developmental and clinical perspectives* (pp. 400–419). New York: John Wiley & Sons.

Waterman, C. K., Dawson, L. J., & Bologna, M. J. (1989). Sexual coercion in gay male and lesbian relationships: Predictors and implications for support services. *The Journal of Sex Research, 26,* 118–124.

Woodman, N. J. (1987). Homosexuality: Lesbian women. In A. Minahan (Ed.), *Encyclopedia of social work* (18th ed., Vol. 1, pp. 805–812). Silver Spring, MD: NASW Press. Copyright 1990, National Association of Social Workers, Inc.

Zimmerman, B. (1992). What has never been: An overview of lesbian feminist literary criticism. In W. R. Dynes and S. Donaldson (Eds.), *Lesbianism* (pp. 341–365). New York: Garland.

Chapter 17

Abramovitz, M., & Newdom, F. (1994, April). Decorating welfare reform. *City Limits,* 22–23.

Affilia: Journal of Women and Social Work. (1986a). *1*(1), 66.

Affilia: Journal of Women and Social Work. (1986b). *1*(2), 2.

Affilia: Journal of Women and Social Work. (1986c). *1*(4), 65.

Akabas, S. H. (1995). The world of work. In N. Van Den Bergh (Ed.), *Feminist practice in the 21st century* (pp. 105–125). Washington, DC: NASW Press. Copyright 1995, National Association of Social Workers, Inc.

American Association of Retired Persons. (1994). *A profile of older Americans.* Washington, DC: Author.

Ames, B. (1995, August/September). Renewed assaults on abortion and reproductive rights. *National NOW Times.* Washington, DC: National Organization for Women.

Avis, J. M. (1992, July). Where are all the family therapists? Abuse and violence within families and family therapy's response. *Journal of Marital and Family Therapy,* 18(3), 225–232.

Bachman, R. (1994, January). *Violence against women: A national crime victimization survey report.* Washington, DC: U.S. Department of Justice.

Bricker-Jenkins, M., & Hooyman, N. R. (Eds.). (1986). *Not for women only: Social work practice for a feminist future.* Silver Spring, MD: NASW Press. Copyright 1986, National Association of Social Workers, Inc.

Burgess, A. W., & Holmstrom, L. L. (1974). Rape trauma syndrome. *American Journal of Psychiatry, 131,* 981–986. Copyright 1974, the American Psychiatric Association. Reprinted by permission.

Chernesky, R. H. (1995). Feminist administration style, structure, purpose. In N. Van Den Bergh (Ed.), *Feminist practice in the 21st century* (pp. 70–88). Washington, DC: NASW Press. Copyright 1995, National Association of Social Workers, Inc.

Code of federal regulations, Vol. 29, Sec. 1604.11.

Commission on Accreditation. (1994). Curriculum policy statement for master's degree programs in social work education. In *Handbook of accreditation standards and procedures* (pp. 134–146). Alexandria, VA: Council on Social Work Education.

Commission Annual Reports. (1995, Fall). *Social Work Education Reporter, 43*(3), 3–12.

Committee on Ways and Means, U.S. House of Representatives. (1993). *Overview of entitlement programs, 1993 green book.* Washington, DC: U.S. Government Printing Office.

Danziger, S. K., & Danziger, S. (1993). Child poverty and public policy: Toward a comprehensive anti-poverty agenda. *Daedalus, 122*(1), 57–85.

Dinerman, M. (1986). The woman trap: Women and poverty. In N. Van Den Bergh & L. B. Cooper (Eds.), *Feminist visions for social work* (pp. 229–249). Washington, DC: NASW Press.

Dressel, P. L. (1992). Patriarchy and social welfare work. In Y. Hasenfeld (Ed.), *Human services as complex organizations* (pp. 205–223). Newbury Park, CA: Sage.

Equal Employment Opportunity Commission. (1995). *Sexual harassment statistics: EEOC & FEPAs combined: FY1989-FY1994.* Washington, DC: Author.

Gibelman, M., & Schervish, P. H. (1995). Pay equity in social work: Not! *Social Work, 40*(5), 622–630.

Gould, K. H., & Bok-Lim, C. K. (1976). Salary inequities between men and women in schools of social work: Myth or reality? *Journal of Education for Social Work, 12,* 50–55.

Jones, R. (1995). The price of welfare dependency: Children pay. *Social Work, 40*(4), 496–505.

Koss, M. P., Leonard, K. E., Beezley, D. A., & Oros, C. G. (1985). Non-stranger sexual aggression: A discriminant analysis of the psychological characteristics of undetected offenders. *Sex Roles, 12*(9/10), 981–992.

Kravetz, D. (1976). Sexism in a woman's profession. *Social Work, 21*(6), 421–426.

Landers, S. (1992, April). Survey eyes therapy fees. *NASW News,* 39–43.

Lerman, L. G. (1983). Legal help for battered women. In J. J. Costa (Ed.), *Abuse of women: Legislation, reporting, and prevention.* Lexington, MA: Lexington Books.

Lewin, T. (1994, October 15). Working women say bias persists. *The New York Times,* p. 8.

Martin, P. Y., DiNitto, D., Norton, D. B., & Maxwell, S. (1984). *Services to rape victims in Florida, 1984: A needs assessment study.* Tallahassee, FL: State of Florida, Department of Health and Rehabilitative Services.

Maypole, D. E. (1986). Sexual harassment of social workers at work. *Social Work, 31,* 29–34.

McNeece, C. A., DiNitto, D. M., DeWeaver, K. L., & Johnson, P. J. (1987). Social work education: No sexual harassment here? *Human Service Education, 8*(2), 20–28.

National Association of Social Workers. (1975). NASW standards for social work personnel practices. Washington, DC: NASW Press. Copyright 1995, National Association of Social Workers, Inc.

National Association of Social Workers. (1994). *Social work speaks* (3rd ed.). Washington, DC: NASW Press.

National Committee on Pay Equity. (1995). *Questions and answers on pay equity*. Washington, DC: Author.

National Institute of Justice Statistics. (1995). *Sexual assault*. Washington DC: Author.

National Organization for Women. (1981). *Strong public support for ERA*. ERA Countdown Campaign. Washington, DC: National Organization for Women.

National Organization for Women. (1992). *Abortion and birth control*. Washington DC: Author.

O'Donnell, S. (1993). Involving clients in welfare policy-making. *Social Work, 38*(5), 629–635.

Pavetti, L. A. (1993). *The dynamics of welfare and work: Exploring the process by which young women work their way off welfare*. Cambridge, MA: Harvard University, John F. Kennedy School of Government.

Perlmutter, F. D. (1994). United States: A feminist health organization. In F. D. Perlmutter (Ed.), *Women and social change: Nonprofits and social policy* (pp. 158–175). Washington, DC: NASW Press.

Pope, K. S., Levenson, H., & Schover, L. R. (1986). Sexual intimacy in psychology training. *American Psychologist, 34,* 29–34.

Rado, S. (1948). Pathodynamics and treatment of traumatic war time phobia (traumatophobia). *Psychosomatic Medicine, 4,* 362–368.

Singer, T. L. (1989). Sexual harassment in graduate schools of social work: Provocative dilemma. *Journal of Social Work Education, 25*(1), 68–76.

Sowers-Hoag, K. M., & Harrison, D. F. (1991). Women in social work education: Progress or promise? *Journal of Social Work Education, 27,* 320–328.

Spalter-Roth, R. M., Hartmann, H. I., & Andrews, L. (1992). *Combining work and welfare: An alternative anti-poverty strategy*. Washington, DC: Institute for Women's Policy Research.

Suarez, Z., Lewis, E., & Clark, J. (1995). Women of color and culturally competent feminist social work practice. In N. Van Bergh (Ed.), *Feminist practice in the 21st century* (pp. 195–210). Washington, DC: NASW Press. Copyright 1995, National Association of Social Workers, Inc.

Sullivan, C. M., Basta, J., Tan, C., & Davidson, W. S., II. (1992). After the crisis: A needs assessment of women leaving a domestic violence shelter. *Violence and Victims, 7,* 267–275.

Sullivan, C. M., & Rumptz, M. H. (1994). Adjustment and needs of African-American women who utilized a domestic violence shelter. *Violence and Victims, 9,* 275–286.

Queralt, M. (1996). *The social environment and human behavior: A diversity perspective*. Boston: Allyn & Bacon.

Urdang, L., & Flexner, S. B. (1973). *The Random House college dictionary*. New York: Random House.

Van Den Bergh, N. (Ed.). (1995). *Feminist practice in the 21st century*. Washington, DC: NASW Press. Copyright 1995, National Association of Social Workers, Inc.

Van Den Bergh, N., & Cooper, L. B. (Eds.). (1986). *Feminist visions for social work*. Washington, DC: NASW Press.

Wilson, M., & Martin, D. (1993). Spousal homicide risk and estrangement. *Violence and Victims, 8,* 3–16.

Chapter 18

Barker, R. L. (1995). Private practice. In R. L. Edwards (Ed.), *Encyclopedia of social work* (19th ed., pp. 1905–1910). Washington, DC: NASW Press. Copyright 1995, National Association of Social Workers, Inc.

Beck, B. M. (1981). Social work's future: Triumph or disaster? *Social Work, 26*(5), 368–371.

Becker, R. (1961). *Study of salaries of NASW members.* New York: National Association of Social Workers.

Briar, S. (1987). Direct practice: trends and issues. In A. Minahan (Ed.), *Encyclopedia of Social Work,* (18th ed., Vol. 1, pp. 393–398). Silver Spring, MD: Author.

Bureau of Labor Statistics. (1986). *Employment projections for 1995: Data and methods* (Bulletin 2253, p. 44). Washington, DC: U.S. Government Printing Office.

Bureau of Labor Statistics. (1991). *Household data survey: Employed civilians by detailed occupation, 1983–1991.* Washington, DC: U.S. Government Printing Office.

Burgess, R. L., & Bushell, D. (1969). *Behavioral sociology: The experimental analysis of social process.* New York: Columbia University Press.

Council on Social Work Education. (1995). *Statistics on social work education in the United States, 1994.* New York: Author.

Downs, W. R., & Rubin, A. (1994). Lacking evidence of effectiveness, should single-case evaluation techniques be encouraged in practice? In W. W. Hudson & P. S. Nurius (Eds.), *Controversial issues in social work research.* Boston: Allyn & Bacon.

Fischer, J. (1973). Is casework effective? A review. *Social Work, 18*(1), 5–20.

Fischer, J., & Corcoran, K. (1994). *Measures for clinical practice, Volumes I & II.* New York: Free Press.

Fisher, B. (1995). Political social work. *Journal of Social Work Education, 31*(2), 194–203.

Germain, C. (1979). *Social work practice: People and environments, an ecological perspective.* New York: Columbia University Press.

Gibelman, M., & Schervish, P. (1993). *Who we are: The social work labor force as reflected in the NASW membership.* Washington, DC: NASW Press. Copyright 1993, National Association of Social Workers, Inc.

Gingerich, W. J., & Green, R. K. (1996). Information technology: How social work is going digital. In P. R. Raffoul & C. A. McNeece (Eds.), *Future issues for social work practice* (pp. 19–28). Boston: Allyn & Bacon.

Haynes, K. S. (1996). The future of political social work. In P. R. Raffoul & C. A. McNeece (Eds.), *Future issues in social work practice* (pp. 266–276). Boston: Allyn & Bacon.

Howard, M. O., & Lambert, M. D. (1996). The poverty of social work: Deficient production, dissemination and utilization of practice-relevant scientific information. In P. R. Raffoul & C. A. McNeece (Eds.), *Future issues for social work practice,* (pp. 277–292). Boston: Allyn & Bacon.

Imershein, A. W. (1986). The impact of Reagan's new federalism on programs and policies in Florida. *Florida Policy Review, 1*(2), 30–37.

Ingersoll-Dayton, B., & Jayaratne, S., (1996). Measuring social work practice effectiveness: Beyond the year 2000. In P. R. Raffoul & C. A. McNeece (Eds.), *Future issues in social work practice* (pp. 29–36). Boston: Allyn & Bacon.

Miller, L. M. (1978). *Behavior management: The new science of managing people at work.* New York: Wiley.

Murdock, S. H., & Michael, M. (1996). Future demographic change and the demand for social welfare services in the 21st century. In P. R. Raffoul & C. A. McNeece (Eds.), *Future issues for social work practice* (pp. 3–18). Boston: Allyn & Bacon.

National Association of Social Workers. (1987). *Salaries in social work: A summary report on the salaries of NASW members, July 1986–June 1987* (p. 7). Silver Spring, MD: Author.

Nurius, P., & Hudson, W. W. (1993). *Human services practice, evaluation & computers: A practical guide for today and beyond.* Pacific Grove, CA: Brooks/Cole.

Raffoul, P. R. (1996). Social work and the future: Some final thoughts. In P. R. Raffoul & C. A. McNeece, (Eds.), *Future issues for social work practice* (pp. 293–300). Boston: Allyn & Bacon.

Rose, S. D. (1980). *A casebook in group therapy: A behavioral-cognitive approach.* Englewood Cliffs, NJ: Prentice-Hall.

Sarri, R. C. (1973). Effective social work intervention in administration and planning roles: Implications for higher education. In Council on Social Work Education, *Facing the challenge,* (pp. 31–32). New York: Author.

Sarri, R. C. (1986). Organizational and policy practice in social work: Challenges for the future. *Policy Science Quarterly, 101*(2), 14–19.

Specht, H., & Courtney, M. (1994). *Unfaithful angels: Social work's abandoned mission.* New York: Free Press.

U.S. Department of Health and Human Services. (1990). *Seventh special report to the United States Congress on alcohol and health* (DHHS Publication No.ADM 90–165). Rockville, MD: Alcohol, Drug Abuse and Mental Health Administration, National Institute on Alcohol Abuse and Alcoholism.

U.S. Department of Labor. (1986). *Quarterly reports.* Washington, DC: U.S. Government Printing Office.

Author Index

Subject Index